THE AMERICAN JOURNAL OF PHYSIOLOGY

VOLUME LIV

BALTIMORE, MD.
1920–1921

CONTENTS

No. 1. November 1, 1920

The Effect on the Composition of the Blood of Maintaining an Increased Blood Volume by the Intravenous Injection of a Hypertonic Solution of Gum Acacia and Glucose in Normal, Asphyxiated and Shocked Dogs. *H. L. White and Joseph Erlanger* 1

The Functional Activity of the Capillaries and Venules. *D. R. Hooker* 30

Studies on the Visceral Sensory Nervous System. I. Lung Automatism and Lung Reflexes in the Frog (R. pipiens and R. catesbiana). *A. J. Carlson and A. B. Luckhardt* 55

The Effect of Adrenalin on Venous Blood Pressure. *Helene Connet* .. 96

Studies on the Visceral Sensory Nervous System. II. Lung Automatism and Lung Reflexes in the Salamanders (Necturus, Axolotl). *A. B. Luckhardt and A. J. Carlson* 122

Changes in Acid and Alkali Tolerance with Age in Planarians. With a Note on Catalase Content. *John W. MacArthur* 138

Studies on the Alkaline Reserve of the Blood of the Insane. *Nobuharu Suitsu* 147

Gastric Tonus of the Empty Stomach of the Frog. Comparative Studies IV. *T. L. Patterson* 153

Studies on the Submaxillary Gland. VI. On the Dependence of Tissue Activity upon Volume-flow of Blood and on the Mechanism Controlling This Volume-flow of Blood. *Robert Gesell* 166

Studies on the Submaxillary Gland. VII. On the Effects of Increased Salivary Pressure on the Electrical Deflections, the Volume-flow of Blood and the Secretion of the Submaxillary Gland of the Dog. *Robert Gesell* 185

Studies on the Submaxillary Gland. VIII. On the Effects of Atropin upon Volume-flow of Blood, Electrical Deflections and Oxidations of the Submaxillary Gland. *Robert Gesell* 204

No. 2. December 1, 1920

The Distribution and Quantitative Action of the Vagi as Determined by the Electrical Changes Arising in the Heart upon Vagus Stimulation. *E. W. H. Cruickshank* 217

The Influence of Glands with Internal Secretions on the Respiratory Exchange. I. Effect of the Subcutaneous Injection of Adrenalin on Normal and Thyroidectomized Rabbits. *David Marine and C. H. Lenhart* 248

Studies on the Visceral Sensory Nervous System. III. Lung Automatism and Lung Reflexes in Reptilia (Turtles: Chrysemys elegans and Malacoclemmys lesueurii. Snake: Eutenia elegans). *A. J. Carlson and A. B. Luckhardt* 261
Studies of the Respiratory Mechanism in Cardiac Dyspnea. I. The Low Alveolar Carbon Dioxide of Cardiac Dyspnea. *John P. Peters, Jr. and David P. Barr* 307
Studies of the Respiratory Mechanism in Cardiac Dyspnea. II. A Note on the Effective Lung Volume in Cardiac Dyspnea. *John P. Peters, Jr. and David P. Barr* 335
Studies of the Respiratory Mechanism in Cardiac Dyspnea. III. The Effective Ventilation in Cardiac Dyspnea. *D. P. Barr and John P. Peters, Jr* 345
Studies on the Brain Stem. IV. On the Relation of the Cerebral Hemispheres and Thalamus to Arterial Blood Pressure. *F. T. Rogers* 355
Experimental Studies in Diabetes. Series II. The Internal Pancreatic Function in Relation to Body Mass and Metabolism. 5. The Influence of Fever and Intoxication. *Frederick M. Allen* 375
Experimental Studies in Diabetes. Series II. The Internal Pancreatic Function in Relation to Body Mass and Metabolism. 6. Gas Bacillus Infections in Diabetic Dogs. *Mary B. Wishart and Ida W. Pritchett* 382
Studies in Experimental Traumatic Shock. I. The Basal Metabolism. *Joseph C. Aub* 388
Studies in Experimental Traumatic Shock. II. The Oxygen Content of the Blood. *Joseph C. Aub and T. Donald Cunningham* 408
Studies in Experimental Traumatic Shock. III. Chemical Changes in the Blood. *Joseph C. Aub and Hsien Wu* 416

No. 3. January 1, 1921

Experimental Studies in Diabetes. Series II. The Internal Pancreatic Function in Relation to Body Mass and Metabolism. 7. The Influence of Cold. *Frederick M. Allen* 425
Experimental Studies in Diabetes. Series II. The Internal Pancreatic Function in Relation to Body Mass and Metabolism. 8. The Influence of Extremes of Age upon the Production of Diabetes. *Frederick M. Allen* 439
Experimental Studies in Diabetes. Series II. The Internal Pancreatic Function in Relation to Body Mass and Metabolism. 9. The Influence of Pregnancy upon Experimental Diabetes. *Frederick M. Allen* 451
Rhythmicity of the Pyloric Sphincter. *Homer Wheelon and J. Earl Thomas* 460
A Difference between the Mechanism of Hyperglycemia Production by Ether and by Chloroform. *Ellison L. Ross and L. H. Davis* 474
Digestibility of Some Hydrogenated Oils. *Arthur D. Holmes and Harry J. Deuel, Jr* 479
Index 489

THE AMERICAN
JOURNAL OF PHYSIOLOGY

VOL. 54 NOVEMBER 1, 1920 No. 1

THE EFFECT ON THE COMPOSITION OF THE BLOOD OF MAINTAINING AN INCREASED BLOOD VOLUME BY THE INTRAVENOUS INJECTION OF A HYPERTONIC SOLUTION OF GUM ACACIA AND GLUCOSE IN NORMAL, ASPHYXIATED AND SHOCKED DOGS

H. L. WHITE AND JOSEPH ERLANGER

From the Physiological Department of Washington University, St. Louis

Received for publication July 3, 1920

The present work was undertaken with the idea of investigating the effect upon the composition of the blood of producing and then maintaining for some hours an expansion of the blood volume through the intravenous injection of a hypertonic crystalloid and colloid in combined solution, in the hope of throwing some light on the mechanism of the processes involved. The solution injected consisted of 18 per cent glucose and 25 per cent gum acacia and is the one that has been found useful in the treatment of traumatic shock (1). Studies of the blood changes produced were carried out under conditions which were varied in a way that might change the permeability of the vessel walls to the tissue fluids and their various constituents.

The literature contains many references to studies, more or less complete, of the blood changes following the intravenous injection of crystalloids, glucose, NaCl, Na_2SO_4 and urea being the substances most commonly used. Brasol (2) found that following intravenous injection of a hypertonic glucose solution the blood was greatly diluted in 2 minutes but that the blood volume had returned to normal within 2 hours. He found that there was no relation between the amount of glucose injected and the per cent of glucose found in the blood 2 minutes later, that the blood sugar was normal 2 hours after the injection, that part of the sugar which leaves the blood can be found in the tissues, but part cannot be found and is perhaps changed to glycogen, lactic acid or "undergoes some other chemical metamorphosis," and that the absolute quantity of protein in the serum remains unchanged. He concludes that the effects produced are purely the results of the increased intravascular osmotic tension due to the injected glucose. Klickowicz (3) obtained similar results as regards blood volume with strong solutions of Na_2SO_4. Leathes (4) finds that the "increase in the volume of the blood caused by the injection of 5 grams of dextrose per kilo is enormous and quite out of proportion to that caused by the volume of the injection. This increase takes place with remarkable rapidity; the volume of the blood is nearly doubled by the time the injection is finished." Gasser and Erlanger (5) followed the blood volume after intravenous injection of 5 cc. of 18 per cent glucose solution per kilo body weight, the injection being made as rapidly as possible. They found that the maximum dilution was attained within 0.5 to 2 minutes and that the blood then began to concentrate, rapidly at first, and then more slowly, and became normal within 5 to 45 minutes. Starling (6) finds hydremic plethora following glucose injection and that the distended vessels begin at once to unload the excess of water. Paton (7) finds that when 4 grams of carbohydrate in 10 cc. of water per kilo body weight are injected intravenously only a small per cent of the amount injected can be recovered immediately from the blood, the time from the beginning of the injection to the end of collecting the sample being 90 to 100 seconds. Hamburger (8) finds that in the horse an intravenous injection of 7 liters of 5 per cent Na_2SO_4 causes a marked dilution of blood serum in respect to its chloride and protein content, a return to normal being accomplished very quickly, within 2 hours. Practically the same effect on protein content of serum follows the injection of 5 liters of 0.5 per cent Na_2SO_4 solution, while the chlorides are diluted as with a hypertonic solution but do not return to normal. The blood volume was not followed in these cases, so no conclusions can be drawn as to whether the return to normal was due to a passage of water out of the blood stream or an entrance of solids into the blood stream. Fisher and Wishart (9) found that blood dilutes as a result of alimentary hyperglycemia. Magnus (10) obtains varying results in his studies of changes in blood composition following the intravenous injection of NaCl solutions, the results depending upon the osmotic tension of the injected solution, although consistent results were not obtained with hypertonic solutions.

The common feature of the experiments discussed above is that the substances injected were crystalloids and, with the exception of those of Fisher and Wishart, the injection was rapid; and the increase in blood volume, with hypertonic solutions, always is very rapid in appearance and of short duration. Woodyatt, Sansum and Wilder (11) injected glucose intravenously over long periods of time at a uniform rate and determined the tolerance rate as 0.8 to 0.9 gram per kilo per hour. Erlanger and Woodyatt (12) injected glucose intravenously at uniform rates varying between 0.57 and 4 grams per kilo per hour for from 20 to 60 minutes into anesthetized animals in shock. The pulse amplitude was uniformly markedly increased, indicating a condition of plethora. A subtolerant dose was as effective as injections made at more rapid rates. In a normal animal an injection lasting 30 minutes at the rate of 1.78 gram per kilo per hour raised arterial pressure only about 5 mm. Hg. but the pulse amplitude increased quite appreciably. The fact that a considerable increase in blood volume is accompanied by only a slight rise in arterial pressure is presumably due to diminution in viscosity of the blood and to vasomotor accommodation. While the blood volume was not followed in these cases it presumably soon fell after cessation of injection to its pre-injection state.

With regard to the entrance of protein into the circulation, Morawitz (13) found restoration of proteins most active in the first few hours after severe hemorrhage. Whipple and co-workers (14) find that after severe hemorrhage the regeneration of plasma proteins is much more rapid on a liberal high protein diet than on a liberal bread and milk diet, and least rapid on fasting. They infer from this that there is an actual new formation of protein and make no mention of the possibility of some of the protein being drawn in from the tissue fluids. They also find that "after the initial depletion of serum proteins the body can almost always regenerate 1 per cent of the total protein during the first 24 hours following the plasmapharesis. This figure is remarkably constant and does not seem to be influenced by diet or fasting . . . . . or the amount of shock. We may perhaps look upon this as the maximum effort of the body to replace these essential serum proteins, an effort which surely depends upon the body protein as it is present in fasting experiments. It will be the same whether there is a marked breakdown of host protein, as evidenced by great increase in urinary nitrogen, or whether this tissue autolysis is minimal." That they do not regard this maximum effort as accomplished by the passage of protein directly into the blood from the tissues but rather as a true rebuilding is shown by their further statement that it "probably represents the absolute maximum production under the greatest stimulus." They present further evidence that the restoration of plasma proteins after hemorrhage is due to a new formation of proteins and that the liver is the chief seat of this process in that restoration is greatly hindered by phosphorus and chloroform poisoning and by an Eck fistula.

A rather careful review of the literature has failed to disclose any references to studies of the body fluids made during a period of prolonged increase of blood volume due to the injection of hypertonic solutions. It is evident that only two means are at our disposal for maintaining an increased blood volume for a comparatively long period, several hours for instance, with fluids other than blood or blood plasma. One is by a continuous injection of a hypertonic or isotonic solution of crystalloids at a rate more rapid than the rate of the blood's fluid loss. In this case the large amount of fluid injected would so dilute the blood that no conclusions could be drawn as to the interchange of water and solutes between tissue spaces and blood stream. The other method is to inject a small volume of a strongly hypertonic solution which will not only draw fluid into the blood stream but hold it there for some time. To accomplish this result a solution containing both crystalloid and colloid is necessary (15). So far as we know the present work represents the first effort made to study changes in the composition of the blood induced in this way.

PROCEDURE

Dogs were used in all experiments. The animals were not prepared by controlling their intake of food or water previous to the experiment. Most of them were fed and watered on the morning of the experiment. In the first seven cases the animal was given 1 grain of morphine an hour before starting the operation; in the case of dog 8, 2 grains were given by mistake. In the remainder of the cases the morphine was omitted because of its disturbing effect on the blood and urinary sugar. In the first four cases strict surgical asepsis was observed throughout the experiment; in the remainder these precautions were relaxed, although the fluid injected and the injecting apparatus were sterile. No differences in results due to these technical differences were observed. Three sets of experiments were performed; the first, a series of nine experiments, on normal dogs; the second, a series of two, on asphyxiated dogs; the third, a series of three, on dogs in shock. The procedure and data of each series are presented separately.

The *procedure in the first series* was to anesthetize the dog with ether, immediately draw a "standard" sample of blood from the femoral artery, then to start the injection into the femoral vein. The dose in all cases was 5 cc. per kilo per hour of an 18 per cent glucose and 25 per cent gum acacia solution, the injection lasting 1 hour and proceeding at a uniform rate. Immediately at the termination of the injection another sample of blood was taken and the dog put back into its cage. Subsequent samples were taken at approximately 2-hour intervals until five samples were obtained. Little or no anesthetic was required while drawing the last three samples. On each sample determinations were made of hemoglobin (16), plasma chlorides (17), plasma total nitrogen and plasma non-protein nitrogen (18), and plasma sugar (18). The nitrogen and chloride determinations were made in duplicate. Direct Nesslerization was at first attempted for both the total and the non-protein nitrogen determinations, appropriate dilutions being made, but it was found that the presence of the large amount of carbohydrate in the samples rendered digestion with the prescribed digestion mixture so difficult that indirect Nesslerization had to be resorted to. In the latter cases of the series the total nitrogen determinations were made by the macro-Kjeldahl method since it was felt that the micro-Kjeldahl with indirect Nesslerization was not sufficienty trustworthy. Figures given in the tables under the heading "total N" are protein nitrogen figures and are obtained by subtracting the non-protein nitrogen figure from the total nitrogen figure as determined by the Kjeldahl. Several dilutions of the filtrate for plasma sugar determinations were made, the dilution being accepted whose reading was closest to 20, the standard being set at 20 on the Dubosq or Bock-Benedict colorimeter. Freezing point determinations were attempted in the first experiment, working with 1.5 cc. of hirudinized plasma in a special tube in the Beckmann apparatus, but it was found that consistent results could not be obtained with this amount of plasma and these determinations were discontinued as it seemed inadvisable to take more blood. In lieu of direct determinations the crystalloid osmotic pressure of the plasma has been roughly estimated by adding the osmotic pressures exerted by the NaCl and glucose present. The calculations were made from published tables of direct osmotic pressure determinations and of freezing point determinations. By using various schemes for utilizing every available drop of plasma it was possible to make all determinations with 13 cc. of blood drawn at each sample. Allowance for blood drawn as samples has been made in the calculations. Dogs 8 and 9 were bled 15 per cent of their blood volume at the time of taking the first sample. In the last few cases the urine was also followed, the bladder being emptied as completely as possible with a small coudé catheter at the time of drawing the blood samples. The results of the first series are given in table 1.

The *procedure in the second series* was to anesthetize the dog with ether (morphine being omitted in these and subsequent experiments), insert a tracheal cannula, draw a standard sample of blood from the femoral artery and empty the bladder. The animal was then made to rebreathe air in a large spirometer until the CO_2 tension of the air in it mounted to about 30 mm. Hg. as determined with Marriott's (19) tubes on samples drawn from the spirometer. The injection was then started, the CO_2 tension being kept around 30 to 35 mm. Hg., fresh air being admitted at intervals when the dog became markedly dyspneic. Dyspnea was moderate to marked throughout the injection. This procedure was introduced in an effort to discover whether asphyxia altered the permeability of the vessel walls. At the conclusion of the injection the second sample of blood and urine was drawn, rebreathing discontinued, the animal put back into its cage and subsequent samples taken as in the first series. The results of the second series are given in table 2.

In the case of dog 10 the injection rate was not accurately timed, at first. Twenty-five cubic centimeters were run in during the first 20 minutes. The injection was then stopped for 10 minutes, the remainder of the injection then proceeding at the proper rate. When the last sample was drawn from dog 10 he struggled quite vigorously and it was necessary to anesthetize him deeply, which is not usually necessary for the last three samples. This anesthesia probably accounts for the high blood sugar value in the last sample of dog 10.

The *procedure in the third series* was to anesthetize the animal, insert a tracheal cannula and connect a manometer with a femoral artery, draw a standard sample and then put the animal into a condition of shock. The condition induced was the so-called mechanical shock of Janeway and Jackson (20), which they produced by temporary partial occlusion of the vena cava regulated so as to keep the blood pressure at 30 to 40 mm. Hg. for 2 hours. The method of obstructing the cava used in the present work was one described by Erlanger and Gasser (21), a clamp being used by which graded compression can be exerted upon the cava between the liver and the diaphragm through a small abdominal incision. The mean arterial pressure was kept at about 40 mm. Hg. for 120 to 135 minutes. At the end of this time the clamp was removed, the second sample drawn, the injection given, a third sample then taken, and the dog kept as long as he would live, samples being drawn at about 2- or $2\frac{1}{2}$-hour intervals. Very little anesthetic was required to keep the dog quiet after shock had been produced. This procedure was employed in an endeavor to ascertain whether the permeability of the vessel walls is altered in shock.

The results of the third series are given in table 3 and in the brief case histories.

DISCUSSION OF RESULTS

Series I. Normal Dogs

1. Blood volume. It is evident that in all cases there is a marked immediate increase in blood volume, amounting to 11 to 16 per cent, which usually slowly returns toward normal. Some slight increase in volume, about 2 per cent, usually persists even after 6 or 7 hours. The combined action of the glucose and acacia in effecting changes in blood volume is interesting. The early high intravascular osmotic tension which causes the rapid increase in volume is due principally to the glucose. The glucose, however, rapidly passes out into the tissue spaces (see plasma sugar figures) but through the influence of the gum acacia the water very slowly leaves the vessels. The persistent increase of blood volume, 2 or more per cent, is less than the amount of water which must be added to the amount of acacia presumably remaining in the blood (22) in order to make it isosmotic to the plasma proteins. It will be noticed, however, that in every case but one, dog 3, where the figures are the same, the total amount of plasma proteins at the close of the experiment is less than that at the start. Part of the injected acacia, then, presumably is taking the place of the removed plasma protein in holding water, and only the remainder can be employed in holding an excess of water above normal blood volume. Quantitative determinations of acacia in the blood would be necessary in order to ascertain just how much acacia is available for maintaining an increased blood volume. Any fraction of the persisting increase in intravascular osmotic tension which might be due to the glucose could not play any part in maintaining the increase in blood volume, since glucose now exists in the tissue spaces in equal concentration, having passed out from the blood stream, and is exerting an equal attraction there. In fact, the blood sugar figures show that the excess of glucose has been entirely removed from the blood stream, and presumably from the tissue fluids, inside of 2 hours. The fate of the glucose will be discussed later.

TABLE 1

Data of series 1, normal dogs

DOG	SAMPLE	TIME	BLOOD VOLUME	PLASMA CHLOR.	SUGAR	N. P. N.	PROTEIN N: Remaining	PROTEIN N: Withdrawn	PROTEIN N: Total	PROTEIN N: Per 100 cc. plasma	URINE: Amount	URINE: Sugar	URINE: Sugar
		hours	*per cent*	*grams per 100 cc.*	*grams per 100 cc.*	*mgms. per 100 cc.*	*grams*	*grams*	*grams*	*grams*	*grams*	*per cent*	*grams*
1	1		100	0.631									
	2	0	118	0.607									
	3	1 5′	112	0.619									
	4	3 15′	105	0.628									
	5	5 25′	106	0.629									
2	1		100	0.612	0.196	32							
	2	0	111	0.581	0.341	31							
	3	2	108	0.602	0.200	31							
	4	4	105	0.608	0.125	32							
	5	6 30′	103	0.610	0.127	31							
3	1		100	0.605	0.192	26	5.05		5.05	0.805			
	2	0	116	0.562	0.247	27	5.41	0.06	5.47	0.685			
	3	2	115	0.582	0.219	26	5.35	0.12	5.46	0.685			
	4	4 10′	113	0.589	0.127	25	5.21	0.18	5.39	0.685			
	5	6 15′	112	0.600	0.133	26	5.06	0.24	5.30	0.675			
4	1		100	0.595	0.282	32	4.53		4.53	0.837			
	2	0	114	0.537	0.564	33	4.11	0.06	4.17	0.622			
	3	2 20′	109	0.558	0.182	32	4.21	0.12	4.33	0.680			
	4	4 30′	105	0.572	0.182	33	4.31	0.18	4.49	0.742			
	5	7 25′	102	0.586	0.170	33	4.40	0.24	4.64	0.794			
5	1		100	0.579	0.232	25	3.94		3.94	0.720			
	2	0	116	0.533	0.381	25	no det.	0.06					
	3	2 5′	113	0.554	0.178	26	3.79	0.12	3.91	0.572	6	4.8	0.29
	4	4 15′	109	0.570	0.167	25	3.89	0.18	4.07	0.623	8	6.0	0.48
	5	6 40′	102	0.574	0.172	26	3.50	0.24	3.74‡	0.624	35	3.2	1.12
Total											49		1.89

6	1		100	0.635	0.222	33	6.46		6.46	0.852			
	2	0	113	0.601	0.500	32	6.08	0.07	6.15	0.660			
	3	2	112	0.618	0.217	33	6.09	0.14	6.25	0.674			
	4	4 25′	106	0.632	0.215	33	6.10	0.21	6.31	0.727			
	5	7 40′	101	0.635	0.204	32	5.96	0.28	6.24	0.772	245		5.6
	Total										245	2.3	5.6
7	1		100	0.582	0.308	31	4.35		4.35	0.833			
	2	0	111	0.560	0.541	30	4.54	0.07	4.61	0.744			
	3	2 10′	106	0.568	0.342	31	4.42	0.14	4.56	0.760			
	4	4 20′	102	0.574	0.250	31	4.16	0.21	4.37	0.774			
	5	7	98	0.579	0.185	30	4.06	0.28	4.34	0.800	20	2.3	0.46
	Total										20		0.46
8*	1		100	0.642	0.400	28	10.01		10.01	1.14	21	1.7	0.35
	2	0	99	0.610	0.606	27	8.72	1.555	10.27	1.03	108	7.1	7.7
	3	2	95	0.630	0.286	28	8.55	1.64	10.19	1.062	80	6.4	5.1
	4	4 10′	89	0.636	0.234	27	7.88	1.73	9.61	1.091	28	4.3	0.55
	5	6 20′	86	0.640	0.220	27	7.54	1.82	9.36	1.115	55	1.0	0.55
	Total after injection										271		14.55
9†	1		100		0.133						200		0
	2	0	106		0.292						10		f. t.
	3	2	97		0.163						14		0.17
	4	4	94		0.133						20		tr.
	5	6 10′	93		0.135						42		0
	Total after injection										86		0.17+

* Dog 8 bled 220 cc. at 1st sample.
† Dog 9 bled 160 cc. at 1st sample.
‡ Evidently some mistake in last determination.

The rather wide variations in the rate of the falling off from the initial increase in blood volume possibly are to be attributed to variations in vasomotor accommodation and in the preexisting water content of the tissue spaces. Scott (23) finds the hemoglobin content increased immediately by a rise in blood pressure produced by various procedures, and lowered by a fall in pressure. He cites evidence indicating that the hemoglobin method gives an accurate picture of relative blood volume; and, as he says, "these results can only be explained by increased pressure forcing fluid out of the blood to the tissue spaces and the passage of fluid back from the tissue spaces to the blood when the pressure is lowered." He did not determine the nature of the interchanged fluid.

At the time of taking the first sample dog 8 was bled approximately 15 per cent of his calculated blood volume, 15 per cent having been about the average initial increase in blood volume following the injection. This was done in order to ascertain whether the interchange of liquids and solids between the blood and the tissues is modified when the plethora that is induced by the injection of a hypertonic solution is prevented by previous hemorrhage. Blood volume figures indicate that the liquid interchange is about as in unbled animals. The question of the departure of the behavior of the solids in this animal from the behavior of the interchanges of solids in animals without previous hemorrhage will be considered below. In the case of dog 9 the 15 per cent depletion of the blood is more than made up by the time of the termination of the injection (blood volume raised to 106 per cent of normal); this volume falls in 2 hours to 97 per cent, then very slowly to reach 93 per cent at the end of 7 hours. The gum acacia is in all probability filling the place of the removed plasma proteins in holding water.

2. Blood composition. The main point of interest is, What is the nature of the fluid drawn into the blood stream and how does its composition change subsequently? A satisfactory answer to these questions should serve to elucidate the processes determining the interchanges.

a. Protein. Any conclusion as to the passage of protein into or out of the blood stream must be based on calculations of the absolute amount of plasma protein in the entire blood stream. If, for instance, it should be found that the curve representing the percentage of plasma protein ran parallel to the curve representing the reciprocal of blood volume, this would not mean that the absolute protein content of the plasma was unchanged, since practically all of the fluid drawn into the blood stream enters the plasma and an increase of 15 per cent in blood volume would mean an increase of over 23 per cent in plasma volume. The method used here of calculating absolute amounts of plasma protein is essentially that used by Magnus (10), some changes in the method being introduced in order to allow for the hemoglobin withdrawn in the samples. It assumes that the blood is 9 per cent of the body weight (24), (25), (26), this figure being used instead of 7 per cent used by Magnus, that the blood is 64 per cent plasma by volume and that all the water drawn into the blood stream enters the plasma. While none of these three assumptions is strictly correct, the first and third are very nearly so and variations in the second will not involve gross errors since the calculations for the additional samples of any one animal are based upon the plasma volume figure obtained in the calculation of the standard blood of that animal. A sample calculation may be given for purposes of illustration.

Sample calculation. Dog 7. Body weight, 9.1 kilos

HEMOGLOBIN				TOTAL NITROGEN*	
Sample number	Reading	Volume per cent uncorrected	Volume per cent corrected	Sample number	Grams N per 100 cc.
1	20.0	100	100	1	0.83
2	22.6	113	111	2	0.74
3	22.0	110	107	3	0.76
4	21.4	107	102	4	0.77
5	21.0	105	98	5	0.80

* The terms "N" or "Total N" refer to protein N, i.e., the non-protein N has been subtracted from the Kjeldahl figure.

Method of correcting blood volume for hemoglobin withdrawn. For each sample 13 cc. of blood are removed. This is 1.6 per cent of the blood volume of this animal, or 1.6 per cent of 819, which is 0.09 × 9100. Since, after the first sample, only 98.4 per cent of the original amount of hemoglobin remains in the blood stream the increase in volume of the blood is only 98.4 per cent of that indicated by the blood's dilution as shown by the hemoglobin readings in the colorimeter. To illustrate, assume that 5 per cent of blood and therefore of hemoglobin is withdrawn from a normal dog, assume that the normal or standard sample reads 20 in the colorimeter, as in our case, and assume further that a second sample drawn subsequent to the withdrawal of 5 per cent blood volume reads 21 in the colorimeter. If we failed to consider the previous loss of the 5 per cent hemoglobin we would infer from this reading that the blood volume had increased 5 per cent, was now 105 per cent of the normal. What has actually happened, however, is that the blood volume has been replaced just to its original state, the diluent being of course hemoglobin-free, so that each unit volume of blood now contains only 95 per cent of its normal amount of hemoglobin. To find the true blood volume we should take 95 per cent of 105 or 100 per cent, in round numbers. To find the true blood volume in any case, therefore, we should multiply the apparent blood volume by the percentage figure of hemoglobin remaining in the blood stream at the time of drawing the sample.

Upon the basis of this treatment of the data we find that in dog 7 the blood volume at the time of drawing the last sample is actually slightly decreased rather than increased, as the hemoglobin readings would seem to indicate, i.e., the decrease in the percentage of hemoglobin in the last sample is not great enough to account for all the hemoglobin removed. We must assume, therefore, that the blood volume has fallen slightly. The decrease, however, is not as great as the volume lost by hemorrhage. This means that some of the fluid drawn in has stayed in but not quite enough to equal the amount lost by hemorrhage. In all the other normal animals the final blood volume even after correction for the withdrawal of blood was slightly above the initial or normal volume.

Using the corrected blood volume figures we may proceed with the *method of calculating total plasma nitrogen*. It may be noted here that the figures for blood volume per cent given in all the tables have been corrected for the amount of blood lost according to the method outlined above.

$0.09 \times 9100 = 819$ cc., blood volume at beginning, blood 1.

$0.64 \times 819 = 524$ cc., plasma 1.

$0.83 \times 5.24 = 4.35$ grams N in plasma 1.

Blood 2 is 111 per cent of blood 1, by volume. The 111 per cent increase has been in the plasma. $0.11 \times 819 = 90$ cc. increase.

Plasma 1 = 524 cc. $524 + 90 = 614$ cc., plasma 2.

$0.74 \times 6.14 = 4.54$ grams N in plasma 2.

Blood 3 is 107 per cent of blood 1. The 7 per cent increase has been in the plasma. $0.07 \times 819 = 57$ cc. $524 + 57 = 581$ cc., plasma 3.

$0.76 \times 5.81 = 4.42$ grams N in plasma 3.

By the same method we get $0.77 \times 5.40 = 4.16$ grams N in plasma 4.

$0.80 \times 5.08 = 4.06$ grams N in plasma 5.

These figures indicate that by the time sample 5 was drawn protein had passed out of the blood stream, i.e., less protein is in the plasma than was there at the beginning. If, however, we add to each plasma N figure the amount of plasma N taken out in that sample and in preceding samples we get the following figures: The amount of N withdrawn with each sample is $0.64 \times 13 \times 0.008 = 0.07$ gm. N, 0.008 being taken as the average amount of N per cc. plasma in this animal. Variations in different samples are not significant in calculations on 13 cc. The effect is of course cumulative; 0.14 gm. will have been removed by the time the third sample is drawn, 0.21 gm. by the time of the fourth, etc.

SAMPLE NUMBER	PROTEIN N		
	N remaining	N withdrawn	Total protein N
	grams	*gram*	*grams*
1	4.35	0.0	4.35
2	4.54	0.07	4.61
3	4.42	0.14	4.56
4	4.16	0.21	4.37
5	4.06	0.28	4.34

These figures show that there is at first a slight increase in the amount of plasma protein but that by the time of the fifth sample this has disappeared, and that the final total plasma protein N is the same as the original figure if the amount withdrawn is added. Different animals show some variations from this behavior.

The figures obtained on the dogs without hemorrhage are not constant. All show that there is a marked decrease in the concentration of plasma protein accompanying the increased blood volume; but two cases, dogs 3 and 7, show that this decrease is not quite so great as the increase in plasma volume, i.e., a slight amount of protein enters the blood stream; while two others, dogs 4 and 6, indicate that a slight amount of protein passes out of the blood. Of these cases, however, the figures for dog 7 are the most reliable, since they were obtained by Kjeldahl determinations, using 2 cc. of plasma, while the others were obtained by indirect Nesslerization, working with 0.05 cc. of plasma. While the figures are not convincing, it appears that there is a slight increase in the absolute amount of plasma protein immediately after the injections. If the amounts of protein withdrawn in taking the samples are added to the amounts remaining we find a greater, though still quite slight, increase and that the amount of plasma protein tends to become constant in most cases at a level slightly above or about the same as the original one.

Scott (27) showed that dilution of the blood *in vitro* with isotonic Ringer's solution causes protein to pass from the blood cells into the plasma. He uses this observation to account for the increase in total plasma protein following hemorrhage or the injection of isotonic Ringer's solution (28). By inferring that slight variations from the proper proportions of the salts in the fluid added to the blood greatly inhibit this transfer of protein, he accounts for the greater increase in plasma protein after hemorrhage.

In order to determine whether or not the increase in total plasma protein which we found could be due to a passage of protein from blood cells to plasma the following experiment was performed. From an 8 kilo dog 140 cc. of blood were drawn into a vessel containing the minimum amount, 0.12 gm. per 100 cc. blood, of potassium oxalate that would prevent clotting. This was stirred and 45 cc. samples immediately put into each of three cylinders. All three were stirred continuously while to one was added 2.5 cc. of the gum-glucose solution at a constant rate over 40 minutes, to the second 2.5 cc. of gum-glucose solution + 5 cc. Ringer's solution with the calcium omitted; the third was merely stirred and used as a control. The second of the above mentioned procedures may be assumed to approximate the conditions obtaining in the intravenous injection *in vivo* of 5 cc. of the gum-glucose solution per kilo body weight or per 90 cc. blood, the 5 cc. Ringer's per 45 cc. blood being the average increase in blood volume over the amount of fluid injected. After the addition of the solutions was completed hematocrit determinations were made on each sample and Kjeldahl nitrogen determinations made on each plasma.

SAMPLE	HEMATOCRIT			PLASMA IN 45 CC. BLOOD	PROTEIN IN PLASMA
	Total	Cells	Plasma		
				cc.	*gram*
1 (45 cc. blood)	10.7	4.2	6.5	27.4	0.259
2 (45 cc. blood + 2.5 cc. g.g.)	11.0	4.1	6.9	28.2	0.260
3 (45 cc. blood + 2.5 cc. g.g. + 5 cc. Ringer's)	11.4	3.6	7.8	30.8	0.257

The results collected in the accompanying table show that there was no exchange of protein between cells and plasma. It seems fair, therefore, to eliminate the blood cells as a source of the increased plasma protein in our *in vivo* experiments.

Kjeldahl determinations were also made on the gum-glucose used in order to determine if it might be a source of N. It was found that 2 cc. of the solution is equivalent to 0.6 cc. tenth normal HCl. Expressed in percentage of N our determination shows 0.168 per cent N in the gum acacia or 0.042 per cent N in the solution injected. Rideal (29) finds gum acacia to contain only 0.031 to 0.082 per cent N. Other observers have reported varying percentages of N, depending upon the source of the gum. The form in which the N exists has never been determined, so far as we have been able to learn. The amount of the solution used for a 10 kilo dog, 50 cc., would contain only 0.021 gm. N, according to our determinations. Corpuscles and injected solution may therefore be disregarded as a source of the increase in plasma N. Our results lead us to the conclusion, therefore, that the injection of the acacia-glucose solution leads in some way to the entrance of protein into the circulation.

The changes in the percentage concentration of plasma protein following the injection are also of interest in that they indicate roughly the changes in the colloidal osmotic tension of the blood. It is seen that the concentration falls markedly immediately after the injection, considerably more than can be accounted for by the blood's dilution due to the injected fluid alone. Let us assume that each 5 cc. of the injected solution contains 4.5 cc. of water. Since 4.5 cc. of water are injected per kilo body weight or per 90 cc. of blood or per 58 cc. of plasma, the plasma is diluted 7.8 per cent by the water injected. The plasma protein percentage, however, invariably falls more than this, averaging about 15 per cent, showing that not only the fluid injected but the fluid drawn in from the tissues dilutes the plasma in respect to its protein content. The plasma protein content in the subsequent hours rises toward normal but never reaches it, this state of affairs co-existing with a slight persisting increase in blood volume. The assumption seems justified that part of the colloidal osmotic tension of the plasma is being supplied by the injected gum acacia.

Magnus reports two experiments with intravenous injection of concentrated (35 per cent) NaCl solution. In one case he finds the total plasma proteins diminished by 7 per cent by this procedure, in the other case increased by 5 per cent. These were on previously unbled dogs and the results are comparable to our results on previously unbled dogs.

Dog 8, *which was bled 15 per cent of his blood volume* before the injection, shows a decrease in total plasma protein at the second sample. When, however, the amount of plasma protein withdrawn by hemorrhage is added to the total amount in the blood at the time the second sample was drawn we find a slight increase in the plasma protein—some protein has passed in.

b. Sugar. It is seen that the initial blood sugar values in the first 8 cases are very high, 0.192 to 0.308 gm. per 100 cc. This is due to the well known action of morphine as a respiratory depressant, the imperfect respiration causing a hyperglycemia. At the close of the injection the figure is still higher, 0.247 to 0.564 gm. per 100 cc., due to the injected glucose. Within 2 hours the figure has usually fallen to or below the initial value. The sugar figures on dog 9 are much the most valuable since here the disturbing effect of the morphine is not present. The initial figure is 0.133, the slight increase above normal probably being due to the ether; the figure immediately at the termination of the injection is 0.292; 2 hours later, 0.163; 2 hours later, 0.133; and the last sample, 2 hours after this, contains 0.135 gm. These figures show that the sugar rapidly passes out of the blood, and is almost back to normal in 2 hours. The fate of the sugar will be considered later.

Since the increased blood volume persists for several hours after the blood sugar has returned to normal it must be concluded that gum acacia remains in the circulation and holds water there. The great difficulty of digestion for nitrogen determinations of all the samples taken subsequent to the injection, even those which had regained a normal blood sugar value, indicates that there was an abnormally large amount of carbonaceous material in the blood and confirms the view that gum acacia remains in the blood for some time.

c. Plasma chlorides. The plasma chlorides were followed because it was felt that their behavior under the conditions of the experiment would be typical of that of the inorganic crystalloids in general. The percentage concentration of plasma chlorides always falls in the second sample, but not in any way to the same extent that the blood is diluted; in fact, the percentage fall in concentration is not even as great as the percentage of dilution of plasma accomplished by the injected fluid. It has been seen above that the plasma is diluted about 7.8 per cent by the injected fluid. The percentage fall of plasma chloride concentration is less than this, averaging about 6 per cent. In other words, the fluid drawn into the blood stream carries with it chlorides in concentration equal to that of plasma and in addition to this inward filtration of chlorides an inward diffusion has started to supply chlorides for the injected fluid. This diffusion continues for several hours, the percentage of plasma chlorides steadily rising and becoming normal in 6 to 8 hours.

d. Non-protein nitrogen. It will be noted that the plasma N.P.N. concentration remains constant with variations in plasma volume, indicating that the vessel walls are more permeable to urea than to NaCl. The constant concentration of N.P.N. means that not only does the fluid drawn in have a N.P.N. concentration equal to that of plasma but also that the diffusion into the blood stream of the N.P.N. necessary to make up the injected fluid to the concentration of N.P.N. existing in plasma is very rapid, being completed by the time of completion of the injection. Urea's greater solubility in lipoids, which are assumed to be present in cell walls, may account for this. An alternative view is that the urea does not diffuse into the blood stream but is secreted into the blood stream at the proper rate to maintain a constant concentration. Our methods and data do not afford us any means of deciding which of these processes actually occurs but the former seems the more probable.

e. Rather rough estimations of the *crystalloid osmotic tension* of the plasma samples, using the method of calculation mentioned above, show that while there may be some attempt on the part of the organism to keep this tension constant, the compensatory mechanism, if such exists, is not adequate to keep pace with the factors tending to vary the osmotic tension.

3. Urine. When morphine had been given sugar always appeared in the urine in rather high percentage, 5 to 6 per cent. In two cases, dogs 6 and 8, a marked diuresis resulted; in two others, dogs 5 and 7, urinary secretion was practically normal in volume. Dog 9, which had no morphine, showed only a trace of sugar and his volume excretion was normal or slightly increased. As to the fate of the injected glucose, it is evident that it does not stay in the blood and that only a small fraction is excreted in the urine, in fact only a trace when morphine is omitted. It will be noted that the injection is so timed that the anesthetized animals receive glucose at the rate of 0.9 gm. per kilo per hour, the unanesthetized dog's tolerance rate (11). No study of the tissue fluids or glycogen depots was made but we may conclude with Brasol that the remainder is "perhaps changed to glycogen, lactic acid or undergoes some other chemical metamorphosis." The observation of Fisher and Wishart (9) that the metabolism is increased 20 per cent accounts for a part of it.

It is evident, confirming the finding of Meek and Gasser (22), that the gum acacia injected with the glucose does not diminish urinary secretion, as is maintained by Kruse (30); in fact in the cases where hyperglycemia was extreme, with blood sugar values around 0.500 gm. per 100 cc., glycosuria occurred with an accompanying diuresis. Two cases with hyperglycemia and glycosuria, dogs 5 and 7, while not exhibiting a diuresis, certainly did not show a suppression of urine. The urine was not followed in the first four cases. In the case of dog 9, where morphine was omitted with the result that hyperglycemia was not so marked and no significant glycosuria occurred, excretion rate of water was normal or slightly increased. Knowlton (31) finds that colloids exerting osmotic pressure, such as gum acacia, inhibit NaCl diuresis but have but little effect on Na_2SO_4 diuresis. Glucose diuresis belongs to the same class as that of NaCl, i.e., it is presumably due to purely mechanical factors, such as hydremic plethora, rather than to a direct action on the kidney cells. We might explain, then, the normal excretion of urine following the injection of the gum-glucose solution, in the absence of morphine, as due to a balance arrived at between the inhibitory action of the acacia and the diuretic action of the glucose, the later gaining the upper hand when, due to morphine, a marked hyperglycemia is produced with a resultant glycosuria.

SERIES II. ASPHYXIATED DOGS

There is evidence that asphyxia increases the permeability of the vessel walls. Bolton (32) holds that permeability is increased by stagnation of blood with decreased O_2 supply, since edema of the neck is produced by ligature of the superior vena cava, despite the absence of any rise in pressure in the jugulars and presumably in the capillaries. Starling (33) also draws the conclusion that the edema under these conditions must be due to increased permeability of walls which allows protein to pass out into the tissues and hold water there.

The present experiments on asphyxiated animals were carried out with these statements in mind. Study of the data (table 2) shows that, owing probably to the asphyxia, the blood sugar figures are very high, 0.133 and 0.244 before and 0.800 and 0.770 immediately after the injection. In both cases the value 2 hours after the injection was below the initial value, the asphyxia having long since worn off. Except for this no significant departure from the behavior in normal animals occurs. The asphyxia introduces so many complicating circulatory factors, however, that we are not justified in concluding that the permeability of the vessel walls is unchanged, although we have no proof that it is. For example, protein might have been drawn in but promptly squeezed out again due to the asphyxial rise in blood pressure. It will be noted that even without morphine here the hyperglycemia is extreme and the glycosuria marked but that the blood sugar rapidly falls to or below the normal. The apparent continuance of the glycosuria after the blood sugar has fallen to normal is probably due to the fact that the bladder was not completely emptied at each catheterization, urine containing sugar which had really been excreted during the period of hyperglycemia being obtained at each sample.

TABLE 2

Data of series 2, asphyxiated dogs

DOG	SAMPLE	TIME	BLOOD VOLUME	PLASMA CHLOR.	SUGAR	N. P. N.	PROTEIN N				URINE		
							Remaining	Withdrawn	Total	Per 100 cc. plasma	Amount	Sugar	Sugar
		hours	*per cent*	*grams per 100 cc.*	*grams per 100 cc.*	*mgms. per 100 cc.*	*grams*	*grams*	*grams*	*grams*	*cc.*	*per cent*	*grams*
10	1		100	0.635	0.133	25	5.25		5.25	0.980	20	0	0
	2	0	111	0.585	0.800	25	5.55	0.08	5.63	0.881	14	6.4	0.9
	3	2	108	0.625	0.118	26	5.57	0.16	5.73	0.920	40	5.8	2.3
	4	4 35′	105	0.620	0.111	25	5.27	0.24	5.51	0.914	6	5.2	0.3
	5	8	102	0.630	0.182	25	5.15	0.32	5.47	0.930	75	3.4	2.6
Total after injection											135		6.1
11	1		100	0.650	0.244	28	4.77		4.77	0.902	160	0	0
	2	0	116	0.592	0.770	29	4.95	0.07	5.02	0.742	18	+	
	3	2 5′	114	0.640	0.171	28	4.94	0.14	5.08	0.761	12	+	
	4	4 25′	110	0.636	0.167	29	4.74	0.21	4.95	0.770	20	+	
	5	6 45′	102	0.642	0.164	28	4.76	0.28	5.04	0.870	135	+	
Total after injection											185		10.1

TABLE 3

Data of series 3, shocked dogs

DOG	SAMPLE	TIME	BLOOD VOLUME	PLASMA CHLOR.	SUGAR	TOTAL N				URINE		
						Remaining	Withdrawn	Total	Per 100 cc. plasma	Amount	Sugar	Sugar
		hours	*per cent*	*grams per 100 cc.*	*grams per 100 cc.*	*grams*	*grams*	*grams*	*grams*	*cc.*	*per cent*	*grams*
12	1		100	0.632		8.30		8.30	1.004			
	2		88	0.642		6.67	0.08	6.75	0.993			
	3		127	0.592		7.54	0.16	7.70	0.770			
13	1		100	0.629	0.154	10.15		10.15	0.976			
	2		84	0.633	0.145	7.64	0.08	7.72	0.980	24	0	0
	3		129	0.550	0.404	8.32	0.16	8.48	0.707	18	0	0
	4	1 52′	124	0.580	0.154	9.16	0.24	9.40	0.826	26	0	0
Total										68		
15	1		100	0.635	0.200	5.74		5.74	0.818	140	0	0
	2		84	0.645	0.220	4.16	0.06	4.22	0.791			
	3		117	0.594	0.444	4.45	0.12	4.57	0.651	10	3.0	0.3
	4	2 10′	114	0.610	0.274	4.40	0.18	4.58	0.672	34	4.2	1.4
	5	4 35′	111	0.640	0.172	4.30	0.24	4.54	0.686	2	4.0	0.08
	6	6 45″	107	0.644	0.141	4.27	0.30	4.57	0.723	0		0
Total after injection										46		1.8

SERIES III. SHOCKED DOGS

Dog 12. Body weight, 14.36 kgm. No morphine. Specimens from pancreas, liver, spleen, large and small intestine and kidney for histological study. B. P. at 9:55 is 160 mm. First sample at 10:10, B. P. then 150. Cava clamped at 10:25, B. P. immediately fell to 40 mm. 11:30, B. P. 40, pulse 120, very little ether required. 12:40, B. P. 40, clamp removed, B. P. rose slowly, reached 50 in 3 minutes, 55 in 6 minutes. Second sample, at 12:52, B. P. fell sharply to 38; injection started at 12:57. B. P. soon fell to 34, respirations of expiratory type, heart very irregular. As injection proceeded respiration and heart action improved, B. P. climbed to 40 in 15 minutes. 1:25, B. P. 60. 1:30, animal tried to vomit, intestines extruded from wound, B. P. fell to 40, rose again to 54 in 5 minutes. 1:50, B. P. 60. 1:55, B. P. 65. 1:57, injection ended. 2:03, 3rd sample. Animal tried to vomit during taking of sample 3, B. P. fell to 42. 2:10, B. P. 34. 2:13, animal died. It will be noted that in this severe grade of shock the loss of 13 cc. of blood almost killed the dog (sample 2) and an additional loss of 13 cc. did produce death (sample 3).

Dog 13. Body weight, 18.05 kgm. 1:00 p.m., B. P. 125. 1:20, B. P. 128, 1st sample drawn. 1:25, cava clamped, B. P. fell to 40 and was maintained there. 1:30, ether discontinued. 3:30, clamp removed, B. P. rose to 60 in 2 minutes, amplitude of fluctuations very great. In 4 minutes B. P. averaged 80. 4:00, 2nd sample, B. P. 100, not affected by drawing 13 cc. blood. Injection started at 4:08, 4:20, B. P. 110. 4:30, B. P. 115, ether required. 4:40, B. P. 120. 4:43, B. P. 125. 5:03, 130. 5:08, injection ended. 5:12, 3rd sample, 5:15, B. P. 110, ether almost continuously since 4:30. 5:50, B. P. 90. 6:00, B. P. 80, 6:10, B. P. 64, pulse regular, ether discontinued. 6:25, B. P. 58. 6:40, B. P. 50. 6:55, B. P. 40. 6:57, B. P. 30. 6:59, 4th sample, animal died immediately. This case illustrates well the type of shock in which the blood pressure is well maintained for some time, masking the true severity of the shock; eventually comes the rather sudden terminal circulatory and respiratory collapse.

Dog 15. Body weight, 12.2 kgm. 10:10, 1st sample. 10:20, B. P. 140. 10:25, cava clamped, B. P. fell to 40 and was maintained there. 12:25, clamp removed. B. P. rose to 100 on removing clamp. 12:30, 2nd sample, B. P. 110. 12:35, injection started, B. P. 110. 12:50, B. P. 130. 1:25, B. P. 125. 1:35, injection ended. 1:37, 3rd sample, B. P. not affected by drawing sample. 2:30, B. P. 110. 3:35, B. P. 100. 3:45, 4th sample, B. P. 90. 6:10, 5th sample, B. P. immediately before sample = 80, immediately after = 65. 6:25, B. P. 60. 6:40, B. P. 55. 7:15, B. P. 45. 8:20, 6th sample, B. P. 35 immediately before, dropped to 30 immediately after, death in few minutes.

It is now believed practically universally that in traumatic shock blood plasma leaves the circulation. Inasmuch as the concentration of the proteins of the plasma remaining in the vessels is not appreciably changed it must be assumed that in shock the permeability of the vessel walls is increased. The present series of experiments was planned in order to ascertain whether the fluids drawn into the blood stream by the hypertonic solution in fatally shocked animals would carry along with them more protein than this procedure brings in when applied to normal animals. Four animals were used, but one died in shock before the injection was completed. The results from the other three are given (table 3). Non-protein nitrogen was not followed in these cases as blood was so valuable and it was felt that this determination could best be omitted. The only respects in which the results of this series differ from those of the normal series are in blood volume and protein content.

1. Blood volume. In accordance with the results of numerous previous observers we find the blood volume greatly diminished in shock. In this series the second or "shocked" sample was taken as the standard for subsequent determinations of hemoglobin and blood volume. As a result of the injection of the gum-glucose solution the blood volume is markedly increased above its shock level, the increase even bringing the blood volume above its initial normal level in all three cases. The volume then gradually falls off until (in the one case which could be followed for several hours, dog 15) at the end of 7 hours after the injection it reaches approximately its initial normal level. This was shortly before the animal died.

2. Plasma protein. The method of calculating the absolute amounts of plasma protein may be illustrated here. The case of dog 12 may be taken.

Body weight 14,360 grams

HEMOGLOBIN*				TOTAL NITROGEN†	
Sample	Reading	Volume per cent uncorrected	Volume per cent corrected	Sample	N per 100 cc. plasma
					grams
1	20.0	100	100	1	1.004
2	17.8	89	88	2	0.993
3	25.6	128	127	3	0.77

* Sample 1 is taken as the standard for reading sample 2, sample 2 as the standard for reading sample 3 and any subsequent samples that may be obtained.

† Since N.P.N. was not followed in shocked animals the figures given here as "total N" are the actual Kjeldahl figures. Practically no change in the relations of the figures is produced by the subtraction of the small constant N.P.N. figure from each total N figure, as was done in the first two series.

Calculation. 0.09 × 14,360 = 1292 cc., blood 1.
0.64 × 1292 = 827 cc., plasma 1.
1.004 × 8.27 = 8.30 gm. N. in plasma 1.
Blood 2 has 88 per cent volume of blood 1, i.e. 12 per cent less.

Assume this has all been taken from the plasma. This probably is not correct because of accumulation of corpuscles in the periphery. This peripheral aggregation of corpuscles, however, would, as is mentioned below, make the calculated exchange of protein even greater if it could be quantitatively considered.

12 per cent of 1292 = 155. 827 − 155 = 672 cc., plasma 2.

6.72 × 0.993 = 6.67 gm. N in plasma 2.

Volume of blood 2 is 88 per cent of blood 1, i.e., 1137 cc.

Volume of blood 3 is 127 per cent that of blood 2.

The extra 27 per cent of 1137 or 307 cc. has entered the plasma.

Plasma 2 = 672 cc. 672 + 307 = 979 cc., plasma 3.

9.79 × 0.77 = 7.54 gm. N in plasma 3. Summarizing in the form of a table we have:

SAMPLE NUMBER	PLASMA N REMAINING	PLASMA N WITHDRAWN	TOTAL PLASMA N
	grams	*gram*	*grams*
1	8.30		8.30
2	6.67	0.08	6.75
3	7.54	0.16	7.70

We find that the absolute amount of plasma protein is greatly diminished in shock, its concentration remaining practically constant or being very slightly diminished. This is in agreement with the refractometric findings of Gasser, Erlanger and Meek (34). With the increase in blood volume determined by the injection the absolute amount of protein rises markedly above its shock level but does not reach the normal level. The concentration falls considerably but not to the same degree as plasma volume is increased. In other words, the fluid drawn in is not so rich in protein as is plasma but neither is it protein-free. Due to the method of following the blood volume these figures probably do not indicate the real magnitude of the changes in total protein. As is well known, the slowed circulation of shock causes red blood cells to accumulate in the capillary area so that the number in the arterial blood, in which the hemoglobin was followed, is relatively small and the estimated blood volume therefore high. And it is to be presumed that the improved circulation following the injection of the gum-glucose solution will return some of the jammed corpuscles to the circulation, causing the blood volume estimation to be too low.

Following the blood changes after the injection, it is found that protein continues to increase even while water is passing back out, the protein concentration rising faster than the plasma volume falls. What may happen is that when the injection is given the fluid drawn in brings with it protein through the abnormally permeable walls, but in lower concentration than it occurs in plasma. Then, as the blood pressure rises, the circulation improves and lymph flow is reëstablished. The lymph flow from the liver and intestines is probably accelerated to a far greater degree than that from the extremities, for two reasons: *a*, In these animals the circulation of both posterior extremities was practically done away with since both femoral arteries and veins were ligated. *b*, Since the capillaries of the liver and intestines are the most permeable it is probable that most of the protein that disappeared from the plasma in the process of the development of shock passed out into the tissue fluids of the liver and intestines. As the circulation to these organs is now improved the normal lymph flow is reëstablished and this lymph flow sweeps along with it back into the blood stream through the thoracic duct the plasma protein which had accumulated in the tissue spaces of the liver and intestines during the induction of shock. Thus protein is entering the blood stream even while blood volume is falling. Such an interpretation of the results accounts for the rapid initial increase in blood volume with an increase in absolute amount, although a decreased percentage, of plasma protein, for the subsequent falling off in volume and for the concomitant continued increase in the absolute amount of protein. The prospect of technical difficulties in collecting lymph over a long period of time has kept us from making direct observations on this latter point.

In the shocked animals, as in the normal and asphyxiated, the final sample shows a percentage concentration of plasma protein lower than that of the initial sample and at the same time the blood volume at the time of the final sample is greater than initially; or, as in the case of dog 15, who was followed for 8 hours, when the blood volume has in time fallen to slightly below its initial normal level, the percentage concentration of plasma protein has fallen to a considerably greater extent. This must mean that here too gum acacia is taking the place of plasma protein in holding water in the circulation.

Starling (35) says "Absorption by the blood vessels as a result, say of artificial hemorrhage, if determined entirely by the osmotic attraction of the plasma colloids for the extravascular fluids, can only bring about a passage of water and salts into the blood vessels. . . . . According to my explanation this (absorbed) fluid should be pure salt solution. That it is more dilute than plasma is clearly shown by experiments but our data do not yet suffice to determine whether the incoming fluid is a weak solution of protein, such as that contained in the tissue spaces, or is a pure salt solution. If it is proved by quantitative results to contain protein, then some other factor, such as back filtration or active absorption by the endothelial cells of the blood vessels, must be involved in addition to the colloid constituents of the circulating blood." The present data point strongly to the conclusion that some protein does pass in directly in the case of shock although it might not be impossible to explain all of our data on the assumption that the protein is carried back into the blood stream by the lymph. The rapidity with which it occurs, however, speaks against this.

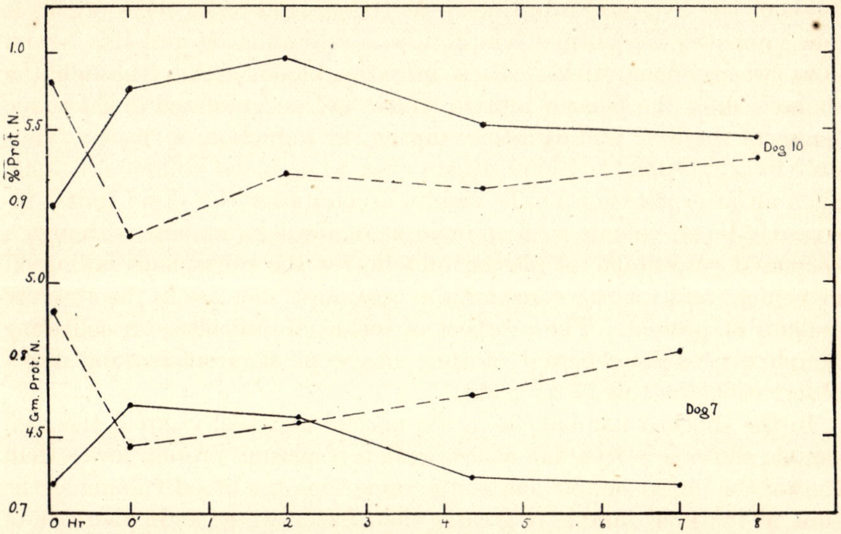

Fig. 1. Changes in total amount (solid line) and per cent (broken line) of plasma protein N in a normal animal, dog 7, and in an asphyxiated animal, dog 10. Time of taking 1st sample is indicated by *0*, the end of the injection by *0'*.

3. Urine. The urine in the case of dog 13, a shocked animal, contains no sugar in spite of the hyperglycemia which far exceeds the normal overflow threshold. This dog was in rather severe shock and the absence of glycosuria is probably due to the fact that no urine was secreted after shock developed. The fact that additional samples of urine could be drawn probably means that the bladder had not been completely emptied of its pre-shock urine. Dog 15 was in better condition and excreted urine containing sugar.

4. Non-toxicity of the acacia-glucose solution. It was our intention in these experiments to produce a grade of shock that would prove fatal in a few hours and in this we succeeded. Some of the animals were almost moribund when the solution was administered. In no case

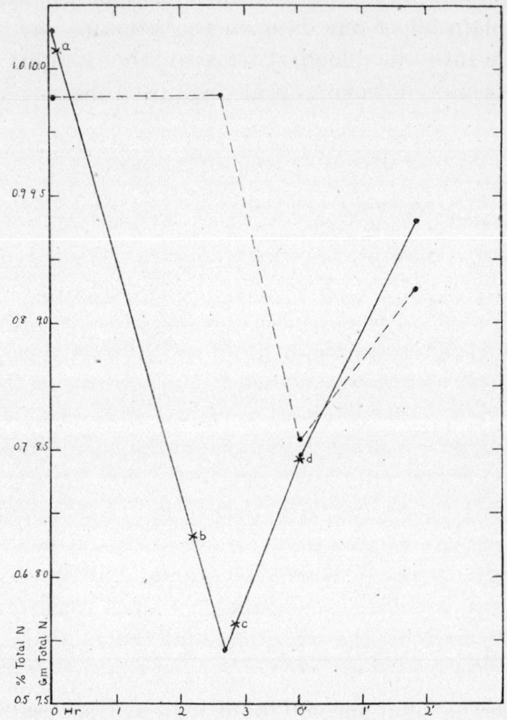

Fig. 2. Changes in total amount (solid line) and per cent (broken line) of plasma total N in a shocked animal, dog 13. Letters designate times of procedures, as follows: *a*—cava clamped; *b*—clamp removed; *c*—injection started; *d*—injection ended. Time of taking 1st sample is designated by *0*, while *1*, *2*, etc., designate hours after taking 1st sample up until end of injection. The end of the injection, when the 3rd sample is taken, is designated by *0'*, while *1'*, *2'*, etc., designate hours after end of injection.

were any untoward effects observed as a result of the injection; the blood pressure, heart action and respiration always were benefited. The rectal temperature was practically unchanged. In one case a slight albuminuria was observed in one sample, but microscopic examination revealed large numbers of spermatozoa. The albuminuria had disappeared in the next sample. Casts, hematuria or hemaglobinuria were never observed. No hemolysis occurred as a result of the injections, some slight laking being present in several plasma samples but it was no more evident in samples taken after the injection than in those taken before. This laking is attributed to the ether. These findings in regard to the non-toxicity of gum acacia are in accord with those of Bayliss (36), who discusses the rather misleading statements of Kruse (30) as to the toxic effects observed after the injection of acacia.

SUMMARY AND CONCLUSIONS

A strongly hypertonic glucose and gum acacia solution was injected intravenously into normal, asphyxiated and shocked dogs, and the resultant changes in blood volume and composition were studied.

The immediate effect was a marked increase in blood volume; in normal and asphyxiated animals the blood volume then gradually fell toward but did not completely return to normal in several hours.

The blood volume, markedly diminished in shock, is increased to above its normal level by the injection and then gradually falls to or below its normal level.

The absolute plasma protein is increased slightly or not at all in normal animals and in asphyxiated animals; in an animal which had been bled there was a slight increase when the amount withdrawn was allowed for. The absolute amount of plasma protein is markedly diminished in shock, is increased by the injection and the increase continues for some time after the injection. It is believed that at least a part of the increase in plasma protein following the injection in shock is due to a passage of protein in through the vessel walls.

Gum acacia seems to take the place of plasma protein in holding water in the circulation.

There is a marked hyperglycemia immediately after the injection in normal animals; this is accentuated by morphine and asphyxia. The blood sugar value falls to or nearly to normal within 2 hours. In shocked animals the blood sugar behaves much as in normal animals. There is only a trace of sugar excreted by normal animals excepting when morphine or asphyxia cause marked glycosuria. Shocked animals without morphine excrete some sugar unless, as a result of the shock, there is a suppression of urine.

The fluid drawn into the blood stream brings with it chlorides in concentration equal to the chloride concentration of plasma but the diffusion into the blood stream of sufficient additional chlorides to bring the chloride concentration of injected fluid up to that of plasma is not complete for several hours.

The entrance of urea into the plasma takes place with such facility that the non-protein nitrogen concentration of the plasma remains constant.

There is no suppression of urine in normal animals as a result of the injection, if anything the rate of secretion is slightly increased.

The crystalloid osmotic tension of the plasma does not remain constant.

No hemolysis, hematuria, hemoglobinuria, albuminuria, cylindruria, fluctuations in body temperature or any other untoward effects were observed as a result of the injections.

The authors wish to thank Dr. W. H. Olmsted, of the Department of Internal Medicine, for his kindness in extending the facilities of his laboratory for carrying out many of the determinations and for several valuable suggestions on points of analytical technique.

BIBLIOGRAPHY

(1) Erlanger and Gasser: Ann. Surg., lxix, 389.
(2) Brasol: Arch. f. Physiol., 1884, 211.
(3) Klickowicz: Arch. f. Anat. u. Physiol., 1886.
(4) Leathes: Journ. Physiol., 1896, xix, 1.
(5) Gasser and Erlanger: This Journal, 1919, l, 104.
(6) Starling: Journ. Physiol., 1899, xxiv, 317.
(7) Paton: Journ. Physiol., 1899, xxiv, 419.
(8) Hamburger: Osmotischer Druck u. Ionenlehre, B. II, 7.
(9) Fisher and Wishart: Journ. Biol. Chem., 1912, xiii, 49.
(10) Magnus: Arch. f. Exper. Path. u. Pharm., xliv, 68.
(11) Woodyatt, Sansum and Wilder: Journ. Amer. Med. Assoc., 1915, lxv, 2067.
Wilder and Sansum: Arch. Int. Med., 1917, xix, 311.
Sansum and Woodyatt: Journ. Biol. Chem., 1917, xxx, 155.
(12) Erlanger and Woodyatt: Journ. Amer. Med. Assoc., 1917, lxix, 1410.
(13) Morawitz: Oppenheimer's Handb. d. Biochem., II, 2, 78.
(14) Kerr, Hurwitz and Whipple: This Journal, 1918, xlvii, 356.
(15) Erlanger and Gasser: This Journal, 1919, l, 119.
(16) Scott: This Journal, 1916, xl, 128.
(17) Van Slyke and Donleavy: Journ. Biol. Chem., 1919, xxxvii, 551.
(18) Folin and Wu: Journ. Biol. Chem., 1919, xxxviii, 81.
(19) Marriott: Journ. Amer. Med. Assoc., 1916, lxvi, 1594.

(20) Janeway and Jackson: Soc. Exper. Biol. Med., xii, 193.
(21) Erlanger and Gasser: This Journal, 1919, xlix, 151.
(22) Meek and Gasser: This Journal, 1918, xlv, 548.
(23) Scott: This Journal, 1917, xliv, 298.
(24) Meek and Gasser: This Journal, 1918, xlvii, 302.
(25) Dawson, Evans and Whipple: This Journal, 1920, li, 232.
(26) McQuarrie and Davis: This Journal, 1920, li, 257.
(27) Scott: Journ. Physiol., 1915–16, l, 128.
(28) Scott: Journ. Physiol., 1915–16, l, 157.
(29) Rideal: Pharm. Journ., 1892, 1073.
(30) Kruse: This Journal, 1919, xlix, 137.
(31) Knowlton: Journ. Physiol., 1911–12, xliii, 219.
(32) Bolton: Proc. Roy. Soc., lxxix, 267.
(33) Starling: Fluids of the body, 164.
(34) Gasser, Erlanger and Meek: This Journal, 1919, l, 31.
(35) Starling: Fluids of the body, 102.
(36) Bayliss: Journ. Pharm. Exper. Therap., 1920, xv, 29.

THE FUNCTIONAL ACTIVITY OF THE CAPILLARIES AND VENULES

D. R. HOOKER

From the Physiological Laboratory of the Johns Hopkins University

Received for publication July 10, 1920

INTRODUCTION

The significance of the blood stream in the capillary bed for the nutritive processes of the body is well recognized. But it is only in recent times that emphasis has been laid on the capillaries as a factor in the dynamics of the circulation. It is the purpose of this paper to present evidence in support of the belief that the capillaries and venules, as well as the arterioles, respond to direct chemical stimulation and also to indirect stimulation through the intervention of nerve fibers. If this proof is established, the functional activity of the capillary and venous beds must henceforth increase in both theoretical and practical importance. In the first place local tissue needs may by direct chemical action control the capillary blood streaming through the part as shown so clearly by Krogh (1) for muscle. In the second place, the capillaries and venous fields being under the influence of the central nervous system, it follows that local vascular reflexes (2) and systemic vascular reflexes undoubtedly depend upon the coöperation of the capillary and venule with the arteriole; that, in other words, the peripheral resistance, both functional and static, includes arteriole, capillary and venule. And in the third place the effective blood volume, both fluid and corpuscular, must be subject to alteration and regulation to a very significant degree.

Most of the work on the function of the capillaries hitherto reported, except the recent paper by Krogh just mentioned, has been done on the frog in which the transparency of the tissues permits microscopic visualization of these vessels. It is possible, however, using Lombard's method of a drop of oil on the skin (3) to extend such studies to the mammal. Furthermore, most of the recent evidence in the mammal bears upon dilatation of capillaries. It may be assumed that a vessel which is shown to dilate must also contract, but the direct evidence has hitherto been lacking. Nor is there much evidence that the blood capillary and the venule are under nervous control.

HISTORICAL

The first evidence that capillaries have the power independently to change their caliber was published in 1858. In that year Lister (4), describing the early stages of inflammation, pictured with camera lucida drawings a very great increase in the caliber of the capillaries in inflamed tissue. This observation was followed by the studies of Stricker published some seven years later (5). Stricker observed the capillaries in the nictitating membrane of the frog to dilate and to constrict. The constriction was less evident than the dilatation and appeared to be due to two processes, one a nuclear swelling and the other an actual contraction of the endothelial protoplasm. These results were obtained in tissue removed from the body and therefore deprived of its blood supply, and Stricker himself is not convinced that they are not due to lethal changes in the tissue. This possibility is supported by figure 4 in his paper, which pictures a change in shape of a capillary vessel which must be extremely unusual if compatible with functional activity. In a second paper published the following year Stricker (6) describes further experiments with the nictitating membrane of the frog removed from the body and examined in the aqueous humor under the microscope. Many of these preparations were entirely unsatisfactory but a few of them gave beautiful responses to stimulation by ammonia vapor. When the tissue was exposed to ammonia vapor for three or four seconds and then examined under the microscope, Stricker saw the capillary lumina almost disappear and then dilate wide enough for a corpuscle to pass. This phenomenon occurred about twice in fifteen minutes. Further, Stricker observed a varicosity on a capillary which moved forward, suggesting peristaltic activity on the part of the endothelial tube. When the capillaries thus under observation contracted they became practically invisible but could be readily seen again after the contraction had passed off. Stricker likewise employed electrical stimulation. The procedure which he used is not clear but with it he obtained repeatedly good results on various specimens. When stimulated, the capillaries would contract almost instantaneously and dilatation would follow a moment or more after the cessation of the stimulus. After a few applications of the stimulus no further response could be obtained. Even better results were had in the case of the capillaries of the tail of the living tadpole. These vessels were found to respond to mechanical, chemical and electrical stimulation. Of these, chemical stimulation was apparently by far the most effective. Stricker regarded these changes as due to a turgescence of the capillary endothelium such that, without change of the outside diameter of the vessel, the lumen was altered in size due to a thickening of the wall (7).

Although Cohnheim (8), among others, contested Stricker's view that the capillaries possess inherent contractility in the sense just defined, confirmatory evidence was quickly forthcoming. Stricker's work was followed by that of Golubew (9), who confirmed the observation that capillaries change their size under varying conditions, and advanced the observation that certain spindle elements on the capillary walls contract into spheres, thus occluding the lumina of the vessels and so functioning as a constriction. This notion of the mechanism of capillary function was supported a few years later by Tarchanoff (10). This author used alcohol, ether, ammonia, ferric chloride and acetic acid as well as heat. These procedures caused the so-called spindle elements to swell and so to occlude the lumina, but it was not uncommon to find that the vessels failed to dilate after the stimulus was removed.

In 1878 Severini (11) published a monographic study of the capillaries in which he states, among other things, that the application of oxygen causes the capillaries to contract, while the application of CO_2 causes them to dilate. Severini appears to be of the opinion that these gases act chiefly on the spindle elements described by Golubew. The observations were made upon the frog but also upon the capillaries in the mesentery of the guinea pig. Tarchanoff was unable to confirm these observations of Severini's, nor was Roy, working with von Mehring in 1879, able to confirm them. In 1879 Roy and Brown (12) published their very important paper describing observations on the capillary blood pressure in the frog. These authors were convinced that the capillaries have the power of independent contractility and that their caliber is not, as was believed by many, due to passive changes. They found that there was little difference in the size of the capillaries of the frog's web before and after the leg was amputated. Dilatation of the capillaries was also observed on the application of chloroform, and it was also noted that the capillaries dilated as the result of Goltz's "klopfversuch." These authors were of the opinion that it is the whole capillary and not the spindle elements of Golubew which contract. They observed that local anemia produced by compression of the area under observation results in a subsequent hyperemia which is accompanied by a dilatation of arterioles, capillaries and venules. This latter phenomenon occurred after section of the sciatic nerve when stimulation of the nerve caused a strong contraction of the arterioles. It is interesting that they observed only a contraction of arterioles on nerve stimulation. Since this procedure failed to elicit changes in the capillaries, they conclude that the functional activity noted in the latter vessels must be due to some local mechanism and they favor the conception that it is due to a direct chemical action upon the endothelium rather than upon the functional existence of what they refer to as peripheral vasomotor ganglia. The latter conception accords with what we now speak of as axon reflexes, which Krogh has recently invoked to explain localized dilatation of capillaries following punctate stimulation (13). More recently Biedl (1894) saw the peripheral vessels (arterioles, capillaries and venules) all contract in the frog's mesentery on the application of salt solution at 45°C., and dilate again when the heat was removed (14).

Mayer in 1885 (15) again observed the endothelium of the capillaries to contract under electrical stimulation. The evidence that the lymphatic vessels throughout the body are contractile is very strong. The phenomenon was observed by Mayer and by Elliott Clark (16) and others in the tail of batrachian larvae. Histological evidence makes it perfectly clear that the lymphatic capillaries are supplied with nerve fibers. These fibers have been observed and pictured a number of times (Kytmanof, 17), and Camus and Gley (18) have obtained graphic records of the functional response of the larger lymphatics to electrical stimulation of nerves. Sabin, in a comprehensive article on the origin and development of the lymphatic system (19), has collected these data in a convincing manner. The lymphatic and blood capillaries are essentially similar in histological structure. The evidence that the blood capillaries are innervated is not so well established as is the case with the lymphatics, nevertheless there appears to be little doubt of the fact. Shäffer states that nerve fibers may be found to follow each individual blood capillary in the rabbit's mesentery (20). Anatomical knowledge therefore furnishes adequate grounds for the expectation, supported by experimental work on the frog, that the mammalian blood capillaries will be shown to be contractile and under the control of the nervous system.

In 1903 Steinach and Kahn (21) published an extensive paper on the contractility of the capillaries. Their observations were directed almost wholly to the effect of direct electrical stimulation in the frog. They used the excised nictitating membrane from the frog and observed, contrary to the findings of Stricker and Biedl, an actual collapse of the whole capillary tube. According to these writers the collapse is due to activity, not of the endothelium as such, but of the perivascular cells described by Rouget (22) and Mayer (15) so that the endothelial capillary tube is collapsed by a passive infolding of the tissue. The venules were also observed to contract.

Analogous results were demonstrated in the omental capillaries of kittens and guinea pigs. The technical procedure used for these animals is not described and capillaries of less than 10 μ were not seen to contract. They believe that the vessels which they actually saw contract belong, however, to the category of capillaries.

Finally, in a frog preparation which is described in great detail, they obtained contraction in the capillaries of the nictitating membrane upon stimulation of the sympathetic fibers which leave the cord in the third, fourth and fifth spinal roots. The latency of contraction was four to five seconds, sometimes twenty seconds, as compared with a latency of one to three seconds by direct stimulation. It was not uncommon to observe rhythmic contractility of the capillaries after the stimulus had ceased. Galvanic was more efficacious than faradic stimulation and it appears that an exceedingly powerful stimulus was required—twelve Daniell cells.

In recent times attention has been again focussed on the functional significance of the capillary bed largely as the result of the work of Dale and his collaborators in the study of histamine shock (23). Dale has advanced the hypothesis that histamine is an endothelial poison which paralyzes the capillary wall so that a marked dilatation occurs. With this dilatation there results a pooling of blood in the capillaries sufficient to account for the marked fall in blood pressure found in conditions of shock. As the result of the work of Bayliss (24) and Cannon (25) and of Abel and Kubota (26), it would appear that a histamine-like substance may be produced in the body as the result of tissue injury sufficient, under certain conditions, to account for the primary symptoms of shock. So that today the opinion is quite widely held that histamine or a histamine-like body plays an important part in functional processes of the body. This applies not only to pathological states such as shock, but Abel and Kubota have advanced the conception that such a substance is significant in normal physiological processes regulating the distribution of the blood.

In an important contribution to this subject, Krogh (1) has recently shown that an enormous increase in patent capillaries may be demonstrated in active muscle as compared with resting muscle. This increase may indeed amount to more than 700 per cent. Krogh noted that electrical stimulation and massage open up many new capillaries and that electrical stimulation enlarges the capillaries already patent. He regards the mechanism for the regulation of the capillary capacity as being in the capillaries themselves; that is, as due to some chemical regulation or else as associated with an axon reflex mediated through the sensory nerve fibers. He observed that scratching the tongue of an urethanized frog with a glass needle caused a local hyperemia with dilatation of the capillaries and arterioles (13). A closed capillary thus made to dilate opens from the venous end with the appearance of a reversed corpuscular flow. When the dilatation reaches the arterial end of the capillary, the blood stream suddenly assumes the normal direction. Since cocaine was found to abolish this reaction, Krogh was forced to the assumption that it was an axon reflex. He found that cocaine also abolishes the dilatation caused by the application of iodine but does not affect the dilatation caused by acids. Section of nerves supplying the part under investigation at first did not affect the response to chemical and mechanical stimulation. For some days after the nerve section the tissues were hyperemic and the capillaries responded normally to stimulation. Later on, however, the hyperemia disappeared and the capillaries reacted only with a very localized response. From these and other observations Krogh concludes that the capillaries dilate and contract independently of the general blood pressure, and that the spread of response in the capillaries is due to a local axon reflex, probably along the sensory fibers.

Another line of evidence for the contractility of the capillary is found in the tache originally described by Marey (27) in the human being. If a blunt-pointed instrument is drawn across the skin a white line is left which turns to red in a few seconds. In certain cases the red line may be bordered with white and develop a definite urticarial wheal. Clinically this condition is regarded as indicative of vasomotor insufficiency. Marey explained it as due to a localized contraction and dilatation of the capillaries. Bloch (28) thought there was no evidence that the capillaries actually contracted. According to him the red represented capillary dilatation while the neighboring pallor was due to a drainage of blood into the vessels which dilated because of the mechanical injury.

Ryan (29) has sought to standardize this test for application in various forms of fatigue. Cotton, Slade and Lewis (30) found the reaction well developed in cases of soldiers with irritable heart and adduced new evidence in support of the belief that it is a capillary phenomenon. The red line and neighboring pallor may still be demonstrated after the circulation in the arm has been shut off with a sphygmomanometer cuff. Hence they conclude that the arterioles and venules cannot participate in the production of the red line because there is no excess pressure available to dilate these vessels. If the arm be raised before the pressure cuff is applied the reaction cannot be demonstrated because the skin is depleted of blood. On the other hand, if the arm be lowered before the pressure is applied, the reaction is vivid because there is an excess of blood in the skin.

These investigators incidentally show that epinephrin constricts the capillaries. When epinephrin is injected into the skin the resulting pallor is to be regarded as due to a contraction of the arterioles which shuts off the blood from the distal capillaries. If such an injection be made, however, after the blood flow in the arm has ceased as the result of occlusion by a blood pressure cuff, pallor is still produced. Since constriction of the arterioles would now have no effect in stopping the flow of blood into the capillaries, the pallor which results must be due to constriction of the capillaries themselves. This observation that the local application of epinephrin constricts the capillaries is especially interesting in conjunction with the work of Sollmann (31) who showed that histamine also locally applied develops an urticarial wheal.

Very recently Thaysen (32) has reported quite remarkable oscillations in the red cell count in a case of polycythemia. On one occasion he recorded an increase from 5.3 million to 10.6 million in the course of twelve hours. His investigations and tests showed that these fluctuations were caused by varying contraction and dilatation of the capillaries and precapillaries of the skin. This writer is reported to believe that careful observations would reveal similar results in other cases of polycythemia in which the vasomotor system is so unstable that the condition might be called one of vasomotor or capillary ataxia. These observations are an extreme instance of the well recognized difficulty in obtaining consistent red cell counts in many clinical cases. It would be of very great interest and importance to know if such fluctuations are indeed due to alterations in capillary tone.

METHOD

The technique followed in the experiments which form the basis of this paper was very simple. Cats were used exclusively. After anesthesia was established the animal was placed on a flat holder so that the back of the head and ears rested on the same plane with the vertebral column. The ear to be observed was shaved and thoroughly cleaned and dried. By means of a heavy thread through the upper lip the head was so held that an ear flattened out against the board. This flattening of the surface was further accentuated by sealing the ear to the board with collodion. A microscope giving a magnification of about 70 × was adapted for adjustment over the animal holder and a strong artificial light arranged to give direct illumination of the area at an angle of approximately 45 degrees completed the equipment. Castor oil was flooded over the field at the outset and occasionally during the observations.

With such an arrangement a flat vascular plexus can easily be found preferably in the neighborhood of the tip of the ear in which the corpuscular flow in the finer vessels can be readily followed for an indefinite period. In this region the skin lies loosely attached to the connective tissue which forms the framework of the ear. There is no muscle other than that in the blood vessels which might indirectly influence the vascular area under observation. Animals with little pigment in the skin are preferable but it is far from impossible to obtain good visualization of the capillary network and venules even when a considerable amount of pigment is present. One sees vessels of various size, capillaries with red cells streaming through in single file up to larger vessels in which the corpuscles are packed in a thick column. The picture is essentially like that seen in the transparent tissues of the frog. Vessels exhibiting pulsation are infrequent; probably the arteries and arterioles take a deeper course while the capillaries, venules and veins lie quite superficially, as is indicated to the unaided eye. The capillaries ramify freely particularly about the hair follicles and considerable areas are readily found in which the network forms a horizontal plane and therefore is easily visualized without change of focus. It should be emphasized that with the magnification employed one does not see the capillary wall; it is only by the presence of the red blood cells that the capillaries are recognized. Consequently when the vessels are emptied of blood the field becomes a blank so far as the smaller vessels are concerned.

Attention may be directed to the fact that our present conception that the red blood cells course through the capillaries in single file rests upon observations of the capillary circulation in the frog. In this animal the corpuscles are extremely large as compared with the same cells in the mammal (frog 22 x 16 μ, cat 6 μ, man 8 μ) so that the reason for the prevalent opinion is obvious. In the mammalian capillary circulation, including that of man (33), corpuscles may sometimes be seen moving in this manner but it is much more usual to find the capillaries with lumina sufficient to allow more than one corpuscle to pass at a time. This difference is doubtless due to the higher rate of metabolism in the mammal. There is likewise a much more rapid movement of the corpuscles in the warm than in the cold blooded animals. Therefore to restrict the capillary, in the mammal, to blood vessels in which the corpuscles move slowly and in single file is not strictly consonant with the facts.

Post-mortem behavior of vessels. If in the preparation as above described ether be poured down the tracheotomy tube and the animal be thus killed, the movement of blood at first comes to a sudden stop. Then the corpuscles clump slightly and shortly begin to move forward in the normal direction. This movement, at first noticeable in the capillaries, extends to the venules and there is a slow and gradual progression of blood toward the larger veins. The appearance is as if no blood entered the capillaries from the arterial side and that a milking process, akin to peristalsis, swept the corpuscles onward toward the vein. When the process is complete it may be found that here and there in the capillary net a few clumped corpuscles are locked as if the constriction of the vessel had failed to carry on the last of its contents.

These events occupy varying lengths of time in different animals. They may develop completely in a few minutes or they may last half an hour or more. The completeness with which the vessels empty is also a varying factor. Sometimes, particularly in old and debilitated animals, the blood may not be moved at all; sometimes the field is swept absolutely free of blood but more often a few clumps of corpuscles are left stranded, particularly in the venules. The stagnation of these clumped corpuscles is significant in that they give direct evidence of the contraction of the venules since their diameter is readily appreciated to be less than was that of the same section of the vessel prior to death.

The condition of the vessels as thus described prevails for some time, fifteen minutes or more. Then a remarkable change occurs for the vessels begin to relax and fill. Close observation reveals that relaxation first develops on the venous side and that the blood flows, slowly at first, then quite rapidly, from vein to venule to capillary, and that by the end of approximately an hour the vascular area is filled again and filled full with the indication that capillaries invisible before death are now widely open.

One further change remains to be mentioned: an indefinite time after the relaxation and filling of the capillaries just described, the vascular net is once more emptied of blood. This change is roughly coincident with the onset of skeletal muscle rigor and after it is once developed there is apparently no tendency to a reversal, at least after four days there was in one instance no sign of blood in the smaller vessels.

The foregoing description of the post-mortem appearances of the peripheral vascular bed is substantiated by the photograph reproduced in figure 1. In the technique of photographing these vessels two major difficulties had to be overcome, especially when applied to the living animal. The first was to provide sufficient illumination without heat to cut down the exposure time so as to avoid accidental movements. This was accomplished by the use of an arc light projection lantern without the bellows and projecting lenses. The lantern was tilted at approximately forty-five degrees and so placed that the light rays were concentrated almost to a focus on the part to be photographed at a distance of about 60 cm. from the source of light. The second difficulty was to overcome the movements of the ear due to respiration which, however slight, were sufficient when magnified to spoil the picture in the requisite exposure of thirty seconds. In some animals the respiration was quiet enough not to be a disturbing factor but in the majority of cases a clear picture could not be obtained. In the latter, resort was therefore had to artificial respiration for a couple of minutes before the picture was taken. The apnoea which resulted was adequate to the requirements.

For observation alone the nictitating membrane has some advantages over the ear. In the cat it usually offers a perfectly white ground on which the vessels stand out with exquisite definition. Arterioles, capillaries and venules are readily recognized and less illumination is required. Probably the vessels have less covering tissue over them. Salt solution instead of oil must of course be used to keep the tissue moist. A thread passed through the cartilaginous edge may serve to spread the membrane over the eye ball.

This area of tissue is, however, ill-adapted for photographs. It suffers more than the ear from respiratory movements and the arterial pulsation both in the vessels of the tissue itself and in the underlying eye ball cannot be overcome. In addition to these difficulties activity in the smooth muscle of the membrane itself cannot be controlled with the result that the focal plane cannot be maintained. Finally, and most important for the work in hand this tissue cannot be easily brought below the heart level. It follows that passive drainage of the vessels may therefore result if the circulation stops.

The area photographed was magnified ninety times in most of the pictures taken. A larger magnification than this led to trouble because slight differences of position of the plate, which could not be avoided, resulted in a poor focus. The vessels were focussed on the grownd glass plate of the camera at the beginning of an experiment and as a rule this focus was not changed. A focal error frequently crept in, however, due it is presumed to changes in turgidity of the underlying tissues so that the results so far as the relative size of a vessel is concerned are not wholly trustworthy in the case of capillaries. Conspicuous changes in the size of the larger vessels may be relied upon because such changes can be readily recognized by the eye when using the microscope without the camera. As to the capillaries, their presence or absence in the picture should be the sole criterion. If a capillary has disappeared or if its continuity is broken it is proper to assume that it has constricted because, as has been stated, the vessels under inspection lay below the heart level and only active constriction could empty them of corpuscular elements.

Using the procedure above outlined, photographic records were obtained from eight cats in which no preliminary steps were taken other than etherization and tracheotomy. The animals were kept under ether until a satisfactory control picture was taken and then sufficient ether was poured down the trachea to cause prompt death. Of these eight animals three failed to show a primary vascular constriction shortly after death and were not observed further, and six showed complete or partially emptied vessels. The latter group all showed a subsequent peripheral vascular dilatation followed later by emptying. In addition a number of other animals were observed, but not photographed, with confirmatory results.

Figure 1 is selected to exemplify these results. If shows the four stages of vascular change. Three minutes after death the venules are constricted and the capillaries largely emptied. Forty-five minutes

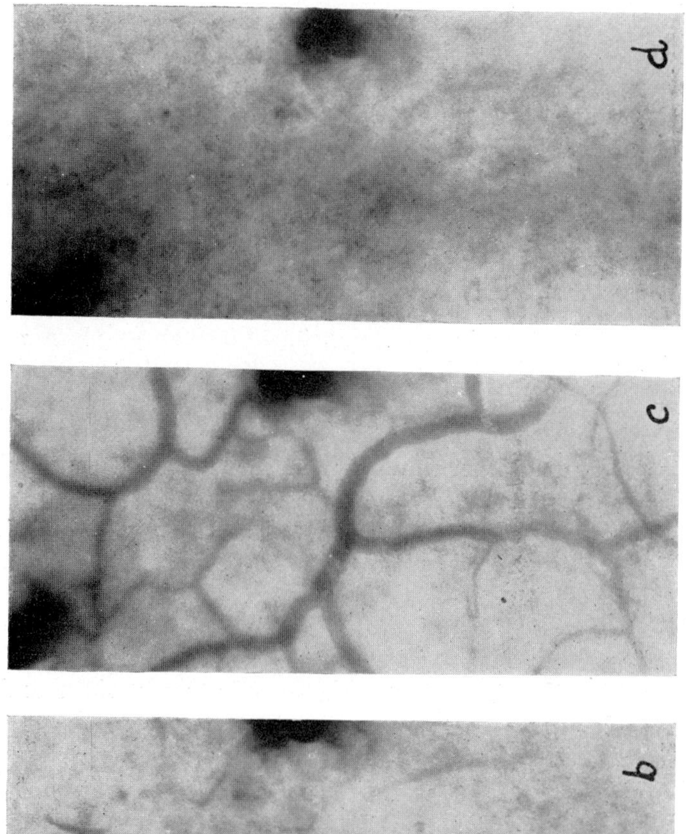

Fig. 1. Post-mortem changes in the peripheral vessels. Magnification 90 ×. Cat. *a*, At 10:28. At 10:36, ether to death. *b*, At 10:39. *c*, At 11:23. *d*, At 12:00. No further change was noted in four subsequent days during which the preparation was preserved. The negatives have not been retouched.

after death the venules are widely dilated and many capillaries are visible. After another period of forty minutes all the blood has been swept out of the vessels and only the shadows of the largest vessels can be found. The data at hand indicate that this last change is permanent since no further alteration was observed to occur for a period of four days.

It may be pointed out here, as was emphasized by Bayliss (20), that there is no inherent difficulty in the conception that the protoplasm constituting the capillary endothelium undergoes change of shape and so mediates a constriction of the vascular lumen. The motility of amoebae and of the white blood cells of higher animals is dependent upon such a change of form and many other similar instances could be mentioned.

That the vascular phenomena above described are not dependent upon the innervation of the vessels was shown in three animals in which death by ether was produced subsequent to section of the cervical sympathetic. In each of these cats the primary constriction was well developed in from one to four minutes. This was followed by dilatation and subsequent constriction in two of the three. In the one which failed to show dilatation the vessels were largely empty three and a half hours after death.

Death by ether subsequent to the intravenous injection of a dose of ergamine phosphate sufficient to cause permanent or transient "shock" (23) is not followed by the same vascular changes. The intact animal or the animal after section of the cervical sympathetic exhibits a primary constriction in the capillaries and venules followed by dilatation and subsequent permanent constriction, as above indicated. If the dose of ergamine is a fatal one or if the animal be killed with ether after partial or complete recovery from "shock," the primary constriction is inconspicuous or wholly absent. In four animals thus observed, two showed no primary constriction whatever and two gave a mere suggestion of it. Furthermore in but one of these animals (a kitten killed by the ergamine) did the constriction subsequent to dilatation develop. In all but this last animal the vessels remained dilated and filled with blood as long as observed (in one case nineteen hours).

These results then clearly support the view advanced by Dale that ergamine phosphate (histamine) is a capillary poison. Additional evidence is found in a single animal in which after histamine and nerve section the vessels similarly failed of the usual response after ether death. In other words, the histamine effect is not dependent upon the integrity of the vascular nerves.

The results thus far presented show that the peripheral vascular bed passes through a number of active changes subsequent to death and that these changes depend upon a local or peripheral function since they are not affected by nerve section and are largely done away with by the injection of an endothelial poison (histamine). Almost at once after death the capillaries, venules and, presumably, the arterioles constrict with the result that the peripheral field is swept more or less completely free of blood. Since the corpuscles can be seen in transit toward the veins, the result is suggestive of peristaltic constrictions running along the vascular tubes. This condition must be looked upon as the first consequence of asphyxia and may well be a significant factor in the asphyxial rise of arterial and venous blood pressure as ordinarily recorded whereby the lesser and minute vessels throughout the body discharge their contents into the larger channels. This passing constriction gives way shortly to a marked dilatation such as is usually associated with the collection of asphyxial and catabolic products. Some time later and roughly coincident with the onset of skeletal muscle rigor a second constriction develops which is apparently permanent in character. Whether this change is due to a rigor contraction of smooth muscle and endothelium, our present knowledge of these tissues is insufficient to determine. In no case were observations continued long enough (never more than four days) for skeletal muscle rigor to pass off, consequently the assertion that the change, assuming it due to rigor, is permanent is somewhat arbitrary. Post-mortem tissue changes, including laking of the blood, may in this length of time, however, have so clouded the field that the vessels could not be seen even though they were filled with blood. Also the blood may clot and so fail to run into the vessels even after their lumina have become patent. It will be noted that this observation does not accord with the livor mortis seen so frequently by pathologists.

Experiments with nerve stimulation. A second point of even greater interest and importance brought out in this research is the effect of nerve stimulation upon the peripheral vascular bed. In this set of observations the animals were usually anesthetized with urethane and the cervical sympathetic nerve dissected out for stimulation. In no instance was it possible to determine, by inspection or by photographs, that section of this nerve altered in any way the caliber of the vessels of the ear. On the other hand, electrical stimulation of the nerve gave unmistakable evidence of constriction in both capillaries and venules and subsequent to stimulation an over-dilatation was

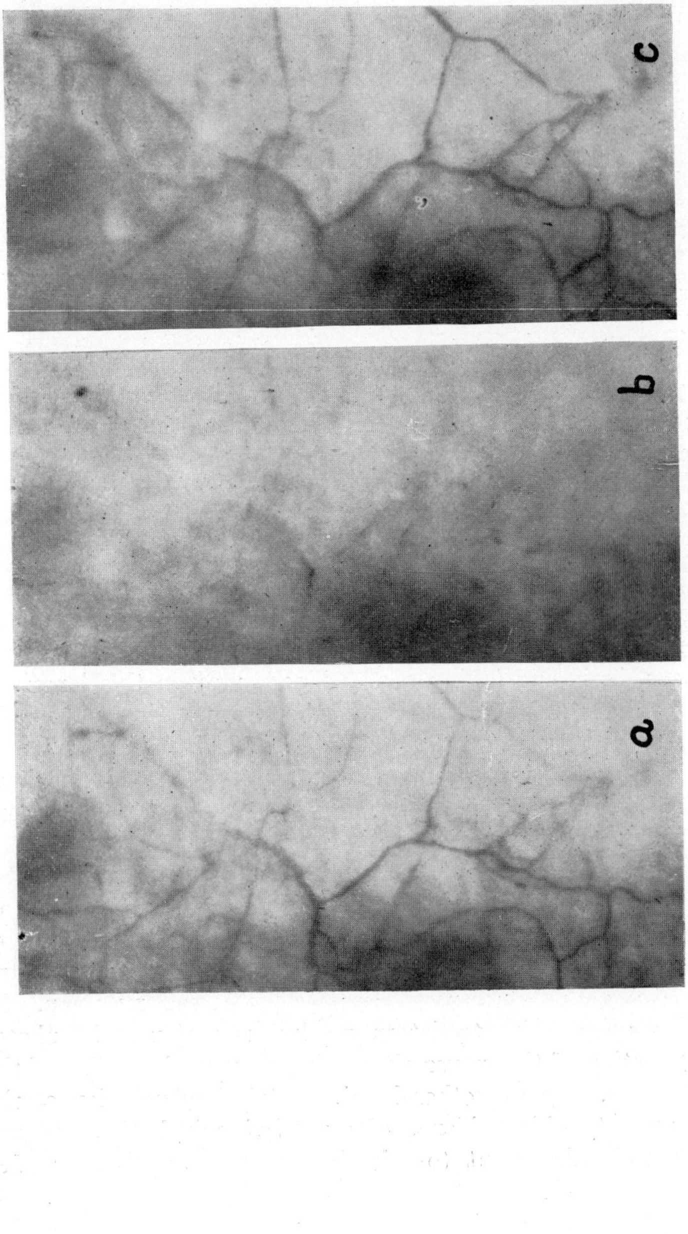

Fig. 2. Constriction of capillaries and venules by electrical stimulation of the cervical sympathetic. Magnification 90 ×. Cat. *a*, Before, *b*, during, and *c*, after stimulation. The negatives have not been retouched.

recognized. These results were so sharp that it was considered necessary to perform but three experiments in each of which the observation was repeated many times. No indication of fatigue was noted since the results were as good five hours after an experiment was begun as at the start. Figure 2 gives the photographs obtained in one of these experiments.

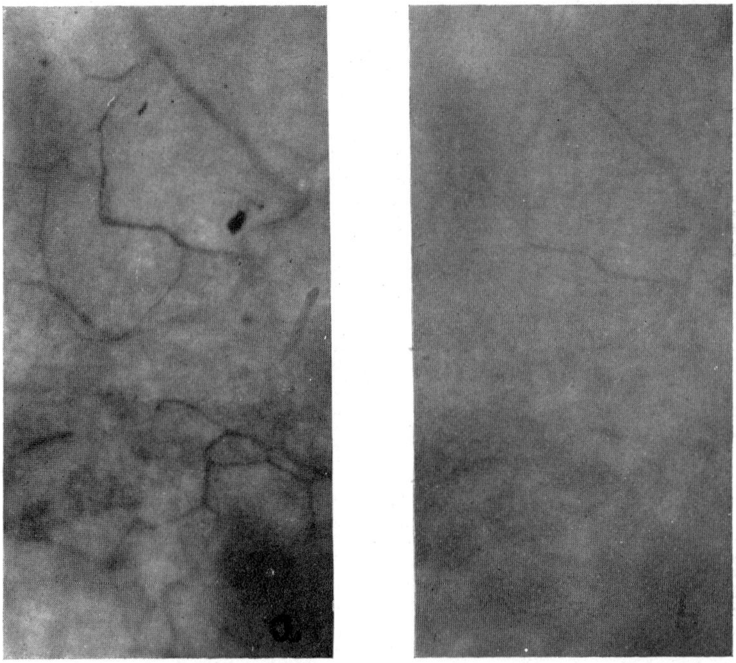

Fig. 3. Constriction of capillaries and venules following the injection of 3 cc. 1: 50,000 epinephrin. Magnification 90 ×. Cat. The cervical sympathetic nerve had been cut. *a*, Before, and *b*, shortly after the injection of epinephrin. The negatives have not been retouched.

This figure shows clearly the constriction and disappearance of the capillaries and venules during electrical stimulation of the cervical sympathetic and their subsequent over-dilatation two minutes after the stimulus was removed. It happens that no larger venule was present in this field but these were repeatedly seen to respond just as conspicuously as shown here for the capillaries. The response of the venules may be appreciated, although not very clearly, in the next figure (fig. 3), which shows the effect of epinephrin injection.

Experiments with epinephrin. Further evidence of the sympathetic innervation of the capillaries and venules was developed from the injection of epinephrin. This substance, selective in action for contractile tissues with sympathetic nerve supply, gave results comparable with those obtained with electrical stimulation of the cervical sympathetic. The effect was the same both before and after section of the sympathetic. Figure 3 is made from photographs taken before and just after the intravenous injection of 3 cc. of 1: 50,000 epinephrin in a cat three and a half hours after the cervical sympathetic had been cut.

The injection of histamine destroys this mechanism. In a cat in which nerve stimulation had given sharp constriction, 6 mgm. ergamine phosphate were injected. As soon as the resultant dilatation of the peripheral vessels was developed, the cervical sympathetic was again stimulated. The strongest stimulating current available failed to elicit the slightest response.

The findings here presented are contrary to our present belief that the active functional peripheral resistance is to be found wholly in the smaller arterioles with smooth muscle in their coats. The evidence given indicates that nerve impulses along vasomotor fibers may play upon the caliber not only of the arterioles but on that of the capillaries and venules as well. We must therefore modify our conception of the peripheral resistance in the matter of functional activity to include the whole peripheral vascular bed including therewith the arterioles, capillaries and venules.

It will be obvious, furthermore, that if the conception in regard to the peripheral resistance here advanced is substantiated, the body possesses a remarkable mechanism for the regulation of the distribution of the blood. For by alterations in the tonic capacity of the capillaries and venules, which is under the control of the central nervous system, circulating corpuscles as well as plasma can be mobilized to a very considerable degree in accordance with the physiological needs of the various tissues both local and general. It would seem also to follow that blood volume and plasma volume determinations must be subject to the same physical mechanism (34).

If, as is highly probable, specific nerve fibers supply the different parts of the peripheral vascular bed (arterioles, capillaries and venules) the play of functional adjustments must be exceedingly complex. Hitherto it has been possible to invoke chemical processes alone to account for many of the exquisite adaptations recognized to occur in physiological adjustments. In the light of the facts here presented we may conceive of a highly organized nervous mechanism adapted to quick and efficient response superimposed upon the primitive chemical methods available to the organism. There is doubtless a happy coaptation between these two major processes of control but on the body surface, exposed to noxious environmental factors, and in the voluntary muscles where quick adjustments of blood supply are constantly demanded, we might expect the nervous regulation to play a significant teleological rôle. In the glands and deeper body tissues generally, on the other hand, where reaction time is of less significance, responses may largely depend upon chemical factors for their instigation.

If the body has at its control such a highly organized device for the disposition and partition of the blood by which extensive capillary beds may be largely emptied of or packed with corpuscular elements or plasma, an explanation is readily found for the uncertainties of blood cell counts and blood volume determinations. Individual capillaries may be opened up or closed or they may be gorged with stagnant inactive corpuscles, as is possible to demonstrate on the finger (32). Mediation of these and similar changes would be accomplished by activation of the arteriole, capillary or venule functioning individually or collectively. It is natural to infer that normally such forces are well balanced and counteract one another so that the volume and corpuscular composition of the blood is held relatively stable, but in time of physiological stress or in disease the alterations which develop might assume considerable proportions. The significance of this mechanism for the nutrition of the tissues will likewise be apparent since it may be presumed to exercise control over the rate at which plasma passes through the capillaries and into the tissue spaces.

The present work does not include a demonstration of nervous regulation of vasodilatation in the capillaries and venules but the evidence justifies the assumption of such an hypothesis. On the other hand, the primary constriction followed by dilatation which occurs after death indicates that chemical regulation may function both in constriction and dilatation. The effects of the injection of epinephrin and of histamine likewise substantiate this conception. These findings accord with the recent clean-cut results obtained by Krogh (1) on the increase in number of patent capillaries in active muscle and the similar results recognized to occur in the early stages of inflammatory processes (4). The work of Gaskell (35), Bayliss (36) and the writer (37) on the chemical regulation of peripheral resistance is thus to be interpreted that chemical factors constrict as well as dilate the finer vessels other than the arterioles.

To further substantiate the fact that nervous impulses actually produce a constriction of capillaries and venules, attention may again be called to the condition of these experiments. The vascular bed under observation lay some 2 cm. below heart level. An occlusive constriction in the arterioles could not therefore passively drain the vessels distal to the constriction and supporting a hydrostatic column. It is conceivable that, if these vessels were under tension due to a *vis a tergo*, they might decrease in size when their filling pressure was shut off but they would not empty. Indeed it was found in an experiment in which the carotid was occluded long enough to bring the blood stream to a standstill in the peripheral vessels, that the capillaries showed no appreciable decrease in size and that the corpuscles did not tend to clump. The latter point is small but significant because when the capillaries are made to contract, as by nerve stimulation, the corpuscles invariably tend to gather together and move along in clumps.

Lister (4) in that splendid paper to which reference has already been made on the "Early Stages of Inflammation" published in 1858, describes an experiment on the frog which is of decided interest in this connection. He was studying with the microscope the behavior of the peripheral vessels in the web of the foot under various conditions and in this experiment he observed that irritation of the cord caused the capillaries and venules to disappear from view. He ascribes this result to an active constriction of the aterioles sufficient to block the passage of the red cells but insufficient to stop the flow of plasma so that the corpuscles floating in the capillaries and venules are washed onward from the field. The red blood cells of the frog are of course relatively large and could presumably be blocked in the manner indicated, but I am inclined to believe that Lister actually saw a constriction of the vessels in question. In the first series of experiments described in the present paper the evidence is clear that, after the heart has ceased to beat, the capillaries and venules can empty themselves not once but twice against an appreciable hydrostatic resistance. The movement and disposition of the corpuscles under these conditions is not to be distinguished from their behavior under the influence of nerve stimulation; the stream stops quite abruptly, the corpuscles congregate in masses and then progress slowly and without definite regularity. This forward movement occurs against a hydrostatic resistance and in spite of the fact that the corpuscles would tend in a stagnant plasma, because of their specific gravity, to settle and adhere to the vessel wall.

Doctor Connet has recently shown in a research done in this laboratory (38) that the injection of epinephrin raises the systemic venous blood pressure. In this work she was able to exclude the slowing of the heart which has hitherto been regarded as sufficient to account for the phenomenon, and reached the conclusion that the substance acts by a direct effect upon the veins in the intact animal just as it has been repeatedly shown to act upon isolated vein preparations. It seems highly probable in view of the results presented here that the rise in venous pressure following the injection of epinephrin demonstrated by Doctor Connet is associated with a constriction of the capillaries and venules as well as of the veins.

Experiments with histamine. With a method available for the study of the capillaries in the mammal it was quite natural that one should be led to a study of the effect of histamine. The attractive hypothesis advanced by Dale (23) that histamine "shock" (and probably traumatic "shock") is due to a specific toxic action upon the capillaries rested upon indirect evidence. It was possible with the preparation at hand to put this hypothesis to a direct test.

References have already been made to the toxic action of histamine on the capillaries and venules in the experiments previously described:—after the injection of histamine post-mortem constriction of these vessels was absent or very slight and no constriction could be obtained by nerve stimulation. In addition to these experiments a number of experiments were performed, seven in all, in which attention was directed primarily to the histamine effect. Ergamine phosphate, 6 mgm. per kilo in salt solution, was injected intravenously in accordance with Dale's technique.

The results were uniformly clean-cut and decisive. Within a few minutes after the injection the capillaries and venules were filled with stagnant blood and definitely dilated. The dilatation was distinctly more conspicuous in the venules. These changes developed in conjunction with the fall in arterial blood pressure and in one experiment in which it was followed with a fall in venous pressure.

Doctor Rich has obtained similar results in the capillaries of the mammalian omentum (39) by a different method. Rich found that flooding the peritoneal cavity with Zenker's fluid gave prompt fixation of the tissue so that it could be removed and studied under the microscope. If the tissue was thus fixed immediately after the intravenous infusion of histamine, marked capillary and venous dilatation and engorgement could be demonstrated. This vascular change was entirely absent in

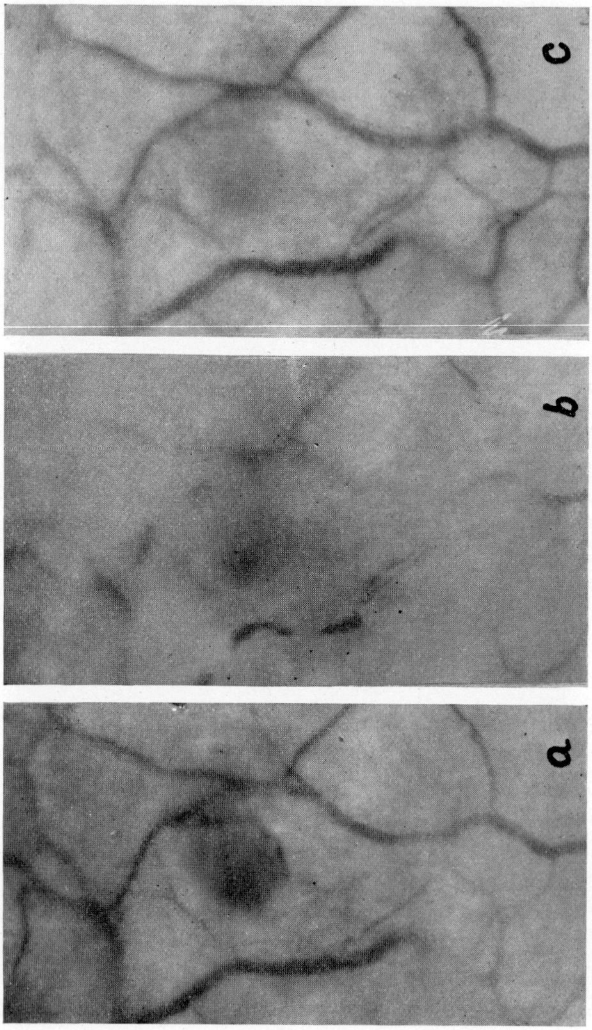

Fig. 4. Effect of histamine on the capillaries and venules. Magnification 90 ×. Cat. *a*, At 10:28. At 10:40, ergamine phosphate (6 mgm. per kilo) was injected. *b*, At 10:50. *c*, At 11:25. The negatives have not been retouched.

control experiments in which salt solution was infused instead of histamine.

Usually, although not invariably in my experiments, this dilatation was preceded by what must be interpreted to be a constriction, under the experimental conditions. This constriction lasted a variable but brief period of time, frequently so short that it could not be photographed satisfactorily. This reaction is especially well exemplified in figure 4 in which the photograph which shows the constriction was taken ten minutes after the injection of ergamine when the arterial pressure was 24 mm. Hg. The arterial pressure was still at 24 mm. Hg. thirty-five minutes later when the last photograph shown in this figure was obtained.

This transitory constriction of the capillaries and venules may not occur throughout the body since Rich was unable to find any evidence of it in the capillaries of the omentum. It may be due to a primary central effect of the poison or, what seems more probable at the moment, it may represent one of those curious reactions according to which a drug or substance depressive in effect at first acts as a stimulus. Such a transitory reversal of effect is not uncommon in perfusing the isolated heart with inorganic salts and I have observed a similar effect in perfusing the respiratory center (40). Burridge (41) has suggested, in the case of the heart, that the condition is associated with the state of aggregation of the colloids.

Although it thus appears possible that histamine may under certain conditions produce its primary "shock" effect while the capillaries and venules of the ear are constricted, these experiments as a whole undoubtedly lend strong support to Dale's hypothesis to explain histamine "shock."

In conclusion it will not be out of place to state that the preparation used in these experiments offers an excellent method of demonstrating the capillary circulation in the mammal to students. A low power microscope (ocular 1 and objective 3), adapted by removal of the stage to fit over the edge of an animal holder and a good light are all the apparatus that is required. The capillary circulation can be similarly observed in the rabbit and presumably also in the dog although the latter animal has not been investigated. The rabbit's ear is, however, distinctly more susceptible to inflammatory processes than is that of the cat.

SUMMARY AND CONCLUSIONS

A method is described whereby the peripheral circulation (particularly the capillaries and venules) in the cat's ear may be observed and photographed. It is thus possible to study in the living mammal the capillary circulation, investigation of which in the intact animal has hitherto been limited to the frog. Making use of this method, the following experimental results were obtained:

1. After ether death the peripheral vessels at first constrict so that they are largely emptied of blood. This constriction which occurs usually within a few minutes lasts but a short time and is followed by a marked dilatation and engorgement. Subsequently and roughly coincident with the development of skeletal muscle rigor, the vessels are again emptied of blood. The latter condition prevails indefinitely (four days at room temperature).

These changes are much less conspicuous or entirely absent if the animal is previously injected with histamine. They are not affected by section of the vasomotor nerve fibers (cervical sympathetic).

It is thus concluded that these post-mortem vascular reactions are independent of the central nervous system and that they are abolished by an endothelial poison.

It is suggested that the first constriction represents a response to asphyxia and may be a significant factor in the asphyxial rise of arterial and venous blood pressure.

2. Section of the vasomotor fibers to the part (cervical sympathetic) did not cause an appreciable dilatation of the vessels but electrical stimulation of these fibers gave clear evidence, by causing constriction, that the capillaries and venules are under sympathetic nervous control. This fact was further substantiated by the injection of epinephrin which caused a similar vascular response.

The reaction to nerve stimulation could not be obtained in an animal poisoned with histamine.

These results indicate that the functional peripheral resistance is not limited to the arterioles but includes the capillaries and venules as well. It is inferred that this resistance is subject to chemical as well as nervous control. This concept involves a reorganization of our present beliefs concerning the peripheral resistance and implies the existence of an efficient physical mechanism for the distribution and regulation of the circulating blood volume and of the supply of nutriment to the tissues.

3. The injection of histamine (ergamine phosphate) causes a prompt and permanent dilatation of both capillaries and venules with stagnation of the corpuscular stream.

This reaction appears to be characteristic and thus confirms Dale's hypothesis that histamine "shock" (and presumably traumatic "shock") is largely dependent upon the reaction of the capillaries. It should be noted, however, that the present results extend this reaction to include the venules as well as the capillaries.

Prior to the dilatation which appears to be the characteristic histamine effect, there is usually a short period when the vessels in the ear are constricted. Neither this transitory effect nor the general histamine effect is influenced by nerve section. Both effects are thus due to the direct action of the substance on the vessels.

It is probable that vessels elsewhere in the body do not show this passing constriction since it may persist for some minutes after the systemic arterial pressure is at shock level and give place to dilatation while the blood pressure level remains unchanged.

BIBLIOGRAPHY

(1) Krogh: Journ. Physiol., 1919, lii, 457.
(2) Hill: Schäfer's Text book of physiology, London, 1900, ii, 166.
(3) Lombard: This Journal, 1912, xxix, 335.
(4) Lister: Phil. Trans., 1858, cxlviii, 645.
(5) Stricker: Sitzungsb. d. kais. Akad. d. Wissensch., 1865, li, 1.
(6) Stricker: Untersuch. z. Naturl. d. Mensch. u. d. Thiere, Giessen, 1866–70, x.
(7) Stricker: Vorlesungen über die allgemeine und experimentelle Pathologie, Wien, 1883, 675.
(8) Cohnheim: Arch. f. path. Anat., 1867, xl, 42.
(9) Golubew: Arch. f. mikros. Anat., 1869, v, 49.
(10) Tarchanoff: Pflüger's Arch., 1874, ix, 407.
(11) Severini: Ricerche sulla innervazione dei vasi sanguigni, Perugia, 1878.
(12) Roy and Brown: Journ. Physiol., 1879, ii, 323.
(13) Krogh: Journ. Physiol., 1919, liii, p. xlvii.
(14) Biedl: Quoted from Steinach and Kahn (see 21).
(15) Mayer: Quoted from Sabin (see 19).
(16) Clark: Anat. Rec., 1909, iii, 183.
(17) Kytmanof: Anat. Anzeiger, 1901, xix, 369.
(18) Camus and Gley: Arch. d. Physiol., 1894, vi, 454.
(19) Sabin: Johns Hopkins Hosp. Rept., 1916, xvii, 347.
(20) Shäffer: Quain's Anatomy, vol. II, part I, p. 346. London, 1912.
(21) Steinach and Kahn: Pflüger's Arch., 1903, xcvii, 105.
(22) Rouget: Arch. d. Physiol., 1873, v, 603.
(23) Dale and Laidlaw: Journ. Physiol., 1919, lii, 355.
Dale and Richards: Journ. Physiol., 1918, lii, 110.

(24) Bayliss: Intravenous injections in wound shock, London, 1918, 108.
(25) Cannon: Journ. Amer. Med. Assoc., 1919, lxxiii, 174.
(26) Abel and Kubota: Journ. Pharm. Exper. Therap., 1919, xiii, 243.
(27) Marey: Ann. d. sci. nat., 4e serie, ix, cashier 2, 1858. Quoted from La Circulation du Sang, Paris, 1881, 377.
(28) Block: Arch. d. Physiol. norm. et path., 1873, v, 681.
(29) Ryan: This Journal, 1918, xlv, 537.
(30) Cotton, Slade and Lewis: Heart, 1917, vi, 227.
(31) Sollmann: Journ. Pharm. Exper. Therap., 1917, x, 147.
(32) Thayson: Ugeskrift f. Laeger, 1920, lxxxii, 473. Quoted from Journ. Amer. Med. Assoc., 1920, lxxv, 70.
(33) Danzer and Hooker: This Journal, 1920, lii, 136.
(34) Smith: This Journal, 1920, li, 221.
(35) Gaskell: Journ. Physiol., 1880, iii, 48.
(36) Bayliss: Journ. Physiol., 1901, xxvi, p. xxxii.
(37) Hooker: This Journal, 1911, xxviii, 361.
(38) Connet: This Journal, 1920, liv, 96.
(39) Rich: Personal communication.
(40) Hooker: This Journal, 1915, xxxviii, 200.
(41) Burridge: Quart. Journ. Exper. Physiol., 1915, viii, 331.

STUDIES ON THE VISCERAL SENSORY NERVOUS SYSTEM

I. Lung Automatism and Lung Reflexes in the Frog (R. pipiens and R. catesbiana)

A. J. CARLSON and A. B. LUCKHARDT
From the Hull Physiological Laboratory, University of Chicago

Received for publication July 12, 1920

This report is the beginning of an investigation and analysis of the reflexes evoked by the visceral sensory nerves in all the groups of vertebrates available for study. The inception to this line of work was the observation on man (7) that strong contractions of the empty stomach produce reflex effects on the cardiac and the vasomotor centers. To date we have studied the reflexes from the visceral afferent system involving the skeletal musculature, the respiratory mechanism, the gastro-intestinal tract, the heart and blood vessels, and the urinary bladder. In some cases our reflex results compelled us to re-investigate the motor mechanisms of the organ involved in the reflex response. This is true especially of the lungs.

We have today fairly comprehensive and accurate knowledge of the efferent nervous mechanism of the viscera, thanks to the work of Gaskell, Langley and others.

On the sensory or afferent side our information is made up largely of gaps and guesses, despite its probable importance in functional integrations in health and disease. This phase of physiology has been studied especially with reference to *conscious* visceral sensations, to witness only the work of surgeons and internists on direct and referred visceral pain, and of physiologists and psychologists on the sensibility (conscious) of the alimentary canal. To our knowledge a thoroughgoing investigation of the sub-conscious reflexes evoked from the visceral sensory nerves in health and disease has not been made. In Gaskell's recent monograph (8) on the involuntary nervous system the afferent component of this system is not even mentioned, and in Sherrington's article on the "Sympathetic Nervous System" in the 1911 edition of the Enclyclopedia Britannica the afferent component is dismissed with the following sentence: "Of the afferent fibers of the sympathetic little is known save that they are, relatively to the efferent, few in number, and that they, like the afferents of the cerebro-spinal system, are axones of nerve cells seated in the spinal ganglia."

EXPERIMENTAL METHODS

1. The lung contractions were registered by means of water manometers (diameter 8–10 mm.) connected with small glass cannulae inserted and tied in the tips of the lungs. For the most delicate lung contractions these water manometers were not sufficiently sensitive, and in the study of these phases a very delicate tambour was employed. In fixing the cannula in the tip of the lung care must be taken so that the direct handling of the lung is minimum and gentle, as direct and rough handling induces prolonged tonic contractions that may involve the whole lung. In animals in poor physiological conditions, the lungs are usually quite atonic, and these contractions due to direct handling (mechanical stimulation) are less in evidence.

In experiments with the glottis open and the frog preparation breathing spontaneously no artificial pressure can be maintained in the lungs, because if the lungs are collapsed through cannulae in the lung tips, the frog promptly fills the lung again up to the original pressure. If this original pressure is slightly exceeded by inflation through the cannula the glottis is promptly opened and the pressure reduced. In the experiments involving the closure of the glottis the lungs were practically always collapsed and empty at the conclusion of this operation In the subsequent inflation of the lungs we always took pains not to exceed the normal pressure maintained by the frog (1–3 cm. water).

Most of the previous investigators of the physiology of the respiratory movements in the frog have used various methods for graphic registration of the throat and flank movements (Martin (16), Wedenskii (26), Langendorff (14), Sherrington (23), Baglioni (3), Soprana (24), Nikolides (20), (21)). Brown (5) and Willem (27) recorded intrapulmonic pressure by means of cannulae in the tip of the lungs. Mochi (17), (18), (19) placed the body of the frog, except head and throat, in a plethysmograph and closed the plethysmograph by sectioning the frog's skin around the neck and tying to the plethysmograph tube. It seems to us that the method of Mochi introduces more trauma and abnormal physiological conditions than a slit through the abdominal wall for placing cannula in the tip of the lungs.

2. For the registration of the variations in the intrapulmonic pressure during normal respiration the animals were usually decerebrated, and slits made through the abdominal wall over the lung tips, of sufficient size to insert cannulae in the lung tips. This incision through the abdominal wall was made with or without local application of cocaine. The animals were then placed, usually without restraint, on a board or preferably in a small dark box. In most cases animals thus prepared would sit quietly for long periods, unless disturbed by external stimulations. In a few animals the abdominal incisions were made under local anesthesia without previous decerebration.

3. In the experiments where it was necessary to separate the lungs completely from the influence of skeletal muscle contractions several methods of procedure were used:

a. After decerebration and fixing the cannulae in the lung tips, the animals being placed in normal position (ventral side down) on the board or in the dark box, the abdominal muscles were cut away and the spinal cord pithed below the brachial plexus. In such a preparation movements of the head, strong respiratory movements (swallowing) or movements of the front legs will alter the intrapulmonic pressure, but the rapidity of these movements is much greater usually than the lung contractions so that the latter can be readily differentiated from the passive effects of the former movements, and in favorable preparations the former movements may be absent over considerable periods, thus giving the lung contractions free play.

b. Without previous decerebration the spinal cord was cut just below the medulla and pithed the entire length caudad, the animal placed on the board dorsal side down, the abdominal wall opened for its entire length by a median incision, and the lungs completely isolated, except for their anatomical connections with the pharynx and esophagus. Animals thus prepared continue to breathe spontaneously for considerable periods if care is taken not to injure the lungs or pharynx and prevent exsanguination. Head and pharyngeal movements are still capable of influencing the intrapulmonic pressure mechanically. The isolated lungs were prevented from drying by a thin layer of absorbent cotton kept moist with Ringer's solution.

4. Closure of the glottis. Our greatest technical difficulty consisted in proper closure of the glottis in experiments where this procedure was essential. The frog has no trachea and bronchi. The glottis opens directly into a rather large tracheal sac which communicates with the base of each lung. This tracheal sac is so closely adherent to the tissues at the base of the heart that we found it impracticable to close the lungs by ligation or compression of this sac without an amount of injury to the heart nerves, and main blood vessels that resulted in quick failure of the circulation. The following experiments were tried without practical success:

(1) Ligation of base of lungs at their junction with the tracheal sac, leaving the lung blood vessels and nerves outside the ligature. This failed because of the impossibility of accomplishing the latter without puncturing the lung wall, or if successful the ligation produced enough anatomical distortion to interfere with the lung circulation.

(2) Closing the tracheal sac or either lung by small wads of cotton pushed through the glottis. This failed mainly because the glottis opening is smaller than the diameter of the tracheal sac or its communication with the lungs. Hence the cotton wad passed sooner or later into the lung cavities.

(3) It was noted, when the median incision exposing and isolating the lungs was carried forward to the level of the base of the heart only, that lateral and dorsal tension exerted by pull on the front legs would prevent air from entering or leaving the lungs by the normal breathing movements. This was evidently due to collapse of the tracheal sac by external compression. This gave us the clew to a method of closing the glottis and blocking the air communication between the two lungs with the least possible trauma or physiological violence. A cotton plug of suitable size, with or without a coating of vaseline, was inserted through the mouth and pushed down the esophagus to the level of the glottis and the tracheal sac. The pressure thus exerted on these structures from the esophagus not only closed the glottis but usually compressed the tracheal sac sufficiently to prevent air communication between the two lungs, especially if in addition the front legs were put under slight dorso-lateral tension.

This mode of procedure sufficed for the degrees of lung contractions accompanying the normal respiratory movements, or induced by reflex stimulation. But it proved inadequate in case of the extreme tetanus of the lungs following section of the vago-sympathetic nerves or pithing of the medulla. These strong contractions always forced the glottis open against the cotton plug in the esophagus. Hence in all the experiments on this phase of lung physiology the glottis had to be closed more firmly. This was done by clamping the rim of the glottis with a slender artery forceps. The mouth being held open, a slender hook was passed through the glottis, under gentle forward traction the rim of the glottis was compressed with a slender artery forceps, a small cotton plug pushed into the esophagus and left in situ together with the forceps. Care must be taken not to place the forceps too far down on the tracheal sac and pharyngeal tissues, as in that case the pulmonary branches of the vagi as well as the lung blood vessels are included in the grip, or placed on such tension that vagus action on the lung and lung circulation are interfered with.

The essential drawback to this procedure is the trauma produced or rather the violent mechanical stimulation of the sensory nerves in the glottis, larynx and pharynx by the compression. Placing the artery forceps in the region described produced something like profound prostration or "shock" in the preparation. Respiratory movements cease for a considerable period, and in the case of animals otherwise in poor condition may not return at all. It is scarcely necessary to add that the results reported, using this method of closure of the glottis, are based on the vigorous preparations in which spontaneous respiration returned.

5. The mucus in the lung cavities can, of course, not be eliminated from the lungs in the normal way under any condition of glottis obstruction. Furthermore, the unavoidable trauma to lungs and tracheal sac in preparation may actually increase the mucous secretion. This lung mucus is a hindrance and a source of error in registering lung tonus and contractions by our method, as strong contractions may force some mucus into the cannula in the lung tips, and this will interfere with the prompt and accurate response of the water manometer to slight variations in the intrapulmonic pressure. It is needless to say that preparations must be discarded in which the lung mucus interferes with accurate recording of lung contractions.

6. Administration of the drugs. All the drugs used, unless otherwise noted, were mixed with varying quantities of Ringer's solution and injected slowly into the abdominal vein. A few injections were made directly into the heart.

7. Prevention of asphyxia after closure of the glottis. It was, of course, essential to maintain circulation and lung ventilation even after closure of the glottis, so that abnormal reflexes and local lung reactions would not be set up by asphyxia. We endeavored to maintain good circulation by ligation of the main blood vessels sectioned in the preparation of the animal and by occasional intravenous injections of small quantities of Ringer's solution. The frog's heart is apparently very sensitive to the mechanical factors of filling, as it ceases to beat entirely or beats very feebly when the blood pressure is very low, but resumes an adequate rhythm on replacing the lost blood with Ringer's solution.

It is well known that the frog in water carries out a considerable proportion of its gaseous exchange through the skin. Under the temperature conditions prevailing in the laboratory during this work the frogs (R. pipiens) would remain under water for 18 to 25 minute periods, come to the surface and make a few vigorous respirations and submerge again for the same length of time. Evidently the filling the lungs with air, supplemented with the skin respiration, met the respiratory needs for 20 to 30 minutes. On the basis of these facts, we always kept the skin of our frog preparations moist with water, and gave occasional artificial respirations, except in cases of extreme lung tetanus when the latter procedure would have been useless.

8. All the tracings reproduced with this report were taken with the same speed of the kymograph. The time record is not always attached to the tracings reproduced, for reasons of economy of print paper. But the reader interested in any question involving the time element as a matter of importance can readily transfer the time tracing, given in a few of the tracings, to the others; 25 cm. of tracing (original size) = 17 minutes.

LUNG TONUS AND LUNG CONTRACTIONS DURING NORMAL RESPIRATION

1. The anatomy of the frog's lung is well known. The reader will recall that the lung is a paired muscular sac, numerous septa on the interior surface dividing this into small spaces or alveoli. The septa extend only a few millimeters from the lung wall, so that the larger part of the lung cavity is a large single air space. There are no bronchi and no true trachea, the tracheal sac having essentially the same structure as the rest of the lungs, and probably carries out the same respiratory function.

Smooth musculature covers the entire wall of the lungs and extends into the smallest septa on the inner surface. More or less definite external muscle strands follow the course of the main pulmonary blood vessels on the lung surface.

The arrangement of the lung musculature is such that contraction (even of the septal musculature) will reduce the size of the lung cavity, or raise the intrapulmonic pressure in case the air in the lung is not free to escape.

The action of the septal musculature would be analogous to that of the bronchial constrictor muscle of the mammalian lung. So far as we know, the mammalian lung has no counterpart to the lung wall musculature in the frog.

After having discovered the striking peripheral motor automatism of the frog's lung we become especially interested in the local nervous tissue in the lung of this animal group. According to the histological investigations of Arnold (1), Smirnow (25), Cuccate and Wolff (28), there are numerous ganglia, as well as isolated ganglion cells (multipolar and bipolar) along the course of the main vago-sympathetic nerve trunks on the surface of the lungs. There are medullated and non-medullated nerve fibers in these nerve trunks. A plexus of fine non-medullated nerve fibers surrounds the strands of lung musculature. The ganglion cells and these nerve plexuses are most abundant at the base of the lungs. Arnold points out that the ganglia and ganglion cells in the frog's lung are histologically identical with those of the frog's heart. They are also probably identical, both as to histology and function, with the ganglionic plexuses (Auerbach) in the wall of the gut, especially as the lung is a diverticulum from the esophagus.

2. The external respiratory mechanism of the amphibians differs from that of all other air-breathing animals in that the air enters the lungs under positive pressure due to the act of swallowing. One might therefore surmise that in the amphibia the respiratory center in the brain is anatomically and physiologically identical with the center for deglutition.

The sequence and coördination of the respiratory acts (buccal movements, closing of nares, expiration and inspiration or swallowing air) have been correctly analyzed and described especially by Langendorff (12), (13), Baglioni, Brown (5) and others, and most recently by Willem (27). We have nothing new to add on that point, and can contribute no new facts bearing on the old and new speculations as to phylogenetic and physiological significance of the buccal movements which proceed rhythmically between the actual renewal of air in the lungs (swallowing).

The types of the respiratory rhythm as revealed by the intrapulmonic pressure in normal and in decerebrated frogs are shown in figure 1. The filling of the lungs by swallowing (upstroke) is preceded by opening of the glottis and escape of some air into the buccal cavity. According to most of the competent and recent investigators, the nares are closed during the whole act so that while the air escapes from the lung it does not actually escape through the nares. Rebreathing is therefore a marked feature of the frog's lung respiration. The buccal movements going on between the swallowing acts and with the nares open, bring fresh air into the buccal cavity.

In exceptional cases there is a perfect synchrony between the buccal movements and the actual air swallowing (fig. 1, *B*). But usually

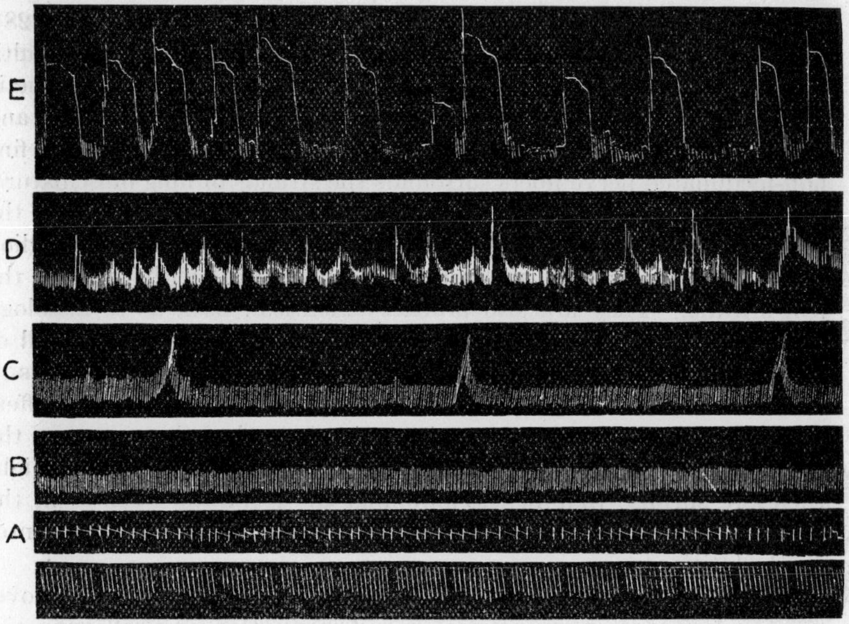

Fig. 1. Records of intrapulmonic pressure in frogs. Tracings *A*, *D*, *E*, taken by water manometer; tracings *B* and *C* by air transmission and tambour. Tracings *A* to *D*, Rana pipiens, animals decerebrated and the tip of one lung exposed by small abdominal incision. No anesthetics, animals sitting quietly in normal posture. Tracing *E* from bull frog (R. catesbiana), tip of lung exposed by small abdominal incision after cocaine, animal sitting quietly in a darkened moist box; time, 5 seconds. Showing varying types of respiration in the frog

All the tracings n this article are reduced to about $\frac{2}{5}$ of the original.

several buccal movements are made between each swallowing act (fig. 1, *A*), and a striking feature of the air swallowing rhythm in most frogs is a periodicity similar to the Cheyne-Stokes breathing in mammals. This has been observed by most of the former investigators on the respiratory movements in the frog (Luschinger and Sakalow (15), Langendorff (12), (13), Wedenskï 26, Sherrington (23), etc.). The frog may go on over long periods swallowing as much air as that which previously escaped through the open glottis, thus maintaining a constant general level of intrapulmonic pressure of 1 to 2 cm. of water. This type may periodically change into one in which during a few powerful air swallowings the amount of air forced in greatly exceeds the quantity that escaped between the time of glottis opening and the swallowing act. In consequence of this the lungs expand and the intrapulmonic pressure rises from the general level of 1 to 3 cm. of water up to a level of 6 to 9 cm. of water. All respiratory movements then cease for periods varying from 5 to 60 seconds and the act is renewed, that is, the quantity of air let out of the lung in each respiratory act is greater than that forced in; the lung shrinks and the intrapulmonic pressure falls to its former general level of 1 to 2 cm. of water (fig. 1, *C, D, E*).

According to our experience, this is the usual type of respiration in the frog. As previously noted by Sherrington and others, decerebration or other methods of preparation are not responsible for inducing it. It is probably a normal rhythm developed in connection with the habitual under-water existence of the animal. During the respiratory pause with high intrapulmonic pressure this pressure, as recorded by the ordinary water manometer, may show an initial rise and then remain at a fairly constant level until the next respiratory act, but if the pause is long the intrapulmonic pressure gradually falls, due, not to escape of air through the glottis, but to relaxation of the tonus of the lung musculature.

3. Active lung contractions and lung inhibitions associated with the respiratory movements.

a. Contractions. The reader's attention is invited to the tracings reproduced in figures 2 and 3. It will be noted, especially on the upper tracing in figure 2, that at the end of the last respiration followed by a Cheyne-Stokes pause, there is a latent period of 1 or 2 seconds followed by a rise in the intrapulmonic pressure that may exceed the maximum upstroke of the final inspiration. When the pause is sufficiently long and registration apparatus sufficiently delicate, it will be seen that this rise in pressure is due to a contraction lasting from 10 to 15 seconds. These contractions are evidently due to the activity of the lung musculature, for we have observed them in animals after isolation of the lungs, fixation or resection of the abdominal and shoulder muscles or destruction of the entire spinal cord below the medulla. Moreover, the changes in the intrapulmonic pressure due to active

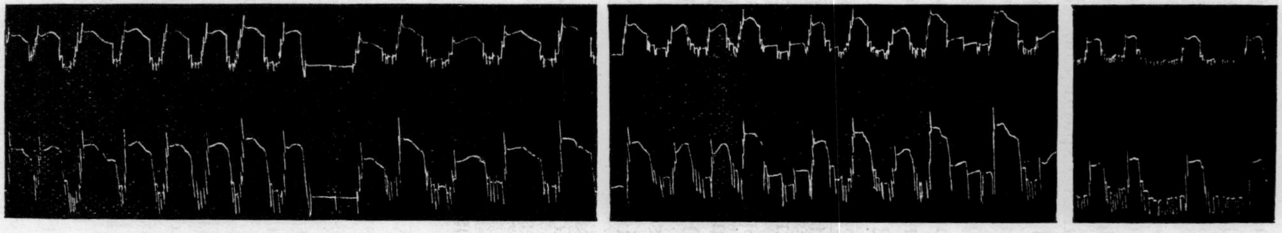

Fig. 2. Tracing of intrapulmonic presure in the bull frog in normal respiration. Frog in normal posture and resting without restraint in dark box. Operation for insertion of cannula in tip of one lung made under local anesthesia. Lower record by water manometer, upper record by delicate tambour. Showing the curve of lung contraction during the respiratory pause following the periodic rapid inspiration. The lung contractions are shown best on the tambour tracings, as this instrument is more delicate than the water manometer.

Fig. 3. Rana pipiens. Water manometer tracings showing contractions of lung following spontaneous respiration (quick up and down strokes). Whole brain exposed, spinal cord cut and pitted below medulla. Cannula in tip of one lung, opposite lung tied off. Glottis open. Animal lost much blood and was breathing irregularly.

contractions or relaxation of the skeletal musculature are more rapid. The contractions are also too slow to be due to passive elastic rebound of the connective tissue of the lung. They are, however, very similar to the quick spontaneous contractions that are seen at times in the hypertonic frog lung after cutting the vagi or complete destruction of brain and spinal cord (fig. 7). The tracing in figure 3 illustrates the fact that these lung contractions may follow single respiratory movements, if the pause between two successive swallowings is of sufficient duration.

It would seem that these contractions of the lung musculature following the active inspiration or attempts at inspiration have not been seen by previous workers, except possibly Graham Brown (5). On

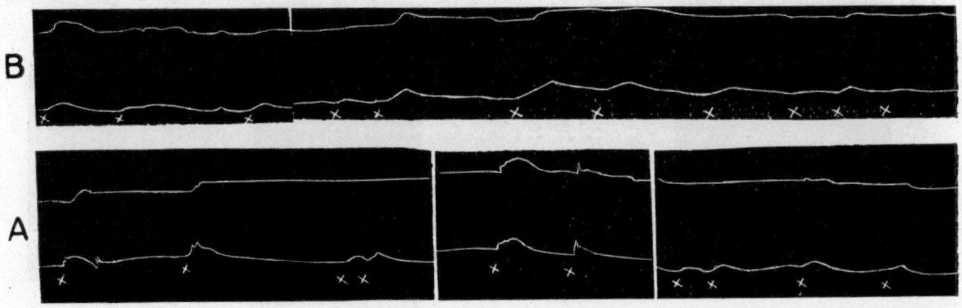

Fig. 4. Water manometer tracings of the contractions of the lung musculature in the frog (Rana pipiens) that follow upon the external respiratory movements. Spinal cord transected and destroyed below the medulla. Lungs isolated and cannulated (tip). Glottis closed with forceps so that there is no communication between the two lungs. *A*, upper tracing equals left lung; lower tracing equals right lung. *B*, same. *X* = pharyngeal respiration or attempt at swallowing air.

some of the tracings published by Brown there is an increased pressure in the lungs shortly before expiration, and Brown suggests that this is due to muscular contractions in the lungs.

The lung contractions do not depend on the change in tension on the lung tissues following a forceful inspiration. The glottis may be closed and the pressure in the lungs raised to that of the normal of 1 to 3 cm. of water, and in such preparations each attempt at respiration, single or a series, is followed by lung contractions (fig. 4). In preparations with the glottis closed the contractions are usually more prolonged than those seen in figures 2 and 3.

We are thus forced to the conclusion that in the frog the normal inspiratory movements lead to active contractions of the lung musculature through associated innervation, either of the motor fibers to the lung or through central depression of the inhibitory fibers controlling a peripheral automatism.

b. Inhibition. In preparations with the glottis closed, and in intrapulmonic pressure approximately normal (1–3 cm. of water), *the active respiratory movements lower the intrapulmonic pressure*, evidently by inhibition of the lung muscle tonus (fig. 5). With the glottis closed no air can enter or leave the lungs. The respiratory movements of the throat and pharynx, especially if they are vigorous, induce slight fluctuations in the intrapulmonic pressure of equal rapidity with the pharyngeal movements. Vigorous movements of the head may induce,

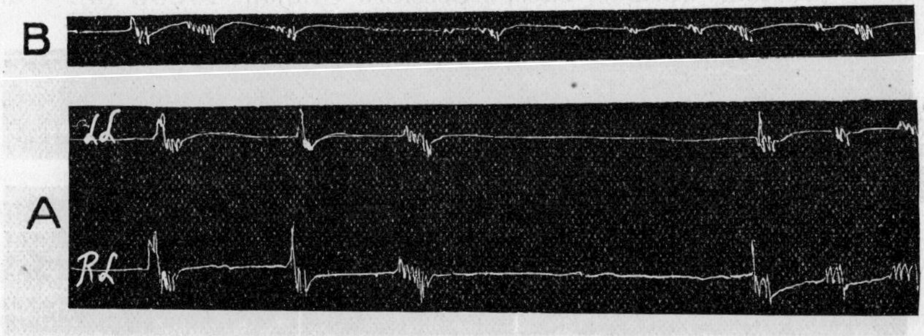

Fig. 5. Water manometer tracings of the intrapulmonic pressure in frogs (R. pipiens). Spinal cord cut and pithed below medulla. Cannula in tip of lung, and glottis closed (imperfectly) by cotton and collodion. *A*, simultaneous record from both lungs of the bull frog. *B*, record from lung of R. pipiens. Showing inhibition of the tonus of the lung musculature during the active respiratory movements. The rapid fluctuations (respiration) on the tracings are due to movements of larynx and head, and not to entrance and exit of air into the lungs.

possibly, stronger positive pressure in the closed lungs synchronously with these movements. It is possible but not probable that the lowering of lung muscle tonus during the rapid and rigorous swallowing movements are due to mechanical stimulation of the lung from this source, since the inhibition cannot be produced by similar fluctuations in intrapulmonic pressure artificially induced, and direct mechanical stimulation of the lungs when strong enough to have an effect causes contractions.

The return of the lung muscle tonus following the period of inhibition is quite similar to the lung contractions described in previous sections and illustrated in figures 2, 3 and 4. So far as we know, this inhibition of the lung musculature has not been noted by previous investigators.

The utility of the correlation is obvious, the relaxation of the lung musculature during inspiration being favorable to the filling of the lungs by the swallowing act.

THE PERIPHERAL MOTOR AUTOMATISM OF THE LUNGS AND THE INFLUENCE OF THE VAGI AND THE CERVICAL SYMPATHETIC NERVES ON THIS AUTOMATISM

1. In preparations with the glottis closed, lungs isolated from the influence of skeletal muscle contractions, section of the vago-sympathetic nerves in the neck, destruction of the medulla, or ligation of the base of the lungs *induces immediately a permanent hypertonus or incomplete tetanus of the lung neuro-muscular mechanism* (figs. 6, 8 and 9). By permanent, we refer, of course, only to the time of observation in these crucial experiments, that is, 2 hours. We found it difficult to maintain the preparation in good physiological condition over longer periods, especially with both lungs contracted down so that the lumen is completely obliterated thus preventing lung ventilation. The circulation also fails gradually.

The hypertonus of the lungs is usually at its maximum shortly after the isolation from the central nervous system, and there may be a gradual fall of the tonus during the observation period of 1 to 2 hours. This gradual fall is probably due to the failure of maintaining adequate circulation in the lungs, that is, to asphyxia.

This remarkable lung reaction is obtained in all frogs in good physiological condition, and the better the condition of the frog the stronger the lung tetanus on sections of the vagi. In frogs in poor condition (infected, starved or moribund from any cause) destruction of the medulla or vagi section causes little or no lung tetanus. In such preparations stimulation of the peripheral end of the cut vagi also fails to influence the lung tonus. Poor physiological conditions in the frog are evidently associated with lung atony, just as these conditions usually involve atony and absence of stomach rhythm in all species of animals so far studied.

We have occasionally found preparations showing marked lung tonus before section of the vagi or destruction of the medulla, that is, a tonus greater than that of normal respiration. We are inclined to ascribe this to the following causes: *a*, temporary depression of the medulla or nervous "shock" due to cutting the spinal cord, strong mechanical stimulation of many sensory nerves; *b*, direct mechanical injury to the

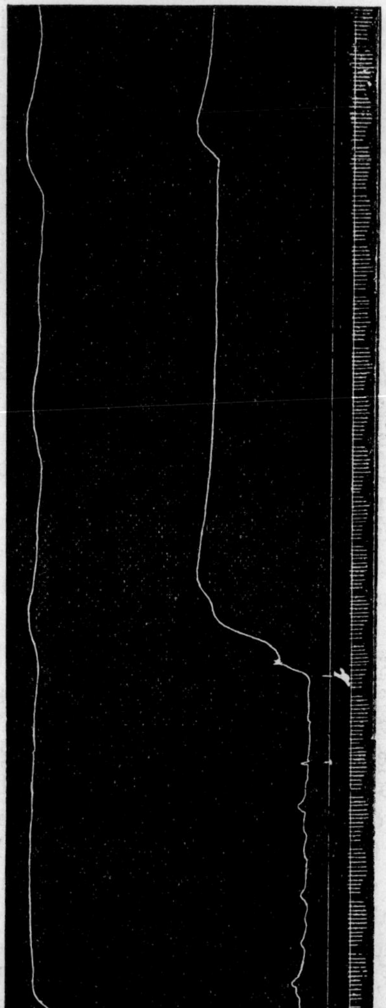

Fig. 6. Water manometer tracings of intrapulmonic pressure of frog (R. pipiens). Spinal cord transected and pithed below medulla. Frog fixed on dorsal side, abdomen laid open and lungs isolated from influence of skeletal muscles. Cannulae in tips of lungs. Glottis closed by forceps, shutting off at the same time air connections between the two lungs without interfering with lung circulation and lung innervation. *a*, Ligation of base of left lung (upper tracing). *b*, Section of right vagus (lower tracing = right lung). Signal line = base line pressure for right lung. Time, 5 seconds. Showing prolonged tetanus or tonus of lung neuro-musculature mechanism on severance of vagi nerves.

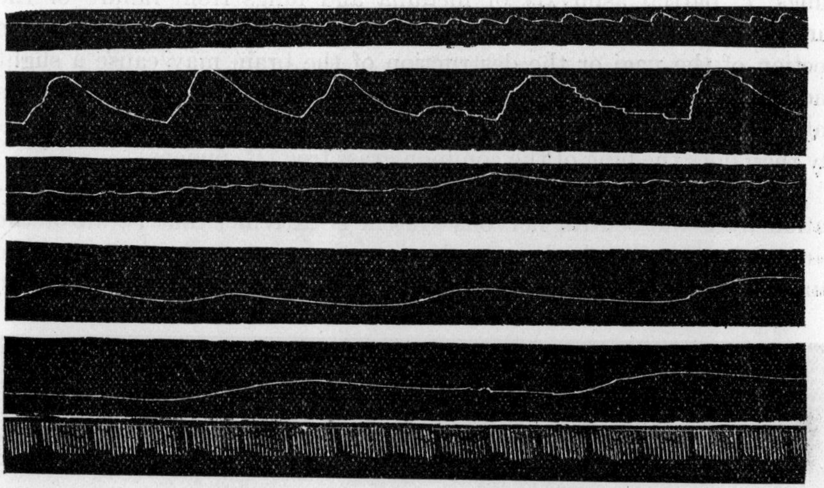

Fig. 7. Water manometer tracing of the intrapulmonic pressure in the frog (R. pipiens). Showing various types of peripheral automatism after isolation of the lungs from the central nervous system (section vago-sympathetic nerves or pithing of brain). Time, 5 seconds.

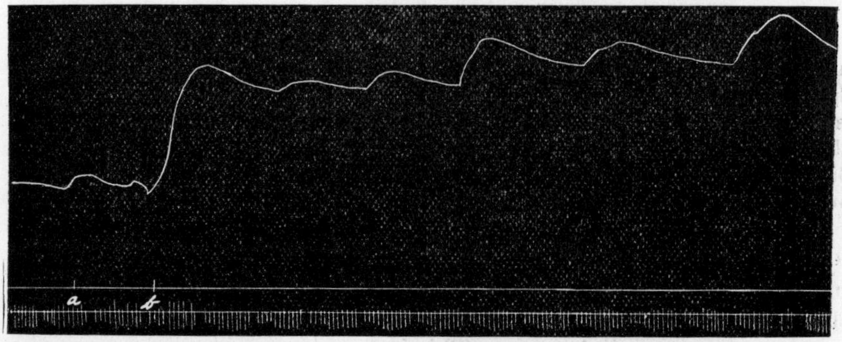

Fig. 8. Water manometer tracing of the intrapulmonic pressure in the frog's lung (R. pipiens), showing the incomplete tetany of the lung following destruction of the brain. Spinal cord cut and pithed below the medulla. Abdomen opened and lungs freed from influence of skeletal muscles. Cannula in tip of lung. Glottis closed by forceps, leaving vagi nerves and lung circulation intact. *a*, Transection of upper jaw. *b*, Crushing of brain (including medulla) by artery forceps. Time, 5 seconds.

lungs; *c*, partial asphyxia of medulla and lungs from failure of the circulation (unavoidable hemorrhage, etc.). In such preparations the section of the vagi or the destruction of the brain may cause a slight increase of the lung tonus (fig. 9). The lung of the bull frog passes into prolonged hypertonus on direct mechanical stimulation more readily than does the lung of the common grass frog (R. pipiens).

In our most vigorous preparation the lung tetanus following isolation from the central nervous system is extreme, that is, all of the air is driven out of the lung cavity into the water manometer and the lung cavity is completely obliterated. Even the traces of mucus are

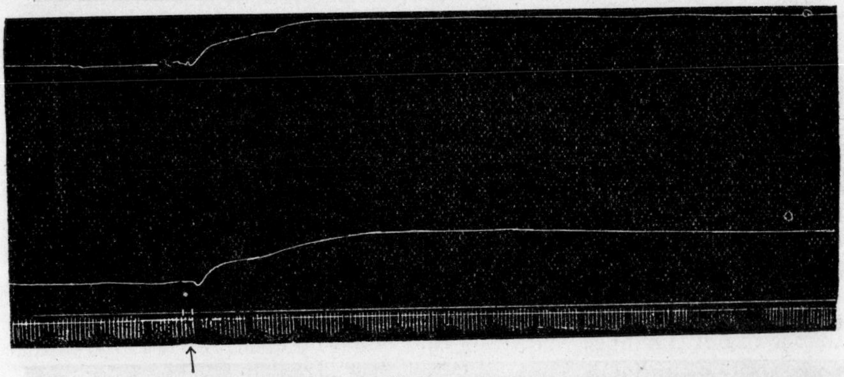

Fig. 9. Water manometer record of the intrapulmonic pressure in the frog's lung, showing moderate tetanus or tonus of the lung on destruction of the brain. Spinal cord cut and pithed below the medulla; frog fixed on dorsal side, and lungs isolated from influence of skeletal musculature. Cannula in tip of lungs; glottis closed by forceps, also shutting off air communication between the two lungs. Signal = crushing of brain with forceps. Signal line = the zero line of water pressure for right lung (lower tracing). Time, 5 seconds.

forced into the cannula in the tip of the lungs. The maximum intrapulmonic pressure thus developed is from 6 to 10 cm. of water above the pressure existing during normal respiration, that is, a total pressure of from 7 to 12 cm. of water. This is not the maximum pressure the lung tetanus is capable of developing. If the lungs are connected with a mercury manometer so that some air still remains in the lung cavity, even under the maximum lung tetanus following vagi section, the intrapulmonic pressure rises to the surprising height of 20 to 40 mm. Hg. (25–50 cm. water).

2. The nature of the peripheral lung tetanus. In most of our preparations the water manometer tracings of the lung tonus following isolation of the lungs from the central nervous system show a straight line indicating a continuous tonic or complete tetanic contraction (fig. 9). The more vigorous preparations exhibit various types of rhythmic contractions superimposed on the continuous hypertonus, at least during the first 15 to 60 minutes following the lung isolation. But even in these preparations the rhythm fails before the complete failure of the tonic state of contraction in later stages of the record. It would thus seem that the appearance of rhythm on the hypertonic state of the lung is a question of physiological condition of the lung motor mechanism.

The usual type of the rhythmic lung contractions is shown in figures 6 and 8, that is, a slow rhythm, the contraction and relaxation requiring 2 to 3 minutes. In general, the more vigorous the preparation the more rapid the rhythmic contractions. In other preparations contractions last only 20 to 30 seconds, and occasionally this faster rhythm may be superimposed on the slower rhythm (fig. 7), both rhythms being in turn superimposed on the continuous hypertonus. Whether these varying types of contractions involve different musculatures cannot be made out by the present method of experimentation. The continuous hypertonus as well as the strong slow rhythm seem to involve the whole lung. The more rapid rhythm is too feeble to be detected by direct inspection of the lung. Nothing that could be interpreted as peristaltic contractions similar to those exhibited by other visceral structures has so far been noted by us, although our water manometer tracings of the lung hypertonus as slow rhythmic contractions suggest many points of similarity to the contractions of the empty stomach as recorded by the balloon method. This may be of significance in connection with the fact that the lung is a diverticulum from the foregut (esophagus).

It appears that this striking lung tetanus or hypertonus following isolation of the lungs from the central nervous system has not been observed by previous investigators, evidently because none have sectioned the vagi after closing the glottis under conditions permitting recording the neuro-muscular tonus of the lungs. Several workers have studied the influence of vagi section on the external respiratory movements of the frog. Mochi states that the lungs remain permanently collapsed and empty when the medulla and vagi are left intact but all the brain anterior to the medulla removed. This is probably an error. Langendorff claims, at least, that the external respiratory movements persist after removal of the brain anterior to the medulla. According to Martin (16) and Mochi (17), (18), (19), stimulation of the optic

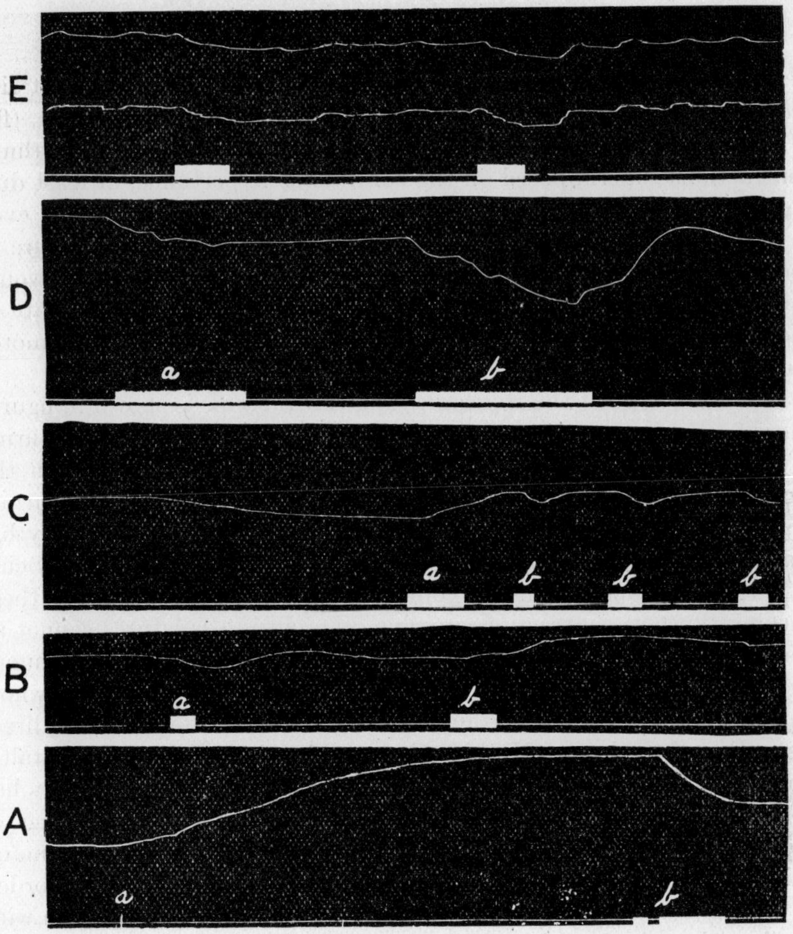

Fig. 10. Water manometer tracings of the intrapulmonic pressure in the frog (R. pipiens). Spinal cord cut and destroyed below medulla; lungs isolated and cannula fixed in tip of lungs. Glottis closed.

A: Right lung: *a*, section of vago-sympathetic nerve; *b*, stimulation of peripheral end of cut nerve with moderately strong tetanizing current.

B: Left lung: left vago-sympathetic nerve sectioned. Stimulation of peripheral end of cut nerve with weak, *a*, and strong, *b*, tetanizing current.

C: Left lung, after section of left vago-sympathetic stimulation of peripheral end of cut nerve with very strong, *a*, and moderately strong, *b*, tetanizing current.

D: Left lung, in very strong tonus after section of left vago-sympathetic nerve. Stimulation of the peripheral end of the cut nerve with weak, *a*, and strong, *b*, tetanizing current.

E: Upper tracing = left lung; lower tracing = right lung. Signal = stimulation of the peripheral end of the cut nerves. Showing inhibitions of lung tonus and contractions on stimulation of the peripheral end of the vago-sympathetic nerve.

lobes accelerates the respiratory movements. This may indicate a subsidiary respiratory center anterior to the medulla. At any rate mere decerebration does not induce lung tetanus in our experience.

Martin (16) states that destruction of the brain and spinal cord leaves the lungs entirely empty of air, but he does not make out or recognize that this is due to a persistent lung tetanus. Babak (2) quotes a number of authors as having shown that after vagi section or lung extirpation the frogs swallow air, periodically, into the stomach, and the air may actually escape by the cloaca. Berti and Marzemin (4) state that section of the vagi peripheral to the superior laryngeal branch results in irregular attempts at lung respiration on elevation of the temperature. Nikolides (20), (21) states that vagi section slows the respiratory movements making them at the same time irregular and stronger. Heinemann (9), one of the earliest observers, states that section of both vagi leads in the course of several days to such abnormal filling of the lungs that some of the viscera are pushed out through the cloaca. But when he opened the abdomen of these frogs the lungs were found collapsed or only partly filled. It is possible that Heinemann's frogs actually swallowed air into the stomach and intestines because of persistently constricted lungs. Soprana (24) states that vagotomized frogs breathe slower and deeper, but die more quickly from asphyxia on elevation of the temperature. According to Pari (22), the vagotomized frog is unable to fill the lungs, the lungs remain collapsed for weeks, and the air is forced into the stomach. It is possible that Pari's permanently collapsed lungs were in reality in a constricted state. But the method of observation did not suffice to record the fact.

It is certain that the force of the air swallowing would fail to cause air to enter the lungs against the maximum state of lung contraction found by us after section of the vagi nerves. But we do not know how long this hypertonus persists in the surviving animal, as all our experiments to date have been crucial. And even if the hypertonus, tonus or tetanus remained as long as the frog continued in good condition, failure of lung respiration may soon operate to place the frog below par in general, in which case there may be depression of the peripheral lung automatism already noted by us in animals in poor condition. The process of physiological readjustment of the peripheral lung motor mechanism may also come into play, similar to the readjustment that gradually takes place in the case of the heart and the respiratory center in the medulla after vagi section.

3. The action of the vagi and the cervical sympathetic nerves on the lung motor mechanism. a. The cervical sympathetic nerves. Section of the cervical sympathetic before its union with the vagus has no effect on the lung tonus (fig. 11), in marked contrast to the effects produced by section of the combined vago-sympathetic nerve. Electrical stimulation of the peripheral end of the cut cervical sympathetic causes slight contraction of the lung on the same side. It is difficult to stimulate the cervical sympathetic nerves, under the conditions of our experiments, and at the same time avoid escape of the current to the vagus

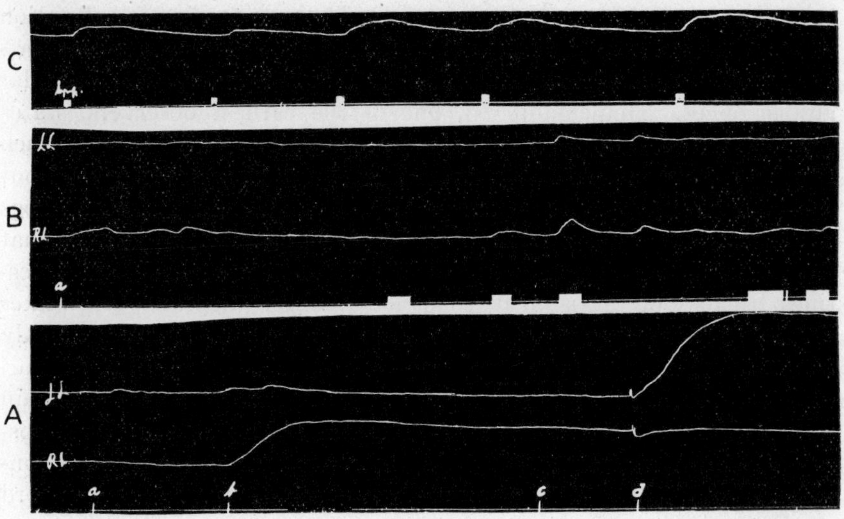

Fig. 11. Water manometer tracings of the intrapulmonic pressure in the frog's lungs (R. pipiens). Frogs decerebrated, animals fixed on dorsal side, lungs isolated from influence of skeletal muscle contraction. Cannula in tip of lungs. Glottis closed.

A: Upper tracing, left lung; lower, right lung. *a*, section right cervical sympathetic; *b*, section of right vagus; *c*, section of left cervical sympathetic; *d*, section of left vagus.

B: Upper racing, left lung; lower, right lung. *a*, section of right cervical sympathetic nerve; signal, stimulation of peripheral end of right cervical sympathetic. In this preparation the left cervical sympathetic and both vagi were intact.

C: Record from left lung, showing lung contractions on stimulation of the peripheral end of the cervical sympathetic nerve with strong tetanizing current, the vagus being intact.

Showing motor fibers to the lungs in the cervical sympathetic nerve, but no effect on lung tonus from section of these motor fibers.

ganglion, or to other sensory nerves, thus inducing reflex effects. Our usual technique was to section the large brachial nerve close to the vertebral column, taking care not to injure the slender sympathetic trunk passing under it; also section the root of the hypoglossal, and after again sectioning these nerves peripherally, handle the cervical sympathetic by the stump of the brachial to which it is attached. We also made it a point to apply the fine pointed electrodes to the cervical sympathetic trunk at least 3 mm. distant from the vagus root. But even with the best of precautions escape of current to adjacent structures could not always be prevented. And we are inclined to explain the *bilateral* lung effects produced by the stimulation of one sympathetic (fig. 11, *B*) as due to escape, and consequent reflexes. It is to be noted further that it requires relatively strong tetanizing currents applied to the sympathetic trunk to secure the lung contractions. Inhibitory effects on the lung were never obtained from the cervical sympathetic nerves.

Our conclusion is that the cervical sympathetic trunk carries motor (but no inhibitory) fibers to the lungs via the vagi. Under the conditions of our experiments the section of these motor fibers has no effect on the lung tonus, showing that this motor mechanism is not in tonic activity, and that the section of the nerves is not a sufficient stimulus for even a transient contraction.

b. The vagi nerves. We have seen that section of the vagus induces permanent hypertonus in the lung of the same side. Stimulation of the peripheral end of the cut vagus with a tetanizing current causes an inhibition of this tonus followed by a return to the former state. The vagus stimulation is thus able to completely abolish (temporarily) the tonus induced by the vagi section. In the preparations showing no lung hypertonus on vagi section owing to peripheral lung atony vagus stimulation usually causes no lung inhibition.

In several such preparations we observed that the vagi also failed to influence the heart rhythm. We can state that the failure of the vagi to act in the normal manner on the lungs and heart in these preparations was not due to mechanical injury to the vagi or to the heart and lungs. The significance of this coincidence requires further investigation. It is well known to laboratory workers in physiology that one frequently encounters frogs in which the vagi stimulation fails to influence the heart. This inhibitory action of the vagus on the lung is obtained with the minimum and up to relatively strong tetanizing currents. The stronger stimuli produce at times motor after-effects, and very strong tetanizing currents may produce contraction only or a brief initial contraction followed by inhibition. This latter result was obtained by strong stimuli, especially in preparations showing less than the maximum lung tonus following vagus section.

Stimulation of the peripheral vagus inhibits not only the tonus but also the spontaneous rhythmic contractions that may be superimposed on the lung hypertonus following isolation from the central nervous system (fig. 10, *E*).

It is thus clear that the vagi and the cervical sympathetic nerves in the frog bear the same physiological relations to the lungs as they do to the heart, that is, motor fibers in the latter and inhibitory fibers in the former to both organs. We shall show later in the section on the action of drugs on the lungs, that some of the motor fibers to the lungs are true vagi fibers, and do not belong to the cervical sympathetic complex.

4. The peripheral lung automatism. We are now in position to analyze more definitely the origin of the motor hypertonus of the lungs after vagi section. It is not due to temporary stimulation of motor fibers. We have shown that section of the sympathetic nerve fibers has no effect. There are some motor fibers to the lungs of pure vagus origin. But cutting of these fibers produces no effect on the lungs, after previous paralysis of the inhibitory vagi fibers by large doses of nicotine. It is not due to mechanical trauma to the lungs. Ligation of the base of the lung may induce lung tetanus by direct trauma or by asphyxia, lung circulation being cut off. But stopping the circulation by excising the heart does not cause lung tetanus, and section of the vagi is done without touching the lungs or the adjacent structures. Moreover, the indirect mechanical disturbance of the pharynx and the base of the lungs is much greater from isolation of the vagi or the cervical sympathetic nerves, and these latter procedures do not bring on lung tetanus. The lung hypertonus is not an asphyxia phenomenon. Excessive lung ventilation, normal or artificial, will not prevent or abort it, if the vagi are sectioned or the brain destroyed. The lung hypermotility is not a temporary motor reflex state induced via the medulla by the powerful afferent impulses induced by the extensive operative trauma, for the lung is found collapsed and maximally contracted in frogs with the brain destroyed, without previous operative injury of any kind, and we know of no other reflex state that may persist for hours after lesion of the reflex path. It is not unlikely, however, that any condition inducing a peripheral lung hypertonus of a degree interfering with the respiratory functions of the lungs would augment the inhibitory action of the medulla on the lungs, probably through sensory fibers from the pulmonary branches of the vagi, a mechanism analogous to that of the depressor nerves and the cardio-inhibitory center.

In the experiments with pithing the medulla we at times obtained a slight temporary inhibition of the lung tonus prior to the typical lung tetanus. The temporary inhibition is evidently due to a transient stimulation of the medulla inhibitory center by the act of destruction. It is not probable that the subsequent lung hypertonus is due to a more lasting traumatic stimulation of the motor fibers, analogous to the effect produced on the heart by strong stimulation of the two sets of fibers in the vagi nerve trunks. This possibility is disproved by the fact that nicotine paralyzes the lung inhibitory nerve mechanism, leaving the motor nerve mechanism intact, and nicotine causes a lung tetanus which is not augmented by subsequent destruction of the medulla or section of the vagi.

Hence we must conclude that in the frog the vagi inhibitory fibers to the lungs are in constant or tonic activity, holding the peripheral motor automatism in check, and that on removal of this check the lungs go into a persistent tetanus or hypertonus. In other words, the lungs of the frog behave like the heart of many species of animals on section of the vagi; the heart beats faster, the lungs become hypertonic to a degree that nullifies their function.

These observations place the lung of the frog in the same category as the heart and the alimentary tract as regards independent peripheral motor automatism. In all these structures we have the same motor tissues, viz., nerve cells, nerve plexuses and musculature. We are therefore confronted by the same problems as regards the nature of the mechanism of the lung automatism that have engaged the attention of the physiologists in connection with the heart and the gut. A question of equal importance is the persistence or modification of this primitive lung automatism, in health and disease, in other groups of lunged animals.

CHANGES IN INTRAPULMONIC PRESSURE AS A RESULT OF THE STIMULATION OF VARIOUS AFFERENT NERVES

No investigations have been made on reflexes into the lung musculature. Most of the previous workers have been engaged in a study of the external respiratory phenomena of the frog. Wendenski (26) noted

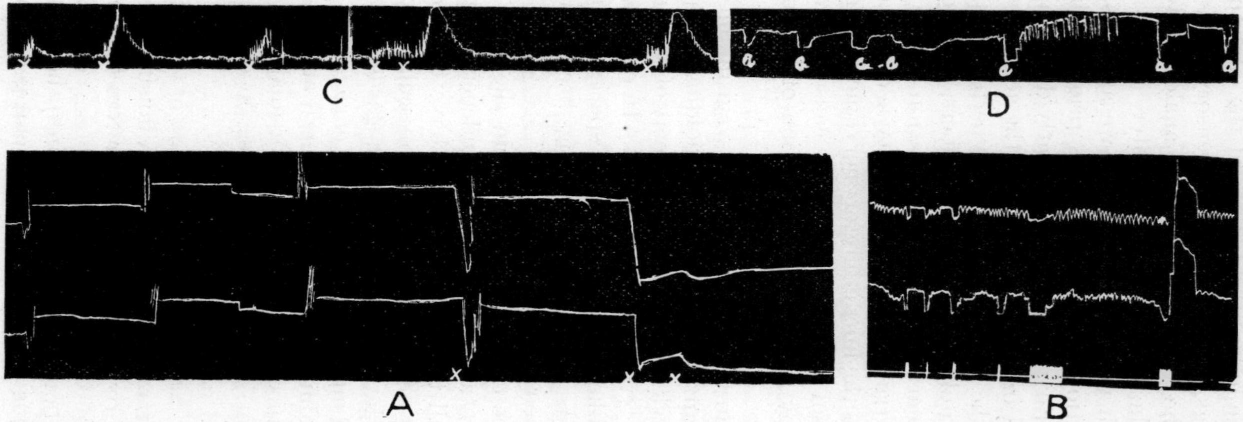

Fig. 12. Water manometer tracings of the intrapulmonic pressure in frogs. Glottis free. Cannula in tip of lungs. Tracings *A*, *B*, *C*, frogs decerebrated. Tracing D, spinal cord cut and destroyed below medulla leaving the brain intact. *A*, Bull frog. Upper tracing, left lung; lower, right lung. *X*, rubbing skin of hind leg.

B: (R. pipiens) upper record, left lung; lower, right lung. Signal, electrical stimulation of the urinary bladder.

C: *X* = gentle stroking of skin of hind leg, resulting in accelerated inspiration.

D: *a* = approach of finger on any moving object within the frog's visual field, followed by inhibition in a state of complete expiration or collapse of lungs.

"expiratory tetany" following weak stimulation of sensory fibers in the vagi. His method as well as that of other workers was not designed to note actual contractions of the lung itself, since in every case previous experimenters worked with an open glottis. However, tracings 15 and 16 of this article, taken from doubly vagotomized frogs, show very slight inspiratory and expiratory excursions of the flanks and long tonus variations obviously due to the strong tonus of the lung and the tonus contractions in the lung as seen by us.

Sensory stimulation of any sort, be it electrical or mechanical, has a powerful effect on the external respiration of the frog by either reducing the intrapulmonic pressure by reflex opening of the glottis, or if the latter is closed by hemostat or pressure by vaselinized cotton at the time of application of stimulus, by reflex lung contraction which will cause the intrapulmonic pressure to rise.

Figure 12 *A* shows at *X* the sudden opening of the glottis in decerebrated bull frog, holding air under considerable pressure, following gentle stroking of the skin of the hind leg. The first part of the tracing shows voluntary respirations (swallowing of air) with maintenance of high intrapulmonic pressure. The prompt collapse of the lung is followed immediately by marked respiratory effects which raised the intrapulmonic pressure to its original level. Stimulation of the skin in another preparation similarly prepared (fig. 12 *C*) not only increased the volume of the respiratory gulps, which were occurring regularly and continuously prior to the stimulation, but induced the animal in every instance to fill the lungs to the maximum capacity in the fashion described in the second section of this paper.

Figure 12 *B* shows a similar collapse of the lungs in Rana pipiens due to opening of the glottis following electrical stimulation of the urinary bladder with a moderately strong tetanizing current.

Tracing *D*, figure 12, was obtained from a frog with brain intact. In this animal the simple approach of the finger or person at *a* led to collapsed lung followed by more or less marked efforts at refilling.

In all tracings reproduced in figure 12 the glottis was open. These preparations, therefore, were not favorable for a study of the pulmonary activity itself (lung contractions or inhibitions) following the stimulation of various afferent nerves. In order to maintain the volume of air constant we closed the glottis by a mosquito forceps or vaselinized cotton and raised the intrapulmonary pressure to a point maintained by the animal under normal conditions and then noted the effect of the stimulation of the afferent nerves.

The ligation of the vagus on one side (mechanical stimulation) in many instances induced reflex contraction of the opposite lung. In the present state of our knowledge it is impossible to state whether record of such a contraction as shown in figure 13 *A* at *X* is due to reflex stimulation of the lung through the motor fibers of the vagus or due to a temporary inhibition of the tonic inhibitory control over the lung via the vagi, leaving the peripheral automatic mechanism in the lung unchecked. A possible answer to this question might be obtained by noting the effect of such stimulation in animals in which the tonic inhibitory mechanism has been previously paralyzed by nicotine. If under these conditions stimulation of the sensory nerves yields the same results the recorded contraction is the result, not of a temporary inhibition of the tonic inhibitory mechanism, but due to the reflex stimulation of the pulmonary motor fibers through the vagi (and sympathetics). Consideration of the law of reciprocal innervation would suggest that under normal conditions both mechanisms are involved in the phenomenon whose graphic record is that of a rise in intrapulmonic pressure.

Irrespective of the mechanism or mechanisms involved in ultimately effecting contractions of the lungs, we can confidently say that stimulation of the skin of the upper mandible, mild mechanical irritation of the anterior nares, mechanical stimulation of the bladder and cloaca, or electrical stimulation of the urinary bladder, mesentery, small intestine, pyloric end of stomach, esophagus and central end of the brachial nerve effect reflex contractions of the lung. These points are shown individually in figure 13 and figure 14, which with the accompanying legends are self-explanatory. The mode of preparation of the animals used in both series is virtually the same with this exception: In the preparations, records of which are illustrated in figure 13, the glottis was clamped by means of a mosquito forceps; in the tracings reproduced in figure 14 the glottis was kept occluded by pressure over it by a piece of vaselinized cotton.

Of these records two deserve particular attention. In figure 13, *D*, is recorded the powerful reflex lung contractions obtained by closure of the glottis by a hemostat. A decided inhibition preceded the contraction.

Tracing *E* in the same figure shows an unusually strong reflex contraction of both lungs as a result of crushing the skin of the lower mandible.

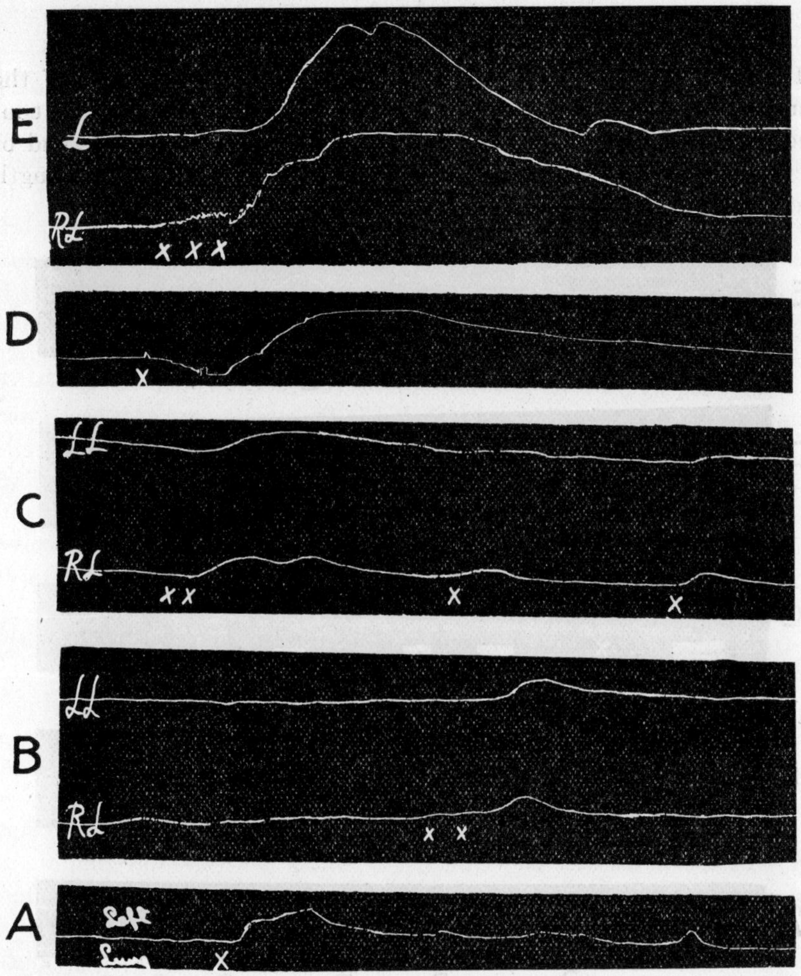

Fig. 13. Water manometer tracing of intrapulmonic pressure in the frog (R. pipiens). Spinal cord cut and destroyed below medulla. Cannula in tip of lungs, abdomen opened and the lungs isolated from abdominal and shoulder musculature. Glottis closed by clamp except in tracing *D*.

A: Left lung; *x*, ligation of right vago-sympathtic nerve, showing reflex contraction of left lung on vagus stimulation.

B: Upper tracing, left lung; lower, right lung. *X*, mechanical stimulation of the skin of the upper mandible, showing reflex lung contraction.

C Upper tracing, left lung; lower, right lung. *XX*, mechanical stimulation of the nares; *X*, mechanical stimulation of the cornea, showing reflex lung contractions.

D: *X*, closure of the glottis with artery forceps, showing temporary reflex inhibition of lung tonus followed by strong contraction.

E: Upper tracing, left lung; lower equals right lung. *XXX*, crushing skin of lower mandible, showing exceptionally strong reflex lung contractions.

In this series of experiments stimulation of the fundic end of the stomach (fig. 14, *D*, "*c*") with the electrical current yielded no reflex contraction of the lung at a time when stimulation of the pyloric end of the stomach and cardiac region of the esophagus with the same strength of current gave uniformly striking results.

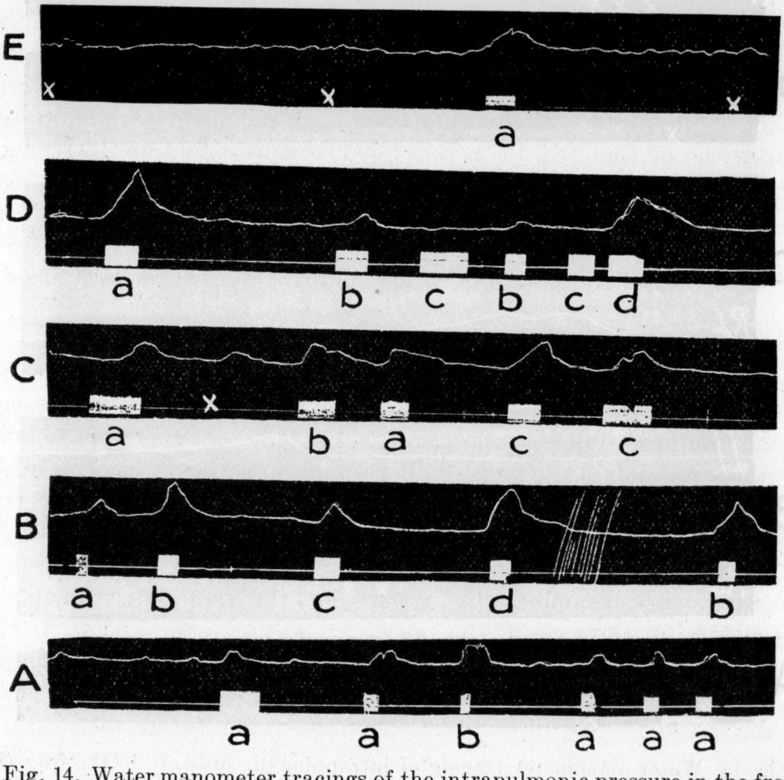

Fig. 14. Water manometer tracings of the intrapulmonic pressure in the frog's lung, showing reflex contractions of the lung musculature. Frogs decerebrated. Abdomen opened, lungs isolated from influence of skeletal muscle contractions. Cannula in tip of lungs, and glottis closed with a plug of vaselined cotton pushed into the pharynx.

A: *a*, mechanical stimulation (stroking) skin of hind leg; *b*, pinching toes of hind leg.

B: *a*, mechanical stimulation of urinary bladder; *b*, electrical stimulation of urinary bladder; *c*, mechanical stimulation of cloaca.

C: Electrical stimulation; *a*, large intestine; *b*, mesentery; *c*, small intestine.

D: Electrical stimulation; *a*, small intestine; *b*, pyloric end of stomach; *c*, fundus of stomach; *d*, esophagus (cardiac region).

E: *a*, electrical stimulation of central end of brachial nerve plexus. *X*, spontaneous respiration (quick up stroke).

In a summarizing sentence we might therefore state that the stimulation of every sensory nerve (afferent visceral or cutaneous) gives rise reflexly to lung contractions.

THE ACTION OF CERTAIN DRUGS ON THE MOTOR MECHANISM OF THE LUNG

Our interest in the action of drugs on the neuro-muscular mechanism of frog's lung had its inception during our study of the physiological action of the vagus on the lung musculature following electrical stimulation of the nerve. Such stimulation gave at outset variable results until we noted that the effects depended to some extent on the strength of the tetanizing current employed, as noted above. At any rate, we had good reason to suspect that the vagus carried both motor and inhibitory fibers to the lung motor mechanism. At this juncture it occurred to us that the use of drugs might be helpful in clarifying the situation.

Nicotine. Mindful of the action of nicotine in abolishing the inhibitory effect of vagus stimulation on the heart without affecting the motor action, we assumed that the drug might act similarly with respect to the inhibitory fibers in the vagus to the lung. If this were so, electrical stimulation of the vagus following the injection of nicotine might give clearer evidence of motor fibers in this nerve than before nicotinization. Since, furthermore, the paralysis of the ganglion cells in the course of the inhibitory fibers to the heart effected by this drug is preceded most commonly by *stimulation*, the same effect might be anticipated in the case of the inhibitory fibers to the lungs. If this were true nicotine ought to cause, on injection, an inhibition similar to, if not identical with, the inhibition of the heart commonly observed as the marked effect of stimulation of the vagus before the injection of the drug, especially if the tonic central inhibitory control exercised over the lungs via the vagi had been abolished by either sectioning of the nerves or destruction of the medulla.

The results obtained exceeded our expectations. Inspection of figure 15 (at *g*) shows that 1 mgm. nicotine when intravenously injected effects a pulmonary inhibition in the lungs released from the tonic inhibitory influence of vagus by section of these nerves (at *a* and *b*) which compares favorably with the inhibition obtained by previously stimulating the nerves with a tetanizing current of moderate intensity (see *e* and *f*).

If, on the other hand, the nicotine is injected intravenously in an animal following ligation and section of but one vagus, as in figure 16,

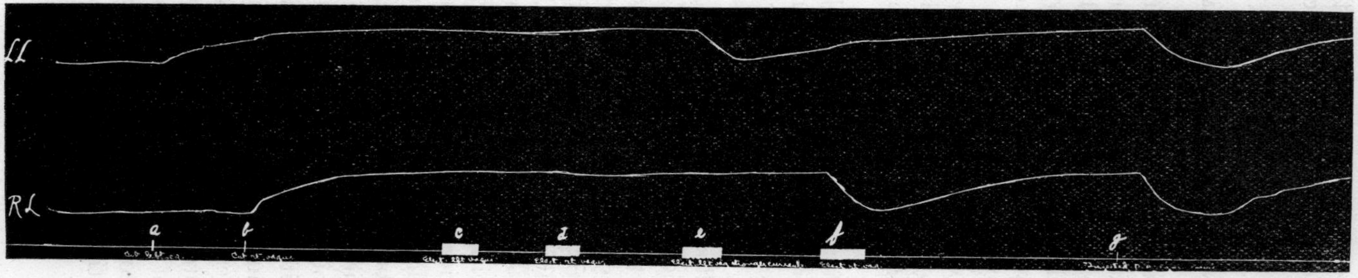

Fig. 15. Water manometer tracings of the intrapulmonic pressure in the frog's lung (R. pipiens). Spinal cord sectioned and destroyed below medulla. Cannula in tip of lungs. Lungs isolated from influence of skeletal musculature. Lower tracing, right lung; upper tracing, left lung. Glottis closed. *a*, Section of left vagus; *b*, section of right vagus; *c* and *d*, stimulation of left and right vagus with very weak tetanizing current; *e* and *f*, stimulation of left and right vagi with stronger tetanizing current; *g*, injection of 1 mgm. nicotine in 5 cc. Ringer's solution into abdominal vein.

Showing nicotine inhibitions of lung muscle tonus identical with the vagi inhibitions.

the immediate effect on the lungs is an inhibition of the tonus of the lung which has been denervated, and an escape from the tonic inhibitory influence exercised by the vagus on the lung which is still connected with its center, as at *c*, where the left lung (upper tracing) shows a rise in tonus occurring in the course of an inhibiton of the right lung, the latter comparing favorably with the inhibition effected by previous stimulation of the vagus (*b*). In this experiment the left vagus has been cut *physiologically* by the drug. If at the time of this drug cutting the vagus through central action is exercising its maximum inhibition on the lung, the effect of the primary stimulating action of the drug would not appear since the lung at the time of drug stimulation is already under maximum inhibitory control. As a matter of fact, in the majority of preparations this is apparently the case, the drug nicotine simply releasing the peripheral automatic mechanism from the maximum tonic inhibitory effect of the center through the vagus. This release is certainly complete for section of the vagus to this lung is without further effect on its tonus. This latter fact would furthermore indicate that the more or less prompt rise of intrapulmonary pressure following section of the vagus without nicotine was due, not to the mechanical stimulation of the motor fibers contained in this nerve, but to the removal of the tonic inhibitory control. That the vagus nerve contains such motor fibers can be shown very satisfactorily in any preparation that has been nicotinized. In figure 16 electrical stimulation of the nerves after nicotine (as at *g*, right vagus, and *h*, left vagus) gives now marked contraction of the lung instead of the usual inhibition before nicotine (*b*).

Figure 17, *A*, is offered as another example of this phenomenon. Following the release of the left lung from tonic inhibitory control exercised over it through central vagal control by section of the left vagus at *a*, 2 mgm. nicotine were injected at *b* with the result that the right lung was now released from its inhibition by the "cutting" action of the drug and the left lung was inhibited by the primary stimulation action of the drug on the inhibitory mechanism of the left lung. Figure 17, *B*, shows the change in effect as a result of electrical stimulation of the vagus nerve following the injection of nicotine. In this experiment stimulation of the vagus at *b* caused pronounced inhibition. The injection of nicotine at *c* was followed by the usual inhibition in the lung which has been released from the tonic inhibitory control by section of the nerve at *a*. Subsequent, however, to this nicotinization, electrical stimulation at *d* caused marked contraction of the lung instead of inhibition.

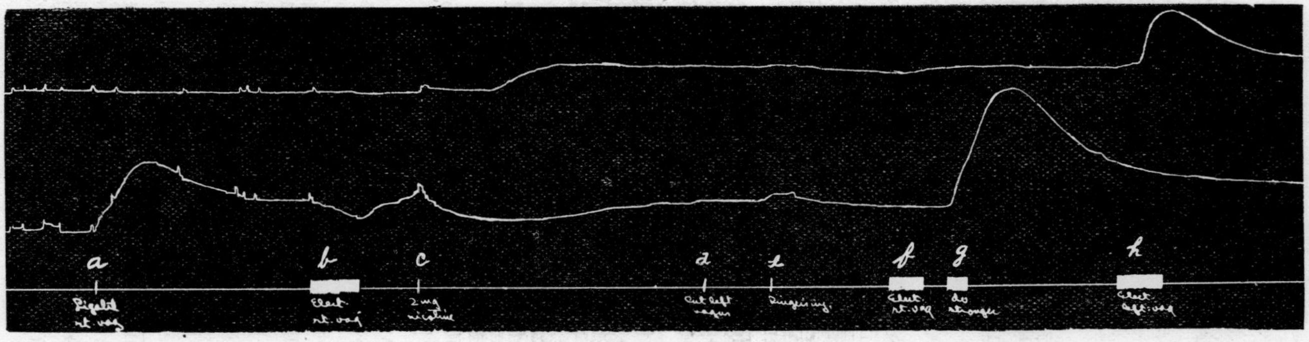

Fig. 16. Water manometer tracings of the intrapulmonic pressure in the frog's lung (R. pipiens). Spinal cord cut and destroyed below medulla; glottis closed; cannula in tip of lungs. Lungs isolated from influence of skeletal musculature. The quick up-strokes on tracings to the left of *C* are due to movements of the larynx in the spontaneous respiratory movements. Upper tracing, left lung; lower, right lung. *a*, Ligation of right vagus; *b*, electrical stimulation of right vagus; *c*, injection of 2 mgm. nicotine in 10 cc. Ringer's solution into abdominal vein; *d*, ligation, left vagus; *e*, injection of 10 cc. Ringer's solution into abdominal vein; *f* and *g*, stimulation of right vagus with weak and strong tetanizing current; *h*, stimulation of left vagus with tetanizing current.

These tracings show the primary inhibitory action of vagus stimulation and nicotine on the lung hypertonus following section of the vagi, the paralysis of inhibitory fibers of the vagi by nicotine thus permitting the full development of peripheral lung tonus, and the reversal of the inhibitory action of the vagosympathetic action after nicotine.

The results are uniformly clear-cut and decisive. By means of this drug nicotine it is possible to differentiate between two types of efferent pulmonary fibers occurring in the vagus, i.e., inhibitory fibers and motor fibers. The former exercise in the normal frog a powerful inhibitory control over the lung and are either more numerous or more readily susceptible to electrical stimulation than the motor fibers. It is only after the abolition of the inhibitory control of the lung by nicotine that

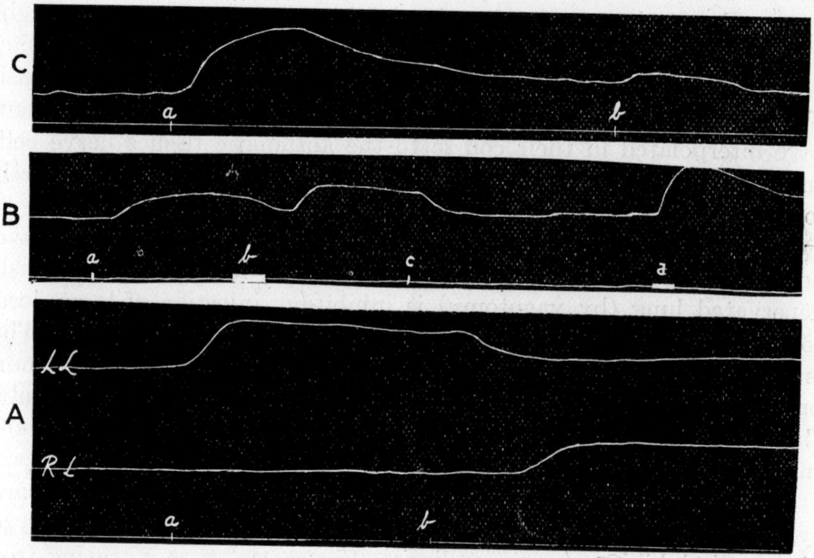

Fig. 17. Water manometer tracings of the intrapulmonic pressure in the frog (R. pipiens). Spinal cord cut and destroyed below the medulla. Glottis closed. Cannula in tip of lungs. Lungs isolated from influence by skeletal musculature.

A: Lower tracing, right lung; upper, left lung. *a*, Ligation of left vagus; *b*, injection of 2 mgm. nicotine in 10 cc. Ringer's solution into abdominal vein. Showing abolition of the tonic vagus inhibition of the lung neuro-muscular mechanism by nicotine.

B: Tracing from right lung. *a*, Ligation of right vagus; *b*, stimulation of peripheral end of right vagus with weak tetanizing current; *c*, injection of 2 mgm. nicotine in 10 cc. Ringer's solution into abdominal vein; *d*, stimulation of peripheral end of right vagus with same strength of tetanizing current as at *b*. Showing inhibition of lung tonus and paralysis of the vagi inhibitory fibers by nicotine.

C: Tracing from left lung. *a*, Injection of 5 mgm. nicotine in 5 cc. of Ringer's solution into the heart; *b*, injection of 1 cc. 1–1000 histamine into the heart. Showing stimulation of the lung by large doses of nicotine and stimulation by histamine after paralysis of the inhibitory nerves by nicotine.

electrical stimulation yields a more or less marked motor effect. Nor are these motor fibers of sympathetic origin running in the trunk of the vagus; for, granting the presence of some motor fibers in this nerve to the lung, the motor response on stimulation of the sympathetic after nicotine is smaller in a given animal than the response from the vagus itself, as noted earlier in the paper. In short, the vagus nerve contains two sets of fibers to the pulmonary motor mechanism of which the inhibitory exerts a tonic predominant control; the motor fibers are apparently not in a state of tonic activity for sectioning of the vagus after cutting the inhibitory fibers in this nerve by nicotine has no further effect on the intrapulmonic pressure. It would appear on the basis of our pharmacological studies that the inhibitory fibers of the vagus have interpolated in their course to the automatic tissues nerve cells on which the drug acts; the motor fibers on the other hand run directly to the automatic tissue.

Large doses of nicotine. Whereas the constant effect of the intravenous injection of small doses (2 mgm.) of nicotine in the previously denervated lung (by vagotomy) is inhibition, injection of large doses (5 mgm. or more) causes pronounced contraction of the lung. This is well shown in figure 17, *C*, where the injection of 5 mgm. caused more or less abrupt contraction followed by slow relaxation. It is probable that the nicotine in this dosage acts as a direct stimulant to the smooth musculature.

Atropine. This drug, even when given in large doses, does not paralyze the endings of the inhibitory fibers to the lungs as it paralyzes the cardio-inhibitory nerve endings. Figure 18, *A*, is a tracing from a frog which had received 1 cc. of a 0.1 per cent solution of atropine sulfate 45 minutes previous to experimentation. Pithing of the brain at *a* was followed by the typical escape of the lung from tonic central inhibitory control. The failure of atropine to paralyze the inhibitory nerve ending in the lung is shown further by the fact that even mechanical stimulation of the nerve at *b* gave powerful inhibition, as did electrical stimulation at *c*. As an after-effect of mechanical or electrical stimulation of the nerve there were pronounced motor effects. The results obtained from the right lung of another frog were somewhat different. Here (fig. 17, *B*) ligation of the vagus caused the usual escape of the lung from the inhibition. On the other hand, mechanical stimulation due to handling of the vagus nerve (at *b*) was followed by contraction. Stimulation of this nerve at *c* with a mild tetanizing current was in this instance followed by contraction instead of the usual inhibition.

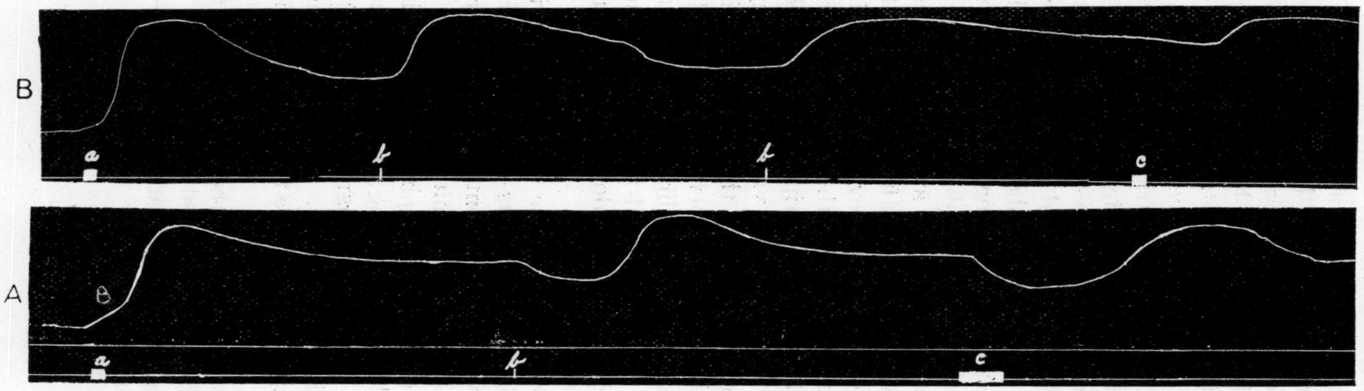

Fig. 18. Water manometer tracings of the intrapulmonic pressure in the frog (R. pipiens). Spinal cord cut and destroyed below medulla. Cannula in tip of lungs. Glottis closed. Lungs isolated from influence of skeletal muscle contractions.

One cubic centimeter of 0.1 per cent solution of atropin sulphate injected into the dorsal lymph sac 45 minutes before animals were prepared for the experiments.

A: Left lung; *a*, brain pith; *b*, mechanical stimulation (pulling) of left vagus; *c*, electrical stimulation of left vagus.

B: Right lung; *a*, ligation right vagus; *b*, mechanical stimulation of right vagus; *c*, electrical stimulation of right vagus with weak tetanizing current. Showing persistence of vagi inhibitory influence on the lung with exaggeration of the motor after effects after atropin in sufficient quantities to paralyze the cardiac vagi fibers.

To meet the objection that in these cases the dosage was too small and that the effects of the drug had worn off before experimentation was begun, we prepared another frog as follows: After decerebration, insertion of the cannula into the tips of both lungs, and clamping of the glottis, we sectioned the left vagus and obtained the usual escape of the lung from the tonic central inhibition control. Stimulation of this nerve gave the usual inhibition. The intravenous injection of $\frac{1}{2}$ mgm. atropine did not effect the result of stimulation of the vagus. We now injected within 1 hour's time in successive doses, 1, 2 and 4 mgm. atropine sulphate. These injections did not change the usual reaction obtained from stimulation of the peripheral vagus. Following the injection of the last 4 mgm., the right lung escaped from central inhibitory control in a manner indistinguishable from section of its vagus nerve. Apparently this huge dose of atropine paralyzed the center, for section of the right vagus was without further effect. Stimulation of its peripheral end, however, yielded even now inhibition followed by contraction of the lung, indicating that the chief action on the lung of atropine in huge doses is not peripheral. Since decided motor after-effects result from stimulation of vagus to the lung in a heavily atropinized frog, we might conclude that the drug likewise has *some effect* in paralyzing the inhibitory nerve endings unless we assume that it sensitizes the motor nerve endings in the vagus. At any rate the peripheral action of atropine and nicotine are quantitatively decidedly different if one compares the dosage in milligrams and the results effected thereby.

Both drugs paralyze the center and likewise act on the peripheral mechanism. Nicotine accomplishes both results quickly and decisively in smaller doses, while atropine acts on the center only in large doses and only renders paretic the inhibitory terminations of the vagus. The frog is apparently quite tolerant to atropine. Eight milligrams injected intravenously into a decerebrated frog at one time suspends external respiration promptly (as does 1 mgm. of nicotine). Examination of the lungs shows them contracted. But almost complete recovery sets in within an hour and at this time the lungs assume their normal size and function.

Atropine in this dosage does not paralyze the terminals of the inhibitory fibers of the lung as it does the vagal nerve endings in the heart. In all of these atropinized preparations stimulation of the vagus nerve was without effect on the heart.

Adrenalin. In the frog the irrigation of the lung itself or injection of adrenalin chloride into the circulation causes inhibition of the automatic quick rhythm of the lungs which appears spontaneously as noted in a previous section of this paper or inhibits the hypertonic activity of the lung following section of the vagus. As illustrations of this effect of adrenalin we offer figure 19, *A* and *B*. The former tracing shows inhibition of the quick rhythm when adrenalin was applied to the lung directly at *X*; the latter, inhibition of the hypertonic state of the lung following vagotomy.

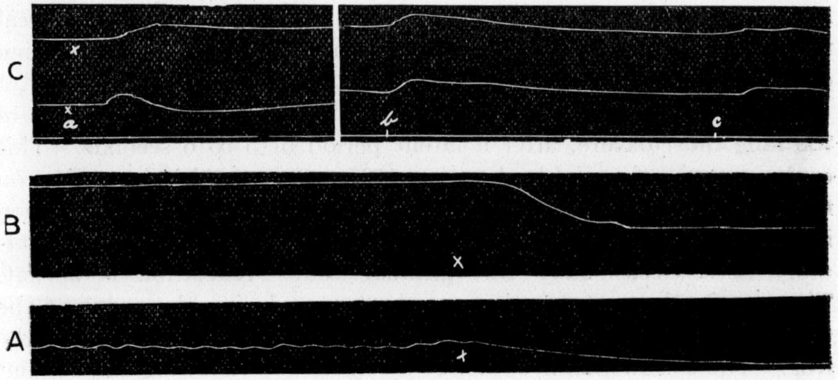

Fig. 19. Water manometer tracings of the intrapulmonic pressure in the frog (R. pipiens). Spinal cord cut and destroyed below medulla. Cannula in tip of lungs. Vagi nerves cut, and lungs isolated from influence of skeletal muscle contraction.

***A:* *X*, application of $\frac{1}{10}$ cc. adrenalin chloride (1–1000) in Ringer's solution to surface of lung.**

***B:* *X*, injection of $\frac{1}{10}$ cc. adrenalin chloride in 2 cc. Ringer's solution into the heart.**

***C:* Upper tracing, left lung; lower tracing, right lung. Intravenous injections of histamine in 2 cc. Ringer's solution; *a*, 0.01 cc.; *b*, 0.02 cc.; *c*, 0.06 cc. 1–1000 histamine hydrochloride.**

Showing inhibition of lung tonus by epinephrin and stimulation by histamine.

Histamine. Figure 19, *C*, and figure 17, *C* at *b* show the effect of histamine-HCl on the neuro-muscular apparatus of the lung when injected intravenously in varying concentrations. In moderately small or large doses it causes invariably a slight contraction of the lung which in amplitude bears no relationship to the dosage. Our experience, as a matter of fact, leads us to believe that successive doses of the drug given within a relatively short period of time have less and less effect because, possibly, of the cumulative poisonous property of this drug.

SUMMARY

1. The actual respiratory movements (opening of glottis and swallowing of air) are accompanied by relaxation of the tonus of the lung musculature, due either to greater action of the inhibitory fibers in the vagi or central inhibition of the motor nerve mechanism, on the assumption that the latter is in tonic activity. This inhibition occurs during the respiratory movements even when no air can enter or leave the lungs. It is therefore of central origin, an effect coördinated with the true respiratory act. From the point of view of utility the inhibition may be designated as a "receptive relaxation." The buccal movements that go on during the period between actual air swallowing do not seem to influence the lung tonus.

2. At the end of the respiratory act there is an active contraction of the lung musculature, after a latent period of 5 to 6 seconds. This contraction is of variable duration (10 to 20 seconds) depending on the respiratory rate and the condition of the lungs. The contraction is usually followed by a gradual tonus relaxation up to the next respiratory act. Occasionally this gradual tonus relaxation is absent. These active lung contractions are best seen during the pause of the Cheyne-Stokes type of breathing, which appears to be normal for the frog. The contraction is cut short by the next swallowing act, so that when the animal is breathing rapidly, the active lung contractions are not in evidence, the lung musculature being in a continuous state of "receptive relaxation." The active lung contractions following a respiratory act can be accounted for by a lowering of the inhibitory influence, thus permitting the peripheral automatism to come into greater play. We have not been able to determine whether motor innervation via vagi and sympathetic nerves also play a rôle as contractions follow the respiratory act even when no air enters or leaves the lungs. It is not a reflex initiated by the stimulation of pulmonary sensory fibers through lung distention. It is probably entirely central in origin and referable to the respiratory center, the inspiratory discharge of this center having the immediate effect of a temporary stimulation of the inhibitory mechanism for the lung tonus, the lung contraction of the end of the inspiration merely signifying excess back swing of the central inhibitory control on its return to the more or less constant level.

3. Section of the cervical sympathetic fibers has no effect on the lung tonus but stimulation of these fibers before they join the vagi

nerves causes lung contractions. The cervical sympathetic nerves contain a few motor fibers, but no inhibitory fibers to the lungs. These motor fibers in the sympathetic do not appear to be in tonic activity, but our experiments on this point are not final.

4. Section of the vagi nerves or destruction of the medulla causes a permanent hypertonus or incomplete tetanus of the lungs. This is due to removal of a tonic inhibitory check on the peripheral lung motor mechanism (peripheral neuro-muscular automatism). Ligation of the pulmonary branches of the vagi produces the same effect. The only part of the central nervous system necessary for this tonic inhibitory control is the medulla. Section and destruction of the entire spinal cord below the medulla has no permanent effect on the tonus mechanism. Decerebration has likewise no permanent effect on it. Destruction of the midbrain causes a temporary diminution of the lung inhibition probably through a "shock" state of the medulla. The afferent aspect of this tonic lung inhibition requires further study. The most important afferent pathway is probably the pulmonary branches of the vagi.

The contractions of the lungs following vagi section are powerful enough to develop a pressure of from 20 to 40 mm. Hg., and if the glottis is not artificially closed all the air in the lung cavity is forced out, the lungs contract down to a solid mass and are thus rendered useless as organs of respiration. All our data on this point are those of acute experiments lasting only 2 to 3 hours. The possible readjustment of this peripheral lung automatism to meet the needs of the animal after double vagotomy is being investigated by long time experiments.

5. Stimulation of the peripheral end of the vagi inhibits the lung tonus induced by vagi section. Strong tetanizing currents applied to the peripheral vagus trunk usually cause strong contractions following the primary inhibition. Nicotine paralyzes the lung inhibitory fibers of the vagi apparently without injury to the motor fibers, so that after nicotine vagus stimulation causes lung contractions only. These contractions are stronger than can be caused by stimulation of the cervical sympathetic nerve. Hence, on the basis of the usual interpretation of nervous action, the vagi carry both inhibitory and motor fibers to the lungs, the former predominating and being tonically active like the cardio-inhibitory mechanism in many animals.

By stimulation of the peripheral end of the vagus we have so far failed to cause a greater tonus relaxation in the lungs than that which existed before vagi section. This means either that the tonic vagi inhibitory action is ordinarily maximal, or that the simultaneous stimulation of the motor fibers in the vagi trunks neutralizes a part of the inhibitory effects.

The efferent actions of the vagi and the cervical sympathetic nerves on the lungs are unilateral. Only occasionally have we seen effects on the lung of the opposite, in case of sympathetic stimulation. This was probably due to escape of current, and not to actual nerve crossing.

6. Reflex contraction of the lungs are induced by the stimulation of the afferent fibers in the vagi, by stimulation of the cutaneous nerves, the sensory fibers in the nares and the cornea, and the sensory fibers in the visceral organs. These lung reflexes could be brought about either by augmented action of the motor nerve mechanism or by depression of the tonic inhibitory mechanism. On the basis of the usual conceptions of reciprocal innervation both factors are probably involved. It is thus clear that practically all afferent nerves have reflex connection with the medullary nuclei controlling the lung tonus and contractions.

7. As stated above, it is possible to differentiate between the motor and inhibitory fibers in the vagus trunk by means of nicotine. This drug in *moderate doses* (2 mgm.) paralyzes not only the respiratory center but also the peripheral inhibitory mechanism so that subsequent stimulation of the vagus causes more or less powerful lung contractions in place of the usual inhibition resulting from stimulation of this nerve before nicotinization. If nicotine is injected in a frog that has suffered bilateral vagotomy with the usual escape of the tonic inhibitory control of the corresponding lung, nicotine effects a marked inhibition of this lung and after a slight interval an escape from central control of the other lung. The escape of the one lung does not occur until the primary and temporary inhibition (stimulation) of the peripheral mechanism in the other is about over. This probably means that the lung still connected with the center before nicotinization is under maximal central inhibitory control since the drug in this instance produces no primary inhibition. Injection of nicotine in any case destroys the central tonic inhibitory control of the lungs similar to destruction of the medulla or double vagotomy. In large doses nicotine causes contraction of the lung musculature probably by direct stimulation of the muscular elements.

8. Atropine in doses large enough to paralyze the cardio-inhibitory fibers of the vagus has no effect on the terminations of inhibitory fibers in the lungs. In fact, even huge intravenous doses (8 mgm.) do not

completely paralyze these terminations. Such doses paralyze chiefly the medullary centers which send out the inhibitory impulses. As a result the lungs contract. But even this center recovers within an hour and again assumes its tonic inhibitory control over the lungs.

9. Histamine in small or large doses (0.01 to 0.07 cc. 1:1000 sol.) causes temporary contraction of the lung musculature.

10. Epinephrin inhibits both the peripheral automatic tonus and the peripheral automatic rhythm if one is present.

BIBLIOGRAPHY

(1) Arnold: Virchow's Arch., 1863, xxviii, 433.
(2) Babak: Handb. d. Vergl. Physiol., 1914, i, 729.
(3) Baglioni: Arch. f. Physiol., 1900, Suppl. Band, 33.
(4) Berti et Marzenini: Arch. d. Fisiol., 1910, viii, 389.
(5) Brown: Arch. f. d. gesammt. Physiol., 1909, cxxx, 193.
(6) Bohr: Skand. Arch. f. Physiol., 1899, x, 74.
(7) Carlson: This Journal, 1913, xxxi, 318.
(8) Gaskell: The involuntary nervous system, London, 1916.
(9) Heinemann: Virchow's Arch., 1861, xxii, 1.
(10) Keith: Nature, 1904, lxix, 511.
(11) Königstein: Arch. f. d. gesammt. Physiol., 1903, xcv, 616.
(12) Langendorff and Seibert: Arch. f. Physiol., 1881, 241.
(13) Langendorff: Arch. f. Physiol., 1887, 285.
(14) Langendorff: Arch. f. Physiol., 1888, 304.
(15) Luchsinger and Sokolow: Arch. f. d. gesammt. Physiol., xxiii, 283.
(16) Martin: Journ. Physiol., 1878, i, 137.
(17) Mochi: Arch. Ital. d. Biol., 1910, liii, 472.
(18) Mochi: Zeitschr. f. Biol. Tech. u. Metb., 1912, ii, 115.
(19) Mochi: Folia Neurolial, 1912, vi, 769.
(20) Nikolides: Centralbl. f. Physiol., 1908, xxii, 753.
(21) Nikolides: Arch. f. Physiol., 1910, 197.
(22) Pari: Arch. d. Fisiol., 1906, iii, 283.
(23) Sherrington: Journ. Physiol., 1891, xii, 292.
(24) Soprana: Arch. Ital. d. Biol., 1904, xlii, 151.
(25) Smirnow: Anat. Anzeiger, 1888, iii, 258; Cuccati: Int. Monatschr. f. Anat. u. Physiol., 1888, v, 194.
(26) Wedenski: Arch. f. d. gesammt. Physiol., 1881, xxv, 129.
(27) Willem: Arch. néerl. de Physiol., 1919, iii, 315.
(28) Wolff: Arch. f. Anat., 1902, 179.

THE EFFECT OF ADRENALIN ON VENOUS BLOOD PRESSURE

HELENE CONNET

From the Physiological Laboratory of the Johns Hopkins University

Received for publication July 15, 1920

A REVIEW OF THE LITERATURE ON VENOUS BLOOD PRESSURE

Regulation of venous pressure by: 1. Peripheral resistance. It is usually stated that, in general, increased peripheral resistance (in the arterioles)—other things being equal—causes a rise in arterial pressure and a fall in venous pressure and that decreased resistance has the opposite effect.

Bayliss and Starling (7) and Plumier (61) advance the idea that an increased peripheral resistance caused by vasoconstriction decreases the capacity of the vascular system and tends to cause a rise of pressure in all parts of the system. What change will occur in the venous pressure will depend upon whether the influence of the decreased flow from arteries to veins causing a fall, or the decreased capacity of the system causing a rise, predominates. The opposite state of affairs holds in case of decreased peripheral resistance. Sometimes the tendency for the venous pressure to rise is exactly counter-balanced by the tendency to fall. Bayliss and Starling (7) cite, as an illustration, the absence of venous pressure change when vasomotor paralysis has been induced by section of the cord just above the first thoracic segment. Plumier (61) also illustrates this point. He finds no change in venous pressure after weak or strong stimulation of the central stump of the vagus, both vagi being sectioned. In the case of weak stimulation, vasodilatation was produced while strong stimulation produced vasoconstriction. In each case, however, the influence of the peripheral resistance on the venous pressure was balanced by the opposite influence of the change in the capacity of the system.

According to Bayliss and Starling (7), sometimes the venous pressure-raising factor in vasoconstriction of the arterioles predominates, as when the splanchnics are directly stimulated or the vasomotor center is stimulated by asphyxia. The objections, as advanced by Hill and Barnard (37) and Plumier (61), to attributing this rise in venous pressure to decreased capacity of the vascular system will be discussed later.

2. Heart rate. The authors mentioned above (Bayliss and Starling, and Plumier) state that a rise in venous pressure is obtained when the heart slows or stops beating because there is a tendency toward equalization of pressure throughout the system, resulting in a fall in arterial and a rise in venous pressure due to the elasticity of the arteries forcing more blood into the veins. Usually in a slowly beating heart the output per minute decreases and hence the heart does not pump into the aorta per unit of time as much as it did before, thus causing a back pressure in the pulmonary veins, which eventually affects the right heart and causes a rise in the vena cava pressure. This would be true especially when there was an increased resistance to the blood-flow in the arteries, as in vasoconstriction.

Bayliss and Starling (7) consider that most of the rise of venous pressure after peripheral stimulation of the vagus is due to the decreased capacity of the system which comes as a result of the anemic stimulation of the vasomotor center following the low arterial pressure brought about by such stimulation. Their proof of this is that only a slight rise is occasioned by stimulation of the vagus when either the cord or the splanchnics are cut. Plumier (61) has a different explanation for this. He considers the slowing of the heart of primary importance and the vasoconstriction of secondary. He says that cutting the cord or splanchnics causes such a marked vasodilatation (arterial pressure in one of Bayliss and Starling's experiments fell from 120 mm. to 60 mm. Hg.) that tendency toward equalization of pressures cannot show the effect that it would, if the conditions of the vascular system were normal. This point is perhaps brought out more clearly by considering what changes take place in the vascular system under asphyxia, produced by removal of artificial respiration in an animal whose chest has been opened. Bayliss and Starling offer an explanation for this rise in venous pressure, similar to that given in connection with vagus stimulation. Plumier (61) attempts to prove his point that vasoconstriction is of only secondary importance, by comparing the effect of asphyxia before and after section of the vagi. With vagi intact the arterial pressure rises only slightly but the heart beat soon becomes very slow, and coincident with this slowing the venous pressure in the inferior vena cava and the external jugular rises markedly. As soon as artificial respiration is renewed and the heart beats faster, the venous pressure falls. In the experiment when both vagi are cut, the arterial pressure rises, due to vasoconstriction, but the venous pressure remains unchanged, until (100 seconds after the beginning of asphyxia) the heart becomes paralyzed and consequently slows, and the blood pressure falls. At this time the venous pressure rises. Furthermore, after artificial respiration has been renewed, the arterial pressure rises, due to continued vasoconstriction, and when it is at its maximum the venous pressure has already fallen to normal.

The difficulty here, it seems to me, is in trying to make either heart-slowing or vasoconstriction alone account for the rise in venous pressure. Bayliss and Starling (7) themselves, when discussing the rise of venous pressure after splanchnic stimulation, say (p. 172): "In experiment 5 one of the vagi was intact and the heart was slowed as usually occurs when the splanchnics are stimulated. One might be inclined to ascribe the rise of venous pressure to this slowing of the heart, were it not that in other experiments where both vagi were divided, we still obtained a slight rise on stimulation of the splanchnics." Evidently, then, the slowing of the heart is responsible for the greater part of the venous pressure rise, if not absolutely all. On the other hand, one cannot see how Plumier can be sure that Bayliss and Starling are wrong in ascribing some of their rise in venous pressure, after asphyxia for instance, to the decreased capacity of the system, since no experiment has been performed in which that factor has been ruled out, granting that Bayliss and Starling's attempt to rule it out, not only ruled it out, but introduced a new factor, that of vasodilatation after section of the cord or splanchnics, which vitiated the comparison. It would seen as though this point might be settled by an arrangement, such as that used by Heard and Brooks (31), for keeping the arterial pressure constant under varying experimental conditions. When, after adrenalin or asphyxia with vagi intact, the change in capacity of the system, due to vasoconstriction, was not allowed to be effective, one could then see how much this factor has to do with the rise in venous pressure on slowing of the heart.

3. "Respiratory pump." According to Hill and Barnard (37) none of the above explanations is adequate in accounting for the rise of venous pressure obtained as a result of various experimental procedures. They attribute the rise which occurs on arrest of the heart under peripheral vagal stimulation to the respiratory spasms produced, and on asphyxia to strong abdominal and general muscular movements, for in curarized animals these rises do not occur, at least in the case of asphyxia. Their curarization was sufficient to abolish natural respiration, but did not interfere with the heart or tone of the arterial system. As regards vagal stimulation, they say (p. 348), "we ourselves unfortunately have not been able to maintain arrest of the heart in the curarized animal for long enough time to settle this point." Yet in figure 12, page 342 of this article, they show a rise in venous pressure in the same animal on stimulation of the vagus before and after the administration of chloroform. "In the first instance the escape of the heart is complete, the respirations are greatly intensified and by the powerful expiratory spasms of the abdominal muscles the venous pressure is greatly raised. In the second case the inhibition is complete while the respirations, weakened by the chloroform, remain unaltered during the standstill of the heart." On examination of the second curve one sees the venous pressure beginning to rise as soon as the beat of the heart is stopped, but while it is rising the animal was changed to the feet-up position. The venous pressure continues to rise until the heart once more begins to beat. This rise of venous pressure evidently cannot be ascribed to the activity of the respiratory muscles since no change in respiration occurs during the standstill of the heart, nor, probably, to the feet-up position which was assumed during the rise of venous pressure.

These authors object to any explanation of these phenomena which assumes that a rise in venous pressure can be brought about by sending more blood into the venous system, as occurs on arrest of the heart, or by decreasing the capacity of the vascular system by arterial vasoconstriction. They believe that the vascular system is not filled to distention and that since the veins can hold all the blood of the body without distention, no increase in amount of blood in the veins or decrease in arterial caliber can cause a rise in venous pressure. To prove that the veins can hold all the blood of the body at zero pressure they cite the condition that exists in the animal after death. Then, since it might be thought that after death the tone of the vascular system had passed off, they attempt to prove their point in a living animal. After stopping the heart by vagus stimulation, they alternately placed the dog in the vertical feet-down and horizontal positions until all the blood had passed from the arteries into the veins, and past the venous valves so that no reversal of flow could take place. They say (p. 346), "In this experiment we produced a positive pressure in the veins and no pressure in the arteries. . . . . Since the arteries are emptied of blood the whole system is not filled to distention . . . . . ." Just because the arteries are much more elastic than the veins and can, when the heart stops beating, empty themselves of blood and produce a greater positive pressure than before in the veins, it does not therefore follow, it seems to me, that the vascular system, while the heart was beating, was not filled to distention.

Furthermore, in refutation of Bayliss and Starling's belief that anemia of the brain in vagal arrest causes vasoconstriction, they say (p. 348), "In our experiments when the heart has escaped from arrest, there has not occurred any great rise of arterial pressure which we should expect to indicate vasoconstriction." Why should one expect any great rise of arterial pressure after the heart has begun to beat again? With the resumption of the heart beat and consequent rise of arterial pressure toward normal, the cause of the vasoconstriction, anemia of the brain, is removed.

"Any appreciable increase of vena cava pressure is due either to the reduction of the capacity of the venous system by the action of the respiratory muscles, or to the failure of the heart in maintaining the systolic output" (p. 350). By this, I presume, is meant the inability of a slowly beating heart to expel per minute as much blood as it receives per minute, thus causing a back pressure in the veins. I fail to see how this could cause a rise in venous pressure if their contention is correct, that the venous system is capable of holding all the blood of the body without distention, especially since it occurs almost immediately on slowing of the heart, before the arteries could have emptied the greater part of their blood into the veins. Of course, it may be contended that the cava is only a part of the venous system and it might become distended when a large amount of blood collected in it, but this hardly seems a valid contention in the case of the immediate rise in venous pressure on arrest of the heart.

4. Chemical mechanism. Roy and Brown (64) in experimenting with the frog's web, tongue and mesentery, found that temporary anemia was followed by dilatation of arteries, capillaries and veins. This dilatation they attribute to a "relative diminution in the lymph of certain of the constituents of the blood, or the presence in increased amount of certain of the products of tissue exchange, or both of these combined" (p. 359). This effect, they say, is independent of cerebrospinal vasomotor effects; it may possibly be due to action on peripheral vasomotor ganglia, but they think it is more probably due to direct action on vessel walls. These causes operate in other congestions and the authors feel that this automatic regulation of the peripheral circulation is of very great importance.

Henderson and Harvey (33), and Henderson (32) develop the idea of a peripheral chemical control of venous pressure "largely through variations in the CO_2 content of the venous blood." CO_2, by relaxing the veins, they believe, removes the resistance to the flow of blood from capillaries to veins, and so causes an increase in venous pressure. They speak of such a relaxation as though it were merely the complete or partial removal of a clip, allowing more blood to flow into a vessel whose caliber remains the same. But if relaxation means more than this; if it means an actual increase in the capacity of a portion of a blood vessel, due to the lessening of vascular tone, it is difficult to see how this relaxation can cause a rise in the pressure in the vessel even though there is an increased amount of blood present.

5. *Nervous mechanism.* In a study of the regulation of the blood supply of the brain in 1890, Roy and Sherrington (65) found that stimulation of the peripheral stump of the vago-sympathetic nerves in dogs produced sometimes a rise, sometimes a fall of general venous pressure. They think that this probably means that the vago-sympathetic trunk contains vasomotor fibers to the veins. As discussed in the section on heart rate, later observers have attributed this rise which peripheral vagus stimulation gives, to the slowing of the heart which is occasioned by such stimulation. Slowing of the heart due to paralysis from asphyxia with both vagi cut has been shown by Plumier to give a rise in venous pressure comparable to the rise caused by peripheral vagus stimulation. This perhaps does not prove that the vago-sympathetic nerves possess no venomotor fibers, but there seems to be perfectly adequate explanation for the venous pressure change without assuming the existence of such venomotor fibers. That Roy and Sherrington sometimes found that stimulation of the peripheral stump of the vago-sympathetic nerves produced a fall in general venous pressure, may possibly have been due to an escape of current to the central end of the nerve through the fluid medium surounding the tissues. One cannot tell what happened to the heart rate in these cases of a fall in venous pressure for no graphs are given or statement made in regard to it.

Thompson (72) in 1893 observed constriction of the superficial veins of the hind limb of dogs and rabbits on stimulation of the sciatic nerve or the spinal cord. The constriction took place in short sections, the diameter of the vein between the segments remaining unchanged. Bancroft (3) confirmed these observations and extended the work.

He observed the appearance of the veins of the hind limb of a cat (rabbits also were used but were not found nearly as satisfactory) before and after section of various nerves, and thus traced out the vasomotor supply. The cell body of the pre-ganglionic fiber lies in the spinal gray matter, the axis-cylinder emerging in the anterior root of the 1st, 2nd, 3rd or 4th lumbar nerve, following the corresponding white ramus into the sympathetic chain, running down it for a certain distance. The cell body of the post-ganglionic fiber lies in the 6th or 7th lumbar sympathetic ganglion, the axis-cylinder running to the veins in the sciatic nerve. Langley's nicotine method was used to determine the position of these ganglia.

The experiments of Gunn and Chavasse (30) and Crawford and Twombly (18) on the effect of epinephrin on isolated veins lend support to the belief that a venopressor nervous mechanism exists in the veins. The details of these experiments will be given later in this paper under the head of adrenalin.

Hooker (41), (42) has demonstrated veno-pressor fibers in a nerve trunk running from the inferior mesenteric ganglion to the veins of the large intestine. A rise in venous pressure in an isolated loop of intestine was induced by stimulation of: *a*, the nerve to the part (peripheral mechanism); *b*, a sensory nerve such as the saphenous (central reflex mechanism); *c*, the central mechanism by asphyxia. Section of the peripheral nerve or destruction of the medulla destroyed the reflex. A probable failure of this mechanism in shock is predicated by Morison and Hooker (55).

A contraction of the veins seems to be the cause of the increased capillary pressure found in the blue-handed type of irritable heart cases as described by Briscoe (9). This is especially illustrated in those patients whose hands were sometimes normal and sometimes blue. The average readings of this class, when the hands were normal, were: venous pressure, 10.6 cm. H_2O; capillary pressure 25.3 cm. H_2O; and when blue were: venous pressure, 10.6 cm. H_2O; capillary pressure, 33.3 cm. H_2O. Whether this contraction of the veins falls under the chemical mechanism theory or the nervous mechanism theory, the author does not state. One presumes, from the article, that it is the latter.

It is not intended in this paper to review in detail the literature on portal venous pressure, as it forms a rather specialized type of venous pressure. A comprehensive review of the literature which has established the presence of a vasomotor mechanism in the radicles of the portal vein, is to be found in Burton-Opitz's (13) and Edmunds' (22) papers.

Effect on venous pressure of: 1. Adrenalin. a. Effect on isolated veins. Dunn and Chavasse (30) have tested the effect of adrenalin (1 to 100,000) on isolated ring preparations from various veins in the sheep (external jugular, mesenteric, superior and inferior cava) and find a constriction similar to that which occurs in the arteries. The external jugular gave a greater response than the superior and inferior cavae. The amount of response of the mesenteric vein could not be compared with that of the other veins, for the temperature in the case of the mesenteric was 41°C., while in the other experiments it was 36°C. From this they judge that the veins probably contain veno-constrictor nerve fibers from the thoracico-lumbar sympathetic nervous system. Crawford and Twombly (18) corroborate these observations, finding constriction of ring preparations from femoral, iliac and saphenous veins of the dog. Their work on roosters is interesting in that they find some veins that contract in adrenalin solutions, and others that do not. Rings of the jugular vein of white Leghorn roosters, taken from the middle of the neck, contract slowly with 1 to 60,000 adrenalin in oxygenated Ringer's solution, but rings from the jugular vein near the head and from the large vein of the wattles gave no response. This argues, they feel, against a vasomotor supply to the cephalic end of the jugular vein and the veins of the wattles, and they suggest that perhaps the absence of vasoconstrictor fibers in wattles may be one of the reasons why they blue so easily.

b. Effect of intravenous injections. Hill (36) found that intravenous injection of suprarenal extract into a dog whose vagi had been divided caused a rise in arterial pressure of 1170 mm. $MgSO_4$ solution, while the vena cava pressure remained unaltered. Plumier (61) attributed the rise in superior and inferior vena cava pressure, which he obtained on intravenous injection of adrenalin in the intact animal (dog), to the slowing of the heart which such an injection occasions. He feels that one does not get as great a rise with say a 0.4 mgm. injection as the slowing of the heart would seem to indicate, but this may be explained by the fact that the increased force of the heart beat tends to reduce the venous pressure. However, after cutting the vagi, unless a very large dose is administered, there is no change or only a slight rise in venous pressure. In both cases there was important vasoconstriction resulting in a considerable rise in arterial pressure, but this decreasing of the capacity of the vascular system, he points out, is not sufficient, in itself, to change the venous pressure. Capps and Matthews (16) find that a small dose (they do not state the amount) of adrenalin does not affect the venous pressure, but a large dose, such as $\frac{1}{8}$ mgm. (2 minims) of 1 to 1000, causes a rise of from 10 to 80 mm., and that coincident with this rise, the heart is markedly slowed. "The rise in venous pressure was coincident with this halting, irregular action of the heart, and it remained high until the normal rhythm returned. We found likewise that, in a slow or inhibited heart-action from exciting the vagus nerve with faradic current, the venous pressure rose. Hence it seems probable, as Plumier (61) states, that the rise in venous pressure after large doses of epinephrin is explained by the halting heart-action rather than by any venomotor stimulation" (p. 390). Bainbridge and Trevan (2) exclude reflex vagus inhibition in their experiments by a small dose of atropin early in each experiment. Under these conditions they find little or no change in vena cava pressure after adrenalin injection into a portal tributary or systemic vein (hepatic artery tied or intact), but a rise in portal pressure due, they think, either to a swelling of the columns of the liver cells narrowing the capillary channels, or constriction of the radicles of the portal vein. Two cubic centimeters of a 1 to 10,000 solution of adrenalin cause a rise in portal pressure equal to 255 mm. of sodium citrate solution. Kuno (50) explains the slight rise in venous pressure which he obtained on injection of adrenalin, with the heart beating faster, by saying, "the contraction of the blood vessels evoked by adrenaline is most distinct in the arterial system so that a large amount of blood might escape into the veins. The pressure in the veins does not therefore fall, on the contrary it rises more or less during action of the adrenaline although the heart works extremely energetically" (p. 232).

As far as I know, no measurements have been made of the effect of adrenalin on venous pressure in man. A word of caution should, therefore, be given about transferring data concerning adrenalin from animals to man. As has been noted above, the rise of venous pressure in dogs has been attributed to the concomitant slowing of the heart. In man, however, adrenalin does not slow, but quickens the heart rate.

Clinical findings reported by Donaldson (21) and Miller (54) indicate that in practically every person (normal or pathological) adrenalin injection causes no change or causes an increase in pulse rate. Only one case of a fall in pulse rate was reported (Donaldson) and this was in a patient much collapsed from hemorrhage. With the subcutaneous injecion of 0.5 cc. of 1 to 1000 adrenalin, used in the "Goetsch" test (29), (57), there is no reaction on the part of normal patients and an increase of ten to fifty beats per minute in patients hypersensitive to adrenalin. This result is further corroborated by the work of Wearn and Sturgis (74) and of Tompkins, Sturgis and Wearn (73). Therefore it would be incorrect to assume that the results obtained by Capps and Matthews (16) on dogs, in their studies on "venous blood-pressure as influenced by the drugs employed in cardiovascular therapy," necessarily apply to man. Similarly, Meek and Eyster's conclusion (53) (based on experiments on unanesthetized dogs with good vagal tone), that adrenalin cannot be the immediate cause of cardiac acceleration which follows moderate exercise, because the heart slows after adrenalin, cannot be held good for man in whom the heart increases its per-minute rate after adrenalin. Still another example of the different way in which adrenalin affects the same structure in different animals is given by Barbour (5), who found that adrenalin caused constriction of human coronary arteries, but relaxation of the coronary arteries of the calf, sheep and pig.

2. Various other influences. Since the experimental work in this paper deals only with the effect of adrenalin on venous blood pressure, it does not seem appropriate to review, in detail, the effect of various other in uences on venous pressure. The following references may, however, serve to make this general review of the subject more complete. The relation of venous pressure to:

a. Gravity. Hill (35); Hill and Barnard (37); Barach and Marks (4)

b. Respiration. Jacobson (46); Wertheimer (75); Hill and Barnard (37); Burton-Opitz (12); Plumier (61).

c. Exercise. Burton-Opitz (11); Hooker (38); Elpers (23); Jones (47); Henderson and Harvey (33). Krogh's (49) recent work on the effect of exercise in opening up new capillary beds, is of interest in this connection.

d. High altitudes. Schneider and co-workers (66), (67), (68), (69); Kellaway's (48) work on the relation of anoxemia to the output of adrenalin may throw some light on the question of the effect of high altitudes on venous pressure.

e. Increased atmospheric pressure. Hill (36).

f. Drugs, other than adrenalin. Hill and Barnard (37); Plumier (61); Burton-Opitz (14); Capps and Matthews (16).

g. Injection of physiological solution. Bainbridge (1); Kuno (50).

Venous pressure work on man. A review of various methods for measuring venous pressure in man is found in an article by Hooker and Eyster (43), in the Johns Hopkins Hospital Bulletin for 1908. The following is a list of articles dealing with these methods:—Oliver, 1898, (58); Frey, 1899, (26); 1902, (27); Gaertner, 1903, (28); von Basch, 1904, (6); Sewall, 1905, (70); von Recklinghausen, 1906, (62); Oliver, 1907, (59); Moritz and von Tabora, 1910, (56); Frank and Reh, 1912, (25); A. A. Howell, 1912, (45); Lombard, 1912 (51); Hooker and Reese, 1914, (44); Hooker, 1914, (39); Brown, 1918, (10); Wiggers, 1918, (76). For comparison with the normal venous pressure values in man, given in the above articles, it may be of interest to note the venous pressure values obtained by Jacobson, 1867, (46), in sheep, and by Burton-Opitz, 1903, (12), in dogs.

Pathological values are given in the articles by Calvert (15); Hooker and Eyster (43); A. A. Howell (45) and Clark (17). Diurnal variations are given by Oliver (60); Hooker (39) and Clark (17); the effect of age and sex on venous pressure by Elpers (23) and Hooker (39), (40), and the effect of temperature by Elpers (23); Hewlett (34) and Hooker (39).

AN EXPERIMENTAL STUDY OF THE EFFECT OF ADRENALIN ON VENOUS BLOOD PRESSURE

Introduction. It is evident from the foregoing discussion that in studying the effect of any drug on venous blood pressure, one must take into consideration the effect of this drug on the various mechanisms, changes in which are known to cause changes in venous pressure. So close is the relationship between the various parts of the circulatory, vasomotor and respiratory systems, that any change in one part usually causes changes in several other parts. Hence, a change in venous pressure must very often be ascribed to the operation of several factors, sometimes supplementing, sometimes antagonizing one another. Sometimes one factor is so predominant than any other is lost sight of. This seems to have been the case in the previous study of the effect of adrenalin on venous pressure. A greatly slowed heart causes a rise in venous pressure. Adrenalin, injected into the blood stream of dogs with good vagal tone, causes slowing of the heart and a rise in venous pressure. Naturally, the conclusion was that the rise in venous pressure was due to the slowing of the heart rate, especially since little change in pressure occurred on administration of adrenalin to these dogs after vagotomy.

It has been demonstrated for sheep by Gunn and Chavasse (30), and for dogs and roosters by Crawford and Twombly (18), that adrenalin chloride causes contraction of isolated vein rings. The work of Bainbridge and Trevan (2) indicates that the radicles of the portal vein in the intact animal contract under the influence of adrenalin. Nerves to the veins of the limb have been demonstrated by Thompson (72) and Bancroft (3), and to the portal vein by Mall (52) and others. The experiments of Hooker (41), (42), demonstrate the existence, in the intestinal veins at least, of a nervous constrictor mechanism, which can be stimulated directly or indirectly. In view of this evidence, one naturally wonders whether or not such a nervous mechanism is functioning when adrenalin chloride is introduced into the circulation, and if the general venous pressure rise occasioned thereby is not, in part at least, due to a constriction of the veins. No evidence, as far as I know, has been found that points to such a mechanism coming into play after adrenalin, except in the case of the portal vein.

It is with these things in mind that the present investigation has been undertaken, to ascertain what factor or factors are responsible for the general rise of venous blood pressure which follows the intravenous injection of a solution of adrenalin chloride.

Experimental procedures. In the course of these experiments about fifty dogs and twenty-five cats were employed, weighing, on the average, 8 kgm. and 2.3 kgm., respectively. The experiments on dogs were carried out under ether anesthesia. The cats were decerebrated according to the method described by Sherrington in his recent laboratory manual (71), an anesthetic, ether, being used only during the procedures prior to the decerebration. The decerebrate cat preparations were always kept on an electric pad throughout the experiment.

Arterial pressure was recorded by a mercury or a Hürthle manometer, sometimes by both. Venous pressure was recorded as follows: brass cannulae (7 cm. long by 1 to 1.5 mm. bore, for cats, and 16 cm. by 2 to 2.5 mm., for dogs), connected with manometers containing 2 per cent sodium citrate, were inserted in the external jugular and femoral veins and pushed in past the valves so that the pressures recorded were those in the superior and inferior cavae. Whenever there was any doubt that the cannulae were not properly inserted, a dissection was made at the end of the experiment. The entrance of the superior cava into the heart was taken as the zero level for pressure. To make sure, from time to time, that no clots had formed, the pressure was raised in the manometer, by means of a pressure bottle, to several centimeters above the pressure existing in the vein and the citrate solution then allowed to run into the vein. This it did promptly, if there was no obstruction. It was always noted on the tracing when such a procedure occurred. Controls were made which showed that injections of such amounts of 2 per cent sodium citrate ($\frac{1}{2}$ to 1 cc.) had no visible effect on the circulatory system, and the amount of fluid injected was insufficient to cause any change in venous pressure.

Simultaneous tracings of arterial pressure, respiration and time relations were made on a smoked paper kymograph. Since the experimenter worked alone, it was necessary to resort to some method of recording, so that venous pressure readings could be made and injections carried out and recorded by one person, and the exact correspondence between the various pressures be noted on the tracing. One lever recorded respiration, another the arterial blood pressure, and a signal magnet, which marked the base line for the arterial pressure (mercury manometer), recorded the duration of the injection and was also connected with a Harvard clock recording half-minutes. In this circuit there was an electric buzzer which signaled every time the marker was recording a half-minute, and at the sound the level of the venous pressure manometers was noted, the pressures later being marked at the proper place on the tracing. On the same line with this marker, and writing only a millimeter or two behind it, a Jacquet chronograph recorded seconds.

Parke, Davis & Company's adrenalin chloride 1 to 1000 solution was used throughout. Before injection, it was diluted with 0.7 per cent sodium chloride to the desired strength, usually 1 to 10,000.

Special experimental procedures, not followed in all experiments, are described in connection with the experimental data obtained from those procedures.

Of course, if small rises of venous pressure are to be considered significant, one must make sure that they are not caused by the introduction of fluid, used in the injection. For this reason, very small amounts of adrenalin solution were slowly injected (in most cases 0.5 to 3.0 cc. in 5 seconds or more), and control experiments were several times made to ascertain how large an amount of 0.7 per cent NaCl had to be introduced to cause any change in venous pressure. One-half to 3.0 cc. were without effect, 5.0 cc. caused a rise of 3 or 4 mm., while 20.0 cc.—a larger amount than was ever employed in adrenalin chloride injections—caused a rise of only 10 or 15 mm. Na citrate solution.

Experimental work on: 1. Changes in peripheral resistance and capacity of the vascular system. Under all conditions studied, adrenalin always caused a rise in arterial pressure due to arterial constriction. The rise was higher for the same dose when the heart rate was increased than when it was decreased, but there was always a rise. Such a constriction, other things being equal, would tend to cause a fall in venous pressure due to the obstruction to the flow from arteries to veins but, on the other hand, the decreased capacity of the system brought about by arterial constriction would tend to raise the pressure in all parts of the circulatory system. In some cases of arterial constriction, as shown by Bayliss and Starling (7) and discussed in the historical review in this paper, the two factors may balance and give no change in venous pressure. There is one factor here which seems to have received little notice in this connection, and that is the rate at which plasma may leave the blood stream under varying arterial pressures. How far this may operate toward compensating the "decreased capacity of the system" factor, is not known. At all events, in the case of adrenalin, when all other causes for change in venous pressure are ruled out, as far as possible, these factors of peripheral resistance and capacity of the system seem to balance, for no change in venous pressure occurs. Chart 1 (I and II) illustrates this point. About a quarter of an hour after the decerebrated cat (chart 1, I) was curarized, according to the procedure described under "respiration," 0.15 mgm. (3 cc.) of adrenalin chloride was injected into the right femoral vein causing no change in vena cava pressure, although the arterial pressure was raised from 34 to 167 mm. Hg.

Chart 1 (III and IV) shows an experiment in which the venous pressure fell after adrenalin, a very unusual occurrence. It is probable that, in this case, the increased peripheral resistance so obstructed the flow from arteries to veins that there occurred a fall in venous pressure. The decrease in heart rate would tend to cause a rise in venous pressure, but this was apparently overbalanced by the factor or factors tending to cause a fall. In any case, it seems evident that the usual rise in venous pressure caused by adrenalin is not brought about, directly, by changes taking place in the arteries, though, as will be explained later, a rise in arterial pressure may assist in causing a rise of venous pressure when it occurs in conjunction with a slowing of the heart.

2. Chemical regulation. It is conceivable that adrenalin may act as a chemical stimulant to venous musculature, independent of any effect

CHART NO. I

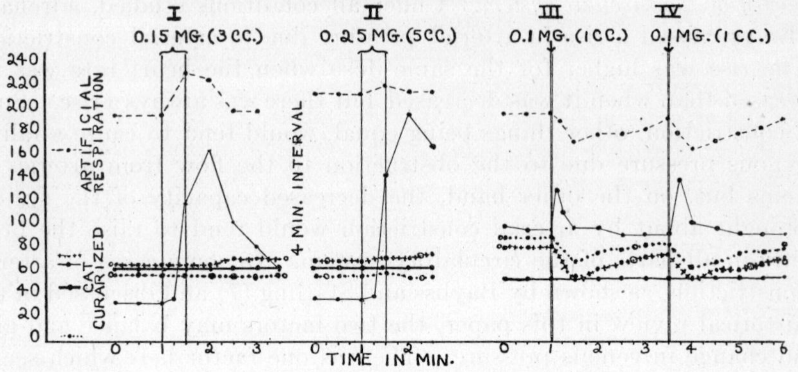

CHART NO. 2

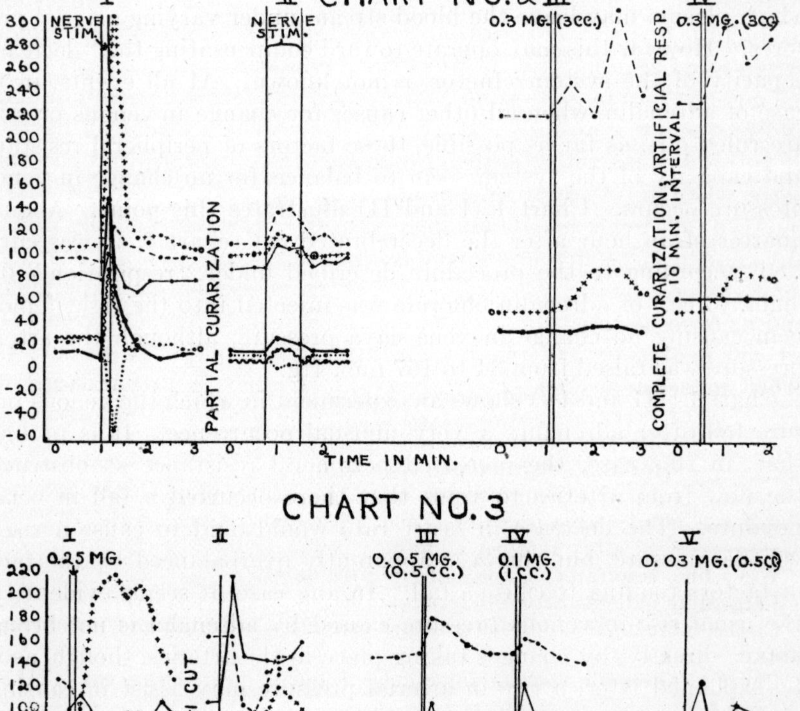

CHART NO. 3

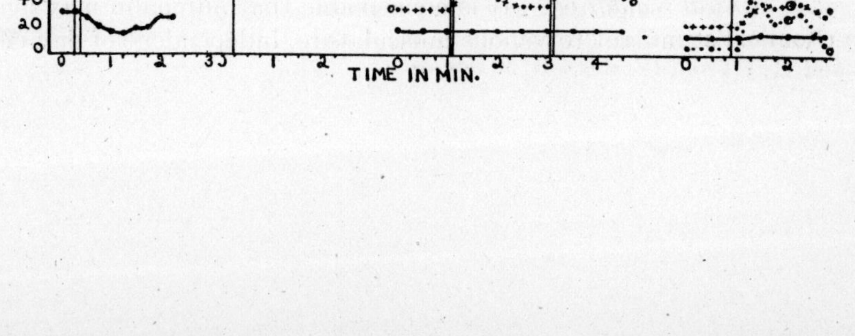

through a nervous mechanism. As far as I know, no work has been done on this subject. However, adrenalin produces an effect upon venous rings similar to that upon arterial rings, and it seems reasonable to assume, until disproved, that in the veins, as has been shown for the arteries, adrenalin acts by stimulating the myoneural junctions of the sympathetic nerve fibers in the vascular musculature.

3. *Respiratory and muscular factors*. The contraction of muscles against the veins, as in exercise, and changes in respiration, are known to be very efficient in causing changes in venous pressure. Take for example chart 2 (II), showing the result of stimulation of the saphenous nerve before and after administration of curare. The dog was not completely curarized, as can be seen from the fact that a slight change in rate and amplitude of respiration was elicited by strong sensory stimulation. The interesting thing is that the venous pressure response seems to bear a definite relation to the amount of respiratory response. When adrenalin chloride is injected in small amounts (usually 0.1 to 0.3 mgm.) there may be no respiratory response, or a decrease in height and frequency of respiration occurs. This change evidently has little or nothing to do with the rise in venous pressure, since that rise takes place when no respiratory variations occur, and a decrease in rate causes a fall, not a rise in venous pressure. However, to fully rule out any change in venous pressure due to muscular contraction or respiratory change, curare was administered in a number of experiments, and as soon as breathing ceased artificial respiration was given. The air was heated to 30°C. before reaching the animal. To be sure that other muscles besides the respiratory muscles were paralyzed, the

------- pulse rate per minute.
——— arterial pressure in mm. Hg.
.... superior cava pressure in mm. 2 per cent sodium citrate.
++++ inferior cava pressure in mm. 2 per cent sodium citrate.
▬▬▬ respiratory rate per minute.
Wavy line, respiratory amplitude (relative only).
Large dots indicate actual determinations.
Circles indicate that venous pressure cannula was tested and found free of clots.

Chart 1. Adrenalin chloride injections: I and II, decerebrate cat 7; III and IV, dog 4 B.

Chart 2. I and II, dog 35 A—Stimulation of saphenous nerve before and after partial curarization; III and IV, decerebrate cat 9—Adrenalin chloride injections, before and after complete curarization; vagi cut.

Chart 3. Adrenalin chloride injections: I and II, dog 1 A, vagi cut between I and II; III and IV, dog 4 B; V, dog 29 A.

minimal nerve stimulus necessary to cause contraction of some skeletal muscle in the fore limb was determined before curare, and then sufficient curare was given to cause this stimulus and other stronger stimuli to become ineffective. In such experiments adrenalin had practically the same effect on the venous pressure before and after curare: chart 2 (III and IV) is an example. Changes in the rate of the artificial respiration seem, also, to be ineffective. It has been noticed a number of times that the venous pressure response to adrenalin is not as marked immediately after the administration of curare as it is later. In a few cases, as shown in chart 1 (I and II), the effect persists. This depressant action on venous pressure response is probably due to an action on the nervous mechanism in the veins. That it usually passes off very rapidly, fits in with the general idea that the primary depressant action of curare on the circulatory system is of very short duration.

When not curarized, occasionally the act of injecting was a sufficient sensory stimulus to cause a muscular response. This muscular response, often seen in a stretching out of the lower limbs and consequent stretching of the abdominal muscles, was not evident on the tracing given by the usual pneumograph. Therefore, instead of recording respiration by means of a rubber bag around the chest, a small rubber balloon was inserted through a small opening into the abdominal cavity near the diaphragm, and the skin closed tightly around the glass tube to which the balloon was attached. The balloon was then blown up until it held about 5 cc. air, and connected with a recording tambour and lever as the bag around the chest had been before. This has the advantage of recording not only respiratory changes but also changes in abdominal pressure which very markedly influence venous pressure, as shown by Hill and Barnard (37).

4. Heart rate and output per minute. Plumier (61), in his work on venous pressure, laid great stress on slowing of the heart rate as a very efficient means of raising the venous pressure. Occasionally the heart suddenly stops beating after an injection of adrenalin. The venous pressure may then rise very high; in one case it rose five times as high as it had after a similar dose of adrenalin when the heart rate was increased. In dogs with good vagal tone, the heart usually slows markedly after adrenalin and the venous pressure rises (see chart 3, I). Even with the vagi cut the pulse rate is often slowed, due probably to a direct action on the heart musculature, as is shown in chart 3 (II). A rather uncertain venous pressure response is often seen in vagotomized dogs when the heart rate is increased after an adrenalin injection.

Such results would lead one to attribute the rise in venous pressure solely to the decreased heart rate as did Plumier (61) and, later, Capps and Matthews (16). Chart 3 (III, IV and V), however, makes one doubt that heart rate is the only factor involved. Work on dogs under ether did not prove satisfactory in clearly demonstrating whether or not a nervous mechanism played some part in venous pressure response to adrenalin. There are several reasons for this. In order to rule out the slowed heart rate, the vagi had to be cut. This caused a very great increase in the depth of respiration which brought about such a marked rise and fall in venous pressure that it was difficult to compare such fluctuations in pressure with the change occurring after adrenalin, since the respiratory variations were then often absent, due to temporary cessation of respiration. Besides, even with the vagi cut, the heart frequently slowed after adrenalin. Still more serious, perhaps, is the possible effect of ether on the nervous mechanism. Ether depresses the arterial vasomotor response to adrenalin, as shown by Berry (8) and Rous and Wilson (63), and could naturally be expected to affect a nervous mechanism in the veins—all the more so because, as shown by Hooker (41), this mechanism is extremely sensitive. If very light ether anesthesia were employed, there would then be the difficulty of muscular and respiratory responses discussed above. Chart 3 (III and IV) shows an unusual experiment in which the ether anesthesia was light, and yet respiration remained constant throughout the experiment. Experiments on decerebrated cats, which needed no anesthetic after the operation, and whose vagal tone is not nearly so marked as dogs', proved to be very satisfactory. Also, it was no small consideration, since curare is very difficult to obtain, that it took only a small amount of curare to curarize a cat, as compared with a dog. Since sensory stimuli have been shown to be effective after curare, it is desirable, for humanitarian reasons, to work on a decerebrated preparation where there can be no question of not giving enough anesthetic during curarization to cause analgesia.

Concerning the influence of change of the heart rate on venous pressure, it should be said that it is really the per-minute output of the heart, rather than the heart rate alone, that is essential. Quoting from Erlanger and Hooker (24), (p. 161), "If the pulse pressure is approximately dependent upon the amount of blood that escapes from the arteries during one cardiac cycle, then it is obvious that the amount that escapes must vary directly as the pulse rate." Therefore, pulse pressure multiplied by pulse rate gives us an expression of the output of the heart per minute. It is possible to increase or decrease the output per minute by increasing or decreasing either or both of these factors, and to keep the output constant by varying the two factors proportionately in the opposite directions. Hence one cannot say that a slowed heart necessarily causes a decreased output per minute, and hence a rise in venous pressure. It is theoretically possible that the pulse pressure might so increase that even with a lower heart rate the output per minute would increase. In the case of adrenalin, however, this possibility seems never to be realized, at least when the pulse rate is greatly reduced. For example, in one experiment, before adrenalin, the pulse pressure was 180 mm. Hg. and the pulse rate per minute 158, making a per-minute output of 28,440. After adrenalin, the pulse pressure was 240 and the pulse rate 20, giving the greatly decreased per minute output of 4800. The slowing in this case was way out of proportion to the increased pulse pressure, and was accompanied by a rise in venous pressure from 25 to 120 mm. Na citrate.

Experiments were performed on dogs, as illustrated in chart 4, in which the vagi were cooled by perfusing ice water through glass tubing in a V around each nerve, and afterwards allowing the nerves to come to room temperature again. The pulse rate, arterial pressure, respiratory rate and amplitude were all affected but very little change in venous pressure took place. When the perfusion of ice water around the nerves was discontinued, the pulse rate decreased from 144 to 108, the venous pressure decreasing also a few millimeters. When the heart stops beating the rise in venous pressure is due to a back pressure in the veins and also to the tendency for equalization of pressures to take place throughout the vascular system. When the heart slows, but does not stop, these factors operate to cause a rise in venous pressure, but to a less extent. If now the arterial pressure rises as the slowing of the heart occurs, as after adrenalin, the mean pressure of the vascular system toward which the various pressures are tending will, of course, be greater, and hence there is a much greater possibility of a large rise in venous pressure. In one experiment, after an adrenalin injection, the heart was slowed about as much as after the cooling of the vagi was discontinued (chart 4, II). In the former case the arterial pressure rose, showing that the capacity of the vascular system was decreased, while in the latter it fell. In the case of adrenalin there may be a nervous constrictor mechanism in the veins at work, but from other experiments on dogs it seems likely that this plays little part in etherized dogs. It seems more probable that the decreased capacity of the system acts in connection with the slowed heart rate to cause a rise in venous pressure.

5. Nervous mechanism. It can readily be seen from the foregoing that one cannot attribute a rise in venous pressure to the activity of a vasomotor mechanism in the veins, unless one is sure that the per-minute output of the heart has not decreased sufficiently to explain the rise. As we have seen, when this factor is ruled out in experiments on dogs under ether, the evidence for the functioning of a nervous mechanism is not very conclusive. In the experiments on decerebrate cats, however, there is clear evidence of such a mechanism. With the vagi intact, we may get the response which is usual in dogs—a rise in venous and arterial pressure and a slowing of the heart, chart 5 (I and II). When, however, the vagi are cut (chart 5, III and IV), there is still a rise in venous pressure. The heart rate is practically unchanged and the pulse pressure increased (as nearly always occurs after adrenalin) so that the output per minute is now increased and the tendency would be for a fall rather than a rise in venous pressure. So also in this experiment, the respirations were decreased in height and frequency which would tend to lower rather than raise venous pressure. The rise, therefore, which one does get under these circumstances seems to be due to a nervous factor, rendered probably less effective in producing a rise because of the factors tending to produce a fall. Chart 6 shows very uniform rises in venous pressure, though in some cases the heart rate is slowed and in some cases increased in frequency. In the experiment shown in chart 7, the respiratory factor is completely controlled by curarization. The vagi are cut in IV and V.

It is interesting to inquire whether or not the seat of this action of adrenalin is central or peripheral. Two different types of experiments were performed to investigate this question. In the first, the cord was sectioned in the cervical region (about at the level of the fifth or sixth cervical vertebra). As is shown in chart 8, this does not destroy the venopressor response to adrenalin, though whether or not any small part of the reaction is of central origin is hard to determine, since the amount of response to a certain dose is not invariable, and so the effect of a dose before cutting the cord is difficult to compare with the same dose just afterwards. The response before and after is quite similar, however.

For the second type of experiment the isolated vein preparation of Hooker (41) was used. In the first of these experiments, Doctor Hooker kindly demonstrated the method to the writer. An isolated loop

CHART NO. 4

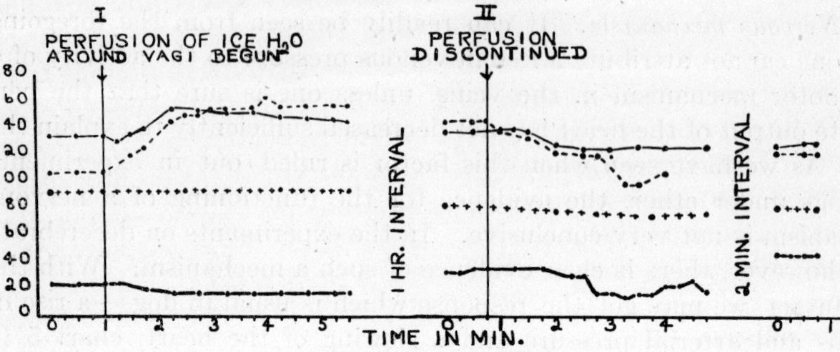

CHART NO. 5

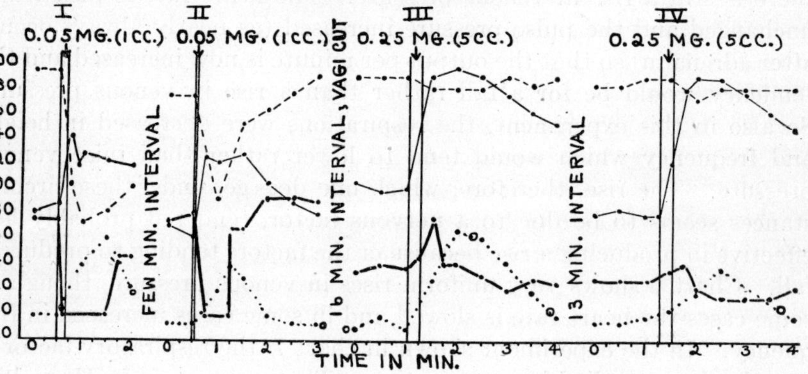

CHART NO. 6

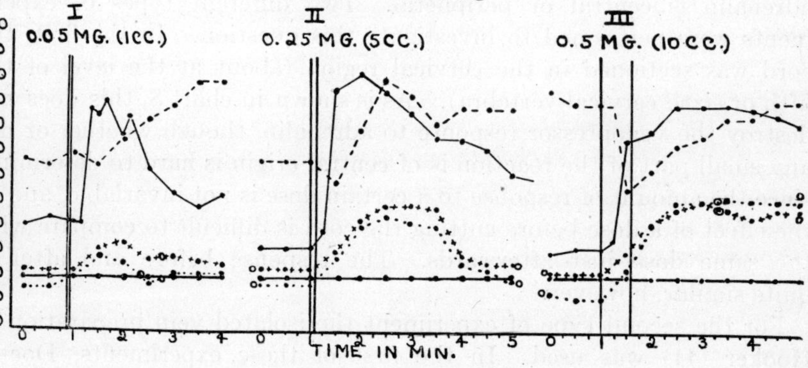

of large intestine in which the inferior mesentery artery and vein had been cannulated, was hung up free from the surrounding intestines. The only connection with the animal was through a nerve running from the inferior mesenteric ganglion to the large intestine and entering the intestine in close proximity to the inferior mesenteric artery. Blood was washed out of the vessels from artery to vein by means of warmed (about 37°C.) Ringer's solution under air pressure of 90 to 120 mm. Hg. The cannulated artery was then disconnected from the air pressure apparatus and allowed to hang freely from the preparation. The vein was then connected with a venous pressure manometer containing warmed Ringer's solution. The zero level was, in most cases, adjusted to the level of the vein in which the pressure was being measured. The vein was distended by a positive pressure of from 30 to 100 mm. Ringer's solution, by means of a pressure bottle. Any change in the caliber of the vein would then be indicated by a rise or fall in the level in the venous pressure manometer. Hooker (42) has shown that, in this preparation, a rise in venous pressure may be elicited, peripherally, by stimulation of the nerve to the part; reflexly, by sensory stimulation; and centrally, by asphyxia. In such a dog, when adrenalin chloride was injected into the saphenous vein in doses from 0.2 to 0.6 mgm., no rise in venous pressure in the isolated vein occurred, but when such injections were followed by asphyxia, produced by closing off the end of the tracheal cannula for two or six minutes, a rise in venous pressure from 15 to 20 mm. occurred, showing that the preparation was still in good condition. This seems to show that the venopressor rise after adrenalin is not due to any central mechanism, controlling the caliber of veins, but to a peripheral effect on sympathetic endings, such as takes place in the arterioles.

- - - - - - pulse rate per minute.
——— arterial pressure in mm. Hg.
.... superior cava pressure in mm. 2 per cent sodium citrate.
++++ inferior cava pressure in mm. 2 per cent sodium citrate.
▬▬▬ respiratory rate per minute.

Large dots indicate actual determinations.

Circles indicate that venous pressure cannula was tested and found free from clots.

Chart 4. Dog 17 A—Vagus nerves cooled.

Chart 5. Decerebrate cat 3—Adrenalin chloride injections, vagi cut between II and III.

Chart 6. Decerebrate cat 6—Adrenalin chloride injections, artificial respiration.

CHART NO. 7

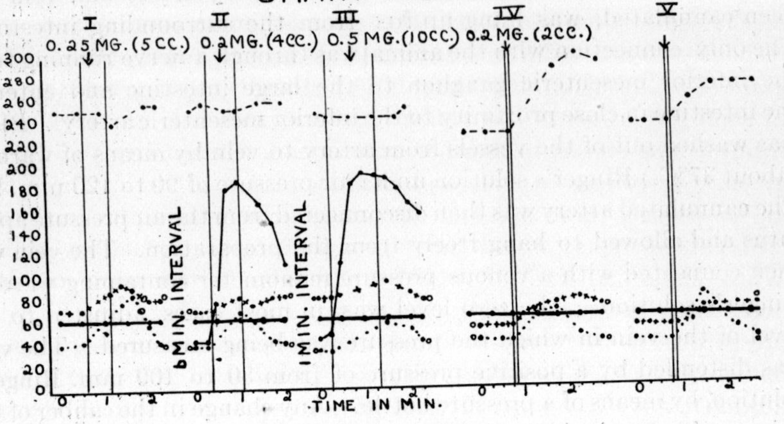

CHART NO. 8

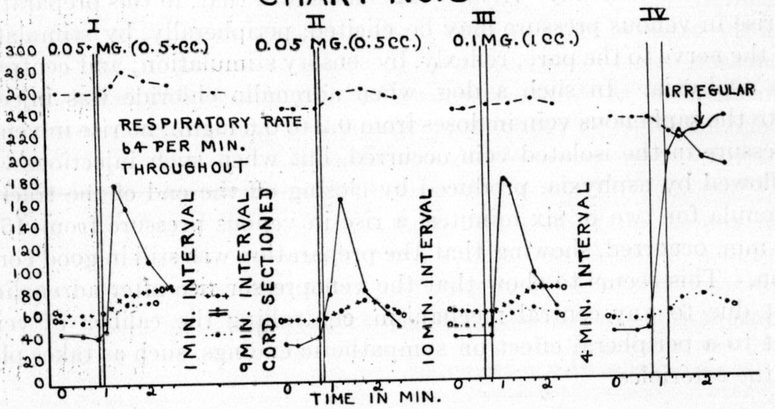

CHART NO. 9

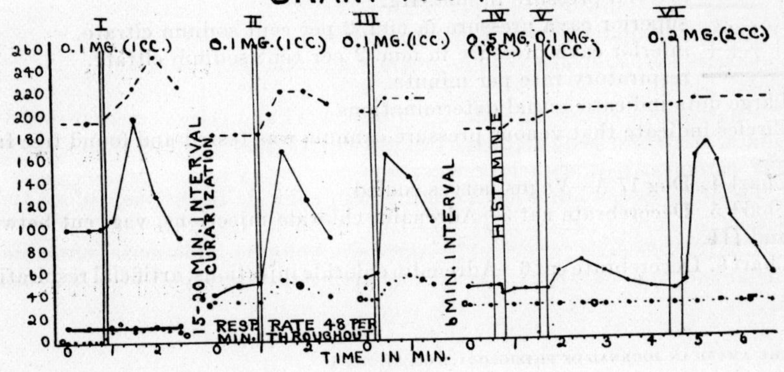

Some experiments which were being carried out in this laboratory suggested that histamine might have an effect on the venopressor mechanism. Chart 9 (I, II, III) shows typical arterial and venous responses to adrenalin in a curarized, decerebrate cat. One-half milligram (1 cc.) of histamine (chart 9, IV) caused a fall in arterial pressure; in some experiments the venous pressure also fell. A more marked reaction was shown in another experiment, where twice the dose was given. According to Dale and Laidlaw (19), had the cat been under an anesthetic, these doses of histamine, from which the unanesthetized cat recovers, would have produced fatal circulatory collapse. When histamine was followed by adrenalin in the same and larger doses than given previously in the experiment, there was no venous pressure response (chart 9, V and VI). The arterial pressure rose, but not nearly as high as before, with the same dose. A second injection, however, gave a typical arterial pressure rise, but still no change in venous pressure. The work of Dale and Richards (20) and Dale and Laidlaw (19) leads them to conclude that relaxation of the capillaries is the cause of the vasodilator effect of histamine. The fall in venous pressure after histamine and the subsequent failure of the nervous mechanism to respond to adrenalin, indicates that histamine has a relaxing effect on venous tone, also, and acts in some way to depress the activity of the venopressor mechanism.

Summary. The various possible factors operating to produce the rise in venous blood pressure which occurs in dogs and cats after intravenous injection of adrenalin are discussed. The two factors chiefly responsible are the decreased heart rate bringing about decreased unit output of the heart, and a vasoconstrictor mechanism in the veins. The

\- - - - - - pulse rate per minute.
——— arterial pressure in mm. Hg.
.... superior cava pressure in mm. 2 per cent sodium citrate.
++++ inferior cava pressure in mm. 2 per cent sodium citrate.
▬▬▬ respiratory rate per minute.
Large dots indicate actual determinations.
Circles indicate that venous pressure cannula was tested and found free from clots.

Chart 7. Adrenalin chloride injections: I, II and III, decerebrate cat 8—Vagi intact; cat curarized; artificial respiration; IV and V, decerebrate cat 9—Vagi cut; cat curarized; artificial respiration.

Chart 8. Decerebrate cat 15—Adrenalin chloride injections, before and after section of cord; vagi cut; cat curarized; artificial respiration.

Chart 9. Decerebrate cat 17—Adrenalin chloride injections, before and after histamine; vagi cut; cat curarized and artificial respiration begun between I and II.

effect of the first factor is accentuated by the fact that the arterial pressure is greatly raised by adrenalin in the doses here used. The first factor has been recognized before. Reasons are given why the second factor was previously overlooked. In dogs with good vagal tone and under an anesthetic, the rise in venous pressure is almost entirely due to the first factor. In cats whose vagal tone is not nearly as strong, the second factor predominates. This nervous mechanism is shown to be acted on peripherally by adrenalin, and to be depressed by ether, curare and histamine, especially the last.

I may take the opportunity here to thank Dr. W. H. Howell and Dr. D. R. Hooker of this University, and Dr. J. L. King of Goucher College, for kindly encouragement and aid in the preparation of this paper.

BIBLIOGRAPHY

(1) Bainbridge: Journ. Physiol., 1915, l, 65.
(2) Bainbridge and Trevan: Journ. Physiol., 1917, li, 460.
(3) Bancroft: This Journal, 1898, i, 477.
(4) Barach and Marks: Arch. Int. Med., 1913, xi, 485.
(5) Barbour: Journ. Exper. Med., 1912, xv, 404.
(6) von Basch: Wiener med. Presse, 1904, xlv, 961.
(7) Bayliss and Starling: Journ. Physiol., 1894, xvi, 159.
(8) Berry: Endocrinology, 1917, i, 306.
(9) Briscoe: Heart, 1918, vii, 35.
(10) Brown: Johns Hopkins Hosp. Bull., 1918, xxix, 93.
(11) Burton-Opitz: This Journal, 1903, ix, 161.
(12) Burton-Opitz: This Journal, 1903, ix, 198.
(13) Burton-Opitz: Quart. Journ. Exper. Physiol., 1912, 329.
(14) Burton-Opitz and Wolf: Journ. Exper. Med., 1910, xii, 278; Proc. Soc. Exper. Biol. and Med., 1910, vii, 70.
(15) Calvert: Journ. Amer. Med. Assoc. 1907, xlviii, 1168; Johns Hopkins Hosp. Bull., 1908, xix, 44.
(16) Capps and Matthews: Journ. Amer. Med. Assoc., 1913, lxi, 388.
(17) Clark: Arch. Int. Med., 1915, xvi, 587.
(18) Crawford and Twombly: N. Y. Med. Journ., 1913, xcviii, 327.
(19) Dale and Laidlaw: Journ. Physiol., 1918–19, lii, 355.
(20) Dale and Richards: Journ. Physiol., 1918–19, lii, 111.
(21) Donaldson: Brit. Med. Journ., 1914, i, 476.
(22) Edmunds: Journ. Pharm. Exper. Therap., 1915, vi, 569.
(23) Elpers: (Kiel), 8°, Dortmund, 1911.
(24) Erlanger and Hooker: Johns Hopkins Hosp. Rept., 1904, xii, 145.
(25) Frank and Reh: Zeitschr. f. exper. Path. u. Therap., 1912, x, 241.
(26) Frey: Illustr. Monatschr. d. ärztl. Polytech., 1899, xxi, 68.
(27) Frey: Deutsch. Arch. f. klin. Med., 1902, lxxiii, 511.
(28) Gaertner: München med. Wochenschr., 1903, l, 2038.

(29) Goetsch: N. Y. State Journ. Med., 1918, xviii, 259.
(30) Gunn and Chavasse: Proc. Roy. Soc. ,1913, lxxxvi B, 192.
(31) Heard and Brooks: Journ. Pharm. Exper. Therap., 1915, vi, 605.
(32) Henderson: This Journal, 1916-17, xlii, 589.
(33) Henderson and Harvey: This Journal, 1918, xlvi, 533.
(34) Hewlett: Amer. Journ. Med. Sci., 1913, cxlv, 656.
(35) Hill: Journ. Physiol., 1895, xviii, 15.
(36) Hill: Proc. Roy. Soc., 1900, lxvi, 478.
(37) Hill and Barnard: Journ. Physiol., 1897, xxi, 323.
(38) Hooker: This Journal, 1909, xxv, 24 (Proc.) (preliminary report); 1911, xxviii, 235.
(39) Hooker: This Journal, 1914, xxxv, 73.
(40) Hooker: This Journal, 1916, xl, 43.
(41) Hooker: This Journal, 1918, xlv, 543.
(42) Hooker: This Journal, 1918, xlvi, 591.
(43) Hooker and Eyster: Johns Hopkins Hosp. Bull., 1908, xix, 274.
(44) Hooker and Reese: This Journal, 1914, xxxiii, 27 (Proc.).
(45) Howell: Arch. Int. Med., 1912, ix, 148.
(46) Jacobson: Arch. f. Anat. u. Physiol., 1867, 226.
(47) Jones: Lancet, 1917, i, 574.
(48) Kellaway: Journ. Physiol., 1918–19, lii, 63 (Proc.).
(49) Krogh: Journ. Physiol., 1918–19, lii, 457.
(50) Kuno: Journ. Physiol., 1917, li, 221.
(51) Lombard: This Journal, 1912, xxix, 335.
(52) Mall: Arch. f. Physiol., Suppl., 1890, 57.
(53) Meek and Eyster: This Journal, 1915, xxxviii, 62.
(54) Miller: Lancet, 1914, ii, 158.
(55) Morison and Hooker: This Journal, 1915, xxxvii, 86.
(56) Moritz and von Tabora: Deutsch. Arch. f. klin. Med., 1910, xcviii, 475.
(57) Nicholson and Goetsch: Amer. Rev. Tuber., 1919, iii, 109.
(58) Oliver: Journ. Physiol., 1898, xxiii, 5 (Proc.).
(59) Oliver: Quart. Journ. Med., 1907–08, i, 59.
(60) Oliver: Blood and blood pressure, London, 1901.
(61) Plumier: Arch. internat. d. physiol., 1909, viii, 1.
(62) von Recklinghausen: Arch. f. exper. Path. u. Pharm., 1906, lv, 463.
(63) Rous and Wilson: Journ. Exper. Med., 1919, xxix, 173.
(64) Roy and Brown: Journ. Physiol., 1879–80, ii, 323.
(65) Roy and Sherrington: Journ. Physiol., 1890, xi, 85.
(66) Schneider: This Journal, 1920, li, 180.
(67) Schneider and Sisco: This Journal, 1914, xxxiv, 1.
(68) Schneider and Sisco: This Journal, 1914, xxxiv, 29.
(69) Schneider, assisted by Cheley and Sisco: This Journal, 1916, xl, 380.
(70) Sewall: Colorado Med., 1905, ii, 219.
(71) Sherrington: Mammalian physiology; a course of practical exercises, 1919.
(72) Thompson: Arch. f. Physiol., 1893, 102.
(73) Tompkins, Sturgis and Wearn: Arch. Int. Med., 1919, xxiv, 269.
(74) Wearn and Sturgis: Arch. Int. Med., 1919, xxiv, 247.
(75) Wertheimer: Arch. d. physiol. norm. et path., 1895, vii, 107.
(76) Wiggers: Journ. Amer. Med. Assoc., 1918, lxx, 508.

STUDIES ON THE VISCERAL SENSORY NERVOUS SYSTEM

II. Lung Automatism and Lung Reflexes in the Salamanders (Necturus, Axolotl)

A. B. LUCKHARDT and A. J. CARLSON

From the Hull Physiological Laboratory of the University of Chicago

Received for publication July 17, 1920

In a previous article (5) we showed that the lung of the frog contracts immediately following the external respiratory act; that the lung musculature can be induced to contract reflexly by the stimulation of any visceral or cutaneous nerve with practically no exceptions; that the lungs of this animal possess a peripheral automatic mechanism which at times shows rhythm but which under normal conditions is kept in a state of inhibition by tonic central inhibitory impulses via the vagi; that these nerves, furthermore, contain not a few motor fibers which apparently exert no marked tonic activity; and that the cervical sympathetic nerves contain but few motor and no inhibitory fibers for the lungs. In addition, we made a brief study of the action of certain drugs (atropine, adrenalin and histamine) on the lungs besides using nicotine extensively in differentiating between the motor and inhibitory nerves contained in the vagus fibers to the lungs.

On completion of this work it seemed quite important to us to investigate the neuro-muscular apparatus and physiology of the nerves of the lungs of other available amphibia to determine whether or not the physiological mechanism discovered in frogs is the same or similar in this class of animals.

METHODS

The only amphibia available for this study were the axolotl and necturus. The general methods of study were those reported in our first article, modified to meet the anatomical peculiarities of the type of animal which we were studying.

In every instance the cord was pithed below the medulla. As in previous work on the frog we cannulated the tips of the lungs exposed by a ventral incision and connected each cannula with either a water manometer or delicate tambour. After recording the normal respirations or respiratory attempts of the animal, we attempted to elicit reflex lung contractions as the result of mechanical and electrical stimulations applied to the animal anterior to the spinal transection. We subsequently closed the glottis with a small mosquito forceps (in axolotl only) and pithed the brain (specifically the medulla) to note any tonic inhibitory influence the vagi nerves might have on the neuromusculature apparatus of the lungs. Stimulation of the same nerves to the lungs next engaged our attention. This was followed by the effect of the intravenous injection of drugs alone or in combination. Because of the poor or imperfect circulation in necturus, as a result of the preparation of the animal for experimentation, for certain purposes we injected the drug deep muscularly, 15 to 20 minutes, before preparing the animal in the manner described above; for we found that even injection of the drug in Ringer's solution by way of the bulbus arteriosus or into the pulmonary artery failed to reach the posterior end of the lung of this animal.

The lungs of necturus are paired sacs, extending from the level of the heart almost to the anal region. There are no alveoli or septa in these lungs. According to Miller (9) the course of the smooth muscle fibers in the lung walls is circular, except at the apex. Both lung artery and lung vein lie superficial to the muscle layer.

Miller has described medullated and non-medullated nerve fibers and nerve nets in the necturus lung. The pulmonary fibers of the vagi enter the base of the lungs in many branches, not along the pulmonary blood vessels, as in the frog, but between the blood vessels. There are many ganglion cells (bipolar and multipolar) in the main nerve trunks and in the nerve plexuses. According to Miller, the non-medullated fibers connect with the ganglion cells. Similar ganglionated nerve plexuses have been described in the lungs of other tailed amphibians, especially by Stirling (11) in the case of the newt. The older anatomical literature is reviewed in detail by Oppel (10). Miller's description of the ganglionated nerve plexuses in the necturus lung is practically identical with the local nervous system of the necturus heart, as studied by one of us (6).

In necturus the glottis or opening from the pharynx into the trachea is exceedingly small, and certainly not suited for rapid filling or emptying the lung sacs with air. We have repeatedly seen these animals attempt to swallow air, the air escaping by the gill slits and in no instance entering the lungs. There can be no doubt that in necturus the gaseous exchange is carried out by the gills, supplemented by the skin, and the rôle of the lung sacs in respiration is an open question. The lung sac of necturus has the same histogenesis as the lung of other vertebrates, although it remains most primitive as regards differentiation. Should these structures be called lungs, especially if they serve mainly or exclusively as "hydrostatic organs?"

In our review of the anatomical and zoölogical literature on amphibian respiration, we came across the surprising fact, apparently well known to zoölogists though not to physiologists, that many species of tailed amphibians have neither lungs nor gills, and in other species without gills the lungs appear to be too rudimentary to function in respiration. The normal condition of these species is that of the frog with the lungs extirpated, that is, the gaseous exchange is carried out entirely by the skin. But several zoölogists (Wilder (12), Lönnberg (8), Camerano (4), Bethge (3) and others) have concluded mainly on anatomical grounds (great vascularity of the mucous membrane of the buccal cavity and upper end of the esophagus), that the pharyngeal cavity serves lung functions, especially in those species having neither lungs nor gills. It appears to be a fact that the so-called buccal respiratory movements (including that of the external nares) are carried out even in those species in which the lungs are absent. But Babák and Kühnova (1) have shown that the brain centers controlling these movements are different from those governing the filling and emptying of the lungs, the latter are, the former are not influenced by asphyxia, which fact seems to throw doubt on the respiratory character of these buccal movements. Lapique and Petetin (7) have also shown, in the case of one species of salamanders devoid of lungs and gills, that the main respiratory organ is in the skin.

None of these questions can be settled except by direct physiological experiments, but we may regard the necturus lungs, provisionally at least, as lungs on the basis of organogenesis. Their motor control also places them in the same category with the lung of the frog and of the axolotl.

Since the entire respiratory apparatus (including the lung) of the necturus is strikingly more primitive than that of the other salamander used in this study, we shall describe the results obtained from necturus first and end with a description of those obtained from the axolotl.

Necturus maculatus. External respiration in this animal is essentially performed by the large gills which under usual conditions are kept in more or less constant motion. Occasionally the animals come to the surface for air which is promptly expelled by an act of swallowing through the gill slits. The lungs of this animal consist essentially of two thin elongated muscular sacs which are well supplied with blood vessels. With but one exception we found them collapsed. In an inflated and atonic condition their diameter is about 1 cm. at their greatest circumference. At their ends they taper off into blunt tips, at their base they communicate with a tracheal sac similar to that possessed by the frog. This sac communicates with the oral cavity through a glottis situated far down in the pharyngeal region. The glottis is exceedingly primitive. It consists essentially of a slit which is quite easily overlooked on direct inspection. We agree with the description of Oppel that the glottis is exceedingly delicate. Taking everything into account we feel that the lungs may serve an excretory function (elimination of CO_2) but are rarely if ever filled with air during any act of external respiration. The lungs receive their innervation through pulmonary fibers carried by the vagi. It was found impracticable to isolate these latter nerves in the neck for direct electrical stimulation. They were isolated at their exit from the skull by a dissection to right and left of the median line after a sagittal section of the skull.

Because of the inaccessibility of the glottis for closure by hemostat as practised in the frog, we prevented communication of the lungs through the glottis with the mouth by dorso-lateral traction and fixation in that position of the fore legs after pinning the animal on its back. A wad of cotton wedged under the neck of the animal at the level of the tracheal sac or put over the tracheal sac and held firmly in that position by the constriction of a rubber band was an additional measure employed in not only closing off the glottis but in preventing intercommunication between the lungs through the tracheal sac.

Axolotl. The lungs of this genus of amphibia are certainly more complex than in necturus. On opening the abdominal cavity one is at first glance struck with the resemblance of the lungs of this animal with the reptilian lung. The upper portions of both lungs are subdivided into alveolar sacs by septa; the lower appendages which extend down the abdominal cavity for a considerable distance are more saclike in their texture. As in the frog and necturus the lungs communicate at their base with the tracheal sac which in turn communicates with the mouth cavity through a well-developed glottis. In the specimens which we used gills were present and functioning. It was equally apparent, especially on opening the abdominal cavity, that the animals could and did make use of the lungs for gaseous exchange. In this animal the vagi could be isolated in the neck as in the frog. The result of our investigation on this form is confined to a study of less than a dozen animals. Although most of the animals were in good condition at the time of experimentation, they deteriorated more quickly than the frog and the necturus similarly prepared. We are confident, however, that our results are characteristic of this form especially since they fit in well with what we observed in the frog and necturus.

All the tracings reproduced with this report were taken with the same speed of the kymograph. A single time tracing showing 5 second intervals will be found at the bottom of figure 1. It can be used in a study of the time relations in all other tracings should the reader care to do so.

RESULTS

1. Necturus maculatus: a. The central inhibitory control of the lungs through the vagi. As mentioned above it was found impossible for anatomical reasons to isolate the vagus nerve or its pulmonary branches in the neck to note the effect of ligation and sections of these nerves on the tonic activity of the lung musculature. Since destruction of the medullary centers in the frog effected the same result, we adopted this expedient in necturus. Having closed the glottis and prevented intercommunication of the lungs as described above we connected the lungs each with a water manometer and destroyed the brain entirely by rapidly pithing it. Figure 1, *A*, shows the effect of such a procedure. The destruction at *a* of the cerebral lobes and midbrain was followed by a temporary escape of the lungs from inhibitory control. The subsequent destruction at *b* of the medullary centers was followed by permanent hypertonic state of the lung as in the frog. In another animal whose cord was not pithed at all but which lay quietly on its back as a result of a rubber band placed tightly about the front legs,[1] ligation of the base of one lung was followed by an immediate escape of this lung from tonic inhibitory control in a manner identical with destruction of the medulla (fig. 1, *B*).

[1] Both in the frog and in the necturus pressing the front legs tightly together with a rubber band renders the animals quiescent, and they will lie quietly on their backs for long periods without attempting to turn to a normal position. This procedure depresses also some of the skeletal reflexes.

It should be noted that in this animal the entire central nervous system was intact and that there was the minimum trauma produced in exposing the tip and base of one lung. Nevertheless, on severing this lung from its physiological connection with the central nervous system, the typical lung tetanus was produced. The results of this type of experiment strengthen our position that the striking peripheral automatism of the amphibian lung is a normal physiological state and not induced by the trauma rendered necessary by the experimental procedures.

From these experiments it would seem to follow that in this animal the lung is kept in tonic inhibition by central vagal control. If now one proceeds further and stimulates the peripheral end of the exposed vagus nerves at the base of the skull as was done in many animals, one obtains temporary escape of the lung from the hypertonic state as is shown in figure 2. This animal suffered at *a* an exposure of the anterior end of the brain by resection of the end of the upper mandible. This operative procedure was followed possibly by a slight inhibition of the lung tonus. The medulla was rapidly pithed at *b* resulting in permanent hypertonus of the lung. Stimulation of the peripheral end of the left and the right vagus at *c* and *d* respectively was in each instance followed by a temporary inhibition of the lung with an unusually rapid return to its hypertonic state. If the peripheral vagus stimulation is of sufficient strength the inhibition of the lung tonus usually puts the lung back temporarily to the identical tonus state prior to the destruction of the medulla. This is additional evidence that the state of the lung tonus in the intact animal is governed by the inhibitory control through the vagi.

Since ligation of the base of the lung effects the same result as destruction of the medulla, namely, an escape of the lung from its state of inhibitory control, it might be expected that electrical stimulation of the base of the lung would cause an inhibition comparable if not identical with stimulation of the peripheral end of the vagus. Figure 3 records the result of such an experiment. The lungs being in a state of hypertonus as a result of destruction of the medulla by pithing, stimulation of the vagus of the right lung at *a* caused an inhibition which is virtually duplicated by stimulation of the base of the left lung at *b*.

It appears to us from these observations that there is no escape from the conclusion that the vagi nerves possess inhibitory fibers for the lung which under normal conditions exercise a maximum inhibitory control over the lungs by tonic impulses from the medullary centers.

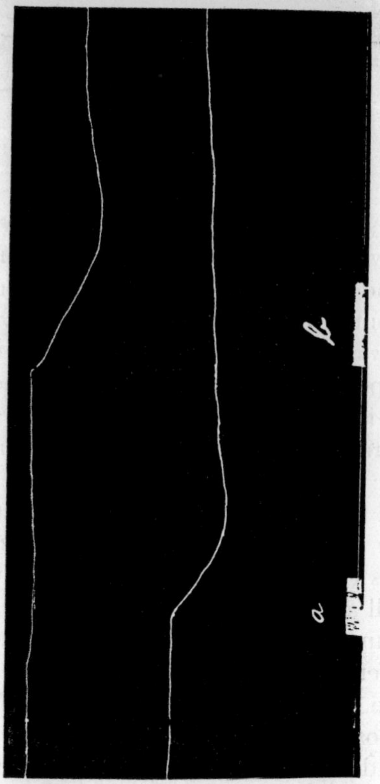

Fig. 3

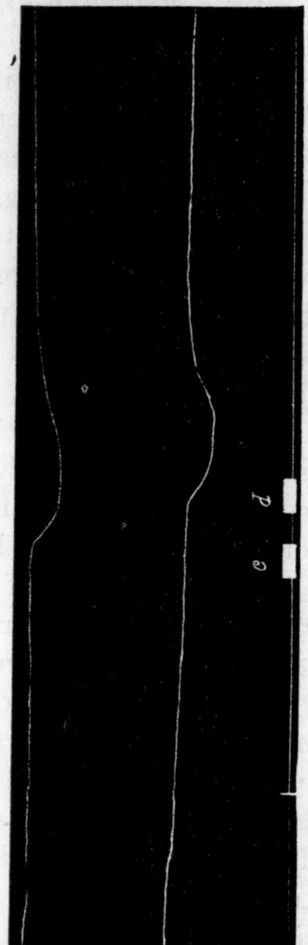

Fig. 2

B

A

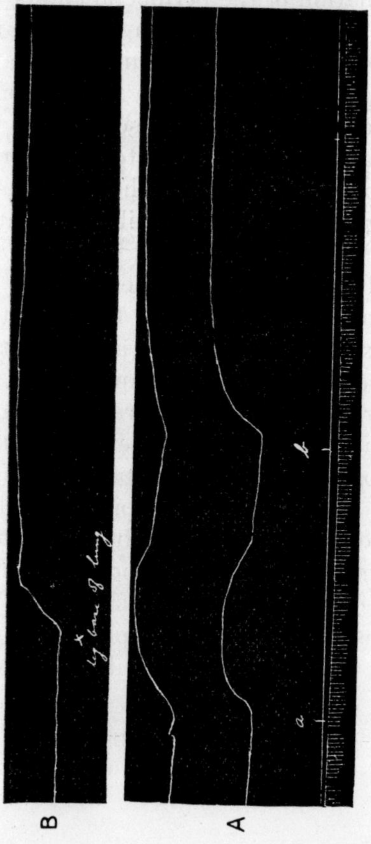

Fig. 1

b. Peripheral lung rhythm. In two instances the lungs of necturus showed a type of tonus rhythm seen occasionally in the frog. Figure 4, *A* and *B*, are records taken from these animals. In figure 4, *A*, this tonus rhythm appeared on pithing the medulla at *a*. Here a fast and later a slow tonus rhythm is written on the curve indicating release of the lung from central vagus inhibition. In figure 4, *B*, the tonus rhythm followed a decidedly rapid inhibition resulting from faradization of the base of the lung at *a* with a strong tetanizing current.

The interpretation of these results is based entirely upon speculation. It is possible that the rhythm which appeared as a result of the destruction of the brain (fig. 4, *A*) arose from occasional inhibitory impulses reaching the lungs through the vagi from more or less intact portions of the medulla which escaped complete destruction during the pithing of the latter. The tetanization with a strong current of the base of the lung in figure 4, *B*, at *a* might have effected changes in the physiological state of the automatic tissue present in the lungs which initiated an occasional and recurring refractory state of this peripheral automatic

Fig. 1. Water manometer tracings of the intrapulmonic pressure in necturus.

A: Spinal cord cut and destroyed below medulla, cannula in tip of lungs. Glottis closed by dorsal traction on front legs. Lungs isolated by ventral median incision; *a*, destruction of cerebral lobes and midbrain; *b*, destruction of the medulla. Showing permanent lung hypertonus on destruction of medulla.

B: Animal rendered quiet by tying rubber band around front legs, placed on dorsal side, no restraint, with water running over gills. Abdominal incision at base and tip of lung; *x*, ligation of base of lung. Showing permanent lung hypertonus identical with that following destruction of medulla. Time tracing: 5 second intervals.

Fig. 2. Water manometer tracings of the intrapulmonic pressure in necturus. Upper tracing, left lung; lower, right lung. Spinal cord cut and destroyed below medulla; cannulae in tips of lungs. Lungs isolated by a ventral median incision. Glottis (trachea) closed by pressure exerted by dorsal traction on front legs.

a, Transverse section of upper mandible exposing anterior end of brain.

b, Pithing brain.

c, Stimulation of left vagus at base of skull.

d, Ditto, right vagus.

Showing hypertonus of lungs induced by destruction of the medulla, and inhibition of this tonus by vago stimulation.

Fig. 3. Water manometer tracings of the intrapulmonic pressure in necturus. Cannulae in tips of lungs. Spinal cord and brain destroyed. Lungs in hypertonus. Upper tracing, left lung; lower, right lung; *a*, stimulation of right vagus at base of skull; *b*, stimulation of base of left lung.

Showing identical inhibitions of the lung tonus by vagus and by direct lung (base) stimulation.

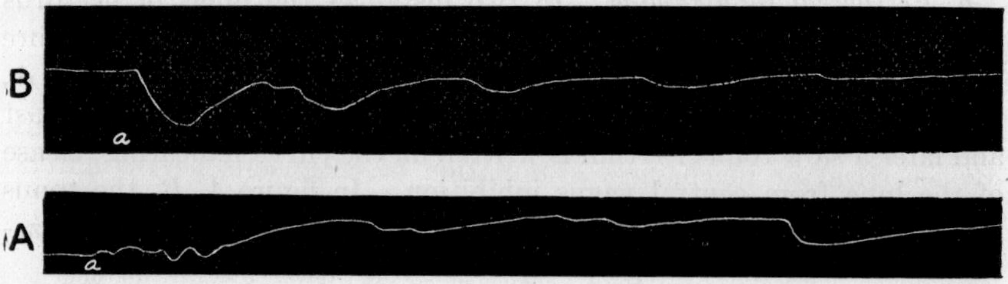

Fig. 4. Water manometer tracings of the intrapulmonic pressure in necturus. Cannula in tip of lung. Spinal cord cut and destroyed below medulla, lungs isolated by ventral median incision.

A: A pithing of the medulla showing a tonus rhythm of the lungs following destruction of the brain.

B: Lung in hypertonus from destruction of the brain; *a*, direct stimulation of the base of the lung with a weak tetanizing current.

Showing primary inhibition of lung tonus followed by a tonus rhythm.

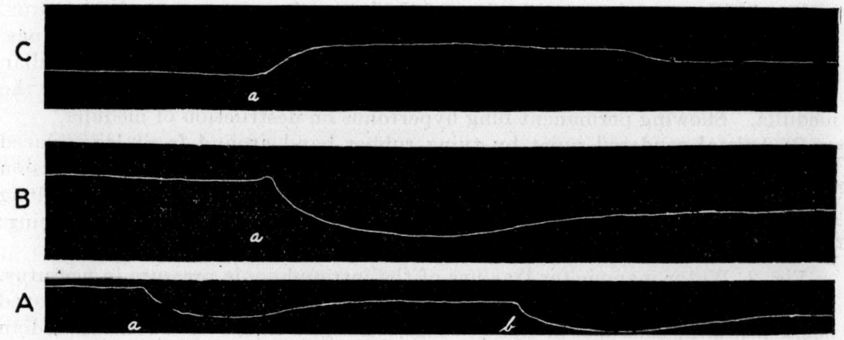

Fig. 5. Water manometer tracings of the intrapulmonic pressure in necturus. Cannula in tip of lung. Brain and spinal cord destroyed, giving the lungs permanent hypertonus.

A: *a*, injection 0.5 cc. adrenalin; *b*, 0.6 cc. of (1:1000) adrenalin in 5 cc. Ringer's into heart. Showing inhibition of lung tonus by adrenalin.

B: *a*, injection of 3 mgm. nicotine into heart, showing inhibition of lung tonus by nicotine.

C: *a*, injection of 0.6 cc. histamine (1–1000) into heart after partial recovery of preparation from a previous injection of nicotine. Showing direct stimulating action of histamine on lungs after paralysis of inhibitory nerve mechanism by nicotine.

mechanism, the inhibition of the hypertonic state of the lung giving rise to the appearance of a rhythm.

c. Reflex lung contractions as a result of cutaneous stimulation. We have been unable to effect reflex contractions of the lungs of the necturus by electrical or mechanical stimulation of cutaneous nerves anterior to the spinal transection.

d. The action of pituitrin, histamine, nicotine and adrenalin on the hypertonus of lung. In most of the work on drugs a cannula was tied into bulbus arteriosus. The drug was diluted with Ringer's and the injections made under moderate pressure through the bulbus. The method was poor even under favorable conditions. Direct intravenous injection was out of the question because active circulation through the lungs was absent in every animal although heart appeared in good condition. Even when the drug was injected under pressure we never felt certain that it reached all parts of the lung. This was due partly to the peculiarity of the pulmonary circulation in this animal and partly to the fact that a good deal of the fluid containing the drug escaped from the vessels ruptured in destroying the brain and isolating the vagi.

Adrenalin. The injection of adrenalin caused a marked inhibition of the hypertonic lung as is recorded in figure 5, tracing *A*, at *a* and *b*.

Pituitrin. According to the commonly accepted view, pituitrin is a direct stimulant of smooth muscle tissue. We were somewhat surprised to find that this drug in small or large doses causes a prompt and marked inhibition. Figure 6, *A*, is a record taken from an animal which suffered destruction of the medulla at *a* followed by a hypertonic state which was markedly reduced by the injection of pituitrin at *b*. The slow recovery is also recorded. No attempt was made to determine the point of action of pituitrin. Pituitrin not only caused a relaxation of the lung; but when weak solutions of this drug were used to irrigate the intestines all intestinal movements ceased after a short latent period. It would seem, therefore, that in these animals pituitrin does not act as a direct muscular stimulant but rather as a stimulant of the inhibitory mechanism.

Histamine. Figure 6, *B*, illustrates at *c* the typical inhibitory effect of this drug in an animal whose lungs were in hypertonus as a result of destruction of the medulla at *b*. Both lungs showed pronounced relaxation with very slow recovery. In all types of animals other than necturus this drug causes a more or less powerful contraction of the lung musculature (turtle, frog). Necturus proved to be an exception

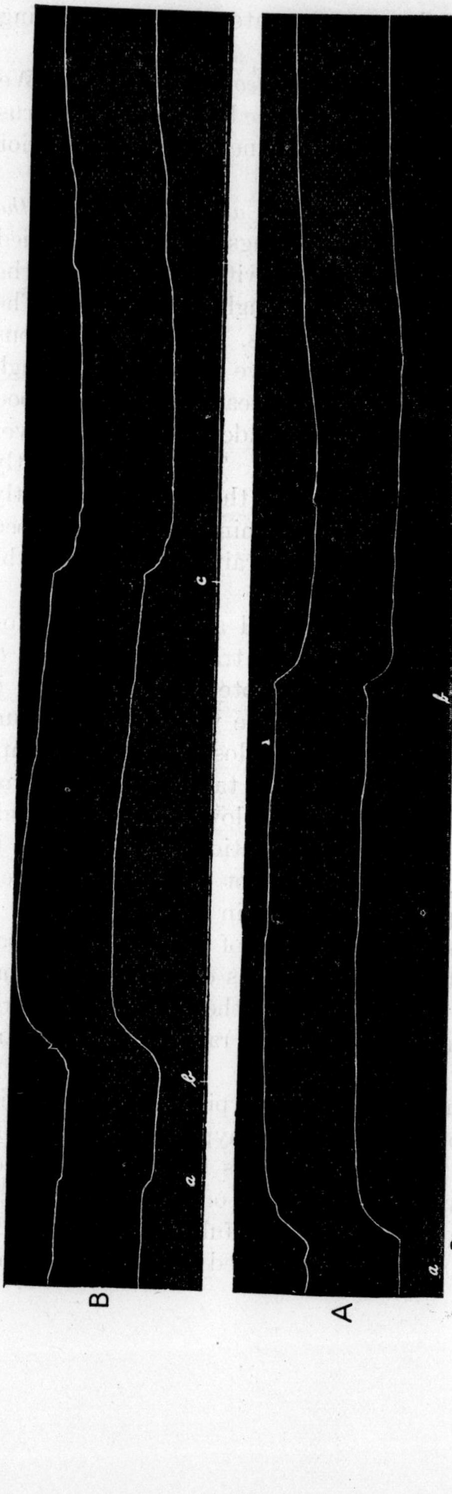

Fig. 6

Fig. 7

to the generally accepted view that the drug supposedly acts as a direct muscular stimulant. The results obtained suggest the possibility that the drug acts primarily on the inhibitory mechanism. We therefore attempted to eliminate the latter by means of nicotine. As a matter of fact we found that the injection of histamine after previous nicotinization effected a contraction of the lung in every instance as is recorded graphically in figure 5, *C* at *a*.

Nicotine. It will be recalled that this drug acted on the frog's lung in a manner similar to section of both vagi. We furthermore showed that in this animal the drug acted by paralyzing the inhibitory center in the medulla as well as the vagus inhibitory terminations in the lungs; for we found that after nicotinization stimulation of the peripheral end of the vagus gives rise to a lung contraction instead of the inhibition seen before giving this drug.

The subcutaneous or deep muscular injections of large (5 to 10 mgm.) doses into the normal intact necturus is in 15 minutes followed by general clonic convulsions with an increase in the rate and amplitude of the gill movements. Tetanus of the gills supervenes and active external respiration comes to an end some time before the general

Fig. 6. Water manometer tracings of the intrapulmonic pressure in necturus. Cannula in tip of each lung. Spinal cord cut and destroyed below medulla. Lungs isolated by ventral median incision. Glottis and tracheal sac closed by mechanical pressure through dorsal traction on front legs.

A: Upper record, left lung; lower, right lung; *a*, pithing of brain; *b*, injection of 0.5 cc. pituitrin in 5 cc. of Ringer's solution into heart. Showing inhibition of lung hypertonus by pituitrin.

B: Upper tracing, left lung; lower, right lung; *a*, section of upper mandible exposing anterior end of brain; *b*, pithing of brain; *c*, injection of 0.7 cc. histamine (1–1000) in 5 cc. Ringer's solution into heart. Showing inhibition of lung hypertonus by histamine.

Fig. 7. Axolotl. Water manometer tracings of the intrapulmonic pressure. Spinal cord pithed and destroyed below level of innervation of front legs. Lungs isolated by abdominal incision; cannula in tip of lungs. Glottis open. Spontaneous respiration (quick movements of lever) except where indicated.

A: a, Gentle mechanical stimulation of gills.
b, Gentle mechanical stimulation of skin of front legs.
c, Gentle mechanical stimulation of skin of mandibles.
d, Strong mechanical stimulation (pressure) of toes of front leg.
x, strong attempt at respiration (swallowing).
B: a, Moderate mechanical stimulation of the gills.
b, Gentle stroking of skin of front leg.
c, Strong mechanical stimulation of the gills.

Showing lung contractions following spontaneous respiratory movements and on stimulation of various sensory nerves.

convulsions cease. The lungs of such animals were found contracted. *Pithing the brain, stimulation of the vagi themselves, or stimulation of the lung itself at its base were without effect.*

If the dose of nicotine injected subcutaneously is reduced still further (2.5 to 1 mgm.) the same symptoms appear in 10 to 15 minutes but are less severe. Pithing of the brain or stimulation of the vagi is again without effect. Direct stimulation of the lung at its base with a strong tetanizing current gives rise to an inhibition of the lung without any or with but feeble return.

From these results it would appear that *a*, the lungs of this amphibian is supplied only with inhibitory fibers through the vagi; *b*, that nicotine paralyzes the respiratory center for the lungs and also the junction between the preganglionic fiber endings and postganglionic cell body, since external respiration ceases with the lungs in hypertonus and since stimulation of the base of the lungs will still yield inhibition when stimulation of the vagus nerve itself gives nothing; *c*, the vagus nerve contains no motor fibers for the pulmonary musculature. Without commenting at this time on the possible significance of this fact, we call attention to the fact that in this most primitive lung which we have studied, the lung is solely under the tonic influence of inhibitory fibers carried by the vagi and motor fibers are apparently absent. We have been unable to elicit a motor response of the lung either by stimulation of the vagi or the lung itself in any normal or nicotinized animal.

The apparent resistance of the peripheral lung mechanism to this drug compared with that of frog may possibly be due to the rather sluggish and imperfect circulation through the lungs.

2. Axolotl. Earlier in this paper we called attention to the fact that the axolotls with which we worked, although possessing gill remnants, were essentially air-breathing animals; and that the lungs were decidedly better developed for that purpose than the lungs of the necturus.

a. Lung contractions at the end of normal respiration. Records were taken of the changes in the intrapulmonic pressure occurring during normal respiration with the glottis open. It can be seen from figure 7, *B*, that every spontaneous respiratory effort (gulp) as indicated in the tracing of the quick movement of the lever is followed by contraction of the lung. These lung contractions compare favorably with those obtained under similar experimental conditions from the frog.

b. Reflex lung contractions. Gentle mechanical stimulation applied to the skin of the mandible, gills or front legs induced lung contractions of reflex origin as is seen in figure 7, *A*, at *a*, *b* and *c*. In these three instances the lung contraction appeared without a preceding attempt at respiration. Subsequent attempts at respiration were followed in each instance by lung contractions in every way similar to those of reflex origin induced by gentle stimulation. It is obvious that the contractions are not the result of changes in the intrapulmonic pressure due to movements of the animal during external respiration; for they occur in the absence of all visible movement of the head region.

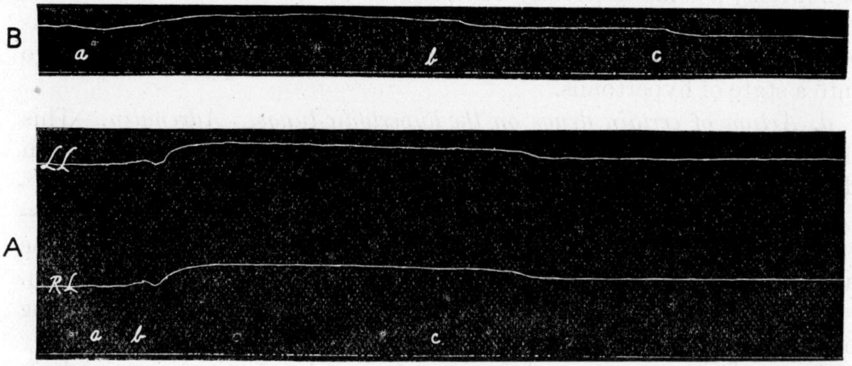

Fig. 8. Axolotl. Water manometer tracings of the intrapulmonic pressure. Spinal cord transected below medulla and pithed posteriorly. Cannula in tip of lungs, lungs isolated by median abdominal incision. Glottis closed by forceps. All injections intravenously (in 2 cc. Ringer solution).

A: Lower tracing, right lung; upper, left lung.

a, Transection of upper mandible exposing anterior end of brain.

b, Pithed brain.

c, Injection of 1 cc. 1:10,000 adrenalin.

B: a, Pithed brain.

b, Injection of 0.01 cc. 1:1000 histamine.

c, Injection of 2 mgm. nicotine.

Showing the inhibitory action of these drugs on the lung hypertonus following destruction of the brain, the latter being equivalent to section of the vagi nerves.

Strong mechanical stimulation of the fore legs or gills may lead to partial or complete opening of the glottis with partial or complete collapse of the lungs as is illustrated in figure 7, *A*, at *d*, and figure 7, *B*, at *a*, *b* and *c*. Strong attempts at respiration after marked stimulation of pain fibers as at *xxx* in figure 7, *A*, were not followed by the filling of the lungs until considerably later. It might be assumed that the strong stimulation interfered temporarily with the central control of the mechanism normally at the service of the animal in filling its lungs with air or depresses the central inhibitory control over the lungs. If the latter is the correct interpretation the animal failed to fill its lungs in spite of violent respiratory attempts because of their hypertonic state. Although we have no direct evidence on this matter the latter interpretation seems to be the more probable one.

c. The central inhibitory control of the lungs through the vagi. It is certain that in the axolotl the medullary centers exert, under normal conditions, a tonic inhibitory control over the lungs as in the frog and necturus; for as a result of the destruction of the medulla which is equivalent to section of both vagi (as in fig. 8, *A*, at *b*) both lungs go into a state of hypertonus.

d. Action of certain drugs on the hypertonic lungs. Adrenalin. This drug temporarily inhibits the hypertonus of the lungs resulting from destruction of the medulla as seen in figure 8, *A*, at *c*.

Histamine. In axolotl the intravenous injection of 1 mgm. of histamine-HCl caused inhibition of the lung musculature not unlike the action of this drug in the hypertonic lung of necturus (fig. 8, *B*, at *b*).

Nicotine. The invariable effect of nicotine on the hypertonic lung of the axolotl is inhibition (fig. 8, *B*, at *c*).

As previously noted we were not only restricted to a few animals in study of this form but found that the physiological state of the animals rapidly declined as the result of our operative procedures. The axolotl furnishes a less hardy physiological preparation than the frog or necturus. As far as our results go they check with those obtained from the frog and necturus.

SUMMARY

1. The vagus center exerts a tonic inhibitory control over the lungs. Destruction of the medulla releases the lung from this control. As a result, the lungs assume a state of more or less permanent hypertonus (necturus and axolotl).

2. Electrical stimulation of the peripheral end of the vagus nerves causes a temporary inhibition of the hypertonic state of the lungs, only on the side of stimulation, during and for some time after the stimulation (necturus and axolotl).

3. The efferent vagi fibers to the lungs are solely of the inhibitory type. We have never seen the slightest indication of a motor response on stimulation of these nerves. Unlike the frog, the vagi of these forms of amphibian life possess few if any motor fibers for the lungs (necturus and axolotl).

4. Electrical stimulation of the base of the lung yields the same results as stimulation of the peripheral end of the vagus (necturus and axolotl).

5. We have been able to elicit reflex lung contractions from gentle mechanical stimulation of cutaneous nerves only in the axolotl. Intense stimulation of sensory nerves (pain) probably prevents filling of the lungs during attempts at respiration because of a hypertonic condition of the lungs due to an inhibition of the inhibitory center.

6. There may appear as a result of destruction of the medulla or strong faradization of the base of the lung a tonus rhythm in the denervated lungs of the necturus. This rhythm has not been seen in axolotl.

7. Adrenalin, pituitrin, histamine and nicotine cause a marked inhibition of the hypertonic condition of the lungs resulting from the destruction at the medulla. Histamine injected into the animal after nicotine causes a contraction of the lung. In axolotl these drugs act in the same direction. Pituitrin was not used in this form; nor was histamine injected after nicotinization of the animal.

BIBLIOGRAPHY

(1) Babák and Kühnova: Arch. f. d. gesammt. Physiol., 1909, cxxx, 444.
(2) Barrows: Anat. Anz., 1900, xviii, 461.
(3) Bethge: Zeitschr. f. Wissensch. Zoöl., 1898, lxiii, 680.
(4) Camerano: Anat. Anz., 1894, ix, 676; Arch. ital. d. Biol., 1896, xxv, 219.
(5) Carlson and Luckhardt: This Journal, 1920, liv, 55.
(6) Carlson: Arch. f. d. Physiol., 1905, cix, 51.
(7) Lapique and Petetin: Compt. Rend. Soc. Biol., 1910, lxix, 84.
(8) Lönnberg: Anat. Anz., 1899, xxii, 545.
(9) Miller: Bull. Univ. Wisconsin, Science Series, II, 1900, 203.
(10) Oppel: Lehrb. d. Vergl. Mikr. Anat., 1905, vi, 277.
(11) Stirling: Journ. Anat. and Physiol., 1882, xvi, 90.
(12) Wilder: Amer. Naturalist, 1901, xxxv, 183.

CHANGES IN ACID AND ALKALI TOLERANCE WITH AGE IN PLANARIANS

With a Note on Catalase Content

JOHN W. MacARTHUR

From the Hull Zoölogical Laboratory, University of Chicago, and the Department of Biology, University of Toronto

Received for publication July 17, 1920

During a study of the effects of certain typical acids, bases and salts upon living planarians (*Planaria dorotocephala*, *P. maculata* and *P. velata*), observations were made which are here reported on account of the wider interest of their bearing upon tolerance of H^+ and OH^- ions, upon the relative efficiency of the mechanism for regulation of neutrality in young and old individuals, and upon the problem of acidosis in general.

Methods. A closely graded series of concentration of the acids (hydrochloric chiefly, also sulfuric and acetic) or alkali (sodium hydroxide) is made up from standardized N or 0.1 N solutions by dilution with aerated well water or other (Lake Michigan or Lake Ontario) water in which the worms live and thrive. The well water, which was used chiefly, has a pH value of 7.5 to 7.6 and an ion and gas content to be published with the larger study above mentioned. Both distilled water and strongly chlorinated tap-water are in themselves injurious to these worms and hence could not well be used for the purposes of these experiments; but similar tests are now being made with *P. maculata* in distilled water, this species being but little affected by distilled water in the period of time required.

Into the series of dilutions of an acid or alkali in 500 cc. or 1000 cc. Erlenmeyer flasks, filled and ready to be plugged with rubber stoppers, are introduced the flatworms, usually ten larger (18 to 20 mm.) and ten smaller (8 to 12 mm.) specimens together, all selected sound from established well-fed cultures. In some cases a similar group of three easily distinguishable sizes was used (22± mm., 15± mm. and 8± mm.). In control flasks all such individuals live practically indefinitely.

The hydrogen ion concentrations, already in a graded series from the method of diluting the normal solution, are measured and corrected at critical points by the colorimetric method with appropriate indicators: thymol-blue, brom-phenol-blue, methyl-red, brom-cresol-purple, phenol-red and phenol-phthalein, and the Hynson, Westcott and Dunning apparatus (1). Certain difficulties were encountered from the fact that glassware requires particularly thorough cleaning after each usage, and because strong acids added to water containing so much carbonate as do these naturally generate CO_2 and such solutions tend to return gradually toward neutrality. But these facts have no great significance here except as they render impracticable a precisely accurate determination of the actual limits of tolerance, as may be made in distilled water and by electrometry. In all cases it was the relative rather than the absolute susceptibility that was sought and that is here emphasized.

Extensive physiological studies of planarians have been made by Child (2), (3), who showed for *P. dorotocephala* by various means that the smallest worms (up to about 6 or 7 mm.) consist of but one zoöid, while the medium-sized ones (12 to 14 mm.) usually possess a second zoöid region, and larger specimens (20 to 25 mm. or more) exhibit at the posterior end a third zoöid or group of very small zoöids, constituting what is essentially a "growing tip." At least the chief, the second and the third of these zoöids were demonstrable physiologically by both "direct" and "indirect" methods in cyanides, but only after fission do the typical head structures of the zoöids become visibly differentiated morphologically. The growing tip is evidently involved repeatedly in the reproductive process; hence as this region grows its zoöids become more independent and acquire a higher rate of metabolic reaction and, like young individuals, are more susceptible to high concentrations and less susceptible to low concentrations of lethal agents (KNC, anesthetics, etc.).

Experimental. The chief observations are recorded and summarized graphically in the accompanying figure. The time records are averages from repeated tests made of each dilution; such averages for separate tests show but small deviations from the general average, but individual deviations are often large and overlapping wherever the curves lie close together. Dr. C. M. Child, to whom the writer is indebted for many opportunities and suggestions in this work, has recently used these experiments as part of a class course at the University of Chicago.

Acids. Immersed in HCl solutions that kill almost instantly (e.g., in acidities greater than about pH = 2) all worms are fixed and preserved intact (range of preservation). In lower concentrations, from pH = 2 down to about pH = 4.5, all individuals are killed and caused to disintegrate, the older somewhat later and more slowly than the younger (range of direct susceptibility and inhibition). In this disintegration all regions of the body are not equally and simultaneously involved, but usually the posterior tip and the head are first attacked

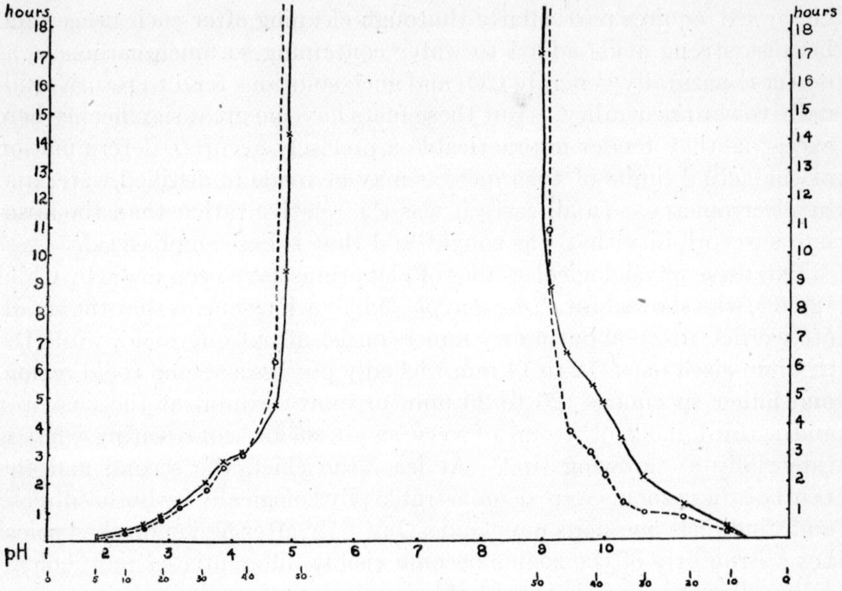

Fig. 1. Time in hours of distinct initial disintegration of young worms ---o---o--- and old worms ——x——x—— in solutions of different pH values (abscissae) up to pH = 10. Small numbers below abscissae indicate volumes of well water added to one of N/10 HCl (left) or NaOH (right).

Below pH = 2 ± is the range of preservation or fixation. Then follows with increasing dilution up to pH 4.4 ± the range of distinct direct susceptibility which grades off by a transition range into the range of acclimation or indirect susceptibility.

With NaOH the range of preservation is evidently absent, direct susceptibility differences between young and old much more marked, and the indirect susceptibility differences less marked than with acids.

and then the regions behind the head in order from in front backward; and, as might be expected from the small differences in direct susceptibility between young and old, the anterior end of a second zoöid is not distinguished. As the acidity approaches pH = 4.5 or pH = 4.6, the age difference in survival time decreases more and more and finally becomes nil, and disintegration does not discriminate between the small and the large. In still more dilute solutions, however (pH = 4.7 to 4.9), where death is delayed for several hours and a certain amount of recovery from the initial inhibitory effects of the agent is possible, the relative susceptibility of young and old individuals is reversed (range of indirect susceptibility and acclimation), and smaller worms disintegrate last or not at all, while larger ones either disintegrate entirely or lose their head region. Posterior zoöids are left intact, and the posterior part of the first zoöid was never seen to disintegrate before the anterior end. Often the young worms live for days or indefinitely after the old are partially or wholly gone. Recovery tests, made by returning young and old alike to fresh water after various periods of exposure to the agent, are even more delicate in their indication of the sites and degrees of injury, and were used to extend and confirm the results obtained by leaving the animals in the agent up to the end of the experiment.

A more or less definite sequence of changes leads up to the final disintegration with acids. After the initial stimulation, during which the flatworm assumes for a time a slender form, moves rapidly and secretes some mucus, it gradually loses its power of adherence to the glass walls of the container and becomes shortened, cylindrical and swollen. This state is soon followed by discoloration or whitening, the loss of color occurring, as noted, first at the sensory tip, margins and ventral surface of the head and gradually extending backwards, often more rapidly on the ventral surface, and in larger individuals beginning early also at the growing tip. The whitening appears to indicate that semipermeability or some similar property of the surface layer has been abolished at the approach of death, for following close upon the loss of pigment occur disintegrative changes of a characteristic kind: as the parts become sticky and adherent to glass the regularity of the external contour is interrupted by small breaks in the continuity of the surface, the protoplasmic granules swell and mass into small clumps or liquid spheres and scatter out into the medium until finally little remains of the old body but a soft white shreddy outline composed of the more resistant connective and supporting tissues quite stripped of all the relatively susceptible epithelial parts.

Results differ in no essential way if sulfuric acid in slightly higher concentrations be substituted for the hydrochloric, or if a considerably greater strength of acetic acid be used—the difference probably being necessary to compensate for the lesser dissociation of the organic acid.

A *change of response* occurs upon addition of acid to the normal medium. The planarians then exhibit a fairly strong negative geotropism, climbing always up the walls of the container, whether in doing so they approach or attain a surface or not. Since strong acids cause a release of CO_2 into the solution, the response may perhaps be considered generally appropriate and adaptive, inasmuch as ordinarily an increase of CO_2 is doubtless associated with an insufficiency of oxygen (to which a similar response is made) and both could doubtless be avoided by rising to a better aerated surface layer.

Alkali. In alkaline solutions the same general results are obtained with certain more or less significant modifications. In the hydroxide (NaOH) stimulation is evidently more marked than in acids, and both whole worms and surviving parts of any size are more active both spontaneously and upon mechanical stimulation up to the very point of death. Alkalies also cause the secretion of a very excessive amount of mucus, which collects, as often as removed, in the bottom of the vessel.

Even quickly killing concentrations do not produce a definite fixation and preservation. Disintegration, if rapid, occurs, by a rather violent process of splitting and bursting of the dorsal surface in darkened lines; if slow, it begins at the margins and dorsal surfaces of the head and the posterior tip, and in larger specimens may also appear at what is presumably the anterior end of the second zoöid.

Results with NaOH differ from those with HCl and resemble more nearly those with KNC in one respect—in the slowly acting concentrations, allowing partial acclimation of the larger animals, death sometimes begins at the posterior end of the first zoöid and proceeds forward, while the head region of the first zoöid and all of the posterior zoöids remain intact for some time or indefinitely. In short the details of disintegration with this alkaline agent resemble those with most "acid dyes," while "basic vital dyes" rather resemble acids in their effect (unpublished work).

By the method of direct susceptibility there is much greater difference in survival time of young and old with NaOH than with HCl, the old surviving about twice as long as the young. The effective range of concentrations for indirect susceptibility, on the other hand, is less extended than with acids.

It will be noted that the range of critical concentrations, within which young animals and young parts only are able to regulate slight H^+ ion alterations, is a comparatively limited one and lies just beyond the limits resisted by all alike. Thus increase of H^+ ion up to pH =

4.9 on the one side or of OH^- ion to about pH = 9.1 on the other come within the normal range for all members of the species; slight additional changes (from pH = 4.9 to pH = 4.8 or 4.7 and from pH = 9.1 to pH = 9.2 or 9.3) can be met by the young individuals and parts alone; still greater changes are beyond the powers of acclimation of any, though the old resist the longer.

The greater tolerance by younger planarians and the posterior zoöid region of such dilute acid and alkaline solutions is almost certainly only another example of the greater power of acclimation to mildly depressing conditions associated so generally with more active metabolism (3). In fact the general principle underlying the indirect susceptibility method is founded on the discovery that organisms or parts of organisms possessing an intenser metabolism can acclimate or acquire tolerance more quickly and more completely than less active organisms or parts to low concentrations of cyanides, narcotics, etc. Child also showed later that the anterior, ventral and median regions (the regions of high direct susceptibility and presumably of most rapid metabolism) in Echinoderm and Annelid embryos, developing in low concentrations of NaOH, alcohol or HCl in sea-water, acclimated or acquired tolerance, or after temporary exposure recovered most quickly and underwent a proportionately accelerated and increased development in the larvae (4).

The explanation of this power of acclimation is not known, but may be in some way associated, as regards acids and alkalies, with differences in protoplasmic conditions, such as the higher percentage water content of metabolically active parts or individuals. If this water carries, as seems probable, at least an equal proportional and a greater total salt content, such inorganic salts of these as are buffer-acting substances (carbonates, phosphates, etc.) would act here much as in mammalian blood, to increase resistance to additional H^+ and OH^- ions in the medium. Or, if a greater proportion of mid-products of protein metabolism, or more ionized protein, be present during rapid metabolism, then these amphoteric substances may serve as acids or bases according as there are excess bases or acids in the medium. Naturally such buffers and metabolites would be protective only against slightly and slowly injurious concentrations; with higher concentrations the projective action is quickly overcome and the agent may diffuse and act most rapidly in the parts with greatest water content.

The acid or alkali effects may of course be produced through injury to some enzyme or enzymes essential to continuance of metabolic processes. Inasmuch as the almost universally occurring enzyme, *cata-*

lase, may eventually be shown to play some rôle in metabolism generally and in oxidation in particular (5), the writer wishes to record here the results obtained from numerous experiments to determine the catalase content or activity of planarians of different ages. It was found that equal weights of crushed young worms (8 to 15 mm.), maturer worms (18 to 20 mm.), and of very old worms (25 to 30 mm.) liberated in 15 minutes at 22°C. from $1\frac{1}{2}$ per cent unneutralized hydrogen peroxide the following quantities of oxygen respectively per gram weight of tissue: 653.3 cc., 460.4 cc. and 317.6 cc. Without a single exception, in many repetitions of the experiment, the rule was found to hold that *the larger (older) the worm the lower is the catalase content.* It is of interest to note that the oxygen consumption of young planarians has been found to be from 15 per cent to 100 per cent greater than that of old ones (6), showing a higher basal metabolism, just as the Benedict method does for man.

Some significance should be attached to the fact that though there are such large differences in direct susceptibility of young and old with alkalies, these differences are small with acids; while, on the contrary, though the differences by indirect susceptibility are small with alkalies, they are larger with acids. *The young are evidently comparatively and absolutely less resistant to alkalies, but relatively more resistant to acids.* With advancing age there would appear to be a decreased relative resistance to acids and an increased relative resistance to alkalies—a set of changes such as would result from a gradual onset of a state of acidosis and the more or less incomplete oxidation of the larger-acid products left from a state of lowered metabolism. MacNider (7) has shown that as age advances the acid-base equilibrium of mammals is more and more easily disturbed or overtaxed; that uranium nitrate, for instance, is more toxic to the old than to the young and produces sooner in the old a condition of true acidosis (8), characterized by a depletion of reserve carbonates in the blood, etc.; and that the aged, after uranium treatment, received intravenously without injury considerably more alkali than did the young.

For all the species used by Child (4) in controlling form and proportions of developing embryos, he found that "the agents which are most effective in producing the differentially inhibited type of form are least effective in producing the types of form characteristic of differential acclimation, and vice versa," his series being effective in producing acclimation types in the order: HCl, alcohol, NaOH, NH_4OH, KNC. Thus acclimation was rapid in acids and alcohol, slow in NaOH and

NH_4OH, and exceedingly slow in KNC. A similar contrasting physiological effect between HCl and NaOH is here shown by other means for fresh-water planarians.

Comparing allied species with *P. dorotocephala* it may be said that in general *P. maculata* has a slightly wider range of normal tolerance, while *P. velata* is distinctly less resistant to acids and more resistant to alkalies.

SUMMARY AND CONCLUSIONS

1. *Planaria dorotocephala* of all ages used tolerate HCl up to about pH 4.9 and NaOH up to about pH 9.2 in the well water (pH = 7.5 to 7.6) in which they live, i.e., they tolerate a range of pH from 4.9± to about 9.2±.

2. Smaller, physiologically younger, individuals are on the average tolerant of a slightly wider range of hydrogen ion concentration (from pH = 4.7 to pH = 9.3) than are larger, physiologically older individuals, this difference of susceptibility being apparently somewhat greater on the acid than on the alkaline side of neutrality. The young possess a greater power of neutrality-regulation than do the old, explanatory suggestions for which are offered.

3. In concentrations of alkali which kill within a few hours susceptibility is reversed in relation to age, the young being very much more susceptible than the old. In similar concentrations of the acids young specimens are likewise on the average more susceptible, but only slightly more so. In other words, high concentrations of OH^- tend to increase and high concentrations of H^+ tend to diminish differences in direct susceptibility between young and old individuals. This suggests a possible increasing average acidity with senescence and decreasing metabolism.

4. Young planarians have about double the catalase content of old planarians per gram weight of tissue.

5. In acid solutions liberating CO_2, in which worms live for some time, they commonly assume, as in conditions of oxygen deficiency, a negative geotropism of an obviously adaptive nature as a normal means of escape from excess CO_2.

6. These facts indicate the necessity of taking into account the factors of age, size and metabolism in defining range of tolerance to agents and conditions.

BIBLIOGRAPHY

(1) Clark and Lubs: Journ. Bact., 1917, ii.
(2) Child: Journ. Exper. Zoöl., 1913, xiv.
(3) Child: Senescence and rejuvenescence, 1915, Chicago.
(4) Child: Journ. Morph., 1916. xxviii, 65; 1917, xxx, 1.
(5) Burge: Science, 1918, xlviii, 327. Also literature of Alvarez and Starkweather, This Journal, 1918, xlvi, 186, and Appleman: Amer. Journ Bot., 1918, v. 207.
(6) Hyman: Biol. Bull., 1919, xxxvii, 388.
(7) MacNider: Science, 1917, xlvi, 643.
(8) Henderson: Science, 1917, xlvi, 73.

STUDIES ON THE ALKALINE RESERVE OF THE BLOOD OF THE INSANE

NOBUHARU SUITSU

From the Wistar Institute of Anatomy and Biology, Philadelphia, Pennsylvania

Received for publication July 19, 1920

These studies were undertaken to ascertain whether or not the alkaline reserve of the blood of the insane shows any significant differences from that found in the blood of normal individuals, and whether or not the blood of the various types of insanity studied vary one from the other in their carbon dioxide combining capacity. During the course of the investigation certain other material was obtained which will be briefly discussed.

The subjects of these studies were patients at the Pennsylvania Hospital, Department for Mental and Nervous Diseases, Philadelphia.

Since Van Slyke, Stillman and Cullen (1) have shown that a slight rise in plasma carbon dioxide tension usually follows eating, the samples of blood to be analyzed were taken at the uniform hour of eleven o'clock in the morning, three and a half hours after breakfast, unless otherwise noted. The blood specimens were drawn from an arm vein with a Record syringe containing a small amount of potassium oxalate. Care was taken to avoid the sucking in of air. After filling the syringe the point of the needle was plunged under paraffin oil contained in a small test tube and 2 cc. of blood expressed and centrifuged. The plasma was then pipetted off and the carbon dioxide capacity determined as described by Van Slyke (2), and Van Slyke and Cullen (3). The determination was carried out two or three times on one and the same sample and the average adopted as the result.

A general comparison of the findings obtained from excited and depressed cases. It is well known that not only mechanical but also psychic activities have great influence upon respiratory and circulatory functions (1), and that the alveolar carbon dioxide tension under ideal normal conditions indicates the level of the blood bicarbonate, but since the alveolar carbon dioxide tension is altered by numerous factors, psychic, physiological and pathological (4), it is not a reliable measure of the blood bicarbonate except when it is certain that both the mechanical and nervous factors controlling respiration are normal.

With these facts in view an attempt was made to determine whether or not any relation existed between the plasma carbonate and conditions of excitement and depression. The figures in table 1 give the plasma CO_2 capacity in twelve cases classed as depressed and ten individuals exhibiting excitement.

It will be seen that in general terms all the values fall within normal limits and that no significant differences can be observed between the two groups. The mere fact that no differences occur in these two groups

TABLE 1

The alkaline reserve of the blood of the excited and depressed insane

Cubic centimeters of CO_2 reduced to 0°, 760 mm. bound as bicarbonate in 100 cc. plasma

EXCITED CASES	DEPRESSED CASES
64.42	72.08
64.42	69.14
63.95	66.36
63.57	66.36
63.48	66.36
62.08	63.54
60.20	59.74
54.38	59.68
51.24	57.39
45.04	55.94
	52.06
	51.18
Average........59.28	61.65

of patients permits the supposition that in long-continued excitations a compensatory reaction occurs sufficient to preserve the normal level of the alkaline reserve of the blood, which one would naturally suppose to be lowered by consequence of the increased activity.

The alkaline reserve of the blood during individual changes in mental condition. A confirmation of the general findings that no evident differences are to be found in the alkaline reserve of the blood of excited or depressed insane patients is afforded by the figures given in table 2. These results represent the analyses of the bloods from single individuals at frequent intervals over periods of several weeks during which there occurred a marked change in mental condition with respect to excitement and relative depression. It is seen that in these cases at least there failed to occur any consistent change in the alkaline reserve of the blood accompanying the change from excitement to depression or vice versa. The four individuals studied were all diagnosed as dementia precox cases.

The variability of the alkaline reserve of the blood of the insane from week to week. During the course of these investigations opportunity was afforded to determine the degree to which the alkaline reserve of the blood varies in the individual from week to week in cases where the general trend of mental condition was uniform.

The results are given in table 3. The variability is given by the value for the average deviation calculated for each individual. An inspection of the table shows that although the absolute amounts all fall within normal limits and no significant differences occur, yet there are differences in the degree of variability to be observed in different individuals. These differences, however, cannot be evaluated since the data are insufficient.

Table 4 is a compilation of the analyses obtained from 112 bloods from 51 individuals arranged in the order of their descending value. The figures represent the cubic centimeters of CO_2 reduced to 0°, 760 mm. bound as bicarbonate by 100 cc. plasma. It is seen that the absolute amounts do not exceed the limits usually attributed to normal bloods save at the extremes. The main fact of interest lies in the relatively low variability of this blood factor which is comparable with that obtained for the average deviation of the blood creatinine nitrogen in similar patients (5).

In table 5 there have been arranged the values representing the average amounts, the average deviation, and the range of fluctuation of the alkaline reserve of the blood according to diagnosis. From the data it is evident that no significant differences obtain in the absolute amounts of the alkaline reserve of the blood in the different types here studied. It should be noted, however, that there is a tendency for the variability of this blood factor to be greater in the mentally disturbed than in normal individuals.

The alkaline reserve of the blood taken three and a half and fourteen hours after eating. Since it is often inconvenient to take samples of blood early in the morning and before breakfast a comparison was made of the alkaline reserve of the blood taken three and a half hours after breakfast, and fourteen hours after the night meal. The data are given in table 3.

TABLE 2

The alkaline reserve of the blood of four dementia precox patients during states of excitement and states of depression

NUMBER	CONDITION	CO_2 REDUCED TO 0° 760 MM. BOUND AS BICARBONATE IN 100 CC. OF PLASMA
		cc.
1	Quiet	50.24
	Excited	64.77
	Excited	63.30
	Quiet	59.68
	Depressed	60.56
	Excited	63.48
2	Excited	60.70
	Excited	63.43
	Depressed	68.51
	Excited	61.07
	Excited	74.80
3	Excited	63.30
	Quiet	60.19
	Quiet	57.78
4	Excited	56.71
	Quiet	54.22
	Quiet	52.49

TABLE 3

The individual variability of the alkaline reserve of the blood of the insane as observed from week to week

Cubic centimeters of CO_2 reduced to 0°, 760 mm. bound as bicarbonate in 100 cc. of plasma

	SET 1	SET 2	SET 3	SET 4	SET 5	SET 6	SET 7	SET 8	SET 9	SET 10	SET 11	SET 12
	58.46	55.34	53.21	70.07	64.30	65.47	62.60	64.12	74.90	59.80	69.20	72.96
	58.15	62.79	63.48	72.00	63.42	64.38	63.51	58.90	73.26	65.46	62.49	73.93
	66.73	62.40	62.56	75.38	65.30	57.74	65.50	59.80	70.10	62.58	66.79	64.38
	65.66	53.92	71.02	75.31	63.36	67.81	61.54	62.56	70.17	63.30	63.30	67.20
	63.42	66.31	63.66	74.85								
	63.44	64.34	63.42	73.57								
	69.14	70.41										
Average....	63.45	62.22	62.89	73.53	64.10	63.85	63.29	61.35	72.11	62.79	65.47	69.62
Variability.	4.0	7.0	5.3	2.3	1.2	4.8	1.9	2.7	2.8	2.3	4.4	5.5

TABLE 4

The carbon dioxide combining capacity of 112 bloods from 51 insane and normal individuals

ALKALINE RESERVE	DIAGNOSIS	ALKALINE RESERVE	DIAGNOSIS	ALKALINE RESERVE	DIAGNOSIS	ALKALINE RESERVE	DIAGNOSIS
75.38	M. D.	66.36	M. D.	63.42	M. D.	58.90	D. P.
75.31	M. D.	66.36	M. D.	63.42	N.	58.62	D. P.
74.90	D. P.	66.31	M. D.	63.42	I. M.	58.46	M. D.
74.85	M. D.	65.66	M. D.	63.36	N.	58.40	D. P.
74.80	M. D.	65.50	D. P.	63.30	D. P.	58.15	M. D.
73.57	M. D.	65.47	D. P.	63.30	D. P.	57.78	D. P.
73.26	D. P.	65.38	N.	63.17	D. P.	57.74	D. P.
72.08	M. D.	65.30	N.	63.09	D. P.	57.39	M. D.
72.00	M. D.	64.77	D. P.	62.79	M. D.	56.71	D. P.
71.04	N.	64.42	M. D.	62.60	D. P.	55.94	M. D.
71.02	I. M.	64.42	S. D.	62.56	D. P.	55.52	D. P.
70.41	M. D.	64.38	D. P.	62.56	I. M.	55.34	M. D.
70.17	D. P.	64.34	M. D.	62.44	M. D.	55.10	?
70.10	D. P.	64.30	N.	62.40	M. D.	54.38	M. D.
70.07	M. D.	64.12	D. P.	62.08	M. D.	54.22	D. P.
69.53	D. P.	63.95	M. D.	61.54	D. P.	53.92	M. D.
69.14	D. P.	53.66	I. M.	61.52	D. P.	53.21	I. M.
69.14	M. D.	63.61	N.	61.33	N.	52.97	D. P.
69.12	D. P.	63.57	N.	61.07	M. D.	52.75	M. D.
69.12	N.	63.57	M. D.	60.70	M. D.	52.65	?
68.60	D. P.	63.54	?	60.56	D. P.	52.49	D. P.
58.51	M. D.	63.54	D. P.	60.20	M. D.	52.06	D. P.
68.32	D. P.	63.54	N.	60.19	D. P.	51.24	D. P.
67.88	D. P.	63.51	D. P.	60.03	N.	51.18	?
67.81	D. P.	63.48	M. D.	59.80	D. P.	50.24	D. P.
67.22	N.	63.48	D. P.	59.74	I. M.	50.20	N.
66.73	M. D.	63.48	I. M.	59.68	D. P.	47.76	D. P.
66.36	M. D.	63.43	M. D.	59.68	D. P.	47.61	?

Average, 62.99; Variability, 7.35; Range, 73.38–47.61.

M. D., Manic depressive; D. P., Dementia precox; I. M., Involutional melancholia; S. I., Senile involution; N., Normal.

TABLE 5

The range of fluctuation, average amounts and average deviations of the alkaline reserve of the blood of the insane according to diagnosis

NUMBER OF CASES	DIAGNOSIS	RANGE	AVERAGE AMOUNT	AVERAGE DEVIATIONS
		cc.	*cc.*	*per cent*
15	Normal	47.61–71.04	62.60	6.6
39	Manic depressive	52.75–75.38	64.42	7.3
8	Involuntary melancholy	51.18–71.02	61.03	7.7
47	Dementia precox	47.76–74.90	61.84	8.2

Sets number 7–8–9 are the values obtained after the shorter fast, and sets 10–11–12 those found after the longer period of abstinence in the same individuals respectively. The investigation extended over eight weeks, the first four weeks of which being the period when the blood specimens were taken once a week after breakfast, and the second four weeks being the period when the samples were taken before breakfast.

It is evident that there are no valid or consistent differences in the bloods taken at these times.

SUMMARY

The results of the studies here reported indicate that:

1. The alkaline reserve of the blood of the insane appears to fall within the limits considered normal for healthy persons.

2. There are no demonstrable differences in the absolute amounts of the alkaline reserve of the bloods from excited or depressed patients here studied.

3. The variability of the plasma carbon dioxide combining capacity seems to be higher in the insane than in the small group of normals here studied.

4. No noteworthy differences obtain in the alkaline reserve of the blood taken three and a half and fourteen hours after eating.

I take this occasion to express my appreciation of the courtesy of Dr. Owen Copp in affording me the facilities of the Pennsylvania Hospital, Department of Nervous and Mental Diseases. The work was carried on under the direction of Dr. Frederick S. Hammett, for whose help and advice I am deeply grateful.

BIBLIOGRAPHY

(1) Van Slyke, Stillman, and Cullen: Journ. Biol. Chem., 1917, xxx, 401.
(2) Van Slyke: Journ. Biol. Chem., 1917, xxx, 347.
(3) Van Slyke and Cullen: Journ. Biol. Chem., 1917, xxx, 289.
(4) Higgins: This Journal, 1914, xxxiv, 114.
(5) Hammett: Journ. Biol. Chem., 1920, xli, 599.

GASTRIC TONUS OF THE EMPTY STOMACH OF THE FROG

Comparative Studies IV[1]

T. L. PATTERSON

From the Hull Physiological Laboratory, The University of Chicago and the Physiological Laboratory, Queen's University

Received for publication July 23, 1920

Sherrington (1) in 1915 called our attention to the reflex postural activity of muscle and nerve as being the main outcome of the functioning of the proprioceptive part of the nervous system for at least the skeletal muscle. He pointed out that the muscle fiber possessed the property of exhibiting different lengths while exhibiting one and the same degree of tension, and that it was not to be regarded as an elastic band. Furthermore, he believes that unstriated muscle, like skeletal muscle, possesses the same properties as is shown by the ease with which the hollow visceral organs, like the bladder and stomach, adapt their size to the volume of their contents and with very little alteration in their intravesical pressure. Under these conditions, visceral tonus is therefore postural configuration. In confirmation of this Hurst (2) found that the relaxation of the rectum was analogous to what Sherrington described as the "lengthening reaction" of the "postural tone" in the skeletal muscles and in the bladder, and which he at an earlier date had described in connection with the stomach and intestine, although he had not actually used the expression "visceral tone." In case of the skeletal muscle the reflex postural action depends normally upon the afferent nerve of the posturing muscle itself, while in the unstriated muscle it is far less dependent on the central nervous system for its adjustment and maintenance.

More recently Grey (3) has shown by slowly filling the empty viscus with warm physiological saline solution and recording the fluctuations in the intragastric pressure that the normal stomach in rabbits and

[1] A preliminary report of this work was made before the 1919 meeting of the American Physiological Society at Baltimore, a brief abstract of which was published in the Proceedings of that society.

cats is capable of adapting its size to the volume of its contents with very small changes in the intragastric pressure. According to this investigator, the mechanism involved in the postural configuration of the stomach is situated in the wall of the viscus itself and concerns solely its musculature together with its intrinsic nervous mechanism, while the extrinsic nerves exhibit no direct influence, but serve rather to regulate the tension of the stomach wall.

The experiments summarized in this report were undertaken with the view of securing further data on the gastric tonus (postural activity —Sherrington, Hurst, Grey) of the neuro-muscular apparatus as applied to the empty stomach. While the term "postural activity" is very applicable to the skeletal musculature it appears to me that it is not well suited for the unstriated musculature which makes up the larger portion of the walls of the hollow visceral organs, therefore the older and simpler terminology of gastric tonus will be used throughout this paper. The results tend to show that the extrinsic nerves exert a partial influence on the tonal activity of the stomach viscus, as well as serving to modify and regulate the gastric activity at least in the frog. This animal is particularly adapted for such a study for it has been shown in a previous paper (4) of this series that the gastric hunger contractions show no periodicity and no appreciable change in gastric tonus, both features of which are present in the higher animals. In contradistinction to the higher animals, the contractions are practically continuous with scarcely any distinction between the digestive peristalsis and the hunger movements.

Among the first to make observations upon the internal pressure of the hollow visceral organs were Mosso and Pellacani (5) who investigated the bladder in man and in the dog. These authors found that the bladder is capable of adjusting its cavity-volume to different quantities of content, which it enfolds with about the same light tension of grasp whether the viscus is nearly empty or well filled. Somewhat similar observations have been made upon the fundic portion of the stomach. Kelling (6) found that within certain limits the intragastric pressure remained unaffected by the quantity of fluid within the viscus and that the intra-abdominal pressure altered very little in the dog before and after the taking of a copious meal, although the intake of the volume of food might amount to 50 per cent of the total contents of the abdomen in the fasting condition. He infers from these latter observations that the additional volume of contents must be accommodated for by a reflex adjustment of the postural contraction of the abdominal muscles. Pike and Coombs (7) in confirmation of the above have reported that the introduction of fluid into the stomach or into the peritoneal cavity of cats causes lengthening of the rectus abdominis muscle while the flow of fluid out of the stomach causes a shortening of the same muscle. These changes in the length of the muscle are small and do not occur if the posterior roots of the spinal nerves supplying the muscle have been cut, or if the spinal cord has been transected at the level of the lower cervical roots. The section of both vagi has no marked effect on the response of the muscle. The authors regard the change in the length of the muscle corresponding to the increase or decrease in volume of the contents of the abdominal cavity as a reflex process dependent upon afferent impulses which falls into line with other known instances of postural activity of muscle and nerve. The observations of Sick and Tedesko (8) and others have shown that the gradual filling of a cat's stomach is not accompanied by a rise in intragastric pressure and that the excised stomach, kept alive in a bath of warm oxygenated Ringer's solution also exhibits the same phenomenon to an unmistakable extent.

Cannon and Lieb (9) have also brought forth evidence that each passing of the cardia by swallowed food is accompanied by a rapid small dilatation of the fundus, and that this dilatation is a reflex operated through the vagus. Rogers (10) has reported that central stimulation of one vagus nerve with the opposite nerve intact in the decerebrate dog and after complete splanchnic section leads to reflex spasmodic contractions of the entire stomach and increased gastric tone. Therefore it would appear that the adaptability of the normal stomach at all times is a form of receptive expression brought about by changes in the intragastric pressure as the volume of its contents slowly increases or decreases.

Experimental procedure. The same general method of experimentation was used in the following experiments on the bullfrog (Rana catesbiana) as that described in the preceding paper (11) of this series, with the exception that the gastric balloon was inflated with a known quantity of air by means of a graduated glass syringe sufficient to maintain a constant pressure of 2 cm. in the water manometer and the number of cubic centimeters of air necessary in the different experiments to produce this constant pressure was recorded. Normal contractions of the empty stomach were obtained from each animal, extending over a period of several days, and then these animals were either vagotomized, splanchnetomized or vago-splanchnetomized (section of both sets of nerves) and the respective observations repeated over a period of from two to three weeks and compared with the normal. The recorded tracings were taken on a slowly moving drum making a revolution in fifty to sixty minutes.

The changes in volume capacity of the stomach as influenced by partial and complete isolation from the central nervous system. The influence of the vagi and splanchnic nerves on the activity of the empty stomach of the frog has been reported in a previous paper (11). According to these results, double vagotomy leads to a sympathicotonic condition of the stomach followed with nearly the normal type of hunger contractions with the exception that they appear to be of a somewhat slower rate and slightly weaker. On the other hand, section of the splanchnic nerves leads to a hypertonic stomach with shallow contractions, showing an increased rate and tending to run into incomplete tetanus, while complete isolation of the stomach from the central nervous system leads to a hypotonic stomach with about the normal type of gastric hunger contractions. Somewhat similar changes have been described by Cannon (12) on cats for the digestive movements and by Carlson (13) on dogs for the movements of the empty stomach.

Although the sectioning of these nerves in various animals has led to certain changes in gastric tonus, as arising from the influence exerted through the extrinsic nerves supplying the stomach, no attempt has been made to analyze the question quantitatively. In order to study the changes in volume capacity of the empty stomach as influenced by partial and complete isolation from the central nervous system, twenty-one animals were used for the various observations recorded herein, as follows,—seven were vagotomized, seven splanchnetomized and seven vago-splanchnetomized. In addition, fifteen other animals were used but as the length of the duration of these experiments was more or less brief due to parasitization or other causes leading to an early death, the data from these were excluded. However, in none of these experiments in which results were obtained were they contradictory to the typical results as tabulated. There were also a few animals of this number excluded because of incomplete nerve section. The following tables have been prepared as showing typical results of the experiments.

The animals used for the observations in the preceding experiments were twelve to thirteen inches in length, extended, and it was found, without exception in this size of animal, that 10 cc. of air introduced by a syringe into the gastric balloon was sufficient to maintain a constant manometric pressure of 2 cm. in the stomach of the normal animal. Larger animals in proportion to size require greater quantities of air to obtain this constant manometric pressure, and vice versa. In one case, a very large frog measuring sixteen inches, the only one used in the series of experiments, 15 cc. of air were necessary to produce

TABLE 1

*Effect of section of the vagus nerves on volume capacity of stomach and contractions**

DATE 1918	CONDITIONS	AIR IN BALLOON	STRENGTH OF CONTRACTIONS	REMARKS
		cc.	*cm.*	
August 7	Stomostomized			
August 10	Normal	10	6.5	
August 11	Normal	10	6.0	
August 12	Normal	10	6.5	
August 13	Vagotomized			Operation O.K.
August 16	Vagotomized	15	6.5	
August 17	Vagotomized	15	8.0	
August 18	Vagotomized	15	6.8	
August 19	Vagotomized	15	7.0	
August 20	Vagotomized	15	8.0	
August 21	Vagotomized	15	6.5	
August 22	Vagotomized	13	6.5	
August 23	Vagotomized	10	6.0	
August 24	Vagotomized	10	4.5	
August 25	Vagotomized	10	5.5	
August 26	Vagotomized	10	5.8	
August 27	Vagotomized	10	6.2	
August 28	Vagotomized	10	5.0	
August 29	Vagotomized	10	4.0	
August 30	Vagotomized	10	3.5	
August 31	Vagotomized	10	Very weak	
September 1	Vagotomized	10	Very weak	
September 2	Vagotomized			Animal died. Autopsy showed both vagi cut

* Work now in progress on lung tonus of the frog shows that double vagotomy leads to practically the same effects as extirpation of the lungs, and this may shorten the life of the animals.

the constant pressure of 2 cm. in the water manometer. The question of the elasticity of the rubber balloon may arise here for, as Osborne (14) pointed out, in thin-walled rubber bags the extensibility of the elastic material is great and its dimensions, including its thickness, alter much under the stretch imposed. Furthermore, a subspherical bag may change in general figure as its size is altered, or changes in the physical consistence of the rubber membrane may occur as inflation and deflation proceeds, all of which would lead to serious complication for the analysis of results. However, in the case of the gastric balloon used 10 or even 15 cc. of air do not fill the rubber balloon, so that the tension of the bag's elasticity complicates the stomach tonus.

TABLE 2

Effect of section of the splanchnic nerves on volume capacity of stomach and contractions

DATE 1918	CONDITIONS	AIR IN BALLOON	STRENGTH OF CONTRACTIONS	REMARKS
		cc.	*cm.*	
August 7	Stomostomized			
August 10	Normal	10	6.0	
August 11	Normal	10	6.7	
August 12	Normal	10	6.5	
August 13	Splanchnetomized			Operation O.K.
August 16	Splanchnetomized	4	0.5	
August 17	Splanchnetomized	4	1.0	
August 18	Splanchnetomized	4	0.8	
August 19	Splanchnetomized	4	0.6	
August 20	Splanchnetomized	4	0.5	
August 21	Splanchnetomized	4	1.4	
August 22	Splanchnetomized	6	0.5	
August 23	Splanchnetomized	10	0.3	
August 24	Splanchnetomized	10	0.4	
August 25	Splanchnetomized	10	0.3	
August 26	Splanchnetomized	10	0.3	
August 27	Splanchnetomized	10	0.2	
August 28	Splanchnetomized	10	Very weak	
August 29	Splanchnetomized	10	Very weak	
August 30	Splanchnetomized	10	Very weak	
August 31	Splanchnetomized			Animal died. Autopsy showed splanchnics cut

In testing out the amount of air necessary to produce the constant manometric pressure it was found without exception in all the animals that a much smaller amount than 10 cc. of air would produce changes in the manometer amounting to 2 or more centimeters but the length of its duration was very short and the pressure soon fell to the zero level or closely approximated it depending on the quantity of air introduced. This is indicative of the ease with which the stomach adapts its size to the volume of its contents.

In female animals filled with large egg masses the number of cubic centimeters of air necessary to produce the constant pressure showed no variations from that of the non-egg-carrying female and the male, although the abdomen was much enlarged. This condition in the egg-carrying female is doubtless accounted for, at least in part, by a reflex mechanism leading to a relaxation of the abdominal muscles, an adaptation similar to the reflex relaxation of the rectus abdominis muscle in increased volume contents of the stomach as has been described by

TABLE 3

Effect of section of the vagi and splanchnic nerves on volume capacity of stomach and contractions

DATE 1918	CONDITIONS	AIR IN BALLOON	STRENGTH OF CONTRACTIONS	REMARKS
		cc.	*cm.*	
October 22	Stomostomized			
October 25	Normal	10	6.5	
October 26	Normal	10	6.5	
October 27	Normal	10	6.9	
October 28	Normal	10	6.7	
October 28	Vagi and splanchnics cut			Operation O.K.
November 2	Vagi and splanchnics cut	15	6.7	
November 3	Vagi and splanchnics cut	15	7.0	
November 4	Vagi and splanchnics cut	15	6.9	
November 5	Vagi and splanchnics cut	15	7.2	
November 6	Vagi and splanchnics cut	15	6.6	
November 7	Vagi and splanchnics cut	15	8.0	
November 8	Vagi and splanchnics cut	15	6.5	
November 9	Vagi and splanchnics cut	15	5.8	Morning
November 9	Vagi and splanchnics cut	13	6.0	Night
November 10	Vagi and splanchnics cut	13	5.0	
November 11	Vagi and splanchnics cut	13	4.4	
November 12	Vagi and splanchnics cut	13	3.5	
November 13	Vagi and splanchnics cut	13	3.4	
November 14	Vagi and splanchnics cut	13	3.5	
November 15	Vagi and splanchnics cut	13	Very weak	
November 16	Vagi and splanchnics cut	13	Very weak	
November 17	Vagi and splanchnics cut	13	Very weak	
November 18	Vagi and splanchnics cut			Animal died. Autopsy showed both vagi and splanchnics cut

Pike and Coombs (7). The animals with very few exceptions were run continuously as soon as recovery was complete after the operation and the fast commenced immediately.

Section of both vagi or the vago-sympathetic nerves (11) in the neck of the frog increases the volume capacity of the stomach temporarily, as shown in table 1, from the normal of 10 cc. to 15 cc. of air. This condition invariably lasts from eight to nine days. Usually on the ninth day following the cutting of the nerves there is a decrease in the

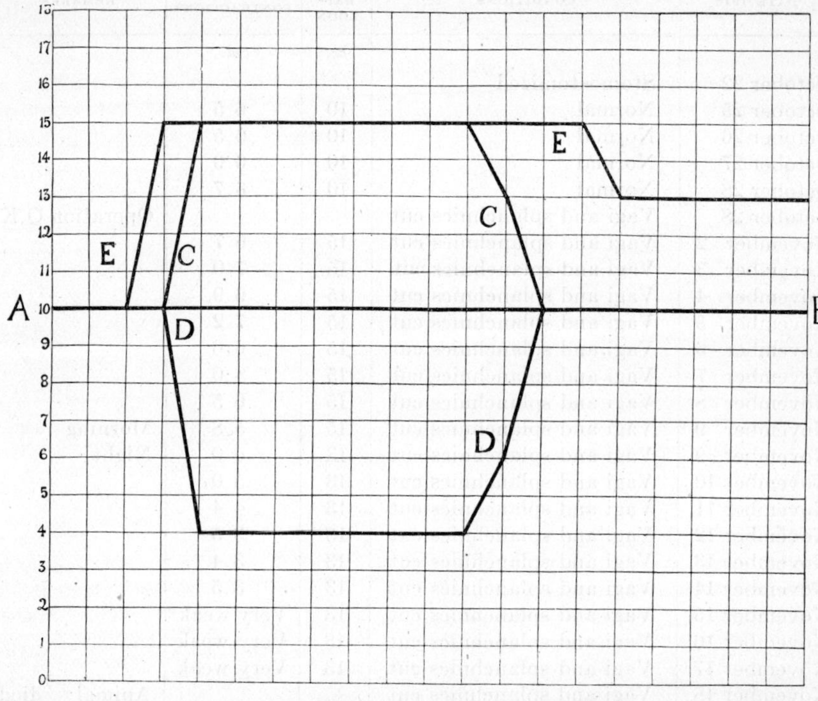

Fig. 1. The spaces left to right indicate the number of days experiment ran. Vertical spaces above and below the heavy line *A B*, representing the normal pressure of 10 cc. of air necessary to maintain a constant pressure of 2 cm. in the water manometer, indicates the positive or negative changes from the constant in the volume capacity of the stomach as influenced by the extrinsic nerves. Curve *C C*, shows effect of sectioning both vagi on stomach. Curve *D D*, effect of splanchnic section. Curve *E E*, combined effect of section of both vagi and splanchnic nerves. Note complete recovery of gastric tonus in first two cases, while in the latter there is only a partial recovery. Heavy line *A B* also indicates negative effect of decerebration on stomach. Figures at left indicate number of cubic centimeters of air in balloon.

intragastric pressure to about 13 cc. of air and on the next day it drops again to the normal or 10 cc. level, and remains there. In other words, the normal tone of the stomach has been reëstablished (fig. 1), and this condition as it exists in the frog may be comparable to the temporary loss of tonus as described by Cannon (12) in cats. The contractions of the empty stomach tend to approach the normal, but on the whole they are of a slightly slower rate and more irregular. The amplitude of the individual contractions may even appear greater than normal and this may be because the contractions start rather suddenly and without any marked preliminary increase in tonus in the fundic end of the stomach.

Section of the splanchnic nerves in the frog markedly decreases the volume capacity of the stomach temporarily, as shown in table 2, from the normal of 10 cc. to 4 cc. of air. This marked diminution in size like the increase after double vagotomy invariably lasts from eight to nine days. Usually on the ninth day following the cutting of the nerves there is an increase in the intragastric pressure to about 6 cc. of air, while on the next day it reaches again the normal or 10 cc. level and remains there. Here again the stomach has reëstablished its gastric tonus (fig. 1). This condition in the frog is much more marked than Carlson (13) found it to be in dogs for just as the number of cardio-inhibitory fibers vary in the vagus of the cat and the dog, so also may not the number of motor fibers in the vagi destined for the stomach vary in different animals? The contractions of the empty stomach are small, showing an increased rate and a tendency to approach incomplete tetanus. This is especially true during the temporary period of high tonal activity when only 4 cc. of air are required to maintain the constant manometric pressure and in one animal 3 cc. of air were found to be sufficient. In a few such animals I have found in the morning following the removal of the balloon the night before such strong gastric and esophageal contraction that it was impossible to introduce the balloon through the short esophagus into the stomach without first introducing a small glass seeker and stretching it. I have even had difficulty in introducing the seeker the first time on one or two occasions because of such marked contraction. This would seem to uphold the views of Cannon (12) and Kelling (6) that the gastric fibers of the vagi function to make the gastric muscles exert a tension.

Section of the vagi and splanchnic nerves in the frog increases the volume capacity of the stomach permanently, as shown in table 3, from the normal of 10 cc. to 15 cc. of air, but in this case there is not a complete recovery. After this complete isolation of the frog's stomach from the central nervous system, the 15 cc. stomach invariably lasts from twelve to thirteen days, which is a longer period than in either the vagotomized or splanchnetomized stomach. Usually on the thirteenth day following the sectioning of these nerves which is accomplished at one operation there is a fall in the intragastric pressure to a 13 cc. level, where there are no further changes (fig. 1). This new and partial readjustment of the hypotonic stomach is evidently determined by the intrinsic local gastric motor mechanism of the stomach wall for the gastric hunger contractions persist after its isolation from the central nervous system. The appearance of the individual contractions is much the same as when the vagi alone are cut. These contractions may exhibit a greater or lesser amplitude and show a tendency toward irregularity. All the animals in the different groups were autopsied to verify more especially the sectioning of the respective nerves. In a few of these animals in which the heart was still beating regularly the effect of vagal stimulation on the stomach was determined. This resulted usually in a phase of inhibition followed by a stronger phase of excitation immediately upon the removal of the stimulus and is in confirmation with the findings of Hopf (15) on frogs. Stimulation of the sectioned splanchnic usually resulted in a relaxation of the body of the stomach, if any change at all occurred, and if the stimulation was repeated several times in succession it seemed to bring about a constriction of the pyloric sphincter and perhaps also that of the cardiac sphincter, a condition which would seem to indicate that the splanchnics might possess a few fibers of the motor type. The stimulation of these two nerves does show, however, that the fibers of neither have degenerated, and since the rate of nerve degeneration differs in different animals and in frogs requires from thirty to one hundred and forty days, depending upon the season of the year (16), there is no possibility of the regeneration of these nerves. The normal functioning of the two sets of nerves to the stomach is indicated by the results of sectioning, as well as by the results of stimulation. In the case of the isolation of the stomach from the influence of the vagi with the splanchnics intact, or vice versa, there is a perfect physiological readjustment of the normal tonus of the gastric musculature. On the other hand, after complete isolation of the stomach (vagi and splanchnics severed) from the central nervous system there is only a partial physiological readjustment of the gastric musculature. This indicates that the extrinsic nerves play a prominent part in the maintenance of gastric tonus, at least in the frog. When the splanchnics are sectioned it must be the motor fibers of the vagi that produce the high and temporary gastric hypertonicity, i.e., hypertonic stomach. When the vagi are cut and the splanchnics permitted to exert their full influence on the gastric musculature it is reasonable to believe that these nerves must possess motor fibers probably to the sphincter muscles and that these areas then act as tonic rings which, in connection with the intrinsic or local reflex mechanism of the gastric wall, are capable of producing a perfect physiological readjustment. Whereas, in the case of the stomach completely isolated from the central nervous system, this intrinsic or local gastric mechanism is incapable of bringing about a complete readjustment and in consequence of this it creates a new level of gastric tonus. Thus, every reflex is in its own measure an integral reaction, and is purposive in that it bears some biological purport for its organism. This physiological readjustment occurred regularly in all the animals, that is, it could be looked for after a lapse of a certain number of days following the sectioning of the nerves. For example, in the case of the vagotomized stomach when this readjustment started I have seen in a few instances the pressure in the manometer increase from the constant level of 2 cm. to 5 or 6 cm., but I have never observed it in the stomach of the normal animal. In the splanchnetomized stomach of the course the first readjustment stage is marked by a fall in the manometric pressure to zero.

The changes in gastric tonus observed throughout this series of experiments are so slight in the normal frog that they are practically unmeasurable. However, tonus is the prime condition for that tension which must be developed before contraction can result and if the tension persists the contraction recurs (17). Furthermore, the importance of the tonic state in the normal functioning stomach is reinforced by the fact that when all the extrinsic nerves are cut the stomach develops in time within itself a tonic state, while the adaptability of the abdominal cavity to the volume of its contents is left to the postural reflex.

The effect of decerebration on the tonus of the stomach. It has been shown by King and Connet (18) that the rate of the gastric contractions is increased in decerebrate guinea pigs and that the stomach becomes hypertonic. According to Rogers (19) the hyperactivity of the crop of the decerebrate pigeon is inhibited by food and water as in the normal bird, while the writer (4) has reported no change in the type of the contractions from the empty stomach of the normal and the decerebrate frog. In order to study the effect of decerebration on the volume capacity of the stomach, observations were made on six decerebrate frogs. The following table has been prepared from a typical experiment.

Decerebration in the frog has no effect on either the volume capacity of the stomach or the amplitude of the individual contractions, as is shown in table 4. There is also no change in the type of contractions, which confirms the work of the previous paper (4). The negative findings in these experiments show that the higher cerebral centers in the frog play no appreciable part in either the maintenance of gastric activity or the tonic state. Since section of the vagi leaves the stomach in a temporary hypotonic condition (15 cc. stomach) while the decerebration effects are negative we may infer that impulses from centers

TABLE 4

Effect of decerebration on volume capacity of stomach and contractions

DATE 1918	CONDITIONS	AIR IN BALLOON	STRENGTH OF CONTRACTIONS	REMARKS
		cc.	*cm.*	
July 26	Stomostomized			
July 31	Normal	10	6.0	
August 1	Normal	10	6.5	
August 2	Normal	10	6.0	
August 2	Decerebrated 4:15 p.m.			Operation O.K.
August 2	Decerebrated	10	6.0	Contractions started again at 5:35 p.m.
August 3	Decerebrated	10	6.3	
August 4	Decerebrated	10	6.0	
August 5	Decerebrated	10	5.2	
August 6	Decerebrated			Animal died. Autopsy showed complete removal of cerebral hemispheres

in the mid-brain and medulla exercise the controlling influence and produce after section of the splanchnics the temporary hypertonic stomach, i.e., high gastric tonus. It may be further implied that there is a dynamic readjustment in the central nervous system which leads to an actual diminution in the inhibitory impulses through the splanchnics after vagal section or an inverse motor condition existing through the vagi after splanchnic section, or else the stomach may bring about its physiological readjustment by an increased resistance or tolerance of the splanchnic or motor impulses over the respective nerves to the gastric mechanism.

CONCLUSIONS

1. The normal stomach of the frog possesses a marked capacity for adapting itself to the volume of its contents with only minimal changes in the intragastric pressure. This is in confirmation with the work of Grey and others.

2. Both the intrinsic and extrinsic nerves take part in the maintenance of gastric tonus as is shown by partial and complete isolation of the stomach from the central nervous system.

3. Section of the vago-sympathetic nerves (double vagotomy) with the splanchnics intact increases the volume capacity of the stomach temporarily, but there is later a complete readjustment.

4. Section of the splanchnic nerves with the vagi intact decreases the volume capacity of the stomach temporarily, but there is again a complete readjustment as above.

5. Section of both the vagi and splanchnic nerves (complete isolation from the central nervous system) increases the volume capacity of the stomach permanently, and in this case there is only a partial readjustment, at least for a period extending over three weeks, and the tonus of the stomach is established upon a new level from that of the normal.

6. Decerebration affects neither the volume capacity of the stomach nor the type of the contractions.

The writer desires to acknowledge his indebtedness to Doctor Carlson for his kindly and valuable criticism.

BIBLIOGRAPHY

(1) Sherrington: Brain, 1915, xxxviii, 191.
(2) Hurst: Seale Hayne Neur. Studies, London, 1919, i, no. 4, 208.
(3) Grey: This Journal, 1918, xlv, 272.
(4) Patterson: This Journal, 1916, xlii, 56.
(5) Mosso and Pellacani: Arch. ital. d. Biol., 1882, i, 96.
(6) Kelling: Zeitschr. f. Biol., 1903, xliv, 161.
(7) Pike and Coombs: This Journal, 1917, xlii, 395.
(8) Sick and Tedesko: Deutsch. Arch. f. klin. Med., 1908, xcii, 146.
(9) Cannon and Lieb: This Journal, 1912, xxix, 267.
(10) Rogers: This Journal, 1917, xlii, 605.
(11) Patterson: This Journal, 1920, liii, 293.
(12) Cannon: This Journal, 1906, xvii, 429; 1911, xxix, 250.
(13) Carlson: This Journal, 1913, xxxii, 369.
(14) Osborne: Proc. Roy. Soc., 1909, B, lxxxi, 485.
(15) Hopf: Zeitschr. f. Biol., 1910, lv, 409.
(16) Bethe: Allgemeine Anatomie und Physiologie des Nervensystems, Leipzig, 1903, 158.
(17) Cannon: Arch. Int. Med., 1911, viii, 417.
(18) King and Connet: This Journal, 1915, xxxix, 123.
(19) Rogers: This Journal, 1916, xli, 555.

STUDIES ON THE SUBMAXILLARY GLAND

VI. On the Dependence of Tissue Activity upon Volume-flow of Blood and on the Mechanism Controlling this Volume-flow of Blood

ROBERT GESELL

From the Departments of Physiology of Washington University Medical School and of the University of California

Received for publication July 27, 1920

INTRODUCTION

This paper has to do with two problems: one the dependence of tissue activity upon volume-flow of blood, and the other the mechanism by which the volume-flow of blood is controlled. While these problems may be considered as distinct from each other, yet they have a certain interdependence which may warrant their discussion in common.

I have previously reported results bearing upon both problems (1), (2). Although no definite conclusions were reached concerning the mechanism of volume-flow control, it was shown that in hemorrhage the organism as a whole suffers from a reduced flow of blood as is indicated by the reduced alkaline reserve of the plasma of the blood. But despite the fact that the organism suffers from a reduced flow of blood we know from the work of others (3), (4) that a tissue may be stimulated to great activity even though the flow of blood may be very low or even absent. This apparent independence of volume-flow and tissue activity is shown in figures 1 and 3, where secretion of saliva is used as the index of tissue activity.

DEPENDENCE OF SECRETION UPON VOLUME-FLOW OF BLOOD

To show the dependence of tissue activity upon volume-flow of blood, using secretion as the index to activity, special methods must be employed. The greatest care must be taken that change in volume-flow of blood be the only variable. When the gland is activated by stimulation of the chorda tympani the periods and strength of stimulation must be equal and periods of rest must be chosen which will avoid the augmenting effect of previous stimulation. Results obtained under such conditions can be compared with results obtained when the blood supply is modified. Such results are shown in figures 1, 2 and 3, in which blood pressure, volume-flow of blood, secretion, electrical deflections, time in seconds and moment of stimulation of the chorda tympani are recorded. The volume-flow of blood was measured with the bloodless method previously described.

Figure 1, *A* and *B*, shows the effects of occluding the carotid artery during a short period of stimulation lasting 14 seconds. In the first record, the artery was unoccluded and stimulation of the chorda tympani produced the usual rapid acceleration of blood flow. In the second, where the artery was occluded, the flow of blood during the period of stimulation was slow but the amount of saliva secreted was not diminished. The results might be taken to indicate that even large fluctuations in volume-flow of blood need not affect the metabolic processes of the gland, were it not for the change in the contour of the electrical deflections which suggests that the glandular processes were modified. On the other hand, the absence of an after-flow of blood following de-occlusion indicates that the gland was not overtaxed by the temporary reduction in the blood-flow.

Figure 1, *C* and *D*, shows the effect of occlusion of the artery during greater activation. The secretion of saliva during occlusion was not reduced, yet the electrical deflection was modified again as in 1, *B*. The difference between the results shown in 1, *A* and *B*, and in 1, *C* and *D*, is that de-occlusion in the latter observations was followed by a markedly accelerated after-flow of blood indicative of an overstrain of the tissue resulting from activation without sufficient blood supply.

Figure 2, *A*, *B* and *C*, shows the effect of more prolonged occlusion of the artery lasting through a period of stimulation of 30 seconds. Even this longer period of occlusion has little effect upon the amount of saliva obtained—16.2 drops during the period of occlusion as compared with 18.2 and 19.2 drops during the preceding and subsequent periods of free flow of blood. In figure 3, *A*, *B*, *C* and *D*, where the periods of stimulation and occlusion were still longer, the reduced flow of blood again had relatively little effect. In fact (*C*) during occlusion 18.4 drops of saliva were secreted compared with 19.0, 19.6 and 20.3 in the preceding and subsequent periods.

Upon the whole, the results indicate that relatively short periods of occlusion of the carotid artery affect little the amount of saliva elicited by stimulation of the chorda tympani. This absence of marked effects may be apparent only and may be due to the fact that the gland at the moment of stimulation has recovered from previous activation and readily liberates its stored material and energy regardless of the momentary decrease in flow of blood during the period of activation. If so, it would be better to study the dependence of tissue metabolism

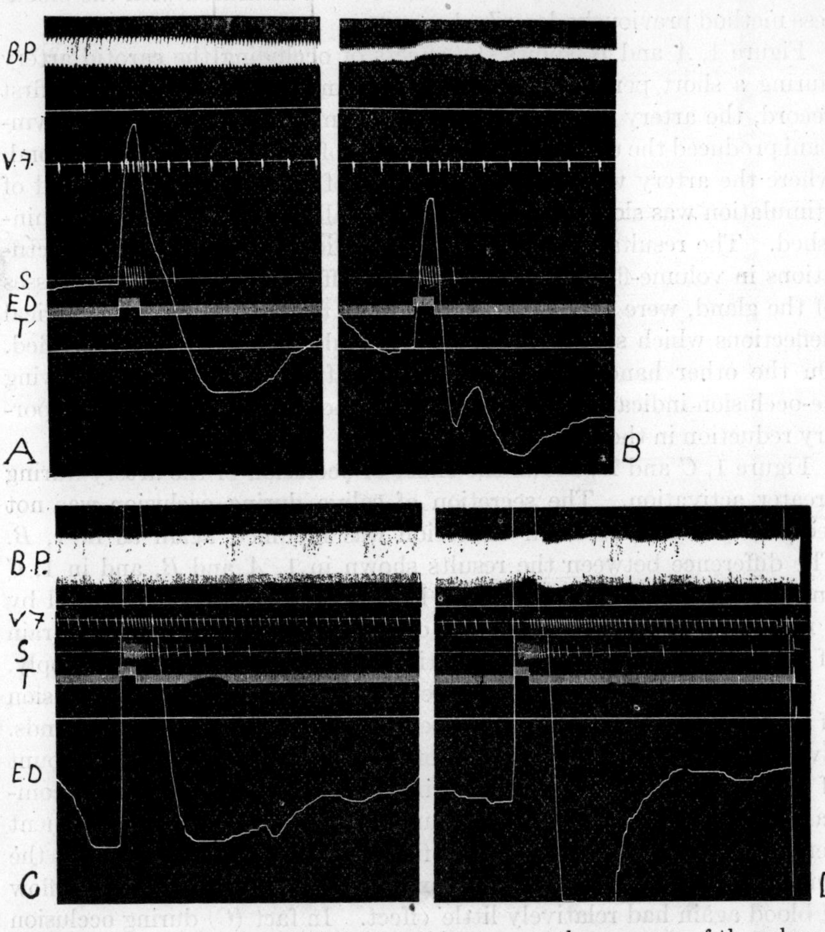

Fig. 1. Effect of occlusion of the carotid artery on the response of the submaxillary gland to stimulation of the chorda tympani. 1*A*, normal; 1*B*, artery occluded; 1*C*, normal; 1*D*, artery occluded; *B.P.*, blood pressure; *V.F.*, volume-flow of blood; *S.*, salivary secretion; *E.*, electrical deflection; *T.*, time in seconds and moment of stimulation of the chorda tympani.

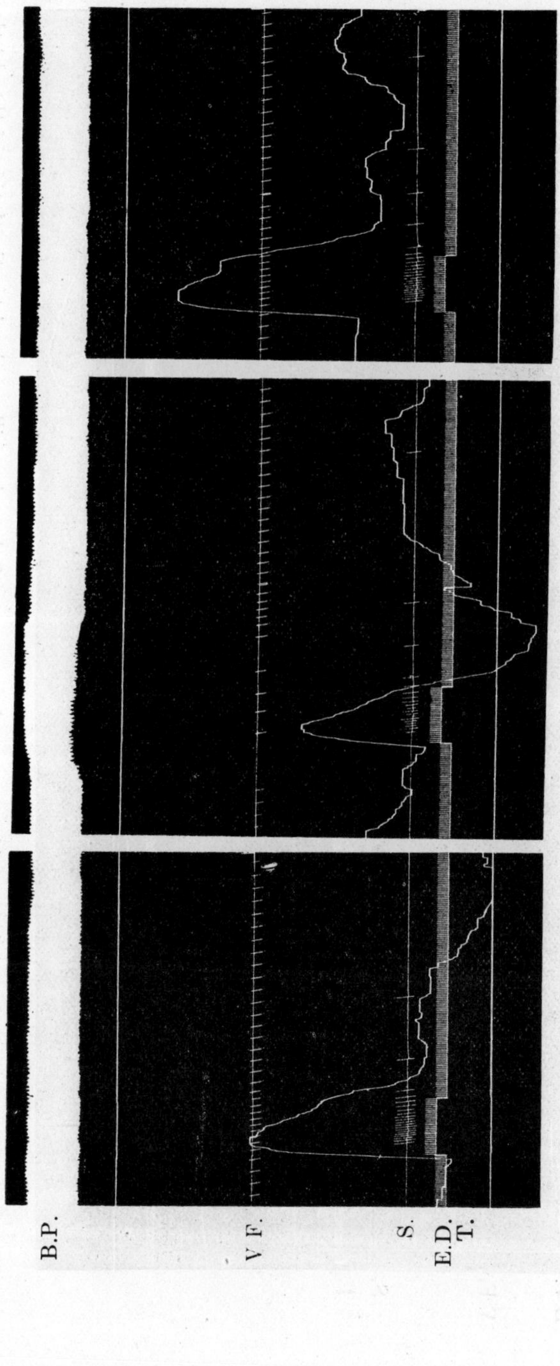

Fig. 2. Effect of occlusion of the carotid artery on the response of the submaxillary gland to stimulation of the chorda tympani. *2A*, normal, 18.2 drops of saliva secreted; *2B*, artery occluded, 16.2 drops of saliva secreted; *2C*, normal, 19.2 drops of saliva secreted.

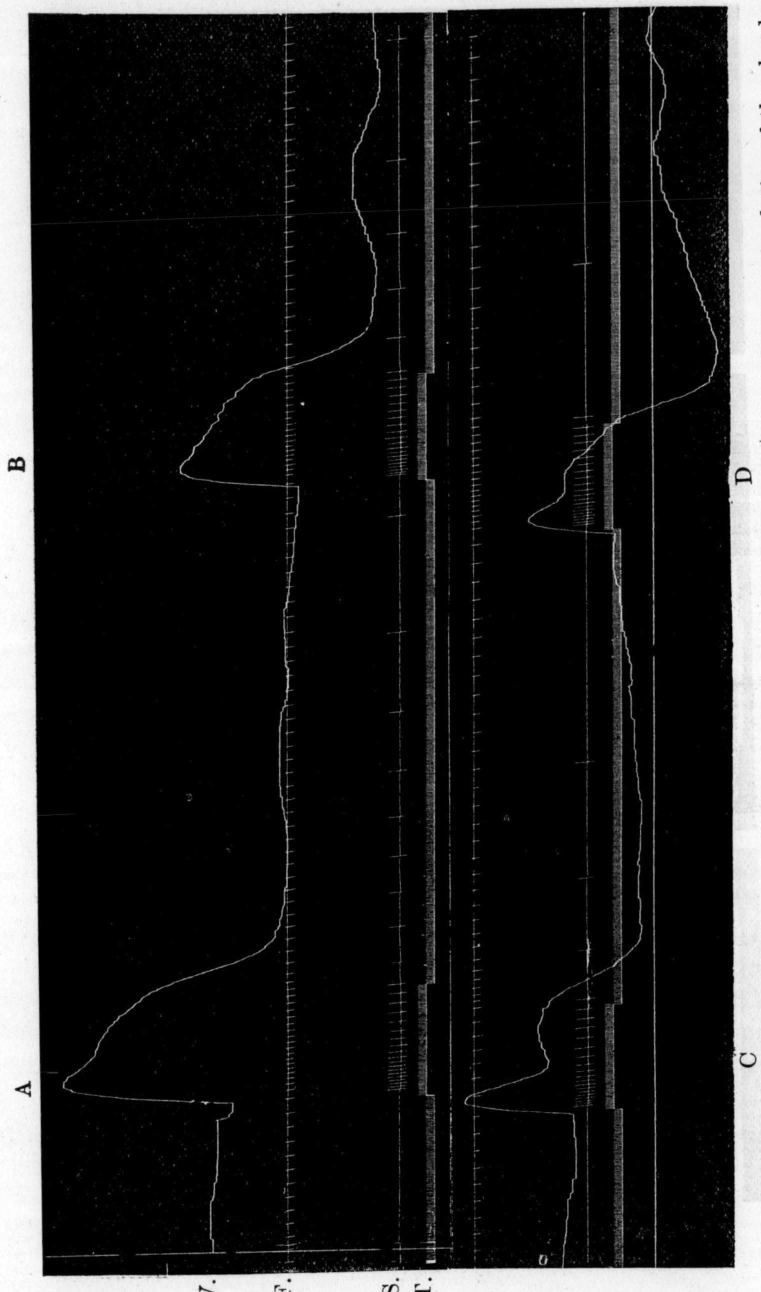

Fig. 3. Effect of occlusion of the carotid artery on the response of the submaxillary gland to stimulation of the chorda tympani. *A*, *B* and *D*, normal records with 19.0, 19.6 and 20.3 drops of saliva secreted; *C*, artery occluded, 18.4 drops of saliva secreted.

upon tissue which has not fully recovered from previous activation; for this purpose the gland might be activated over a longer period of time, and the blood supply modified during this period of activation, that is while activity and recuperation are going on hand in hand.

A series of such experiments is shown in figure 4, *A*, *B*, *C*, *D* and *E*. In figure 4, *A*, *B* and *C* the gland was activated by the injection of pilocarpin and the flow of blood was restricted in three ways: in *A* by obstruction of the carotid artery; in *B* by injection of adrenin; and in *C* by stimulation of the vago-sympathetic. In every instance the slowing of the flow of blood affected the response of the gland to the stimulation of pilocarpin. The objection might be raised that we not only interfered with the blood supply but also with the supply of pilocarpin which stimulates the gland. This objection can not hold in the experiment represented in figure 4, *D* and *C*, where the gland was activated by stimulating the chorda tympani. In 4, *D*, the flow of blood was decreased during stimulation by occluding the artery. The volume-flow of blood was not recorded but the moments of occlusion and de-occlusion are evident in the blood pressure tracing. It will be noted that the effect of occlusion became progressively greater as occlusion continued, suggesting that stored up saliva may be easily liberated, whereas the storage and liberation of new saliva required a greater flow of blood. The slowing of the secretion is undoubtedly due to the slowing of the blood stream and not to fatigue of the gland from prolonged stimulation, as is indicated by the subsequent acceleration of secretion upon de-occlusion of the artery. In this record secretion continued for some time after cessation of stimulation. Occlusion of the artery during this after-secretion again retarded secretion. The effects of injection of adrenin during prolonged stimulation of the chorda tympani were quite as striking—see figure 4, *E*.

The gland from which figure 5 was obtained was extremely sensitive to changes in volume-flow of blood. The period of stimulation of the chorda tympani lasted from *A* to *B*. The close parallelism between secretion and volume-flow of blood is very evident. Short irregular fluctuations which were not due to occlusion of the artery also are to be seen.

Figure 6 is taken from the same experiment as figure 5. It shows again the effect of volume-flow of blood upon the threshold of stimulation for secretion. Stimulation of the chorda tympani elicited an increased volume-flow of blood and though no visible secretion occurred it excited the gland, as is evidenced by the electrical deflection. That

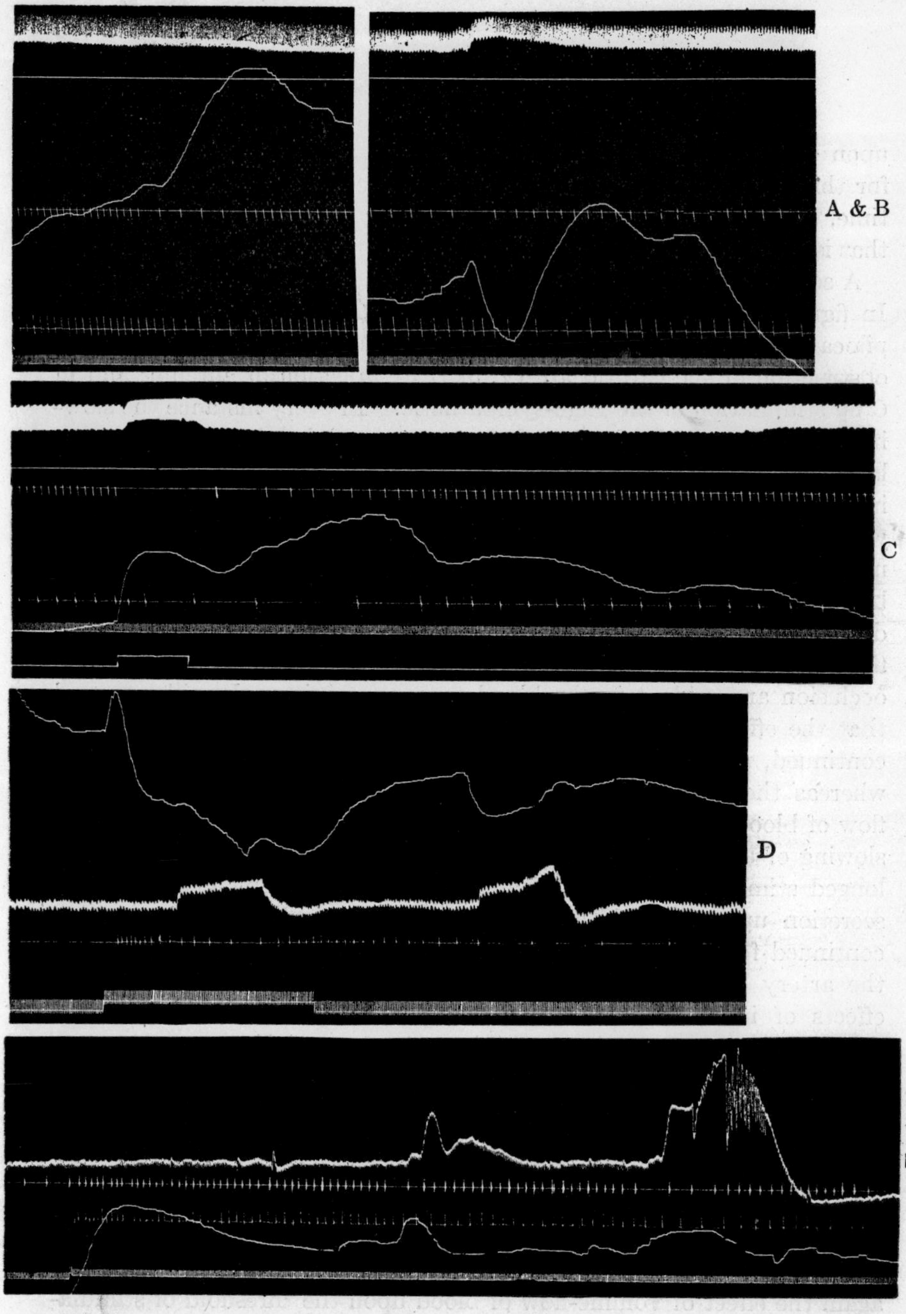

Fig. 4. Effect of interfering with the blood supply to the submaxillary gland during prolonged activity. In *A*, *B* and *C*, the gland was activated by the injection of pilocarpin and the blood flow interfered with by arterial occlusion, injection of adrenin and stimulation of the vagosympathetic respectively. In *D* and *E* the gland is activated by stimulation of the chorda tympani and the flow of blood interfered with by arterial occlusion and the injection of adrenin.

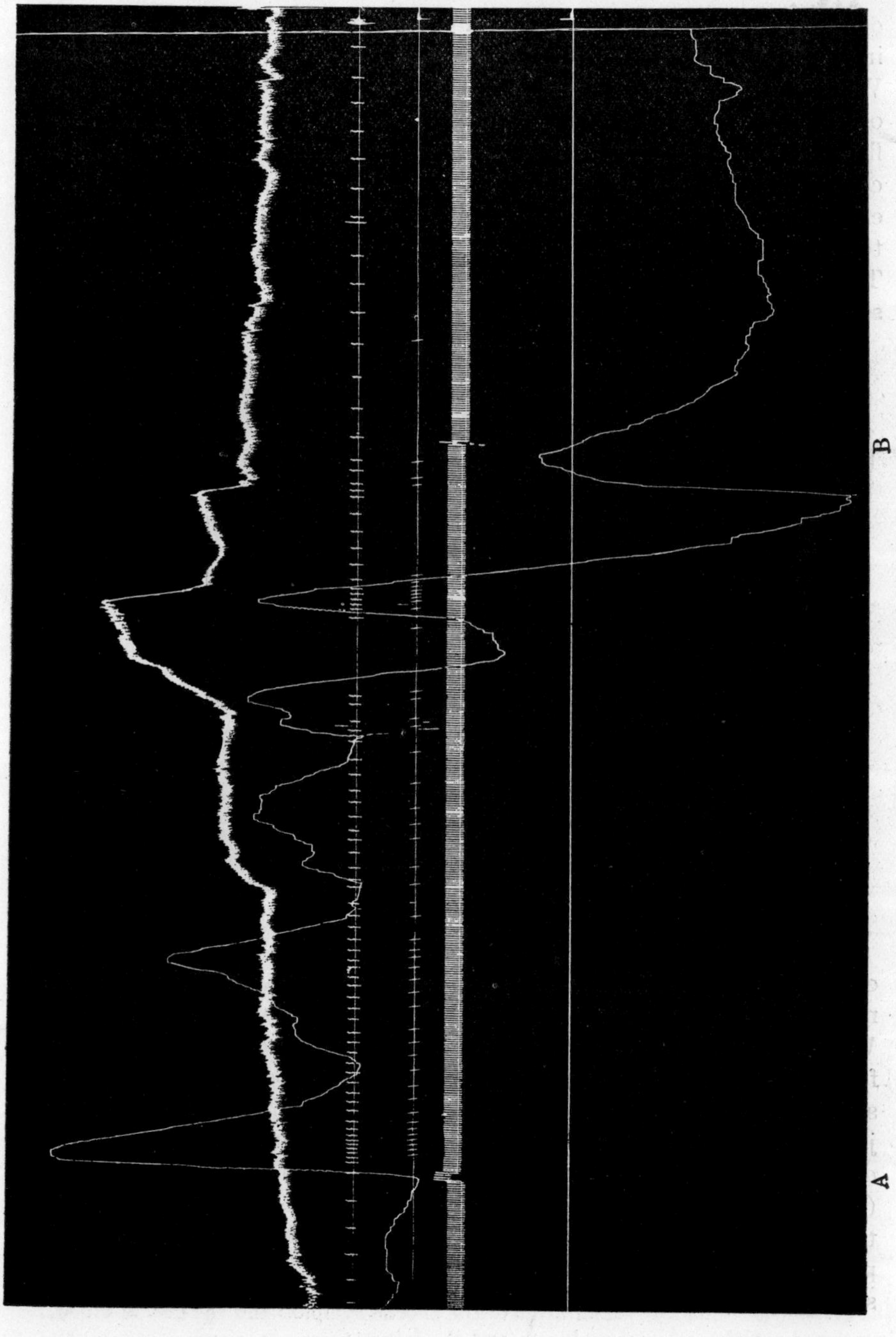

Fig. 5. Relation of secretion to volume-flow of blood.

occlusion of the carotid artery during excitation affected the processes in the gland is indicated by another change in the electrical deflection. When the artery was de-occluded about 20 seconds after the cessation of stimulation a rapid flow of blood occurred. This accelerated blood flow was accompanied by a copious secretion. The fact that an accelerated blood flow was associated with secretion some time after the effects of stimulation had wholly or at least partially worn off, seems to indicate that secretion in this instance occurred in two definite stages. The results are in line with the observation that the elicitation of visible secretion requires a stronger stimulus than does the elicitation of an

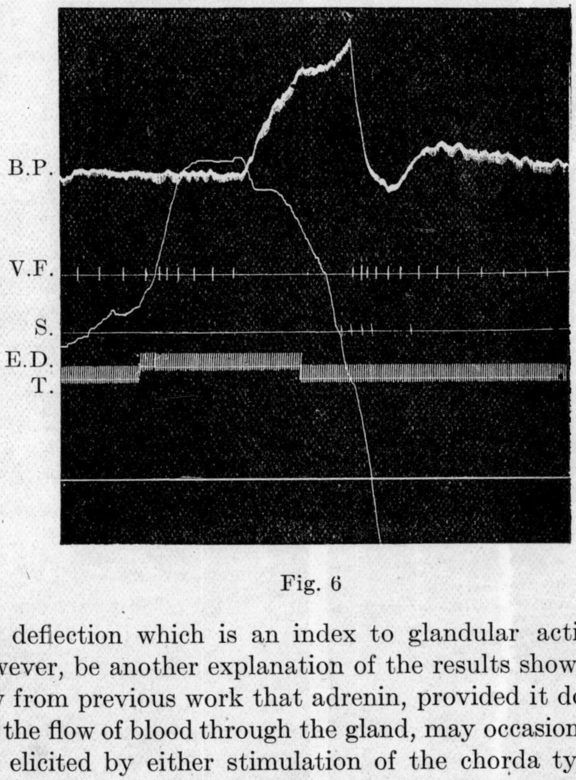

Fig. 6

electrical deflection which is an index to glandular activity. There may, however, be another explanation of the results shown in figure 6. We know from previous work that adrenin, provided it does not interfere with the flow of blood through the gland, may occasionally augment secretion elicited by either stimulation of the chorda tympani or injection of pilocarpin. It is possible that the short period of arterial occlusion led to an asphyxial discharge of adrenin into the circulation (5) sufficient to augment secretion. Unfortunately results similar to those seen in figure 6 were not obtained frequently enough to make possible the determination of the factor underlying the accelerated secretion.

THE MECHANISM CONTROLLING THE VOLUME-FLOW OF BLOOD

It is well known that after atropinization of an animal stimulation of the chorda tympani may accelerate the volume-flow of blood through the submaxillary gland without eliciting visible secretion. This observation is used as evidence of the presence of vasodilator fibers in the chorda tympani. But Barcroft (6) pointed out that even though there be no visible secretion resulting from stimulation of the chorda tympani, oxidations in the gland may be increased. The accelerated flow of blood may, therefore, be due to liberation of dilator metabolites rather than to stimulation of dilator fibers.

The fact that stimulation of the chorda tympani, too weak to produce visible secretion, may elicit an increased volume-flow of blood is likewise cited as evidence for the presence of dilator fibers in that nerve. But the fact that such an increase in volume-flow of blood is accompanied by an electrical deflection also makes possible the explanation of dilatation through dilator metabolites (1).

Since these methods, which indicated the existence of dilator fibers, fail to yield crucial data concerning the mechanism of volume-flow control, I attempted in a previous research to throw further light on the problem by a variety of indirect methods (1). The results obtained were summarized as follows:

> As to the existence of vasodilator nerves the question which initiated this research nothing definite can be said. We have no proof that such nerves do not exist, neither have we proof that metabolites can not adequately control the volume-flow of blood. All that can be said is, that if the dilator fibers do control the volume-flow of blood, this flow may be augmented still more by an accumulation of metabolites. Many observations might apply to both theories, some however point more strongly to the metabolite control.

It was shown in that research that with conditions constant the flow of blood is very finely adjusted to the activity of the gland. By plotting the superbasal flow of blood on the ordinates against progressively increasing amounts of salivary secretion on the abscissas we found superbasal flow of blood to be a linear function of superbasal metabolism. Such accelerated flow accompanying tissue activity is undoubtedly a purposive reaction to make good the excess of liberated energy, but does not help toward determining the mechanism of volume-flow control. This reaction of accelerated flow of blood is studied to advantage by plotting continuous curves of glandular activity and volume-flow elicited by stimulation of the chorda tympani. This method not only brings out in another way the parallelism of the two phenomena but in addition shows the time relation of the two processes.

Figure 7 shows the effect of stimulation of the chorda tympani of 12 seconds duration in 7, *A*, and of 60 seconds in 7, *B*. The activity of the gland (secretion) is plotted on the ordinates in solid black against time on the abscissas. Volume-flow of blood is plotted as a line. The portion of the curve of volume-flow of blood preceding stimulation of the chorda tympani represents the basal flow of blood or the flow of rest; the curve above that level represents the superbasal flow. Though in each instance the increased flow of blood followed stimulation

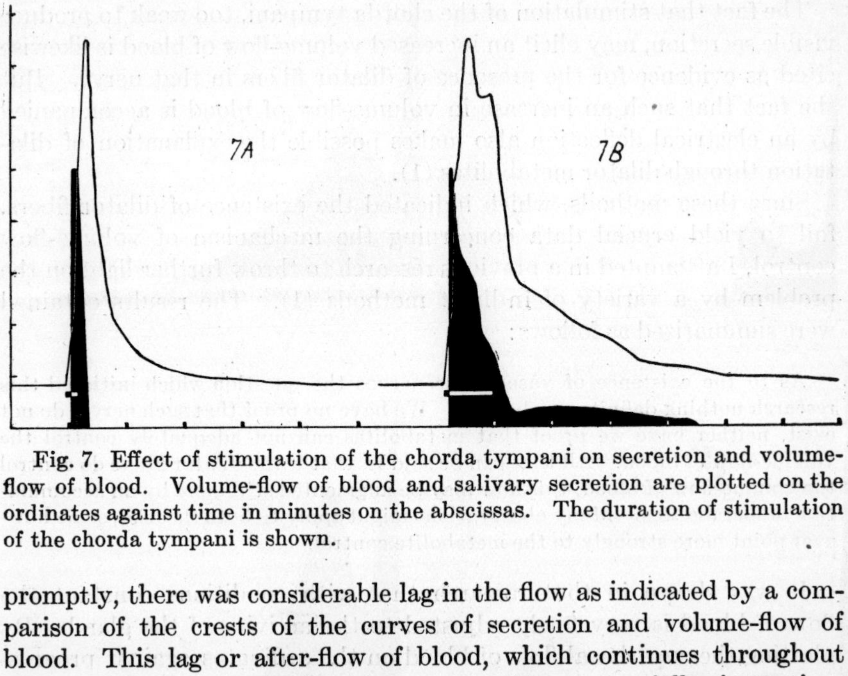

Fig. 7. Effect of stimulation of the chorda tympani on secretion and volume-flow of blood. Volume-flow of blood and salivary secretion are plotted on the ordinates against time in minutes on the abscissas. The duration of stimulation of the chorda tympani is shown.

promptly, there was considerable lag in the flow as indicated by a comparison of the crests of the curves of secretion and volume-flow of blood. This lag or after-flow of blood, which continues throughout the experiment, is suggestive of a recuperative process following activation, and is in agreement with the findings of Barcroft and Hill on oxidation and heat formation associated with tissue activation.

Figure 8 shows results obtained in other experiments. The graphs were obtained from four different animals. Graphs *A* and *B* show the relation of volume-flow of blood to prolonged activity of the gland elicited by prolonged excitation of the chorda tympani. The usual effect of such stimulation upon secretion is a rapid acceleration followed by a decrease which in turn gives way to a secondary increase. The parallelism between secretion and volume-flow of blood is striking.

Graph 8, *C* and *D*, shows the same relation, but the fluctuations in secretion differ from those in graph 8, *A* and *B*, in that they are elicited by short periods of stimulation. Secretion elicited by stimulation of

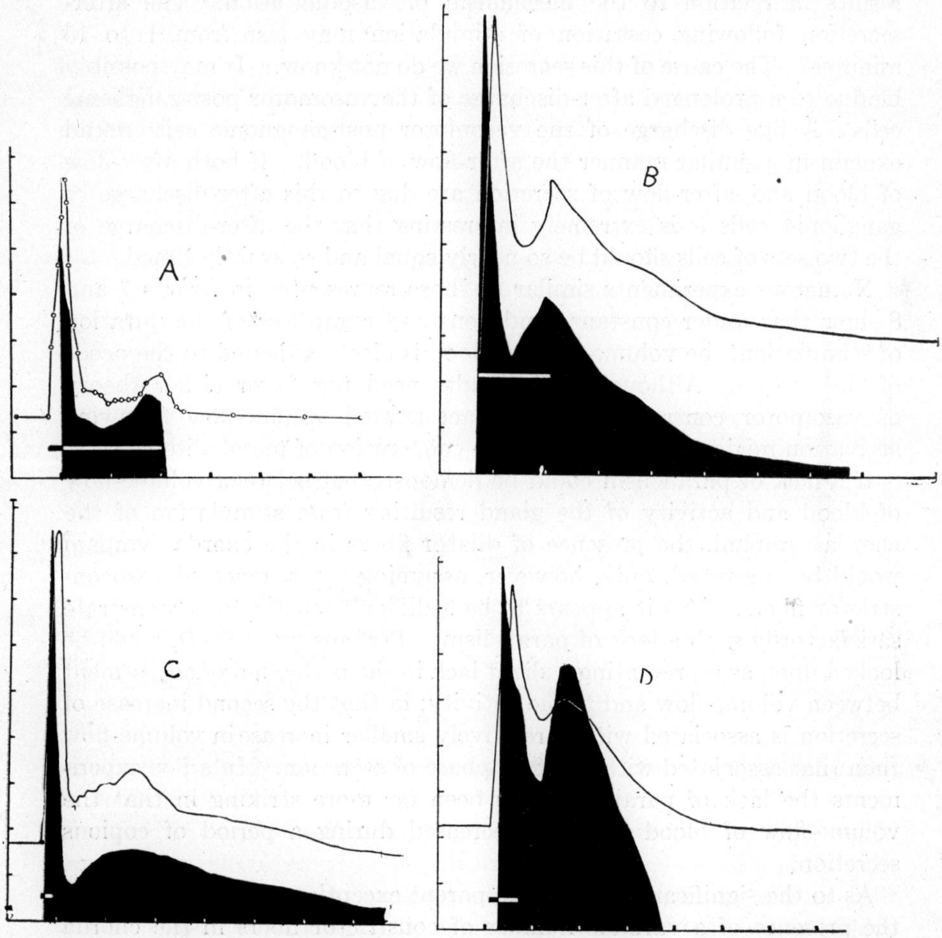

Fig. 8. Effect of stimulation of the chorda tympani on secretion and volume-flow of blood. Volume-flow of blood and salivary secretion are plotted on the ordinates against time in minutes on the abscissas. *A* and *B* show the relation of volume-flow of blood to prolonged secretion elicited by prolonged stimulation of the chorda tympani. *C* and *D* show the relation of volume-flow of blood to prolonged secretion elicited by a short period of stimulation of the chorda tympani.

the chorda tympani as a rule stops promptly upon cessation of stimulation, but not infrequently, the secretion slows only to accelerate before ultimately decreasing. Such results are represented in graph 8, *C* and *D*. The volume-flow of blood here, too, is closely adjusted to the activity of the gland. It is interesting to consider the significance of these results in relation to the mechanism of vasodilatation. The after-secretion following cessation of stimulation may last from 1 to 15 minutes. The cause of this secretion we do not know. It may possibly be due to a prolonged after-discharge of the vasomotor post-ganglionic cells. A like discharge of the vasomotor post-ganglionic cells would explain in a similar manner the after-flow of blood. If both after-flow of blood and after-flow of secretion are due to this after-discharge of ganglionic cells it is extremely interesting that the after-discharge of the two sets of cells should be so nearly equal and so exactly timed.

Numerous experiments similar to those represented in figures 7 and 8 show that under constant conditions and regardless of the duration of stimulation, the volume-flow of blood is nicely adjusted to the needs of the tissues. Although such results need not favor either theory of vasomotor control, the lag of accelerated volume-flow following activation might suggest at least the coöperation of metabolite control.

If a lack of parallelism could be demonstrated between volume-flow of blood and activity of the gland resulting from stimulation of the chorda tympani, the presence of dilator fibers in the chorda tympani would be suggested, only, however, assuming the absence of vasoconstrictor fibers. But it appears to be a difficult matter to demonstrate satisfactorily such a lack of parallelism. Perhaps graph 8, *D*, could be looked upon as representing a slight lack in the perfection of adjustment between volume-flow and tissue activity, in that the second increase of secretion is associated with a relatively smaller increase in volume-flow than that associated with the first phase of secretion. In a few experiments the lack of parallelism has been far more striking in that the volume-flow of blood actually decreased during a period of copious secretion.

As to the significance of these apparent exceptions, it is obvious that the presence of a variable number of constrictor fibers in the chorda tympani might change the relation between glandular activity and volume-flow of blood elicited by stimulation of the nerve. Fröhlich and Loewi (7), believe that such fibers exist. They obtained a decreased flow of blood, such as is described above, when the chorda tympani was stimulated. In their experiments nitrites were administered for the purpose of producing a maximum dilatation, thereby permitting effective stimulation of the constrictor fibers running in the chorda tympani. Bayliss (8) failed to obtain the decreased flow of blood under the conditions given by Fröhlich and Loewi and furthermore failed to confirm the results by stimulation of the cervical sympathetic nerve of the cat, which is known to contain constrictor fibers.

I attempted to determine the presence of constrictor fibers running in the chorda tympani by selective stimulation of these fibers produced by hemorrhage. I recorded the volume-flow of blood from both submaxillary glands during progressive hemorrhage. On one side the chorda tympani and the vago-sympathetic were cut and on the other side only the vago-sympathetic. Since one gland was connected with the central nervous system through the chorda tympani and the other gland was completely isolated, if constrictor fibers are present in the chorda tympani we might expect a difference in the curves of basal flow of the two glands (basal flow of blood plotted on the ordinates against mean blood pressure upon the abscissas). A comparison of the curves of basal flow of blood failed to indicate the presence of constrictor fibers in the chorda tympani.

The results shown in figure 9 are more helpful in explaining the difference between the results of Fröhlich and Loewi and of Bayliss. In this figure the curve of secretion and of basal-flow of blood and of salivary secretion elicited by short periods of stimulation of the chorda tympani at various levels of blood pressure during progressive hemorrhage are plotted. The period of stimulation in each case lasted about 20 seconds. The curve beginning on the abscissas is the curve of secretion. The other is the curve of blood flow. The horizontal portion preceding stimulation of the chorda tympani represents the flow of rest or basal-flow and the remaining portion the secretory or super-basal flow of blood. Record *A* was obtained during normal blood pressure. In record *D* the pressure had fallen to about 40 mm. Hg.

From the work of Barcroft we know that during secretion water is abstracted from the blood flowing through the gland. As the basal-flow of blood diminishes with decreasing pressure the basal and super-basal-flow of blood decrease and the configuration of the curves changes in a way indicative of this abstraction of water, for it will be noted that in the final stages of hemorrhage the flow of blood during secretion is actually less than the flow of rest. The irregularities of the curves of blood flow in graphs *B* and *C* apparently are the result of abstraction of water from the blood, but only when the blood pressure is too low to take sufficient advantage of the dilatation which presumably occurs, does the abstraction of water reduce the flow below that of rest. This reduction gives the appearance of constriction.

The exceptions to the proportionality of tissue activity and volume-flow of blood, therefore, can not be said to be real, but figure 10 shows results which may possibly be of significance. This figure shows the effect of reducing in steps the strength of a prolonged and continuous stimulation of the chorda tympani. The period of stimulation lasted

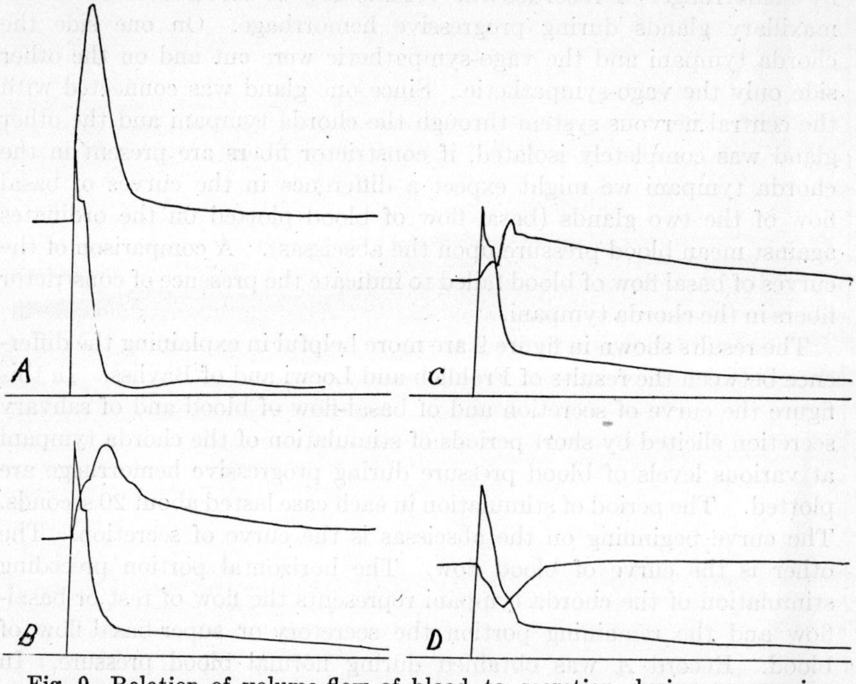

Fig. 9. Relation of volume-flow of blood to secretion during progressive hemorrhage.

approximately 7 minutes. Figure 10, *A*, shows the usual results of such a procedure and figure 10, *B*, the unusual results. In figure 10, *A*, it will be noted that at the points *B*, *C* and *D*, where the strength of current was decreased, volume-flow of blood and secretion showed proportional changes. Not so in figure 10, *B*. For some reason the response of the gland to the same procedure was strikingly different. The chorda tympani was stimulated at *A* and the strength of stimulation kept constant up to *B*. During this period the usual relations between volume-flow of blood and secretion obtain. At *B* the strength of stimulation was suddenly decreased and, barring the smaller variations

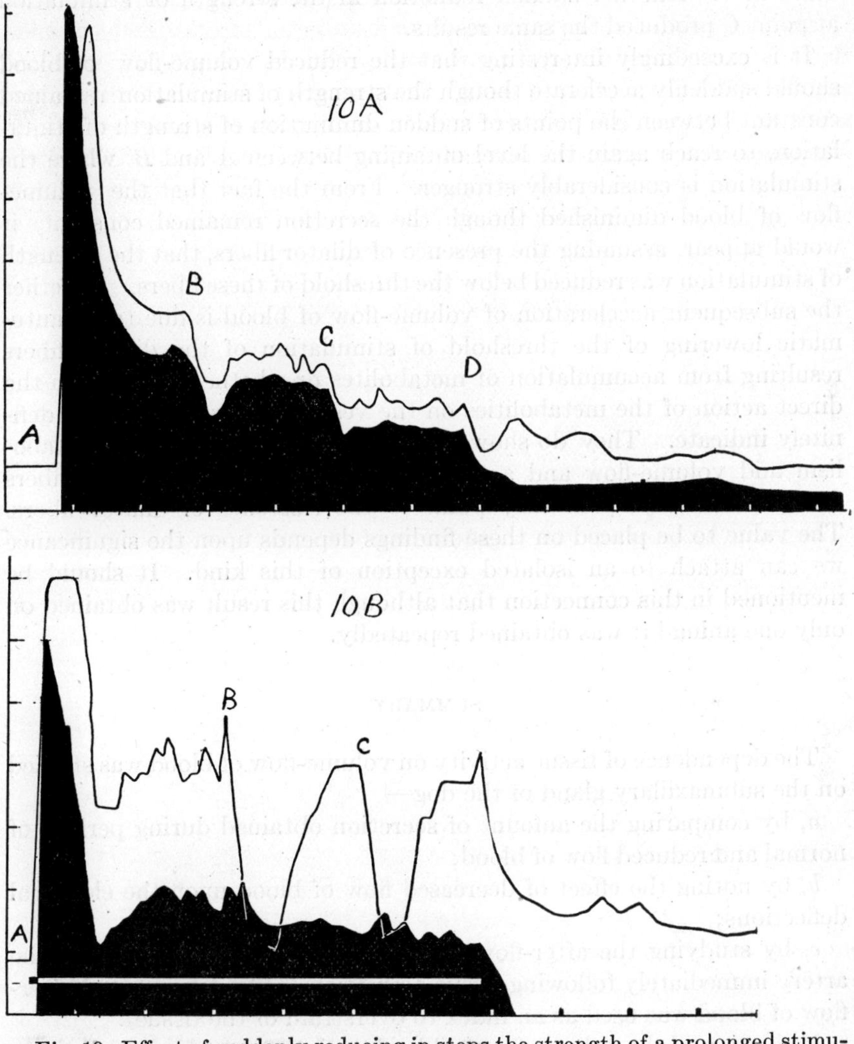

Fig. 10. Effect of suddenly reducing in steps the strength of a prolonged stimulation of the chorda tympani.

in rate of secretion, there was little if any change of rate. On the other hand the volume-flow of blood was enormously reduced—almost to the basal flow of blood. Though the strength of stimulation and rate of secretion remained constant up to point C, the flow of blood remained reduced for a short period only, coming back again to the original super-basal flow. Another sudden reduction in the strength of stimulation at point C produced the same results.

It is exceedingly interesting that the reduced volume-flow of blood should suddenly accelerate though the strength of stimulation remained constant between the points of sudden diminution of strength of stimulation, to reach again the level obtaining between A and B where the stimulation is considerably stronger. From the fact that the volume-flow of blood diminished though the secretion remained constant, it would appear, assuming the presence of dilator fibers, that the strength of stimulation was reduced below the threshold of these fibers. Whether the subsequent acceleration of volume-flow of blood is due to an automatic lowering of the threshold of stimulation of the dilator fibers resulting from accumulation of metabolites or whether it is due to the direct action of the metabolities on the vessels, the results do not definitely indicate. They do show a lack of parallelism between metabolism and volume-flow and accepting the absence of constrictor fibers in the chorda tympani they point to the existence of dilator fibers. The value to be placed on these findings depends upon the significance we can attach to an isolated exception of this kind. It should be mentioned in this connection that although this result was obtained on only one animal it was obtained repeatedly.

SUMMARY

The dependence of tissue activity on volume-flow of blood was studied on the submaxillary gland of the dog—

a, by comparing the amount of secretion obtained during periods of normal and reduced flow of blood;

b, by noting the effect of decreased flow of blood upon the electrical deflections;

c, by studying the after-flow of blood following de-occlusion of the artery immediately following tissue activation. (An exaggerated after-flow of blood was used as an index to overstrain of the tissue).

Reduction of the volume-flow of blood during a short period of stimulation of the chorda tympani, from 10 to 30 seconds, did not decrease the amount of secretion.

The glandular processes, however, were affected by such procedure, for the electrical deflections were invariably altered.

Reduction of the volume-flow of blood during a period of more intense stimulation, but also of short duration, although it did not reduce the amount of secretion elicited, resulted in a more prolonged flow of blood as well as an altered electrical deflection.

With more prolonged stimulation of the chorda tympani the various glands responded differently to arterial occlusion. On some glands occlusion of the artery for a period of about 1 minute was without effect upon secretion, while in others a noticeable reduction in secretion occurred.

The temporary independence of tissue activity of volume-flow of blood as evidenced by secretion is probably apparent only and is due to the recovery of the gland between periods of stimulation and to the relative independence of the process of liberation of secretion on volume-flow of blood.

The dependence of tissue activity upon flow of blood is better shown by reducing the flow through a tissue which has already been activated for some minutes, that is, in a tissue in which recuperation and activity are going on hand in hand.

Such methods showed a very close dependence of tissue activity upon volume-flow of blood. The results substantiate the views previously published on the significance of hemorrhage and reduced flow of blood from other causes in the onset and sustentation of the condition of traumatic shock.

Prolonged stimulation of the chorda tympani usually produced fluctuations in secretion during the period of stimulation: first a rapid secretion followed by a decrease, then another acceleration giving way to a final decrease at the end of stimulation. Similar fluctuations were produced by a short period of stimulation lasting only a small part of the period of secretion. Whether the stimulation was long or short, the volume-flow of blood and the secretion ran parallel with each other. The significance of the findings is discussed.

The close parallelism between tissue activity and volume-flow of blood offered difficulties in demonstrating definitely the existence of dilator fibers.

One experiment showing a lack of this parallelism indicates the presence of dilator fibers in the chorda tympani.

Data are presented indicative of chemical regulation of blood flow.

Experiments are cited pointing to the absence of constrictor fibers in the chorda tympani.

BIBLIOGRAPHY

(1) Gesell: This Journal, 1919, xlvii, 438.
(2) Gesell: This Journal, 1919, xlvii, 468.
(3) Carlson: This Journal, 1908, xx, 180.
(4) Langly and Fletcher: Phil. Trans., 1888, clxxx, 109.
(5) Cannon: This Journal, 1919, li, 399.
(6) Barcroft: The respiratory function of the blood, Cambridge University Press, 1914.
(7) Fröhlich and Loewi: Zentralbl. Physiol., 1906, xx, 229.
(8) Bayliss: Journ. Physiol., 1908, xxxvii, 256.

STUDIES ON THE SUBMAXILLARY GLAND

VII. On the Effects of Increased Salivary Pressure on the Electrical Deflections, the Volume-flow of Blood and the Secretion of the Submaxillary Gland of the Dog

ROBERT GESELL

From the Departments of Physiology of Washington University Medical School and the University of California

Received for publication July 27, 1920

In studying the electrical deflections of the submaxillary gland of the dog I noted that stimulation of the chorda tympani produced a greater and more prolonged after-flow of blood when the salivary duct was obstructed than when unobstructed (see figs. 4, 5 and 8). In so far as these observations aid in elucidating the mechanism of the control of volume-flow of blood they pertain to the problem of papers II, III, IV, VI and VIII of this series. The observations, however, will be considered from a broader point of view, namely, in their relation to the general problem of the physiology of the salivary glands.

The data will be discussed under the following heads:

1. Effects of increased salivary pressure upon the electrical deflections of the gland.

a. Occlusion of the salivary duct during secretion elicited by the injection of pilocarpin.

b. Occlusion of the duct synchronous with secretion elicited by the stimulation of the chorda tympani.

c. Backward injection into the salivary duct of the resting gland.

2. Effects of increased salivary pressure upon the volume-flow of blood through the gland.

a. Occlusion of the salivary duct during secretion elicited by the injection of pilocarpin.

b. Occlusion of the duct synchronous with secretion elicited by the stimulation of the chorda tympani.

c. Backward injection into the salivary duct of the resting gland.

3. Effect of increased salivary pressure upon secretion.

a. Occlusion of the duct during secretion elicited by the injection of pilocarpin.

b. Occlusion of the duct synchronous with secretion elicited by stimulation of the chorda tympani.

c. Backward injection into the salivary duct of the resting gland.

d. Effect of occlusion of the duct during secretion elicited by the stimulation of the chorda tympani upon secretion elicited by subsequent stimulation of the chorda tympani and vago-sympathetic.

e. Effect of backward injection in the resting gland upon subsequent secretion elicited by stimulation of the chorda tympani or vago-sympathetic before and after atropinization.

1. EFFECTS OF INCREASED SALIVARY PRESSURE UPON THE ELECTRICAL DEFLECTIONS OF THE GLAND

a. Occlusion of the duct during secretion elicited by the injection of pilocarpin. When the submaxillary gland is activated by the injection of pilocarpin a definite electrical deflection occurs and when the secretion approaches a constant rate the two electrodes tend again to assume a constant difference of potential as is evidenced by the horizontal direction of the recorded electrical deflection. If the salivary duct is now occluded a typical disturbance of this equilibrium occurs which is shown in figure 1, *A*, *B*, *C*, *D* and *E*. The first effect of occlusion was an upward deflection which gave way in a few seconds to a downward deflection. De-occlusion produced the reverse effect. The downward deflection accompanying occlusion was suddenly accelerated and changed as suddenly into an upward deflection. The contour of the deflection differed considerably from time to time and from animal to animal as is obvious from figure 1, *A*, *B*, *C*, *D* and *E*, yet the four phases were present in all. The electrical deflection elicited by occlusion and de-occlusion of the duct may therefore be looked upon as more or less accurately indicating the sequence of certain glandular processes set up by these procedures.

b. Occlusion of the salivary duct synchronous with secretion elicited by the stimulation of the chorda tympani. If the chorda tympani is stimulated at regular intervals with stimuli of equal strength and duration equal amounts of saliva may be elicited and electrical deflections of the same contour may be obtained, provided, the period of rest intervening between stimulations is of such duration as to prevent the augmenting effect of previous excitation. When such constant results were obtained it was found that occlusion of the salivary duct along with stimulation of the chorda tympani produced a definite change in the electrical deflection as is seen in figures 2 and 3. These figures show five sets of observations—2, *A*, *B* and *C*, and 3, *A* and *B*. In any single set of observations the chorda tympani was stimulated at equal intervals of time with equal strength of stimulation and the duct occluded equal lengths of time. But in the different sets of observations the periods and strength of stimulation, the periods of rest and of occlusion of the duct were variable. This variability must in part

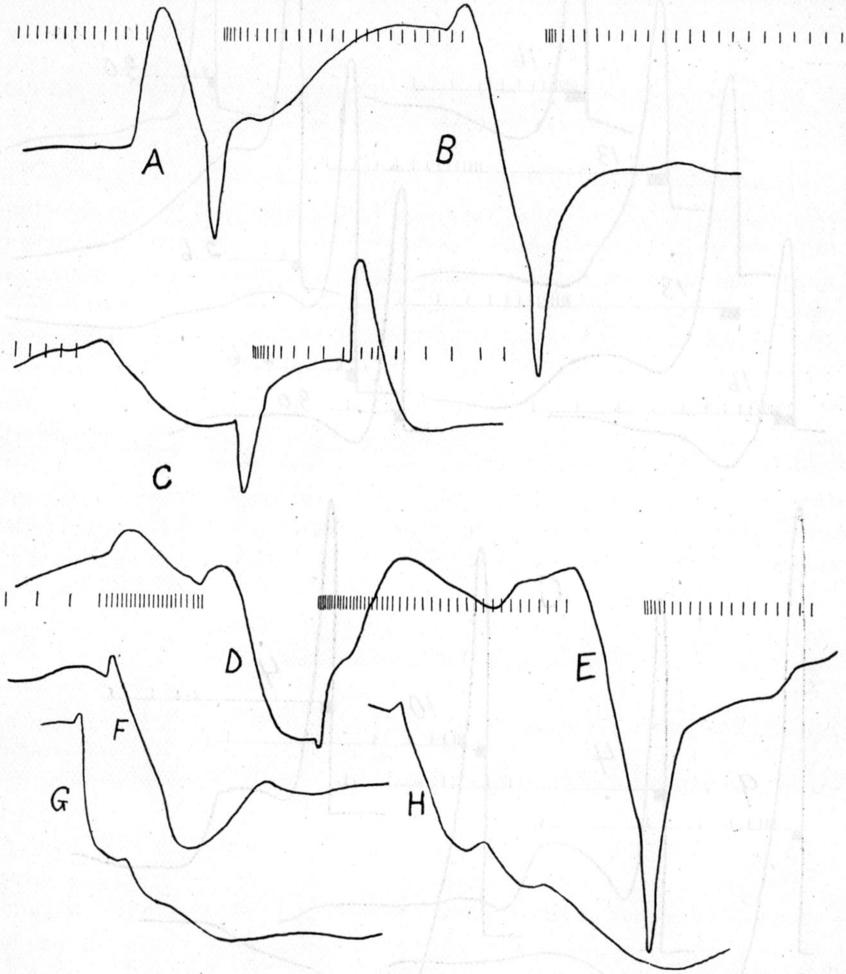

Fig. 1

account for the differences of the deflections. Bearing the variability of the conditions of the experiments in mind it is quite remarkable that the changes in contour produced by occlusion of the duct should be as uniform as they are.

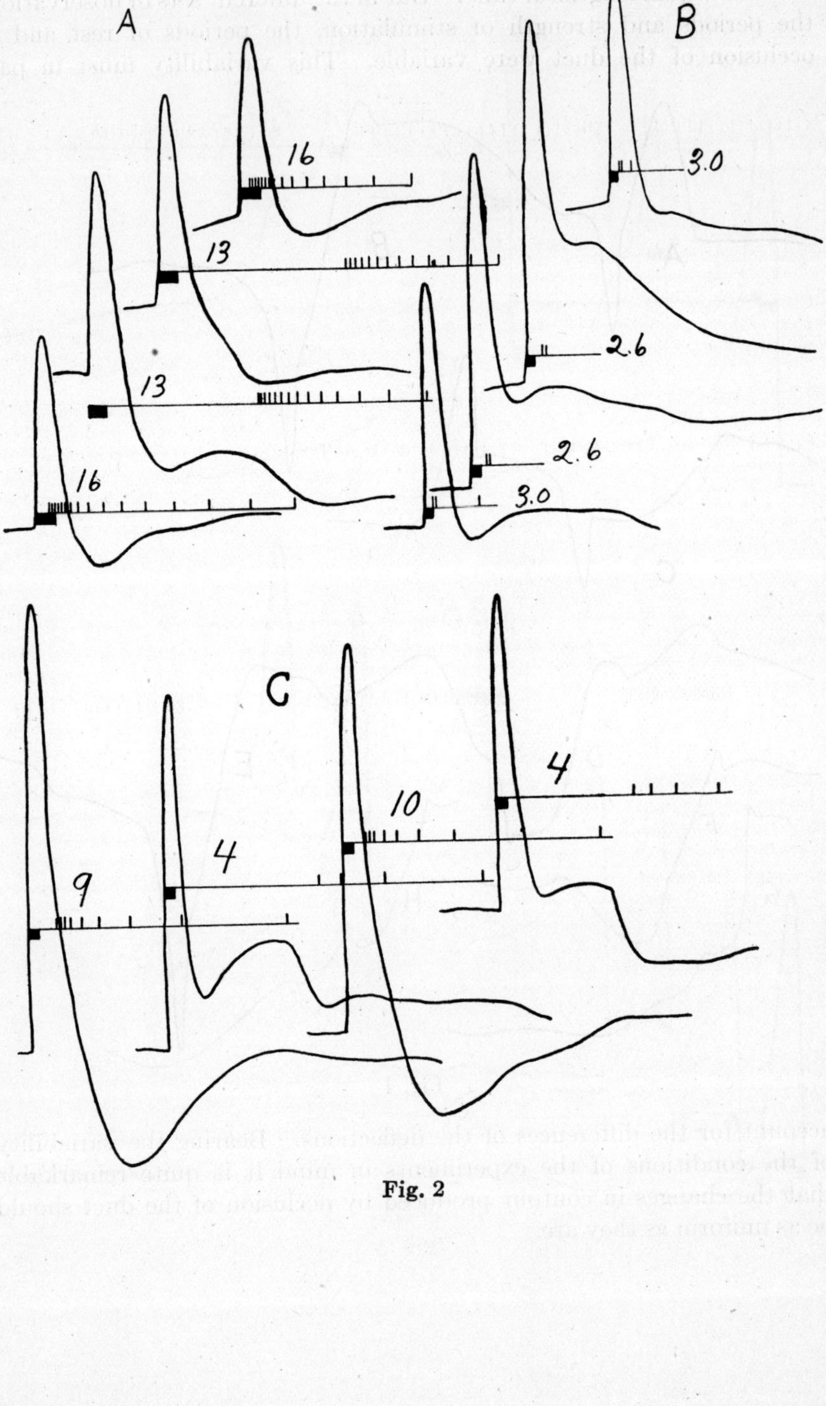

Fig. 2

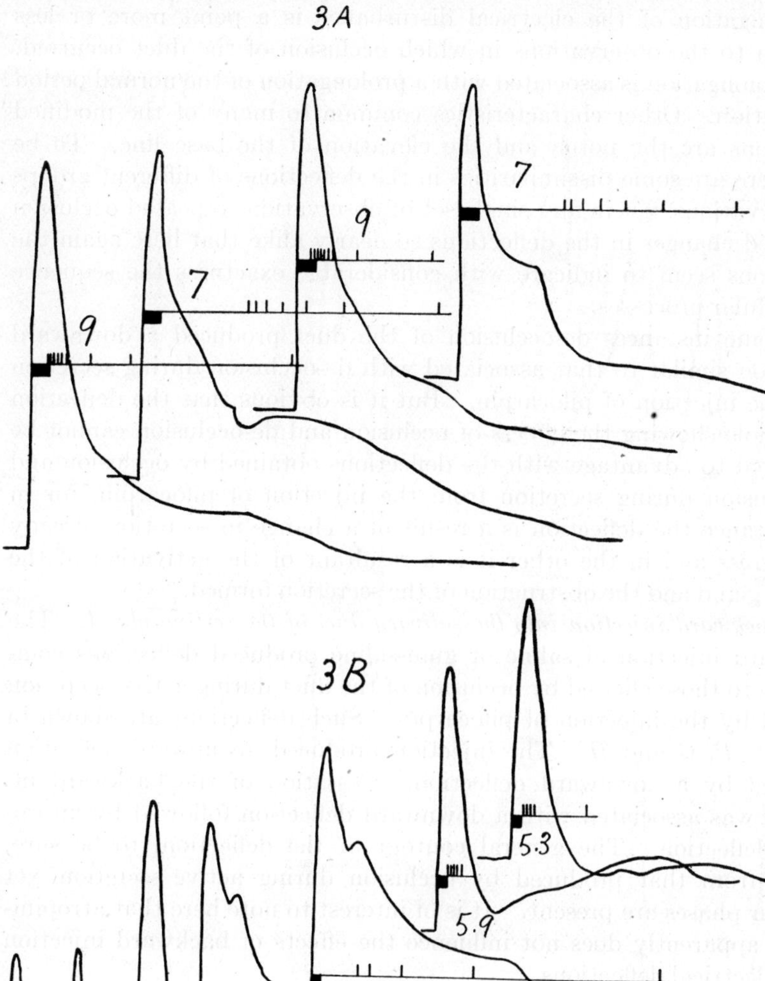

Fig. 3

Prolongation of the electrical disturbance is a point more or less common to the observations in which occlusion of the duct occurred. This prolongation is associated with a prolongation of the normal period of secretion. Other characteristics common to many of the modified deflections are the notch and the elevation of the base line. To be sure there are some dissimilarities in the deflections of different groups of observations, yet in any single set of observations repeated occlusion produced changes in the deflections so nearly alike that here again the deflections seem to indicate with considerable exactness the sequence of glandular processes.

In some instances de-occlusion of the duct produced a downward deflection similar to that associated with de-occlusion during secretion from the injection of pilocarpin. But it is obvious that the deflection as a whole showing the effects of occlusion and de-occlusion cannot be compared to advantage with the deflections obtained by occlusion and de-occlusion during secretion from the injection of pilocarpin, for in one instance the deflection is a result of a change in secretion already in progress and in the other it is a resultant of the activation of the resting gland and the obstruction of the secretion formed.

c. Backward injection into the salivary duct of the resting gland. The backward injection of saline or gum-saline produced deflections comparable to those elicited by occlusion of the duct during active secretion elicited by the injection of pilocarpin. Such deflections are shown in figure 1, *F*, *G* and *H*. The injection produced an upward deflection followed by a downward deflection. Cessation of the backward injection was associated with a downward deflection followed by an upward deflection. The general contour of the deflection, to be sure, differs from that produced by occlusion during active secretion, yet the four phases are present. It is of interest to note here that atropinization apparently does not influence the effects of backward injection upon electrical deflections.

2. EFFECTS OF INCREASED SALIVARY PRESSURE UPON THE VOLUME-FLOW OF BLOOD THROUGH THE GLAND

a. Occlusion of the salivary duct during secretion elicited by the injection of pilocarpin. Occlusion of the salivary duct during secretion resulting from the injection of pilocarpin as a rule retarded the flow of blood during the period of occlusion, as is shown in figure 5, *A*. On de-occlusion the flow accelerated again to reach or surpass the flow preceding occlusion. The de-occlusion flow of blood in figure 5, *A*, only approximated the pre-occlusion flow, but in consideration of the fact that the volume-flow of blood as a rule is proportional to the activity of the gland and of the fact that the de-occlusion secretion was considerably slower than the pre-occlusion secretion, the results suggest that even in this observation occlusion in reality produced an accelerated after-flow of blood.

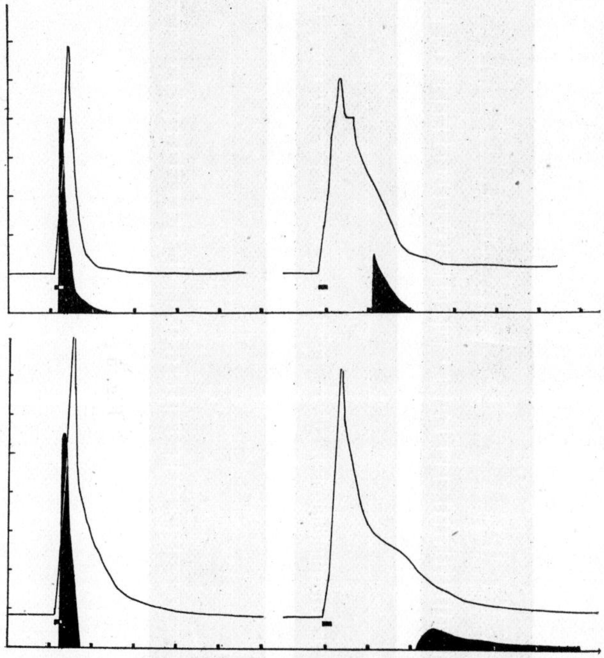

Fig. 4

b. Occlusion of the duct synchronous with secretion elicited by stimulation of the chorda tympani. The above results are substantiated by the universally accelerated after-flow of blood noted on de-occlusion of the duct after occlusion synchronous with secretion elicited by stimulation of the chorda tympani (see figs. 4 and 6). A comparison of record *B* of figure 6, in which occlusion of the duct occurs, with records *A* and *C*, in which there was no occlusion of the duct, shows the accelerated flow of blood. The results of two such experiments are plotted in figure 4 in which secretion (solid black) and volume-flow of blood (single line) are plotted on the ordinates against time in minutes

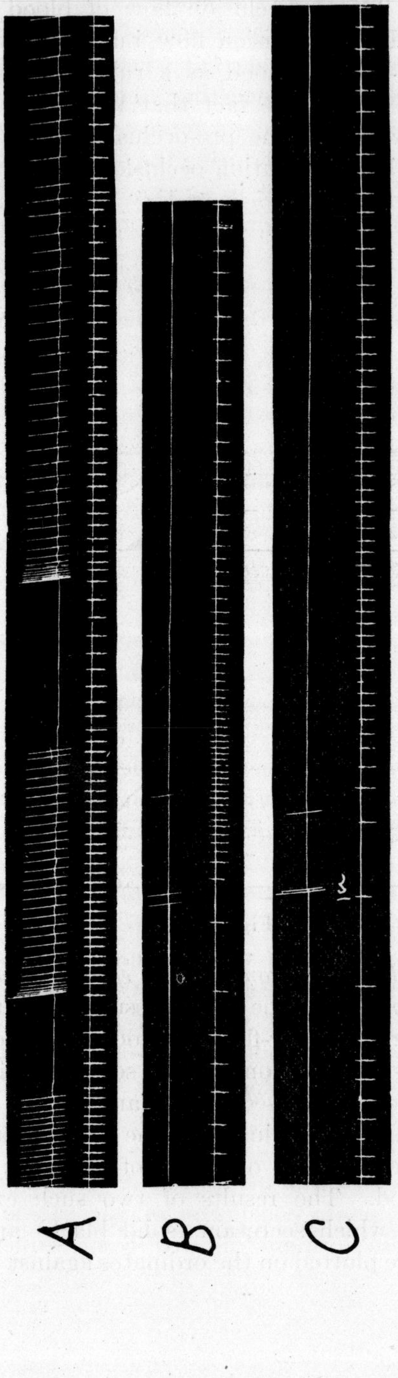

Fig. 5

on the abscissas. The duration of stimulation of the chorda tympani is marked by the rectangle near the abscissas at the beginning of the record. The extra-flow of blood elicited when the duct was occluded greatly exceeded the extra-flow occurring when the duct was not occluded. Though the two experiments represented in this figure show little reduction of the flow of blood during the occlusion of the duct, such slowing not infrequently occurred, in agreement with the results produced by occlusion of the duct during secretion elicited by the injection of pilocarpin.

c. Backward injection into the salivary duct of the resting gland. Backward injection into the salivary duct of the resting gland produced comparable results to those obtained by increasing the salivary pressure in the two ways discussed above (see fig. 5, *B* and *C*). During the period of increased salivary pressure the flow of blood was greatly reduced. On cessation of injection, which is indicated by the salivary record, the volume-flow of blood accelerated to remain accelerated for several minutes above the basal-flow of blood preceding injection.

3. EFFECT OF INCREASED SALIVARY PRESSURE UPON SECRETION

a. Occlusion of the duct during secretion elicited by the injection of pilocarpin. De-occlusion of the salivary duct after occlusion during secretion elicited by the injection of pilocarpin was followed by a momentary rapid acceleration of secretion which within a few seconds usually gave way to a rate of secretion below that obtaining before occlusion (see fig. 5, *A*). How much of the momentary accelerated secretion was due to the emptying of distended ducts, to the passage of saliva which escaped into the tissue spaces back into the ducts, to the liberation of secretion accumulated in the cells themselves due to failure to overcome the increased salivary pressure in the ducts, the experiments do not show. The retarded secretion following de-occlusion suggests some form of tissue damage resulting, possibly, from backward filtration. The effect which occlusion of the duct has upon the rate and amount of secretion following de-occlusion depends largely upon the duration of occlusion, the rate of the pre-occlusion secretion and the variability common to the glands themselves. Some saliva is always unaccounted for in the compensatory secretion.

b. Occlusion of the duct synchronous with secretion elicited by stimulation of the chorda tympani. Occlusion of the salivary duct during stimulation of the chorda tympani followed by subsequent de-occlusion produced variable results, depending again upon the rate of secretion elicited by stimulation, the duration of occlusion of the duct and the peculiar reaction of the gland itself. Various results from several animals are shown in figures 2 and 3. The records in each case are arranged in their proper sequence. Figure 2, *A* and *B*, which is compiled from two different animals, shows the effects of prolonged occlusion of a copious secretion and a momentary occlusion of a scant secretion. In figure 2, *A* the chorda tympani was stimulated at regular intervals of 4 minutes with a constant strength of stimulation lasting 16 seconds. With the duct unobstructed each stimulation elicited 16 drops of secretion as is shown in the first record of that series. In the following two records where the duct was occluded for 2.5 minutes 13 drops of saliva were secreted following de-occlusion, that is, only 3 drops of secretion were lost. In the final control when the duct was unoccluded 16 drops were again elicited. In the following record, 2, *B*, a scant secretion of only 3 drops of secretion was elicited by a relatively weak stimulus lasting 5 seconds. The duct was occluded only 10 seconds. It will be noted that occlusion of such scant secretion for only 10 seconds resulting in a loss of about 13 per cent of the secretion and producing a definite change in the electrical deflection, stands in striking contrast to the loss of only 3 drops out of a larger total of 16 drops of secretion obstructed for 2.5 minutes. The results in figure 2, *B* indicate that the storage capacity of the ducts of a gland weighing approximately 7 gm. may be little over 2 drops and that if an amount greater than 2 drops is obstructed, enough back pressure may be developed to interfere with further secretion. If that is true, where were the 13 drops of the experiment represented in 2, *A* stored?

c. Backward injection into the salivary duct of the resting gland. An index to the capacity of the ducts as it pertains to this problem may be indicated by the after-flow of secretion following backward injection of gum-saline in the resting gland. When a small amount of fluid was injected and then retained by occlusion of the duct, subsequent de-occlusion within 40 to 80 seconds was usually followed by several drops of after-flow. Not infrequently there was no after-flow whatever; but the usual flow of 2 to 4 drops suggests again that the ducts may accommodate, for a short time at least, approximately 3 drops of saliva.

d. Effect of occlusion of the duct during secretion elicited by the stimulation of the chorda tympani upon secretion elicited by subsequent stimulation of the chorda tympani and the vago sympathetic. The effects of occlusion of the duct during secretion elicited by the stimulation of the chorda tympani upon secretion elicited by subsequent stimulation of the chorda tympani and vago sympathetic are shown in figure 6. This figure gives the results of two sets of observations, *A-D* and *W-Z*. The record of the first set shows secretion and volume-flow of blood; the record of the second set electrical deflections as well. The chorda tympani was stimulated at regular intervals with stimuli of equal strength and duration. Equal amounts of secretion were elicited with each stimulation under normal conditions. During one such period of stimulation the salivary duct was occluded and the effect upon the subsequent stimulation noted. In record *A* a total of 12 drops of saliva was secreted. Since 3 of these drops were secreted slowly after the cessation of stimulation, only 7 drops were rapidly secreted during the period of stimulation. In record *B* the duct was occluded during stimulation of the chorda tympani and several minutes after stimulation the duct was de-occluded whereupon only one drop of saliva fell from the cannula. Next, record *C*, the chorda tympani was stimulated with the duct de-occluded; 13 drops of saliva were secreted, of which 11 drops appeared within the 10-second interval of stimulation. In record *D*, the final control, 6 drops of saliva were secreted rapidly. It follows from these results that occlusion of the duct during secretion increased the subsequent secretion by 4 or 5 drops.

The augmenting effect of occlusion upon secretion is shown still better in observations *W*, *X*, *Y* and *Z*, due to the fact that after-secretion was absent. In record *W* stimulation of the chorda tympani for a period of 10 seconds elicited 4 drops of saliva. In record *X* the duct was occluded during stimulation. A rapid flow of blood occurred. There was no flow of saliva on de-occlusion of the duct. In the following record, *Y*, stimulation elicited 8 drops of saliva or double the amount in record *W*. In the final control approximately 3 drops were again secreted. Note the electrical deflections.

The effects of occlusion of the salivary duct during secretion elicited by stimulation of the chorda tympani on subsequent secretion elicited by stimulation of the vago sympathetic appear to be identical with those just described (see fig. 7). The lower broken line on which time is marked in seconds indicates when the chorda tympani was stimulated and the upper line when the vago-sympathetic was stimulated. The results of alternate stimulation of the chorda tympani and vago-sympathetic without occlusion of the duct are shown in the upper tracing; with occlusion, in the lower tracings. Without previous occlusion of

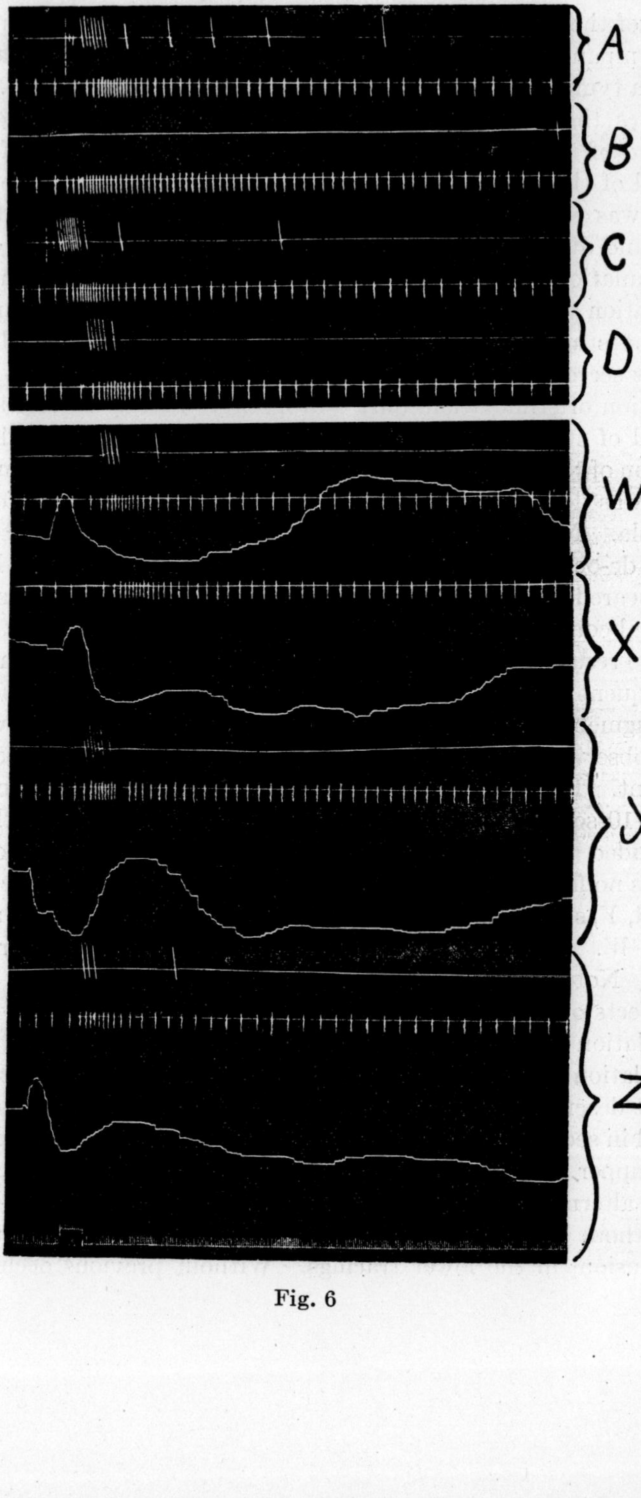

Fig. 6

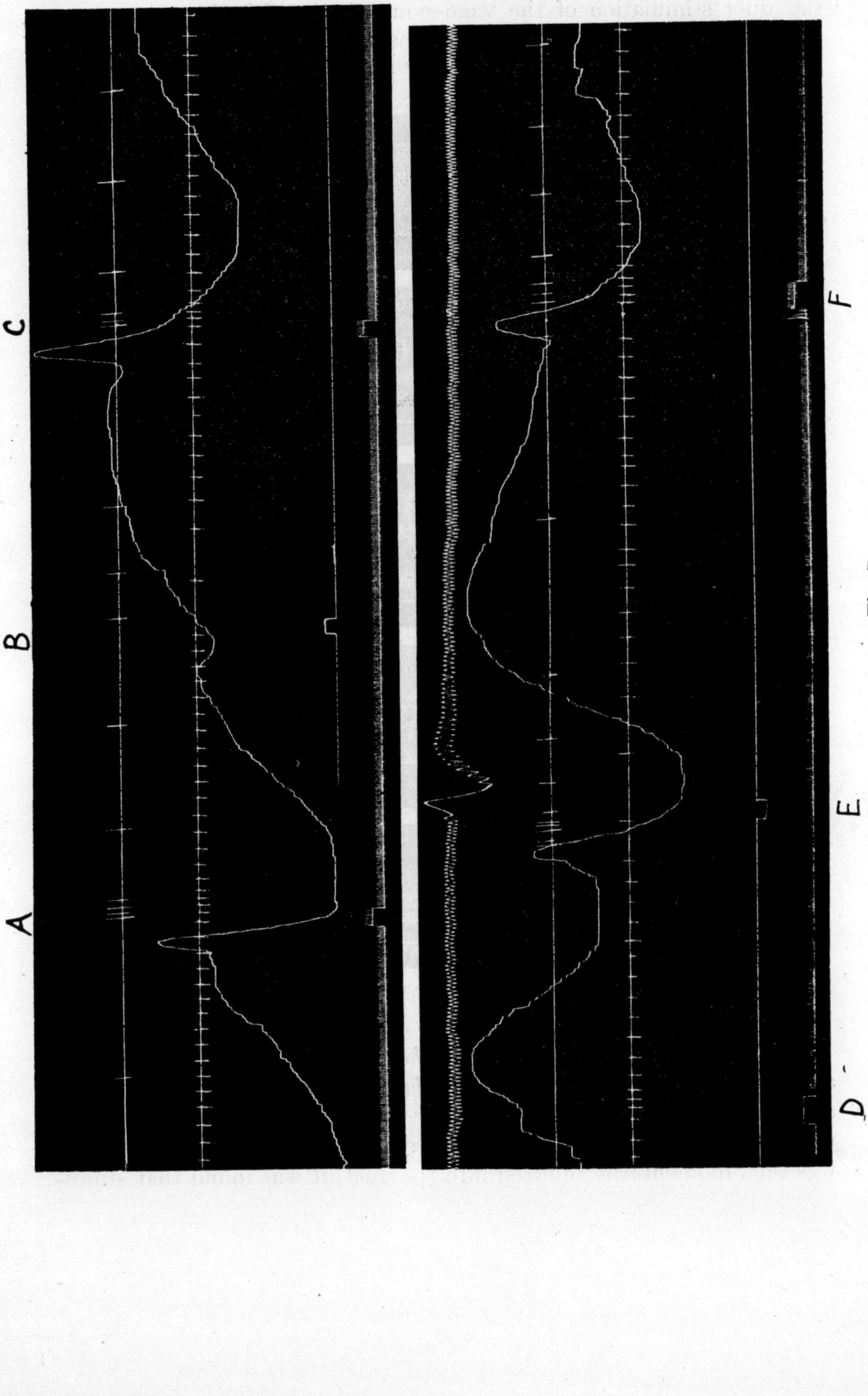

Fig. 7

the duct stimulation of the vago-sympathetic elicited a slow scanty secretion of only 3 drops, but with previous occlusion a secretion of 8 drops.

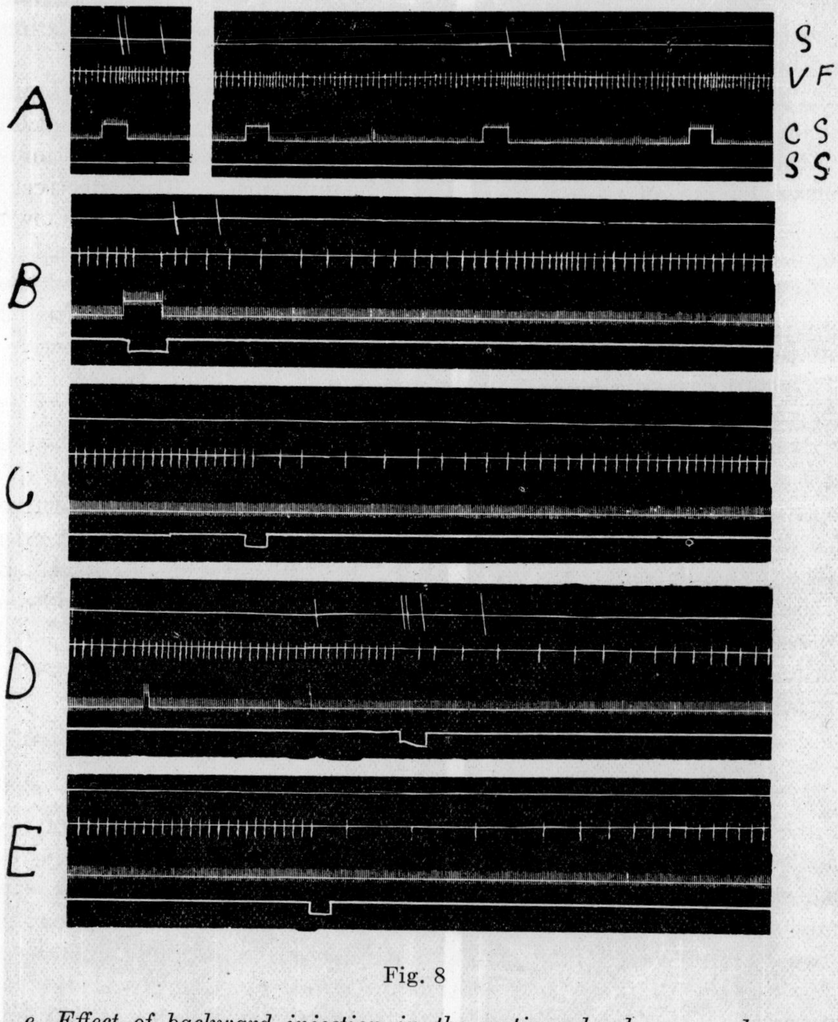

Fig. 8

e. Effect of backward injection in the resting gland upon subsequent secretion elicited by the stimulation of the chorda tympani or vago-sympathetic before and after atropinization. When equal amounts of saliva were elicited at regular intervals by equal stimulation and gum-saline was then momentarily injected into the duct, it was found that stimulation of the chorda tympani 1 to 5 minutes following the injection elicited a greater amount of secretion and that the latent period of secretion was reduced by several seconds. The same reduction in latent period was noted when stimulation of the chorda tympani was preceded by occlusion of the duct during secretion elicited by stimulation of the chorda tympani.

The experiment represented in figure 8 shows the effect of atropin upon the results described above. In record *A*, the first stimulation of the chorda tympani elicited 3 drops of saliva. Following that stimulation 1 mgm. of atropin was injected intravenously. This effectively paralyzed the chorda tympani for the prevailing stimulus, as is shown by the absence of secretion with the second stimulation. Gum-saline was then injected backwards through the duct into the gland and the duct de-occluded within a minute. The next stimulation elicited 2 drops of secretion though the subsequent stimulation was ineffective. In record *B*, a continuation of the experiment, the chorda tympani and vago-sympathetic were simultaneously stimulated producing 2 drops of secretion. The accelerated volume-flow of blood shortly following was a result of the injection of 11 mgm. of atropin. Stimulation of the vago-sympathetic following that injection in record *C* was ineffective so far as secretion is concerned, but reduced the flow of blood. In record *D*, gum-saline was injected into the duct between the breaks on the time record. One drop left the cannula on de-occlusion. Subsequent stimulation of the vago-sympathetic yielded 4 drops and final stimulation none. Similar results have been obtained after the intravenous injection of 350 mgm. of atropin.

DISCUSSION

From the work of Langley we know that during rest some of the constituents of salivary secretion are elaborated and stored ready for subsequent secretion. It appears that even after the glandular cells are well stocked with zymogen granules, secretion may yet occur in two definite stages, final elaboration followed by ultimate liberation. Various observations point in that direction, e.g., the observation of Langley on the augmenting effect of stimulation of the chorda tympani upon the secretion elicited by subsequent stimulation of the sympathetic fibers. Stimulation of the chorda tympani too weak to elicit secretion may produce a definite electrical deflection. In the preceding paper it was noted that a gland subjected to a subnormal flow of blood failed to secrete during the period of stimulation of the chorda tympani, whereas it secreted 20 to 30 seconds after cessation of stimulation when the flow of blood through the gland was suddenly accelerated. The observation in the present paper, that a gland may continue to secrete for a period of 4 or 5 minutes after the cessation of stimulation, as is shown in the de-occlusion experiments, is likewise of significance; as is also the fact that injection of atropin in amounts sufficient under usual experimental conditions to paralyze the secretory endings of the chorda tympani, fails to prevent a discharge from the gland on stimulation of the chorda tympani after a previous injection of gum-saline into the duct of the gland.

Unfortunately we do not understand the reaction of the gland to increased salivary pressure. The fact that a storage of more than 2 drops of saliva in the ducts embarrasses the gland and that 13 drops of saliva may be secreted after the duct is occluded for a period of 2.5 minutes indicates that at least not all of the after-secretion following de-occlusion is due to an expression of saliva contained within the distended ducts. The slowness of the secretion would also speak against this. Yet we have some evidence pointing to the contractility of the salivary ducts; for example, when the gland is secreting at an even rate as a result of an injection of pilocarpin, a short stimulation of the chorda tympani results in a momentary acceleration of secretion followed by a compensatory slowing which in turn gives way to a rate approaching the initial rate.

We know that when secretion occurs against a high resistance much of the saliva is filtered backward into the interspaces of the gland. The extreme slowness of secretion in certain instances following de-occlusion of the duct suggests the passage of this saliva back into the ducts. So far as I know we have no evidence that an increased salivary pressure results in filtration of saliva back into the secreting cells themselves or prevents the liberation of saliva which is already in these cells. Since "secretion" may be elicited following backward injection after atropinization sufficient to paralyze secretion, there is the possibility that under more normal conditions fluid is filtered backward into the cells, this fluid being later liberated. A part of the excess fluid within the cells may be liberated by a passive mechanism on the reduction of the salivary pressure accompanying de-occlusion, but the passive mechanism may not be sufficient to liberate all of the excess fluid or secretion and this may then be actively liberated upon stimulation of the chorda tympani. It seems not improbable that this active liberation may be the result of active contraction of certain constituents of the secreting cells themselves. This problem needs further investigation and will be reported upon later. The results so far indicate only that atropin in certain stages of atropinization paralyzes primarily the function of elaboration of secretion leaving the function of liberation more or less intact.

As to the nature of the changes in volume-flow of blood produced by increased salivary pressure we can say that they are not of a central reflex origin if all the vasomotor nerves to the gland run in the chorda tympani and vago-sympathetic, for these changes in flow occurred after section of both nerves. The decreased flow obtaining during the period of increased pressure may well be a mechanical effect of compression of the capillaries and venules, for it obtains during stimulation of the chorda tympani when the factors normally producing dilatation are at work, as well as when the gland is at rest. On de-occlusion of the duct the compressing pressure vanishes and the flow of blood not only returns to normal but greatly exceeds the normal. When this accelerated flow was first noticed with occlusion accompanying stimulation of the chorda tympani it was thought that possibly more energy was required for secretion against a high pressure and that the accelerated flow of blood supplied this needed energy. The accelerated flow resulting from backward injection into the duct of the resting gland is contradictory to this view. The accelerated flow does not seem to be due to a specific chemical irritation of the saliva itself for it occurs after injection of inert solution, such as saline and gum-saline. Whether a backward filtration into the secreting cells would bring about increased volume flow of blood we do not know. The only suggestion we have at present to account for the accelerated flow is the tissue damage resulting from backward filtration into the tissue spaces and possibly into the cells themselves.

SUMMARY

Occlusion of the duct of the submaxillary gland of the dog during secretion elicited by the injection of pilocarpin produced characteristic electrical deflections.

Injection of gum-saline into the duct produced somewhat comparable deflections.

Occlusion of the duct along with stimulation of the chorda tympani modified in a more or less typical way the usual electrical deflection obtained by stimulation when the duct was not occluded.

Occlusion of the salivary duct during secretion elicited by the injection of pilocarpin retarded the flow of blood. The after-flow of blood was at times accelerated.

Backward injection of gum-saline into the salivary duct of the resting gland retarded the flow of blood during the period of increased pressure. Release of that pressure resulted in an accelerated flow of blood at times lasting many minutes.

Occlusion of the duct during secretion elicited by stimulation of the chorda tympani frequently retarded the flow of blood. De-occlusion was followed by a markedly accelerated after-flow of blood.

De-occlusion of the salivary duct during secretion elicited by the injection of pilocarpin was followed by a short period of accelerated secretion. This accelerated secretion never compensated fully the absence of secretion during the period of occlusion.

De-occlusion of the duct several minutes subsequent to injection of gum-saline into the duct was followed by an after-flow from the duct of 0 to 4 drops.

Occlusion of the salivary duct along with stimulation of the chorda tympani was followed upon de-occlusion by a secretion less in amount than that normally elicited with the duct unoccluded. The amount of saliva unaccounted for varied considerably with the animal, the duration of occlusion and the amount of secretion obstructed.

De-occlusion of the duct after obstructing for several minutes a temporary secretion elicited by stimulation of the chorda tympani may be followed by a slow secretion lasting 4 to 5 minutes.

Occlusion of the duct during secretion elicited by the stimulation of the chorda tympani increased the amount of saliva elicited by subsequent stimulation of the chorda tympani or vago-sympathetic. The latent period of secretion was also reduced by several seconds.

Backward injection of gum-saline into the resting gland increased the amount of secretion elicited by subsequent stimulation of the chorda tympani or vago-sympathetic and reduced the latent period of secretion.

Injection of atropin sufficient to check secretion elicited by the stimulation of the chorda tympani or vago-sympathetic may fail to prevent secretion with similar stimulation after backward injection into the salivary duct.

If all the nerve fibers reaching the submaxillary gland run in the chorda lingual and vago-sympathetic the changes in volume-flow of blood resulting from increased salivary pressure are not of a central reflex origin.

The decreased volume-flow of blood during the period of increased salivary pressure is probably due to mechanical occlusion of the capillaries or venules.

It is suggested that the accelerated flow of blood following de-occlusion is a result of tissue damage from backward filtration into the tissue spaces, and possibly into the cells themselves.

The effects of occlusion of the duct upon secretion elicited by stimulation of the chorda tympani suggests that secretion may occur in two definite stages. The effects of atropin on augmented secretion following backward injection of gum-saline into the duct suggests the same inference.

STUDIES ON THE SUBMAXILLARY GLAND

VIII. On the Effects of Atropin upon Volume-flow of Blood, Electrical Deflections and Oxidations of the Submaxillary Gland

ROBERT GESELL

From the Departments of Physiology of the Washington University Medical School, St. Louis, and the University of California, Berkeley, California

Received for publication July 27, 1920

When the chorda tympani is stimulated definite effects are produced in the submaxillary gland among which are: secretion of saliva, an augmented flow of blood, a change in the electrical condition of the gland and an accelerated oxidation. This paper considers briefly some of the effects of the intravenous injection of atropin upon these processes.

The work is a continuation of the study of electrical deflections of the submaxillary gland and has a bearing upon the problems of vasomotor control. In paper II of this series (1) the nature of the electrical deflections elicited by stimulation of the chorda tympani was discussed. It was pointed out that such factors as the type of lead, the strength and duration of stimulation, the period of rest, etc., all influence the kind of deflection obtained. It is essential then to keep these factors in mind in connection with the effects which atropin produces upon electrical deflections elicited by stimulation of the chorda tympani.

We know from the work of others the effect which atropin has upon secretion of saliva. These effects, when noted in this work will, therefore, be discussed only in their connection with the changes in volume-flow of blood, the electrical condition of the gland and oxidations.

Atropin influences the electrical response of the gland profoundly as was shown by Bayliss and Bradford (2). I have obtained like results.

Figure 1 shows the effect of the injection of 1.5 mgm. of atropin. Record *A*, shows the effects of stimulation of the chorda tympani with both vago-sympathetics intact before the injection of atropin. Record *D*, shows the effects of stimulation after double vago-section and atropinization. Records *B* and *C*, show the effects of section of the left and right vago-sympathetics respectively. Atropinization abolished

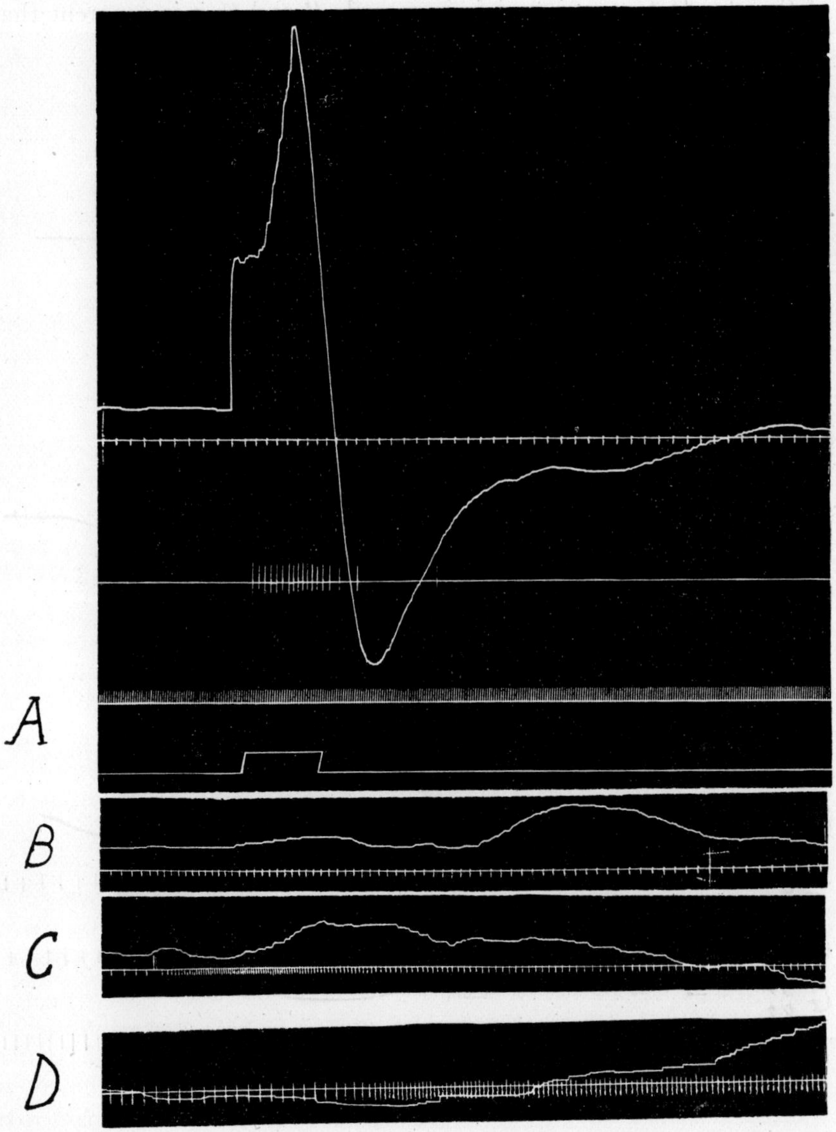

Fig. 1

both the secretion and the electrical deflection elicited by stimulation of the chorda tympani, and from records *B* and *C*, it is apparent that

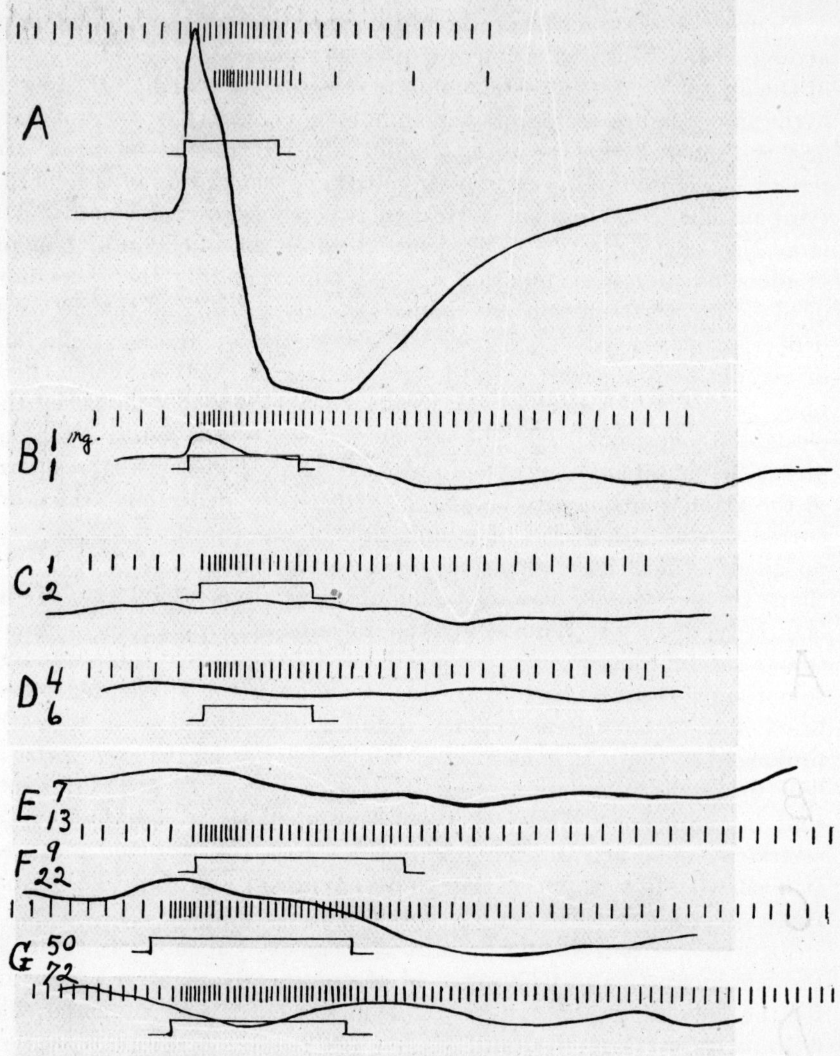

Fig. 2

volume-flow of blood per se was of little if any significance in the development of electrical changes. In record *A*, where the volume-flow of blood was least affected the largest electrical deflection occurred, and in records *C* and *D*, where the flow was enormously accelerated, both passively and actively, there was practically no change in the electrical deflection.

Figure 2 shows the effects of repeated injections of small amounts of atropin, each injection occurring several minutes before stimulation of the chorda tympani. The amounts injected are noted on the record —the upper figure represents the amount injected prior to stimulation and the lower figure the total amount injected at that moment. In record *A*, before the injection of any atropin, stimulation of the chorda tympani elicited a copious secretion, a copious flow of blood and a large electrical deflection. In record *B*, after the injection of 1 mgm. of atropin, similar stimulation elicited approximately the same flow of blood but the secretion was reduced to only ½ drop and the electrical deflection was nearly abolished. The injection of another milligram of atropin before record *C*, although exerting no further visible effect upon the volume-flow of blood, paralyzed secretion and abolished the electrical deflection. The subsequent records followed the injections of 4, 7, 9 and 50 mgm. of atropin respectively. The electrical response of the gland continued to be absent, at least the deflections which occurred during the period of stimulation of the chorda tympani were no greater than those which occurred during the periods of rest. At times the accelerated flow of blood resulting from stimulation of the chorda tympani was reduced by the injection of atropin as is apparent from a careful comparison of records *A* and *B* of figure 3. It is of interest to note in connection with figure 2 that although the accelerated superbasal flow of blood was slightly reduced, the after-flow was greatly prolonged so that the sum total of the effects was a greater superbasal flow for equal stimulation after the administration of atropin. Note that in the lower records the basal flow of blood is considerably accelerated. The acceleration was not due to a rise of blood pressure. It occurred after section of the chorda tympani and the vago-sympathetic and therefore was peripheral in origin.

Figures 3, 4 and 5 show results of other experiments. In figure 3, the administration of 0.08 mgm. of atropin nearly paralyzed secretion for the prevailing stimulus, only 1 drop was elicited as compared with 6 drops before atropinization. It likewise reduced the superbasal flow of blood. The electrical deflection was still very distinct. In figure 4, taken from a different animal, a similar injection abolished secretion entirely. The electrical deflection was still prominent and the superbasal flow of blood during the period of stimulation was hardly affected,

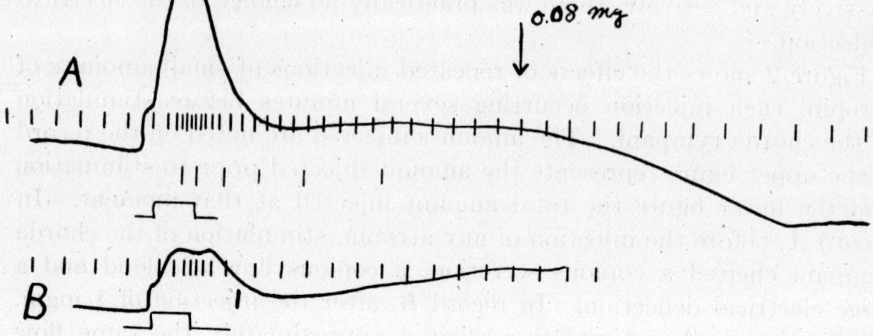

Fig. 3

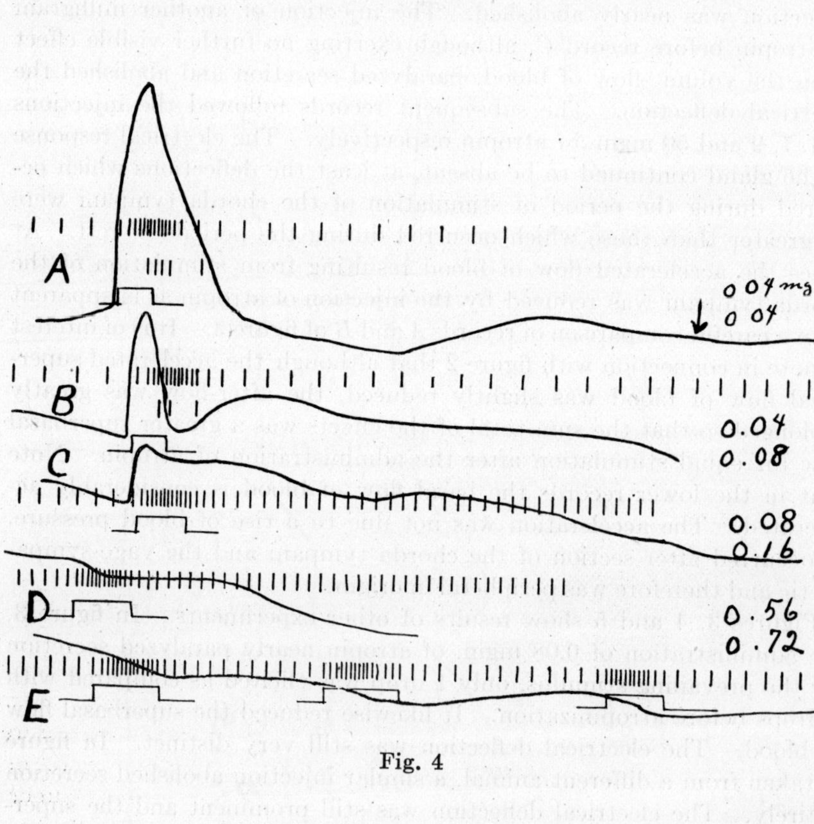

Fig. 4

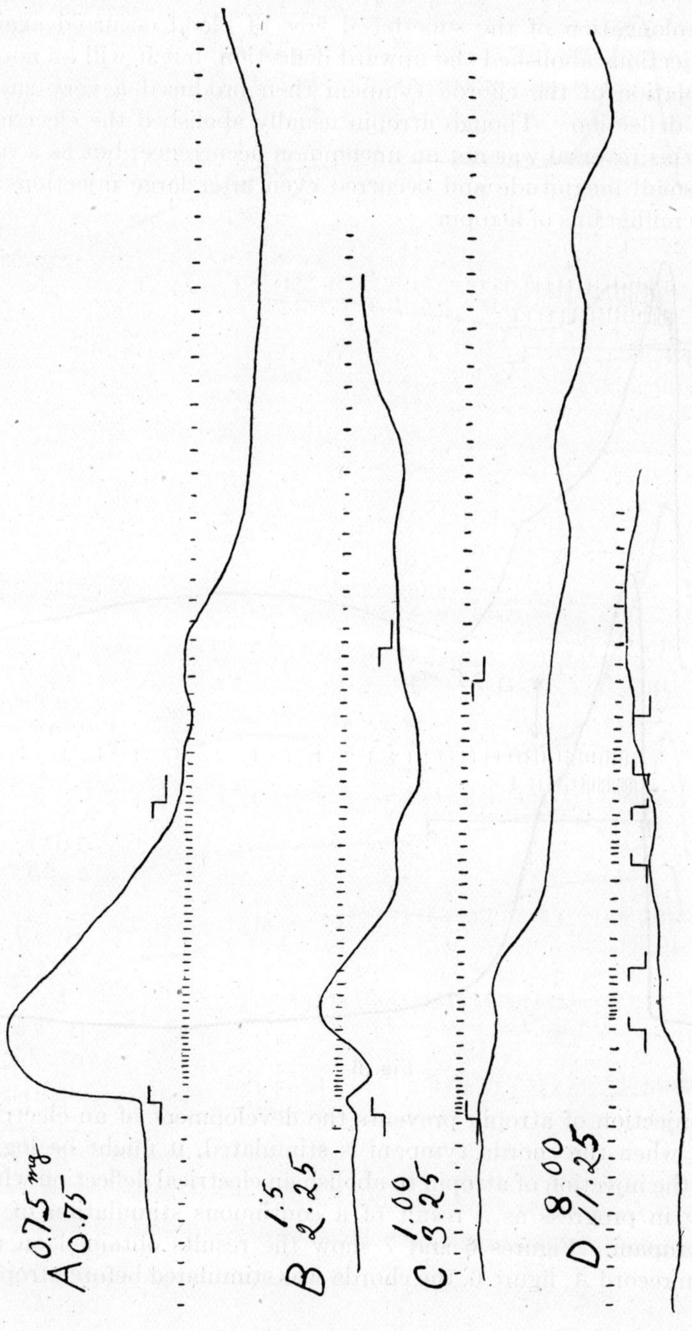

Fig. 5

but the prolongation of the superbasal flow of blood occurred again. Further injections abolished the upward deflection, but it will be noted that stimulation of the chorda tympani then produced a very small downward deflection. Though atropin usually abolished the electrical deflection this reversal was not an uncommon occurrence; but as a rule it was of small magnitude and occurred even after large injections of 30 or more milligrams of atropin.

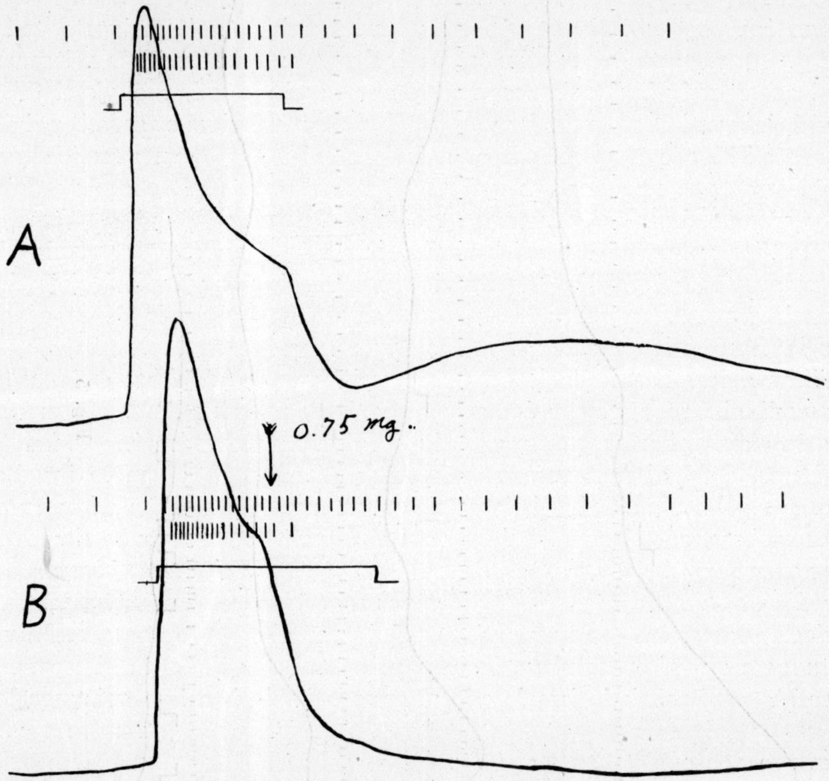

Fig. 6

If the injection of atropin prevents the development of an electrical deflection when the chorda tympani is stimulated, it might be logical to expect the injection of atropin to abolish an electrical deflection which is already in progress as a result of a continuous stimulation of the chorda tympani. Figures 6 and 7 show the results obtained on this point. In record *A*, figure 6, the chorda was stimulated before atropini-

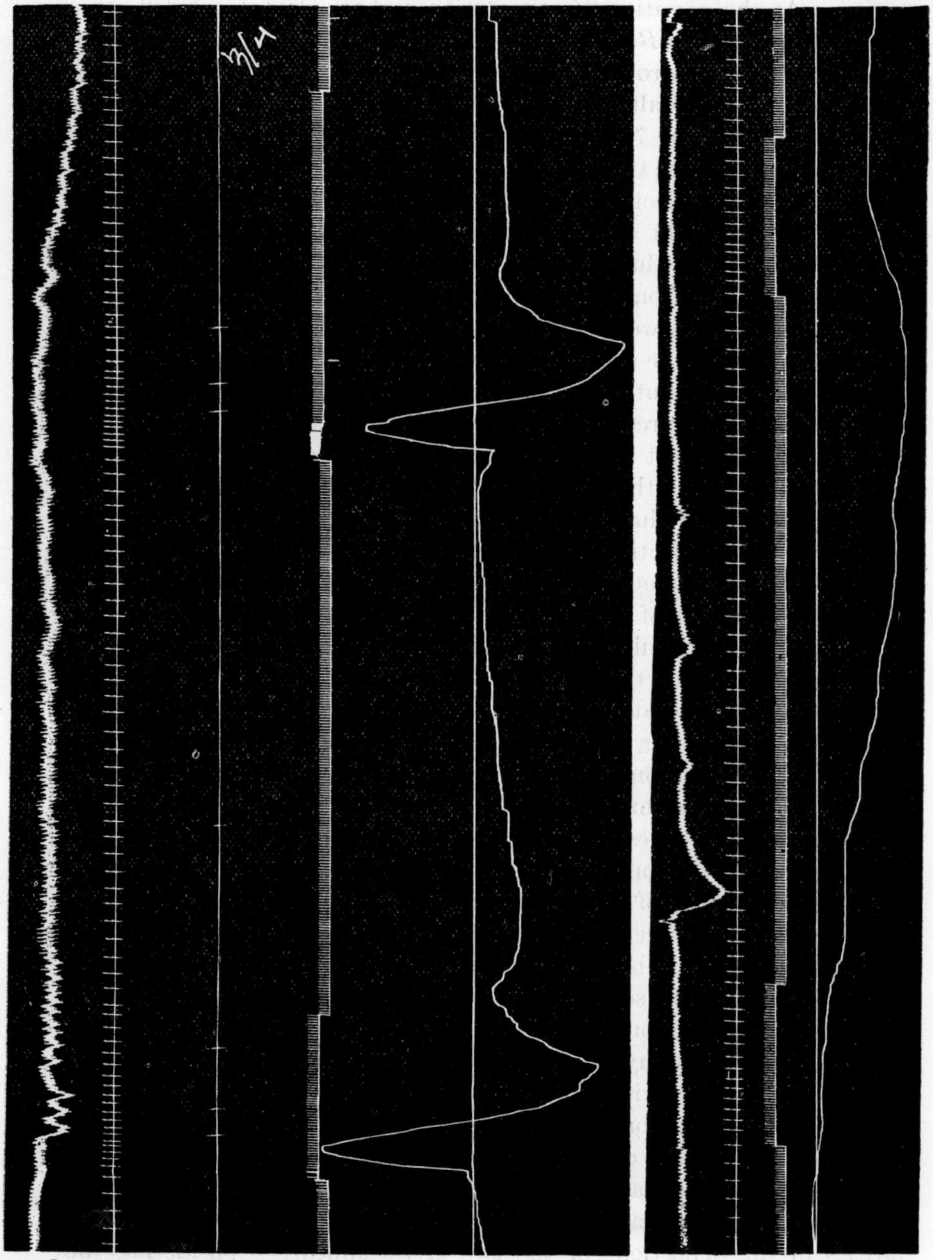

Fig. 7

zation. At the cessation of stimulation a sharp downward deflection occurred. In record *B*, atropin was injected during the period of stimulation. When the atropin reached the gland the same sharp downward deflection occurred, although the stimulation of the chorda tympani continued. In figure 7, record *B*, where the atropin reached the gland at relatively the same time interval as cessation of stimulation in record *A*, the electrical deflections were nearly identical. From the electrical deflections one might conclude, neglecting the volume-flow of blood, that atropinization during stimulation of the chorda tympani and cessation of stimulation call forth the same effects.

It is obvious that we know too little about electrical phenomena in living tissues to arrive at such a definite conclusion, yet I have tried in an indirect way to put this conclusion to the test. It should be possible to grade the strength of stimulation, or perhaps more correctly stated, the end effect of stimulation, in two ways—mechanically by regulating the strength of shock delivered by the induction coil, and physiologically by reducing the effectiveness of stimulation of constant strength by the injection of graded doses of atropin. A comparison of the electrical, secretory and vasomotor response of the gland with these two methods of gradation of stimulation seemed worth while attempting. The results obtained on two animals are shown in figures 8 and 9. The chorda tympani was stimulated at regular intervals with stimuli of equal duration. In the first observation in both experiments the stimulation was too weak to elicit visible secretion. The strength of stimulation was then increased with each observation up to an arbitrary maximum. That maximum was then kept constant for the remaining series of observations, but prior to each stimulation small amounts of atropin were injected, as small as 0.05 mgm. Each increase in strength of stimulation elicited an increase in the amount of secretion and a decided change in the electrical deflection. After the maximum strength of stimulation was reached each injection reduced the amount of secretion and elicited just as decided changes in the electrical deflection. The records show the results obtained and hardly need a lengthy discussion. To be sure, the corresponding deflections obtained with increasing and decreasing activation as indicated by the secretion are not superimposable, yet if we carefully compare the tracings of figure 8 keeping three factors in mind—the magnitude of the upward deflection, the reversal of the deflection to a downward deflection, and roughly, the general contour—definite similarities in the deflections of the two series appear. Considering the fact that identical deflections can be obtained only when many factors remain perfectly constant and that two series of deflections—one ob-

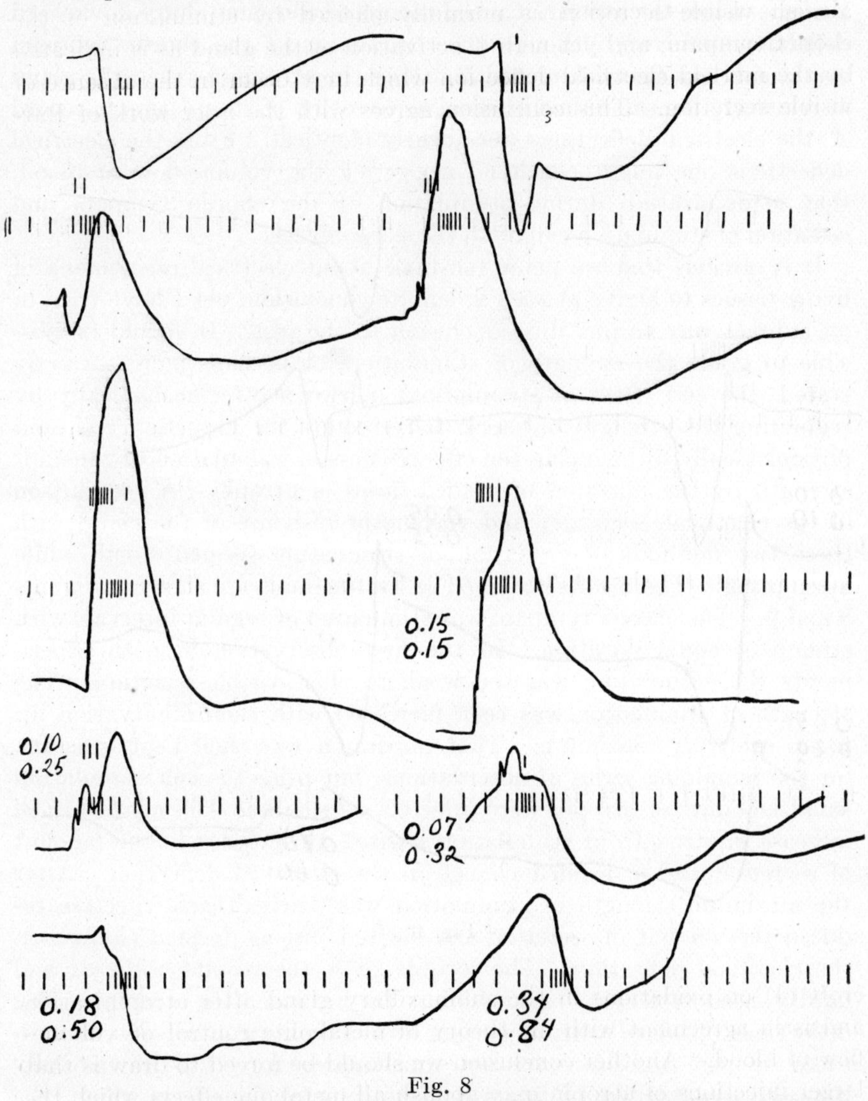

Fig. 8

tained with increasing strength of electrical stimulation and the other with decreasing strength of electrical stimulation—show dissimilarities, as demonstrated before, it is significant that the two series of deflections as obtained in this research have as many points in common as they do.

If the electrical method detects minute changes in metabolic activity we should be forced to conclude that a small injection of atropin may abolish visible secretion as normally elicited by stimulation of the chorda tympani, and yet permit activation of the gland as is indicated by the marked electrical deflection which may occur in the absence of visible secretion. This conclusion agrees with the later work of Bar-

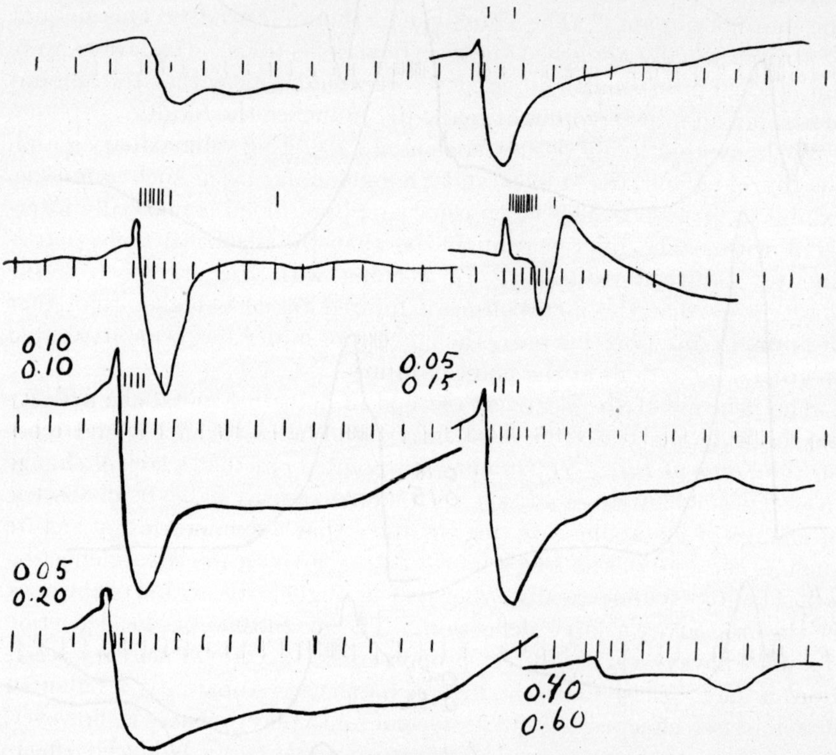

Fig. 9

croft (4) on oxidations in the submaxillary gland after atropinization and is in agreement with his theory of metabolite control of volume-flow of blood. Another conclusion we should be forced to draw is that larger injections of atropin may abolish all metabolic effects which the chorda tympani has upon the submaxillary glands. This conclusion agrees with the earlier results of Barcroft (3) on oxidations in the submaxillary gland after atropinization. If correct, it reduces the importance of metabolite control, this control then only complementing the control by the vasomotor nerves.

In some experiments in which I have measured the oxidations of the gland as affected by stimulation of the chorda tympani after the injection of 3 to 5 mgm. of atropin (5), I found that although occasionally oxidations were increased as much as 15 per cent above the oxidations during rest, as a rule, oxidations were not increased by stimulation of the chorda tympani. (The Van Slyke method was used.) This amount of atropin usually abolished the electrical deflections. Oxidations were not studied after smaller injections. It would appear that the amount of atropin administered might markedly influence the results.

We know that living tissues, such as the secreting submaxillary gland, the thyroid gland, the kidney, and a nonglandular tissue such as muscle, exhibit electrical changes when their supply of blood is markedly interfered with. The inference might be that the electrical deflection is due to disturbed oxidation. In keeping with this inference is the observation that the metabolism of injured tissue is higher than that of normal tissue; on this basis the current of injury has been attributed to greater oxidations at the point of injury.

The delicacy of the electrical method of detecting metabolic activity has been demonstrated in many ways by Waller (6) in his researches on the *Signs of Life*. Yet it must be pointed out that a lack of change in electrical condition of a tissue need not necessarily indicate an absence of change of metabolic rate, for we know that a symmetrical structure such as the web of the frog's foot does not give an electrical deflection when excited symmetrically, whereas the single layer of skin of the back of the frog gives a large deflection. The magnitude of the deflection does not always vary in direct proportion to the rate of salivary secretion; in fact, occasionally the reverse happens. Apparently a balanced action of two effects of stimulation comes into play. There is, however, no evidence that symmetry of structure or perfectly balanced effects come into play more after atropinization than before.

BIBLIOGRAPHY

(1) Gesell: This Journal, 1919, xlvii, 411.
(2) Bayliss and Bradford: Proc. Royal Soc., 1886.
(3) Barcroft: The respiratory function of the blood, 1914, Cambridge University Press.
(4) Barcroft: Journ. Physiol., 1901, xxvii, 31.
(5) Gesell: Not published.
(6) Waller: The signs of life, New York, 1903.

THE AMERICAN
JOURNAL OF PHYSIOLOGY

VOL. 54 DECEMBER 1, 1920 No. 2

THE DISTRIBUTION AND QUANTITATIVE ACTION OF THE VAGI AS DETERMINED BY THE ELECTRICAL CHANGES ARISING IN THE HEART UPON VAGUS STIMULATION

E. W. H. CRUICKSHANK

From the Physiological Department of Washington University, St. Louis

Received for publication July 3, 1920

In a survey of the literature upon the vagus nerves, one can not but be struck by the fact that so many workers in this field have paid so little attention to a clear discrimination between the right and left vagi. General conclusions have been drawn, with regard to vagus activity, which are applicable only to the left vagus, and in the earlier publications no attempt even was made to differentiate between vagus and accelerator nerves, so that functions peculiar to different nerves have been assigned to both vagi.

The idea that the vagus nerves may or may not exert contralateral effects was not put to the test of experiment till 1911, when Garrey (1) carefully considered the matter, using the whole and partially split heart of the turtle and recording his results graphically. His conclusions, which are very definite, are as follows. He asserts first, that the origin of the beat is to be found in the right caval veins, the inherent rhythmicity of which he showed to be greater than that of the sinus and auricles and then he shows that, in the whole heart, the right vagus affects chronotropically, through its action on the right veins, every part of the organ, while the left vagus may affect the whole, including the right veins, but that usually it affects the left veins, the sinus and the auricles, producing quiescence by decreasing the excitability, conductivity and contractility of the auricles, leaving the rhythm of the right veins unaffected. In the "ascidian preparation" of the turtle's heart, in which the beat travelled from right to left, very clear conclusions were arrived at, namely, that the right vagus stopped the whole preparation, while the left inhibited the left auricle and right auricle, the right basal veins still continuing to beat at their original rhythm. This, according to Garrey, is due to the fact that the left vagus does not affect the pace-maker, but acts upon structure similar to that upon which normal cardiac impulses act. The essential point determined is that the vagi act chronotropically on their respective sides, upon those parts which initiate the rhythm. This is the basis of the homolateral view of the action of the vagi, which has been so strongly brought forward by Garrey who, however, showed that such effects were not so clearly marked with regard to the auricles, and he states "that the experiments bring out clearly that in auricles as well as in veins and sinus the vagus effects may cross to the contralateral side."

Robinson and Draper (2), from an investigation of the action of the vagus nerves upon the human heart, corroborate previous findings on the mammalian heart, namely, that the predominant action of the right vagus is a control of rate, through its inhibitory action upon the normal pace-maker of the heart, and that of the left nerve is primarily a control of conduction from auricle to ventricle, through a direct inhibitory effect upon the conducting system and that in gauging the difference upon conductivity of the right and left vagi, the factor of heart rate must be taken into account. Again, with regard to auriculo-ventricular dissociations, it was shown that these are not caused by diminution in the conductivity, but are essentially due to the inherent high rate of rhythmicity of the ventricles, dissociation occurring as soon as vagus stimulation reduced the auricular rate below that at which the ventricles will contract by their own inherent rhythmicity. This viewpoint is supported by experiments of Rothberger and Winterberg (3) who demonstrated true nodal rhythm by stimulation of the right vagus and left accelerator nerves.

Cohn (4) in 1912 stated that negatively chronotropic effects may be obtained upon stimulation of the left vagus and he made this significant statement "that it is doubtful whether the distribution that has been described is as refined as is necessary to explain the results" he obtained.

With regard to the importance of heart rate in gauging dromotropic effects of the vagi, attention is drawn to a paper by Robinson (5) in 1916, in which he shows that there is no constant difference between the right and left vagus nerves in their action upon conductivity between the auricles and ventricles during auricular fibrillation.

The first report upon the electrical changes in the heart due to vagus stimulation was made by Gaskell (6). The type of experiment which he describes depends upon the peculiar arrangement of the vagus nerve in the tortoise heart, where a branch of the vagus runs with the coronary vein from the sinus to the base of the ventricle. This "coronary" vagus being free, the sinus and left auricle could therefore be cut off without damage to the nerve supply of the right auricle, thus allowing of a quiescent preparation. A demarcation current having been produced by "thermic section" and the right vagus stimulated, a deflection was obtained in the same direction as that of the injury current, indicating increased positivity of the uninjured part. These experiments were carried out by means of a d'Arsonval galvanometer.

Gotch (7) in 1887, using a capillary electrometer, could not obtain this vagus effect, the position of the meniscus, upon vagus stimulation, remaining at the position obtaining during diastole. It was suggested by Burdon Sanderson (8), during a discussion of this subject, that the capillary electrometer was probably not sufficiently sensitive to detect such slight changes of potential as had been detected by Gaskell by means of a much more sensitive instrument.

Einthoven (9) in 1908 criticised Gaskell's results and doubted their accuracy because, by means of the string galvanometer he was unable to detect any changes of potential whatsoever. That Gaskell was correct was clearly demonstrated in 1911 by Meek and Eyster (10), who with an Edelmann galvanometer, using the tortoise heart prepared according to Gaskell's method, obtained uniformly positive results. Theirs was an exceptionally clear corroboration of the Gaskell phenomenon, as evidenced by a rapid deflection of the string and its slow return to the original position. If the heart were beating, this prolonged slow fall of the string to its original level would be cut short by the first beat following upon inhibition and the return of the base line to the zero position would be rapid. That this happens in the beating heart was shown by Samojloff (11), who used the same type of instrument. The hearts of decapitated frogs were utilized, an injury current was produced by the application of a drop of 1 per cent KCl to the apex of the heart, and leads taken, one from the apex the other from an uninjured part of the heart. A monophasic variation was obtained with each beat, and upon stimulation of the right vagus the zero line was deflected in the direction of the injury current; the deflection was slow and emphasis was laid upon the fact that the return of the string did not begin until a contraction supervened.

PART I

Electrical changes associated with the action of the vagi

The fundamental principle involved in determining these changes depends upon the following acceptation.

With a demarcation current or injury current. In normal muscle excitation is evidenced by an increased negativity of the part involved and electrodes can be so arranged that such negativity gives rise to an upstroke of the string of the galvanometer. When in the heart an injury current is produced, the injured surface becomes electrically negative to the uninjured part and the difference of potential thereby occasioned gives rise to a deflection of the string in a direction opposite to that which denotes excitation in normal muscle. A wave of excitation passing over such a field would produce at the positive or uninjured part a decrease of its positivity with respect to the injured spot and therefore cause a rise in the direction of, but smaller than, that due to a normal contraction. If the vagus nerve be stimulated, its effect is to reduce the condition of negativity and therefore relatively increase the positivity, the result being a deflection of the string in the same direction as that of the injury current.

In the normal or uninjured condition. To obtain monophasic variations from the action of the heart muscle, one electrode must be placed on the heart, the other on a part of the body wall sufficiently removed from the heart to allow of the activity of all parts of the heart muscle being marked by an upward deflection. If now the electrical changes of the heart, due to its activity, are not totally inhibited, these will show themselves as upstrokes of reduced amplitude, arising from a zero line at a lowered level.

It may be assumed that whatever occasions the beat produces a sudden catabolic change, a change dependent upon a previous building up of excitability or, to use Gaskell's term, a process of assimilation. There is no reason to suggest that such a process of assimilation should be of such a sudden nature as that of the catabolic discharge or dissimilation; the deflection caused by the one may be wholly different from that caused by the other, the factor chiefly concerned being that of velocity. It is supposed that these anabolic changes are inaugurated by vagus action and therefore that electrical stimulation of the vagus increasing these, it should be possible, using a galvanometer of sufficient sensitivity, to detect the changes in potential arising therefrom.

During inhibition the heart suffers an alteration of its excitability and its activity is depressed. It may therefore be feasible to accept the interpretation of Samojloff's curves, that contractions may be resumed at an increased level of anabolism, provided the process has reached completion and stopped, as otherwise it is difficult to conceive of contractions supervening during a process which is essentially of the nature of an inhibition. If the building up of excitability or the inhibitory process has not reached its maximal development, then, to explain the breaking through of heart beats, one must assume that the vagi and the contractions act upon different mechanisms in the cardiac muscle. Gaskell (12), McWilliam (13), (14), and Roy and Adami (15) state that excitability is diminished during inhibition but all that they can prove is, that the heart in inhibition was inexcitable, and that, during a period when it was establishing a necessary condition such that the subsequent stimulus should produce a contraction, that is, a condition of excitability. Therefore their diminished excitability is associated with what may be regarded as a refractory period of inhibition. Just as there is a refractory period in catabolism so one postulates a similar condition in anabolism. This would support the idea suggested that the upstroke is indicative of the true inhibitory period, i.e., the time till maximal deflection is reached, after which the excitability of the tissue is such that stimuli may be effective, which stimuli, however, may be delayed over a longer or shorter period, according to the degree of diminution of conductivity, which is a manifest effect of both vagi.

The results of the experimental work to which reference has just been made, demonstrate clearly the occurrence of electrical changes in the heart during vagus stimulation. These changes then may be employed to determine the distribution of the vagi in the heart, to demonstrate the action of these nerves upon its various parts and to decide if possible by what means vagal impulses are propagated. To do this a preparation of the whole and also of the partially split heart has been used.

Experiments carried out with the d'Arsonval galvanometer

From previous work done, using the string galvanometer for determining the electrical changes occurring in the heart upon vagus stimulation, it was found that, in the normally beating heart, the string galvanometer is too sensitive an instrument to withstand the action current of the heart, when the string is slackened to that extent which is necessary to give definite evidence of the positive variations. With sensitivities such that 1 m.v. gives deflections from 5 to 10 cm., the results are in many cases not convincing. It was therefore determined, seeing that it was impossible to carry out these experiments upon a quiescent heart, to utilize a very sensitive d'Arsonval galvanometer and, by means of a rheotome, to place it in circuit with the heart only, during the very brief period of its quiescence between beats.

Methods

The rheotome. This consisted of a brass segmented wheel having one continuous central contact and two, one on either side of the former, in which there was placed a different length of fiber, so that by adjustment of these, any length of non-conducting material could be readily obtained. Thus by using three contacts, the two external being connected, a definite period of time could be obtained during which the galvanometer could be thrown into the circuit. This period was chosen so that the ventricular, auricular and sinus effects could be eliminated. The circumference of the rheotome was 500 mm., the gap was, after experiment, cut down to 45 mm.

The quiescent period of the heart. To throw the galvanometer into circuit at this point of the cardiac cycle, a simple make and break device was arranged whereby the relaxation of the ventricle completed the circuit between six storage cells and a solenoid, which lifted the catch checking the rheotome wheel. This allowed the wheel to rotate, the retaining pawl being so placed that immediately it was lifted upon ventricular relaxation, the galvanometer was put in circuit with the heart. The rotation of the segmented wheel was so arranged by a switch upon the power table, that one revolution was just completed within the period of the cardiac cycle. The pawl, which was dropped upon contraction breaking the circuit, stopped the wheel for a very brief moment, depending upon slight variations in the heart rate.

It was found that in the majority of cases it was necessary, in order to obtain a quiescent period, to cool the heart, because, in a heart beating at the rate of thirty per minute, the sinus was in action sometimes during a ventricular contraction, or following so closely upon ventricular contraction that the rheotome method was rendered of no avail. The sinus was cooled by means of a blind perfusion cannula, through which was maintained a continuous flow of ice-cooled water of a temperature of about 10°C. The cooled point was maintained upon a definite spot on the sinus, a spot previously determined as being the seat of highest rhythmicity.

The sensitivity and calibration of the galvanometer. The d'Arsonval galvanometer used in these experiments was the type "R" of the Leeds & Northrup Company, which had a sensitivity of 5×10^{-10} amperes per mm. and a voltage sensitivity of 0.5 mm. per microvolt, with a period of 5 seconds. Calibration of the instrument, with the rheotome running, gave readings for 0.1 m.v. of 7.3 cm. in 5 minutes and a return to 0.5 cm. from zero in 6.0 minutes. Therefore a deflection of 7.3 cm. = 0.1 m.v. and is equal, without the rheotome to a deflection of 22 cm. From this it is seen that to obtain full values with the rheotome method, it would be necessary for the vagus effect to last 5 minutes. From the rate of rise of the curves and from their magnitude it will be seen that the "vagus" effect is a very marked one, is maintained and is dissipated quickly by subsquent beats.

A difficulty which arises with the rheotome method is, after vagus stimulation, to cut out the prolonged beats of the auricle which usually encroach upon the quiescent period of the heart, even abolishing it, and so cause a sudden return of the beam of light, which may reach its original position or pass beyond it in two or three steps. One can, however, by operating the rheotome with a key, cut out the auricular beats occurring immediately after inhibition, the solenoid circuit being broken upon the first sign of movement in the basal veins.

Compensation of the injury current. With a very slowly moving coil galvanometer, with the time of stimulus very short, namely 0.18 second when the rheotome was making thirty revolutions to the minute, the response to small currents may be so small as scarcely to be noticed. In compensating, therefore, one must accurately gauge the period of the heart cycle in which no electrical effects from auricular beat are allowed to encroach upon the period of quiescence. The sinus effect is so small that deflections caused thereby can be ignored, but small inclusions of auricular effects would simulate over-compensation. This, as well as the opposite effect of under-compensation, must be guarded against, because the latter, if not accurately gauged, will give deflections in excess of those due to vagus stimulation, since a deflection denoting an increased positivity is an extension of that of the injury current.

Type of reading obtained. It is essential, if maximal deflections are to be obtained, to stimulate the vagus, maintaining the quiescence of the heart, till there is no further increase in the amplitude of the deflection. This may necessitate a vagus stimulation up to from 60 to 80 seconds, although maximal deflections are usually obtained well within this period. The type of reading resulting from this method is shown on the tracings, these records having been made by a device of Gesell (16), in which the beam of light can be followed and the curve recorded upon a moving drum. The record is in the form of a series of steps which are of varying sizes and are in the form of curves as shown in several tracings. It was not practical to follow accurately these fine swinging movements of the beam of light. The first few initial steps are steep; they then rapidly become less and less in size till, at the plateau of the curve, the small pendular movements synchronous with each revolution of the rheotome only are in evidence. The plateau may be maintained for a longer or shorter period and is, unless the rheotome is controlled by hand, suddenly terminated by the first auricular contraction.

Type of reading without the rheotome. In the partially split heart, where the wave of contraction sweeps from right to left, it is of course possible to prevent auricular or ventricular effects of the side under observation, from affecting the galvanometer, but it has been found that after 2 or 3 hours, when the activity of the heart has become considerably lessened, the ventricle has little effect upon the galvanometer, the sinus none at all and the auricular contractions show as small deflections, with a total amplitude of from 1 to 1.5 cm. With such a weakly contracting heart, beating at about sixteen per minute, the mean of these deflections can be taken, because the beats are usually so weak that any cumulative effect takes a considerable time to show any alteration in the mean level of the beam of light. Thus the changes occurring upon vagus stimulation are quite easily discernible.

The whole heart

Table 1 shows that the right vagus is always markedly active upon the right auricle and in many cases very slightly less so upon the left auricle. The point of note with regard to the left auricle is that, in about a fourth of the cases, the right vagus is more effective than the left, and generally the left vagus is always less marked in its action upon the left auricle than is the right vagus upon the right auricle, while upon the right auricle the left vagus is, with three exceptions, decidedly weaker in action than either the right or the left vagus acting upon its respective side. The tracings reproduced here as figures 1 to 5, with attached explanatory notes, illustrate the basis upon which these conclusions rest. All were obtained through the d'Arsonval galvanometer.

TABLE 1

Results with the d'Arsonval galvanometer, with an injury current

	RIGHT VAGUS		LEFT VAGUS		REMARKS
	Right auricle	Left auricle	Left auricle	Right auricle	
	cm.	*cm.*	*cm.*	*cm.*	
1	4.5	3.5	5.5	3.0	Heart cooled. Rheotome rate 24 revolutions per minute
2	7.5	5.0	4.0	3.5	Heart quiet with muscarine; no rheotome
3	4.5	4.0			
4		10.5	5.5		Heart rate 16 per minute
		11.5	5.0		Temperature 10°C.
5		9.0	8.0		Without rheotome; heart quiescent; right auricle cut away
		8.5	9.5		
		8.5	11 0		
		9.0	9.5		
6	2.5			1.0	Gaskell's preparation; coronary vagus intact
	1.5			0.5	
7		0.8	1.0		Sinus cut off from right auricle; coronary vagus intact; left auricle quiet for short periods
		1.0	1.5		
8		7.8	8.8		Heart rate 15 per minute, temperature 10°C.
9		8.5	6.0		Heart rate 20 per minute; heart cooled
		6.5	5.5		
10	6.5	6.5	4.5	3.5	Heart rate 20 per minute; heart cooled
11	6.5	5.0	4.0	4.5	Heart rate 20 per minute; heart cooled
12	6.2	5.5	4.5	5.0	Heart rate 20 per minute; heart cooled
13	3.5	2.5	3.3	2.8	Heart rate 20 per minute; heart cooled
14	5.5	3.0	2.5	2.0	Heart rate 20 per minute; heart cooled
15	2.0		2.0		Heart completely split
16	3.5		2.0		Heart completely split
	2.0		1.0		
17	4.8		3.3		Heart completely split
	4.0		2.5		
18	5.5	5.5	4.2	4.0	Heart cooled
19	2.2	1.8	1.9	1.6	Heart cooled
20	2.5			2.0	Heart cooled
21	3.3	2.0	3.2	2.0	Heart cooled
22	2.1	1.0	2.2	0.6	Heart cooled
23	1.8	1.2	1.4	0.9	Heart cooled
24	1.6			0.8	Heart cooled
25	2.9	2.0	1.9	1.2	Without the rheotome
26	2.6	2.3	2.1	2.0	Without the rheotome

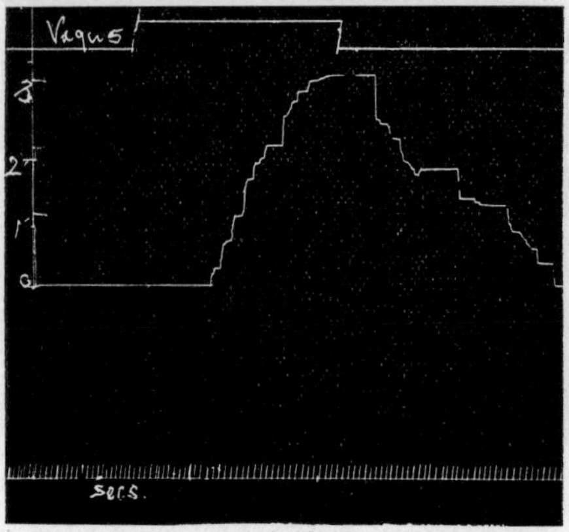

Fig. 1. Whole heart; right auricle, injury current; right vagus stimulation. This is a typical result of the rise and fall during the quiescent period of the heart. Here the only part of the curve not due to vagus activity is the first downstroke occasioned by the commencing auricular beat. The vagus was stimulated for 36 seconds, the deflection obtained being 3.2 cm.

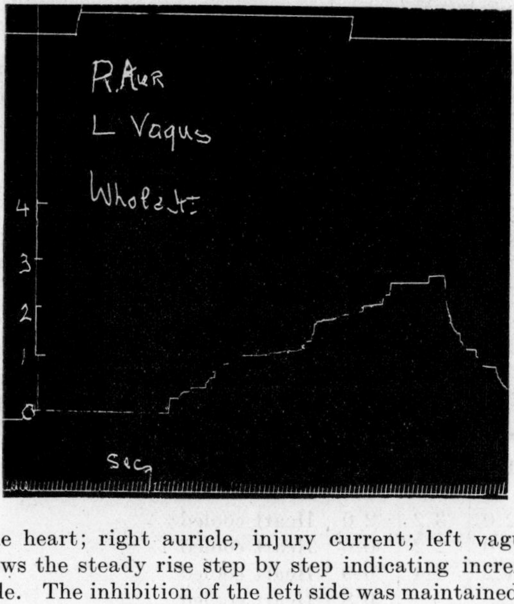

Fig. 2. Whole heart; right auricle, injury current; left vagus stimulation. This record shows the steady rise step by step indicating increased positivity of the left auricle. The inhibition of the left side was maintained for a period of 58 seconds, while stimulation of the vagus lasted for 60 seconds, producing a maximal deflection of 2.6 cm.

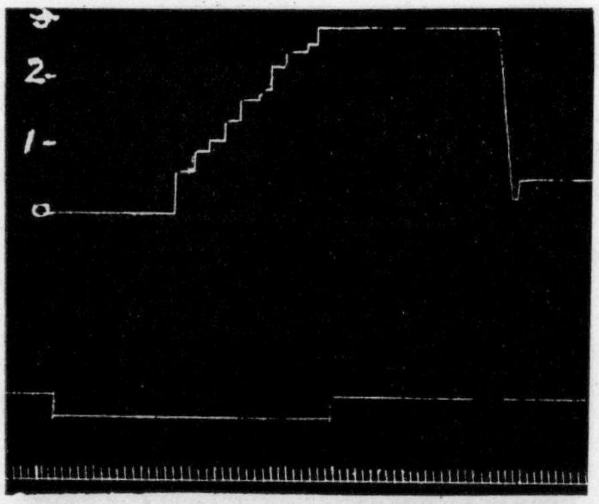

Fig. 3. Whole heart; left auricle, injury current; left vagus stimulation. This is a very good example of the steady step-like movement of the beam of light. The vagus was here stimulated for 36 seconds, the duration of the rise was 24 seconds and the maximal deflection was 2.7 cm.

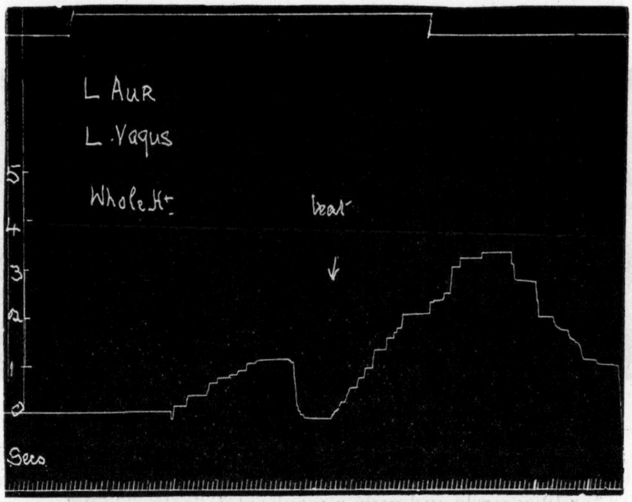

Fig. 4. Whole heart; left auricle, injury current; left vagus stimulation. This tracing is of interest in showing the effect of one beat of the heart breaking through in a short inhibition, which is then followed by a steeper and longer rise giving a total deflection of 3.2 cm. Stimulation of the vagus was continued for 64 seconds and there was no apparent sign of shifting of the electrodes or temporary stoppage of stimulation to account for the single beat.

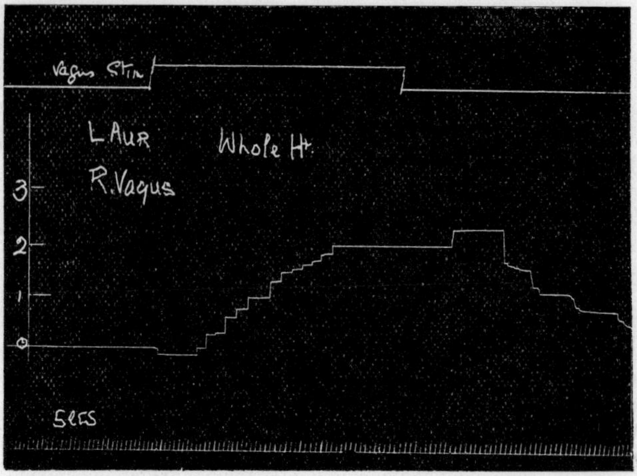

Fig. 5. Whole heart; left auricle, injury current; right vagus stimulation. The total deflection of 2.0 cm. was obtained in 30 seconds. The rise and fall are both typical, the fall below the original base line being due, probably, to a diminution of the demarcation current.

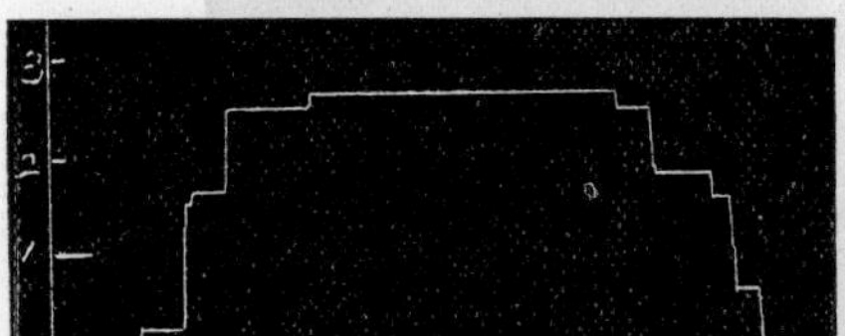

Fig. 6

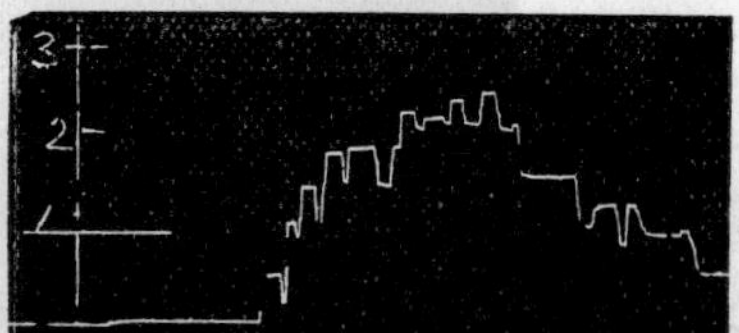

Fig. 7

Fig. 6. Partially split heart; rheotome; right auricle, injury current; right vagus stimulation. In this case the injury current was not compensated. The vagus acted for 12 seconds and gave a maximal deflection of 2.6 cm.

Fig. 7. Partially split heart; rheotome; right auricle, injury current; right vagus stimulation. Here the pendular movements were followed as accurately as possible. This record shows exactly the type of movement which is performed by the beam of light upon the scale, as the galvanometer responds to every brief impulse which it receives with each revolution of the rheotome. The inhibition was maintained for 26 seconds and the rise was completed in 15 seconds, the total deflection being 2.3 cm.

The partially split heart

With the rheotome. The type of results obtained from the partially split heart when the d'Arsonval galvanometer is put into circuit by means of the rheotome is seen in figures 6 and 7 and table 2, and described in the legends to the figures.

Types of deflections obtained without the rheotome. Using the rheotome, the results have, in the case of the action of the vagi on the contralateral sides of the heart, been invariably negative. In fact there is to be seen a slow movement of the beam of light in the direction opposite to that

TABLE 2

Results with the d'Arsonval galvanometer, with an injury current; split heart

	RIGHT VAGUS		LEFT VAGUS		REMARKS
	Right auricle	Left auricle	Left auricle	Right auricle	
	cm.	*cm.*	*cm.*	*cm.*	
1		3.0 2.0	1.5		These readings correspond with those obtained previous to sagittal section. Therefore (?) faulty section
2	4.5	0.0	6.5	0.0	
3	4.0	0.0	5.0	0.0	
4		0.5	3.5	0.0	
5		1.0	4.0	0.0	
6		0.0	5.0	0.0	
7	3.5	0.0	2.0	0.0	
8	3.0	0.0	2.5	0.0	
9	5.0	0.5	3.5	0.0	
10	2.0	0.0	2.0	0.0	
11	2.8	0.0	4.4	?	
12	3.3	0.0	3.2	0.0	

indicating a positive variation, due either to a diminution of the injury current or to the effects of weak contractions from parts of the heart, other than the auricle under obsevation. The best and most decisive results in the partially split heart have been obtained, without the rheotome, 2 to 4 hours after opening the pericardium and about ½ hour after making the sagittal section, because by this time the beats, running from right to left, have lost much of their vigor and rapidity.

The current of injury is not compensated and from the tracings (figs. 8 to 13) it will be seen, that the movements, due to contractions, are very small indeed.

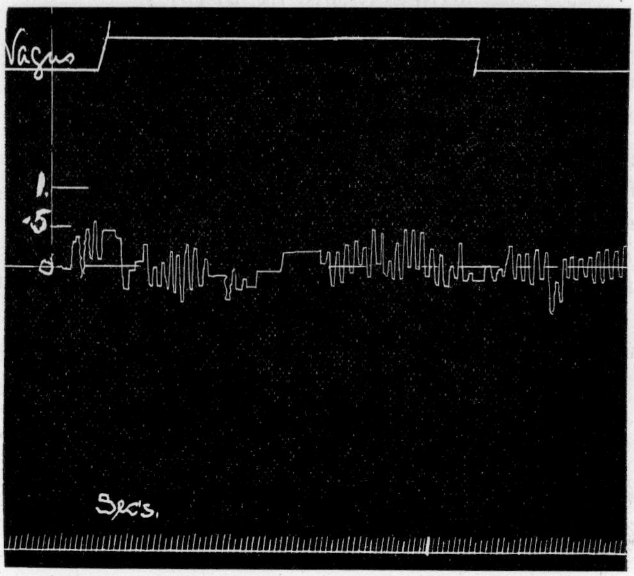

Fig. 8. Partially split heart; without rheotome; right auricle, injury current; left vagus stimulation. The movements of the beam of light were successfully followed in this case and it will be noted that there is neither inhibition of the right auricular beat nor alteration of the base line due to a stimulation of the left vagus lasting 52 seconds.

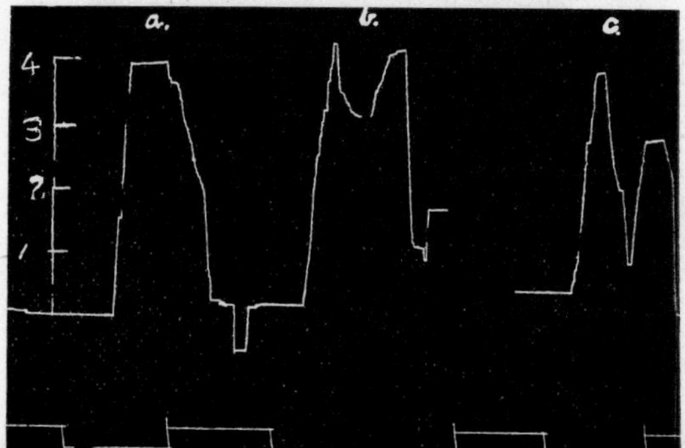

Fig. 9. *a*, *b*, *c*. Partially split heart; without rheotome; right auricle, injury current; right vagus stimulation. These three are typical of results obtained without the use of the rheotome. The height and rapidity of the deflections are comparable to those obtained by Gaskell, and show a definite electro-positive change. The deflections have a maximum of 3.8, 4.0 and 3.3 cm. with a time of 3.0, 4.0 and 3.5 seconds, respectively. The tendency, even in a weakly beating heart, for the "vagus" effect to be repeated, is seen in these tracings.

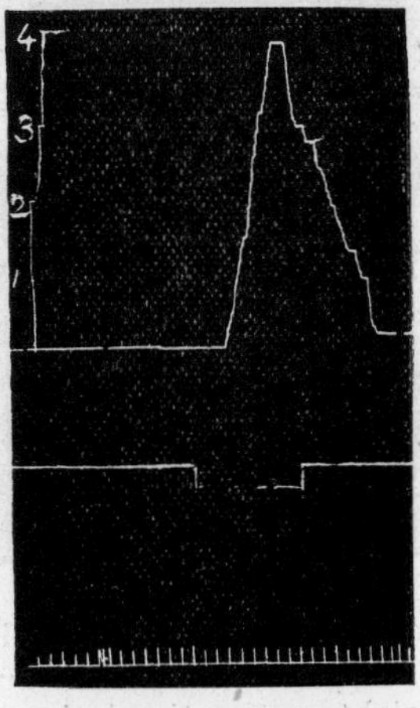

Fig. 10. Partially split heart; without rheotome; left auricle, injury current; left vagus stimulation. The action of the left vagus upon its own side, as graphically shown here, is similar to that obtaining in the whole heart. The response is rapid and the time taken to attain a maximal deflection of 3.8 cm. is 4.0 seconds.

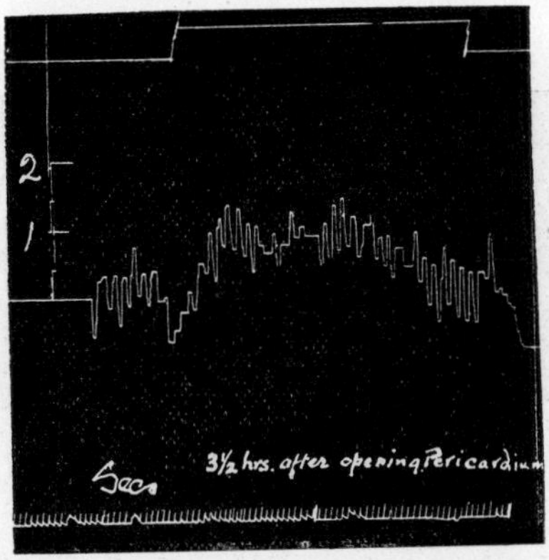

Fig. 11. Partially split heart; without rheotome; left auricle, injury current; left vagus stimulation. This shows activity of the left vagus upon the left auricle three and one-half hours from the commencement of the experiment. The pendular movements are due to the right auricular beats.

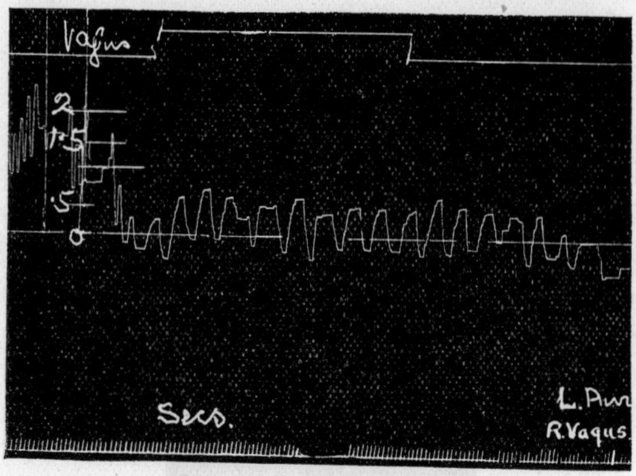

Fig. 12. Partially split heart; without rheotome; left auricle, injury current; right vagus stimulation. The survival of the left auricular contractions in the partially split heart, upon right vagus stimulation, is clearly seen here. The more rapid beats due to the right auricular rhythm are seen at the beginning of the tracing and their almost immediate inhibition upon right vagus stimulation is clearly shown, the slower left auricular rhythm remaining. That in this "ascidian" preparation the right vagus has no effect upon the uniform position of the base line, which is the mean of the auricular deflections, is demonstrated in this experiment, where the right vagus stimulation lasted for 58 seconds.

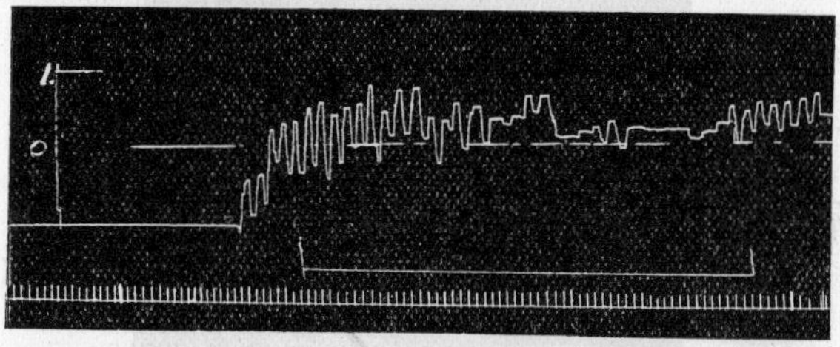

Fig. 13. Partially split heart; without rheotome; left auricle, injury current; right vagus stimulation. The fact that the right vagus has no action on the left auricle in the partially split heart is again shown here. After the deflection of the injury current was obtained, the movements of the beam of light were followed and the right vagus stimulated for 60 seconds. No alterations in the base line took place. The right auricular contractions were inhibited and the latter half of the tracing shows only the left auricular deflections, which with their slower rhythm come into evidence toward the end of the tracing. This occurs after a period of stand-still of very brief duration, during which time the inherent rhythmicity of the left auricle becomes established.

PART II

The quantitative effects of the vagi

The foregoing results with their demonstration of crossed vagal effects suggested a quantitative study of these.

To determine what quantitative vagus changes may occur on both sides of the heart the graphic method was used and the curves plotted on coördinate paper. As the rheotome revolved at a rate of either twenty or thirty revolutions per minute, and as both vagi, in most of the experiments, completely stopped the heart, the repeated contacts were made at regular intervals, thereby giving one a means of comparing the rate of deflection of the beam of light step by step, each step denoting a definite period of time during which the galvanometer was in circuit with the preparation. To arrive at some idea as to the intensity of the vagus action, it is necessary to compare the deflections, using as a standard a definite period of time during which the nerves are stimulated, and to do this the most convenient method is to take a number of steps or a number of revolutions of the rheotome, but not more than that required by the lowest curve to attain its maximal deflection. Without the rheotome, to take a definite height as a standard and compare the time required to reach it, would be admissible, but with the rheotome a standard height precludes any comparative conclusions, because it manifestly gives the slower effect the advantage of a greater number of contact periods.

The curves are plotted for the position of the beam of light either every 5 seconds or for every revolution of the rheotome; the abscissae denote time in seconds and the ordinates deflections in centimeters. The stimulation of the vagus, marked by a signal, was usually continued till the maximal effects were obtained, the time was recorded by a Jacquet chronograph and the records were made by Gesell's method already referred to. The results obtained can best be presented as descriptions of the curves.

Figure 14. Here the right vagus was stimulated for 36 seconds, and the electrical change commenced 13 seconds after stimulation began, and in 38 seconds the maximal deflection had been obtained. The curve both in its gradient and height is typical of the right vagus effect. In 15 seconds the beam of light had risen 2.9 cm., after which the change became more and more gradual, till 10 seconds later, the maximal deflection of 3.3 cm. was attained, where it was steady for 5 seconds and then fell at first quickly, later more and more slowly

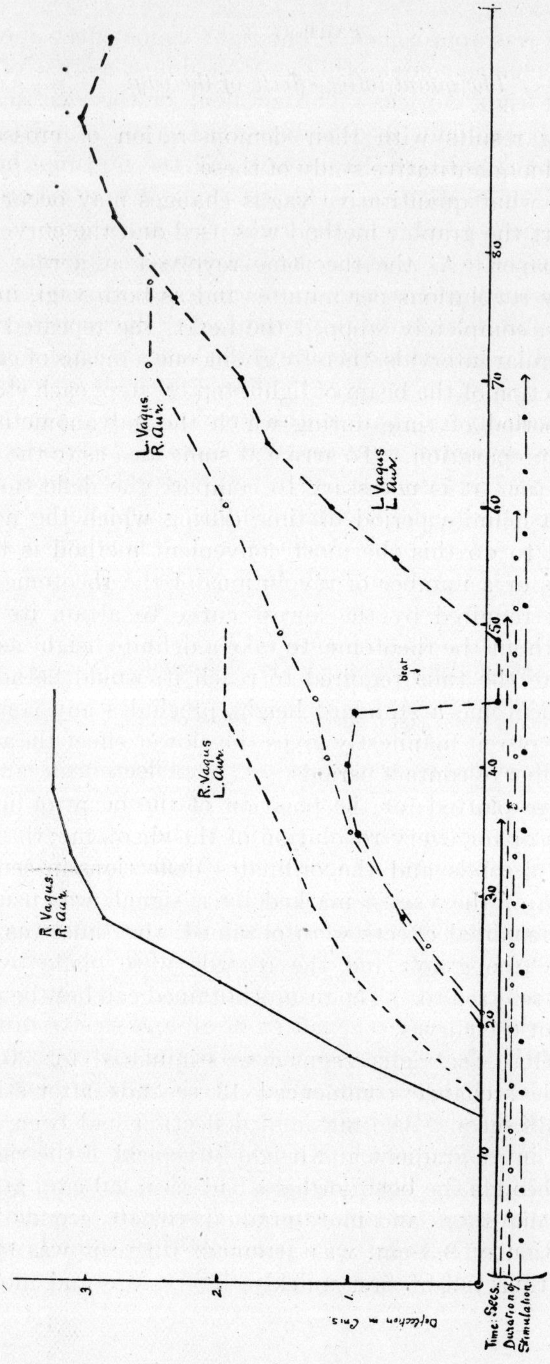
R. Vagus R. Aur.
L. Vagus R. Aur.
L. Vagus L. Aur.
R. Vagus L. Aur.
beat
Deflection in Cms.
Time: Secs.
Duration of Stimulation

Fig. 14

as the base line was approached. The right vagus effect upon the left auricle shows a change commencing as soon almost as that of the right vagus upon the right auricle. The gradient of the electrical change is less marked though quite as definite as that of the homolateral effect. The total stimulation lasted 52 seconds and the maximal height of 2 cm. was reached in 30 seconds. The left vagus in this experiment had a longer latent period but, like the right vagus, the period was practically the same for both sides, 20 and 21 seconds respectively. This is the case previously mentioned, in which a beat was interpolated 24 seconds after inhibition had been produced. The action current of the heart caused an immediate return of the beam of light to just below zero, inhibition was again produced and in 5 seconds it is evident and much more markedly so than in the previous rise. Comparing the left vagus effect upon the right and left auricles, it is seen from this figure that the second rise due to the left vagus is steeper than that of the left vagus effect upon the right auricle. This is the usual result obtained, though not without exception. The maximal rise and the time taken for each vagus on both sides of the heart are as follows:

	cm.
Right vagus acting upon right auricle for 18 seconds	3.3
Right vagus acting upon left auricle for 30 seconds	2.0
Left vagus acting upon left auricle for 40 seconds	3.2
Left vagus acting upon right auricle for 49 seconds	2.0

Figure 15. For comparative purposes the deflections occurring upon each of five consecutive revolutions of the rheotome are plotted. The marked ascendancy of the right vagus upon the right side of the heart is well shown; also from the graph of the second rise of the left vagus upon the left side, which has been traced in for comparison in the position of the original rise, it can be seen that the very definite effect upon its own side is greater than the right vagus effect upon the left both in maximal deflection and in rapidity of its rise. The left vagus action upon the right side is the least marked of all and this record, with the second curve of the electro-positive change of the left vagus transcribed, sums up very clearly the various effects occasioned by both vagi, each acting upon both sides of the heart.

Noting the deflections after five revolutions of the rheotome, the heart being inhibited by both vagi and the time interval between the stimuli being the same for all, namely, 2 seconds, the galvanometer being in circuit with the heart for a period of 0.18 second, we have the following results:

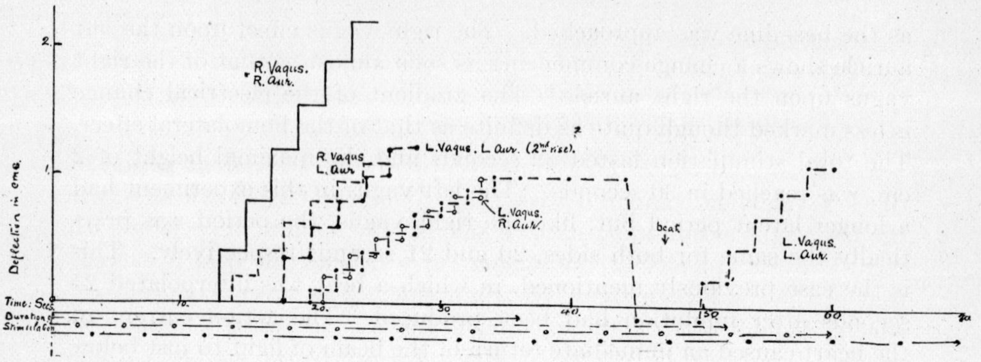

Fig. 15

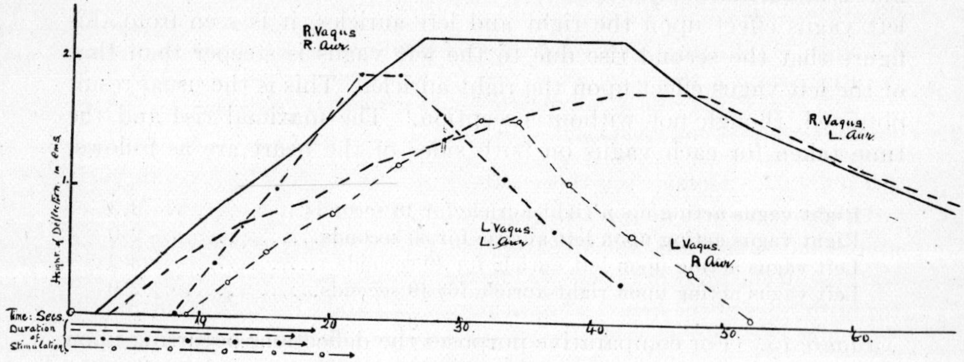

Fig. 16

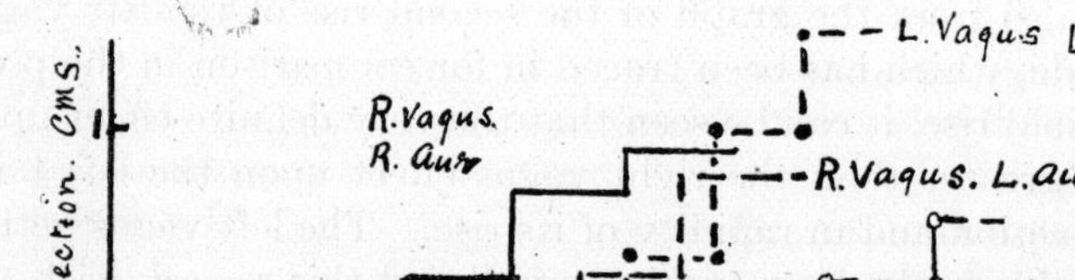

Fig. 17

	cm.
Right vagus acting upon right auricle	1.9
Right vagus acting upon left auricle	0.9
Left vagus acting upon left auricle	1.1
Left vagus acting upon right auricle	0.7

Figure 16. As in the preceding record, the greater latent period of the left vagus as compared with that of the right is shown and here the left vagus action upon its own side is very definite, especially with regard to the velocity of the change, in which in this case it exceeds that of the right vagus upon the right side. The slower contralateral effects, though of scarcely less magnitude are noteworthy, when one recalls what has been suggested with reference to the anatomical distribution of the vagi. The maximal deflections and the time taken for their completion are as follows:

	cm.
Right vagus acting upon right auricle for 25 seconds	2.2
Right vagus acting upon left auricle for 39 seconds	1.8
Left vagus acting upon left auricle for 14 seconds	1.9
Left vagus acting upon right auricle for 22 seconds	1.5

Figure 17. Comparing these effects in four steps of $2\frac{1}{2}$ seconds each, with the exception of the left vagus upon the left auricle in which each step equals 2 seconds, one sees from the record that they are very similar to those in the preceding case. The right vagus was very active, having, for both sides of the heart, a latent period of 2 and 3 seconds respectively. The difference in the velocity of the change effected is not so marked in the first 10 seconds as subsequently; yet the difference in the gradient of the activities of the left vagus upon the left and the right auricle is well marked. The latent period of the left vagus, while greater than that of the right, is, comparable to the right vagus, practically the same for both sides of the heart, namely 8 and 9 seconds for the left and right sides respectively. In this experiment the stimulation of the nerves lasted approximately 20 seconds in each case. The deflections from five revolutions of the rheotome were as follows:

	cm.
Right vagus acting upon right auricle	0.9
Right vagus acting upon left auricle	0.7
Left vagus acting upon left auricle	1.0
Left vagus acting upon right auricle	0.6

Figure 18. This is a record of the only instance in this series in which stimulation of the left vagus nerve did not stop the heart beat but caused a progressive slowing of the rate from 30 to 15 beats per minute

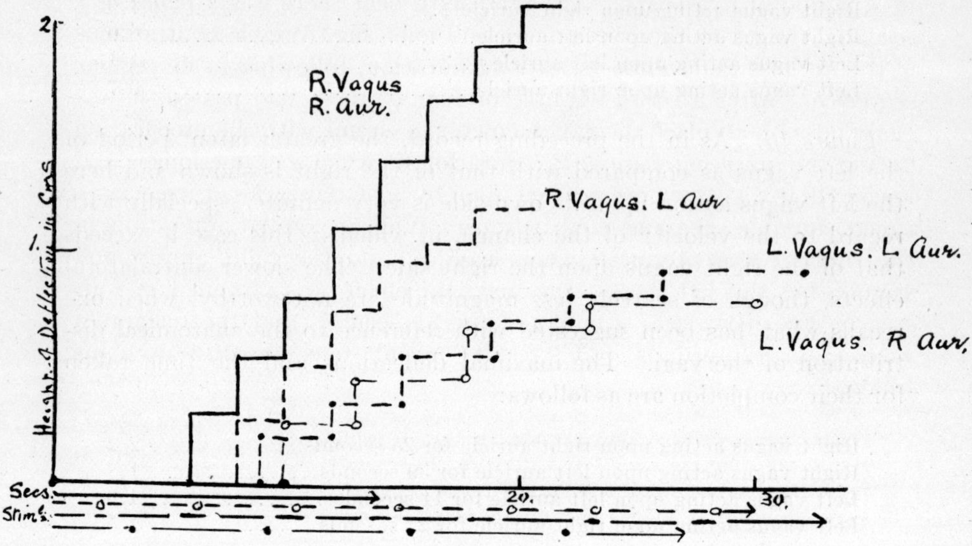
2.
1.
Height of Deflection in Cms
R.Vaqus
R. Aur.
R.Vaqus. L Aur
L.Vaqus. L. Aur.
L.Vaqus. R Aur.
Secs.
Stim's.
20.
30.

Fig. 18

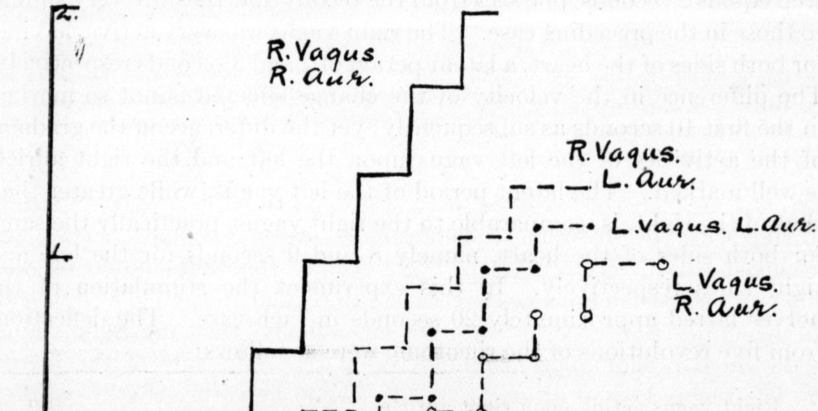
2.
1.
R.Vaqus
R. Aur.
R.Vaqus.
L. Aur.
L.Vaqus. L.Aur.
L.Vaqus.
R.Aur.
Secs.
10
20.

Fig. 19

in a period of five beats. After the sixth beat there was a pause of 7 seconds, the heart then became tumultuous, big, forcible contractions of the auricles and ventricle, of long duration, following in no regular sequence. After a series of three or four of these had passed, it was again possible to place the galvanometer in circuit with the preparation during the quiescent period, the duration of which became longer and longer till it was again encroached upon by a similar series of irregularly timed, forcible, heaving contractions. While a similar alteration in the rhythm was produced when leading from the right auricle and stimulating the left vagus, the maximal effect was obtained in four steps. The nerve was stimulated for 31 seconds and the maximum reached in 12 seconds. The results for all four activities were as follows:

	cm.
Right vagus acting upon right auricle for 14 seconds	2.1
Right vagus acting upon left auricle for 10 seconds	1.2
Left vagus acting upon left auricle for 32 seconds	1.6
Left vagus acting upon right auricle for 12 seconds	0.8

Figure 19. These curves denote the positive variation obtained with six revolutions of the rheotome, this number being that taken by the smallest curve, left vagus acting upon right auricle, to reach its maximal height.

	cm.
Right vagus acting upon right auricle	2.0
Right vagus acting upon left auricle	1.3
Left vagus acting upon left auricle	1.2
Left vagus acting upon right auricle	1.0

Figure 20. In this case the maximal deflections were recorded step by step with the rheotome revolving once every 2 seconds. The vagi produced complete stoppage of the heart in the times noted on the chart and the deflections were remarkably regular in their rise and bear out what previous records have shown, namely, that the right vagus is the most predominant in action upon the right side of the heart, the left vagus less so on the left side, while here the usually parallel effects of the right vagus upon the left auricle and the left vagus upon its own side, are clearly demonstrated. The deflections for fifteen steps, that is for 30 seconds, were as follows:

	cm.
Right vagus acting upon right auricle	4.5
Right vagus acting upon left auricle	3.6
Left vagus acting upon left auricle	3.6
Right vagus acting upon right auricle	2.7

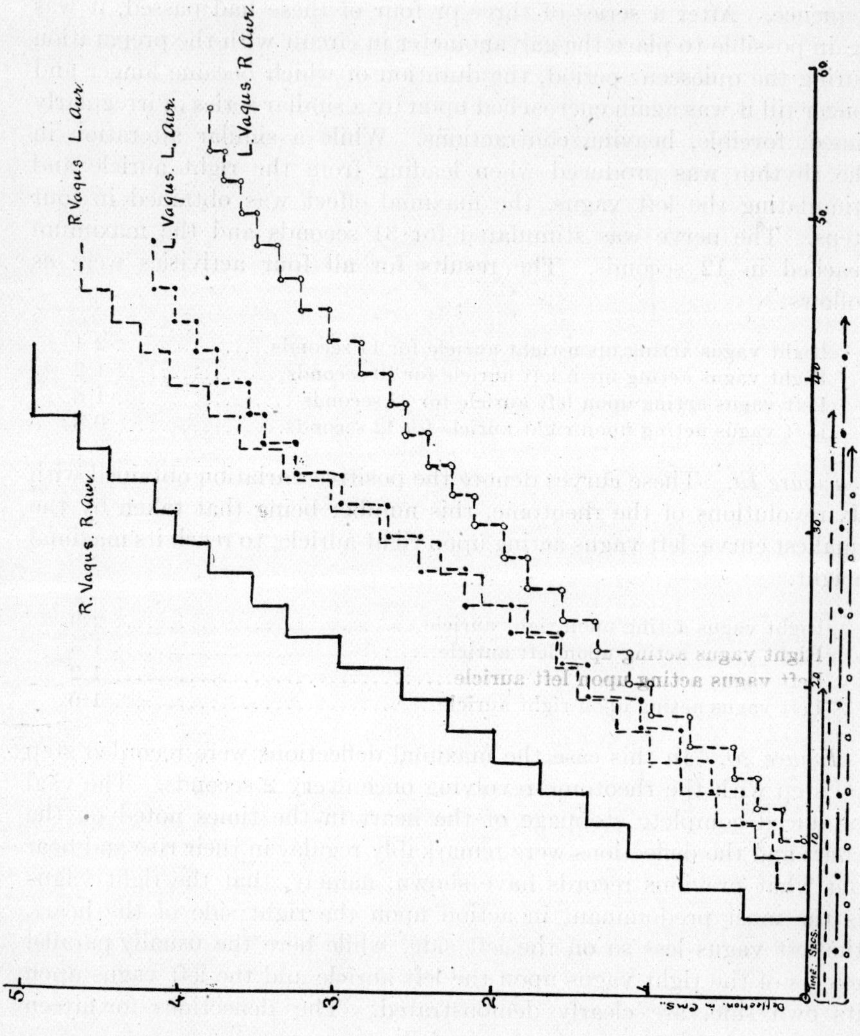
R. Vagus. R. Aur.
R Vagus L. Aur.
L. Vagus L. Aur.
L. Vagus R Aur
Deflection in cms.
Time Secs.
5
4
3
2
1
10
20
30
40
50
60

Fig. 20

Results without the rheotome. Figures 21 and 22. These records are given as typical of the curves obtained with a practically quiescent heart, in which deflections caused by electrical changes of weak contractions could be disregarded. These results are from hearts which have been bloodless for from 3 to 4 hours. The curves are plotted for the position of the beam of light every second and the duration of the stimulus is practically 10 seconds in all cases. One again sees the dominant effect of the right vagus, with a latent period of 5 seconds and

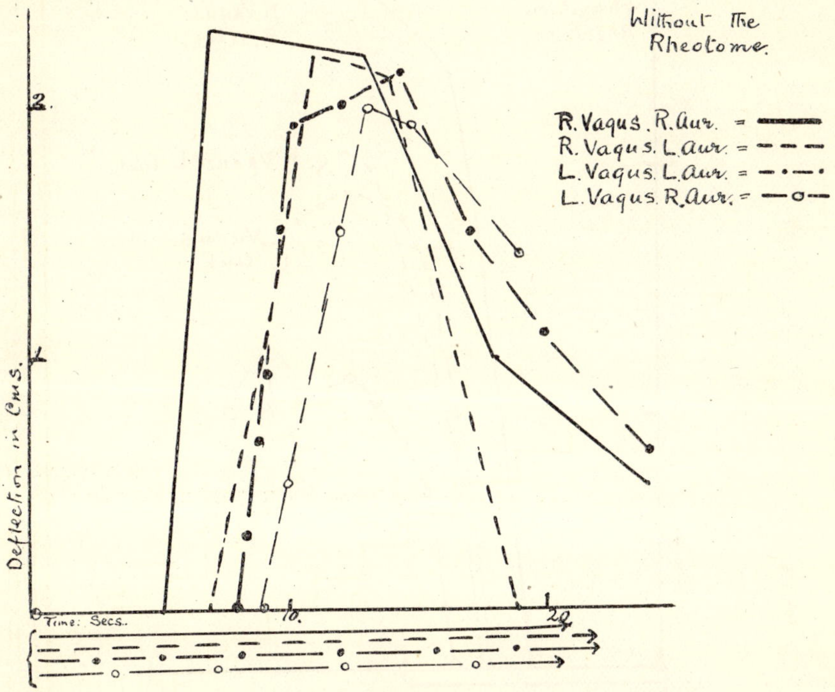

Fig. 21

7 seconds for the respective sides of the heart in both cases. The maximal height is 2.6 cm. and 2.9 cm. respectively. The right vagus effects upon the left auricles are remarkably alike in both cases, the time taken to reach the maximum being 6 and 5 seconds, and the maximal height attained being 2.3 and 2.0 cm., respectively. Such an effect, compared with that obtained from the left vagus acting upon the left auricle, shows the resemblance between the crossed effects of the right vagus and the homolateral effects of the left vagus, with regard to the elec-

trical changes they produce in the left auricle. The rapidity with which the change is produced in the left auricle is greater for the left than for the right vagus. From the latent periods and the heights of the curves, one sees that the crossed effects are slightly less rapid in their inception and in the velocity of their action. It is possible that the

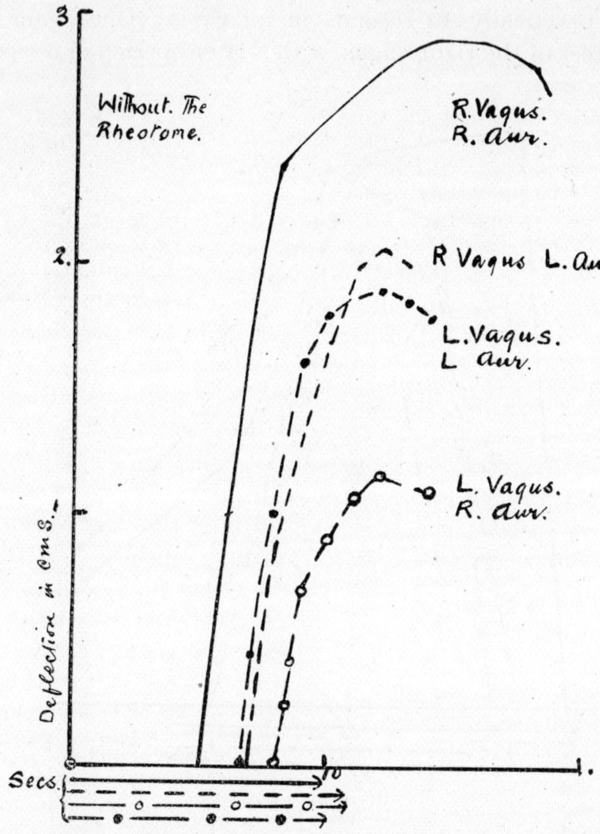

Fig. 22

latent period, in obtaining crossed effects, is directly proportional to the degree of the contralateral distribution of the vagi. From the usually short lapse of time, 1 to 3 seconds, occurring in the production of the crossed effects, either by the right or the left vagus nerves, one must conclude that, anatomically, the crossed distribution of each vagus may, in many instances, be a liberal one.

With regard to the quantitative effects of the vagi upon the whole heart, the results may be summed up in a table of the various effects reduced to a percentage of the sum total:

Right vagus acting upon right auricle	40.9	26.6	35.0	36.3	31.2	30.0
Right vagus acting upon left auricle	20.4	21.9	21.4	23.6	25.0	24.3
Left vagus acting upon left auricle	23.6	30.1	29.5	21.8	25.0	25.7
Left vagus acting upon right auricle	15.0	20.3	14.2	18.1	18.7	20.3

This gives an average result of:

Right vagus acting upon right auricle	30 to 40
Right vagus acting upon left auricle	20 to 25
Left vagus acting upon left auricle	25 to 30
Left vagus acting upon right auricle	15 to 20

DISCUSSION

The experiments carried out with the d'Arsonval galvanometer described in the first part of this paper, corroborate the work of previous investigators with regard to the presence, in the heart muscle, of electrical changes, which are brought about by stimulation of the vagus nerves. It has been shown that these changes can be produced by each vagus nerve acting upon the opposite side of the heart. From the figures quoted in table 1 and from records shown of experiments upon the whole heart, it is evident that the action of the vagi is not mainly homolateral. As far as the vagus effect is distinguished by an increased positivity, by a change in potential, one must conclude that each vagus nerve exerts its greatest effect upon its own side, and upon the opposite side an effect which, generally, is definitely less than, but may, in the case of the right vagus, be almost as great as that of its homolateral action. In comparing the two vagi, it is seen from these results that the right vagus produces a much greater contralateral effect than does the left; that the effect of the right vagus upon the left auricle is generally less than that of the left vagus upon its own side. In only two cases did the left vagus acting upon the right auricle produce an effect greater than that of the homolateral action of the right vagus. It is seen that the contralateral effect of the left vagus is undoubtedly the weakest or least marked of all four activities studied.

These results do not substantiate Garrey's conclusions with regard to the preponderantly homolateral effects of the vagi. There may be a tendency to over-emphasize the homolateral view. In Garrey's case this may have resulted from his assumption that the beat originated in the right caval vein and from the fact that he could find no chronotropic effects thereon with left vagus stimulation. He states "that the left vagus is less effective upon the normal rhythm of the heart than the right vagus, due to the fact that it does not innervate the right basal vein;" and again he states "that crossed effects can be obtained, in some cases even to chronotropic effects, on the right veins by action of the left vagus."

If the left vagus can affect the center of rhythmicity in the left side of the partially split heart, is it not, from these results and from Garrey's suggestion, justifiable to conclude that the left vagus can or may, as a usual function, affect the pace-maker or center or centers of rhythmicity in the right auricle in the whole heart?

That such may be the case, more or less marked according to the degree of crossed distribution, is strongly suggested by the results recorded above, in which, in almost every case, left vagus stimulation quickly arrested the beat of the heart. As there were no evidences of block one must conclude that this is due to an effect upon the center of rhythmicity and that to stop the heart the vagus must act upon all heart tissue which is inherently rhythmical. Thus only, in those cases of complete stoppage, can left vagus inhibition be explained and this point of view demands a contralateral distribution of both vagi. With regard to the partially split heart, it is shown from the figures in table 2 and from the tracings briefly referred to, that here only are the effects of the vagi strictly confined to their respective sides.

This raises the question of the conduction of crossed effects which, according to Garrey, occurs by means of nerve. In the turtle, the crossed effects obtained in the whole heart must pass to the auricle by way of nerve fibers located in the tissue of the sinus. If the vagus effects were the result of a general conduction by means of both muscle and nerve, then, seeing that the muscle wave spreads around the sagittally split heart from right to left, there should be no reason why the vagus effect should not so pass.

In the partially split heart right vagus stimulation stops the whole initially, then the left sinus assumes a controlling rhythmicity for the left side, and if the right side be maintained in inhibition for some time, the beats originating in the left sinus will travel from left to right, but they will not pass from the ventricle to the right auricle. The passage of such contraction impulses shows that no vagus control is exercised upon the ventricle in the turtle. Also, it must be concluded that in the partially split heart no vagus effects can be transmitted across from the right to the left side of the heart, since there is no alteration in the electrical potential of the injury current of the left auricle when the right vagus is stimulated.

In concluding that the ventricular muscle of the turtle plays no part in transmitting vagus effects, it must be borne in mind that the reason may not necessarily lie in the ventricular tissue but in the inability of junctional tissue to transmit these effects. That vagus effects do not spread by way of the ventricle would not preclude such spread from right auricle to left auricle through cardiac tissue proper. Erlanger (17) and Erlanger and Hirschfelder (18) have shown that, after clamping the bundle of His in the dog and thereby producing partial or complete heart block, it is possible to demonstrate some action, though slight, of the vagus upon the ventricle. This goes to show that vagal impulses to some extent travel by routes other than those which subserve normal physiological conduction of the cardiac impulses.

That these impulses may not be associated with ordinary nerve fibers is suggested by the work of Meek and Leaper (19), who show that conduction in the heart, either by nerve fiber or by skeletal muscle, manifests no marked difference in the degree of compression necessary to destroy it. Garrey, in a study of the dissociation of inhibitory nerve impulses, states, "that if normal physiological conduction from sinus to auricle proceeds along nervous paths the blocking of these paths should at the same time block other nervous paths, including all vagus fibers which pass to the auricle through the clamped area, and through this area only." He shows that this is not the case; that compression sufficient to establish complete sino-auricular block, may not interfere with the passage of vagus impulses. This would indicate that if vagus effects are to be transmitted they must pass by way of tissue peculiar to them. That such effects do not spread through muscle tissue is proved by the larger effect upon the corresponding side in the whole heart. This rules out the idea that junctional tissue may be the cause of a non-transmittal of these effects in the partially split heart.

From these results one is led to the conclusion that there is no case for the spread of vagus effects by non-specific tissue, either muscular or nervous, but only by tissue hypothetically peculiar to vagus conduction. It would seem, from the results both in the normal and partially split heart, that for crossed effects in the whole heart, it is not a case of strong or weak stimuli affecting muscle fibers or nerve network, but rather a case of stimuli efficient enough to pass along paths of vagus conduction, the degree to which contralateral function is served depending upon the richness of the anatomical distribution.

With regard to the distribution of both vagi, evidence for a rich contralateral supply to the heart is borne out by this work and in support of this view reference has been made to the work of Cohn and of Robinson. The latter investigator showed that in gauging the action of the vagi upon cardiac conductivity, the rate of the heart had to be taken into account. From this it is seen that, in judging both of chronotropic and dromotropic effects of the vagi, the factor of greatest importance is the action of both right and left vagus nerves upon the center or centers of rhythmicity.

If it is assumed that the vagus acts by reducing the general reactivity of the tissue it happens to innervate directly, then the observation frequently recorded in the literature that left vagus stimulation often blocks the transmission of the contraction wave may be accounted for upon the basis of differences in the distribution of the two vagi with respect to the pacemaker. If in a given case the left vagus innervates the whole of the base of the heart excepting the pace-maker while the right vagus acts upon both parts equally, then stimulation of the left vagus will reduce reactivity and consequently the conductivity of the auricles, but not the rate of impulse initiation. The result would simulate the diminution in conductivity. Stimulation of the right vagus would produce the same reduction in reactivity and of the same parts but at the same time would slow impulse initiation. As a result the interval between successive impulse conductions might become long enough to permit the subjacent tissues, despite their lowered reactivity, to carry every impulse that came from the pace-maker. If the beats could be maintained at their original rate while the right vagus was being stimulated, a diminution of conductivity similar to that produced by left vagus stimulation would become manifest.

CONCLUSIONS

It is concluded that the positive variation of the demarcation current that develops during vagus stimulation is a phenomenon, not due to, although usually associated with, stoppage of the heart. This is shown by the facts:

1. That in the quiescent heart the electro-positive change is obtained.
2. That no electro-positive change is obtained, when in the partially split heart the left auricle temporarily stops beating upon right vagus stimulation.

Thus, looking at the question from two totally different standpoints, we have clear evidence that the electrical change indicative of inhibition is not occasioned merely by the cessation of muscle activity.

It is also concluded that in the turtle the distribution of the vagi through the base of the heart is bilateral, but is not uniform in all parts. In general the relative intensity of action is as follows: Right vagus on right auricle > right vagus on left auricle = left vagus on left auricle > left vagus on right auricle.

The greater tendency, noted in the literature, of stimulation of the left vagus to produce block is not necessarily due to a selective action of this nerve upon the conducting system; the result can be explained quite as well through the relatively slight action of the left nerve upon the pace-maker, which is located on the right side of the heart, while the reactivity of the remainder of the heart is reduced.

I am greatly indebted to Doctor Erlanger for his continued interest in this problem, and for much helpful and very suggestive criticism.

BIBLIOGRAPHY

(1) Garrey: This Journal, 1911, xxviii, 330.
(2) Robinson and Draper: Journ. Exper. Med., 1912, xv, 14.
(3) Rothberger abd Winterberg: Arch. f. d. gesammt. Physiol., 1911, cxli, 343.
(4) Cohn: Journ. Exper. Med., 1912, xv, 49.
(5) Robinson: Journ. Exper. Med., 1916, xxiv, 605.
(6) Gaskell: Journ. Physiol., 1887, viii, 404; also Ludwig's Festschrift, "Beiträge zur Physiol.," 1887, 114.
(7) Gotch: Journ. Physiol., Proc., 1887, viii, 24.
(8) Burdon: Journ. Physiol., Proc., 1887, viii, 26.
(9) Einthoven: Arch. f. d. gesammt. Physiol., 1908, cxxii, 517.
(10) Meek and Eyster: This Journal, 1912, xxx, 271.
(11) Samojloff: Zentralbl. f. Physiol., 1913, xxvii, 575.
(12) Gaskell: Phil. Trans. Roy. Soc., London, 1882, clxxiii, 993.
(13) McWilliam: Journ. Physiol., 1885, vi, 192.
(14) McWilliam: Journ. Physiol., 1888, ix, 167, 345.
(15) Roy and Adami: Phil. Trans. Roy. Soc., London, 1892, clxxxiii, 199.
(16) Gesell: This Journal, 1919, xlvii, 1.
(17) Erlanger: This Journal, 1909, xxv, p. xvi.
(18) Erlanger and Hirschfelder: This Journal, 1906, xv, 165.
(19) Meek and Leaper: This Journal, 1911, xxvii, 308.
(20) Garrey: This Journal, 1911, xxviii, 249.

THE INFLUENCE OF GLANDS WITH INTERNAL SECRETIONS ON THE RESPIRATORY EXCHANGE

I. Effect of the Subcutaneous Injection of Adrenalin on Normal and Thyroidectomized Rabbits

DAVID MARINE and C. H. LENHART

From the Department of Experimental Medicine and the Department of Surgery, Western Reserve University, Cleveland

Received for publication July 29, 1920

The demonstration by Asher and Flack (1), (2), (3) that stimulation of the laryngeal nerves in rabbits with intact thyroids increases and prolongs the rise in blood pressure following the intravenous injection of a given amount of adrenalin has provided the first concrete evidence of a thyroid-adrenal relationship. The Goetsch (4) test in exophthalmic goiter and in clinical conditions resembling exophthalmic goiter, as tuberculosis, cardiac neuroses, etc., is a practical diagnostic application of Asher and Flack's original observations. The effect of the subcutaneous injection of adrenalin on the respiratory exchange in man was studied in 1912 by Fuchs and Roth (5), who found a slight increase in the oxygen intake and carbon dioxide output which they looked upon as negligible and an increase in the respiratory quotient. Later work by Bernstein (6), by Peabody and his co-workers (7), by Tompkins, Sturgis and Wearn (8) and by Sandiford (9) have clearly established that in normal men adrenalin injected subcutaneously in 0.5 cc. to 1.0 cc. (1–1000) doses causes an increase in the respiratory exchange. The studies of Tompkins, Sturgis and Wearn and of Sandiford are the more recent and extensive. The former, working with soldiers, were able to demonstrate the increase in twenty-seven of thirty-four cases. The latter studied forty-six cases including exophthalmic goiter, simple goiter, myxedema, Addison's disease and four normals. She concludes that the subcutaneous injection of 0.5 cc. 1–1000 adrenalin invariably causes an increase in the oxygen intake and the carbon dioxide output.

La Franca (10), working with dogs, found that phloridzin causes a marked decrease in the respiratory exchange, while adrenalin causes a marked increase both in the respiratory quotient and in the oxygen consumption. Hari (11) using curarized dogs and injecting adrenalin intraperitoneally observed a decrease in the oxygen consumption and a rise in the respiratory quotient. Lusk and Riche (12), studying the effect of adrenalin on the power of the animal to oxidize glucose, noted an increase in the respiratory exchange in two normal dogs. Wilenko (13) used urethanized rabbits and found no change in the respiratory quotient or the oxygen consumption.

In view of Asher and Flack's observation it has seemed to us of importance to compare the effects of the subcutaneous injection of adrenalin in normal and thyroidectomized animals and also to compare the effect on the same animal before and after thyroidectomy. The results of these experiments are given in the following pages.

Method. Rabbits have been used because it is possible to remove the thyroids without any physical interference with the function of the iind parathyroids and also because accessory thyroid tissue is less common than in dogs, cats or rats. We have used a Haldane (14) apparatus, modified by substituting Williams' absorbers and a motor-driven pump. This apparatus is readily adapted for the use of rabbits and is simple and accurate.

All rabbits were deprived of food for 15 to 16 hours before beginning the experiments. The adrenalin (P. D. Co., 1–1000) was not assayed. The dose was arbitrarily fixed at 0.5 cc. per kilogram. Each experiment consists of an hour period although in most instances the observations were repeated two or more times without interruption. This makes it possible to compare the results by hours or by longer units of time.

This study includes observations on six rabbits which had been kept in the laboratory for several months under the same conditions before being used in this work. Three rabbits (R 3–203, –205, –206) were "normal." Three had had thyroidectomies—one (3–208) 51 days before beginning the studies and two (3–201 and 3–204) during the studies. The detail figures obtained in each of these animals have been arranged in tables 2, 3, 4, 5, 6 and 7. For the brief discussion which follows, only the figures for the O_2 consumption per gram of body weight per hour will be considered. These have been averaged and arranged in table 1.

a. Controls (*before administration of adrenalin*). The average O_2 consumption for the five rabbits with intact thyroids was 0.607, 0.572, 0.524, 0.477 and 0.436 gram per gram of body weight per hour.

before the administration of adrenalin. These figures might be termed the basal rates and show the usual "normal" variations for different animals though the rate is relatively constant for a given animal. Rabbit 3–208 which had been thyroidectomized 51 days before beginning the observation shows the ordinary effect of thyroidectomy on metabolism first described in man by Magnus-Levy (16).

With rabbits 201 and 204 it is possible to compare the O_2 consumption before and after thyroidectomy. The figures given in table 1 represent the first series of observations before thyroidectomy and the last after thyroidectomy (30 and 31 days). The decrease in O_2 consumption following thyroidectomy is striking. Reference to tables 6

TABLE 1

Average O_2 consumption per gram per hour in cubic centimeters

RABBIT NUMBER	CONDITION OF THYROID	CONTROL	FIRST HOUR AFTER 0.5 CC. ADRENALIN PER KILOGRAM	SECOND HOUR AFTER 0.5 CC. ADRENALIN PER KILOGRAM	THIRD HOUR AFTER 0.5 CC. ADRENALIN PER KILOGRAM	FOURTH HOUR AFTER 0.5 CC. ADRENALIN PER KILOGRAM	
203	Intact	0.607	0.637	0.697	0.789	0.680	0.708
205	Intact	0.436	0.528	0.549	0.595		
206	Intact	0.524	0.545	0.605			
208	Thyroidectomy 51 days	0.355	0.344	0.417	0.433	0.457	
204	Intact	0.477	0.651	0.610	0.530		
204	30 days after thyroidectomy	0.348	0.326	0.498	0.366		
201	Intact	0.572	0.530	0.681			
201	31 days after thyroidectomy	0.402	0.396	0.502	0.480		

and 7 show that the decrease in the rate of metabolism following thyroidectomy is very slow—several days being required before the change becomes manifest. This may be due to the fact that the thyroid hormone is very stable and is normally needed in exceedingly small amounts.

These observations are in harmony with the clinical observations that the onset of symptoms of myxedema in thyroidectomized animals is slow and also that there is usually a latent period of 24 to 48 hours following the feeding of desiccated thyroid before an increase in the metabolic rate can be demonstrated. They are at variance with the effects on blood pressure as reported by Asher and Flack (loc. cit.) and by Levy (17). These authors showed that in acute experiments

TABLE 2

Rabbit 3–203. Thyroids intact

EXPERIMENT NUMBER	DATE	WEIGHT	DURATION	O_2 INTAKE	CO_2 OUTPUT	$\frac{CO_2}{O_2}$	O_2 PER GRAM PER HOUR	ADDITIONAL DATA
		grams		*grams*	*grams*		*cc.*	
1	5– 4–20	2125	3:20– 4:20 p.m.	1.570	2.210	1.02	0.516	Normal control
8	5– 6–20	2095	3:10– 4:10 p.m.	1.670	2.090	0.91	0.557	Normal control—1st hour
9	5– 6–20	2095	4:18– 5:18 p.m.	2.000	2.350	0.85	0.667	Normal control—2nd hour
19	5–11–20	2080	10:04–11:04 a.m.	2.170	1.990	0.67	0.729	Normal control—1st hour
20	5–11–20	2080	11:08–12:08 p.m.	2.170	2.090	0.70	0.740	Normal control—2nd hour
34	5–15–20	2025	10:36–11:36 a.m.	1.550	1.790	0.84	0.565	Normal control
36	5–15–20	2025	2:55– 3:55 p.m.	2.000	2.650	0.96	0.690	2:48 p.m. Injected subcutaneously 0.5 cc. adrenalin (P. D. Co. 1:1000) per kilogram
42	5–18–20	2030	9:35–10:35 a.m.	1.620	1.950	0.87	0.558	Normal control—1st hour
43	5–18–20	2030	10:35–11:35 a.m.	1.650	1.680	0.73	0.568	Normal control—2nd hour
44	5–18–20	2025	1:15– 2:15 p.m.	1.860	2.440	0.95	0.642	1st hour following adrenalin injection. 1:05 p.m. Injected subcutaneously 0.5 cc. adrenalin (P. D. Co. 1:1000) per kilogram
45	5–18–20	2025	2:15– 3:15 p.m.	2.330	2.720	0.85	0.804	2nd hour following adrenalin injection
46	5–18–20	2025	3:15– 4:15 p.m.	2.350	2.410	0.75	0.811	3rd hour following adrenalin injection
47	5–18–20	2025	4:15– 5:15 p.m.	1.970	2.300	0.85	0.680	4th hour following adrenalin injection
48	5–18–20	2025	5:15– 6:15 p.m.	2.050	2.140	0.76	0.708	5th hour following adrenalin injection
77	6– 4–20	2100	10:55–11:55 a.m.	1.710	1.870	0.79	0.569	Normal control
78	6– 4–20	2095	1:40– 2:40 p.m.	1.740	2.140	0.89	0.580	1.35 p.m. Injected subcutaneously 1.05 cc. adrenalin (P. D. Co. 1:1000) per kilogram. 1st hour following adrenalin injection
79	6– 4–20	2095	2:40– 3:40 p.m.	1.770	2.110	0.85	0.590	2nd hour following adrenalin injection
80	6– 4–20	2095	3:40– 4:40 p.m.	2.300	2.800	0.88	0.768	3rd hour following adrenalin injection

TABLE 3

Rabbit 3–205. Thyroids intact

EXPERIMENT NUMBER	DATE	WEIGHT	DURATION	O_2 INTAKE	CO_2 OUTPUT	$\frac{CO_2}{O_2}$	O_2 PER GRAM PER HOUR	ADDITIONAL DATA
		grams		*grams*	*grams*		*cc.*	
92	6–11–20	2180	9:30–10:30 a.m.	1.320	1.540	0.85	0.423	Control
93	6–11–20	2180	10:30–11:30 a.m.	1.330	1.370	0.75	0.426	Control
94	6–11–20	2170	2:50– 3:50 p.m.	1.750	2.400	0.99	0.564	2:42 p.m. Injected subcutaneously 0.5 cc. adrenalin (P. D. Co. 1:1000) per kilogram. 1st hour following adrenal injection
104	6–21–20	2135	9:30–10:30 a.m.	1.300	1.390	0.78	0.426	Control
105	6–21–20	2135	10:30–11:30 a.m.	1.440	1.590	0.80	0.471	Control
106	6–21–20	2115	1:40– 2:40 p.m.	1.490	2.090	1.02	0.492	1:31 p.m. Injected subcutaneously 0.5 cc. adrenalin (P. D. Co. 1:1000) per kilogram. 1st hour following adrenalin injection
107	6–21–20	2115	2:50– 3:50 p.m.	1.660	2.210	0.97	0.549	2nd hour following adrenalin injection
108	6–21–20	2115	4:00– 5:00 p.m.	1.800	2.060	0.83	0.595	3rd hour following adrenalin injection

TABLE 4

Rabbit 3–206. Thyroids intact

EXPERIMENT NUMBER	DATE	WEIGHT	DURATION	O_2 INTAKE	CO_2 OUTPUT	$\frac{CO_2}{O_2}$	O_2 PER GRAM PER HOUR	ADDITIONAL DATA
		grams		*grams*	*grams*		*cc.*	
81	6– 4–20	2390	9:45–10:45 a.m.	1.960	1.970	0.73	0.573	Control
82	6– 4–20	2390	10:45–11:45 a.m.	1.610	1.770	0.80	0.471	Control
84	6– 4–20	2380	2:20– 3:20 p.m.	2.050	2.350	0.83	0.602	1:15 p.m. Injected subcutaneously 0.5 cc. adrenalin (P. D. Co. 1:1000) per kilogram
								2nd hour following adrenalin injection
86	6– 4–20	2325	5:01– 6:01 p.m.	2.160	2.030	0.68	0.650	4th hour following adrenalin injection
100	6–19–20	2400	10:05–11:05 a.m.	1.710	2.090	0.89	0.498	Control
101	6–19–20	2400	11:05–12:05 p.m.	1.900	2.080	0.80	0.553	Control
102	6–19–20	2390	2:10– 3:10 p.m.	1.670	2.250	0.98	0.488	2:00 p.m. Injected subcutaneously 0.5 cc. adrenalin (P. D. Co. 1:1000) per kilogram.
								1st hour following adrenalin injection
103	6–19–20	2380	3:40– 4:40 p.m.	2.060	2.920	1.03	0.605	2nd hour following adrenalin injection

TABLE 5

Rabbit 3–208. R. and L. Thyroidectomy 3–22–20

EXPERIMENT NUMBER	DATE	WEIGHT	DURATION	O_2 INTAKE	CO_2 OUTPUT	$\frac{CO_2}{O_2}$	O_2 PER GRAM PER HOUR	ADDITIONAL DATA
		grams		*grams*	*grams*		*cc.*	
24	5–12–20	2445	11:53–12:53 p.m.	1.020	1.140	0.81	0.292	Control
25	5–12–20	2440	2:00– 3:00 p.m.	1.160	1.450	0.91	0.332	1:55 p.m. Injected subcutaneously 0.5 cc. adrenalin (P. D. Co. 1:1000) per kilogram. 1st hour following adrenalin injection
26	5–12–20	2440	3:00– 4:00 p.m.	1.110	1.020	0.67	0.318	2nd hour following adrenalin injection
33	5–14–20	2410	4:35– 5:35 p.m.	1.450	1.590	0.80	0.421	Control
37	5–17–20	2500	10:21–11:21 a.m.	1.530	2.100	1.00	0.428	Control
38	5–17–20	2500	11:21–12:21 p.m.	1.400	1.990	1.03	0.392	Control
39	5–17–20	2495	1:43– 2:43 p.m.	1.390	2.020	1.06	0.393	1:33 p.m. Injected subcutaneously 0.5 cc. adrenalin (P. D. Co. 1:1000) per kilogram. 1st hour following adrenalin injection
40	5–17–20	2495	2:43– 3:43 p.m.	1.510	2.160	1.04	0.423	2nd hour following adrenalin injection
56	5–20–20	2450	9:35–10:35 a.m.	1.320	1.580	0.87	0.377	Control
57	5–20–21	2450	10:35–11:35 a.m.	1.160	1.440	0.90	0.331	Control
58	5–20–20	2450	11:35–12:35 p.m.	1.040	1.350	0.94	0.297	Control
59	5–20–20	2445	2:00– 3:00 p.m.	1.220	1.510	0.90	0.349	1st hour following adrenalin injection. 1:51 p.m. Injected subcutaneously 0.5 cc. adrenalin (P. D. Co. 1:1000) per kilogram
60	5–20–20	2445	3:00– 4:00 p.m.	1.580	1.650	0.76	0.452	2nd hour following adrenalin injection
61	5–20–20	2445	4:00– 5:00 p.m.	1.630	1.680	0.75	0.466	3rd hour following adrenalin injection
115	6–23–20	2530	9:40–10:40 a.m.	1.170	1.680	1.04	0.323	Control
116	6–23–20	2530	10:40–11:40 a.m.	1.220	1.540	0.92	0.337	Control
117	6–23–20	2525	1:20– 2:20 p.m.	1.090	1.590	1.06	0.302	1:16 p.m. Injected subcutaneously 0.5 cc. adrenalin (P. D. Co. 1:1000) per kilogram. 1st hour following adrenalin injection
118	6–23–20	2525	2:20– 3:20 p.m.	1.720	2.090	0.88	0.476	2nd hour following adrenalin injection
119	6–23–20	2525	3:20– 4:20 p.m.	1.450	1.680	0.84	0.401	3rd hour following adrenalin injection
120	6–23–20	2525	4:20– 5:20 p.m.	1.650	1.660	0.73	0.457	4th hour following adrenalin injection

TABLE 6

Rabbit 3-204. Thyroidectomy 5-21-20

EXPERIMENT NUMBER	DATE	WEIGHT	DURATION	O_2 INTAKE	CO_2 OUTPUT	$\frac{CO_2}{O_2}$	O_2 PER GRAM PER HOUR	ADDITIONAL DATA
		grams		*grams*	*grams*		*cc.*	
49	5-19-20	2425	9:22-10:22 a.m.	1.710	1.960	0.83	0.493	Control
50	5-19-20	2425	10:22-11:22 a.m.	1.600	1.840	0.84	0.461	Control
52	5-19-20	2375	1:40- 2:40 p.m.	2.210	2.680	0.88	0.651	1:33 p.m. Injected subcutaneously 0.5 cc. adrenalin (P. D. Co. 1:1000) per kilogram. 1st hour following adrenalin injection
53	5-19-20	2375	2:40- 3:40 p.m.	2.070	2.690	0.94	0.610	2nd hour following adrenalin injection
54	5-19-20	2375	3:40- 4:40 p.m.	1.800	2.240	0.90	0.530	3rd hour following adrenalin injection
66	5-24-20	2330	10:10-11:10 a.m.	1.500	1.750	0.85	0.450	Removed most of R. and L. thyroid lobes 5-21-20. Control
67	5-24-20	2330	11:10-12:10 a.m.	1.830	1.840	0.82	0.549	Control
68	5-24-20	2225	1:55- 2:55 p.m.	1.300	1.660	0.93	0.409	1:46 p.m. Injected subcutaneously 0.5 cc. adrenalin (P. D. Co. 1:1000) per kilogram. 1st hour following adrenalin injection
69	5-24-20	2225	2:55- 3:55 p.m.	1.690	2.110	0.91	0.531	2nd hour following adrenalin injection
70	5-24-20	2225	3:55- 4:55 p.m.	2.030	2.010	0.72	0.638	3rd hour following adrenalin injection
71	6- 2-20	2400	9:20-10:20 a.m.	1.180	1.370	0.84	0.344	Control
73	6- 2-20	2400	1:50- 2:50 p.m.	1.220	1.860	1.11	0.355	1:15 p.m. Injected subcutaneously 0.5 cc. adrenalin (P. D. Co. 1:1000) per kilogram. 1st hour following adrenalin injection
74	6- 2-20	2400	2:50- 3:50 p.m.	1.420	1.770	0.91	0.414	2nd hour following adrenalin injection
75	6- 2-20	2400	3:50- 4:50 p.m.	1.390	1.680	0.88	0.405	3rd hour following adrenalin injection
96	6-18-20	2490	10:55-11:55 a.m.	1.240	1.540	0.90	0.348	Control
97	6-18-20	2485	2:05- 3:05 p.m.	1.160	1.630	1.02	0.326	1:57 p.m. Injected subcutaneously 0.5 cc. adrenalin (P. D. Co. 1:1000) per kilogram. 1st hour following adrenalin injection
98	6-18-20	2485	3:05- 4:05 p.m.	1.770	2.010	0.83	0.498	2nd hour following adrenalin injection
99	6-18-20	2485	4:05- 5:05 p.m.	1.300	1.710	0.91	0.366	3rd hour following adrenalin injection

TABLE 7

Rabbit 3-201. Thyroidectomy 5-21-20

EXPERIMENT NUMBER	DATE	WEIGHT	DURATION	O_2 INTAKE	CO_2 OUTPUT	$\frac{CO_2}{O_2}$	O_2 PER GRAM PER HOUR	ADDITIONAL DATA
		grams		*grams*	*grams*		*cc.*	
62	5-22-20	2360	3:15- 4:15 p.m.	1.960	2.000	0.74	0.581	Control
63	5-22-20	2360	4:15- 5:15 p.m.	1.900	1.830	0.70	0.563	Control
64	5-22-20	2360	5:30- 6:30 p.m.	1.790	2.530	1.03	0.530	5:19 p.m. Injected subcutaneously 0.5 cc. adrenalin (P. D. Co. 1:1000) per kilogram; 1st hour following adrenalin injection
65	5-22-20	2360	6:30- 7:30 p.m.	2.300	2.320	0.73	0.681	2nd hour following adrenalin injection
87	6-10-20	2840	9:20-10:20 a.m.	1.460	1.950	0.97	0.359	Control
88	6-10-20	2840	10:20-11:20 a.m.	1.170	1.480	0.92	0.295	Control
89	6-10-20	2825	1:50- 2:50 p.m.	1.340	2.290	1.33	0.332	1:45 p.m. Injected subcutaneously 0.5 cc. adrenalin (P. D. Co. 1:1000) per kilogram urinated in chamber. 1st hour following adrenalin injection
91	6-10-20	2825	4:15- 5:15 p.m.	2.020	2.230	0.81	0.513	3rd hour following adrenalin injection
109	6-22-20	2860	9:20-10:20 a.m.	1.750	2.230	0.93	0.428	Control
110	6-22-20	2860	10:20-11:20 a.m.	1.550	1.850	0.87	0.386	Control
111	6-22-20	2860	11:35-12:35 p.m.	1.610	2.130	1.10	0.394	Control
112	6-22-20	2840	2:00- 3:00 p.m.	1.610	2.470	1.11	0.396	1:54 p.m. Injected subcutaneously 0.5 cc. adrenalin (P. D. Co. 1:1000) per kilogram. 1st hour following adrenalin injection
113	6-22-20	2840	3:10- 4:10 p.m.	2.040	2.650	0.94	0.502	2nd hour following adrenalin injection
114	6-22-20	2840	4:21- 5:21 p.m.	1.950	2.300	0.86	0.480	3rd hour following adrenalin injection

lasting only a few hours the effect of adrenalin on blood pressure was markedly decreased by thyroidectomy. The cause of these time differences between the effect of adrenalin on blood pressure and on metabolism in animals with and without thyroidectomy is not clear.

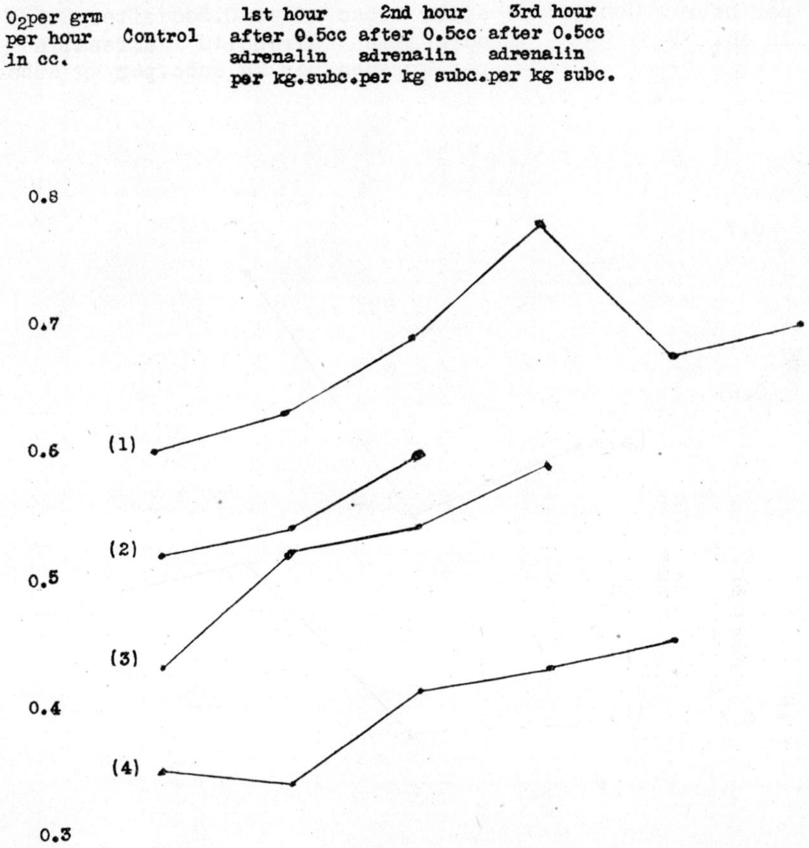

Fig. 1. Average O_2 consumption per gram per hour in cubic centimeters. *1*, Rabbit 203, thyroids intact; *2*, rabbit 206, thyroids intact; *3*, rabbit 205, thyroids intact; *4*, rabbit 208, thyroids removed (51 days).

b. After adrenalin administration. In each case 0.5 cc. per kgm. (P. D. adrenalin 1–1000) unassayed stock adrenalin was injected subcutaneously in the flank. The observations were recorded in hourly periods following the injection. In all instances a rise in the O_2 consumption was noted. The changes are shown graphically in text figures 1, 2 and 3. It occurs as well in the thyroidectomized animals as in "normals." This is brought out best in figures 2 and 3 when the effect of adrenalin before and after thyroidectomy may be compared in

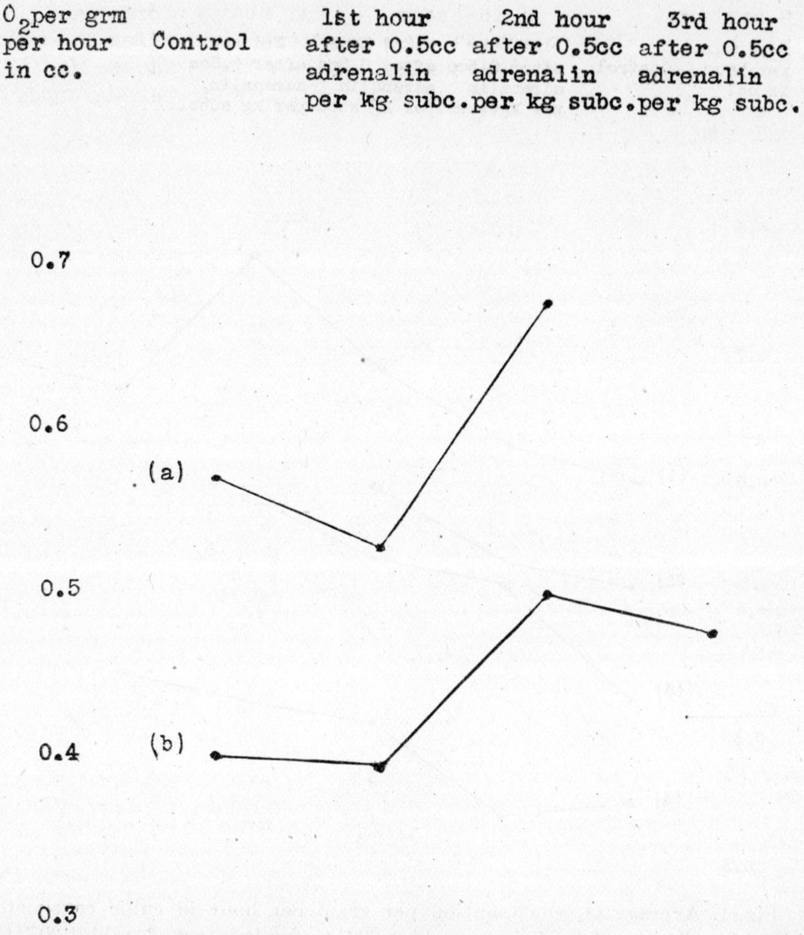

Fig. 2. Rabbit 201. Average O_2 consumption per gram per hour in cubic centimeters. *a*, Thyroids intact; *b*, thyroids removed (31 days).

the same animal. The percentile rise in O_2 consumption appears to be little changed by thyroidectomy. These results confirm Sandiford's observations in human myxedema. The adrenalin effect lasts for hours. We have observed it for five hours, though usually the greatest increase is reached in the third hour. There is some evidence that in the thyroidectomized animals the onset of the increased rate of metabolism is delayed and also the reaction is of shorter duration as

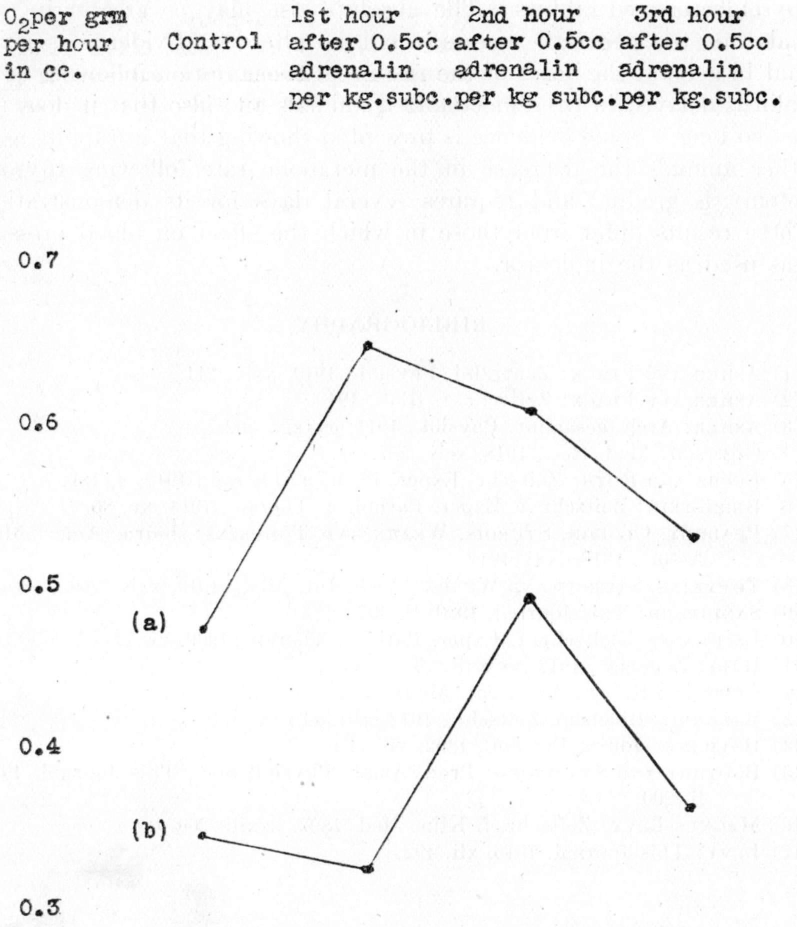

Fig. 3. Rabbit 204. Average O_2 consumption per gram per hour in cubic centimeters. *a*, Thyroids intact; *b*, thyroids removed (30 days).

shown in figures 2 and 3. Another observation on the effect of adrenalin in thyroidectomized animals is that frequently there is a decrease in O_2 consumption during the first hour after adrenalin. This was also observed in "normals" but very rarely.

SUMMARY

Our results on rabbits confirm those of Sandiford on man. Adrenalin causes a rise in the oxygen consumption both in normal and thyroidectomized rabbits. The absolute rise may be greater in normals but the percentile rise may not be altered. Evidence is given that in general the onset of the rise in O_2 consumption following adrenalin is delayed in thyroidectomized animals and also that it does not last so long. Some evidence is presented showing that in rabbits as in other animals the decrease in the metabolic rate following thyroidectomy is gradual and requires several days for its demonstration. These results differ from those in which the effect on blood pressure was used as the indicator.

BIBLIOGRAPHY

(1) Asher and Flack: Zentralbl. Physiol., 1910, xxiv, 211.
(2) Asher and Flack: Zeitschr. f. Biol., 1910, lv, 83.
(3) Asher: Arch. gesammt. Physiol., 1911, cxxxix, 562.
(4) Goetsch: Med. Rec., 1918, xciv, 567.
(5) Fuchs and Roth: Zeitschr. Exper. Path. u. Therap., 1912, x, 187.
(6) Bernstein: Zeitschr. f. Exper. Pathol. u. Therap., 1914, xv, 86.
(7) Peabody, Clough, Sturgis, Wearn and Tompkins: Journ. Amer. Med. Assoc., 1918, lxxi, 1912.
(8) Tompkins, Sturgis and Wearn: Arch. Int. Med., 1919, xxiv, 269.
(9) Sandiford: This Journal, 1920, li, 407.
(10) La Franca: Zeitschr. f. Exper. Path. u. Therap., 1909, vi, 1.
(11) Hari: Zeitschr., 1912, xxxviii, 23.
(12) Lusk and Riche: Arch. Int. Med., 1914, xiii, 673.
(13) Wilenko: Biochem. Zeitschr., 1912, xlii, 44.
(14) Haldane: Journ. Physiol., 1892, xiii, 419.
(15) Boothby and Sandiford: Proc. Amer. Physiol. Soc., This Journal, 1920, li, 200.
(16) Magnus-Levy: Zeitschr. f. Klin. Med. 1897, xxxiii, 269.
(17) Levy: This Journal, 1916, xli, 492.

STUDIES ON THE VISCERAL SENSORY NERVOUS SYSTEM

III. Lung Automatism and Lung Reflexes in Reptilia (Turtles: Chrysemys elegans and Malacoclemmys lesueurii. Snake: Eutenia elegans)

A. J. CARLSON and A. B. LUCKHARDT

From the Hull Physiological Laboratory of the University of Chicago

Received for publication August 3, 1920

LITERATURE

The first observations on the contractility of the reptilian lung on direct stimulation of the pulmonary tissue was made by Paul Bert (1). He showed furthermore that the musculature of the lung was under the motor control of the vagus nerve. These findings have been abundantly corroborated by the subsequent researches of various investigators of whom François-Franck (2) deserves particular mention.[1] Francois-Franck (3), (4) published a number of papers dealing with the comparative physiology of the reptilian lung. The results of these studies are incorporated in two monographs which as far as they touch our work are the most comprehensive and important contributions on the subject. In most forms the vagus is found to exercise a motor control over the lung of the same side. In one lizard (lézard ocelle) the lungs possess in part a crossed innervation the vagus exercising not

[1] Some 32 years after the original observations of Bert, Maar (Skand. Arch. f. Physiol., 1902, xiii, 269) published an article on the gaseous exchange in the lungs of turtles following ligation and stimulation of the vagi and sympathetic nerves under various experimental conditions. This author apparently was not familiar with the fact that the lungs of the turtle are muscular organs innervated through motor fibers carried by the vagus. The possibility that changes in gaseous exchange (increased oxygen consumption and increased CO_2 following ligation of the vagus) might be accounted for by contraction of the lung (mechanical stimulation of motor fibers) never occurred to this investigator. Practically all positive findings which he attributes to section and stimulation of fibers having a secretory or inhibitory effect on gaseous exchange might be explained by the activity or inactivity of the lung musculature and the passive influence of the circulation through the lungs.

only a homolateral but also a contralateral control over the lungs. François-Franck (5) states that the vagi and not the sympathetic nerves contain the motor fibers for the lungs. Jackson and Pelz (7), on the other hand, state that stimulation of the sympathetic in the neck region with a weak current causes dilatation of the lung and that stronger currents may give a contraction even more promptly and vigorously than stimulation of the vagus itself. In some preparations François-Franck (4), (5) found that electrical stimulation of the vagus in the neck gave rise to a contraction which was preceded by an inhibition. According to his experimental analysis this inhibition is only apparent. He attributes it to a movement of neck muscles. If the muscles of the neck were not involved during peripheral stimulation of the vagus no inhibition preceded the contractions. Personally, we have never obtained an inhibition of the lung on direct stimulation of the peripheral vagus. We have, however, in innumerable instances observed an inhibition preceding lung contractions of central origin. We shall return to this point later in a discussion of this phenomenon.

Kahn (8) and François-Franck (5) have described and pictured rhythmical contractions of the lung due to central discharges from the bulbar nuclei; for they stopped on section of the vagi. Kahn in his analysis on turtles which had suffered high spinal transection showed that these lung contractions followed the external respiratory act; François-Franck noted these rhythmical undulations in the intrapulmonic pressure even in curarized animals but only when the bulbar centers and the vagi were intact. He was never able to obtain a tonus rhythm in any lung separated from its center. He found on electrical stimulation of the peripheral end of the vagus that a secondary contraction may appear on the completion of first; or if the peripheral vagus was tetanized for some time a series of contractions might appear during the period of tetanization simulating tonus variation of the lung. In both instances, however, he was probably dealing with incomplete tetany of the lung rather than with discharges from a peripheral nervous automatic mechanism as a result of the vagus stimulation.

A tonus rhythm appearing in a lung whose extrinsic nerves have been cut would suggest a peripheral nervous mechanism possessing automatic activity. On the anatomical side we have the observations of Leydig (9) and Schulze (10) that the lungs of some turtles possess not only ganglionic swellings on the course of the nerve fibers but actual accumulations of ganglion cells. On the physiological side Fano and Fasola (2) have asserted that the oscillations of tonicity in the lungs of the turtle, Emys europaea, persist after complete isolation of the lungs from their nervous center although they admit that under normal conditions part of the tonicity is due to impulses reaching the lung through their extrinsic nerves. Since such a peripheral automatism of the lung did not reveal itself in the turtle studied by François-Franck (tortue grecque) and only occasionally in our own preparations it would seem that the question of a peripheral automatic mechanism in the lung may depend on the species as well as on the physiological condition of the animal under observation.

The published reports of lung contractions as a result of the stimulation of various afferent nerves in the reptilia are very meager. Certainly François-Franck, who made a most extensive study of the physiology of the reptilian lung, refers only incidentally to rhythmical lung contractions set up by stimulation of afferent fibers carried by the vagi (3). In his second monograph (4) on the lizard (lézard ocelle) he describes a similar contraction of one lung following ligation of the vagus of the opposite side (mechanical stimulation). Since in this preparation there was intercommunication between the lungs and since he showed that in this species of reptiles the vagus contained motor fibers not only for the lung of the same side but also for the lung of the opposite side, it is possible to explain his supposed reflex contraction on ligation of the vagus nerve to direct motor effects on the opposite lung or to the passive distention of the lung of the opposite side of ligation of the vagus. Both factors would give a record which might be interpreted as an active reflex contraction of the opposite lung.

Prevost and Saloz (10) are the only investigators who, by a method inferior to our own, have described reflex contractions of the lungs of the turtle (tortue grecque). They found that trauma to the carapace, mechanical stimulation of feet, tail, neck and anal region, caused marked contractions of the lungs.

Coombs (12) has recently shown that stimulation of the optic lobes or the medulla in the turtle induced contractions in the lung, provided the vagi are intact. This seems to indicate that the motor innervation to the lungs passes exclusively by the vagi nerves, unless the sympathetic nerves were sectioned by her method of lung isolation.

EXPERIMENTAL PROCEDURE

The solution of the problems under investigation required an accurate recording of the lung tonus and lung contractions with the least possible injury to or interference with the normal respiration and other processes of the animal. In other words, the necessary aim and requirement so far as possible was to secure *physiological experiments.*

1. Preparation of the animal. No anesthetics were used. Prior (1 to 24 hours) to any dissection or other procedures that would cause pain, the animals were decerebrated by quickly drilling through the skull a little to the side of the median line, introducing a suitable probe through this opening and after cutting off the cerebrum from the midbrain by the transverse stroke virtually pithing the former. By using a small drill and going 2 to 4 mm. lateral to the median line, the median sinus is left intact and profuse hemorrhage avoided. By our method of pithing the cerebrum very little hemorrhage was produced, so that from this factor alone there was little or no impairment to the general circulation or interference with the blood supply of the medulla and midbrain. A small iron hook was introduced into the trephine hole in the skull, by means of which the head was secured to the post as shown in figure 1. The hook being placed in an insensitive spot, the head and neck were thus fixed without the complications from continued irritation of clamps or ligatures about head and neck.

By means of a small drill, holes were made near the edge of the plastron anteriorly and posteriorly, and by strings through these holes in the ventral plate the animal was secured on the turtle stand in the manner shown in figure 1. In the species of turtles worked on, there is a sufficient margin of the ventral plate at both ends for drilling the hole and securing the animal on the stand in its normal posture without touching or injuring the skin.

A few animals were worked on without decerebration. In this case the spinal cord was transected in the neck before any operations were undertaken on the body of the animal.

For convenience of dissection the turtle stand with the animal attached was turned upside down and held in that position by a suitable support while the trachea, the carotids, the jugular vein, the cervical sympathetics, etc., were isolated, balloons introduced into the stomach (via esophagus) and the cannulae and other devices placed in position in the neck and anterior thoracic region.

Isolation of the lungs and other viscera was made by removal of the necessary regions of the dorsal carapace. Cutting through and removing parts of the dorsal carapace is attended with considerable hemorrhage unless care is taken not to injure the intercostal arteries and veins when the calcareous part of the body wall is sawed through or clipped off with strong bone forceps. If suitable care is exercised in this regard, the diploic veins controlled by surgical wax and the intercostal vessels ligated before cutting away the peritoneum and other structures that adhere closely to the calcareous part, the entire body cavity can be laid open from the dorsal side, with very little immediate and with no chronic hemorrhage.

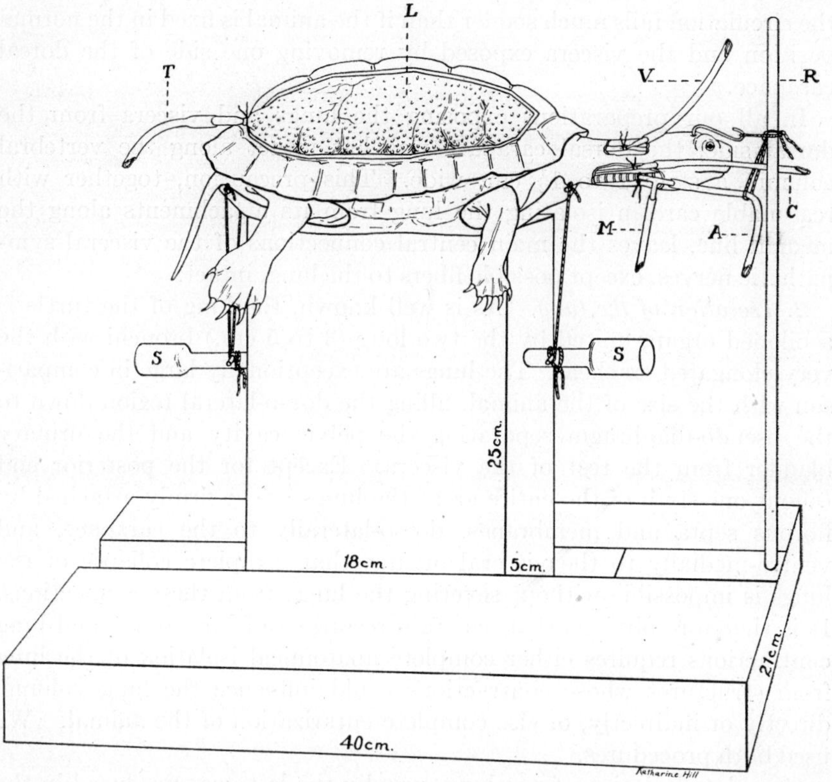

Fig. 1. Diagram of preparation and fixation of the turtle for recording lung contractions. *A:* tube to T-tracheal cannula for spontaneous or artificial respiration in the intact lung. *C:* Cannula in the carotid artery for recording the blood pressure and heart activity. *L:* Lung, isolated, except for pulmonary vagi and blood vessels, bronchus ligated off. Inflated in its normal position in the body cavity. *M:* Tube to manometer for recording the spontaneous respirations. *R:* Flexible steel rod for fixation of the head. *S:* Screws for the fixation of turtle to the top of stand by strings through holes in the plastron. *T:* Cannula and rubber tubing from tip of isolated lung to recording tambour. *V:* Cannula in the jugular vein for intravenous injections.

In a few experiments where it was desired to avoid the injury to visceral sensory nerve connections involved in isolating one lung from the dorsal side, the lungs were exposed and isolated by fixing the animal dorsal side down, removing the entire plastron and dissecting away the liver and greater part of the gut in the way described by Jackson and Pelz (7). In animals fixed on the dorsal side and plastron removed the circulation fails much sooner than if the animal is fixed in the normal position and the viscera exposed by removing one side of the dorsal carapace.

In all our preparations exposing the lungs and viscera from the dorsal side, the dorsal carapace was left intact along the vertebral column, a strip 1 to $1\frac{1}{2}$ cm. wide. This precaution, together with reasonable care in isolating the lung from its attachments along the median line, leaves the main central connections of the visceral sympathetic nerves, except possible fibers to the lung, intact.

2. Isolation of the lung. As is well known, the lung of the turtle is a bilobed organ, united by the two long (3 to 5 cm.) bronchi with the very elongated trachea. The lungs are exceptionally large in comparison with the size of the animal, filling the dorso-lateral region down to the pseudo-diaphragm separating the pelvic cavity and the urinary bladder from the rest of the viscera. Except for the posterior end (about one-sixth of the entire area) the lungs are so firmly attached by fibrous septa and membranes, dorso-laterally to the carapace, and ventro-medially to the visceral organs, that complete collapse of the lungs is impossible without severing the lungs from these connections. It is therefore obvious that accurate recording of lung tonus and lung contractions requires either complete anatomical isolation of the lung from structures whose contractions could influence the lung volume, directly or indirectly, or else complete curarization of the animal. We used both procedures.

Complete isolation of one lung, usually the left, was produced in the following way. The animal being decerebrated, fixed on the turtle stand, as described above, the dorsal carapace over the lung was removed, all the septa and membranes suspending the lung in the body cavity were severed, care being taken not to injure the bronchus, or the pulmonary vagi and blood vessels entering the lungs along the bronchus. In this dissection the lung was not handled directly with forceps or other instruments. It was handled by means of the many membranes and tendons attached to it. It is not necessary to remove these structures close to the lung surface since they can have no effect on the lung tonus and lung contractions after being severed from their normal connections with the rest of the body. This applies even to the large flattened striated muscle closely adherent and attached to the anterior end of the lung. Directed median- and antero-laterally over the dorsal lung wall and being innervated by fibers from the brachial nerve plexus, the contraction of this muscle reduces the size of the lung cavity and thus serves as a muscle of expiration (fig. 24), supplementing the expiratory muscles of the flank and the walls of the body cavity. This muscle is probably identical with the one described by Fano and Fasola as occurring in Emys europaea (2).

This operation and isolation of the left lung does not cause collapse of the right lung or vice versa. There is naturally some interference with the adequate ventilation in the lung of the intact side by the lowering of the intra-abdominal pressure and the incapacitation of the respiratory flank muscles on the side of the operation, but the animal is usually capable of filling and emptying the lung on the intact side to meet the respiratory needs of the body, especially if one takes care not to puncture the delicate septa partially separating the left and the right side body cavities along the line of the great retractor muscle of the neck.

In figure 2 are shown by diagram the main vago-sympathetic nerve connections. The pulmonary vagi branches, usually two or more in number, are of sufficient size and length to be easily handled for experimental purposes; and the bronchus may be ligated and cannulated without injury to the pulmonary nerves or vessels, and the pulmonary vessels may be ligated or cannulated without injury to the nerves.

There is a persistent tendency on the part of some anatomists and zoölogists, as well as physiologists, to speak of the "bronchioles" or bronchial musculature of the turtle's lung. This is entirely misleading. In species of turtles worked on by us the bronchus terminates peripherally, not by the mode of branching into smaller and smaller divisions (bronchioles), but abruptly in the general lung cavity. We are told by the anatomists that the numerous septa subdividing the lung cavity into irregular chambers have strands of smooth muscle fibers like the external walls of the lungs. But the smallest passages between these chambers are of larger diameter than the trachea itself. These passages and septa are alveolated. If these internal septa and irregular passages are to be termed "bronchioles" on the basis of their musculature, the entire lung of the turtle is composed of "bronchioles." These subdivisions in the turtle lungs are alveolar spaces and not part of the dead space similar to the mammalian bronchioles.

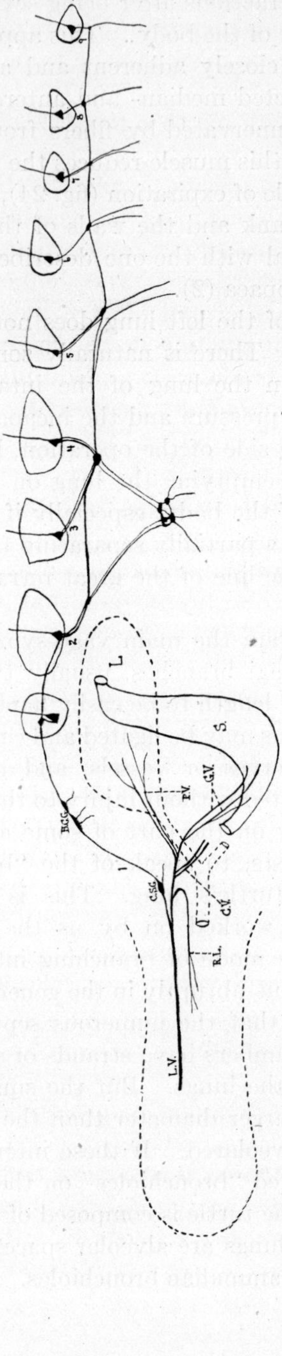

Fig. 2. Diagram of the vago-sympathetic nervous system (left side, ventral view) of the turtle. The diagram of the sympathetic system is not completed posteriorly (sacral region). *L:* Left lung (greatly reduced). *S:* Stomach. *L.V.:* Left vagus. *R.L.:* Recurrent laryngeal nerve. *C.V.:* Cardiac vagi branches. *G.V.:* Gastric vagi branches. *P.V.:* Pulmonary vagi branches. *C.S.G.:* Cervical sympathetic ganglion. *B.S.G.:* Sympathetic ganglia in close association with the brachial nerve plexus. *1:* Cervical sympathetic nerve. *2* to *9:* Nerve connections from the spinal ganglia to the peripheral sympathetic ganglia and nerve plexuses.

3. Recording of the lung contractions. The lung contractions were recorded graphically by water manometers or delicate tambours through air transmission in either case, suitable cannulae being tied either into the bronchus or the free end (posterior tip) of the isolated lung, the isolated lung being distended with air to a pressure of $1\frac{1}{2}$ to 3 cm. of water. In such a preparation active voluntary respiration in the lung on the intact side will still cause passive changes in the intrapulmonic pressure in the isolated lung through the movements of the viscera (on which the isolated and inflated lung rests) especially as a result of very vigorous expiratory movements. We eliminated this source of error in two ways. The isolated and inflated lung was suspended outside the body cavity without traction on the pulmonary nerves or interference with the lung circulation. Or a metal plate was adjusted to the body cavity on the operated side, fixed rigidly to the cut edge of the carapace, except anteriorly, and the isolated and inflated lung placed on this rigid floor, where visceral movements could not influence it. This method can be adjusted so as not to cause traction on the pulmonary nerves, or interference with the pulmonary circulation. The best, and possibly the most physiological method of eliminating these passive lung factors, is partial curarization, that is, doses of curare that will completely paralyze the skeletal muscles, but leave the muscles of respiration largely intact. In our animals this dose varied from $\frac{1}{8}$ to $\frac{1}{4}$ cc. of 1 per cent solution of curare injected intravenously. Turtles subjected to these doses of curare go on breathing regularly though not vigorously, leg and neck movements are abolished, and the gentle respiratory movements on the intact side either do not mechanically influence the isolated and inflated lung on the operated side at all, or else this passive influence is regular or so slight that it is no source of error in the work.

When all these dissections were completed and connections for recording made, the dorsal opening in the carapace was covered with a thick layer of cotton moistened in Ringer's solution, except during such phases of the work as required direct inspection of or working with the isolated lung or its local nerve and blood supply.

4. Artificial respiration. In all cases of complete curarization, artificial respiration was carried out periodically, usually in the intact lung. For that purpose a T-cannula was usually inserted in the trachea. This tracheal cannula was also used in studying the reflex influences of pressure changes in the intact on the isolated lung. The venosity of the blood in the isolated lung was a satisfactory criterion of the need of artificial respiration. Needless to say, artificial respiration was also resorted to in the animals not curarized, if it appeared that the spontaneous respiration through the lung on the intact side did not suffice to avert asphyxia.

It is well known that the reptilia execute the same buccal respiratory movements as the amphibia, although actual swallowing of the air into the lungs does not occur. However, in labored respiration as in mild or severe asphyxia, the reptilia carry on actual swallowing movements as a part of the respiratory act. These swallowing movements may thus be used as an index of external respiration, or rather attempt at external respiration, in animals with the respiratory muscles immobilized by transection or pithing of the spinal cord.

5. *Maintenance of efficient circulation.* If we start with an animal vigorous and in good condition, and care is taken to avoid all but the minimum hemorrhage in the experimental procedures, a good circulation will be maintained as shown by direct blood pressure records or by direct inspection of the isolated lung, for 12 to 24 hours or even longer. In feeble animals the circulation fails much earlier. The circulatory failure is due, not to the failure of the heart, but to low blood pressure evidently due to *transudation of the blood plasma into the lymph and tissue spaces.* This is not ordinary oozing of blood from cut surfaces or hemorrhage due to injured vessels. In a turtle preparation in this condition intravenous injection of Ringer's solution improves the circulation only temporarily, the added fluid soon passes out of the blood vessels into the lymph and tissue spaces, and repeated Ringer's solution injections then render the preparation more edematous.

It is not unlikely that this phenomenon is analogous to the passage of plasma from the blood to the tissues in traumatic shock in mammals, as reported by some investigators.

6. *Additional preparations of the animal for studying some of the lung reflexes.* The turtle preparation described above requires no additional dissection for the study of the lung reflexes induced by inflation or deflation of the intact lung, stimulation of the nares, the cloaca, the penis, the skin or the skeletal nerves. It is even possible by careful manipulation to get at and stimulate the bladder, the rectum, ureter, large and small intestine, etc., through the opening in the dorsal carapace made for the isolation of the lung, without altering the tension on the lung wall mechanically. In the artificial stimulation of the central end of the pulmonary, gastric and vagi branches on the side opposite to the lung under observation it is usually necessary to make

a small opening in the dorsal carapace on that side and partially collapse the intact lung. In the same way inflation of the urinary bladder or the rectum, direct stimulation of the gall bladder, stomach, etc., requires an opening of the carapace posteriorly on the side opposite to the lung under observation, if one is to avoid mechanical errors.

7. On the basis of our own results, and with due regard to methods used by previous investigators on various phases of reptilian respiratory physiology, we feel that a turtle prepared as above with minimum trauma, fixed in normal position without trauma, one lung isolated for accurate observation, the other intact and used in normal spontaneous respiration, is as near its normal physiological state as the necessities of the problem permit. Most phases of lung physiology in the turtle cannot be satisfactorily studied with the animal fixed with the dorsal side down, owing to the special anatomical conditions.

The serious and unavoidable difficulties, apart from that of a laboratory located in a city obtaining turtles in prime condition, are *a*, depressor effects or "central shock" due to sensory effects involved in the operative trauma; *b*, "peripheral shock" or gradual failure of the circulation due to passage of the blood plasma out of the blood vessels into lymph and tissue spaces. It is generally held that reptiles show little or no spinal or traumatic shock, and this was our main reason, besides that of avoiding anesthesia, for working out the visceral reflexes first in this form. Shock, spinal and general, may be minimal but is certainly not absent in the turtle.

8. *Experimental procedure on the snake.* No satisfactory work on the contraction of the lung in these animals can be done without virtually removing the lung from the body, complete pithing of the spinal cord, or complete curarization, thus immobilizing the body. Curarization is, of course, not applicable in experiments on the relation of the lung contractions to the external respiratory act. Hence we used the method of complete pithing of the spinal cord after transection of the cord two or three segments below the medulla. The animal was then fixed, dorsal side down, the lung exposed and isolated by a ventral median incision, taking care to avoid hemorrhage. The recording cannula was inserted in the tip of the lung rather than in the trachea. The trachea was ligated after isolation from the vagi and the neck blood vessels. This preparation is suited only for studying the relation of the respiratory movements to the lung contractions, the vagi action on the lungs, and the lung reflexes evoked from the head region of the animal. In the pithed snake the external respiratory movements appear in the form of attempts at swallowing air just as in the turtle.

In the species of snake used by us the lung is not a paired organ. Alveoli and septa are present in the anterior third of the lung only, the posterior two-thirds of the lung being a delicate apparently muscular sac very much like the primitive lung of necturus. There being only one lung, the necessary artificial respiration had to be carried out periodically in the lung while suspending the recording. This fact renders the snake much less suitable than the turtle for the study of lung motor physiology.

The musculature of the snake lung is very much less developed than that of the turtle. Even delicate water manometers are not sufficiently sensitive for recording the lung contractions. The snake preparations also deteriorate very much faster than does the turtle. Because of these several handicaps the work on the snake was only carried to the point of establishing the identity of the fundamental facts of lung motor physiology in these two groups.

THE RHYTHMIC CONTRACTIONS OF THE LUNGS DURING NORMAL RESPIRATION AND AFTER PARTIAL AND COMPLETE CURARIZATION

1. Typical records of the active lung contractions that follow each external respiratory act or a group of respirations are reproduced in

Fig. 3. Water manometer tracings of the intrapulmonic pressure in the turtle. Animals decerebrated. *A:* Record from left lung; dorsal shell removed on left side, lung isolated except nerve and blood vessel connections. Cannula in left bronchus. The spontaneous respiratory movements at *a* passively influencing the isolated lung. Each group of respiratory movements is followed by contraction of the isolated lung. *B:* Tracing from the same animal as in *A*, 24 hours later after recovery from curare. Record from the intact (right) lung. Cannula in trachea. Each group of respirations is followed by contraction of the lung. *C:* Tracing from left lung, isolated as in *A*, after intravenous injection of a dose of curare ($\frac{1}{4}$ cc. of 1 per cent, to paralyze skeletal muscles). Signal equals gasping or swallowing movements. These are followed by lung contractions. *D: c*, left lung isolated as in *A*; *b*, right lung in normal attachments. *a*, carotid blood pressure (Hg.); signal equals respiratory movements; $\frac{1}{4}$ cc. curare injected intravenously leaving slight respiratory movements of mouth and flanks. Showing lung contractions following respiratory movements. *E* and *F:* Spontaneous contraction of lungs after a large dose of curare ($\frac{1}{2}$ cc. 1 per cent) completely paralyzing all striated muscles. *E*, lung isolated as in *A*. *F*, lung in normal attachment. Showing rhythmic lung contractions in the absence of external evidence of respiration. *G* and *H:* Water manometer records from inflated balloon in the stomach of the turtle; shell intact; stomach atonic and quiescent, but showing beginning of feeble rhythm at *c*; *a*, spontaneous respiratory movements, quick up and down stroke, followed by lung contractions; *b*, shown as diminished tension in the stomach because of the lowered intra-abdominal pressure created by the active lung contraction, the shell being intact. Time, 5 seconds.

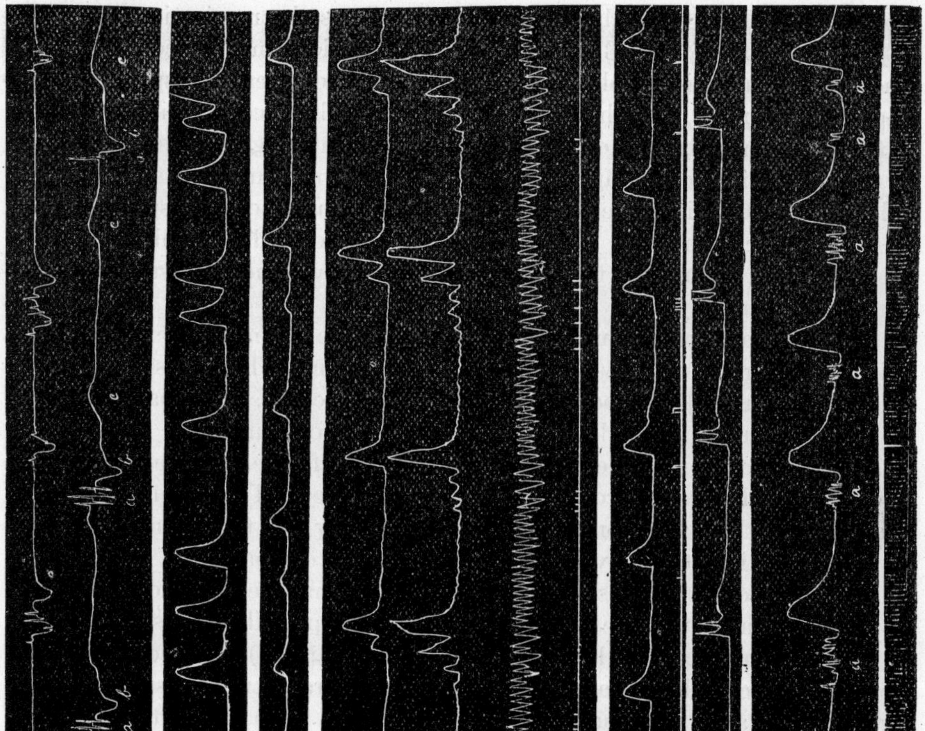

Fig. 3

figure 3, *A*, *B*, *C*. The lung contraction follows the respiration after a latent period of 1 to 3 seconds. In preparations in poor condition the latent period is usually much longer. If the external respiratory movements are of the Cheyne-Stokes type, the lung contraction does not appear until the end of the last respiration in the group, especially if the respirations come fairly close together, except in marked asphyxia. The lung contractions are usually absent when the external respiration is rapid and continuous. This absence appears to be due to inhibition of the center controlling the lung contractions by some process in the external respiratory act.

Under certain conditions acts of external respiration may be executed without being followed by a contraction of the lung. This is especially the case in animals in poor condition from any cause, in preparations in partial traumatic shock from the operative procedure, or if for any reason, such as apnea, the external respiration is feeble. By feeble we mean feeble discharges from the respiratory center. The general relation obtains that the stronger external respiratory act, the stronger the lung contractions that develop during the respiratory pause.

Graphic records of this strong lung rhythm may be obtained from an inflated balloon in the stomach of the turtle, provided the stomach is relatively quiescent and in low tonus (fig. 3, *G* and *H*). The external respiratory act induces passive changes in the intragastric pressure (fig. 3, *G*, *a*) just as in mammals, except reverse, that is, in the turtle expiration causes increased intragastric pressure and vice versa. The active lung contractions appear on the gastric balloon records as waves of negative pressure or lowered tonus, owing to the lung contraction increasing the general intra-abdominal negative pressure.

Tracings showing the lung rhythm as it appears after complete curarization are reproduced in figure 3, *E* and *F*. If a paralyzing dose of curare is injected intravenously in a preparation breathing spontaneously and regularly and exhibiting lung contractions as in figure 3, *A*, the brief central stimulation phase of the curare action, as shown by violent body movements and cardiac arhythmia, is followed by complete quiescence of the lungs lasting for one-half to two hours. This is not due to peripheral paralysis of the pulmonary motor nerve fibers. It is evidently due to paralysis of the medullary centers by curare. Reflex lung contractions can be secured before the spontaneous rhythm appears. But when the spontaneous lung rhythm reappears, it continues for hours or indefinitely provided suitable artificial respiration is carried out at intervals and a fairly efficient circulation maintained.

Fig. 4. Water manometer tracings of the rhythmical contraction of the turtle's lung after complete curare, abolishing skeletal and respiratory movements. Tracings *A* to *D* taken successively about 90 minutes apart. Time, 5 seconds. Showing the usual increased rate and amplitude of the lung contractions with increasing asphyxia of the brain.

The fact that the lung rhythm appears in completely curarized animals shows that it is not due to reflexes evoked by acts of external respiration. It shows further that central and efferent nervous processes of the external respiration go on during the curarized state, because these lung contractions are side events in the normal respiratory act.

These lung contractions following the external respiratory act have been studied and described by Francois-Franck (3), (4) in several species of reptilia. They are evidently identical with the active lung contractions following the respiratory act in frogs and salamanders, recently reported by us (13) and (14). It may be of some interest to note that in this regard the lung physiology of amphibia and reptilia is similar or identical, despite the fact that the mechanisms for effecting lung ventilation in these two groups of animals are entirely different.

2. As already noted, the lung contractions develop during the respiratory pause, and if the respirations come close together they may not appear at all, except in states of marked asphyxia. In fact, a lung contraction once begun may be weakened or cut short by an act of external respiration coming on before completion of the contraction. It would thus appear that while a single respiratory discharge from the respiratory center will, as a side effect, induce a lung contraction after a characteristic latent period, several respiratory discharges following in succession closer than this latent period of the lung contraction interferes with this development in such a way that the lung contraction follows the last respiratory act only. We have made very great efforts to determine the mechanism of this interference by satisfactory experiments.

On most of our tracings from the isolated lung, the animal breathing spontaneously by the lung on the intact side, there appears a tonus relaxation of the isolated lung during the period of external respiration, that is, prior to the active lung contraction. This may be seen in figure 3, *A*, and figure 6, *A*. If all purely mechanical factors were excluded, this would indicate a central inhibition of the lung tonus by discharges from the respiratory center prior to the central processes initiating the lung contractions. Francois-Franck (4), (5) has called attention to the fact that on stimulation of the peripheral end of the incompletely isolated vagus the lung contraction produced by this stimulation may be preceded by an apparent inhibition of the lung tonus, in reality due to mechanical factors developed in the body cavity as the result of the contractions of some muscles of the neck. Furthermore, if the isolated and inflated lung presses against any structure in the body cavity with a force equal to or greater than the internal pressure maintained in the lung ($1\frac{1}{2}$ to 2 cm. water) and if these structures are so moved by the act of spontaneous inspiration that the pressure on the outside of the lung is decreased, the net result would be an apparent inhibition of the tonus of the isolated lung during the external respiratory acts. We endeavored to eliminate this source of error by complete curarization, by section of the spinal cord below the medulla, and by suspending the isolated lung partly outside the body cavity. In completely curarized preparations there is, of course, no external respiratory act, but the facts cited above go to show that the discharge from the respiratory center, after an initial paralysis, is resumed and continues rhythmically. Despite this fact inhibition of the lung tonus prior to the lung contractions rarely if ever appears on the tracings from our completely curarized animals. This may be due, however, to a depression of the medullary centers by the drug (direct chemical action, or indirect by altering or diminishing afferent skeletal nervous impulses) to such an extent that the tonus motor action of the medullary centers on the lung is abolished. Without such tonic motor action there could be no relaxation of lung tonus by central inhibition. This negative result on completely curarized animals is therefore no criterion of what the discharges from the respiratory center may do in the direction of central inhibition of lung tonus, when such central motor tonus is present.

We have secured tracings from animals partly curarized, from animals with section of the spinal cord in the neck, and from animals without curare or spinal cord transection, but with the observed lung suspended outside the body cavity, *indicating a central inhibition of the lung tonus by the discharge from the respiratory center, an inhibition prior to the motor innervation of the lung.* A tracing illustrating this fact is shown in figure 6, *B*. Water manometers are usually not delicate enough to disclose the inhibition. This inhibition is probably proportional to the amount of central motor tonus in the lungs.

From the point of view of utility or teleology this inhibition would be expected, as greater relaxation of the lung tonus means less resistance to lung inflation, and active lung contraction would counteract the inspiratory effort. The possible utility of the active lung contraction following the respiratory act is another matter. Useless, useful or harmful, it is there, and we are at present concerned only with the mechanisms of its initiation and control.

3. We desire to point out, however, that the above described relations of the external respiratory act to the active lung contractions are similar to the relation of the swallowing act to the peristalsis of the esophagus. If the swallowing acts are sufficiently far apart, each swallowing is followed by a peristaltic wave of the esophagus initiated from the medulla. If the swallowing acts are repeated at very brief intervals esophageal peristalsis follows the last swallowing act only. The parallel between swallowing-esophageal peristalsis and respiration-lung contraction appears complete, despite the very diverse functions of the two mechanisms. The lung has the same organogenesis as the esophagus, and the primitive mechanism for external respiration is swallowing, the active lung contractions following the respiratory act (air swallowing) serving probably a real respiratory function. As the mechanism of external respiration changes with the reptilia the organogenesis and primary nervous relations of the lung remaining the same, *the lung inhibition and contractions associated with the respiratory act may represent inherited mechanisms useless, if not at times actually harmful to animals provided with this later respiratory device. It may be a vestigial mechanism on the road to elimination in the process of evolution.*

4. The influence of asphyxia on the bulbar center for the lung rhythm appears to run parallel with the influence of asphyxia on the respiratory center. In curarized preparations permitted to go into varying degrees of asphyxia the lung rhythm increases in rate and intensity to the point of incomplete lung tetanus parallel with increasing asphyxia (fig. 4). It is clear that asphyxia increases the lung tonus by central motor action. The lung rhythm does not end in this state of incomplete tetanus. If the state of asphyxia is permitted to continue, the incomplete tetanus stage is followed by feebler lung contractions appearing at greater and greater intervals (5 to 10 minute intervals in some cases) before the final quiescence. This probably represents the well-known final feeble activity of the respiratory center when the asphyxia is carried beyond the point of stimulation to that of actual impairment of the center.

Further evidence of this complete parallel is furnished by the type of experiments illustrated in figure 5. Here artificial respiration through the intact lung, normal, *A*, and denervated, *B*, both preparations being completely curarized, inhibits the tonus and rhythm in non-asphyxiated preparations, *A*, evidently by inducing apnea, and diminishes the tonus and incomplete tetanus in the asphyxiated preparation, evidently by decreasing the asphyxial condition of the blood.

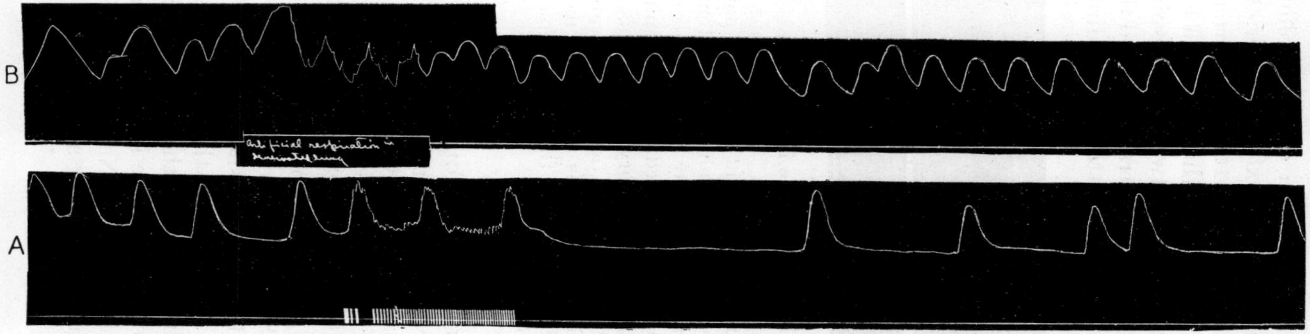

Fig. 5. Water manometer tracings of the intrapulmonic pressure in the turtle. Animals decerebrated and completely curarized; record from left lung isolated except pulmonary vagi branches and lung blood vessels. Cannula in tip of lung. *A:* right lung intact; signal, artificial respiration in right lung, showing inhibition of lung rhythm of the isolated lung. *B:* right lung intact but isolated from central nervous system by section of right vagus in neck. Signal, artificial respiration in right lung. Showing inhibition of the incomplete tetanus of the left isolated lung, through aeration of the blood.

In non-curarized preparations, in which one can follow the action of the respiratory center by means of the external respiratory acts, contractions of the isolated lung, not related to any external respiration, may appear during asphyxia. It appears that asphyxia may occasionally disorganize the normal correlation between the respiratory center and the vagi center controlling the lung contractions, and that asphyxial conditions are capable of stimulating the latter centers directly.

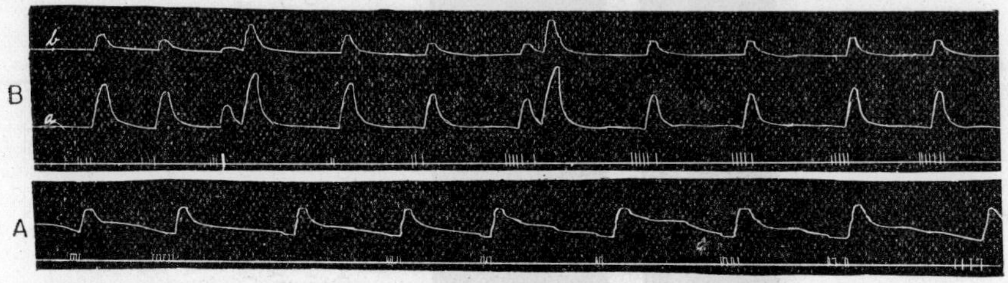

Fig. 6. Tracings of the intrapulmonic pressure in the turtle. Left lung, isolated except pulmonary nerves and blood vessels. Left bronchus ligated. Cannula in tip of lung. Animals decerebrated. Right lung left in normal relations. *A:* signal, spontaneous respiration. Showing inhibition of tonus of isolated lung during respiratory movements followed by strong contraction of lungs. Water manometer. *B:* animal partially curarized, having respiratory muscles in feeble activity. Signal, spontaneous respiratory movements. Both tracings from left isolated lung. *a*, record from delicate tambour; *b*, water manometer. Showing lung contractions following spontaneous respiratory movements, preceded by tonus inhibition, as revealed by tambour, the water manometer not being delicate enough to register the tonus inhibition.

THE RÔLE OF THE EFFERENT PULMONARY VAGI FIBERS AND THE VARIOUS PARTS OF THE BRAIN IN THE GENESIS OF THE RHYTHMIC LUNG CONTRACTIONS

1. In the species of turtle studied by us the spontaneous lung contractions are of central origin, and the motor innervation is through the vagi, as shown by Kahn (8) and François-Franck (5) for the common land turtle of Europe. This may be shown by experiments such as reproduced in figure 7, *A*. In that case the animal was completely curarized, graphic records being taken of the lung contractions both from the isolated and the intact lungs. The intact lung has, of course, its sympathetic nerve connection intact. Nevertheless section of the vagus nerve on the side of the intact lung abolishes the strong contractions in that lung at once and forever. The section of one vagus

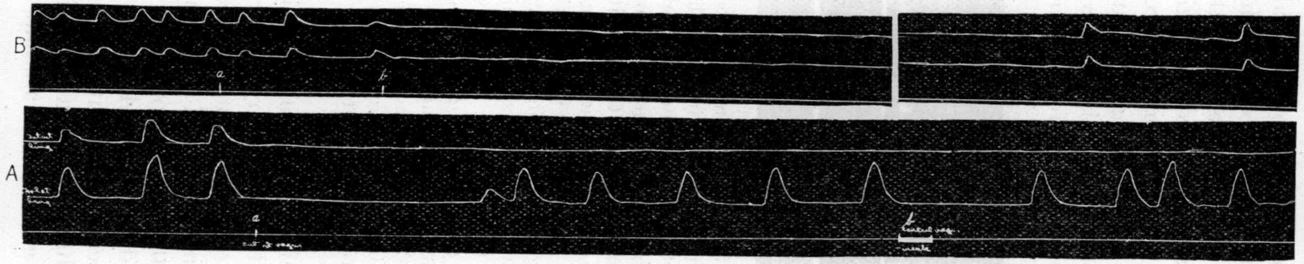

Fig. 7. Water manometer tracings of the intrapulmonic pressure in the turtle. *A* and *B:* upper tracing in each case, right or intact lung; lower, left or isolated lung. Animal completely curarized, after previous decerebration. *A: a,* section of right vagus in neck showing complete abolition of rhythmic lung contractions in right lung and temporary inhibition (reflex) of contraction of left lung. *b,* stimulation of central end of right vagus with weak tetanizing current, showing reflex inhibition of the left lung, that is, inhibition of the medullary center. *B: a,* beginning isolation of spinal cord in the neck. *b,* section of spinal cord in neck, showing reflex inhibition ("shock") of the medullary center governing the rhythmic lung contractions.

stops the contraction of the lung on the opposite side temporarily through stimulation of afferent inhibitory fibers in the vagus trunk depressing the medullary centers. It is thus clear that the motor innervation of the lung rhythm is solely through vagi nerves. The same fact can be illustrated by the use of atropine. Atropine paralyzes the vagi motor fibers in the lungs. The tracing reproduced in figure 8, *C*, was secured from the left lung of a completely curarized preparation, the lung being isolated from the body except for the pulmonary blood

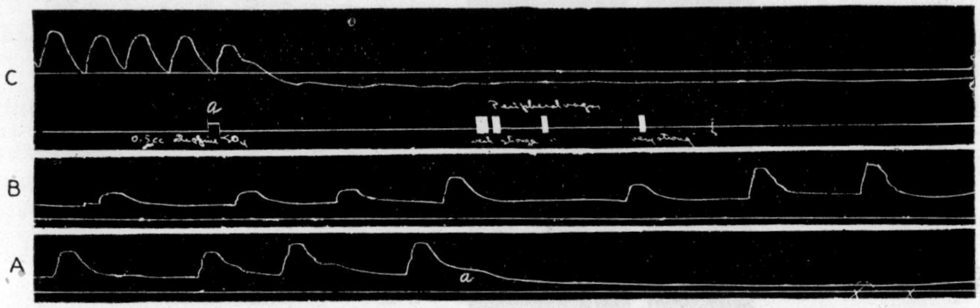

Fig. 8. Water manometer tracings of the intrapulmonic pressure in the turtle. Animals decerebrated. Left lung isolated, cannula in tip; right lung in normal relations. *A* and *B*, showing lung contractions following the spontaneous respiratory movements. *A: a*, section of right vagus in neck, followed by temporary inhibition (central) of the tonus and contractions of the opposite lung, also temporary inhibition of the respiratory movements. The latter reappear at *X*, but are not followed by lung contractions. Tracing *B* is continuation of *A* after a 6 minute interval, the lung contractions gradually regaining normal vigor. *C:* animal completely curarized; lung in strong tonus and contractions, probably from partial asphyxia. *a*, intravenous injection of $\frac{1}{2}$ mgm. atropine sulphate followed by permanent inhibition (peripheral action) of lung tonus and contractions. Signal shows vagus stimulation is without effect on lung.

These tracings indicate a tonic condition of the medullary center controlling the lung motor tissues. This center is more profoundly influenced by depressant impulses ("shock"?) than is the respiratory center.

vessels and pulmonary vagus branches. Intravenous injection of 0.5 mgm. atropine sulphate abolished the lung rhythm promptly just as it abolished the motor action of the vagus on the lung musculature.

The reader's attention may again be directed to the fall in lung tonus induced by peripheral vagus paralysis of atropine and by afferent depressor impulses acting on the medulla (fig. 8, *A* and *C*). The tracings in figure 8 show at least that under some conditions (partial asphyxia) the medulla-vagi-lung motor mechanism is in a state of tonic activity, in which the stronger rhythmic contractions are superimposed much like the constant tonus and the occasional peristaltic contractions of the gut. We have so far been unable to demonstrate this tonic activity under more nearly normal conditions; but our results point in the direction of some normal motor tonus.

2. The inhibition of the contractions of the lung on the opposite side induced by section of one vagus (afferent inhibition of a central automatism) is usually more prolonged than shown in figure 7, *A*. In preparations not curarized it can be shown that section of one vagus temporarily inhibits both external respiration and the tonus and contractions of the lung on the opposite side, the external respiratory acts returning sooner than the lung contractions.

Section of the spinal cord in the neck also produces a very prolonged inhibition of the medullary center initiating the lung rhythm (fig. 7, *B*). This central inhibition or shock is shown not only by the temporary abolition of the spontaneous rhythm, but also by the lowering of the excitability of these centers to reflex stimulation leading to lung contractions.

3. As reported by many previous investigators, stimulation of the peripheral end of the vagus nerve in the turtle causes contraction of the lung musculature (fig. 9, *C*). We have never seen any inhibitory effects on the lung in the turtle from stimulation of the peripheral vagus. This appears to us significant in view of the fact that in the frog the predominant action of the vagi on the lungs is inhibitory, and in the most primitive amphibian lung (necturus) all the efferent lung nerve fibers appear to be inhibitory.

In the species of turtle studied by us the motor action of the vagi on the lungs is strictly unilateral. Single induction shocks (make or break) applied to the peripheral vagus will not cause lung contractions unless exceedingly strong. Weak tetanizing currents applied to the vagi induce an incomplete tetanus or rhythm that seems to indicate a certain degree of refractory state in the peripheral mechanism. Strong tetanization of the vagi will, however, induce curves of complete tetanus closely resembling those of an ordinary muscle nerve preparation (fig. 9, *C*).

In view of the identity of origin and certain similarities in the nervous control of the lung and the alimentary canal, we made some comparisons between the vagi motor action on the lungs and on the stomach (fig. 10). The latent period of the vagi motor action on the stomach is very much longer than its motor action on the lung. The turtle's stomach cannot be tetanized by vagus stimulation; the lungs can be tetanized. The third marked difference is the quick failure of vagus motor action on the stomach on repeated stimulation in comparison with the repeated tetany of the lungs that may be induced by vagus stimulation. These differences may be due, in part, to the fact that in the turtle the vagi carry inhibitory efferents to the stomach in addition to the motor, while the efferent vagus lung action is solely motor. The differences also suggest that the gut has retained more of its primitive automatism (independent peripheral nervous system) while the

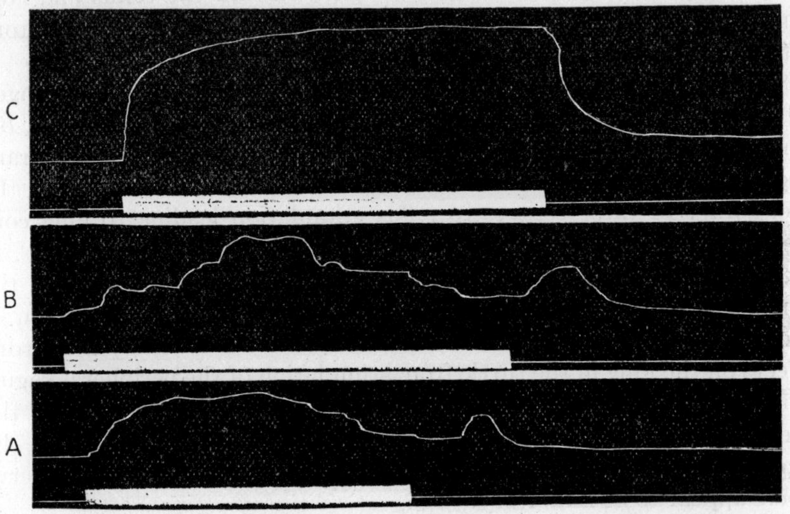

Fig. 9. Water manometer tracings of the contractions of the isolated lung of the turtle. Animal decerebrated and completely curarized; left lung isolated except for pulmonary vagi fibers and blood vessels. Cannula in left bronchus. Stimulation with moderately strong tetanizing current, *A*, optic lobes, *B*, medulla, *C*, peripheral end of left vagus, showing incomplete and complete tetanus of the lung musculature.

differentiation in the lung has been toward the more simple relations of a muscle nerve preparation.

4. In 1878 Martin reported that stimulation of the optic lobes in the frog accelerates the external respiratory movements. Since that time several investigators have concerned themselves with the problem of accessory respiratory centers above the level of the medulla. Recently Coombs (12) reported that stimulation of the optic lobes or the medulla in the turtle with weak tetanizing current causes lung contractions via the vagi nerves.

As we have shown, the normal rhythmic contractions of the turtle lung are side events in the external respiratory act. This being the case, we would expect lung contractions from stimulation of any part

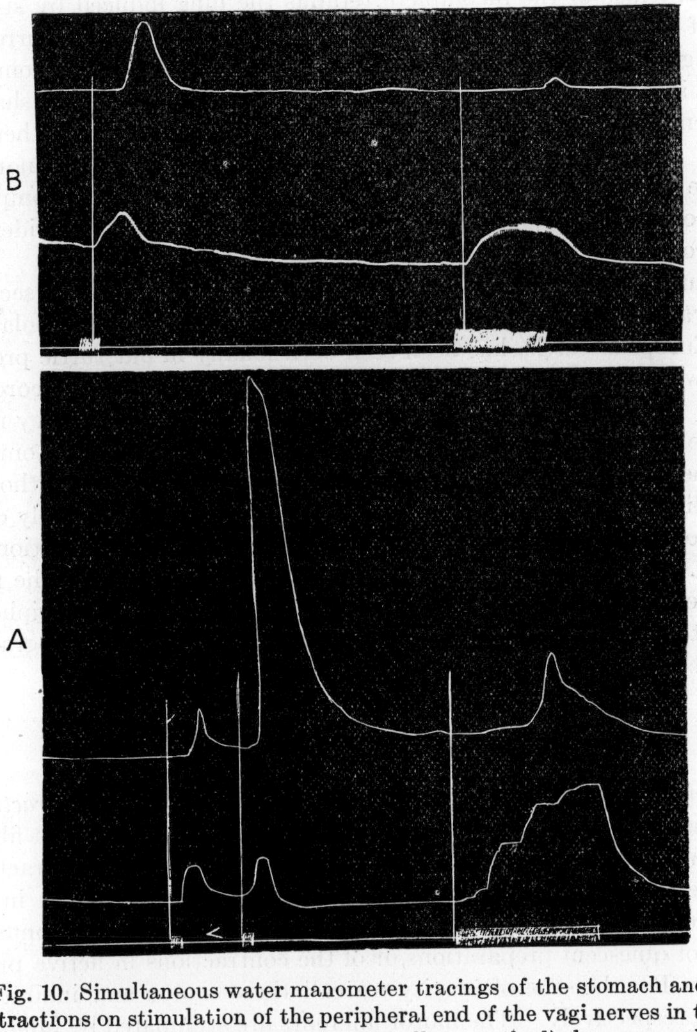

Fig. 10. Simultaneous water manometer tracings of the stomach and the lung contractions on stimulation of the peripheral end of the vagi nerves in the turtle. In *A* and *B*, upper record from stomach (balloon method); lower record from left lung, isolated except for the pulmonary blood vessels and vagi fibers; cannula in left bronchus. Signal, stimulation of peripheral end of left vagus with the tetanizing current. Showing longer latent period, more rapid fatigue and absence of tetanus in the gastric response to vagus stimulation.

of the central nervous system that has motor connections with the medullary respiratory center. This has turned out to be a fact, at least as regards the optic lobes. In figure 9, *A* and *B*, are reproduced typical tracings of the incomplete tetanus the lung induced by stimulation of the optic lobes and the medulla with weak tetanizing currents. The lung contraction curves induced from the optic lobes and from the medulla in completely curarized turtles are practically indistinguishable. Both centers fail quickly under this type of stimulation and there is a single after-discharge (lung contraction) that appears more normal than the contractions induced directly by the stimulation. Complete tetanus of the lungs cannot be induced by central stimulation, evidently because of central refractory states.

A tonus rhythm or spontaneous contraction of the lung after section of the vagi nerves similar to that described by Fano and Fasola (2) in the European turtle, has been seen occasionally in our turtle preparation, when we used an exceedingly delicate tambour as a recording device. The contractions are feeble but slow and regular. They may persist for hours (fig. 23, *A*). It is probable that a peripheral automatic motor mechanism of the lung is present in all species of turtle, although it may differ in degrees in various species; but it requires not only delicate recording devices but, above all, animals in prime condition to reveal it. It is certain that parallel with the development of the new type of external respiratory mechanism in the reptilia, the peripheral lung motor automatism, so prominent in the amphibia, has retrograded or has been changed to one of primarily medullary origin.

LUNG REFLEXES

1. Lung reflexes from sensory stimulation of the respiratory tract: a. The pulmonary branches of the vagi contain two kinds of afferent fibers acting on the medullary center, one type causing reflex lung contraction in a quiescent preparation, or acceleration of the contractions in an active preparation. The other type causing inhibition of the tonus in the case of quiescent preparations or of the contractions in active preparations. For the sake of brevity we call these motor and inhibitory afferents, respectively. The motor afferents are stimulated by inflation as well as by deflation of the lung (fig. 11) or by the weak tetanizing current. Strong tetanizing currents, on the other hand, stimulate the inhibitory afferents. In all these experiments the lung inflation and deflation, and the direct stimulation of the central and of the pulmonary

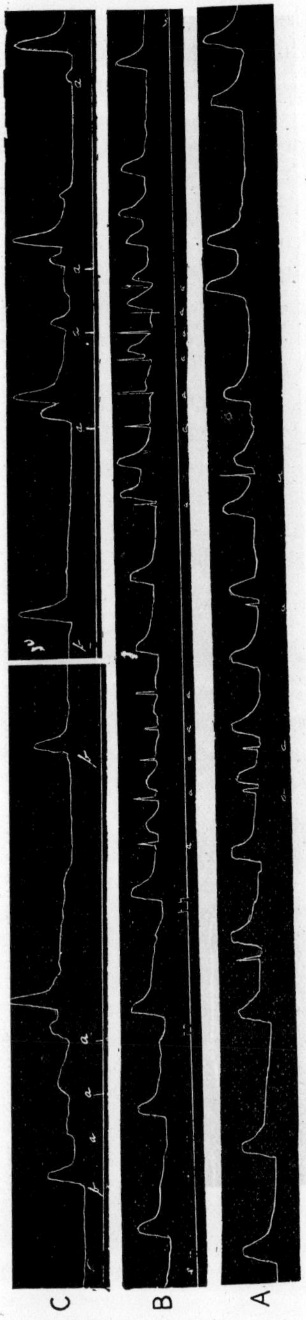

Fig. 11. Water manometer tracings of the intrapulmonic pressure in the turtle. All records from the left isolated lung; cannula in tip of lung. Animals decerebrated. Right lung intact. *A*: Animal completely curarized and showing contractions of isolated lung. *a*, single inflations (positive air pressure) in the intact lung, showing reflex contractions of opposite lung. *B*: animal not curarized. Signal, spontaneous respiration; *a*, single inflation of right or intact lung, showing reflex contractions and also evidence of central refractory state. *C*: Animal completely curarized, spontaneous lung rhythm absent; *b*, single inflation (positive pressure); *a*, single deflation of right or intact lung, showing reflex contraction into opposite lung both from deflation and inflation.

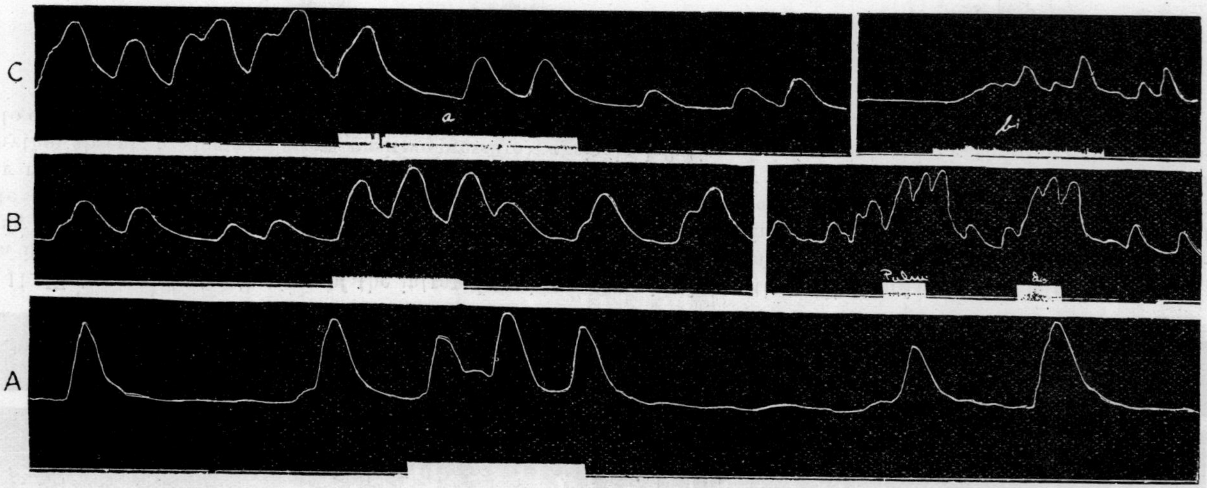

Fig. 12. Water manometer tracings of the intrapulmonic pressure in the turtle. Animals decerebrated and completely curarized. Records from left lung, isolated, except for pulmonary blood vessels and nerves. Cannula in tip of lung; bronchus ligated. *A* and *B:* stimulation of central end of pulmonary branches of right vagus with weak tetanizing current, showing reflex augmentation of the spontaneous lung rhythm. *C:* stimulation of central end of pulmonary vagi (right) with strong tetanizing current, showing inhibition of the spontaneous lung rhythm, *a*, and initiation of this rhythm in the quiescent preparations *b*.

vagi, we used, of course the lung and vagus on the opposite side to the lung serving to record the contractions. In no case did we note the inhibitory afferents being stimulated by lung inflation or lung deflation.

Typical tracings showing the reflex lung contraction on lung inflation and deflation are given in figure 11. Tracings showing the opposite reflex effects on weak and on strong tetanization of the central end of the pulmonary vagi are reproduced in figure 12. The pulmonary motor afferents can also be stimulated by other mechanical means, for example, rubbing the collapsed lung of one side between one's fingers induces reflex contraction in the opposite side via the medulla.

Reflex lung tetanus cannot be produced by lung deflation or inflation, that is, the active change in the intrapulmonic pressure, and not the state of continued inflation or collapse that acts as stimulus to the motor afferents.

In preparations not curarized, but breathing normally by means of the intact lung, single inflation of the intact lung during a respiratory pause usually gives a reflex lung contraction; but if the inflation is made shortly after completion of a spontaneous contraction by the isolated lung, the reflex may not be elicited. The same is true if a series of lung inflations is produced with very short intervals between each inflation. These facts evidently point to a condition of refractory state of the medullary reflex center, unless the phenomenon can be due to simultaneous stimulation of the inhibitory pulmonary afferents.

In turtle preparations in good condition deflation of one lung by suction through the trachea invariably initiates or accelerates the external respiratory movements. Lung inflation, on the other hand, may start a respiratory movement or it may temporarily inhibit the external respiration. It is thus evident that stimulation of the pulmonary motor afferents by lung inflation may initiate reflex lung contractions by acting on the medullary motor center directly, the discharge of the respiratory center not being a necessary link in the chain.

We have found that a single inflation of the intact or isolated lung aerates the blood, accelerates the heart and by so doing improves the circulation through the medullary centers because of the increase in the general arterial pressure. It is certain however that the contraction of the isolated lung following one or more inflations of the intact lung does not occur because of the improved circulation of a more highly oxygenated blood through the medullary lung center; for this reflex contraction persists not only following the inflation of a lung the pulmonary vessels of which have been occluded by a temporary ligature but can be elicited for a considerable time after the complete excision of the heart. On the other hand, it is not obtained from the isolated lung following a single or several inflations of the denervated but otherwise intact lung of the opposite side.

We designate the reflex inhibition of lung tonus and contraction by strong tetanization as due to a separate type of sensory fibers, the inhibitory afferents, at the same time keeping in mind the possibility that this inhibition may in reality be due to abnormally strong or

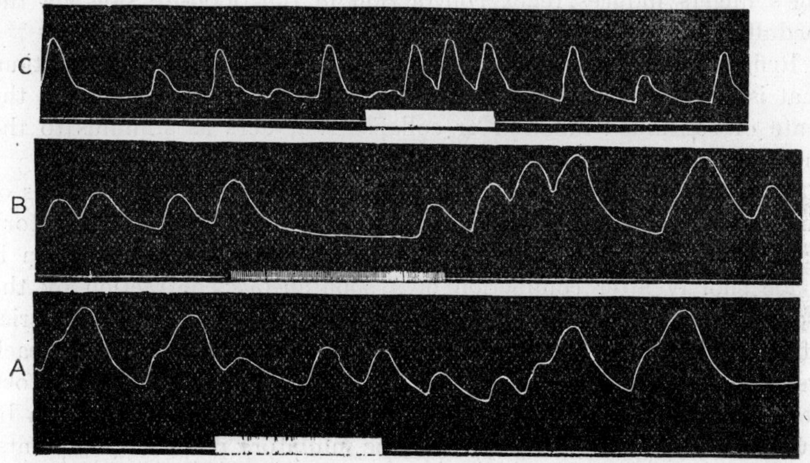

Fig. 13. Water manometer tracings of the intrapulmonic pressure in the turtle. Animals decerebrated and completely curarized. Records from left lung isolated except from pulmonary blood vessels and vagi branches. Cannula in left bronchus. *A* and *B:* stimulation of central end of recurrent laryngeal nerve, showing reflex inhibition of the lung rhythm. *C:* stimulation of central end of gastric branches of right vagus, showing reflex augmentation of the lung rhythm.

abnormally rapid series of impulses over the motor afferents impinging on the central automatic mechanism. This stimulation also inhibits the external respiratory movements.

b. Stimulation of the central end of the inferior or recurrent laryngeal nerves causes invariably reflex inhibition of the lung tonus and contractions (fig. 13, *A* and *B*). At no time was reflex lung contraction obtained from the central end of this nerve. Motor afferents for the lung reflex are either absent or the inhibitory afferents are so predominant that the action of the former type is entirely suppressed on simultaneous stimulation of the two types.

Observations on the effects of external respiration of stimulation of the central end of the inferior laryngeal were not made but in connection with this reflex depression of the lung contraction mechanism we can state that mechanical tension or pulling on the trachea causes profound depression of the respiratory center (fig. 14). Mechanical stimulation of the larynx and glottis (rubbing with blunt probe) on the other hand induces strong lung contractions.

c. Mechanical stimulation (gentle rubbing) of the posterior nares causes very powerful lung contractions. If the stimulation is long-

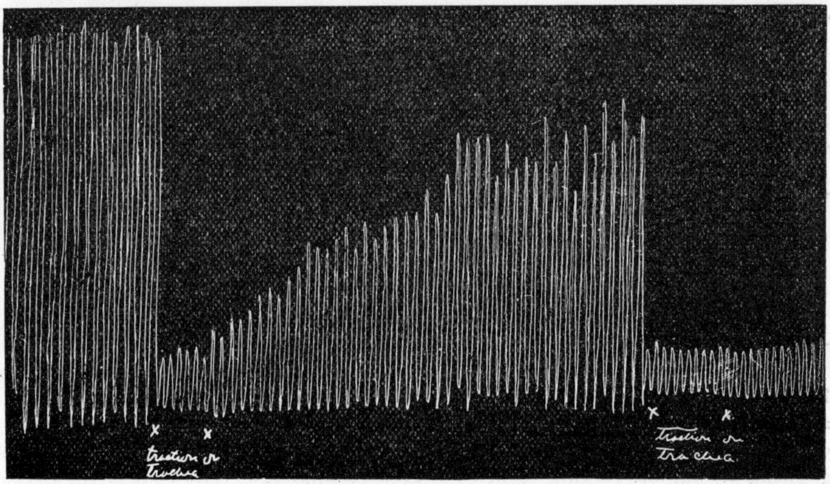

Fig. 14. Tracing of respiratory movements (water manometer) in the turtle. Animal decerebrated; cannula in trachea, rapid respiration due to partial asphyxia; x–x', strong forward traction on trachea, inducing a temporary depression of the respiratory center, probably through stimulation of the recurrent laryngeal nerves.

continued the lung goes into incomplete tetanus. This stimulation initiates lung contractions in quiescent preparations and accelerates the rhythm in active preparations. When the nares are thus stimulated in decerebrated but non-curarized preparations such stimulation induces most violent respiratory efforts and general struggling.

In general the reflex lung contractions evoked from the nares are more powerful than those produced by stimulation of any other region of the respiratory tract. It is one of the last lung reflexes to disappear as the preparation deteriorates from circulatory failure, and other causes, in long continued experiments. Reflex lung contractions from the nares can be obtained in preparations with the medullary center in such poor condition ("reflex shock") that the spontaneous external respiratory act is not accompanied by lung contraction, all of which point to the fact that the sensory nerve fibers of the posterior nares make strong motor connection with the medullary center controlling the lung contraction. Stimulation of the posterior nares with chemical irritants were not tried.

2. Lung reflexes from spinal sensory nerves: Weak tetanizing of the central end of any spinal nerve causes reflex lung contraction. Most of the tests were made with the sciatic and the large brachial nerves. Weak stimulation accelerates the rhythm in an active preparation and

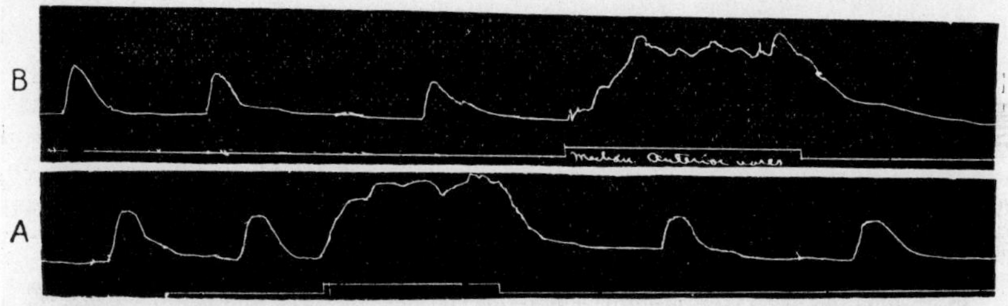

Fig. 15. Water manometer tracings of the intrapulmonic pressure in the turtle. Records from isolated left lung, cannula in left bronchus, pulmonary vagi fibers and blood vessels being intact. Animal decerebrated. *A*, animal completely curarized; *B*, animal not curarized. Signal, mechanical stimulation of the nares, showing incomplete tetanus (reflex), of greater amplitude than that of the rhythmical lung contractions.

initiates a rhythm in quiescent preparations (fig. 16, *A*, fig. 17, *A*). Strong stimulation induces incomplete lung tetanus (fig. 16, *B* at *x-x'*, fig. 17, *C*). In quiescent preparations the incomplete lung tetanus may be followed by brief periods of apparently spontaneous lung rhythm (fig. 17, *B*).

If the preparations are in good condition gentle rubbing of the skin causes lung contractions. Pinching, crushing or cutting the skin causes powerful motor reflexes into the lung (fig. 16, *C*), even when the reflex excitability is not at its maximum. Strong lung contractions are likewise induced by mechanical (rubbing with a blunt probe) or electrical stimulation of the cornea.

Reflex inhibition of the lung tonus or the rhythmical contractions were not obtained from the spinal sensory nerves by any mode of stimulation.

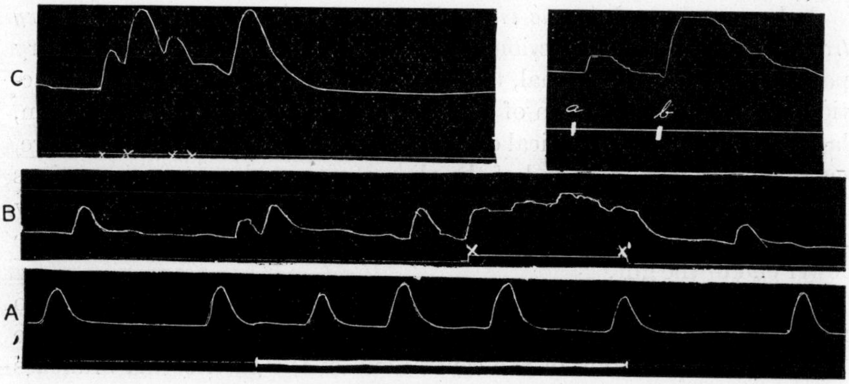

Fig. 16. Water manometer tracings of the intrapulmonic pressure in the turtle. Animals decerebrated and completely curarized. Records from left lung, isolated except for pulmonary blood vessels and vagi nerves. Cannula in tip of lung, bronchus ligated; *A:* light stimulation; *B:* stronger stimulation of central end of sciatic nerve, showing acceleration and incomplete tetanus of lung rhythm. *C: a,* stroking of skin of hind leg with finger; *b,* pinching toes of hind leg, *x,* cutting skin of hind leg. Showing reflex lung contraction on stimulation of cutaneous nerves.

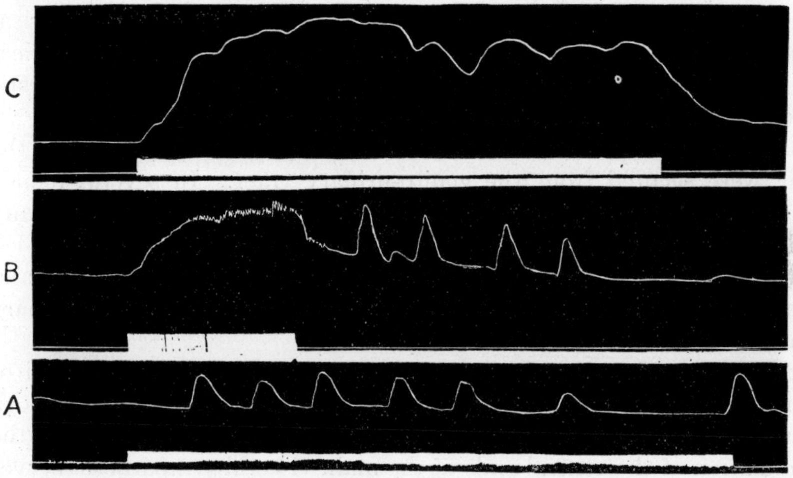

Fig. 17. Water manometer tracings of the intrapulmonic pressure in the turtle. Animals decerebrated and completely curarized. Records from left lung, isolated, except for pulmonary blood vessels and nerves. Left bronchus ligated; cannula in tip of lung. Preparations showing no spontaneous medulla-lung rhythm. Signal, stimulation of central end of sciatic nerve with tetanizing current. Showing reflex development of lung rhythm and lung tetanus.

3. Lung reflexes from the visceral sensory nerves: a. The alimentary tract. Reflex lung contractions may be obtained from practically every part of the alimentary canal, the most powerful being the lung contractions following stimulation of the lower end of the gut (cloaca, rectum, large intestine). Mechanical distention with balloon, rubbing, pressure, cutting or crushing this end of the alimentary canal causes contractions in the lung. (fig. 18, *B*, *C*, *Da*, *Dd*; fig. 19, *a*, *c*). In fact, one may induce incomplete tetanus of the lungs by strong stimulation of the lower end of the gut.

Mechanical or electrical stimulation of the small intestines also induces lung contractions (fig. 19, *b*, *d*). Similar lung reflexes are induced by stimulation of the central end of the gastric vagi branches (fig. 13, *C*), and by direct stimulation of the esophagus. But the contractions of the empty stomach, even when most vigorous, do not influence the lung motor mechanism.

Inhibition of the lung tonus and contractions were not seen as a result of artificial stimulation of the gut. But it seems clear that the afferent nerves of the alimentary canal, especially the oral and anal ends, make motor connections with the lung medullary centers.

b. The genito-urinary tract. Powerful lung contractions are induced by mechanical distention, pinching, crushing, tearing or electrical stimulation of the urinary bladder (fig. 18, *A*; fig. 19, *c*, *b*). Electrical or mechanical stimulation of the ureters, penis, prepuce and testis also produces motor reflexes into the lungs (fig. 18, *Dc*; fig. 19, *f*, *j*). As in the case of the alimentary tract, no reflex inhibitions into the lung were secured from the genito-urinary tract. In several female specimens the ovaries and the oviducts were stimulated, without any reflex influence on the lungs. Stimulation of the kidneys also yielded nothing definite in the way of lung reflexes. The most powerful and consistent lung reflexes in this group are those elicited from the urinary bladder.

c. The visceral sympathetic nerves. Outside the alimentary, the genito-urinary and the respiratory tracts no systematic or long-continued work was made on possible lung reflexes from the viscera, except for the stimulation of the central ends of the main visceral sympathetic nerves and connections. We may note, however, that the stimulation of the central end of the cardiac vagi branches has no effects on the lung. Reflex lung contractions were, on the other hand, obtained from the gall bladder, liver (fig. 19, *g*), and from the spleen.

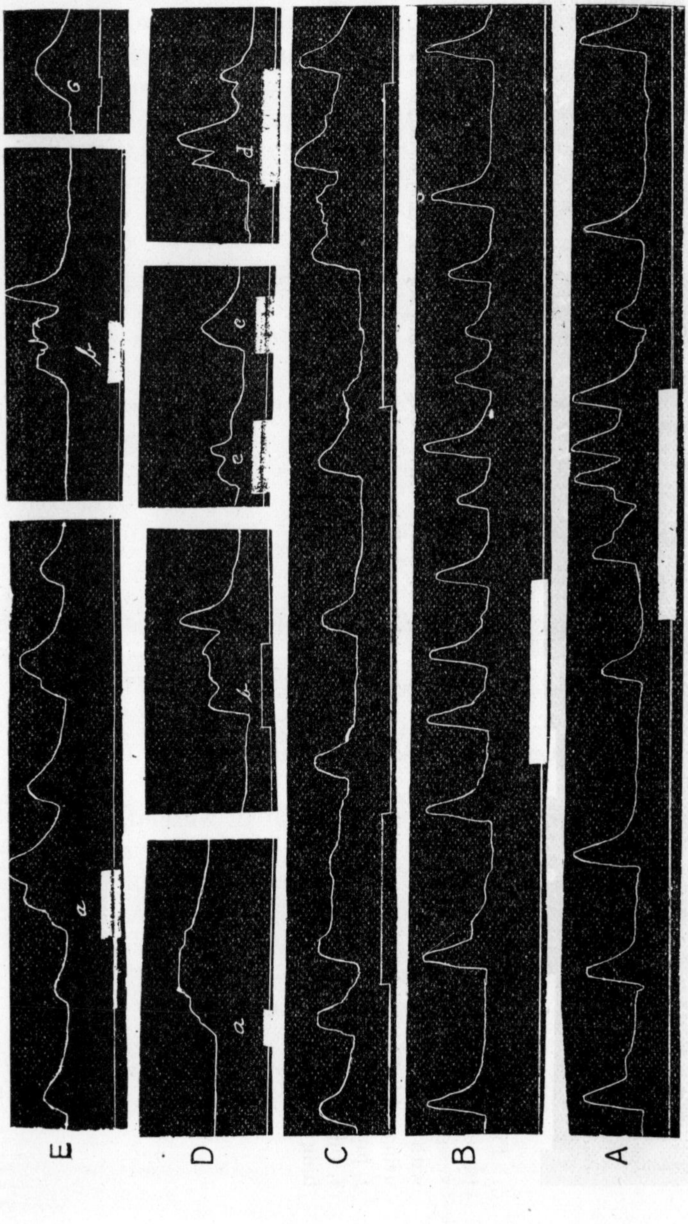

Fig. 18. Water manometer tracings of the intrapulmonic pressure in the turtle. Animals decerebrated and completely curarized. Records from left lung, isolated except for pulmonary blood vessels and vagi branches. Cannula in left bronchus. *A*: signal, distention of urinary bladder with balloon. *B*: signal, distention of rectum and large intestine by balloon, showing reflex augmentation of the lung rhythm. *C*: signal, mechanical stimulation of cloaca, showing reflex increase of lung rhythm. *D*: preparations showing no spontaneous lung rhythm; *a*, mechanical stimulation of cloaca; *b*, mechanical stimulation (pinching) of urinary bladder; *c*, mechanical stimulation (pinching) of penis; *d*, mechanical stimulation (pressing between fingers) of large intestine, showing reflex lung contractions. *E*: *a* and *b*, mechanical; *c*, electrical, stimulation of cornea, showing reflex lung contractions.

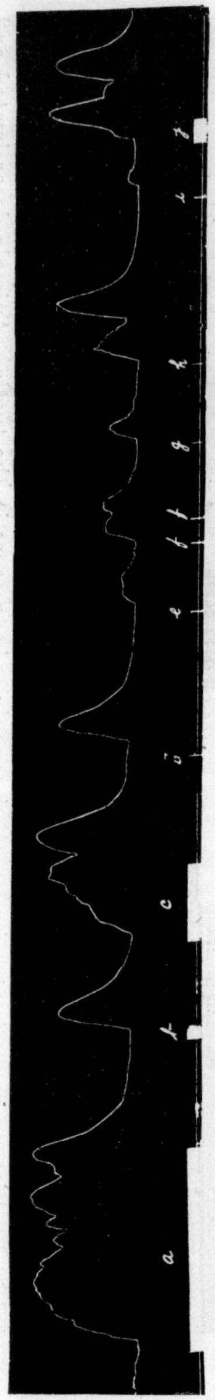

Fig. 19. Water manometer tracing of the intrapulmonic pressure in the turtle. Animal decerebrated and completely curarized. Tracing from left lung, isolated except for the pulmonary branches of the vagus and the blood vessels. Cannula in left bronchus. Preparation showing no spontaneous lung rhythm. *a*, Stimulation of rectum with strong tetanizing current; *b*, stimulation of small intestine, with strong tetanizing current; *c*, stimulation of urinary bladder, with strong tetanizing current; *d*, rubbing small intestine between fingers; *e*, cutting large intestine; *f*, pressing testes between fingers; *g*, rubbing urinary bladder between fingers; *h*, tearing wall of urinary bladder; *i*, rubbing tip of right lung between fingers; *j*, strong electrical stimulation of the right ureter. Showing reflex lung contractions and lung tetanus from stimulation of visceral sensory nerves.

The stimulation (electrical) of the central end of the visceral sympathetic nerves was made in a great many preparations, some in good, some in poor reflex conditions. The results are positive, that is, the stimulation of the visceral sympathetic nerves gives reflex lung contractions (fig. 20). The reflex lung contractions are particularly powerful from nerves *2*, *3* and *4* (fig. 2), these probably representing the group of splanchnic sympathetic nerves of the higher animals.

Reflex inhibitions of lung tonus and of lung contractions were never seen as results of stimulation of the central end of the visceral sympathetics.

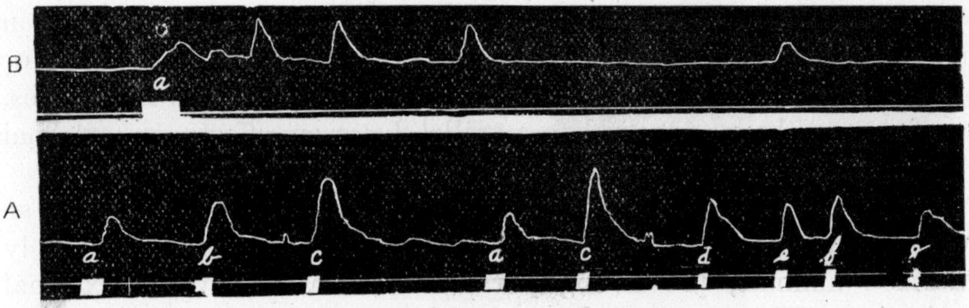

Fig. 20. Water manometer tracings of the intrapulmonic pressure in the turtle, showing reflex lung contractions on stimulation of the central end of various sympathetic nerves. Animals decerebrated and completely curarized. Record from isolated left lung; cannula in left bronchus. Preparations showing no spontaneous lung rhythm. *A:* stimulation with tetanizing current; *a*, nerve 2 (see fig. 2); *b*, nerve 3; *c*, nerves 2 and 3; *d*, nerve 4; *e*, nerve 5; *f*, nerve 6; *g*, nerve 7. *B:* *a*, stimulation with tetanizing current of nerves 2 and 3, showing reflex initiation of a temporary lung rhythm.

Results at times positive at times negative were obtained from the central end of the cervical sympathetic (fig. 2). In some preparations the stimulation of this nerve induced what appeared to be a reflex lung contraction, in other preparations, in equally good reflex condition, the stimulation had no effect on the lung. It appears, therefore, that afferent components in the cervical sympathetic nerve trunk are few in number and variable in their central action, at least as regards their influence on the medullary centers controlling lung tonus and lung contractions.

As the preparations are deteriorating the lung reflexes evoked from the visceral sympathetic nerves usually fail sooner than those called forth by stimulation of the spinal sensory or the afferent nerves of the respiratory tract itself. The cloaca, rectum and urinary bladder are an exception to this rule, the lung reflexes evoked from these organs usually persisting to the end of all reflex response of the animal.

4. The influence of visceral sensory nerves on the respiratory center. We have shown that, excepting the inferior laryngeal (inhibition), the cardiac vagi (no action), the cervical sympathetic (inconstant), and strong stimulation of the pulmonary afferents (inhibition), sensory stimulation, spinal and visceral, induces reflex lung contractions. Since lung contraction is a normal adjunct to the external respiratory act it is pertinent to ask whether these lung reflexes are not secondary to the initiation or acceleration of discharges from the respiratory center. What effects have these sensory stimuli on the rate and intensity of the external respiratory movements? The turtle appears to be no exception to the rule that stimulation of spinal sensory nerves accelerates or initiates external respiration. As regards the spinal sensory nerves, therefore, we have a complete parallel between effects on external respiration and on lung contractions. Both are positive.

In regard to the visceral sensory stimulation the results are not so clear. In the first place much of our reflex work was done on completely curarized animals, preventing parallel observation on the external respiration. We can state, however, that so far as our observations go, stimulation of the abdominal sympathetic nerves induces reflex contraction of the respiratory muscles as an invariable result. But discrepancies appear when we come to the stimulation of some of the visceral organs, especially the cloaca, rectum and urinary bladder. As already pointed out the mechanical or electrical stimulation of these organs causes reflex lung contractions and never any inhibition, at least in curarized preparations. But the same type of stimulation of these organs in non-curarized preparations may cause pure inhibition of the external respiration, as witness the tracing reproduced in figure 21. We are dealing here with two possibilities, viz., *a*, stimulation of some of the visceral sensory nerves induces opposite effects on the two medullary centers depressing the respiratory center and stimulating the lung motor center; or *b*, the visceral afferents may have both effects on the two centers, the end result (depression or stimulation) depending on the intensity and rate of the artificial stimulation, the central action of curare tending to reveal only the stimulation action on the lung motor mechanism. Further work is required to establish either or both of these possibilities.

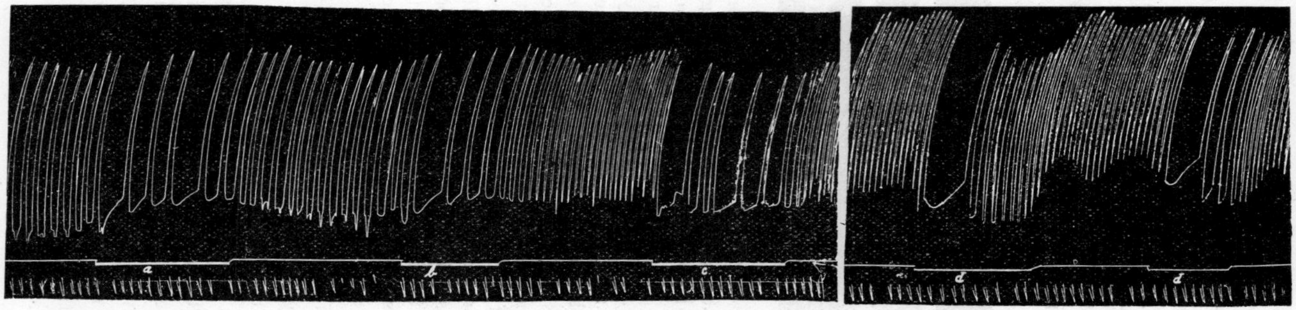

Fig. 21. Water manometer record of respiratory movements in the turtle; animal decerebrated; dorsal shell removed on left side; left lung isolated and left bronchus ligated. Right lung intact; cannula in trachea. *a*, Distention of rectum and lower part of large intestine by inflation of small balloon; *b*, electrical stimulation of the rectum; *c*, distention of urinary bladder by inflation of small balloon; *d*, electrical stimulation of urinary bladder, showing reflex inhibition of respiratory movements by stimulation of afferent nerves in large intestine, rectum and urinary bladder.

RESULTS ON THE SNAKE

1. Spontaneous lung contractions. If the external respiratory acts are not too close together, each act of external respiration is followed by a contraction of the lung. These lung contractions are feeble and of very short duration (fig. 22, *A*). If the attempts at external respiration come close together lung contractions appear only occasionally or rather during the respiratory pauses (fig. 27, *Ca*).

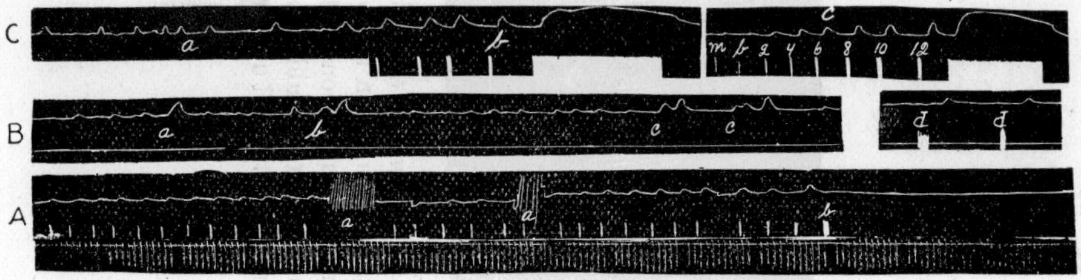

Fig. 22. Tracings (delicate air tambour) of the intrapulmonic pressure in the snake. Spinal cord cut and pithed below the medulla. Lung isolated; cannula in tip, trachea ligated. *A:* signal, spontaneous respiratory movements, showing lung contractions following each attempt at respiration; *a*, artificial respiration through cannula in tip of lung; *b*, pithing of brain followed by cessation of lung contractions. *B: a*, mechanical stimulation of skin of the head; *b*, mechanical stimulation of the cornea; *c*, mechanical stimulation of nares; *d*, electrical stimulation of central end of left vagus—showing reflex lung contractions. *C: a*, lung contractions following spontaneous respiratory efforts; *b*, tetanizing of both peripheral vagi; *c*, stimulation of the peripheral vagi with increasing number of electrical shocks—showing that motor discharge to lungs following respiratory movements is nearly maximal, as brief tetanizing of vagi produces only slightly greater lung contractions and that the vagi-lung muscle reacts to electrical stimulation like an ordinary nerve-muscle preparation. Time, 5 seconds.

These lung contractions in the snake appear to us too feeble to be of any value in the respiratory exchange of the lung.

2. Lung reflexes. Reflex lung contractions can be induced by the stimulation of the central end of one vagus, the other vagus being intact, and by stimulation of the nares, the cornea and the skin of the head region (fig. 22, *B*). The lung contraction following stimulation of the central end of one vagus is invariably preceded by an act of respiration, that is, a discharge from the respiratory center. The other reflex lung contractions may appear without being preceded by attempts at external respiration.

3. Rôle of the pulmonary vagi. Section of both vagi abolishes the lung contractions associated with the acts of external respiration. Stimulation of the peripheral end of either vagus causes contractions of the lung. These lung contractions appear to be confined to the upper third of the lung, that is, to the alveolated part or lung proper. It is a singular fact that, with one exception, all the paired lung reptilia thus far investigated, the lung motor action of the vagi is strictly unilateral, while in this species of snake both vagi act on the one lung. And it appears that the one-lunged condition of most snakes is due not to fusion of the original pair but to atrophy of one of the pair.

The lung motor fibers in the vagi of this snake can be stimulated with single induction shocks more readily than in the turtle. There is also less evidence of a tendency to an all-or-none motor response in the snake lung. In fact so far as our experiments go the vagus lung musculature behaves much like an ordinary nerve preparation.

Lung inhibitions from stimulation of the peripheral vagi were never observed. Destruction of the brain or section of both vagi neither decreased or increased the peripheral lung tonus. The lung vagi motor mechanism is either not in tonic activity or our method of preparing the animal abolishes this tonic activity through central "shock."

While our work on the snake was limited to eleven rather small specimens, the results indicate the essential parallel of the lung motor physiology in the snake and the turtle, namely, the vagi motor control and lung reflexes from the head origin of the animals. We have never observed a peripheral lung motor mechanism in the snake after section of the vagi.

THE DIRECT INFLUENCE OF THE SYMPATHETICS ON THE LUNG MOTOR TISSUES

Jackson and Pelz (7) have published tracings apparently showing strong inhibition of the lung tonus on stimulation of the central end of the cervical sympathetic nerve. These investigators also state that strong stimulation of this nerve may induce lung contractions of greater amplitude than that caused by stimulation of the peripheral end of the vagus. We have made great efforts to verify the results of Jackson and Pelz, particularly in view of the rôle which such inhibitory efferents may play in the lung reflexes.

We have been unable to follow nerve branches from the cervical sympathetic into the lung as figured by Jackson and Pelz. The sympathetic pulmonary branches described by them appear identical with the motor fibers from the brachial plexus to the striated muscle attached to the anterior and dorsolateral wall of the lung.

Stimulation of the central end of the cut cervical sympathetic may induce respiratory movements followed by lung contractions, provided the spinal cord and the vagi are intact. Or if the cervical sympathetic trunk is stimulated near its course past the brachial plexus, contractions of the striated lung muscle, previously referred to, may be produced by an escape of current to its motor fibers. These are the only motor effects on the lung that we have seen following the stimulation of the central end of the cervical sympathetic nerve, and neither are due to stimulation of sympathetic efferents.

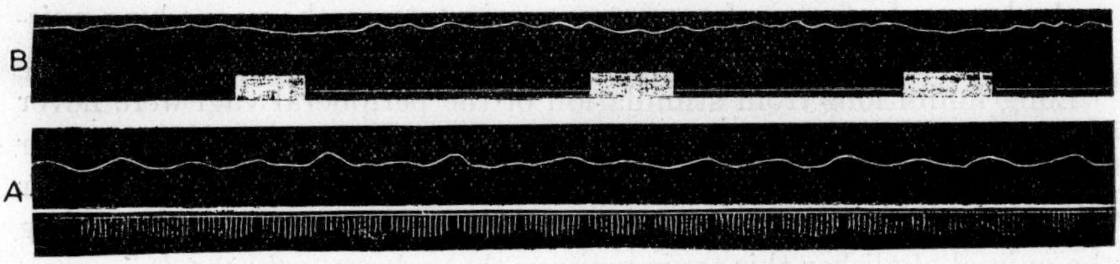

Fig. 23. Tambour tracings of the intrapulmonic pressure in the turtle. Animals decerebrated, fixed dorsal side down, plastron removed; stomach, liver and heart excised; vagi sectioned. Cannula in bronchus. *A:* Tracing showing a tonus rhythm in the lung independent of the vagi-medulla motor mechanism. *B:* Signal indicates stimulation of the central end of the cervical sympathetic nerve, showing slight inhibition (possibly reflex) of the peripheral lung tonus rhythm, developed after vagus section. Time, 5 second interval.

If the course of the sympathetic fibers to the lung in the reptilia is the same as in the amphibia and the mammals, these fibers should join the vagi in the neck or thorax and reach the lung via the pulmonary fibers of the vagi. We have stimulated the peripheral end of the cervical sympathetic nerve before its union with the vagus in very many preparations without any effect on the lung motor mechanism.

In one preparation only did we note any *inhibitory* effect on the lung from stimulation of the central end of the cervical sympathetic nerve. This preparation was decerebrated, fixed on the dorsal side, plastron removed, and eviscerated according to the method of Jackson and Pelz. A peripheral tonus rhythm appeared in the lung after section of the vagi. Tetanization (weak and strong) of the central end of the cervical sympathetic nerve induced some inhibition of this tonus

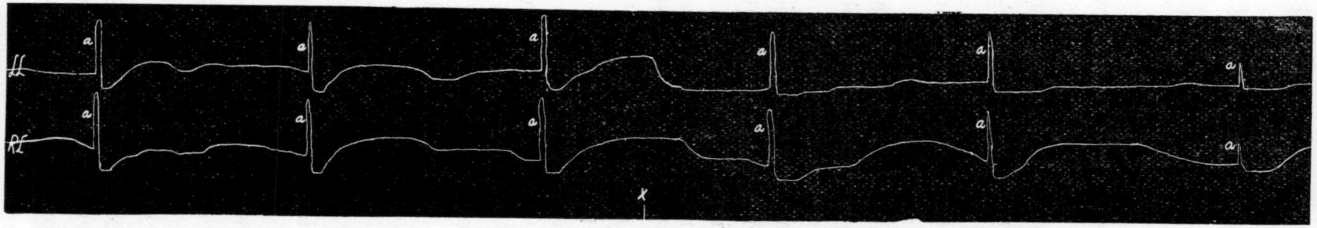

Fig. 24. Water manometer tracing of the intrapulmonic pressure in the turtle. Animal decerebrated, fixed dorsal side down; plastron removed; heart, liver, stomach and intestines excised; striated muscle on the anterior end of lung and its nerve connections left intact. *LL:* left lung; *RL:* right lung; *a*, spontaneous contraction (normal expiration) of the striated expiratory muscle on the surface of the lung, followed, during the respiratory pause, by prolonged tonus contractions of the lung musculature (asphyxia); *x*, section of the left vagus in the neck followed by cessation of the lung contractions, the respiratory contraction of the striated muscle on the lung persisting.

rhythm (fig. 23, *B*). Reflexes through the spinal cord were not excluded in this experiment.

The actual presence of sympathetic efferents to the reptilian lung is, therefore, an open question.

SUMMARY

1. Under normal conditions the external respiratory act inhibits the lung tonus by central action, and is followed by a contraction of the lung during the respiratory pause. These lung contractions are of central origin, the peripheral motor path being the vagi nerves (confirming Kahn and François-Franck).

2. The medullary center controlling the lung tonus and the lung contractions is not identical with the respiratory center, although normally associated with it in function in such a way that discharge from the respiratory center first depresses and then stimulates the lung motor center. The two centers are influenced in the same direction by asphyxial states, the lungs being put in a condition of incomplete tetanus by asphyxia, but one center may act, automatically or reflexly, without the other; and the lung motor centers are more profoundly influenced by afferent depressor nervous impulses (traumatic "shock").

3. The lung contraction developed during the respiratory pause is not a reflex depending on the muscular and other movements in the external respiratory act, as they persist after complete curarization, transection of the spinal cord in the neck, pithing the cord, or complete isolation of the lungs, save for the pulmonary vagi and blood vessels.

4. After section of the vagi a feeble tonus rhythm may appear in the lungs, but the strong contractions associated with external respiration are permanently abolished. Stimulation of the peripheral end of the vagi causes contractions and tetanus of the lungs, confirming the original observation of Bert. This vagus-lung action is unilateral. Stimulation of the peripheral vagus reveals no inhibitory action on the lung motor mechanism. Stimulation of the optic lobes or the medulla, the vagi being intact, causes lung contractions or incomplete lung tetanus (confirming Coombs). The lung tetanus is less complete than on direct stimulation of the peripheral end of the vagi, thus showing a central refractory state.

5. The physiological relation of the respiratory and the lung motor centers have a complete parallel in the relations of the activity of the swallowing center to the medullary mechanism controlling esophageal peristalsis. The action of the motor fibers of the vagi on the lung motor

tissues appears to be more direct and less complicated than the motor action of the vagi on the stomach, although there is some evidence of a tendency to an all-or-none response and rhythm in case of weak tetanization of the peripheral ends of the vagi even in the case of the lungs.

6. Inhibition as a primary act on the lung motor center in the medulla is produced by trauma to the vagi, stimulation of the central end of the inferior laryngeal nerve, and by strong stimulation of the central end of the pulmonary vagus. Trauma to the body causes a profound depression ("shock") of the lung motor center following an initial stimulation.

7. Reflex lung contractions or incomplete lung tetanus can be induced from stimulation of the sensory nerves of the respiratory tract (excepting the inferior laryngeal), that is by inflation, by deflation, or mechanical pressure on the lung of the opposite side, by weak tetanization of the pulmonary afferents, mechanical stimulation of the larynx and the nares. It is thus clear that the normal respiratory act by lung inflation and deflation will by itself induce a lung contraction reflexly. This afferent component from the lung is not necessary for the discharge of the lung motor center associated with the respiratory rhythm, but may act as a cumulative factor. The lung contractions and lung tetanus induced reflexly from mechanical stimulation of the posterior nares are particularly striking.

8. Mechanical and electrical stimulation of the alimentary tract (esophagus, gastric vagi, large and small intestine, rectum, cloaca) and the genito-urinary tract (urinary bladder, ureters, penis, prepuce, testes) induces reflex lung contractions or lung tetanus, the lung tetanus caused by stimulation of the cloaca, rectum and urinary bladder being particularly marked. Reflex lung contraction can also be evoked from stimulation of the gall bladder and the spleen.

9. Stimulation of the central ends of the visceral sympathetic nerves causes reflex lung contractions.

10. Stimulation (mechanical or electrical) of the cutaneous nerves, the cornea and the central end of the sciatic or brachial nerves induces reflex lung contractions or lung tetanus, depending on the strength of the stimulation.

11. The conclusions in regard to lung motor rhythm, its central and peripheral control, and the lung motor reflexes evoked from the head and neck region of the animal, apply both to the turtle and the snake. The lung reflexes from the viscera below the neck were not studied in the snake.

12. It would thus appear that the predominant reflex control of the lungs in these animals, at least under our experimental condition, is motor, thus differing entirely from the amphibia, where the predominating control (automatic and reflex) of the lung motor mechanism is inhibitory.

BIBLIOGRAPHY

(1) Bert: Leçons sur la physiologie comparée de la réspiration, Paris, 1870.
(2) Fano and Fasola: Arch. ital. d. Biol., 1894, xxi, 338.
(3) François-Franck: Arch. d. Zoöl. Exper., 1908, ix, 31.
(4) François-Franck: Arch. d. Zoöl., Exper., 1909, x, 547.
(5) François-Franck: Compt. Rend., 1906, lxi, 6.
(6) François-Franck: Compt. Rend. Soc. Biol., 1906, lxi, 127.
(7) Jackson and Pelz: Journ. Lab. Clin. Med., 1917, iii, 344.
(8) Kahn: Arch. f. Physiol., 1902, 29.
(9) Leydig: Lehrb. d. Histologie d. Mensch. und d. Tiere, Frankfurt, 1857 (as quoted by Oppel).
(10) Prevost et Saloz: Arch. Internat. de Physiol., 1909, viii, 327.
(11) Schulze: Stricker's Handbuch der Lehre von den Geweben d. Mensch. u. d. Tiere, Leipzig, 1871 (as quoted by Oppel).
(12) Coombs: This Journal, 1920, l, 511.
(13) Carlson and Luckhardt: This Journal, 1920, liv, 55.
(14) Luckhardt and Carlson: This Journal, 1920, liv, 122.

STUDIES OF THE RESPIRATORY MECHANISM IN CARDIAC DYSPNEA

I. The Low Alveolar Carbon Dioxide of Cardiac Dyspnea

JOHN P. PETERS, Jr. and DAVID P. BARR

From the Russell Sage Institute of Pathology, in affiliation with the Second Medical Division, Bellevue Hospital and the Department of Medicine, Cornell University Medical College

Received for publication August 9, 1920

It has been shown by many observers, working with various methods, Beddard and Pembrey (1), Porges, Leimdoerfer and Markovici (2), Peabody (3), Pearce (4)—that the alveolar carbon dioxide tension is usually found to be low in cardiac dyspnea. The causes and meaning of this phenomenon have never been clear. In cardiac dyspnea, in contradistinction to most conditions that are associated with a low alveolar CO_2, no proportionate reduction of the alkaline reserve of the blood has been found.

In 1917 one of us (5) studied the relation of the carbon dioxide tension of alveolar air to the bicarbonate concentration of venous plasma. A low alveolar CO_2-tension did not prove to be a constant characteristic of cardiac dyspnea. The alveolar CO_2 was sometimes normal. But it was always lower than normal in relation to the alkaline reserve of the blood as determined by the Van Slyke method. Van Slyke (6) found that in normal subjects the alveolar CO_2-tension maintained a fairly constant relation to the plasma bicarbonate. If the milligrams of CO_2 chemically bound in 1 cc. of plasma is multiplied by the constant 35, the result will be found to agree with the alveolar CO_2-tension (Haldane) expressed in mm. Hg. with about a 10 per cent variation. That is:

$$(\text{Alveolar } CO_2 \text{ in mm. Hg.}) \div (\text{mgm. } CO_2 \text{ chemically bound by 1 cc. of plasma} \times 35) = 100 \pm 10.$$

This observation we corroborated. That such a ratio should obtain in normal resting subjects seems reasonable. To a certain extent it must represent the $H_2CO_3/NaHCO_3$ ratio, if the alveolar CO_2 can be assumed to be a measure of the arterial CO_2-tension and the bicarbonates of venous plasma an indication of the bicarbonates of whole blood.

In most normal resting subjects such assumptions will give rise to no serious errors. The difference between the carbon dioxide content of the arterial and the venous blood is not large and is comparatively constant. In pathological conditions which interfere with the general circulation or the ventilation of the blood in the lungs, a disturbance of these factors and consequently of the ratio may be expected.

In normal resting subjects the alveolar CO_2/plasma bicarbonate ratio varied between 0.90 and 1.10. In cardiac decompensation with dyspnea and in some very advanced pulmonary conditions we obtained ratios consistently below 0.85. To draw any definite conclusions as to the cause of the phenomenon was impossible. We suggested that it might be an expression of some defect of the normal mechanism for the elimination of carbon dioxide and pointed out the possibility of connecting this with the pulmonary changes which had been demonstrated by Siebeck (7), Peabody (8) and others.

Before any interpretation of the low alveolar CO_2[1] of cardiac decompensation is attempted it is obviously necessary to ascertain whether the method employed is applicable and whether the results obtained can be said to represent the true alveolar tension. The prel minary work was done with the Fridericia pipette (9). This has given rise to some criticism. Repetition with a more orthodox Haldane method has given substantially the same results. Although Pearce (4) has criticised the use of the Haldane method, observations by his own method are substantially in agreement with ours.

Siebeck (7), after a careful study of the respiratory mechanism in cardiac insufficiency, came to the conclusion that all determinations of the alveolar CO_2 were useless in this condition. According to Siebeck (7) the alveolar aeration in cardiac dyspnea is very imperfect, in consequence of which the expiratory air contains an excess of unchanged inspiratory air. Apparently he means that attempts to deduce the arterial CO_2-tension from the values obtained by the Haldane alveolar method are unwarranted. But it is perfectly possible to

[1] Although the reduction of the alveolar CO_2-tension is not absolutely constant, few patients fail to show it. In these few the carbon dioxide capacity of the plasma is distinctly high, while in most instances it is at or slightly below the normal level. It seems proper and simpler, for this reason, to speak of the low alveolar CO_2 of cardiac dyspnea.

consider the alveolar CO_2 on its own merits as a functional entity without any deductions about arterial CO_2-tension. However well grounded the anatomical conceptions of Haldane with regard to the origin of the alveolar air in the normal lung may be, it is quite conceivable that in pathological or physiological disturbances, conditions may be so altered that any anatomical term loses its original significance. Here a functional conception proves of greater value.

A normal expiration may be divided into two parts. The first part is practically useless from the standpoint of respiration; it merely serves to empty the dead space (the nose, mouth, pharynx, larynx, trachea and bronchi) of the room air with which it was filled by the last inspiration. In normal resting subjects the volume of this dead space is fairly constant, varying about an average of 130 cc. Behind this lies a mass of air of nearly constant gaseous composition throughout its whole extent and in close contact with the blood in the pulmonary circulation. This is the air which serves for the effective exchange of gases between the blood and the outside air, and it is a sample of this air that the Haldane method attempts to obtain.

The first object of these studies was to find out whether samples obtained by the Haldane method represented the effective respiratory air. We have employed other methods in order to determine whether they give results in agreement with the Haldane values.

Our studies have been confined to three methods: the Haldane (10), the Plesch (11) and the Henderson (12) venous CO_2. Pearce's (13) method has been omitted because its use in severe dyspnea presents considerable difficulties and also because it demands an amount of apparatus that renders it less adaptable as an ordinary clinical procedure.

THE HALDANE METHOD

The Haldane technique for obtaining alveolar specimens, although criticised for various reasons, is still considered the standard technique for the determination of the arterial CO_2-tension in normal subjects. It has not been generally adopted for clinical studies because of a popular opinion that it is difficult or impossible to obtain good samples in any but highly trained subjects. This we have not found to be the case. We are inclined to believe the observer needs more training than the subject.

In these studies we have adhered in all essential respects to the orthodox Haldane technique, introducing only slight modifications which tend to diminish subjective errors. One of these is by no means original and consists of the introduction of a three-way brass stop-cock designed by Mr. G. F. Soderstrom and shown in figure 1. This makes it unnecessary for the patient to close the tube with his tongue. Furthermore, no attempt has been made to collect inspiratory and expiratory specimens, as Haldane advises. Instead, samples have been obtained from the end of a forced expiration begun as soon as possible after the completion of a normal inspiration. When the respirations

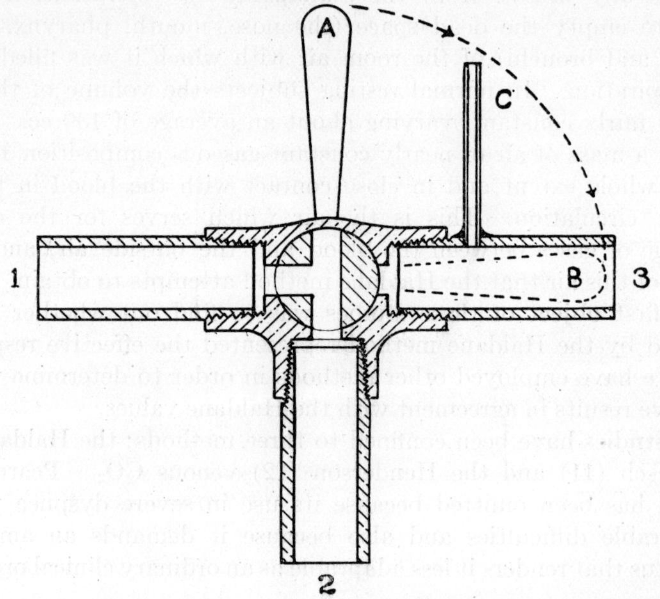

Fig. 1. Three-way stop-cock. *1*, tube for attachment of mouth-piece; *2*, tube leading to spirometer or left open to outside air; *3*, tube for attachment of Haldane tube, with side-arm *C*, to connect with gas sampling tube.

are rapid, as they are in cardiac dyspnea, it is almost impossible to turn the valve at the proper moment to differentiate inspiratory and expiratory alveolar air with any degree of certainty. The propriety of using an expiratory specimen also seems questionable. The prolongation of expiration during dyspnea may be equivalent to holding the breath for the duration of an extra respiration. We have tried to make the subjects force the air out rapidly enough so that the expiration is not considerably longer than a normal one. The specimens as obtained by this method are not all from expirations initiated at the same point in the respiratory cycle, but at various points in the expiratory phase between full inflation and deflation of the lungs.

In detail the procedure is as follows: The rubber mouth-piece with the stop-cock and tube in place is first put in the patient's mouth with the stop-cock open to the air. He is encouraged to breathe through it to convince him that it will not "shut off his breath." After he has gained sufficient confidence the tube is removed from his mouth and a simple spring nose-clip applied to his nose. When he is sure he can breathe through his mouth alone without difficulty the mouth-piece is replaced in his mouth. He is then instructed how to deliver a sample on command and without altering his normal respirations. The sampling tube is then attached to the side-arm of the stop-cock. The operator stands at the right of the bed supporting the tube with his left hand, with his right on the handle of the stop-cock. When he feels that the breathing is normal and regular he tries to accustom himself to its rhythm, so that he may give the signal at the right moment. The signal is given and the stop-cock turned at the same moment. At the end of the forced expiration the cock is turned to the outside air again before the subject has had time to gasp for breath. The operator soon learns to know whether there has been a subjective error in the technique on his own part or that of the patient.

From an inexperienced subject we are accustomed to take several specimens. Although some of the first will occasionally be obviously too low, it is generally possible to get good agreement on the third or fourth attempt in even the most obtuse subject, as may be seen in tables 1 and 2. In a total of 48 observations on 25 patients, involving the collection and analysis of 127 samples, all but four patients gave duplicate samples that varied by 0.4 per cent or less, an accuracy that compares favorably with that found in trained subjects. Patients with cardiac dyspnea proved no exception to this rule. Three of the four patients (A. R., J. J. F. and D. W.) who gave unsatisfactory results on the basis of this criterion, exhibited Cheyne-Stokes breathing. The fourth (P. O. S.) was very ill, somewhat irrational and showed a slight respiratory irregularity.

The results obtained by the Haldane method are in accordance with those previously obtained with the Fridericia tube. The values are comparatively low and much lower than should be expected from the level of plasma bicarbonates. Two obvious criticisms of the method might be made:

1. That the volume of the expiration is too small to clear the patient's dead space.

TABLE 1

Variations in duplicate Haldane specimens in subjects without respiratory or cardiac disorders

SUBJECT AND CONDITION	ALVEOLAR CO_2	MAXIMUM OBSERVED VARIATION	MAXIMUM ACCEPTED VARIATION*	AVERAGE ALVEOLAR CO_2
	per cent			*mm.*
D. P. B., normal	6.16 5.94	0.22	0.22	43.1
	5.25 5.31	0.06	0.06	37.4
	5.72 5.74	0.02	0.02	40.6
	5.39 5.26	0.13	0.13	37.9
	5.16 5.40	0.24	0.24	37.6
	5.39 5.57	0.18	0.18	39.0
	5.60 5.60	0.00	0.00	38.7
	5.39 5.60	0.21	0.21	39.2
	5.45 5.50	0.05	0.05	38.8
	5.62 5.51	0.11	0.11	39.1
	5.32 5.24 5.58	0.34	0.34	38.6
J. P., normal	(5.28) 5.64 5.74 5.45	0.46	0.29	39.9
	5.94 5.85	0.09	0.09	41.6

TABLE 1—*Concluded*

SUBJECT AND CONDITION	ALVEOLAR CO_2	MAXIMUM OBSERVED VARIATION	MAXIMUM ACCEPTED VARIATION*	AVERAGE ALVEOLAR CO_2
	per cent			*mm.*
J. P., normal	5.88	0.26	0.26	40.5
	5.62			
	5.35	0.15	0.15	37.5
	5.20			
Capt., normal	6.24	0.07	0.07	44.4
	6.31			
W. S. M., normal	4.70	0.12	0.12	34.8
	4.82			
P. K., gastric neurosis	5.88	0.25	0.25	41.2
	5.61			
	5.86			
Jno. K., diabetes mellitus	4.24	0.16	0.16	30.1
	4.19			
	4.35			
	4.07	0.05	0.05	28.4
	4.06			
	4.02			
C. P., pernicious anemia	3.98	0.11	0.11	28.2
	3.91			
	4.02			
H. R., polycythemia	4.94	0.32	0.32	34.7
	5.11			
	4.79			

* Values in parenthesis in this and the following table have been discarded for the most part on the basis of internal evidence, only.

2. That the low values are produced by subjective errors; preliminary forced inspirations or gasping at the end of expiration.

To rule these out we attached the Haldane tube to a Tissot spirometer which was equipped with a calibrated recording device which will be described later. By this means we were enabled to obtain a graphic record of the respiration during the entire time that the stopcock was turned, and could at the same time measure the volume of the

TABLE 2

Variations in duplicate Haldane specimens with values for alveolar CO_2 and plasma bicarbonates in patients with cardiac disease

NAME AND DIAGNOSIS	ALVEOLAR CO_2	MAXIMUM OBSERVED VARIATION	MAXIMUM ACCEPTED VARIATION	AVERAGE ALVEOLAR CO_2	ALVEOLAR CO_2 CALCULATED FROM PLASMA BICARBONATE	DIFFERENCE BETWEEN CALCULATED AND OBSERVED ALVEOLAR CO_2	REMARKS
	per cent			*mm.*	*mm.*	*mm.*	
J. W., cardionephritic	4.71 4.75 4.76	0.05	0.05	34.6	39.7	5.1	Hypertension. No dyspnea, hyperpnea nor other signs of decompensation
J. A., cardionephritic	(5.21) 6.01 5.76 5.99	0.80	0.25	42.3	49.7	7.4	Hypertension, no dyspnea, cyanosis nor other signs of decompensation at rest
	4.38 3.98 4.25	0.40	0.40	30.0	41.5	11.5	Slight dyspnea and cyanosis. Lungs show râles at right base
A. J., shell shock	4.59 4.43 (4.03)	0.56	0.16	32.5	46.8	14.3	Effort syndrome. No organic cardiac nor pulmonary condition. Discrepancy probably due to over-ventilation
	4.86 4.78	0.08	0.08	33.6			

J. M. L., chronic cardiac	5.43 5.39	0.04	0.04	38.5			No symptoms nor signs of decompensation. Lungs clear
	5.11 5.35	0.24	0.24	37.2			
A. R., cardionephritic	3.96 4.23 4.78 4.21	0.82	0.82	30.6	31.9	1.3	Hypertension, signs of chronic uremia. Variations in alveolar samples probably due to Cheyne-Stokes breathing
R. W., chronic cardiac	5.69 5.90 5.67 5.78	0.23	0.23	41.0			No dyspnea, cyanosis nor other signs of decompensation
	5.79 6.12	0.33	0.33	42.4			
	6.10 6.22 6.52	0.42	0.42	44.7			
J. C., chronic cardiac	4.65 4.43 4.39	0.26	0.26	32.0			No dyspnea, cyanosis nor other signs of decompensation while at rest. The low alveolar values obtained in the first observation probably due to overventilation
	5.09 5.33 5.37 5.38	0.29	0.29	38.5	43.9	5.4	

TABLE 2—*Continued*

NAME AND DIAGNOSIS	ALVEOLAR CO_2	MAXIMUM OBSERVED VARIATION	MAXIMUM ACCEPTED VARIATION	AVERAGE ALVEOLAR CO_2	ALVEOLAR CO_2 CALCULATED FROM PLASMA BICARBONATE	DIFFERENCE BETWEEN CALCULATED AND OBSERVED ALVEOLAR CO_2	REMARKS
	per cent			*mm.*	*mm.*	*mm.*	
J. J. F., chronic cardiac	4.62 5.08 5.12 4.43	0.69	0.69	34.2	45.5	11.3	
D. W., cardionephritic	(3.08) 4.07 (3.22) 3.59	0.99	0.48	27.3	30.2	2.9	Aortic regurgitation with hypertension. Dyspnea and orthopnea with Cheyne-Stokes breathing. Slightly irrational. Great variations largely due to inadequate coöperation. Low values eliminated by graphic records. Dyspnea probably due to acidosis and not to cardiac disease
P. O. S., chronic cardiac	5.85 5.06 5.27 5.53	0.79	0.79	40.1	52.3	12.2	Extreme decompensation, dyspnea, orthopnea, and Cheyne-Stokes breathing
J. B., chronic cardiac	4.55 4.45	0.10	0.10	32.1	44.8	12.7	Moderate hyperpnea, some cyanosis. Slight edema. Lungs clear. No subjective dyspnea
	4.04 4.18	0.14	0.14	29.3			
	4.21 4.01	0.20	0.20	29.3			

W. W., cardionephritic	3.84 4.15	0.31	0.31	28.5			Moderate dyspnea and orthopnea while at rest. Some signs of fluid in right pleural cavity. Râles over base of left lung
	4.08 4.00 3.97 3.98	0.11	0.11	28.6	43.7	15.1	
J. D. B., chronic cardiac	3.11 3.55	0.06	0.06	25.4			Considerable dyspnea and hyperpnea and orthopnea. Moderate cyanosis
	3.35 3.69	0.34	0.34	25.3	41.7	16.4	
	3.85 3.82 3.90 3.89	0.08	0.08	27.6	46.6	19.0	
	4.51 4.62 4.64 4.34	0.30	0.30	32.2			
J. R., chronic cardiac	4.59 4.56 4.64	0.08	0.08	32.8	48.0	15.2	Severe dyspnea, orthopnea, edema, right hydrothorax
C. D., chronic cardiac	5.10 4.89	0.21	0.21	35.9	46.9	11.0	Severe dyspnea and orthopnea, slight cyanosis. Slight dulness at base of right lung
	4.43 4.75 4.53	0.32	0.32	32.5			

TABLE 2—*Concluded*

NAME AND DIAGNOSIS	ALVEOLAR CO_2	MAXIMUM OBSERVED VARIATION	MAXIMUM ACCEPTED VARIATION	AVERAGE ALVEOLAR CO_2	ALVEOLAR CO_2 CALCULATED FROM PLASMA BICARBONATE	DIFFERENCE BETWEEN CALCULATED AND OBSERVED ALVEOLAR CO_2	REMARKS
	per cent			*mm.*	*mm.*	*mm.*	
Jos. C., cardionephritic	5.36 (4.95) 5.53 5.43	0.58	0.17	38.7	47.8	9.1	Hypertension, auricular fibrillation, marked dyspnea and orthopnea. Some cyanosis. Deformity of right chest
	5.97 5.75 6.06	0.31	0.31	42.2	49.7	7.5	
	(5.78) 6.22 6.60 6.31 6.18	0.82	0.42	44.9	52.2	7.3	
S. I., chronic cardiac	4.01 3.65 3.91	0.36	0.36	27.4	47.6	20.2	Extreme dyspnea, orthopnea, cyanosis and edema, right hydrothorax, râles over remainder of lungs
D. O. C., chronic cardiac	4.21 4.12	0.09	0.09	29.7	40.9	11.2	Considerable cyanosis, orthopnea, and dyspnea. Signs of fluid in right pleural cavity
	3.61 3.83	0.22	0.22	26.5			Cyanosis and dyspnea more marked

D. O. C., chronic cardiac	3.61 3.99 3.67	0.38	0.38	26.7			Condition unchanged
	3.70 3.92 (4.43) 3.56	0.87	0.36	26.6	38.2	11.6	Pleural fluid has increased. Dyspnea more marked
	3.97 3.61	0.36	0.36	23.6			Fluid in both pleural cavities
	3.52 3.82 3.70	0.30	0.30	26.2			Condition unchanged
J. M., chronic cardiac	3.52			25.0	40.9	15.9	Extreme cyanosis. Moderate dyspnea, considerable hyperpnea, right hydrothorax
	4.87 5.03	0.16	0.16	34.8	52.0	17.2	No dyspnea, moderate hyperpnea, cyanosis still marked. Hydrothorax diminished
J. K., chronic cardiac	3.26 3.13 3.03 3.03	0.23	0.23	22.0	37.8	15.8	Extreme cyanosis, slight dyspnea, considerable hyperpnea, few râles scattered over both lungs
	4.24 4.86 4.56	0.62	0.62	32.5			Dyspnea gone, cyanosis slight, still some hyperpnea. Lungs clear
C. C., chronic cardiac	3.95 3.68 3.91	0.27	0.27	27.4			Marked cyanosis. Little dyspnea. No orthopnea. Considerable hyperpnea

TABLE 3

Relation of alveolar CO_2 to volume of expiration

SUBJECT	VOLUME OF EXPIRATION	ALVEOLAR CO_2
	cc.	*per cent*
J. C., chronic cardiac compensated	1016	5.09
	823	5.33
	807	5.37
	790	5.38
W W., chronic cardiac decompensated	797	4.08
	864	4.00
	615	3.97
	665	4.35
	385	4.32
R. W., chronic cardiac compensated	710	5.90
	452	5.67
	645	5.78
	758	6.10
	651	6.22
	516	6.52
J. D. B., chronic cardiac decompensated	1081	4.51
	1290	4.62
	758	4.64
	986	4.34
A. R., cardionephritic. Periodic breathing	505	3.96
	535	4.23
	430	4.78
	505	4.21
D. W.,* cardionephritic. Periodic breathing	(758	3.08)
	677	4.07
	(629	3.22)
	952	3.59

* See figure 2.

expiration. Table 3 shows the values obtained from six experiments done in this way. From the first five experiments it is evident that the expiratory volume is sufficient to clear completely any but an enormously increased dead space. If the dead space were increased to this degree, however, the alveolar CO_2-tension should vary with the expiratory volume. This relation does not obtain. In only one instance, the second observation on R. W., is any such relation even suggested, and in this case the total variation is only 0.23 per cent.

In none of these cases is there any indication in the graphic records of inspiratory activity during the time that the stop-cock was open. That the method is capable of showing such subjective errors is demonstrated in the record of D. W. (fig. 2). This patient presented symptoms of uremia with Cheyne-Stokes respiration. His tracings show that the low values obtained from the first and third samples were due

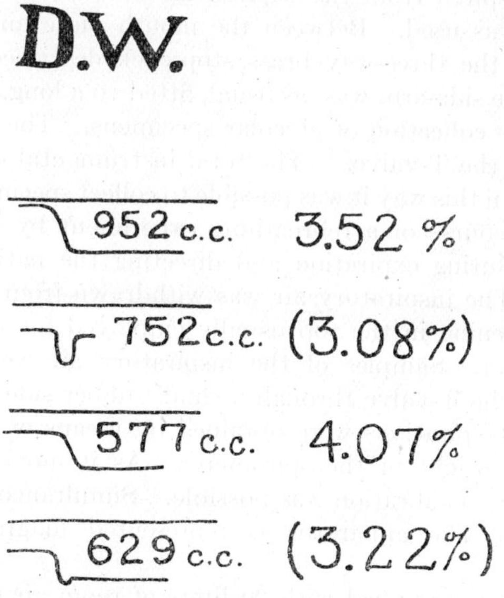

Fig. 2

to inspirations while the valve was open and before the samples had been withdrawn. The discrepancy in the two remaining values seems to depend on the fact that one was obtained during an apneic, the other during a dyspneic period.

The low alveolar CO_2 is not due to subjective errors on the part of the patient nor to any considerable increase in the volume of the dead space.

The alveolar CO_2 after rebreathing. One of the most striking characteristics of decompensated cardiac patients is the intolerance to an increase of CO_2 in the inspired air (14).

It has been shown by Haldane (15) and others that when a person rebreathes air the alveolar CO_2-tension and the ventilation increase as the CO_2 in the inspired air rises. When the alveolar CO_2-tension has risen to a certain point the patient becomes extremely dyspneic and uncomfortable. This we may call the point of intolerance to CO_2. If the alveolar CO_2 be low in cardiac dyspnea at rest it seems reasonable to suppose that it should also be relatively low after rebreathing to the point of intolerance.

For the rebreathing experiments a 100-liter Tissot spirometer, accurately balanced and calibrated at all levels, was employed. To separate the inspired from the expired air a two-way T-valve of the Douglas type was used. Between the mouth piece and this T-valve was interposed the three-way brass stop-cock described above. The opening with the side-arm was, as usual, fitted to a long, wide-bore rubber tube for the collection of alveolar specimens. The other arm was connected with the T-valve. (The total instrumental dead space was about 50 cc.) In this way it was possible to collect specimens of alveolar air during the course of a rebreathing experiment by merely turning the stop-cock during expiration and directing the patient to breathe out forcibly. The inspiratory air was withdrawn from the spirometer through the opening in the top usually employed for the insertion of the thermometer. Samples of the inspiratory air were drawn from this tube near the T-valve through a small rubber side arm. Graphic records of the respirations were obtained by means of a pen attached to the counter-weight of the spirometer. As it moved in a vertical plane only, direct calibration was possible. Simultaneous time records were obtained. The apparatus is represented diagrammatically in figure 3.

The spirometer was filled with 20 liters of room air for each experiment. A larger amount was found to prolong the experiment unduly and to introduce a considerable element of fatigue. Smaller amounts rendered the succession of events too rapid to permit the introduction of all the necessary procedures and accurate analysis of the results obtained.

The minute volume attained in the rebreathing experiments was calculated from the average tidal air and the respiratory rate during the last half-minute of the experiment, except in one or two cases where the limit of tolerance was reached so rapidly that it was necessary to use a shorter terminal period for purposes of calculation. Of course, assuming that the minute volume increases continuously throughout

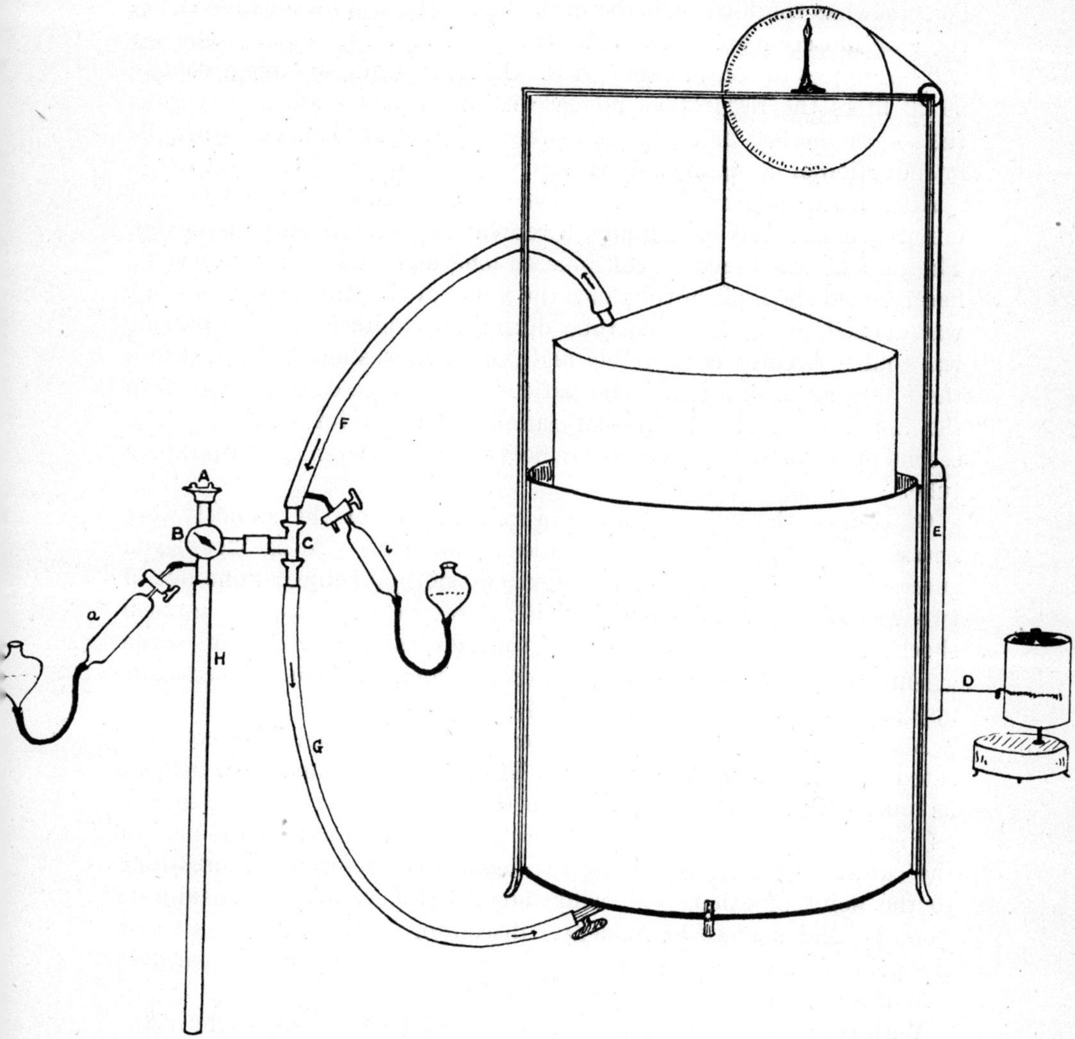

Fig. 3. *A*, mouth-piece; *B*, 3-way stop-cock; *C*, Douglass valve; *F*, inspiratory tube; *G*, expiratory tube; *E*, counterweight of spirometer; *D*, recording pen; *H*, Haldane tube; *a*, sampling tube for alveolar air; *i*, sampling tube for inspiratory air.

the course of the experiment, the values obtained in this way must be somewhat too low. On the other hand, the respirations never become absolutely regular, and calculations based on too small a number will be subject to considerable error. In rebreathing so large a volume as 20 liters the respiratory increase is sufficiently gradual to permit the use of the last half-minute, in the majority of instances, with the introduction of no significant error.

After a satisfactory determination of the resting alveolar CO_2 and minute volume had been made, a rebreathing experiment was begun. The patient was urged to continue as long as he felt able. When he had reached the limit of tolerance the valve of the three-way stop-cock was opened to the Haldane tube during an expiration. The patient was told to breathe out forcibly and the valve was again closed before the following inspiration. The patient was at once disconnected from the apparatus and the alveolar sample removed for analysis. The second operator at the same time removed a sample from the inspiratory tube.

Of course, the coördination and coöperation of the subject were necessary and there were opportunities for mistakes. Altogether eleven successful experiments were made on two normal subjects; one out of two was successful in a patient with a gastric neurosis; one in shell shock; three in two compensated cardiacs; and five out of seven attempted in four patients with cardiac decompensation. The results appear in summarized form in table 4.

A very striking difference is apparent at once between the decompensated cardiac cases and the others. The former were unable to tolerate as much CO_2 in the inspired air and their alveolar CO_2 did not rise to as high a level. This was due to no lack of will power on the part of the cardiacs because in one or two cases they continued rebreathing to the point of exhaustion, while none of the compensated subjects went beyond a state of moderate discomfort. The alveolar CO_2 at the point of intolerance is therefore lower in decompensated cardiacs than it is in normal persons.

With the exception of A. J., the shell shock patient, the height of the alveolar CO_2 at which intolerance was reached bore a general relation to the preliminary alveolar CO_2-tension. In this one case the low resting alveolar CO_2 was due to over-ventilation. This was clearly shown by the fact that his initial reaction to rebreathing was a reduction of the minute-volume, instead of an increase.

TABLE 4

The effect of rebreathing on the alveolar CO_2

NUMBER AND NAME	RESTING ALVEOLAR CO_2	AT END OF REBREATHING EXPERIMENT: Inspiratory air CO_2	AT END OF REBREATHING EXPERIMENT: Alveolar CO_2	DIAGNOSIS AND REMARKS
	per cent	*per cent*	*per cent*	
1. D. P. B.		8.36	8.52	Normal adult. Continued rebreathing to point of considerable discomfort
	6.05	8.01	8.16	
		7.93	8.21	To discomfort
	5.28	8.06	8.30	To discomfort
	5.73	7.84	7.95	To slight discomfort
		6.86	7.53	To slight discomfort
2. J. P.		7.90	8.32	Normal adult. To considerable discomfort
		7.95	7.98	To extreme discomfort
		6.90	7.27	To discomfort
		6.86	7.05	To considerable discomfort
3. P K.	5.78	6.61		Gastric neurosis
	5.50	6.07	6.85	To moderate discomfort. No exhaustion
4. T. deC.	5.50	5.90	7.30	Chronic cardiac valvular disease, compensated
	5.70	6.59	7.27	Rebreathed to point of moderate discomfort
5. J. M. L.	5.23	7.54	7.92	Chronic cardiac. Compensated. Continued rebreathing to point of considerable discomfort
6. A. J.	4.51	6.26	6.30	Shell shock with effort syndrome. To moderate discomfort only
	4.72	6.30	6.89	
7. J. A.	5.92	5.74	6.36	Chronic cardiac, valvular disease, compensated while at rest. Rebreathed to point of considerable discomfort with some exhaustion
		4.52	7.34	
8. J. B.	4.50	3.70		Chronic cardiac valvular disease. Moderate dyspnea while at rest. In the first two experiments continued only to mild discomfort. In the last experiment considerable discomfort. Somewhat exhausted
	4.50	3.92	5.55	
	4.11	5.17	6.26	

TABLE 4—*Concluded*

NUMBER AND NAME	RESTING ALVEOLAR CO_2	AT END OF REBREATHING EXPERIMENT		DIAGNOSIS AND REMARKS
		Inspiratory air CO_2	Alveolar CO_2	
	per cent	*per cent*	*per cent*	
9. Jos. C....	5.93	3.88	6.68	Cardio-nephritic with cardiac decompensation. Considerable dyspnea and hyperpnea. Continued to point of considerable discomfort. Somewhat exhausted
10. C. D....	5.00	2.13	5.10	Chronic cardiac, valvular disease with marked decompensation. Continued to point of marked exhaustion
	4.57	2.89		
11. D. O. C.	4.17	2.94		Chronic cardiac, valvular disease with decompensation. Continued rebreathing to point of discomfort with some exhaustion
		2.53	5.72	

In cardiac dyspnea, then, the alveolar CO_2 is low at the point of intolerance. The relation of the alveolar CO_2 at this point to the resting alveolar CO_2 is similar to that found in normal persons. This is further evidence that the air in the lungs in cardiac dyspnea really presents a diminished CO_2-tension.

THE PLESCH METHOD

Modifications of the Plesch method of obtaining samples of alveolar air have been employed extensively in cardiac disease and other pathological conditions by numerous workers. Both Porges (2) and Peabody (3) used it for their studies on cardiac dyspnea. With this method, the subject rebreathes a limited volume of air, usually 600 to 1000 cc. a number of times, usually from 5 to 10, in a period of time usually between 20 and 30 seconds, which is supposed to be less than the duration of a single complete circulation of the blood. With normal resting subjects it gives values that lie a little higher than those obtained by the Haldane method and is assumed to represent the tension of CO_2 in the venous blood.

Usually the rate and depth of the respirations and the duration of rebreathing can be varied within rather wide limits with only a slight variation in the analyses obtained. This might reasonably be expected even if the theoretical basis of the method were entirely wrong. It has been shown that in normal subjects at rest, lung volume, carbon dioxid output, arterial CO_2-tension and venous CO_2-tension vary within narrow limits absolutely and in relation to one another.

The assumption that such an empirical method is equally applicable to the study of a condition in which all these factors are greatly disturbed, is hardly justifiable.

We have made a few observations on normal subjects and on patients with cardiac disease (see table 5) in which we tested the effect of varying

TABLE 5

Results of varying time and number of respirations on Plesch-alveolar CO_2

	NORMALS				J. M. L. COMPENSATED CARDIAC	DECOMPENSATED CARDIACS					
	D. P. B.			J. P.		S. I.	D. O. C.		W.W.	J. B.	
5 respirations in 25 seconds	6.17	6.04	5.24	6.29	6.08	4.48	4.85	5.41	4.70	5.03	4.82
10 respirations in 25 seconds	6.53	5.97	5.90	6.22	6.76	4.62	4.92	5.88	5.41	5.14	5.53
5 respirations in 35 seconds	6.43	6.35	5.89	6.34	6.90			5.99	5.67	5.63	5.81
10 respirations in 35 seconds	6.34	6.41	5.88	6.43	6.92	4.70		6.29	5.99	5.50	
Average value	6.37	6.19	5.73	6.32	6.67	4.60	4.89	5.89	5.44	5.33	5.17
Maximum variation	0.36	0.44	0.66	0.21	0.84	0.22	0.07	0.88	1.29	0.60	0.99
Haldane alveolar CO_2	5.28	5.33		5.61	5.41	3.86	3.72	3.75	4.34	4.11	4.11
Difference between Plesch and Haldane	1.09	0.86		0.71	1.26	0.74	1.17	1.99	1.10	1.22	1.06

the time and rate of rebreathing within certain limits. The time limits chosen were 25 and 35 seconds; the number of breaths 5 and 10. The apparatus used was essentially the same as that recommended by Peabody (16): a three-way brass stop-cock described above, which connected the subject either with the outside air or a rebreathing bag containing 1000 cc. of room air. The bore of the valve and tubing was 1.75 cm., the instrumental dead space, including the rubber mouthpiece, 30 cc. Rebreathing was always begun after a forced expiration and the patient was directed to make a maximum respiratory effort with each breath.

In the case of J. P. the total difference obtained within the limits of variation of time and number of respirations employed was 0.21 per cent. In D. P. B. the differences were greater: from 0.36 to 0.66 per cent. Moreover, in one experiment on the latter (no. III) it appears that the duration of the experiment has less influence than the number of respirations. In the cardiac patients studied the differences were slightly larger, in one case 1.29 per cent. Again variations in the number of respirations appear almost as important as variations in time. One would be rather at a loss to know which values to accept under these conditions.

Of course 35 seconds and 10 breaths are both in excess of the limits usually employed. The objection may be raised that we have not limited the element of time and the number of breaths sufficiently. To us it seems essential to determine whether limitation of experimental factors produces an equivalent limitation of variation in all subjects. One is not justified in producing an apparent constancy in results by an arbitrary limitation of experimental variations.

THE HENDERSON-LAURENS METHOD

Y. Henderson (12) has recently published a method for the determination of the venous CO_2-tension. It does not differ in principle from previous methods, but demands less effort and intelligence on the part of the subject and is therefore more applicable to clinical studies. It depends on the principle of intermittent rebreathing. Laurens (17) has pointed out that it is necessary to regard certain precautions in rebreathing because diffusion of CO_2 is more perfect during respiratory motions than it is while the chest is motionless. Our technic has been modified, therefore, to meet his requirements.

The apparatus used was the same as that employed in the Plesch studies. The rebreathing bag was filled with about 2000 cc. of expiratory air. In most cases a second observation was made in which the bag was filled with a mixture of air with 6.5 to 10 per cent CO_2. While the patient was breathing room air quietly through the valve, he was ordered to give a maximum expiration. When his lungs were completely deflated the stop-cock was turned. He then filled his lungs with a mixture from the bag by a deep inspiration, retained the air in his lungs about 10 seconds and expired into the bag forcibly. The stop-cock was then turned to the room again and he resumed normal respirations. After a sufficient interval to permit the respirations to return to normal the same procedure was repeated. After each respiration the mixture in the bag was tested for CO_2. The rebreathing was continued until analyses after successive respirations showed that the CO_2-tension had reached a practically constant level. In normal subjects this level is reached after about 7 rebreathings and the level attained in rebreathing expired air and CO_2 rich mixtures is the same.

The results of these studies are shown in table 6. Not all of the experiments are entirely satisfactory; but a more or less constant level is reached in cardiac subjects as well as in normals.

There is a surprisingly close agreement between the venous alveolar values obtained by the Henderson-Laurens method and the average of the values obtained by the Plesch method. The application of the Plesch method, in the simple form usually employed, to the physiologic study of cardiac disease, seems hardly warranted. The limitation of the number of respirations and the duration of rebreathing is more or less arbitrary and based on the study of normal subjects only. The use of an average value obtained from a series of observations in which both time and number of respirations has been varied seems preferable. In normal and cardiac subjects values so obtained agree with those obtained by at least one other venous method.

The difference between the Henderson and the Haldane alveolar CO_2 is greater in subjects with cardiac dyspnea than in normal persons or cardiac patients without dyspnea. In spite of this the actual values found by the Henderson method in cardiac dyspnea are slightly lower than normal. This is again evidence that the carbon dioxide tension of the air in the lungs is reduced in cardiac dyspnea.

It is not possible to argue that the difference between the Henderson and the Haldane alveolar CO_2 represents the difference of CO_2-tension between arterial and venous blood. The Haldane values can not be interpreted as a measure of the arterial CO_2-tension until the criticisms of Siebeck have been answered. The only way to answer them is by the direct determination of the arterial CO_2-tension. The objections to the application of alveolar methods to the determination of the carbon dioxid tension of venous blood are even greater. Christiansen, Douglas and Haldane (18) have pointed out that direct determination of the venous carbon dioxid tension by these methods is impossible. The peculiar effect of oxygen on the carbon dioxid dissociation curve of the blood necessitates the introduction of a correction for the oxygen unsaturation of venous blood. An average correction can be applied in the case of normal persons without any considerable error. In

TABLE 6

Comparison of Henderson-Laurens with Haldane method and its application to cardiac dyspnea

SUBJECT AND CONDITION	REBREATHING EXPIRED AIR: Number of rebreathings	REBREATHING EXPIRED AIR: CO_2 found in bag	REBREATHING CO_2-AIR MIXTURE: Mixture rebreathed CO_2	REBREATHING CO_2-AIR MIXTURE: Number of rebreathings	REBREATHING CO_2-AIR MIXTURE: CO_2 found in bag	CALCULATED VENOUS ALVEOLAR CO_2	PLESCH ALVEOLAR CO_2	HALDANE ALVEOLAR CO_2	DIFFERENCE BETWEEN HENDERSON AND HALDANE	ALVEOLAR CO_2 CALCULATED FROM PLASMA BICARBONATE
		per cent	*per cent*		*per cent*	*mm.*	*mm.*	*mm.*	*mm.*	*mm.*
D. P. B., normal	2	5.25				44.9	45.8	37.9	6.9	
	3	5.74								
	4	6.17								
	5	6.28								
	4	5.69				45.1	45.4	37.6	7.5	
	5	6.21								
	6	6.26								
	7	6.38								
			6.64	6	5.79	43.4		39.0	4.4	
	7	6.14		7	5.82					
	8	6.07		8	5.86					
	9	6.13		9	6.01					
			7.55	6	5.97	42.7		39.3	3.4	
	7	5.95		7	5.88					
	8	6.23		8	5.93					
	9	6.06								
	7	5.80	10.02	5	5.99	41.9		39.2	2.7	
	8	5.84		6	6.03					
	9	5.79		7	5.91					

J. P., normal	2	6.13				43.8	45.0	39.9	3.9	
	3	6.13								
	5	6.20								
			10.34	3	7.02	48.6				
				4	7.01					
	7	6.67		5	6.93					
	8	6.83		6	6.86					
	9	6.83		7	6.77					
	8	6.14	6.96	5	6.34	44.8				
	9	6.23		6	6.28					
	10	6.21		7	6.34					
			7.14	5	5.99	41.9		42.3	4.0	
	7	5.82		6	5.98					
	8	5.76		7	5.95					
J. A., chronic cardiac compensated	4	6.45				46.6		42.3	4.3	49.7
	5									
	6	6.53								
	7	6.52								
J. C., chronic cardiac compensated	7	5.59	10.0	7	6.53	44.9		37.7	7.2	
	8	5.75		8	6.45					
	9	6.00								
J. M. L., chronic cardiac compensated	3	6.25				48.4	47.5	38.5	9.9	
	4	6.66								
	5	6.74								
R. W., chronic cardiac compensated			7.64	7	6.44	47.8		42.4	5.4	
	8	6.44		8	6.72					
	9	6.52		9	6.72					

TABLE 6—*Concluded*

SUBJECT AND CONDITION	REBREATHING EXPIRED AIR		REBREATHING CO_2-AIR MIXTURE			CALCULATED VENOUS ALVEOLAR CO_2	PLESCH ALVEOLAR CO_2	HALDANE ALVEOLAR CO_2	DIFFERENCE BETWEEN HENDERSON AND HALDANE	ALVEOLAR CO_2 CALCULATED FROM PLASMA BICARBONATE
	Number of rebreathings	CO_2 found in bag	Mixture rebreathed CO_2	Number of rebreathings	CO_2 found in bag					
		per cent	*per cent*		*per cent*	*mm.*	*mm.*	*mm.*	*mm.*	*mm.*
J. B., chronic cardiac decompensated	2	5.07				38.9	38.4	29.3	9.6	
	3	5.48								
	4	5.43								
	5	5.25								
Jos. C., chronic cardiac decompensated	4	6.11				45.2		38.7	6.5	47.8
	5	6.35								
	6	6.39								
	7	6.30								
	6	6.77	8.92	5	6.99	48.9		44.9	4.0	52.2
	7	6.34		6	7.06					
	8	6.40		7	6.95					
W. W., chronic cardiac decompensated	7	5.64	6.44	7	5.36	38.7		28.6	10.1	43.7
	8	5.45		8	5.33					
	9	5.43		9	5.59					
D. O. C., chronic cardiac decompensated	3	5.29				40.6	42.1	26.7	13.9	38.2
	4	5.71								
	5	5.56								
	6	5.74								
	7	4.89	7.79	7	5.43	36.0		25.3	10.7	
	8	4.92		8	5.15					
	9	5.04		9	5.07					
Averages (normal subjects and compensated cardiacs)................						45.0		39.2	5.4	
Averages (decompensated cardiacs)..................................						41.4		32.3	9.1	

patients with cardiac decompensation, however, the oxygen unsaturation of the venous blood is much greater (19) and more variable. The use of a standard correction factor may therefore involve considerable error.

SUMMARY AND CONCLUSIONS

The Haldane method of obtaining alveolar air has been employed in the study of a series of cardiac patients with dyspnea with no greater variation in results than is found in studies of trained normal subjects. The carbon dioxid tension of alveolar air thus obtained has been found consistently low in comparison with the carbon dioxid capacity of venous plasma. The comparatively low values are not due to technical or subjective errors nor to any considerable increase in the volume of the dead space. The patient with cardiac decompensation maintains his alveolar CO_2 at a lower level than does the normal and the level to which he will permit it to rise under the influence of rebreathing is proportionately reduced.

The Plesch method gives variable results according to the number of respirations and the duration of rebreathing. If, however, an average of a series of observations in which these factors have been varied is employed the results agree with those given by the Henderson method for venous alveolar CO_2. The values found by these methods are somewhat lower in decompensated cardiac subjects than in normal persons; but are high in relation to the values given by the Haldane method.

No attempt has been made to translate alveolar CO_2-tension into terms of arterial or venous CO_2-tension. The alveolar air has been considered entirely from a functional standpoint as that portion of the air in the lungs which is available for the exchange of gases between the blood in the pulmonary circulation and the outside air. If the term "alveolar air" is used in this sense, it may be said that the alveolar CO_2-tension of subjects with cardiac dyspnea is low in comparison with the carbon dioxid capacity of the plasma. As the latter is variable, but seldom abnormally high, the alveolar CO_2-tension is usually not only relatively but absolutely diminished.

BIBLIOGRAPHY

(1) Beddard and Pembrey: Brit. Med. Journ., 1908, ii, 580.
(2) Porges, Leimdoerfer and Markovici: Zeitschr. f. klin. Med., 1913, lxxvi, 446.
(3) Peabody: Arch. Int. Med., 1916, xvi, 846.

(4) Pearce: Journ. Lab. Clin. Med., 1917, ii, no. 12.
(5) Peters: This Journal, 1917, xliii, 113.
(6) Van Slyke, Stillman and Cullen: Journ. Biol. Chem., 1917, xxx, 401.
(7) Siebeck: Deutsch. Arch. f. klin. Med., 1912, cvii, 253.
(8) McClure and Peabody: Journ. Amer. Med. Assoc., 1917, lxix, 1954.
(9) Fridericia: Berl. klin. Wochenschr., 1914, li, 1268.
(10) Haldane and Priestley: Journ. Physiol., 1905, xxxii, 225.
(11) Plesch: Zeitschr. f. exper. Pathol. u. Therap., 1909, iii, 380.
(12) Henderson: Journ. Biol. Chem., 1917, xxxii, 325.
(13) Pearce: This Journal, 1917, xliii, 73.
(14) Peabody: Arch. Int. Med., 1917, xx, 433.
(15) Campbell, Douglas, Haldane and Hobson: Journ. Physiol., 1914, xliii, 303.
(16) Peabody: Arch. Int. Med., 1914, xiii, 497.
(17) Laurens: This Journal, 1918, xlvi, 147.
(18) Christiansen, Douglas and Haldane: Journ. Physiol., 1914, xlviii, 244.
(19) Lundsgaard: Journ. Exper. Med., 1918, xxvii, 219.

STUDIES OF THE RESPIRATORY MECHANISM IN CARDIAC DYSPNEA

II. A Note on the Effective Lung Volume in Cardiac Dyspnea

JOHN P. PETERS, Jr. and DAVID P. BARR

From the Russell Sage Institute of Pathology, in affiliation with the Second Medical Division, Bellevue Hospital, and the Department of Medicine, Cornell University Medical College

Received for publication August 9, 1920

That the vital capacity of the lungs is reduced during cardiac decompensation is a well-established fact (1), (2). A few experiments have been conducted to find out whether this reduction is associated with a change in the total air containing space of the lungs and to ascertain the effect of such a change on the functional efficiency of the respiratory mechanism.

METHODS

The problem has been approached in two distinct ways: *a*, by the application of the Lundsgaard (3) method for measuring the lung volume by rebreathing oxygen; *b*, by a study of the effect of continuous rebreathing of air on the volume of the tidal air and the comparison of the latter with the vital capacity.

The lung volume of a few normal and pathological cases was measured by the Lundsgaard (3) method of rebreathing oxygen. A graphic record of the preliminary respirations and the vital capacity was obtained with a Tissot spirometer by means of a combination of valves similar to that used for rebreathing experiments and described in the preceding paper (4). A rebreathing bag containing a measured amount of oxygen was attached in place of the Haldane tube. In all cases the subject commenced rebreathing from the position of complete expiration. The volume of the residual air was calculated from the gas mixture in the bag at the end of the observation. The volume of the vital capacity was obtained from the graphic record. The values thus obtained were compared with those obtained by the Lundsgaard (3) method of chest measurement.

TABLE 1

Vital capacity and lung volume

NAME AND CONDITION	DATE	VITAL* CAPACITY	RESIDUAL AIR*	LUNG* VOLUME	METHOD OF DETERMINATION: Volume of O_2 rebreathed	METHOD OF DETERMINATION: Number of respirations	METHOD OF DETERMINATION: Time of rebreathing	REMARKS
		cc.	*cc.*	*cc.*	*cc.*		*seconds*	
1. D. P. B., normal	*Lundsgaard measurements*	*3332*†*	*1478*†*	*4810*†*				Low Lundsgaard measurement probably faulty and due entirely to excessively short sternum
	v/19	4429	1662	6091†	3000	7	18	Ratio V. C./Surface Area = 2.73
	v/21	4328	1551	5879†	3000	7	15	
	v/22	4239	1715	5954†	2050	7	17	
		4284	1632	5916†	2010	7	15	
2. J. P., normal	*Lundsgaard measurements*	*3704*	*1609*	*5313*				
	v/22	3772	1621	5393	3000	7	17	
		3876	1723	5599	2000	7	17	
3. J. C., chronic cardiac	*Lundsgaard measurements*	*2980*	*1460*	*4390*				Young boy of 18 with early rheumatic endocarditis
	vi/10/19	2345	1560	3905	2070	7	18	Compensated at rest
		2432	1515	3947	2070	7	18	No dyspnea nor hyperpnea at rest. Lungs clear

4. J. A., chronic cardiac	*Lundsgaard measurements*	*2930*	*1460*	*4390*				Chronic cardio-nephritic. Hypertension. Cardiac hypertrophy. Blood pressure 210
	v/16/19..........	2430						No dyspnea nor hyperpnea while at rest. Lungs clear
	vi/7/19..........	1242 1329 1418	1214 1250	2456 2579	2020 1500	7 7	19 17	Some hyperpnea even when at rest in bed. Lungs clear except showers of râles at right base
5. A. R., chronic cardiac	*Lundsgaard measurements*	*3640*	*1740*	*5380*				At time of examination was found to have very little hyperpnea. Also had a reduction of the plasma bicarbonate. The hyperpnea was probably due to the reduction of the alkaline reserve and not to cardiac factors. Chest clear. Periodic breathing
	vi/27/19..........	1489 1789	1744	3233	1510	7	17	
6. W. W., chronic cardiac	*Lundsgaard measurements*	*4698*	*2315*	*7013*				Moderate hyperpnea. Some dulness and râles at extreme bases on both sides
	vi/24/19..........	1174	2320	3494	1500	7	14	
	vi/25/19..........	1452	2190	3642	1535	7	20	

TABLE 1—*Concluded*

NAME AND CONDITION	DATE	VITAL* CAPACITY	RESIDUAL AIR*	LUNG* VOLUME	METHOD OF DETERMINATION: Volume of O_2 re-breathed	METHOD OF DETERMINATION: Number of respi-rations	METHOD OF DETERMINATION: Time of rebreathing	REMARKS
		cc.	*cc.*	*cc.*	*cc.*		*seconds*	
7. R. W. chronic cardiac	*Lundsgaard measurements*	*3930*	*1870*	*5800*				No dyspnea when at rest. Some impairment of resonance at extreme right base
	vi/23/19	1714	1264	2978	2050	7	17	
		1064	1244	2308	2000	7	17	
	vi/24/19	1869						
	vi/30/19	2080	1091	3171	2040	7	17	
8. D. O. C., chronic cardiac	*Lundsgaard measurements*	*3540*	*1800*	*5340*				
	iv/29/19	1303						Marked dyspnea when at rest. Some signs of fluid at right base
	vi/2/19	920	757	1677	2020	7	Very rapid	Some fluid in right chest
		985	799	1784	1040	15	17	
	vi/6/19	1193	873	2066	1060	15	Very rapid	Dyspnea more marked. Fluid to angle of right scapula; 1450 cc. removed just after experiment
	vi/9/19	1068	887	1955	990	12	17	Dyspnea less marked. Fluid above angle of right scapula. Some dulness at extreme left base
		1132	861	1993	1000	15	17	

* In each case the values for the normal lung volume as determined by the Lundsgaard method of chest measurement are reported first, in italics. Below them appear the values obtained by the rebreathing method.

† The great discrepancy between the observed and the calculated lung volumes of DPB seems to be due to a very short sternal measurement. The relation between his vital capacity and surface area is quite normal, 2.73. In the light of the work of Dryer and that of West it appears that the surface area is a better criterion from which to calculate the vital capacity. Unfortunately we have not sufficient data to permit recalculations on this basis.

The apparatus and method employed in the rebreathing experiments were described in the first paper of this series (4). By a study of the tidal air of normal subjects and cardiac patients after the continuous rebreathing of air from a spirometer, we hoped to gain some information on the effect of the reduction of vital capacity on the functional efficiency of the respiratory mechanism.

RESULTS

The results of the lung volume determinations are collected in the first three columns of table 1. In each case the normal lung volume, as calculated by the Lundsgaard (3) method of chest measurement is reported first, in italics. Below it appear the values obtained from the rebreathing experiments. In the fourth, fifth and sixth columns are given the conditions of the experiments: the volume of oxygen taken in the rebreathing bag; the number of respirations and the duration of the rebreathing.

The first two subjects were normal. The third had chronic cardiac valvular disease without decompensation. His vital capacity, residual air and lung volume were almost normal. Number 4, at the first observation, in the absence of dyspnea, showed only a slight reduction of the vital capacity. Three weeks later, with a recurrence of dyspnea, his vital capacity was found to be only half as large. His residual air was not far from normal. Unfortunately his residual air was not determined at the time of the first observation.

Number 5, A. R., had hypertensive nephritis with some edema and signs of uremia: drowsiness and Cheyne-Stokes breathing. He showed no considerable hyperpnea, although his plasma bicarbonate was reduced. His chest was entirely clear. His vital capacity was very small but his residual air practically normal.

The last three were decompensated patients with dyspnea and showed very low vital capacities. The volume of the residual air was also considerably below normal in the last two. With the exception of the last patient, who had a massive hydrothorax, the physical signs found in the chest were insignificant in comparison with the diminution of lung volume.

These results indicate that, in patients with cardiac dyspnea, the total volume of air in the lungs which can be detected by the usual methods is considerably less than that found in normal persons. The largest part of the reduction in lung volume is due to a diminution of the vital capacity. The residual air is unchanged or slightly reduced.

The results of the rebreathing experiments are given in table 2. The subjects are arranged from above downward according to the magnitude of their vital capacities, which appear in column 1. In column 2 is given the normal vital capacity as calculated from the Lundsgaard (3) chest measurements. In column 3 is shown the average resting tidal air and in column 4 the tidal air at the end of a rebreathing experiment. The last we have called the "maximum tidal air" because it is the largest respiratory volume which the subject will exchange under the influence of the strongest respiratory stimulus that can be applied, carbon dioxid.

TABLE 2

Vital capacity and tidal air

NUMBER AND NAME	VITAL CAPACITY	CALCULATED VITAL CAPACITY LUNDSGAARD	RESTING TIDAL AIR	TIDAL AIR AT END OF REBREATHING	DIAGNOSIS AND REMARKS
1. D. P. B...	4537	3332*	580	2407	Normal
2. J. P.......	3953	3704	372	1929	Normal
3. T. deC....	3839			1249	Cardiac. Compensated
4. P. K......	3503		371	1192	Gastric neurosis
5. A. J......	2729		389	980	Shell shock. Effort syndrome
6. J. B......	2519		737	1236	Cardiac. Slight dyspnea and hyperpnea
7. J. C......	2432	2980	421		Cardiac. Compensated
8. J. A......	2430	2930	439	1116	Cardiac. Compensated
9. C. D......	2145		315	581	Cardiac. Severe decompensation
10. J. M. L...	1789		390	1309	Cardiac. No dyspnea nor hyperpnea
11. A. R......	1789	3640	604		Nephritic. Mild acidosis
12. R. W.....	1714	3930	244		Cardiac. Some dyspnea
13. J. J. F....	1704		304		Cardio-nephritic. Mild acidosis
14. W. W.....	1452	4698	469		Cardiac. Some dyspnea
15. D. O. C...	1303	3540	423	638	Cardiac. Marked dyspnea
16. S. I.......	1248		375		Cardiac. Severe dyspnea
17. J. M......	1197		475		Cardiac. Extreme cyanosis. Some dyspnea
18. Jos. C....	1182		385	492	Cardiac. Marked dyspnea

* See note, table 1.

Peabody (5) found the average resting tidal air slightly reduced in cardiac dyspnea. This our figures do not show. If such a reduction exists it is small in proportion to the enormous reduction found in the vital capacity.

The maximum tidal air, on the other hand, varies almost directly with the vital capacity and the ratio between the two shows the same range of variation in cardiac patients with dyspnea as in normals (0.35 to 0.55). Number 10 is the only exception to this rule. In his case the "maximum tidal air" was very large in proportion to the vital capacity. It was noted in the course of the experiment on this patient that he could not be induced to exert himself to the full extent of his strength when he blew into the spirometer. The low vital capacity, in this instance, may be only an expression of lack of effort on the part of the patient. This was completely overcome under the stimulus of carbon dioxid and he showed a normal "maximum tidal air," although he did not continue rebreathing to the point of exhaustion.

In the case of the decompensated cardiac patients, however, there was no lack of effort apparent during the determination of the vital capacity. Moreover, two of them continued rebreathing to the point of extreme exhaustion. The reduction of the "maximum tidal air" and the vital capacity may be a functional matter, due to reflex inhibition. If so, this inhibition is so profound that it can not be overcome by the strongest stimulus which can be applied. The increase in the tidal air which normally occurs in response to the stimulus of carbon dioxid is limited by the lowered vital capacity.

DISCUSSION

Siebeck (1), in 1912, measured the lung volume in a series of cardiac patients by a rebreathing method. His studies showed that in cardiac dyspnea the residual air was relatively increased, although the absolute values he obtained seem to have been lower than normal. The reserve air and the complementary air were both decreased. These results are substantially the same as ours. However, Siebeck regarded them as questionable because he was unable to obtain the same constancy in his rebreathed mixtures in cardiac patients as in normals. In the latter the concentration of hydrogen in the rebreathing bag became constant after 5 respirations. In subjects with cardiac dyspnea the concentration continued to change even after 10 respirations. This Siebeck considered to be due to improper diffusion of air in the lungs. He concluded that the actual volume of residual air was greater than that indicated by the rebreathing methods.

As Sonne (6) has shown, the residual air can be measured with only an approximate degree of accuracy even in the normal person. Whether Siebeck is right in believing that the amount of air present is greater than that found, we are unwilling to argue. In two or three cases the number of respirations, the time and the volume of air rebreathed were varied without significant changes in the values obtained. This does not agree with Siebeck's findings. But any air that may be present and undetected must be peculiarly useless for respiratory purposes. A functional conception of the lungs is of more value than a purely anatomical one. In a normal person residual air determinations may be considered as measurements of the volume of air space in the fully deflated lungs, which is available for the rapid diffusion of gases. In this sense, certainly, the residual air is not increased in cardiac dyspnea. Since the vital capacity is decreased the effective volume of the lungs must be diminished.

Whether this diminution is due to a true anatomical lesion or not, we are unprepared to say. In some instances hydrothorax plays a part, but it is by no means an essential part. This we may assume not only because of the absence of physical signs of fluid, but also because of the rapidity with which the vital capacity increases as compensation is established (7).

Just what effect such a diminution of the lung volume may have on the gas exchange must be largely a matter of speculation until the cause of the diminution is determined. If it is not due to a true anatomical lesion it is quite possible that some or all of the blood in the pulmonary vessels is not in gaseous equilibrium with the alveolar air. This might, in part at least, explain the discrepancy between the alveolar CO_2 and the CO_2-combining capacity of the plasma.

This discrepancy Pearce (8) has attributed entirely to the effect of stasis in the general circulation. He has drawn a fine distinction between the causes of the low alveolar CO_2-tension in congenital heart disease, pneumonia and acquired heart disease. In congenital heart disease part of the venous blood does not pass through the lungs, and in consequence is given no opportunity to rid itself of the CO_2 which it has received from the tissues. In consequence the arterial blood is a mixture of aërated and unaërated blood. If there were no compensatory reaction a true carbon dioxid acidosis would occur. The respiratory mechanism, however, responds to the stimulus of the carbon dioxid. The alveolar CO_2-tension and the CO_2-tension of the blood which does pass through the pulmonary circulation is reduced sufficiently to restore the CO_2-tension and hydrogen-ion concentration of the arterial blood to normal.

In patients with pneumonia in whom Pearce found the same discrepancy between the alveolar CO_2-tension and the plasma bicarbonates, he advances a similar explanation. In this case, although all the blood passes through the pulmonary circulation, he supposes that part of the blood passes through non-aërated portions of the lungs. On what seems to us insufficient evidence, he denies the possibility of such a condition in acquired cardiac disease. But certainly the reduction of the effective lung volume renders it not only possible, but not improbable. Even if Siebeck is right and this diminution is not due to a decrease in the actual air-containing space in the lungs, a certain part of this air must be unavailable for the rapid diffusion of gases and that portion of blood in the pulmonary circulation which comes in contact with this air must be less effectively ventilated than normal.

That the blood flow is retarded in decompensated cardiac disease is probable in the light of Harrop's (9) observation of an increase in the difference of the oxygen content of arterial and venous blood.

That this is the sole factor in the production of the low alveolar CO_2 remains to be proved. It is doubtful whether the method of Christiansen, Douglas and Haldane (10), which was employed by Pearce for the determination of the rate of blood flow, can be interpreted quantitatively in cardiac dyspnea. In this method it is assumed that the CO_2-tension of the alveolar air is the same as that of the arterial blood. That such a relation obtains in cardiac dyspnea demands definite proof. The use of respiratory methods that are designed to determine the venous CO_2-tension is also open to question when applied to conditions in which the venous oxygen unsaturation is excessive. Christiansen, Douglas and Haldane showed that the effect of oxygen on the carbon dioxid dissociation curve necessitated the introduction of a correction for the oxygen unsaturation even in normal persons. The extent of this correction in cardiacs can only be guessed.

Although the effect of the small effective lung volume on the exchange of gases between the blood and the alveolar air remains largely a matter of speculation, its effect on the mechanics of respiration is fairly clear. Here we have to deal only with the vital capacity, the portion of the lung volume available for ventilation of the lungs.

Apparently the reduction of vital capacity which occurs during cardiac dyspnea has little effect in limiting the respiratory exchange during rest. The volume of the resting tidal air is not diminished. On the other hand, the amount by which the tidal air can increase under the stimulus of carbon dioxid seems to be distinctly limited by the reduction of the vital capacity. The reserve of the mechanical apparatus of respiration is therefore greatly diminished.

CONCLUSIONS

1. In cardiac patients with dyspnea no evidence of an increased residual air was obtained by the Lundsgaard method.

2. As the vital capacity is diminished, this means that the effective lung volume, the volume of air in the lungs available for the exchange of gases, is diminished.

3. The maximum volume of tidal air attained under the stimulus of continuous rebreathing is lower than normal in cardiac dyspnea. The reduction in the maximal tidal air bears a close relation to the reduction in vital capacity.

BIBLIOGRAPHY

(1) Siebeck: Deutsch. Arch. f. klin. Med., 1912, cvii, 253.
(2) McClure and Peabody: Journ. Amer. Med Assoc., 1917, lxix, 1954.
(3) Lundsgaard and Van Slyke: Journ. Exper. Med., 1918, xxvii, 65.
(4) Peters and Barr: This Journal (no. I of this series).
(5) Peabody, Wentworth and Barker: Arch. Int. Med., 1917, xx, 468.
(6) Sonne: Journ. Physiol., 1918, lii, 75.
(7) West: Paper read before the Section on Medicine of the New York Academy of Medicine, April, 1920.
(8) Pearce: Journ. Lab. Clin. Med., 1917, ii, no. 12.
(9) Harrop: Journ. Exper., Med., 1919, xxx, 241.
(10) Christiansen, Douglas and Haldane: Journ. Physiol., 1914, xlviii, 244.

STUDIES OF THE RESPIRATORY MECHANISM IN CARDIAC DYSPNEA

III. The Effective Ventilation in Cardiac Dyspnea

D. P. BARR and JOHN P. PETERS, Jr.

From The Russell Sage Institute of Pathology, in affiliation with the Second Medical Division, Bellevue Hospital, and the Department of Medicine, Cornell University Medical College

Received for publication August 9, 1920

In the previous papers of this series (1), (2) it has been shown that the effective lung volume is decreased during the dyspnea of cardiac decompensation. The alveolar CO_2 tension, as determined by the Haldane method, is usually low and always lower than the concentration of the bicarbonate in the venous plasma would indicate. We have shown that the air obtained by Haldane's method is probably true alveolar or exchange air. In this paper we shall present evidence to substantiate this contention and shall discuss the influence of a low alveolar CO_2 tension and of a diminished lung volume upon the effective ventilation in relation to the dyspnea of heart disease.

Peabody, Wentworth and Barker (3) find that, although the level of metabolism is normal or only moderately increased during cardiac decompensation, the minute volume of respiration is much greater than in normal individuals. The increase is accomplished by a more rapid respiratory rate with a moderate diminution in the volume of each expiration. The percentage of CO_2 in the expired air is diminished.

Peabody recognizes that the greater observed minute volume may represent no increase in the amount of effective air breathed. The tidal air consists of two parts. The dead space, which fills the upper respiratory tract is practically atmospheric air and is of no value in the ventilation of the functioning portions of the lungs. It is only the remainder of an expiration, the exchange air, which is effective for purposes of respiration. In any given expiration, the relative proportion of dead space to exchange air will determine the efficiency of ventilation. If, as Peabody assumes, the volume of the dead space is not changed during decompensation while the volume of tidal air is diminished, the amount of effective air in each expiration will be diminished.

It is possible to arrive at a rough estimate of the effective minute volume by subtracting an average dead space value from the volume of the tidal air and multiplying the remainder by the respiratory rate. Different observers, Haldane and Priestley (4), Krogh and Lindhard (5) and Pearce (6), have found the volume of the dead space in normal resting subjects to vary between 100 and 200 cc. with an average of about 130 cc. Since there is no evidence that the dead space is changed in cardiac dyspnea and experiments reported in a previous paper (1) indicate that it cannot be greatly above the normal values, 130 cc. has been used as the average volume of the dead space for purposes of calculation.

To determine the effective ventilation, we made a considerable number of observations on the minute volume of normal individuals and of compensated and decompensated cardiacs. The method did not differ from that of Peabody except that a nose clip and rubber mouthpiece were substituted for the Siebe Gorman mask. The instrumental dead space was 30 cc. The expiratory air was collected in an accurately balanced Tissot spirometer for periods varying from five to ten minutes, the volume of expiration and the number of respirations being recorded for each minute. Volumes were reduced to standard conditions of 760 mm. Hg. and 0°C. To these observations we applied the following formula:

(Tidal Air − 160[1]) Respiratory Rate = Effective Minute Volume

The results are tabulated in table 1.

For the purpose of comparing our results with those of Peabody we have calculated the effective minute volume from his figures. The dead space of the Siebe Gorman mask which he used has been estimated at about 50 cc. Averages of the results are given in table 2.

The results of the two experiments are in practical agreement. In the decompensated cases, the minute volume of respiration is greater and the respiratory rate is increased. The volume of the tidal air is sometimes slightly diminished but this is by no means invariable as is shown by the large tidal air of J. B. and J. D. B. (table 1). The effective minute volume is much greater during decompensation.

It might be argued that the increase in effective ventilation is due to the higher level of metabolism and the consequent increase in CO_2

[1] To the average dead space of the individual has been added the instrumental dead space of 30 cc.

production which is observed in many dyspneic cardiac patients. That this is not true can be demonstrated by calculations from Peabody's figures (table 3).

Figures for surface area show that the average size of the patients in the two groups is practically identical. Differences either in the production of CO_2 or in the effective ventilation cannot be due to discrepancies in size. The CO_2 production per minute is only 5.1 per cent greater in the decompensated cases. The volume of effective air breathed per minute is 30.3 per cent higher than in the cases without

TABLE 1

SUBJECT	MINUTE VOLUME	TIDAL AIR	RESPIRATIONS PER MINUTE	EFFECTIVE MINUTE VOLUME	DIAGNOSIS AND REMARKS
	cc.	*cc.*			
D. P. B.	6,900	532	13.0	4,822	Normal adult
	6,789	580	11.7	4,913	
	6,040	592	10.2	4,406	
	6,751	668	10.1	5,131	
J. P.	5,524	372	14.9	3,148	Normal adult
	4,898	389	12.6	2,885	
	7,127	520	13.7	4,943	
G. C. D.	6,386	484	13.2	4,277	Normal adult
	6,243	488	12.8	4,198	
P. K.	4,659	293	15.9	2,115	Gastric neurosis. No sign of cardiac or pulmonary disease
	7,764	371	20.9	4,420	
Cap.	7,866	333	23.6	4,083	Normal adult. Respirations rapid and variable. Obviously over-ventilating
J. A.	6,474	439	14.8	4,106	Chronic cardiac valvular disease. No dyspnea while at rest in bed
	7,611	408	18.6	4,626	
J. M. L.	4,553	390	11.6	2,675	Chronic cardiac valvular disease. No dyspnea while at rest in bed
	6,133	438	14.0	3,893	
R. W.	5,826	244	23.9	2,003	Chronic cardiac valvular disease. Breathing quietly while at rest in bed. Rapid and superficial during experiment
J. W.	7,680	410	18.7	4,675	Chronic nephritis. Hypertension. No dyspnea while at rest in bed
Average	6,401	442	15.2	3,973	

TABLE 1—*Concluded*

SUBJECT	MINUTE VOLUME	TIDAL AIR	RESPIRATIONS PER MINUTE	EFFECTIVE MINUTE VOLUME	DIAGNOSIS AND REMARKS
	cc.	*cc.*			
J. B.	13,170	737	17.9	10,310	Chronic cardiac valvular disease. Dyspnea and cyanosis while at rest
	10,210	612	16.7	7,540	
Jos. C.	13,590	385	35.3	7,936	Chronic nephritis with hypertension. Severe cardiac decompensation with marked dyspnea
	14,140	350	40.3	7,638	
C. D.	9,982	315	31.8	4,916	Chronic cardiac valvular disease. Severe dyspnea and orthopnea
S. I.	6,930	375	18.5	3,970	Chronic cardiac valvular disease. Massive hydrothorax. Dyspnea and orthopnea
D. O. C.	8,069	423	19.1	5,020	Chronic cardiac valvular disease. Marked cyanosis and moderate dyspnea while at rest. Right hydrothorax
W. W.	9,528	469	20.3	6,279	Chronic cardiac valvular disease. Moderate dyspnea while at rest
J. R.	11,393	311	36.7	5,542	Chronic cardiac valvular disease. Marked dyspnea and orthopnea while at rest
	10,110	357	28.3	5,575	
P. O. S.	9,087	279	32.6	3,879	Chronic cardiac valvular disease. Right hydrothorax. Marked dyspnea and orthopnea while at rest
J. D. B.	14,310	821	17.4	11,501	Chronic cardiac valvular disease. Marked dyspnea and orthopnea while at rest
	12,800	538	23.8	8,996	
J. M.	8,652	475	18.2	5,733	Chronic cardiac valvular disease. Extreme cyanosis and some dyspnea while at rest
	9,843	496	19.8	6,653	
Average	10,788	463	25.1	6,766	

dyspnea. Only a small part of the increase in effective ventilation can be accounted for by a greater CO_2 production.

Furthermore, since the dyspneic cardiac breathes a much greater amount of CO_2, each volume of his effective or alveolar air must contain a smaller percentage of CO_2.

TABLE 2

	COMPENSATED CARDIACS	DECOMPENSATED CARDIACS
Minute volume (cc.*)	5,901	8,521
Tidal air (cc.)	466	398
Respiratory rate	13.2	21.8
Effective minute volume (cc.)	3,530	4,600

* Minute volumes have been recalculated from the CO_2 produced per minute and the percentage of CO_2 in the expired air.

TABLE 3

	COMPENSATED CARDIACS	DECOMPENSATED CARDIACS
Surface area (square meters)	1.72	1.77
CO_2 production per minute (cc.)	196	206
Effective minute volume (cc.)	3,530	4,600

It is possible to show more directly the probability of a reduced alveolar CO_2 tension. In the paper describing their method of obtaining alveolar air, Haldane and Priestley (4) indicated a means of determining the volume of the dead space. The data necessary for the calculation were the volume of an expiration, the percentage of CO_2 in the expired air and the percentage of CO_2 in the alveolar air. These were combined in the following formula:

Formula I

$$\text{Tidal air} - \frac{\text{Tidal air} \times \text{per cent } CO_2 \text{ in expired air}}{\text{Per cent } CO_2 \text{ in alveolar air}} = \text{Dead space}$$

By a simple inversion of their formula, the percentage of CO_2 in the alveolar air can be deduced.

Formula II

$$\frac{\text{Tidal air} \times \text{per cent } CO_2 \text{ in expired air}}{\text{Tidal air} - \text{Dead space}} = \text{Per cent } CO_2 \text{ in alveolar air}$$

Both of these formulae were applied to observations on a number of normal individuals and on cardiacs in varying degrees of decompensation. Minute volume determinations were made as in the previous experiments. At the close of an observation, the air was thoroughly mixed in the spirometer and a sample was taken for analysis. Haldane

TABLE 4

SUBJECT	MINUTE VOLUME	RESPIRATIONS PER MINUTE	TIDAL AIR	CO_2 IN EXPIRED AIR	ALVEOLAR CO_2 CALCULATED FROM DEAD SPACE FORMULA	ALVEOLAR CO_2 OBSERVED HALDANE METHOD	ALVEOLAR CO_2 CALCULATED FROM PLASMA BICARBONATE	DEAD SPACE CALCULATED FROM: Observed alveolar CO_2	DEAD SPACE CALCULATED FROM: Alveolar CO_2 calculated from plasma	DIAGNOSIS AND REMARKS
	cc.		*cc.*	*per cent*	*per cent*	*per cent*	*per cent*	*cc.*	*cc.*	
D. P. B.	6,040	10.2	592	3.92	5.39	5.39		130		Normal adult
	6,751	10.1	668	4.16	5.47	5.40		123		
J. P.	4,898	12.6	389	3.84	6.52	5.89		105		Normal adult
	7,127	13.7	520	4.29	6.14	5.75		132		
Cap.	7,866	23.6	333	3.27	6.29	6.31		130		Normal adult
G. C. D.	6,386	13.2	484	3.42	5.11	6.39		195		Normal adult
	6,248	12.8	488	4.04	6.01	6.63		161		
J. W.	7,680	18.7	410	3.03	4.98	4.85	5.60	124	158	Chronic cardiac valvular disease. No dyspnea while at rest
Average	6,625	14.4	486	3.75	5.74	5.83		138		
J. R.	11,396	36.7	311	2.16	4.44	4.60	6.73	139	181	Chronic cardiac valvular disease. Dyspnea and orthopnea while at rest
	10,110	28.3	357	2.33	4.26	3.95		115		
J. D. B.	14,310	17.4	821	2.14	2.66	3.11	5.53	226	473	Chronic cardiac valvular disease. Moderate dyspnea and cyanosis
	12,800	23.8	538	2.69	3.82	4.53		189		
J. M.	8,652	18.2	475	2.40	3.62	3.39	5.76	109	247	Chronic cardiac valvular disease. Extreme cyanosis, moderate dyspnea
	9,843	19.8	496	2.72	4.02	4.96	7.41	195	284	
P. O. S.	9,087	32.6	279	2.30	5.39	5.69	7.40	136	162	Chronic cardiac valvular disease. Severe decompensation with dyspnea and orthopnea
Average	10,885	25.2	469	2.39	4.03	4.32		159		

samples of alveolar air were taken before and after the minute volume determinations. A specimen of blood was drawn from an arm vein for determination of the bicarbonates in the plasma. The results obtained from the plasma were converted into terms of percentage of alveolar CO_2 according to the method of Van Slyke (7).

In formula II, average dead space values were employed for the calculation of the probable percentage of CO_2 in alveolar air. The results are recorded in table 4 (column 6). They agree closely with the results of direct observation by the Haldane method (column 7) and consequently in the decompensated cardiac lie far below the value indicated by the plasma (column 8).

In formula I, the observed alveolar CO_2 per cent and the percentage indicated by the plasma have been applied to calculate the probable dead space. Substitution of the observed values give volumes of dead space which are within the range of normal (column 9) while substitution of percentages indicated by the plasma give decidedly improbable results (column 10).

Formula II has also been applied to Peabody's figures. Averages are given in table 5.

TABLE 5

	COMPENSATED CARDIACS	DECOMPENSATED CARDIACS
Tidal air (cc.)	466	398
CO_2 in expired air (per cent)	3.35	2.44
Calculated alveolar CO_2 per cent (using dead space of 180 cc.)*	5.72	4.70

* Average dead space of 130 cc. to which is added the extra dead space of 50 cc., the capacity of the Siebe Gorman mask.

Both in Peabody's figures and in ours, the percentage of CO_2 in the alveolar air is lower during decompensation.

DISCUSSION

In this series of papers the question of the concentration of CO_2 in alveolar air during cardiac decompensation has been approached from several angles. Of the direct methods, that of Haldane which has been found applicable to dyspneic patients gives values for alveolar CO_2 percentage much lower than it does in normal individuals. Duplicate samples, however, show quite as close agreement in dyspneic cardiacs as in trained normal subjects. Experiments have shown that the low content is not due to subjective errors nor to an increased dead space. After breathing increasing percentages of CO_2, the alveolar CO_2 percentage of dyspneic cardiacs is still relatively lower than it is in normal individuals under the same circumstances. The percentage, moreover, is not increased by increasing the depth of expiration. An expiration of maximum depth contains no greater concentration of CO_2 than does one of a volume just sufficient to clear the dead space. Whether the specimen of air obtained by the Haldane method is from the alveoli or from other portions of the lungs is not of great importance in the present discussion. Whatever the anatomical source of the sample may be, it is the only air which by the greatest effort the decompensated cardiac can expire. It is the only air which can be functionally effective in the elimination of CO_2 from the body. If this is true the CO_2 contained in this air should completely account for the total CO_2 elimination. In this paper it has been shown by the use of Haldane's dead space formula that the percentage of CO_2 found in the Haldane specimen is the percentage theoretically required to account for the CO_2 eliminated.

The accumulated evidence, both direct and circumstantial, indicates that the percentage of CO_2 is low in the effective air of dyspneic cardiac subjects. The cause of this important phenomenon is not clearly understood. Its chief importance in the present discussion lies in its effect upon the ventilation in cardiac disease.

A low percentage of CO_2 in the effective air necessitates a larger effective ventilation to accomplish CO_2 elimination. Even when the metabolism is normal, the decompensated cardiac exhibits hyperpnea. As long as he lies quietly in bed, this usually involves an increase in the rate of respiration with little or no change in the volume of each respiration. Under these circumstances the low effective lung volume, which is the constant accompaniment of decompensation, is not a factor of great importance in the causation of dyspnea. It probably exerts a greater influence during conditions involving a greater production of CO_2.

Concerning the mechanism of ventilation during exercise, we have accumulated no direct evidence. A good indication of the response is furnished, however, by experiments upon the rebreathing of CO_2. Under these circumstances the cardiac is subjected to a most powerful stimulus to respiration. The mechanism should, by analogy, be similar to that occurring during exercise or any other condition involving a rapid production of CO_2 within the body. It has been shown that the cardiac maintains a relatively low alveolar CO_2 percentage during rebreathing. To accomplish this he must breathe a larger volume of effective air. Under the stimulus of CO_2, the volume of the tidal air increases both in cardiacs and in normal individuals. The increase, however, is in proportion to the vital capacity. In both groups the tidal air reaches a maximum at one-third to one-half of the volume of the vital capacity. Thus, a normal individual with an original vital capacity of 4000 cc. may show under the stimulus of CO_2 a tidal air of 1500 to 2000 cc. In a decompensated cardiac whose vital capacity may be only 1500 cc. the tidal air will not rise above 500 to 750 cc. with maximum CO_2 stimulation. The volume of respiration is strictly limited. Any attempt to increase it is accompanied by marked subjective dyspnea.

Two factors in cardiac disease help to explain the dyspnea which is its most constant subjective symptom. The low percentage of CO_2 in the effective air makes an increase in ventilation essential. The diminished effective lung volume makes any large increase difficult or impossible. The first is active under all conditions while the cardiac is decompensated. The second exerts its chief influence when the production of CO_2 in the body is increased.

CONCLUSIONS

1. Air obtained from decompensated cardiacs by the Haldane alveolar method is true exchange air. It corresponds to the alveolar air obtained by the same method in normal resting subjects. It is the only air effective for the elimination of CO_2.
2. During cardiac dyspnea, the bicarbonate content of the plasma gives no indication of the percentage of CO_2 in the exchange air.
3. The minute volume of effective or exchange air is increased during cardiac decompensation.
4. This is not explained by the higher level of metabolism.
5. The greater effective ventilation is necessitated by the low concentration of CO_2 in the exchange air.
6. Great increases in ventilation are impossible because of the diminished effective lung volume of decompensated cardiacs.

BIBLIOGRAPHY

(1) PETERS AND BARR: This Journal, this series, no. I.
(2) PETERS AND BARR: This Journal, this series, no. II.
(3) PEABODY, WENTWORTH AND BARKER: Arch. Int. Med., 1917, xx, 468.
(4) HALDANE AND PRIESTLEY: Journ. Physiol., 1905, xxxii, 240.
(5) KROGH AND LINDHARD: Journ. Physiol., 1917, xliii, 73.
(6) PEARCE: This Journal, 1917, xliv, 391.
(7) VAN SLYKE, STILLMAN AND CULLEN: Journ. Biol. Chem., 1917, xxx, 401.

STUDIES ON THE BRAIN STEM

IV. On the Relation of the Cerebral Hemispheres and Thalamus to Arterial Blood Pressure

F. T. ROGERS

From the Hull Physiological Laboratory, University of Chicago

Received for publication August 9, 1920

In a previous report (1) attention has been directed to the poikilothermous condition that follows the removal of the cerebral hemispheres and thalamus in birds and mammals. In an attempt to discover the causes of this condition it was suggested that possibly a general fall of arterial blood pressure with resulting cutaneous dilatation of the blood vessels might be an essential factor. To test this point a method was devised for measuring the arterial pressure in the pigeon and studies of the blood pressure made before and after reduction to the cold-blooded condition. These tests did not give the anticipated results but led to the discovery that the removal of the cerebral hemispheres, which alone does not reduce the bird to the cold-blooded condition, leads to a permanent slight fall in arterial tension. The plan of the work was therefore extended to a study of the arterial pressure in the normal pigeon, the normal variations, effects of various procedures on the normal pressure, and then, the effect of various types of brain lesions on the arterial pressure.

Asher (2) in his review of the vasomotor mechanism, in 1902 wrote: "There are no known facts which indicate the presence of vasomotor centers in the parts of the brain above the medulla oblongata. The higher cerebral centers influence the vasomotor tone exclusively in a reflex manner through the medullary vasomotor center." This interpretation is based on the original experiments of Ludwig's students, Dittmar and Owsjannikow. These classic experiments in 1872 and 1873 demonstrated the localization of the vasoconstrictor centers in the floor of the fourth ventricle.

Since then innumerable studies have demonstrated that reflex influences from the cerebral hemispheres above and the spinal nerves below may play on this center. (Literature cited by Sachs.) It has become common knowledge that loss of the cerebral hemispheres does not necessarily disturb the arterial pressure in acute experiments. It therefore came somewhat as a surprise to find that in a series of decerebrate birds, kept for several weeks or months after removal of the cerebrum, the arterial pressure was uniformly lower than in normal birds.

Porter showed in 1907 that in curarized rabbits and cats removal of the cerebral hemispheres in acute experiments leads to a profound fall in the blood pressure without depression of the reflex excitability of the vasomotor center.

If a blood pressure tracing be made on a dog before and after decerebration by Sherrington's method, it is frequently found that the pressure is somewhat less after decerebration than before. The complications however of the muscular rigidity that follows, render difficult the interpretation of the effects of the operation on the vasomotor center.

All these experiments are acute traumatic experiments subject to all the uncertainties of shock effects. In the birds many of these difficulties can be obviated, for they can be kept alive easily, for an indefinite time after the operation, and spastic paralytic phenomena are wholly lacking provided the hemispheres only are removed. In the pigeon therefore we have a warm-blooded animal which easily withstands the shock of cerebral ablation, lives indefinitely thereafter, and in which the permanent effects on the blood pressure can be studied.

There was the further inducement that the pigeon in comparison with the mammals combines a relatively low type of cerebral development with the warm-blooded condition and it was hoped that some light would be thrown on the nature of the nervous mechanism of heat regulation in its earlier development.

Methods. The measurements of arterial pressure were at first made in the ordinary way of cannula and mercury manometer. It was soon found that a more convenient and just as reliable method was furnished by substituting a hypodermic needle for the cannula and this method was used in all the work here reported. All measurements have been made on the brachial artery using a hypodermic needle, size 19 or 20 with a bore of about 1 mm. diameter. This furnishes a tube which when inserted into the artery slightly stretches it and fits tightly enough to allow no escape of blood. (In very large birds it may be necessary to use a larger needle.) This was connected to an ordinary small size mercury manometer made of glass tubing 4 mm. in diameter, with stiff-walled rubber tubing. In order to avoid any errors due to possible mechanical effects of friction or differences in level between the bird and the level of the mercury, the manometer was set in a fixed position with the level of the mercury in the plane of the tip of the breast muscles when the bird was fastened on its back. The same manometer, two needles of the same size, and the same size and length of rubber connections, were used throughout the series. Hence any mechanical errors will be nearly uniform throughout the comparative series of pressure determinations. Clotting of the blood was prevented by using 7 per cent sodium citrate throughout the apparatus. A lesser concentration was not always satisfactory, but with citrate solution of this concentration the tracing can be continued indefinitely through all variations of blood pressure of zero to 200 mm. When the needle was removed from the artery the blood vessel was doubly ligated. This causes no apparent trouble to the bird, so the collateral circulation must be extensive. In only one case did gangrene follow the ligation and in this case the ligature involved both brachial artery and vein. All readings were made with the birds under ether anesthesia; no other drugs were used in this study. This introduced, of course, the effects of the anesthetic added to that of the cerebral lesion. No other method however seemed available for it is important that there be no struggles by the animal as these will promptly change the level of the arterial pressure. In order to check these variations due to the action of the anesthetic the routine procedure was adopted of etherizing the bird, putting it on its back with wings spread and the needle inserted in the artery. The pressure was then raised in the manometer to a value a little less than the anticipated pressure. Some care was necessary here not to exceed the arterial pressure and thereby kill the bird by forcing citrate into the circulation. This happened twice in the series of experiments. The arterial pressure was then recorded for all depths of anesthesia, varying from light to deep, using rigidity as an index of light, and abolition of the corneal reflex as index of deep anesthesia. The readings of pressure given in the tables are, therefore, those of the extreme variations under anesthesia, but not including variations due to struggles of the animal. In many cases the pressure maintained a nearly constant level and only one figure is given in such cases.

In order to determine whether or not there were errors due to possible differences in size of the arteries of the two wings, readings were made on a series of birds comparing specifically the pressures in each of the two brachial arteries, in the same bird, allowing intervals of several days between determinations, during which time the birds were kept confined in the cages used throughout the series of experiments. These readings (table 5) agree closely. Of course in the case of specific anatomical anomalies such a comparison would be of no value. One such case has been seen, namely, a double instead of a single brachial artery. In a series of determinations however this

TABLE 1

Arterial pressure in normal pigeons

Anesthesia variations

NUMBER OF PIGEON	ARTERIAL PRESSURE	NUMBER OF PIGEON	ARTERIAL PRESSURE
	mm.		*mm.*
4	122–142	190	104–114
	114–118	188	94-120
	116–118	158	110–130
	150–160	156	154–176
	122–132	178	92–140
153	108–142	161	78–130
170	136	163	108–116
172	103–118	162	106–108
171	135	179	122–160
	116	169	100–110
177	96–108	193	96–98
181	92–108	193	96–102
	126–152	194	122–140
185	116	194	106–124
164	134–176	195	110–148
182	92–118	195	104–128
184	88–128	159	150–170
183	86–112		104–120
186	102–118	168	122–144
187	90–110		

Average pressure, 118 mm.

Average limits of variations, 109–130 mm.

The figure 109 is the average of all the lower of the two readings given for the majority of the animals. Similarly 130 is the average of the higher reading given. The figure 118 is the average of these extremes combined with the single figure given for several birds.

factor is neutralized in the averages given, and by the consideration that the arteries of both wings were used indiscriminately throughout the series of determinations.

Normal blood pressure. The average arterial blood pressure in the brachial artery under ether anesthesia of thirty-nine normal adult pigeons was found to be 118 mm. (table 1). The extreme limits for all stages of anesthesia were 78 to 176 mm. The average limits for the series are 109 to 130 mm. (fig. 1).

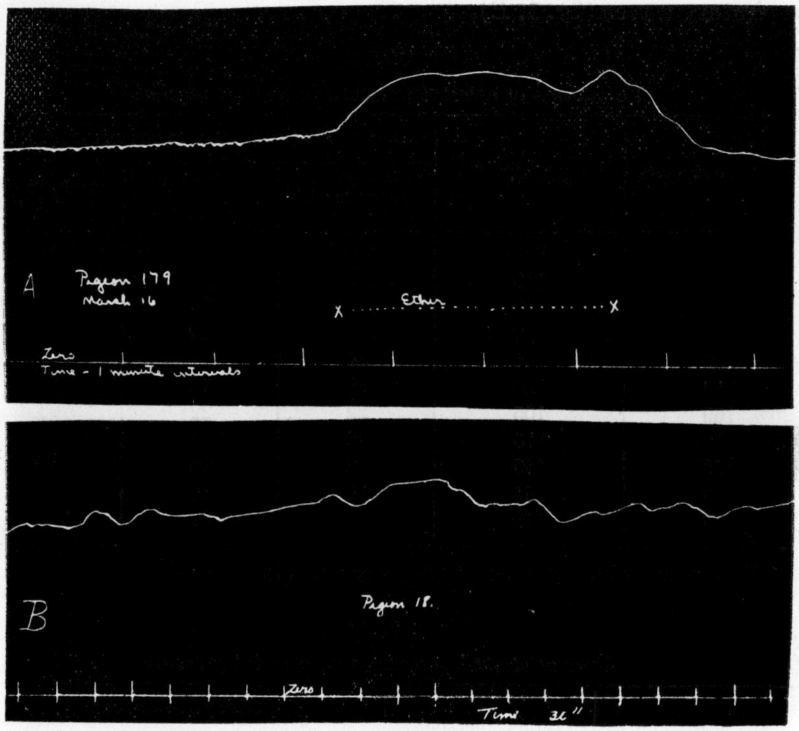

Fig. 1. Arterial pressure in normal pigeons, ether anesthesia. *A:* Light anesthesia: *x–x* more ether given so as to put bird in a state of deep anesthesia. Time in one minute intervals. *B:* Traube-Hering waves in pigeon under light anesthesia. Time in 30 second intervals.

Note: All figures of blood pressure are reduced one-half, except figure 3, which is reduced one-third. A true scale for measuring pressure in these tracings is given in figure 4.

Mechanical stimulation of the brachial nerves, ammonia to the nostrils, and asphyxia, produced the usual types of vasomotor responses. The effects of these procedures are given in table 2 and figures 2 and 3. Electric stimulation of these nerves was not employed. Mechanical stimulation of the nerves by pinching with forceps or traction caused brisk changes in arterial pressure, both pressor and depressor effects.

A lowering of blood pressure by cardiac inhibition seemed particularly easily elicited by traction of the brachial nerves. Traube-Hering waves of pressure have been frequently observed as also have been the shorter respiratory waves (fig. 1, B).

TABLE 2

Variations of arterial pressure in normal pigeons

NUMBER OF PIGEON	AVERAGE NORMAL PRESSURE	RANGE OF VARIATIONS OF PRESSURE INDUCED BY		
		Mechanical stimulation brachial nerves*	Ammonia to nostrils (rise in pressure)	Asphyxia (increased pressure)
	mm.	*mm.*	*mm.*	*mm.*
	110	14		24
	130		34	
	110		40	
153	125	30		
158	120	50	16	24
169	105	22	22	
178	116	12		
179	140	8	26	22
156	164	16	16	
170	110		32	

* This includes both pressor and depressor effects.

TABLE 3

Effects of slight hemorrhage on arterial pressure

NUMBER OF PIGEON	AMOUNT OF BLOOD LOST	ARTERIAL PRESSURE	
		Before bleeding	10 minutes after bleeding
	cc.		
159	5	150–170	126–128
173	1	110	102–118
155	2	130–150	134–148

The removal of small amounts of blood leads to a fall followed by quick recovery (table 3). Thus the loss of 1 to 2 cc. of blood in the normal pigeon leads to a fall quickly followed by compensatory changes which bring the pressure back to normal. The loss of 5 cc. of blood causes much more profound effects but in ten minutes the blood pressure has again reached the average level although below the previous level in the same bird (pigeon 159, table 3).

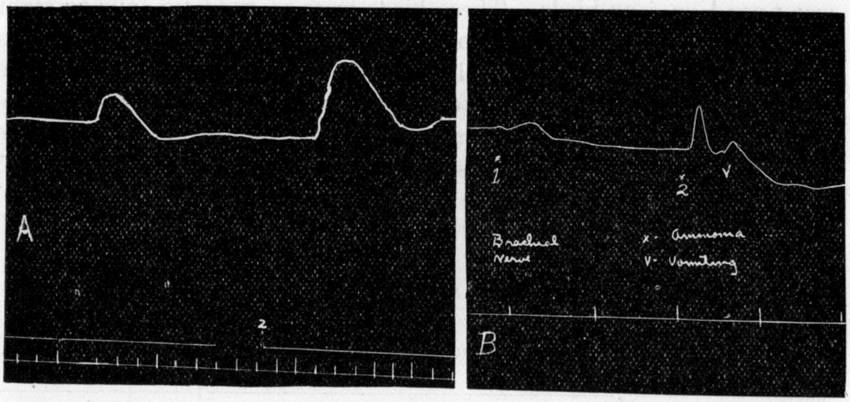

Fig. 2. Blood pressure, normal pigeons. *A: 1,* mechanical stimulation of brachial nerves; *2,* ammonia vapors to nostrils. *B:* Deeper anesthesia than in *A. 1,* mechanical stimulation of brachial nerves; *2,* ammonia to nostrils; *V,* vomiting.

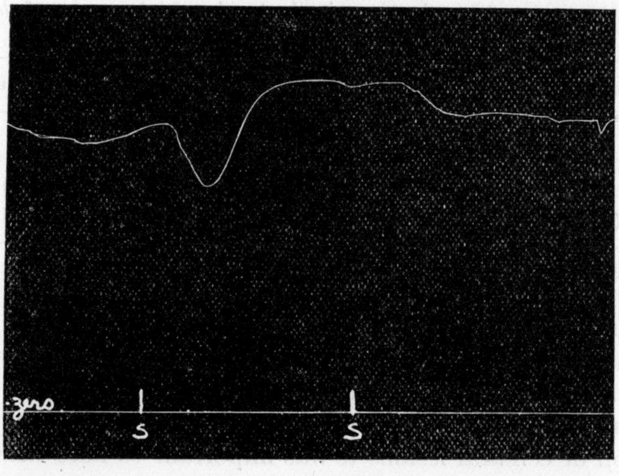

Fig. 3. Blood pressure, normal pigeon. Depressor effects following mechanical stimulation of brachial nerves.

The effect on blood pressure of deprivation of food—but not water—was tested on four birds. These birds were starved for four to eight days. At the end of that time the arterial pressure was normal in three of the birds and slightly lowered in one of them (table 4). The effects of confinement were tested by comparing the pressures of three birds which had been in the laboratory cages for over a year. The average pressure of these birds (six determinations, table 5) was 115 mm. compared with the average pressure of 118 mm.

TABLE 4

Influence of starvation on arterial pressure. Cerebrum intact

NUMBER OF PIGEON	STARVATION PERIOD	ARTERIAL PRESSURE	
		Before starvation	After starvation
	days	*mm.*	*mm.*
183	7	88–112	80–86
184	7	104–114	120–122
182	8	90–108	95–98
164	4	116–135	120–126

TABLE 5

Comparative pressure determinations in the two brachial arteries of the same birds (birds have been in laboratory cages for one year)

NUMBER OF PIGEON	TIME BETWEEN MEASUREMENT	RIGHT WING	LEFT WING
	days	*mm.*	*mm.*
193	3	96–98	96–103
194	3	122–140	106–124
195	3	104–128	110–148

Average pressure in these birds, 115 mm.

By this series of determinations of arterial pressure on thirty-nine normal adult pigeons the average pressure has been determined, the normal variations noted, and the effects of such factors as anesthesia, starvation and the routine reflexes observed. Preliminary to the production of cerebral lesions it was important to note whether or not the loss of the small amount of blood necessary to the operation would alter the level of the arterial pressure. As noted in table 3, the loss of 2 cc. of blood is so quickly compensated for as to justify the conclusion that if in operating not more than 2 cc. is lost the normal level of arterial pressure is maintained.

Effects of decerebration. A description of the varying conditions that follow the removal of the hemispheres or hemispheres and thalamus, or partial lesions of both, has been given elsewhere (7). It will suffice here to state that the classic picture of decerebrate behavior in the pigeon is obtained only if the thalamus be not traumatised in the process of decerebrating (8), (9). Thalamic injury is associated with temperature disturbances, with the behavior of the animal varying as its body temperature changes. The technique of decerebration is therefore important in a comparative series of studies on the rôle of these two parts of the brain. The general anatomy of this region of the brain is described in a previous paper (1). In decerebrating the upper part of the skull above the cerebral hemispheres was removed taking care not to puncture the dura mater. After a little practice this is easily done. A bridge of bone over the very small longitudinal sinus was left intact so as to diminish bleeding and to serve as a support for the skin after removal of the brain substance. The dura was then cut longitudinally and reflected, the anterior cerebral arteries were cauterized and the hemispheres removed in toto. In this way the operation can be completed with the loss of less than 1 cc. of blood. If more than 2 cc. of blood was lost in operating it is indicated in the history of the animals. If the thalamus was to be destroyed, this was done with an electro-cautery, after removal of the hemispheres. The autopsy findings in the brain with histologic description of the parts of the brain remaining after recovery from this type of injury have been described in the preceding report to which reference has been made (7).

It is common knowledge that the removal of the hemispheres sometimes leads to a slight immediate fall in blood pressure which has been attributed to shock, hemorrhage, mechanical stimulation, etc. The same effect is true of the pigeon. In order to avoid these acute effects, the birds have been kept for time intervals of one week to four months after decerebration before the arterial pressure was measured (table 6 and fig. 4). These studies have been carried out on fifteen pigeons, allowing time intervals for recovery from any acute shock effects. In ten of these birds the arterial pressure was measured before decerebration; in five this was not done. For the latter animals some indication of the change in pressure may be gathered by comparing with the average normal arterial pressure value given above.

The average pressure after decerebration, thalamus being left intact, allowing three to seventy-five days for recovery, in fifteen pigeons, was found to be 99 mm., in comparison with the average pressure in thirty-nine normal pigeons, of 118 mm. This reduction seems to be uniform and constant, and continues for months after loss of the hemispheres. It is not due to loss of blood at the time of decerebration for the amount of blood lost was so slight that compensation quickly occurs in the normal animal. It is not due to failure of compensation in the decerebrated bird, for when pressure tracings were made allowing the blood to force the mercury from the zero level, it rises to the level of arterial pressure as quickly in the operated birds as in the normal ones. (Compare figs. 5 and 8 A.) With decerebration plus thalamic lesions, slower compensation may be a factor (see below). This fall in pressure is not due to mere disturbances of food supply for, as tested in normal

TABLE 6

Effects on arterial pressure of removing the cerebral hemispheres, thalamus not traumatised

NUMBER OF PIGEON	TIME FOR RECOVERY*	ARTERIAL PRESSURE Before decerebration	ARTERIAL PRESSURE After decerebration	REMARKS
	days	*mm.*	*mm.*	
179	5	120	102	Much bleeding at time of operation
178	5	120–144	120	Good condition
156	5	154–176	96–112	Good condition
158	8	108–128	96–110	Good condition
168	16	118–124	92–120	Good condition
106	75		96–108	Good condition
155	3	126–136	96– 98	Good condition
166	16	120–122	104–114	Good condition
167	5	116–124	96–102	Good condition
152	16	82– 98	90– 95	Good condition
162	3	104–108	88– 94	Good condition
157	5		80– 84	Good condition
116	11		86– 90	Good condition
	21		96	Good condition
	6		87	Good condition

* The words "time for recovery" indicate the time interval elapsing between the removal of the cerebral hemispheres and the final blood pressure determinations. The words "good condition" indicate that the bird exhibited no skeletal muscle incoördination, body temperature was normal, feathers fluffed in the characteristic decerebrate manner and the bird exhibited decerebrate restlessness. Any variation from these characteristic effects usually indicate thalamic or medullary disturbances or incomplete decerebration.

birds (table 4), complete starvation for periods of three to eight days did not cause greater variations in pressure than the normal anesthesia variations. It might be due to one or more of the following factors.

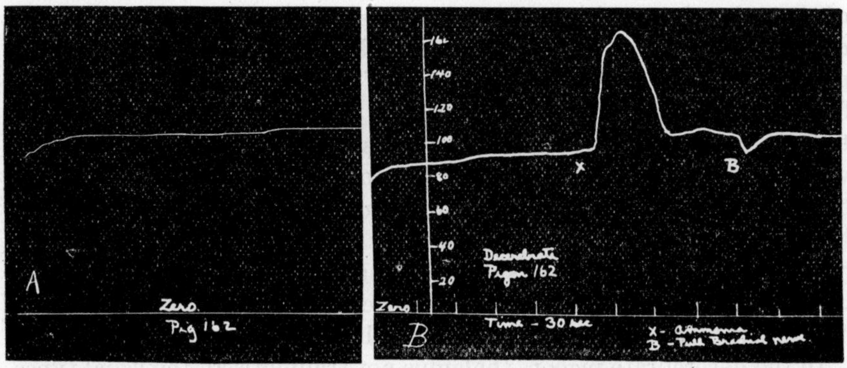

Fig. 4. Blood pressure, pigeon 162: *A:* before, and *B:* eight days after removal of the cerebral hemispheres. Thalamus intact and body temperature normal. Time in 30 second intervals. *B:* *x*, ammonia to nostrils; *b*, mechanical stimulation of brachial nerves.

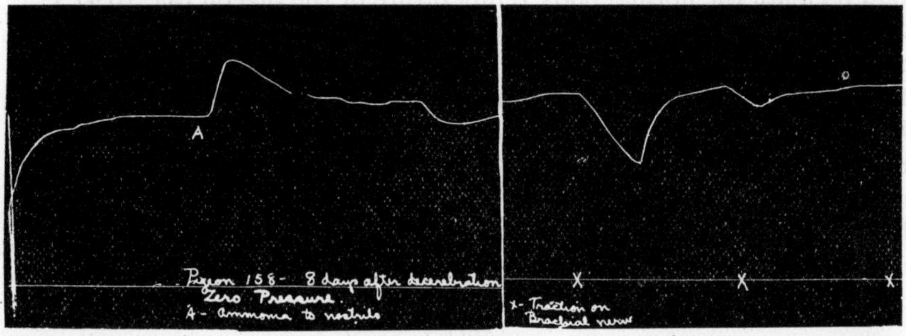

Fig. 5. Blood pressure, pigeon 158, eight days after decerebration. *A:* ammonia to nostrils; *X:* mechanical stimulation of brachial nerves, repeated three times. There was no preliminary increase in pressure in manometer before making this tracing, so the mercury was forced up from the zero line wholly by the arterial pressure.

First, metabolic depression following loss of the hemispheres associated with decreased activity of the animal; or second, loss of a tonic activity of the hemispheres on the vasoconstrictor centers; or possibly due to depressed skeletal muscle tone with resulting capillary dilatation.

In order to test the first of these possibilities the blood pressure determinations were made on a normal pigeon before and after blinding and starvation. Blinding the bird by excision of the eyes brings about a condition of quiet and lessened muscular activity that simulates that of decerebration. The combination of starvation for four days associated with this inactivity of blindness did not lower the average arterial pressure (see table 4, pigeon 164). Of course prolonged starvation for a long period of time will alter the pressure, witness pigeon 183, table 4, and pigeon 188, table 9. Inasmuch as all decerebrate birds were fed by hand and kept in as good condition as possible, it seemed that one week of absolute starvation would represent as great a metabolic disturbance as might be induced by loss of the hemispheres. The result of this test therefore suggested that the fall in arterial pressure is due to the loss of reflex or tonic influences from the cerebrum on some part of the blood pressure regulating mechanism.

In the decerebrate pigeon, thalamus not traumatised, the usual types of vasomotor reflexes may be elicited by stimulation of spinal nerves, ammonia, etc. (fig. 5). Asphyxia produces the usual rise in pressure.

Decerebration with destruction of the thalamus. Combined decerebration and thalamic cauterization abolishes the ability to maintain and regulate the normal body temperature of the pigeon (39° to 41°C.). As stated in the introduction, it was thought that possibly this condition might be due to a generalized fall in blood pressure. As is evident from table 8, this is not the case. If the body temperature of such a bird is kept near the normal level by keeping the bird in an incubator at 30°C. the arterial pressure of such a bird is very near the pressure of the warm-blooded decerebrate pigeon. Thus the average values of blood pressure, decerebrate pigeons (body temperature normal) and decerebrate-thalamic destruction (cold-blooded animals) are as follows:

TABLE 7

BIRDS	NUMBER OF BIRDS	BODY TEMPERATURE	ARTERIAL PRESSURE
		°C.	*mm.*
Normal	39	39–41	118
Decerebrate	14	39–41	99
Decerebration and thalamus destroyed	7	34–41	99
Decerebration and thalamus destroyed	7	26–33	87

It is conclusively evident from this table that the loss of temperature regulation is not due primarily to a lowered arterial pressure, but that the changes of arterial pressure are secondary to the body temperature changes. As the body temperature rises or falls the blood pressure does likewise (table 8 and fig. 6). To this rule one exception was found, pigeon 174. In this animal the pressure did not fall as the body temperature fell, but acted in an inverse manner. Attempts were made to duplicate this but were unsuccessful. This was a bird in which the operation of decerebration was associated with much bleeding. The writer is inclined to attribute the high arterial pressure in this bird to a possible intracranial pressure complication or incomplete destruction of the thalamus.

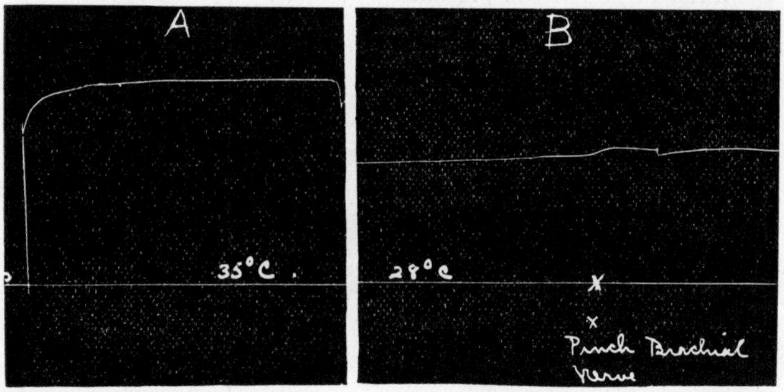

Fig. 6. Blood pressure in pigeon 191. Poikilothermous bird; decerebrate and thalamus destroyed. *A:* Body temperature of pigeon, 35°C. *B:* Body temperature of pigeon, 28°C. *x*, mechanical stimulation of brachial nerves.

In the poikilothermous pigeon the vasomotor reflexes vary in intensity as the body temperature varies (figs. 6 and 7). Both pressor and depressor effects were obtained by stimulation of the brachial nerves. As the body temperature falls the pressor reflexes particularly decrease in intensity. The depressor effects seemed to be due to cardiac inhibition and were present at low body temperatures at which the pressor effects were very much reduced (compare figs. 6 and 7). Ammonia to the nostrils caused a rise in pressure which is associated with respiratory distress. This effect was present at all body temperatures tested (28° to 41°C.), but was more sluggish at lower temperatures than at normal body temperature (compare figs. 5, 7 and 8).

TABLE 8

Arterial pressure in pigeons rendered poikilothermous by destruction of cerebrum and thalamus

NUMBER OF PIGEON	DATE	PROCEEDING	TIME FOR RECOVERY	BODY TEMPERATURE	ARTERIAL PRESSURE
			days	*°C.*	*mm.*
191	June 22	Operation		39	
	June 28	Blood pressure	6	35	93
	June 28	Blood pressure	6	28	58
175	March 9	Operation		39	
	March 14	Blood pressure			
		1 p.m.	5	36	102–106
		6 p.m.	5	28	83–86
174	March 5	Operation, much bleeding		40	
	March 10	Blood pressure			
		2 p.m.	5	34	121
		4 p.m.	5	31	124
		6 p.m.	5	29	124–134
114	February 7	Operation		39	
	February 22	Blood pressure	15	29	92
	March 8	Blood pressure	29	41	85
	March 13	Bird dead			
113	February 7	Operation		3	
	February 20	Blood pressure	13	28	92
		Operation	3	29	78
		Operation	29	41	85
176	March 9	Operation		39	
	March 12	Blood pressure	3	29	76
	March 13	Dead			
180	March 18	Operation, much bleeding		39	
	March 29	Blood pressure	11	34	102–106
169	March 1	Blood pressure tracing, followed by operation on brain		39	100–110
	March 4	Blood pressure	3	31	72–76

Body temperatures of the operated birds fixed by varying the temperatures of bird cages.

Average arterial pressure—body temperature 34–41°C.—was 99 mm.

Average arterial pressure—body temperature 28–31°C.—was 87 mm.

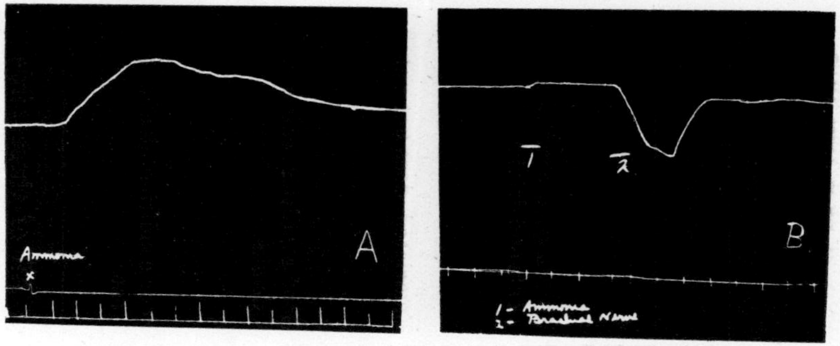

Fig. 7. Blood pressure, poikilothermous pigeons. *A:* Pigeon 169. Body temperature 31°C. Time in 15 second intervals; *x*, ammonia to nostrils. *B:* Pigeon 175. Body temperature 28°C. *1*, ammonia to nostrils; *2*, traction on brachial nerves.

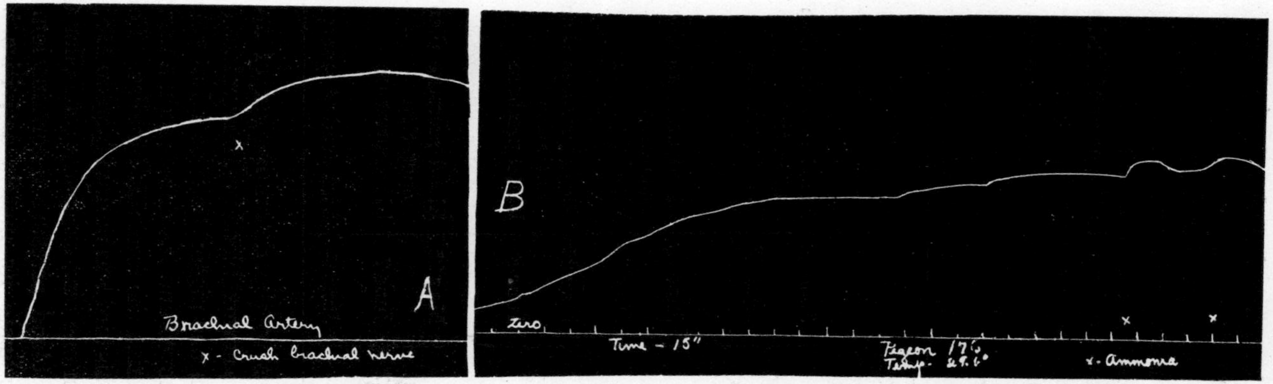

Fig. 8. Comparison of the time rates at which the pressure rises from the zero level of the manometer wholly under the influence of the arterial pressure. *A:* Normal pigeon, body temperature 39°C.; *x*, stimulation brachial nerves. *B:* Poiki othermous pigeon, body temperature 29°C.; *x*, ammonia to nostrils.

Compensation after loss of a small amount of blood occurs more and more slowly as the body temperature is more and more depressed (fig. 8). In this figure the pressure in the manometer was at zero when the artery was connected with it. The slow rise to the level of arterial pressure is in marked contrast to the quick ascent and maintenance of level in the normal bird.

Effects of localized lesions. The major part of the cerebral cortex had been destroyed by electro-cauterization in three birds a year previous to the determination of arterial pressure. All of these birds gave normal blood pressure values (table 10).

TABLE 9

Effects on arterial pressure of removing one cerebral hemisphere

NUMBER OF PIGEON	DATE	PROCEEDING	ARTERIAL PRESSURE	REMARKS
			mm.	
190	June 10	Blood pressure then operation	98–118	
	June 23	Blood pressure	96–122	Bird in good condition—eats and drinks
188	June 8	Blood pressure then operation	92–102	
	June 23	Blood pressure	80–96	Emaciated, does not eat
186	May 25	Blood pressure then operation	100–118	
	June 8	Blood pressure	108–120	Good condition, eats and drinks
187	May 25	Blood pressure then operation	94–110	
	June 7	Blood pressure	82–92	Poor condition, does not eat
	June 9	Bird dead of starvation		

In one pigeon both occipital poles of the cerebral hemispheres were removed and the dorso-median part of the thalamus cauterized without severing the forebrain bundles. Four months later the arterial pressure in this bird was normal (pigeon 118, table 10).

In one bird extensive cerebellar traumatism was done a year before the blood pressure determination. The bird regained its ability to coördinate its muscle activities in the usual way. Blood pressure determination in this bird showed a lower arterial tension (pigeon 193, table 10). At autopsy the bird was found to be tubercular.

In a series of four birds the right cerebral hemisphere only was removed (table 9). After this operation some birds promptly recover and in a few days feed themselves in a normal way. The principal

TABLE 10

Arterial pressure after minor brain lesions

NUMBER OF PIGEON	DATE	OPERATION	ARTERIAL PRESSURE	REMARKS
			mm.	
118	April 28	Occipital cortex removed; thalamus cauterized		
	August 28	Blood pressure tracing	120	Bird in good condition
72	August 17, 1918	Cortez cerebri cauterized		
	July 3, 1920	Blood pressure tracing	122–140	Bird in good condition
73	August 17, 1918	Cortex cerebri cauterized		
	July 3, 1920	Blood pressure tracing	104–148	Bird in good condition
62	February 19, 1919	Cortez cerebri cauterized		
	July 3, 1920	Blood pressure tracing	102–124	
193	May 15, 1919	Gross traumatism of cerebellum		
	July 6, 1920	Bird recovered. Blood pressure tracing	96–102	Bird is tubercular

obvious disturbance in such an animal is complete blindness (at least temporarily) of the opposite eye. In some cases these birds go into a condition resembling complete decerebration (probably due to vascular disturbances in the remaining hemisphere). These animals will not feed themselves, assume a decerebrate attitude and die of starvation unless fed by hand. In this series of four birds two recovered and two died of starvation. The blood pressure readings in the two birds that recovered were normal. The combination of hemi-decerebration and starvation led to lower blood pressure.

It was found, therefore, that no localized cerebral or thalamic injury led to permanent depression of the arterial pressure. Complete loss of either hemispheres, or hemispheres and thalamus, leads to distinct arterial depression.

Artificial stimulation of cerebral cortex. Electric stimulation of the cortex of the cerebral hemispheres gave a slight rise in blood pressure with no movements of the skeletal muscle. Stimulation was done under light ether anesthesia. Stimulation of the thalamus causes a sharp rise in arterial pressure, but also leads to muscular activity. Whether this rise is a true vasomotor reaction or a mechanical one due to striated muscle contraction was not determined, but Sachs and others have shown that vasomotor reflexes are readily induced by artificial stimulation of the thalamic nuclei.

DISCUSSION

The results given above lead to the suggestion that the cerebral hemispheres exert a continuous tonic activity on the mechanism whereby arterial pressure is maintained. Whether this be through the vasomotor, skeletal or some other systems individually or combined is not determined. Porter's findings on curarized decerebrate rabbits indicate a tonic action on the vasoconstrictor centers. The relatively slight influence of the cerebral hemispheres on the skeletal muscle of the pigeon[1] suggests that in this case lowered blood pressure is also due to a loss of vasomotor tone rather than to changes in the skeletal muscle.

The possibility of a depression of arterial pressure due to unknown changes in metabolism, after loss of the cerebrum, can not at present be excluded. Some evidence has been presented that this alone is not sufficient to bring about the vascular changes described, witness the negative effects of starvation, inactivity, etc. These experiments however do not conclusively exclude a contributing metabolic factor

[1] There are no cortical motor points in the cerebral hemispheres of the pigeon except possibly for the eye (Ferrier). Electric stimulation of the exposed cortex in the unanesthetized pigeon causes no muscular movements. Removal of the hemispheres likewise leads to no paralysis. These facts suggest that the fall in arterial pressure is not due to secondary changes in skeletal muscle.

after brain injury. Further studies in metabolism after cerebral lesions must be made in spite of the negative results reported by various observers.

However this may be, the inference can not be avoided that any functional depression of the cerebral hemispheres should be followed by lowered arterial tension. This might be due to sleep, anesthesia or destruction (provided there be no increase in intracranial pressure). Certainly there are differences in detail of the mechanisms in each case but it is noteworthy that in each case of cerebral depression there is lowered arterial pressure. No localized cerebral vasomotor centers are postulated. Indeed localized injuries of either hemispheres or thalamus caused no change of arterial pressure. The lowering of arterial pressure described follows the loss of large amounts of cerebral substance rather than the loss of particular areas of the hemispheres or thalamus. To this extent, this report reaffirms for the vasomotor mechanism, the old teaching of Flourens that, in the bird, the effects of cerebral injury are due not to the loss of local centers but are proportional to the quantity of brain tissue rendered non-functional.

SUMMARY

A method is described for studying the blood pressure in the pigeon.

The average pressure in the brachial artery of thirty-nine normal adult pigeons, under ether anesthesia, was 118 mm. mercury. The average limits of variations, due to variations in anesthesia, were 109 to 130 mm. Pressor and depressor effects on the blood pressure may be readily induced by stimulation of the spinal nerves. Ammonia to the nostrils causes a sharp rise in blood pressure. Respiratory waves and Traube-Hering waves of blood pressure occur as in mammals. The loss of small quantities of blood is quickly followed by compensatory changes bringing the pressure back to normal.

Starvation for three to seven days does not appreciably alter the pressure in normal birds.

Removal of the cerebral hemispheres in fifteen birds led to a fall of the average arterial pressure to 99 mm. (loss of 17 per cent). This lowered pressure persisted for time intervals up to four months after decerebration and never regained the level before operation. Removal of the cerebral hemispheres and thalamus leads to a similar or greater fall in arterial pressure varying as the body temperature varies. The greater the fall in body temperature, the greater the depression of the arterial pressure.

The poikilothermous condition in the bird, following excision of the thalamus, is not primarily due to lowered arterial pressure.

In the pigeon rendered poikilothermous by combined decerebration and destruction of the thalamus, the vasomotor responses to mechanical stimulation of spinal nerves, ammonia to the nostrils, and compensatory recovery of pressure after slight hemorrhages, are all depressed or take place more slowly, varying with the depression of body temperature.

The arterial pressure is not appreciably disturbed by removal of a single cerebral hemisphere, localized lesions of both hemispheres, or localized thalamic lesion (without cerebral destruction) provided these injuries are not associated with starvation.

These experiments suggest that the cerebral hemispheres and thalamus exert a continuous tonic stimulating action on the subcortical blood pressure regulating mechanism. This action is not one of localized cerebral centers but varies according to the amount of brain substance destroyed, rather than the particular area destroyed.

BIBLIOGRAPHY

(1) Rogers: This Journal, 1919, xlix, 271.
(2) Asher: Ergebn. d. Physiol., 1902, ii, 346.
(3) Owsjannikow: Ludwig's Physiologische Arbeiten, Leipzig, 1872–1874.
(4) Dittmar: Ludwig's Physiologische Arbeiten, Leipzig, 1873.
(5) Sachs: Journ. Exper. Med., 1911, xiv, 409.
(6) Porter and Storey: This Journal, 1907, xviii, 181.
(7) Rogers: Journ. Comp. Neurol., 1919, xxxi, 17.
(8) Schrader: Arch. f. gesammt. Physiol., 1889, xliv, 175.
(9) Munk: Über die Funktionen der Grosshirnrinde, 2nd ed., Berlin, 1890.

EXPERIMENTAL STUDIES IN DIABETES

Series II. The Internal Pancreatic Function in Relation to Body Mass and Metabolism[1]

5. The Influence of Fever and Intoxication

FREDERICK M. ALLEN

From the Hospital of the Rockefeller Institute for Medical Research, New York

Received for publication August 10, 1920

The accuracy with which the metabolism of cold-blooded animals can be regulated through the temperature was one of the reasons for the attempt to produce diabetes in them at the outset of this investigation. When the production of a satisfactory type of diabetes proved impossible, the research was thrown back entirely upon mammalian experiments, where the disturbing factors are greater. Some observations were made concerning the effects of fever and of external cold.

No discussion of the literature will be undertaken, beyond reference to a review (1) of the earlier literature, and a more recent paper by Freund and Marchand (2), which show that elevation of body temperature is generally accompanied by elevation of blood sugar, but terminal collapse may be accompanied by hypoglycemia; the rise of body temperature in itself tends to increase sugar tolerance, and lowered tolerance or glycosuria are attributable to intoxication or sometimes to pancreatic damage. Infections are known to be one of the worst agencies in aggravating human diabetes. The effect of aseptic elevation of temperature seems not to have been tested. It was desired in the present research to compare several forms of infectious and non-infectious fever in their influence upon partially depancreatized dogs. The only results actually permitted by circumstances consisted in records of a number of animals which acquired chance infections, and one research concerning the gas bacillus. The observations will be classified according to the site of the infections.

[1] The first four papers of this series are published in the American Journal of the Medical Sciences.

Distemper. For this purpose canine distemper is closely comparable to human tuberculosis. Diabetes plainly increases the susceptibility of dogs and still more of puppies to this infection, in the sense that they both acquire it and succumb to it more easily. Tuberculosis seriously lowers the food tolerance and increases the tendency to glycosuria and hyperglycemia in human patients even in the earlier non-febrile stages, and this effect becomes still greater in the febrile stage. In numerous observations in dogs covering all stages of distemper and all degrees of diabetic tendency, precisely the opposite effect has been found. It is true that distemper is characterized by early failure of appetite and digestion. The resulting emaciation constitutes a very radical undernutrition treatment, and a similarity thus exists to Joslin's frequently quoted Case R (3), in which the emaciation of tuberculosis on a regulated diabetic diet evidently improved the assimilation. But the infection has been observed in dogs with definitely known tolerance, which continued for some time to take a diet close to the limits of tolerance. There have been other examples such as dog C3-77, 1 year old, weighing 10.5 kilos, and subjected on April 13, 1916, to the removal of all but $\frac{1}{22}$ to $\frac{1}{23}$ of the pancreas (estimated remnant 1 gram).[2] Glycosuria began immediately and by April 17 had reached 2.9 per cent, fasting. It then ceased as the first signs of distemper appeared in the form of conjunctivitis. The dog refused food and wasted away in the usual manner till killed on May 7, at a weight of 6.3 kilos. The pancreas remnant weighed 1.35 grams. The islands showed very slight vacuolation in a few cells, such as might persist from the initial glycosuria, but far less than would result from 3 weeks of active diabetes. The remnant was so small and the diabetic tendency so strong that sugar-freedom on fasting would have been impossible if the infection had introduced any aggravation, but the result seemed to be identical with that in a non-infected animal.

Pneumonia. Dog B2-18, after removal of $\frac{12}{13}$ of the pancreas on December 2, developed moderate glycosuria on diets containing carbohydrate, in a cold environment. December 6 the dog was found to be unwell and febrile, but continued to eat the diet through the illness to December 9, and the glycosuria continued unchanged. Death occurred from double pneumonia on December 13. The autopsy urine contained 1.65 per cent sugar. The vacuolation in the pancreatic islands was similar to that of non-infected dogs at the same stage.

[2] All operations were performed under ether anesthesia.

Dog C3-73 similarly underwent operation leaving $\frac{1}{10}$ to $\frac{1}{11}$ of the pancreas on April 3, and died of pneumonia on April 18. The final urine on April 17 contained heavy sugar, but death was apparently preceded by anuria.

Dog D4-72 was left with a remnant of $\frac{1}{9}$ to $\frac{1}{10}$ of the pancreas on January 12, and died of pneumonia on January 19. The appetite continued and the glycosuria was not appreciably changed with the onset of fever. Nothing was eaten after January 17. The autopsy urine still contained a trace of sugar. There was thus a diminution resembling the effect of ordinary fasting, not the great increase which usually accompanies infection in any severe human case.

Cat A1-93 was left with a remnant of $\frac{1}{5}$ to $\frac{1}{6}$ of the pancreas on January 21, and died of pneumonia on January 26. Because of refusal of food, there was only a transitory trace of glycosuria, as would be the case in a non-infected cat fasting after such an operation.

Other examples might be given in which infection failed to cause glycosuria when the removal of pancreatic tissue was not quite sufficient to produce it in a non-infected animal, and still others in which extreme prostration prevented glycosuria which must otherwise have occurred. In no instance was any evidence of aggravation of diabetes seen.

Pleurisy. Dog B2-22 had been used in another department for collection of leukocytes by intrapleural injections, and on December 8, $\frac{9}{10}$ of the pancreas was removed without knowledge of the existence of a large purulent pleurisy. Fever, malaise and other symptoms were found after the operation. The dog ate small quantities of bread and milk on December 9 and 10, and glycosuria of 2 to 3 per cent continued to December 12. Death occurred with sugar-free urine on December 13.

Subcutaneous abscesses. In connection with subcutaneous injections and other procedures a considerable number of abscesses have been observed in dogs with various degrees of diabetic tendency. The infections themselves have been of varying magnitude, from small collections causing no systemic symptoms to large ones accompanied by depression, anorexia and fever above 105°F. The organisms present were sometimes identified as staphylococci, streptococci or mixed bacilli. The same rule held as above, namely, that glycosuria might cease with fasting and prostration, or in less extreme cases might continue unchanged, but a marked aggravation such as is familiar in human cases was never seen.

Infected glands. Dog D4-92 on February 5, 1917, was subjected to removal of all but $\frac{1}{8}$ to $\frac{1}{9}$ of the pancreas. Bread and soup were eaten on February 8, and 100 grams glucose added on February 9, still without glycosuria. Thereafter nothing was eaten and remarkable symptoms of confusion and ataxia appeared, increasing on February 12 to general convulsions and suggesting rabies. The dog was chloroformed on February 13, and the brain examination was negative for meningitis or Negri bodies. The autopsy otherwise was negative except for a little creamy pus found oozing from between the pectoral muscles, leading to caseous-appearing glands in and about both axillae. The type or origin of the infection was not determined. Glycosuria remained absent.

Rabies. Several partially depancreatized dogs died of rabies. One of these was dog B2-02, which, as previously mentioned (4), had been carefully studied and was known to have latent diabetes. No glycosuria resulted in any instance. The negative results were of interest in a condition attended with such pronounced nervous excitation, and in which convulsions may give rise to very marked hyperglycemia (5).

General peritonitis. This naturally involves cessation of glycosuria in most cases because of fasting and prostration. With sufficiently large experience, examples are encountered which indicate that the infection in itself does not alter the glycosuria. Some such were described previously (6), and the following have been observed since.

Dog B2-13. November 24, 1913, removal of $\frac{13}{14}$ of pancreas. There was glycosuria of 0.25 per cent in 60 cc. of urine following operation, and 0.2 per cent in 330 cc. after eating 150 grams meat on November 27. Otherwise there was fasting and freedom from glycosuria up to death from peritonitis on November 29.

Dog B2-21. December 4, 1913, partial pancreatectomy leaving a remnant of $\frac{1}{13}$ to $\frac{1}{14}$. After bread feeding on December 5, heavy glycosuria began, and continued to death from peritonitis on December 11. Bread was eaten daily to December 9. The autopsy urine was 100 cc., with 2.85 per cent glucose. The pancreatic islands showed the slight vacuolation proper to this early stage of diabetes.

Cat A1-82. December 19, 1913, removal of $\frac{7}{8}$ of pancreas. The cat refused food but acted well and cleaned her fur up to December 22, and died of peritonitis December 23. Glycosuria began with a faint reaction on December 21, rose to 2.5 per cent on December 22, and was 4 per cent in the last 55 cc. of urine on December 23. The pancreatic islands showed incipient vacuolation in a minority of cells.

Cat A1-87. January 8, 1914, removal of $\frac{5}{6}$ of pancreas. There was slight continuous glycosuria with very little eating from January 9 to death from peritonitis on January 12. The islands were free from visible vacuolation, as would be expected in a non-infected animal with such brief and mild diabetes.

Peritoneal and pancreatic abscesses. In addition to previous examples (6), the following may be mentioned.

Dog D4-65. December 21, 1916, an Eck fistula was unsuccessfully attempted, and some sutures were left on the veins. January 2, 1917, $\frac{9}{10}$ of the pancreas was removed. The dog was lively and immediately developed glycosuria on bread feeding. This ceased on January 8, and was restored by addition of 100 grams glucose daily. On January 10 emaciation, fever and weakness first became noticeable, but the diet was still eaten without change in the heavy glycosuria. With a change of diet to 1 kilo of beef lung on January 12 glycosuria immediately ceased. Beginning January 14 food was refused, and the dog was killed January 15, at a weight of 9.8 kilos as opposed to an original 13.5 kilos. A grape-sized abscess of creamy pus at the site of the Eck operation was the only discoverable cause of death. It had not altered the course of the diabetes from what is the rule with non-infected dogs under the same conditions.

Dog D4-57. December 7, 1916, removal of $\frac{4}{5}$ of the pancreas. The usual complete absence of diabetes was demonstrated thereafter. March 1, 1917, additional tissue was removed, possibly sufficient for mild diabetes. Malaise, fever and complete refusal of food followed. Glycosuria was absent on March 2, 3 and 4, but present just before death on March 5 to the extent of 0.8 per cent in 182 cc. of urine. The plasma sugar at this time was 0.625 per cent, CO_2 capacity 69.2 vol. per cent. Autopsy showed the pancreas remnant to be riddled with small abscesses, and though there was no necrosis the inflammatory injury had evidently brought on a severe degree of diabetes which would otherwise have been lacking. Infection has never been found to produce acetonuria or other evidences of acidosis in any animal.

Dog F6-14 was subjected to removal of about $\frac{2}{3}$ of the pancreas in three successive operations. January 31, 1918, an attempt was made to produce diabetes by circulatory stasis of the remnant, as described in a later paper. Only slight and transitory glycosuria resulted on a diet of bread and soup with 100 grams glucose. February 8, operation showed an abscess containing about 5 cc. of creamy pus between the pancreas and the duodenum. The cavity was cleaned and stasis repeated. Glycosuria was still impossible to maintain, and on March 9 stasis was applied for a still longer time, no infection being found. Glycosuria was then continuous up to March 19 on bread diet with 100 grams of glucose, but ceased then on plain bread and soup feeding. March 20 the abdomen was again opened, and the pancreas was found buried in a large mass of adhesions, which when delivered outside and opened was found to contain a very large abscess. The pancreas remnant, which in its whole length formed one wall of the abscess, was much inflamed but not digested. Nothing was done except the cleaning up of the infection, and the tolerance continued exactly as before; i.e., glycosuria was absent on bread feeding and present with addition of 100 grams of glucose. On April 10 the abdomen was again opened, and a tiny abscess in the omentum appeared as the only remains of the previous infection. Stasis was again applied to the pancreas remnant, and the dog died within 24 hours, whether from infection or from pancreatic intoxication was undetermined.

The long history of this animal, with alternate presence and absence of a low grade infection, seems to prove that in this instance the infection had no important influence upon the tolerance.

Other examples of this sort might be given. There was particular interest in the cases in which diabetes was produced by inflammation instead of by simple resection, because of the supposed closer imitation of the clinical etiology. It was conceivable that inflammation might damage the islands in function as well as in structure, so as to render them more susceptible to toxic influences. The negative results raised a question concerning some fundamental difference between clinical and experimental diabetes, or a mere difference of constitutional reaction to infection on the part of man and animals. The above general observations sufficed positively to exclude any such marked aggravation of diabetes in animals as occurs regularly in human cases with the fever and intoxication accompanying infection. There remained the need of making a more exact test of the tolerance in experimental diabetes as influenced by infection, and this opportunity was afforded by the experiments with the gas bacillus reported in the next paper. These seemed to indicate that the difference between clinical and the experimental diabetes may be one of degree rather than of kind.

CONCLUSIONS

1. The serious aggravation of diabetes, which occurs almost invariably in human cases in the form of a strongly increased tendency to glycosuria and acidosis, is never seen in dogs. Even when the infection is an abscess bordering or invading the pancreatic tissue, no influence is evident beyond that explainable by direct injury of parenchyma. This contrast between clinical and experimental diabetes is very marked, but according to the more exact tolerance tests in the succeeding paper it may represent a difference of degree rather than of kind.

2. Infection and fever have also no specific influence in diminishing the diabetic tendency of dogs. Care is necessary in interpreting such observations, in order not to confuse the direct influence of fever or infection with the consequences of fasting or prostration, which tend so strongly to suppress glycosuria in dogs. One suggestion of a constitutional difference between species may be found in the tendency of human patients to acidosis and of dogs to cachexia.

3. The aggravation of human diabetes is a reaction to intoxication rather than to fever, as shown by its occurrence in the afebrile stage

of tuberculosis and by other evidence. The present observations concerning infectious fever, with the previous ones concerning the pyrexia of exercise in dogs, prove that no specific aggravation of diabetes or lowering of tolerance results from the metabolic alteration attendant upon elevation of body temperature in experimental animals.

BIBLIOGRAPHY

(1) Allen: Studies concerning glycosuria and diabetes, 1913, 38, 563, 564.
(2) Freund and Marchand: Deutsch. Arch. klin. Med., 1913, cx, 120.
(3) Benedict and Joslin: Carnegie Inst. Washington, Pub. no. 176, 1912, 55. Also Joslin: Treatment of diabetes mellitus, 2nd ed., 1917, 409.
(4) Allen: Journ. Exper. Med., 1920, xxxi, 384.
(5) Allen and Wishart: Journ. Biol. Chem., 1920, xliii, 140.
(6) Allen: Studies concerning glycosuria and diabetes, 1913, 482 (dog 66); 492–495; 760 (dog 179).

EXPERIMENTAL STUDIES IN DIABETES

Series II. The Internal Pancreatic Function in Relation to Body Mass and Metabolism

6. Gas Bacillus Infections in Diabetic Dogs

MARY B. WISHART and IDA W. PRITCHETT

From the Hospital of the Rockefeller Institute for Medical Research, New York

Received for publication August 10, 1920

In the course of this diabetic research four dogs died of gas bacillus infection. Two of these instances were merely post-operative peritonitis, with the gas bacillus predominating.

Another was dog E5-74, a bulldog mongrel, aged 5 years, in splendid condition, weighing 20.7 kilos. July 3, 1917, two-thirds of the pancreas were removed, and most of the remnant was cut off from duct communication.[1] On July 20, the remnant was subjected to circulatory stasis for $1\frac{1}{2}$ hours. Glycosuria was present on bread diet with addition of 150 grams of glucose daily up to July 30, when it ceased, and the dog was turned loose in the yard with other dogs on bread diet. The behavior meantime was normal. About August 5, swelling in the neck became noticeable and the dog was slightly depressed. August 7, the swelling was much larger, and a deep abscess was opened surgically, releasing a considerable quantity of thick bloody pus containing gas bubbles. Cultures from some of the necrotic debris gave a pure growth of B. aerogenes capsulatus. Death occurred August 9, after still greater invasion of the neck. There was no glycosuria or vacuolation of pancreatic islands, though both these conditions might have been prevented by the terminal emaciation and cachexia.

Dog B2–49, a female mongrel aged 3 years, in medium nutrition at a weight of 25.4 kilos, underwent partial pancreatectomy on March 27, 1914, leaving a remnant of $\frac{1}{4}$ to $\frac{1}{5}$ about the main duct. As previously mentioned (1), prolonged carbohydrate over-feeding was used in the attempt to break down tolerance, 300 or 400 grams glucose

[1] All operations were performed under ether anesthesia.

being added to the diet of bread and soup daily. There was neither glycosuria, diarrhea nor any evident ill-health, until the animal was unexpectedly found dead on May 9. There were adhesions in the right pleura, from supposedly sterile intrapleural injections in another department long before the animal was taken for diabetic work, and these probably furnished the start of the infection. Gas bacilli were found abundantly in smears and cultures from the principal viscera, seemingly alone. The greatest change was in the spleen, which was blown up to resemble a lung. The pancreas remnant was normal and free from vacuolation. In other words, neither the prolonged sugar feeding nor the infection produced any change in either islands or acini in this non-diabetic animal.

A study of gas bacillus infections was in progress at this time under the direction of Dr. Carroll G. Bull. As gas bacillus infections are rare in dogs, it was decided to follow up the above accidental observations by experiments upon diabetic dogs with a view to two questions; first, whether such animals are abnormally susceptible to such infections by reason either of the excess of circulating sugar or a specific diabetic lowering of resistance; second, whether an aggravation of the diabetes is demonstrable by such infections. The conditions were favorable for both problems; for the first problem because the growth of the gas bacillus is notably favored by the presence of sugar, and some test was thus afforded of the theory of excess of sugar as the cause of diabetic susceptibility to infection; for the second problem because of the proof (2) of the production of a soluble toxin by the gas bacillus, so that a systemic effect capable of influencing the diabetes might be expected from a local infection. Accordingly experiments with intramuscular injections of pure cultures of the Welch bacillus were performed upon three diabetic dogs. The dosage used was intended to produce the maximum possible local effects and general intoxication without excessive prostration. Still larger doses might have overwhelmed the animals suddenly and completely, but would thus have demonstrated nothing of value for either bacteriology or diabetes.

In the first experiment (table 1) glycosuria practically ceased with the anorexia accompanying infection on September 12, as usual with dogs and in contrast to the usual aggravation of symptoms in human patients with infection. Nevertheless a lowering of tolerance was shown by the heavier glycosuria when the diet was taken on September 13. Illness and fasting again resulted in sugar freedom after the injection of September 14, but a more marked lowering of tolerance was evident in

TABLE 1

Dog E5–88. Male; Welsh terrier mongrel; old but strong, in excellent nutrition; weight 11.25 kilos. August 24, 1917, removal of pancreatic tissue weighing 18 grams. Remnant about main duct estimated at 1.6 grams ($\frac{1}{12}$ to $\frac{1}{13}$). The diabetes was checked by undernutrition and fasting, so that at the time of the experiments the dog weighed 9.5 kilos and took a bread and soup diet with very slight glycosuria.

DATE	RECTAL TEMPERATURE	URINE		REMARKS
		Volume	Glucose	
1917	*°C.*	*cc.*	*per cent*	
September 10		660	0.3	Bread and soup diet
September 11	38.7	450	0.4	
September 12		510	Trace	At 10:45 a.m. injected 0.1 cc. per kilo of broth culture of Welch bacillus intramuscularly right thigh. Marked local edema and swelling. Dog depressed; ate nothing
10:00 a.m.	38.8			
1:15 p.m.	39.7			
3:30 p.m.	40.7			
5:30 p.m.	40.4			
September 13				Thigh still swollen. Dog unwell but took entire diet, part forcibly
9:00 a.m.	39.7	880	2.6	
September 14				9:30 a.m., injected 0.3 cc. per kilo of broth culture of Welch bacillus intramuscularly left thigh. Much local swelling. Dog ill and feverish; refused diet but ate a little meat
9:00 a.m.	38.3	670	2.8	
September 15	39.8	320	1.4	Refused all food
September 16		425	0.3	Refused all food. Great edema and crepitation, extending into scrotum
September 17		510	Trace	Refused food
September 18		650	0	Refused food
September 19		420	0	Refused food
September 20		400	Trace	Ate a trifle of meat and bread
September 21	39.5	450	0	Ate very little of meat
September 22		480	Trace	Ate more meat. Much swelling and gas in leg
September 23		460	0.6	Acting better. Ate more meat
September 24		400	1.2	Ate some bread and meat
September 25		500	2.1	Ate full diet
September 26		700	2.9	Ate full diet
September 27		630	3.4	Ate full diet
September 28		610	3.1	Ate full diet
September 29	38.8	1200	2.2	Both thighs have discharged necrotic material, leaving granulating ulcers. Dog lively and vigorous

the glycosuria from meat alone on September 22 and 23, and the heavier glycosuria thereafter on the regular bread diet.

Dog E5–89. Male; mongrel; age 3 or 4 years; good condition; weight 14 kilos. August 24, 1917, removal of pancreatic tissue weighing 25 grams. Remnant about main duct estimated at 1.6 gram ($\frac{1}{16}$ to $\frac{1}{17}$). Severe diabetes being thus produced, the glycosuria was raised to a maximum by a diet of bread and soup with 100 grams of glucose daily.

September 7, at a weight of 12.6 kilos, 0.25 gram additional pancreatic tissue was removed for microscopic examination.

September 14, at the same weight, 0.1 cc. broth culture of Welch bacillus per kilo was injected intraperitoneally, in order to test whether under these conditions of maximum glycosuria and hyperglycemia infection would be possible. The rectal temperature rose within an hour to 39.4°C. After 6 hours it was 39.5°, and the next morning 39.6°. It then subsided, and after one day of slight malaise the dog continued to eat his diet. The glycosuria continued unchanged except for a diminution on the one day of anorexia.

September 24, an injection of 0.3 cc. of broth culture per kilo was given intramuscularly in one thigh. The usual local and general symptoms occurred in intense form. September 29, with very large swelling and gas formation present in the leg, a blood culture was taken and proved negative. The dog regained a little appetite, taking small amounts of meat and bread daily, but great anemia was shown by blood examinations, the corpuscle volume being only 10 to 12 per cent. Death occurred October 5. Glycosuria remained heavy throughout, including the autopsy urine. The gross autopsy showed no visceral changes suggestive of gas bacillus invasion. Cultures of blood and tissues were also negative for this organism.

The pancreas remnant, normal in appearance and consistency, weighed 1.7 grams. Microscopically, the tissue removed August 7 showed a very early stage of vacuolation of islands. The remnant at autopsy showed a late stage of the process; islands were scarce and small, and the great majority of the cells (probably all of the beta cells) were maximally vacuolated.

In this experiment the production of a general infection with the gas bacillus proved impossible notwithstanding the severe diabetes and intense glycosuria. The intraperitoneal injection failed entirely. The intramuscular injection caused extensive sloughing which destroyed most of the musculature of the limb, but death resulted only from the immediate and subsequent toxic effects and not from systemic invasion.

Dog E5–90. Male; mongrel, age 3 or 4 years; medium nutrition; weight 10.25 kilos. August 24, 1917, removal of pancreatic tissue weighing 20.3 grams. Remnant about main duct estimated at 1.6 gram ($\frac{1}{13}$ to $\frac{1}{14}$). On bread diet there was a diminishing glycosuria which ceased August 31, probably because of hypertrophy of the pancreas remnant, which subsequently at autopsy was found to weigh 5.4 grams. Beginning September 8 the addition of 100 grams glucose restored a heavy glycosuria, and the tolerance was brought down so as to produce a permanent mild diabetes. During October sugar freedom was maintained on a diet of 500 grams lung and 100 grams suet, except for occasional days on which it was proved that bread and soup diet would promptly bring back a mild glycosuria.

October 25, an intravenous glucose tolerance test was performed, by injection of 25 cc. of 10 per cent solution of Merck anhydrous glucose every 15 minutes (1 gram per kilo per hour, on 10 kilos weight) for 3 hours, according to the method described elsewhere (3). Catheterization was performed and blood samples taken before the first injection and at hourly intervals thereafter as shown in table 2.

October 26, 4 cc. of a heavy broth culture of the Welch bacillus were injected intramuscularly in the right thigh. The rectal temperature rose to 41.1°C. that evening and was 39.6° the next morning. The dog refused food and there was no glycosuria. By October 31 there was partial recovery and part of the diet was eaten. The weight had fallen from 10 kilos to 9.75.

TABLE 2

BLOOD			URINE						REMARKS
Plasma sugar			Volume			Glucose			
October 25	November 1	December 18	October 25	November 1	December 18	October 25	November 1	December 18	
per cent	*per cent*	*per cent*	*cc.*	*cc.*	*cc.*	*grams*	*grams*	*grams*	
0.164	0.133	0.122				0	0	0	Before injection
0.333	0.400	0.384	5	41	14	0.034	0.450	0.320	End of 1st hour
0.323	0.400	0.500	14	42	50	0.080	1.150	2.000	End of 2nd hour
0.213	0.216	0.455	95	14	26	Faint	0.360	0.680	End of 3rd hour
0.081			400	150	30	Slight	0.690	0	Next morning

November 1, an intravenous glucose test was performed, identical with the dosage on October 25. A lowering of tolerance was indicated by both the blood and urine analyses.

November 14, 4 cc. of the gas bacillus culture were injected in the other thigh. Local edema, gas formation and necrosis occurred as before, but the general symptoms were less. The temperature on the morning of November 15 was 38.8. The dog ate well and showed a spontaneous glycosuria of 2.15 per cent in 340 cc. urine. The following day it was 0.48 per cent in 530 cc. urine, and then disappeared.

Later the dog was unwell and ate poorly, probably on account of secondary infection of the sloughing area in the leg. No further glycosuria developed, and by December 18 the animal was again in good general health at a weight of 10 kilos, though a large open ulcer was still present.

December 18, the animal was given the same intravenous glucose injections as before. A reduced tolerance was still indicated, either because of the ulcer or because the lowering due to infection was permanent, as it is in many human cases.

An accidental or spontaneous fall of tolerance is probably excluded by the fact that the dog was kept on the lung and suet diet till March 27 without glycosuria. He was then used for other experiments, and no further tolerance test was made.

CONCLUSIONS

1. Intramuscular injections of pure cultures of B. aerogenes capsulatus produced local necrosis and gas formation in partially depancreatized diabetic dogs. Systemic or peritoneal infection was not obtained. The observations failed to indicate any lowering of resistance in these animals due either to the diabetes itself or to the excess of sugar in the body fluids. The latter point is further emphasized by the fact that the reactions were essentially similar in the first dog with mild glycosuria, in the second dog with heavy glycosuria, and in the third dog free from glycosuria. These results agree with the general experience that such animals ordinarily bear operations well and their wounds heal normally.

2. A lowering of tolerance by infection was demonstrable both by feeding and by intravenous glucose tests. Though this influence is less in animals than in human patients, the difference seems to be one of degree rather than of kind.

BIBLIOGRAPHY

(1) Allen: Journ. Exper. Med., 1920, xxxi, 394.
(2) Bull and Pritchett: Journ. Exper. Med., 1917, xxvi, 119.
(3) Allen and Wishart: Journ. Biol. Chem., 1920, xlii, 415.

STUDIES IN EXPERIMENTAL TRAUMATIC SHOCK

I. The Basal Metabolism

JOSEPH C. AUB

With the Technical Assistance of K. Sandiford

From the Laboratory of Physiology in the Harvard Medical School

Received for publication August 12, 1920

The marked loss of body temperature is one of the most striking features of traumatic shock. To study this, as well as to investigate the relationships of metabolism and ventilation to the sudden changes in blood pressure, was the purpose of these experiments. The problem was approached through the gaseous exahange.

The literature upon this subject is very meager. Guthrie (1), reported no consistent findings in either O_2 absorption or CO_2 output with animals under ether anesthesia. Henderson, Prince and Haggard (2), in a preliminary note, mention a marked drop in metabolism in two dogs in shock, but give no details of experiments. Roaf (3), working on decerebrate cats, states that his experiments tend to show that fall of blood pressure does not markedly reduce the production of CO_2.

Methods. Cats were used that had not eaten for 24 hours. They were anesthetized by urethane given by mouth, 8 cc. of a 25 per cent solution per kilo of body weight, and only when fully anesthetized were they stretched out on an animal board. The temperature was recorded through a rectal thermometer graduated to tenths, and was kept as nearly constant as possible by means of an electric heating pad.

The operation consisted of inserting a trachea cannula and cannulae in two arteries, usually both carotids, and also usually one in the external jugular vein. One carotid cannula was then attached to a mercury manometer and blood pressure tracings begun. In some experiments 10 cc. of arterial blood were now removed; in most cases blood was taken only after several respiration samples had been obtained.

The inspired air was room air. The samples of expired air were obtained in two 8-liter copper spirometers. The valves used were Tissot valves, attached directly on the T-shaped glass tracheal cannula. The air sample was promptly withdrawn from the spirometer and preserved under pressure in the usual type of glass sampling tube. Gas analyses were made in the Haldane apparatus, and careful checks of room air were made before samples were analyzed. Urinary nitrogen determinations were not made (4).

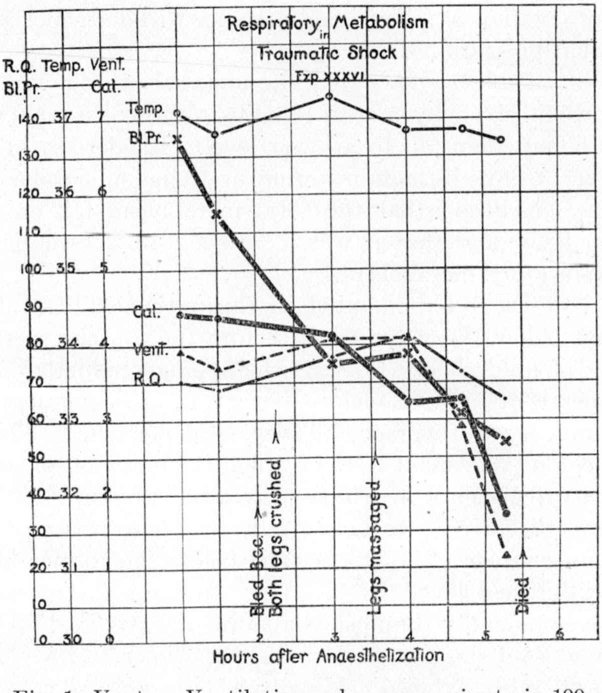

Fig. 1. Vent. = Ventilation volume per minute in 100 cc.
Cal. = Total calories per hour.
R. Q. = Respiratory quotient.

To produce shock the thigh muscles of both hind legs were thoroughly crushed (5). When the blood pressure fell below 70 mm. Hg. systolic and stayed below that level, the animal was considered to be in a state of shock. No attempt was made to measure blood flow, as all extra manipulation was rigidly avoided.

The experiments may be grouped as follows:

I. Normal controls. Table 1.

II. The simple traumatizing of muscle tissue and the study of respiratory metabolism before and after the resulting drop in blood pressure. Tables 3 and 4.

III. The production of traumatic shock and the subsequent raising of the blood pressure by transfusion with cat's blood. Table 5.

IV. The effect on metabolism of hemorrhage when it alone caused a marked fall of pressure. Table 2.

V. The production of a low blood pressure without shock by increasing pericardial pressure. Table 6.

Discussion. Table 1 shows that the metabolism following urethane anesthesia when given by mouth remains quite constant for $4\frac{1}{2}$ hours at least. It may then fall to a lower level. Raeder (6) kept rabbits alive for over 3 days by administering urethane subcutaneously. He came to the conclusion that the total metabolism fell only about 2 per cent an hour, and that it was a satisfactory anesthetic to use in studying respiratory metabolism.

The level of the basal metabolism during shock has fallen in all but one case below the value found before the muscles were crushed. In six cases of mild shock (table 3) the average reduction in calories was -19 per cent, and in eight cases of severe experimental shock (tables 4 and 5) the average fall was -30 per cent. This average does not include experiment LIII in which the metabolism rose. Likewise in five experiments in which pericardial pressure was increased (table 6) and the blood pressure so reduced, there was a prompt drop (fig. 2) to an average of -31 per cent below the former height. In general the "critical level" of blood pressure for the metabolism, as with the development of diminished alkaline reserve, is at 75 or 80 mm. Hg. At that level the metabolism may be within normal limits or it may be considerably reduced. Usually when a normal value is found, the blood pressure has been stationary or rising; but when the metabolism figures are reduced the blood pressure is falling. With a pressure below 75 mm. Hg., the calorie production has, with but one exception, been reduced.

While the reduced blood pressure undoubtedly has a great deal to do with the fall of metabolism, it is probably not the whole story. Experiment XXXIV, table 2, shows that a low blood pressure, following hemorrhage alone, may be associated with only a slight drop in metabolism. With a blood pressure of 55 to 62 mm. Hg. immediately after bleeding the metabolism was only −10 per cent; and in the third period, although the rising blood pressure had been below 80 mm. Hg. for 45 minutes, the metabolism was only −1 per cent. So also in the last period after the pressure had been 50 mm. Hg. for 20 minutes, but was rapidly rising at the time the period was taken, the metabolism was only −7 per cent.

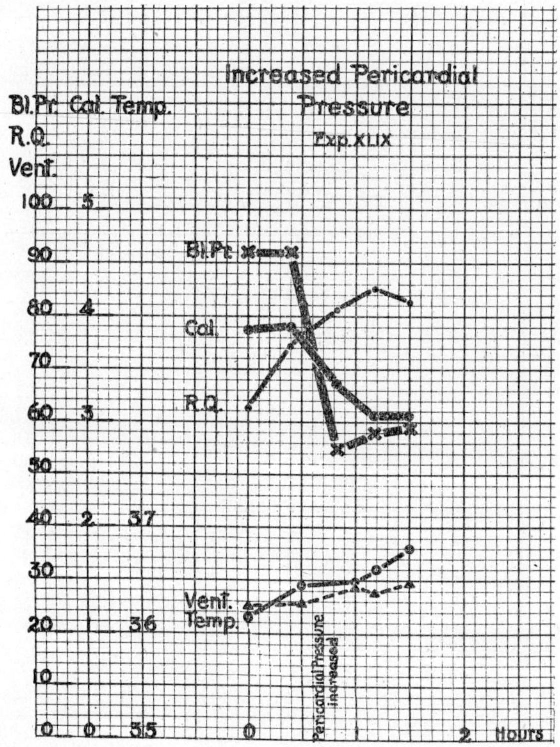

Fig. 2. Vent. = Ventilation volume per minute. The figure should be multiplied by ten.

There are also examples of blood pressures above the critical level associated with reduced metabolism. In experiment XXXIII, table 2, the second period shows a sudden drop of 22 per cent in metabolism 20 minutes after bleeding 15 cc., while later a return to normal limits occurred even though muscle injury was done. This bleeding only caused an immediate drop in blood pressure from 110 to 90 mm. Hg.,

TABLE 1

Respiratory metabolism; controls

Experiment number, weight, date	Time of period	Respiratory exchange per minute: CO_2	Respiratory exchange per minute: O_2	Respiratory quotient	Calculated calories per hour: Calories	Calculated calories per hour: Variation	Respiratory rate per minute	Respiratory volume per minute	Rectal temperature	Blood pressure	Time of anesthetization	Remarks
		cc.	*cc.*			*per cent*		*cc.*	*°C.*	*mm. Hg.*		
Experiment XXVI, 3/28/19, 3200 grams, ♂	11:35	19.4	28.3	0.69	7.83		62	583	38.0	95–105	10:52	
	12:07	21.2	27.9	0.76	7.90			615		110		
	12:50	20.2	28.6	0.71	8.03		44	587	37.0	120–110		
	2:00	19.9	27.7	0.73	7.78	−1	46	606	36.5	110		
	3:00	22.0	28.8	0.76	8.18	+4	*	694	36.8	115–120		
	4:00	19.7	26.1	0.75	7.38	−6	46	474	36.8	120		
	5:10	18.7	26.6	0.70	7.45	−5		447	37.6	110		6 hours, 20 minutes after anesthesia
Experiment XXVII 3/31/19, 3100 grams, ♂	12:23							478	36.8	160	11:30	Blood CO_2 comb. P. 47.1
	1:23	19.8	25.9	0.76	7.35		20	369	36.4	150		
	2:25	19.8	26.1	0.76	7.39			427	36.6	130		
	3:30	18.7	25.8	0.72	7.25	−2		366	37.0	135		
	4:25	18.9	25.5	0.74	7.19	−2		342	37.0	135		Blood CO_2 comb. P. 53.8
	5:25	17.8	24.4	0.73	6.84	−7	27	328	36.5	115		6 hours after anesthesia
Experiment XLVI, 7/15/19, 1800 grams, ♂	11:03	12.1	14.1	0.85	4.10		51	483	36.4	108	10:10	
	11:22	11.3	14.8	0.77	4.19		53	457	36.4	106		
	12:02	9.7	13.3	0.73	3.73	−10	48	357	36.6	95		
	1:15	10.2	13.8	0.74	3.88	−6	45	414	36.8	102		
	2:02	10.1	13.5	0.77	3.81	−8	48	376	36.8	110		
	3:33	8.7	11.7	0.75	3.30	−20	44	350	36.2	100–90		5 hours after anaesthesia
	4:19	8.6	12.2	0.71	3.43	−18	45	380	36.4	100		
	5:11	8.1	11.4	0.71	3.20	−23	43	357	36.8	95		7 hours after anesthesia

Experiment LIX, 12/12/19, 3500 grams, ♀	11:09	17.0	24.6	0.69	6.91			659	38.2	107	9:50	
	11:30	18.5	25.2	0.73	7.07		44	809	38.0	105		11:50–12:00, Bled 25 cc. and transfused with 30 cc. citrated blood
	3:02	13.3	21.1	0.63	5.92	−15	36	443	38.0	100		
	3:25	14.8	22.0	0.67	6.15	−12	38	492	37.9	106		$5\frac{1}{2}$ hours after anesthesia
Experiment L, 3/17/20, 3000 grams, ♂	2:00	18.6	26.9	0.69	7.55			577	37.4	100	1:00	Cat had severe dyspnea before observations started
	2:20	19.5	25.3	0.77	7.18		36	554	37.3	100		
	3:00	19.1	23.5	0.81	6.75	−8	36	540	37.3	90		2:10, Blood samples taken, and blood replaced by transfusion
	4:00	19.1	24.9	0.77	7.08	−4	36	524	37.6	94		
	4:57	19.3	25.1	0.77	7.13	−3	36	547	37.6	115		
	5:36	17.6	24.6	0.72	6.89	−6	36	455	37.5	122		
	6:00	17.0	24.0	0.71	6.73	−8		409	37.5	112		
Experiment LVIII, 4/27/20, 2900 grams, ♂	12:47	14.5	19.3	0.75	5.46		24	594	37.4	100	11:35	1:00, Cat vomited
	1:11	15.1	21.7	0.70	6.10		22	474	37.5			2:10, Bled 25 cc. and blood replaced by transfusion. Cat vomited
	2:25	18.8	25.0	0.75	7.07	+21	20	595	37.5	110		
	3:34	17.4	24.3	0.72	6.81	+18	32	548	37.6			
	4:15	17.0	23.4	0.73	6.56	+13	32	525	37.9	120		3:20, Cat vomited
Experiment LXIX, 5/27/20, 2700 grams, ♀	12:25	18.4	23.6	0.78	6.71			465	37.8	127	11:15	12:55, Bled 25 cc. and blood replaced by transfusion
	12:40	14.3	19.6	0.73	5.51		18	362	37.5	118		
	1:20	15.3	20.3	0.75	5.73		24	396	37.9	106		
	2:27	15.5	20.4	0.76	5.78	−3	27	417	37.9	95		Blood clotted repeatedly in cannula during experiment
	3:06	17.2	21.9	0.78	6.25	+5	28	473	38.0	104		
	3:43	14.0	20.0	0.70	5.60	−6	22	399	38.0	104±		
	4:10	14.1	19.1	0.74	5.38	−10	30	461	38.1	110±		
Experiment LXX, 6/1/20, 3000 grams, ♀	11:37	14.2	21.5	0.66	6.03		22	467	37.4	144	10:30	
	12:47	18.6	25.1	0.74	7.08		40	700	37.6	138±		
	1:34	18.5	25.0	0.74	7.03	+7		666	37.7	145		
	2:15	18.2	23.4	0.78	6.67	+2	44	660	38.4	140±		Cat overheated
	3:45	19.1	28.0	0.68	7.85	+20	40	719	37.7	156		

* Dyspnea.

TABLE 2

Respiratory metabolism; hemorrhage

Experiment number, weight, date	Time of period	Respiratory exchange per minute: CO_2	Respiratory exchange per minute: O_2	Respiratory quotient	Calculated calories per hour: Calories	Calculated calories per hour: Variation	Respiratory rate per minute	Respiratory volume per minute	Rectal temperature	Blood pressure	Time of anesthetization	Blood CO_2 combining power	Remarks
		cc.	*cc.*			*per cent*		*cc.*	*°C.*	*mm. Hg*			
Experiment XXXIV, 4/19/19, 2700 grams, ♀	11:15	14.7	20.4	0.72	5.73		44	523	36.2	102	9:45	48.3	Experiment shows effect of hemorrhage alone
	11:35	13.0	18.4	0.71	5.15	−10	40	464	36.3	55–62			Period taken 5 minutes after bleeding 17 cc.
	12:15	14.4	19.8	0.71	5.65	−1	47	482	36.3	75–80			
	12:45	15.2	19.1	0.80	5.45	−5	46	536	36.4	82			
	1:45	15.0	20.2	0.74	5.69	−1	51	506	35.6	110			Blood pressure 50, 5 minutes before last observation. Period taken 20 minutes after bleeding
	2:30	14.8	18.6	0.80	5.32	−7	40	637	35.8	65–85		52.0	
Experiment XLIII, 5/15/19, 2600 grams	12:12	13.0	19.5	0.67	5.47		28	3402	37.1	130–120	11:30		Spontaneous drop of blood pressure
	12:40	10.9	16.6	0.66	4.66	−15	29	3080	37.0	95			1:30, Bled 10 cc. (pressure below 70 one hour). No trauma
	1:5	11.8	17.1	0.69	4.80	−12	32	3364	37.0	85			
	3:2	11.7	16.8	0.70	4.70	−13	29	4087	37.1	80			

Experiment XXXIII, 4/15/19, 3000 grams, ♂	10:50	18.4	25.3	0.73	7.10		38	440	35.9	115	9:35	43.5	
	11:37	16.5	19.1	0.86	5.55	−22	34	364	35.6	95			Bled at 11:15, 15 cc.
	12:34	17.8	23.1	0.77	6.56	−8	28	407	35.3	78–70			
	1:38	17.9	23.3	0.77	6.63	−7	32	469	36.0	82–84			Legs smashed 12:00–12:08
	2:3	18.1	23.0	0.77	6.68	−6	35	544	35.7	80–83			
	2:37	17.1	21.4	0.80	6.15	−13	36	559	35.9	80		43.5	
Experiment XXXV, 4/22/19, 2400 grams	12:0	14.4	22.0	0.66	6.16		30	482	36.7	105	11:0		Controls vary 14 per cent. Average taken
	12:20	14.7	18.5	0.80	5.28		25	461	36.6	90			
	12:45	14.2	16.7	0.85	4.85	−15	30	533	36.6	60–67		43.3	12:40, Bled 10 cc.
	1:47	14.4	15.4	0.94	4.56	−20	46	629	36.5	75			Effect of hemorrhage
	2:47	16.8	16.2	1.04	4.54	−21	46	1433	36.5	78–63			2:12, Both legs smashed. Traube-Hering waves developed at once
	3:48	10.6	13.1	0.81	3.76	−34	40	670	36.7	50		31.9	Cat died at 4:20 in profound shock

and at the time of observation the blood pressure was 95. It was, however, not rising. In experiment XXX, table 3, where blood pressure fell from 170 to 108 mm. Hg. after severe trauma, the metabolism still fell 14 per cent and 29 per cent; and in experiment XXXI, table 3, even though blood pressure after trauma was 85, the heat production was reduced −21 per cent and −24 per cent. The temperature in these last two experiments, however, was not satisfactory. Likewise in experiment XXXII, the metabolism fell 23 per cent even though the blood pressure was 100. In experiment XXXVI, table 4, fourth period, though the blood pressure was 80–75 in an animal rapidly developing shock, the metabolism was −26 per cent of the normal level. The explanation of these differences is obscure. After hemorrhage the blood pressure may be low for a time without marked drop in metabolism. After muscle injury the metabolism may be reduced before a great fall in blood pressure has occurred. Possibly the observations of Gesell (7) will satisfactorily account for these facts. He found that in the early stages of shock from tissue abuse there is usually a marked reduction of the "volume flow" of blood in peripheral organs, although blood pressure is only little changed, and he reports one instance of increased volume flow after hemorrhage though the blood pressure was falling. The *volume flow of blood* determines the oxygen delivery to the tissues, and this may vary to some degree without corresponding variation in blood pressure.

The reduction of blood pressure by increasing pericardial pressure, as described by Cannon (8), is due to mechanical venous obstruction, and is similar in its action to the methods described by Janeway and Jackson (9) and by Erlanger and Gasser (10). When the blood pressure is reduced by this procedure, the metabolism, as calculated from the respiratory gases, shows a marked prompt reduction to the level found with similar blood pressures in experimental shock (table 6). The respiratory quotient is also similar in that it rises. The prompt reduction of metabolism by this method of merely hindering the venous return to the heart is evidence that some mechanical factor such as retarded blood flow is the cause of the reduced metabolism. This is emphasized by the rapidity of the appearance of the reduction, which by this method seems to occur without delay.

The rapid appearance of diminished alkaline reserve in shock, as shown by the lowering of the blood CO_2 combining capacity, should not reduce metabolism but, if anything, should tend to raise it slightly, as shown by studies (11) in conditions where a similar drop in the reserve may occur.

A feature of the results is the rather low average respiratory quotient. In forty-seven observations in Raeder's publication (6) and in sixty-two normal observations in this series, the average respiratory quotient was the same—0.75. Wilenko (12) in ten periods with cats partly anesthetized by 1 gram urethane per kilo by mouth, had an average respiratory quotient of 0.79 in his controls. This rather low value, as also the work of Underhill (13), and the presence of a hyperglycemia (paper III), all suggest a decreased oxidation of carbohydrate under urethane anesthesia. This point will be more fully discussed in a future publication. Here it is sufficient to say that the control experiments demonstrate that the height of the basal metabolism remains constant under urethane for 4½ hours. Inasmuch as we are dealing with relative changes in each animal, the low respiratory quotient in the control periods does not affect the eventual conclusions. The tendency as shock develops has been for the respiratory quotients to rise—the average for twenty-one observations being 0.81, an effect, probably, of increased ventilation and the resulting pumping out of CO_2.

Having the animal anesthetized makes the determination of the basal metabolism a great deal simpler, for voluntary movements and emotional excitement are removed as factors which might raise the metabolism. The abnormality of some of the respiratory quotients reported here could practically all be traced to irregularities in breathing just prior to or during the observation. A period of hyperpnea previous to the observation gave a low respiratory quotient, and with hyperpnea during the period, the respiratory quotient was always elevated. In cats the breathing under urethane is apt to vary in quantity rather markedly and, as a result, no great stress may be laid upon respiratory quotients. Then, too, there is the factor of rapidly decreasing alkaline reserve with the marked fall of blood pressure, as shown by Cannon (14), and whether this is due to an accumulation of lactic acid or to a disappearance of alkali into the tissues, the effect would probably be a temporary pumping out of extra CO_2 into the expired air. The effect of this change in balance might well affect the dissociation curves of hemoglobin for oxygen and for CO_2 (15). With the low blood pressure found in shock, the effect on the exchange of substances between blood and tissue fluids may be considerably disturbed, and these factors might distort the relationship between the O_2 absorbed and the CO_2 given off in the lungs. As a result, little stress may be laid on the respiratory quotients obtained, because of the

TABLE 3

Respiratory metabolism in shock; mild shock

EXPERIMENT NUMBER, WEIGHT, DATE	TIME OF PERIOD	RESPIRATORY EXCHANGE PER MINUTE		RESPIRATORY QUOTIENT	CALCULATED CALORIES PER HOUR		RESPIRATORY RATE PER MINUTE	RESPIRATORY VOLUME PER MINUTE	RECTAL TEMPERATURE	BLOOD PRESSURE	TIME OF ANESTHETIZATION	REMARKS
		CO_2	O_2		Calories	Variation						
		cc.	*cc.*			*per cent*		*cc.*	*°C.*	*mm. Hg.*		
Experiment XXVIII, 4/2/19, 3100 grams	12:30	23.3	27.1	0.86	7.87		56	857	37.4	100–90	11:00	
	1:00	21.3	25.0	0.85	7.25		78	762	37.2	85		One leg crushed at 1:10 mildly
	2:30	19.6	26.9	0.73	7.61	+1	166	1287	38.2	80		Cat overheated
	3:50	16.5	24.0	0.69	6.72	−10	145–90	874	37.3	75		No severe shock developed
Experiment XXX, 4/7/19, 4000 grams, ♂	11:15	28.5	37.4	0.76	10.59		175	1823	37.5	165	10:10	
	11:40	31.0	39.4	0.79	11.23	+6	195	2400	37.3	150		11:30, Bled 15 cc.
	12:12	27.6	33.8	0.82	9.38	−14	146	2046	36.9	150		12:00, Both legs smashed
	2:00	24.7	32.6	0.76	9.33	−14	116	1504	36.9	112		1:40, Both legs resmashed
	2:50	22.2	26.9	0.83	7.74	−29	80	1120	36.5	108		No real shock developed
Experiment XXXI, 4/10/19, 3300 grams	10:33	20.8	24.9	0.84	7.20		22	509	36.5	150	9:42	Regulation of temperature bad
	11:20	18.6	22.6	0.83	6.51		28	475	36.5	95–100		Legs smashed 11:47 and 12:13
	11:55	17.3	22.0	0.79	6.29	−8	37	484	36.0	85–100		
	12:54	16.3	20.2	0.81	5.78	−15	34	476	35.4	70–65		Suggestive of shock
	1:45	15.3	18.7	0.82	5.44	−21	43	462	35.1	85		Recovering spontaneously
	2:27	13.7	18.5	0.75	5.21	−24	45	568	35.7	85		Temperature low
	3:22	15.6	18.3	0.85	5.30	−23	52	725	36.0	76		

Experiment XXXII, 4/12/19, 2700 grams	12:24	15.2	22.6	0.68	6.33		22	408	36.3	135	11:15	
	12:44	19.0	24.5	0.78	6.96	+10	22	496	36.2	135		1:07, Right leg smashed
	1:17	16.8	22.5	0.75	6.36	−4	15	386	36.2	130		1:40 and 2:12, Left leg smashed
	3:02	16.4	17.2	0.95	5.13	−23	32	627	36.2	100		No shock pressure but metabolism fell
Experiment XXXIX, 5/5/19, 2800 grams, ♂	11:35	17.2	23.5	0.73	6.61		29	424	37.5	135	10:45	
	11:55	16.1	22.5	0.72	6.30	−5	27	389	37.4	120		12:22, Bled 9 cc. Blood pressure fell to 80; rose rapidly
	12:45	16.1	21.5	0.75	6.07	−6	19	467	37.9	100–95		
	1:53	15.3	19.8	0.77	5.61	−13	28	547	37.4	80–87		1:05, Both legs smashed; shock just developing
Experiment LVII, 12/10/19, 4600 grams, ♀	12:05	22.3	31.0	0.72	8.70		18	613	38.9	128	10:30	
	12:25	21.6	30.9	0.70	8.67		20	608	38.8	120		1:10, Left leg smashed
	2:48	22.1	27.5	0.80	7.87	−9		950	38.3	73		Very mild shock
	3:11	21.1	24.5	0.86	7.11	−18	29	1241	38.6	72		Blood pressure never below 70

TABLE 4

Respiratory metabolism; severe shock

EXPERIMENT NUMBER, WEIGHT, DATE	TIME OF PERIOD	RESPIRATORY EXCHANGE PER MINUTE		RESPIRATORY QUOTIENT	CALCULATED CALORIES PER HOUR		RESPIRATORY RATE PER MINUTE	RESPIRATORY VOLUME PER MINUTE	RECTAL TEMPERATURE	BLOOD PRESSURE	TIME OF ANESTHETIZATION	BLOOD CO_2 COMBINING POWER	REMARKS
		CO_2	O_2		Calories	Variation							
		cc.	*cc.*			*per cent*		*cc.*	*°C.*	*mm. Hg.*			
Experiment XXXVI, 4/26/19, 2400 grams	11:48	11.1	15.8	0.70	4.44		40	391	37.1	135	10:45		Bled 8 cc. at 12:55
	12:20	10.6	15.6	0.68	4.38		36	369	36.8	100–130			Both legs smashed 1:00–1:05
	1:45	11.1	14.4	0.77	4.10	−7	34	408	37.3	75			
	2:45	9.4	11.4	0.82	3.23	−26	36	409	36.9	80–75			Traube-Hering waves
	3:30	8.2	11.3	0.73	3.28	−26	30	292	36.9	60–63			Traube-Hering waves
	4:08	4.0	6.1	0.65	1.71	−61	19–13	1162	36.7	55–40			Cat died 4:19 as period ended
Experiment XXXVII, 4/28/19, 3600 grams, ♂	1:10	19.8	26.5	0.75	7.48		28	470	36.5	152–140	12 N		1:55, Bled 10 cc. without loss of blood pressure
	1:30	22.2	28.3	0.78	8.06	+8	32	493	36.6	110–120			
	2:00	21.6	28.9	0.75	8.16	+5	27	546	37.0	130		41.4	2:25–3:25, Smashed both legs
	3:35	21.1	25.7	0.82	7.39	−5	26	594	37.5	110			
	5:50	15.6	18.5	0.84	5.35	−31	25	464	36.5	67–60		27.1	Profound shock just developing. 6:20, Cat died
Experiment XXXVIII, 5/1/19, 2400 grams	11:45	13.4	17.7	0.76	5.00		30–26	362	36.2	140	11:00		
	12:17	13.5	18.0	0.75	5.08		28–50	377	36.3	100			1:00, Bled 8 cc.
	1:12	11.5	16.5	0.70	4.63	−8	30	400	36.2	80			1:35 and 1:55, Both legs smashed. Shock developing
	2:22	16.4	20.2	0.81	5.80	+15	72–66	1212	36.4	80			
	3:25	10.4	12.5	0.83	3.61	−28	46	720	35.6	65			Shock
	3:45	7.1	9.8	0.73	2.74	−46	22	377	35.7	60			

Experiment XLIV, 5/17/19, 2800 grams, ♂	12:20	19.2	24.6	0.78	7.00		26	3857	37.4	120	11:25		Bled 9 cc. at 12:00 and blood replaced
	1:25	20.9	24.9	0.84	7.21		30	3861	37.4	100			
	1:45	22.7	26.4	0.86	7.67		32	4273	37.5	90			Legs smashed at 2:03
	2:45	23.2	23.7	0.98	7.09		29	6431	36.5	75			Severe shock since 3:00
	3:33	14.1	16.7	0.85	4.82	−34	34–30	4590	37.4	65–60			
Experiment LVI, 12/5/19, 4300 grams, ♂	11:41	23.2	32.0	0.73	8.98			959	38.7	126	10:15		12:45, Bled and transfused. 12:50, Leg smashed
	12:02	24.9	32.0	0.78	9.06			856	38.3	140–132			
	3:19	31.4	30.3	1.03	9.06	0		3295	38.3	75–70			Extreme hyperpnea
	3:36	24.5	24.3	1.01	7.26	−20		3628	38.3	64–59			Extreme hyperpnea

TABLE 5

Respiratory metabolism; shock and transfusions

Experiment number, weight, date	Time of period	Respiratory exchange per minute		Respiratory quotient	Calculated calories per hour		Respiratory rate per minute	Respiratory volume per minute	Rectal temperature	Blood pressure	Time of anesthetization	Remarks
		CO_2	O_2		Calories	Variation						
		cc.	*cc.*			*per cent*		*cc.*	*°C.*	*mm. Hg.*		
Experiment XLI, 5/8/19, 3200 grams, ♂	11:50	15.9	23.1	0.69	6.47		*	599	36.3	145	10:50	Respiration rapid-irregular
	12:15	18.6	25.7	0.72	7.21		114–78	956	36.1	110		Respiration rapid and shallow. 12:55, Bled 10 cc.
	2:55	20.9	26.2	0.80	7.50	+7	78–86	1186	36.3	95		1:10–15, Both legs smashed
	3:30	12.2	18.0	0.68	5.04	−28	50–48	775	35.6	50–63		3:28, 4 cc. blood from right femoral vein. Shock developed at 3:30
	3:45	15.0	20.3	0.74	5.73	−18	41	1365	36.2	67		
	4:30	13.3	16.1	0.83	4.64	−33	27	797	35.4	105		Transfused with 20 cc. blood and 15 cc. mammalian Ringer 4:00. Temperature low. Traube-Herring waves
	4:45	12.9	19.3	0.67	5.40	−23	38–34	727	35.3	80–95		
Experiment XLVII, 7/17/19, 2600 grams, ♀	1:22	17.2	22.0	0.78	6.27		51	571	37.1	92	11:00	Legs smashed at 2:40
	2:20	14.6	21.6	0.67	6.07		63	660	36.7	105		No shock yet
	3:43	14.8	21.6	0.69	6.06	−2	64	692	36.3	82		Shock developing rapidly
	4:05	16.1	17.7	0.91	5.20	−16	83	967	36.4	75–65		
	4:17	12.3	15.7	0.78	4.47	−28	72–176	944	36.2	50–70		
	4:48	13.5	17.7	0.75	4.98	−19	40	493	35.2	95–105		4:25–40, 70 cc. blood transfused. Low temperature unexplained except by transfusion
	5:19	12.7	21.0	0.61	5.88	−5	46	476	36.3	110		
	5:38	14.1	19.7	0.72	5.53	−10	42	482	36.5	105		

Experiment XLVIII, 7/22/19, 2700 grams, ♂	11:45	11.8	18.0	0.66	5.04		37	366	36.3	108	10:20	Normal
	12:12	13.7	18.4	0.74	5.18		36	363	36.2	95		
	12:35	14.8	18.1	0.82	5.20		35	391	36.0	105		
	2:25	11.4	14.5	0.79	4.13	−20	27	395	36.3	60		Onset of true shock level
	2:49	11.8	13.9	0.85	4.03	−22	26–64	550	36.3	65		Respiration increasing rapidly
	3:30	17.2	22.3	0.77	6.34	+23	30	424	36.2	130		3:03–15, 65 cc. blood transfused
	4:02						40	426	36.2	115		Analyses discarded
	4:35	12.7	18.6	0.68	5.23	+2	40	524	36.2	100–115		
Experiment LIII, 11/24/19, 4400 grams, ♂	11:40	23.4	31.8	0.73	8.97			941	38.4	112	10:50	
	12:23	21.7	30.8	0.71	8.63		56	1069	38.3	110		12:55–1:20, Bled, transfused and legs smashed
	2:50	28.1	36.1	0.78	10.28	+17	+	2866	38.3	66		Shock
	3:00	26.8	36.6	0.75	10.35	+18	†	3330	38.4	62		3:08–17, Bled 15 cc. Transfused 101 cc.
	3:24	22.2	31.3	0.71	8.77	0	39	901	38.6	116		
	3:35	20.1	30.8	0.65	8.63	−2	36	927	38.5	124–136		
Experiment LII A, 11/4/19, 4200 grams	11:41	18.6	26.5	0.70	7.43		18	447	36.8	130	10:35	
	12:07											
	12:27	17.7	21.4	0.83	6.17	−17		441	36.8	98		2:00–07, Left leg smashed
	2:50	16.1	19.6	0.82	5.65	−24	16	411	36.9	80		2:50, Cat going into shock
	3:03	17.5	19.3	0.91	5.67	−24	14	463	36.8	74		Cat in shock
	4:01	17.9	20.4	0.88	5.95	−20		327	36.4	100		3:45, 67 cc. blood transfused after bleeding 20 cc.
	4:27	16.1	21.8	0.74	6.15	−17		517	36.6	118		Cat has recovered from shock

* Irregular.

† Intense dyspnea.

TABLE 6

Respiratory metabolism in shock; pericardial pressure

EXPERIMENT NUMBER, WEIGHT, DATE	TIME OF PERIOD	RESPIRATORY EXCHANGE PER MINUTE		RESPIRATORY QUOTIENT	CALCULATED CALORIES PER HOUR		RESPIRATORY RATE PER MINUTE	RERPIRATORY VOLUME PER MINUTE	RECTAL TEMPERATURE	BLOOD PRESSURE	TIME OF ANESTHETIZATION	BLOOD CO_2 COMBINING POWER	REMARKS
		CO_2	O_2		Calories	Variation							
		cc.	cc.			per cent		cc.	°C.	mm. Hg.			
Experiment III, 10/5/18, 2900 grams, ♀	10:48	12.5	17.0	0.74	4.77		25	406	34.5	145–150	9:15		
	12:11	10.5	11.0	0.96	3.30	−31	varied		35.4	60			12:08, Blood pressure reduced by pericardial pressure
	2:12	10.2	12.5	0.81	3.60	−25	32	527	34.0	60			
Experiment VI, 10/11/18, 7000 grams, ♀ Dog	10:36	57.7	65.8	0.88	19.21		43	2190	34.0	120		50	11:10, Blood pressure reduced by pericardial tension
	11:13	35.8	38.9	0.92	11.48	−41	46	2060	34.5	60		43	
	12:24	41.7	41.2	1.01	12.30	−36	52	2710	34.5	60		37	
	2:23	33.6	30.6	1.10	9.15	−52	48	2950	32.7	60		34	Temperature of dog low
Experiment VII, 10/12/18, 12,930 grams, ♀ Dog	11:07	58.4	77.5	0.77	21.91		46	2280	35.2	120		47	
	11:46	57.8	70.1	0.82	20.19	−8	68	3560	35.2	100		43	Blood pressure reduced gradually by increasing pericardial tension
	12:27	47.8	51.5	0.93	15.22	−31	51	3300	34.8	80		36	
	12:42	38.1	40.9	0.93	12.11	−45	45	3080	34.3	60		30	
	1:20	44.1	45.1	0.98	13.50	−38	33	2450	32.3	80		32	Very low temperature
Experiment XLV, 7/2/19, 2800 grams, ♂	1:06	17.2	24.4	0.71	6.84		64	632	37.0	95	10:30		Variation of 6 per cent. Average taken
	1:40	16.1	23.0	0.70	6.45		62	644	37.4	90			
	2:05	13.2	17.1	0.77	4.86	−27	59	516	37.5	45–55			Taken immediately after increased pericardial pressure
													2:46, Cat died

Experiment XLIX, 7/25/19, 2500 grams, ♂	3:34	8.6	13.8	0.62	3.89		43	252	36.2	90	11:15		Cannula in pericardium
	3:58	10.3	13.9	0.74	3.90		46	258	36.4	93			4:24, Intrapericardial pressure increased by gum-salt solution
	4:25	9.5	11.7	0.81	3.37	−13	38	285	36.5	55			
	4:44	9.0	10.6	0.85	3.07	−21	40	278	36.6	58			
	5:03	8.8	10.6	0.83	3.06	−21	42	296	36.8	59			Cat killed
Experiment LIV, 12/11/19, 3300 grams, ♂	12:00	16.3	23.8	0.69	6.67			478	38.0	142–116	10:20		A control experiment to show recovery after a low blood pressure
	12:19	17.8	24.3	0.73	6.82			544	38.0	108			
	2:14	17.2	23.2	0.74	6.55	−3	32	516	38.3	112			At 1:11, Blood pressure reduced to 60. At 2:10, pericardial pressure removed
	2:37	16.4	21.4	0.77	6.06	−10		549	38.3	110			

extremely complicating factors which may be influencing them. However, the oxygen absorption from the lungs must represent the amount of oxygen available for metabolic uses in the tissues, inasmuch as the blood leaves the heart normally saturated with oxygen (16). That this absorbed oxygen represents the amount used by the body seems highly probable; as otherwise there would be an accumulation of oxygen in the tissues, a condition which seems decidedly unlikely. In all these observations, therefore, the oxygen absorption has been used as the basis of comparison, and the CO_2 assumes a relatively unimportant rôle through its influence on the respiratory quotient.

The reduced metabolism affords an explanation for the marked reduction of body temperature in shock, which may go as low as 87.8°, or even 76.1° in cervical spine lesions, according to Weil (18) and to Volkmann (17). This investigation, however, does not indicate that the reduction is usually a forerunner of the onset of shock, or that it is a causative factor in the production. In fact, in two experiments the metabolism just before the onset of shock was slightly elevated above the normal level.

The volume of respiration per minute has likewise been studied. The average ventilation per minute of the control observations was 557 cc. in twenty-one experiments; the average after crushing the muscles and before the onset of a shock blood pressure level was 860 cc. in ten experiments, (a variation of +54 per cent from the control observations), and after the onset of shock it was 635 cc. in thirteen experiments. This variation is hardly enough to account for the onset of shock, in these muscle trauma experiments, by the acapnia theory advanced by Henderson and Haggard (19), (20). Besides, rapid breathing with a higher ventilation rate per minute than in shock has been repeatedly seen under urethane anesthesia without the onset of spontaneous shock. These data also show that the fall of the metabolic rate was not due to changes in either the volume or exertion involved in respiration.

With the metabolism so much reduced by shock, it naturally became of interest to know the effect of transfusion of a sufficient amount of blood to bring about recovery. Table 5 shows five such experiments in three of which the metabolism returned to normal limits, while in experiment XLI the metabolism remained low. In experiment XLVIII, the figures for the first period after transfusion were above the normal determinations. Experiment LIV in table 6 shows the effect of reducing the pressure to shock level by pericardial pressure.

Periods III and IV were taken directly after releasing the pressure, and showed a normal rate. It therefore seems that making the circulation adequate causes the low metabolism of shock to disappear promptly.

CONCLUSIONS

1. Ethyl carbamate (urethane) is a satisfactory anesthetic for the study of gaseous metabolism in animals over short periods of time.
2. Experimental traumatic shock causes a marked fall in the rate of basal metabolism to 70 per cent of the original level. The degree of fall is dependent upon the severity of the shock produced.
3. A similar fall of the metabolic rate may be rapidly accomplished by interfering with the circulation by increased pericardial pressure.
4. The effect of hemorrhage is not constant. It may temporarily lower, or have no immediate effect on the metabolic rate.
5. Recovery from shock after blood transfusion is usually associated with a prompt return of the metabolic rate to a normal level.

BIBLIOGRAPHY

(1) Guthrie: Journ. Amer. Med. Assoc., 1917, lxix, 1394.
(2) Henderson, Prince and Haggard: Ibid., 965.
(3) Roaf: Quart. Journ. Exper. Physiol., 1912, v, 31.
(4) Benedict and Carpenter: Carnegie Inst. of Wash., no. 261, 203.
(5) Cannon and Bayliss: Rept. of Shock Committee, English Medical Research Committee, 1919, no. 26, 19.
(6) Raeder: Biochem. Zeitschr., 1915, lxix, 257.
(7) Gesell: This Journal, 1918, xlvii, 468.
(8) Cannon: Comp. rend. d. l. soc. d. biol., 1918, lxxxi, 850.
(9) Janeway and Jackson: Soc. Exper. Biol. and Med., 1915, xii, 193.
(10) Erlanger and Gasser: This Journal, 1919, xlix, 151.
(11) Atkinson and Lusk: Journ. Biol. Chem., 1919, xl, 79.
Aub and DuBois: Arch. Int. Med., 1917, xix, 865.
(12) Wilenko: Biochem. Zeitschr., 1912, xlii, 44.
(13) Underhill: Journ. Biol. Chem., 1911, ix, 13.
(14) Cannon: Rept. of Shock Committee, English Medical Research Committee, 1917, no. 25, 85; Journ. Amer. Med. Assoc., 1918, lxx, 531.
(15) Henderson, L. J.: Journ. Biol. Chem., 1920, xli, 401.
(16) Aub and Cunningham: This Journal, 1920, liv, 408.
(17) Volkmann-Zwichau: Münchener. Med. Wochenschr., 1917, lxiv, 1215.
(18) Weil: Ibid., 338.
(19) Henderson: This Journal, 1910, xxvii, 152.
(20) Henderson and Haggard: Journ. Biol. Chem., 1918, xxxiii, 365.

STUDIES IN EXPERIMENTAL TRAUMATIC SHOCK

II. The Oxygen Content of the Blood

JOSEPH C. AUB and T. DONALD CUNNINGHAM

From the Laboratory of Physiology in the Harvard Medical School and the Medical Clinic of the Peter Bent Brigham Hospital[1]

Received for publication August 12, 1920

In studying the basal metabolism of experimental traumatic shock it became clear that the reduction of the calories utilized was dependent upon some undetermined factor. This was suggested by the fact that the fall in metabolic rate did not always coincide with the fall in blood pressure. Other observers have noted that there were marked changes in the circulation before a shock level of blood pressure was approached. Gesell (1) showed a slowing of blood flow through the salivary gland before a fall in pressure had developed. Yandell Henderson, (2) while working with shock induced by intestinal trauma in dogs, found a markedly decreased O_2 content in the venous blood, which he thought followed the failure of the venopressor mechanism and demonstrated a true anoxemia.

These observations suggested that the determination of the oxygen of the arterial and venous blood, as well as the blood flow during the development and recovery from traumatic shock, might give evidence as to the cause of the fall of metabolism (3).

Method. The animals used were cats, and the methods used for inducing traumatic shock and determining metabolism were similar in all respects to those previously described (3). The values for blood oxygen were obtained by the methods of Van Slyke (4).

The blood was withdrawn in two ways: *a*, by inserting a needle in a branch of the femoral artery and vein, and so entering the larger vessels without causing any stasis; *b*, the more satisfactory way, by inserting thin catheters down the right carotid artery and right superficial jugular vein until they reached the heart. The blood was collected in glass syringes, under paraffine oil, and put into tubes under oil (5).

[1] This is study no. X of a series on the physiology and pathology of the blood from the Harvard Medical School and allied hospitals.

By this method blood could easily be obtained without exposure to air. In order not to disturb the blood volume in the experimental animal, the amount removed for analysis was promptly replaced by an equal amount of citrated cat's blood. Thus fairly large samples of arterial and venous blood could be obtained without permanently affecting the blood pressure or blood volume.

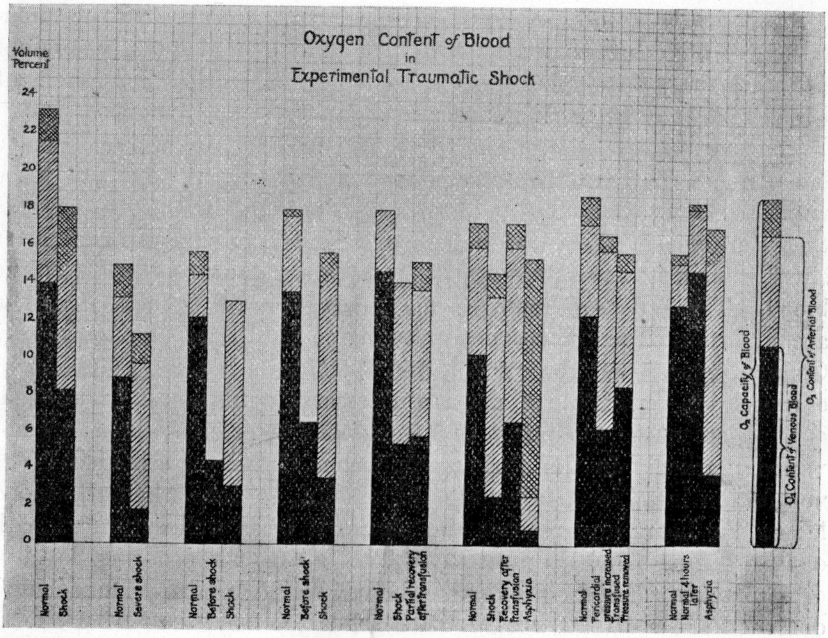

Fig. 1. Normal = Animal under urethane anesthesia.
Before shock = After muscle trauma, but before a true shock level of blood pressure had been established.
Asphyxia = Clamping off trachea completely for 4 or 5 minutes.

After shock had been established for about 30 minutes, as shown by a fall of blood pressure to 60–70 mm. Hg., the blood samples were taken and were immediately followed by a large transfusion of blood, as much as 100 cc. being given in an attempt to relieve the shock. In one case this accomplished a permanent recovery of blood pressure to its original level. In cases where a few minutes' delay followed the taking of the blood samples from the shocked animals, only slight recovery of blood pressure followed the transfusion.

Discussion. Figure 1 shows graphically the more important changes which occur in the oxygen of the blood in traumatic shock. The most striking effect is seen in the oxygen content of the venous blood, which falls very markedly in shock—not only in actual content of oxygen but in percentage of saturation.[2] This is well shown in all the experiments in table 2, but possibly most notably in experiments LIII and LV, and is also present in a control experiment LIV, table 1, where a low pressure was obtained by mechanically interfering with the circulation. The changes observed in profound shock are also present as the shock is developing, and to lesser degree after the improvement which follows large transfusions.

The oxygen capacity of the blood in shock has invariably become less than in the normal sample. This fall in capacity does not agree with the observations of Henderson (2), who found in four experiments that the oxygen of the arterial blood rose 1.5 volume per cent after shock. This he interpreted as demonstrating a concentration of the blood. The fall here reported may, however, be explained by the accumulation of red blood corpuscles in the capillaries, as observed by Cannon, Fraser and Hooper (6), and therefore a relative reduction of corpuscles in venous blood, and not necessarily a dilution of the plasma.

The percentage saturation of hemoglobin in arterial blood has not varied markedly in the various conditions of the experiments. The ventilation is at least adequate throughout, so that when the blood leaves the heart and reaches the tissues it is as well saturated with oxygen during shock as normally. The fall from the normal level of oxygen takes place in the venous blood, which confirms Henderson's observations, and this occurs before shock as well as during shock. In experiment LVI, while the blood pressure was, and had been, 104–94 mm. Hg. for $1\frac{1}{2}$ hours after the muscle injury, the oxygen content of the venous blood had fallen from 12.27 to 4.55 volumes per cent. So also in experiment LVII, although the blood pressure was 84 mm. Hg. after the muscle injury, the oxygen content of the venous blood had fallen from 13.68 to 6.64 volumes per cent.

A similar, though less marked, decrease in the oxygen content of the venous blood is seen after recovery by transfusion as seen in experiment LIII, table 2. That this is sufficient to indicate a true asphyxia in the tissues cannot now be proved because the head of oxygen pressure necessary for normal oxidation is not yet definitely known. How-

[2] The percentage of saturation as used in this paper, represents the oxygen content of venous blood divided by the oxygen capacity of the arterial blood.

ever, the very small amount of oxygen present (with the attendant low partial pressure) makes a true anoxemia possible.

It is true, however, that the venous blood may be as low in oxygen in severe anemia as it is in shock, but in this condition the oxygen of the arterial blood is likewise reduced. Morawitz and Rohmer (7) found that in three human cases of very severe anemia, where the oxygen-carrying capacity of the blood was 4.5 per cent or less, the venous blood had an oxygen content as low as 0.67 per cent, and they assumed an increased blood flow to explain the normal metabolism which is still found in these cases. Lundsgaard (8), also studying patients with anemia, found the venous blood contained as low as 1.16 volume per cent of O_2 in a case with an oxygen-carrying capacity of 5.93 per cent. He concludes that the tissues extract oxygen from the blood with equal readiness whether there is a large oxygen reserve in the blood, "or practically no reserve, as in anemia." These cases, however, had very low oxygen capacities, and therefore the low O_2 content of the venous blood meant a less complete dissociation[3] of hemoglobin and O_2 than would a similar figure in a normal blood. It is the amount (percentage) of this dissociation which must influence the partial pressure of the dissolved oxygen, and this latter is the important factor in the migration of oxygen into the tissues. The oxygen content of normal blood may, therefore, be three or four times that of anemic under the same partial pressure of O_2. As a result, under similar conditions, one would expect to find a much larger figure for the total venous content of oxygen in these shock experiments than would be found in anemia, because anemic blood has less hemoglobin. In fact, the *percentage* saturation of the venous blood in these anemia cases, (16 per cent and 20 per cent), is about the same as in the cases of severe shock, in spite of the lower venous *content*.

A more direct control of the value of the oxygen content found in these experiments are the figures obtained in animals after 4 or 5 minutes of complete asphyxia, for here, just before death, the oxygen value of the venous blood was not very much lower than that found in shock. This is of course indirect evidence, for the matter of greatest importance to the tissue is the oxygen content of the arterial blood. Still, the oxygen content of the venous blood must give a satisfactory

[3] This dissociation is approximately represented by the "per cent of saturation" column in tables 1 and 2. It is approximate, because the small amount of oxygen dissolved in the plasma would be about the same in anemic and normal bloods.

indication of conditions in the venous end of the capillaries, and in the asphyxia experiments must surely indicate an oxygen content which is entirely inadequate for the use of the tissues.

The explanation of this marked anoxemia lies most probably in a slowed blood flow which has been demonstrated in shock, and which can be very well demonstrated in these experiments by the method used by Means and Newburgh (9). In brief it is based on the formula:

$$\text{Volume output of heart per min.} = \frac{\text{cc. } O_2 \text{ absorbed through lungs}}{\text{Volume per cent oxygen utilization of blood}}$$

Using this formula we can calculate the blood flow of several of our cases. The results are shown in tables 1 and 2. It is clear that the blood flow becomes markedly slowed before the onset of a shock level of blood pressure, and that this slowing precedes the fall in metabolism, demonstrated in paper I.[4] This is demonstrated in experiments LVI and LVII. It may therefore be assumed that the fall in metabolism is a secondary manifestation of the decreased blood flow, and of the markedly reduced oxygen content of the venous blood, and is probably due to a true anoxemia. This suggestion is further borne out by the similar findings following increased pericardial tension (exper. LIV), for this must suddenly decrease the rapidity of blood flow. There is a much increased oxygen utilization in the blood and there is also a very prompt fall in the level of the basal metabolism (3), although the only disturbing factor is in the circulation, and no toxic effect from tissue injury can be involved. Verzar (10) has also shown that when perfused muscles are given inadequate oxygen supply the height of their metabolism falls.

Under these conditions we may add another factor to the vicious cycles described by Cannon (11). Krogh (12) has shown that as an oxygen want develops in contracting muscles, many empty capillaries fill with blood, a change which reduces the distance necessary for the diffusion of gases into the tissues. Thus, as anoxemia develops, the capillary bed would increase in volume. This would further decrease the already slowed blood flow, and the slower the flow the greater would probably become the oxygen consumption per cubic centimeter of blood, and hence the decrease in oxygen of venous blood.

[4] Experiment LIII does not show so striking a drop as the other two. It was abnormal, however, in being the only observation which showed a rise in metabolism during shock, instead of a fall. This was probably due to the intense dyspnea.

TABLE 1

Normal controls

Number, weight, date	Time of sample	O_2 of arterial blood: Capacity	O_2 of arterial blood: Content	O_2 of venous blood: Content	O_2 of venous blood: Consumption	O_2 of venous blood: Saturation	Hemoglobin calculated	CO_2 combining power	Blood pressure	Metabolic rate O_2 absorbed per minute	Blood flow per minute	Remarks
		vol. per cent	*vol. per cent*	*vol. per cent*	*vol. per cent*	*per cent*	*per cent*	*vol. per cent*	*mm. Hg.*	*cc.*		
LIX	11:57	15.93	15.38	13.12	2.26	82.4	86.1		92	24.9	1103	Transfused 30 cc. after bleeding
3.5 kgm.	4:07	18.68	18.35	14.93	3.42	79.9	100.7		110	21.5*	630	Transfused 45 cc.
12/12/19	4:24	17.33		3.89		22.4			50			After 4 minutes asphyxia
LXIX	12:55	15.7	16.41	11.80	4.61	75.2	83.6		110	21.6	469	
2.7 kgm.	4:35	15.0	16.38	9.50	6.88	63.3	82.4		108	19.5	284	
5/27/20												
LVIII	2:10	20.92	19.67	14.30	5.37	68.4	113.0		100	20.5	383	
2.9 kgm.	4:35	21.87	17.88	13.47	4.41	61.6	117.0		120	23.8	539	
4/27/20												
LXII	2:45	17.5?	18.0	9.90	8.1	55.0	89.0		100	23.2	283	
2.6 kgm.	5:00	18.4	18.0	9.10	8.9	49.5	93.0		155	22.9	253	
5/14/20												
LIV	12:47	18.96	17.45	12.50	4.95	65.9	102.0	57.4	112	24.0	485	Normal
3.3 kgm.	1:50	16.9	16.07	6.37	9.70	37.7	91.0	46.8	60			Blood pressure reduced by pericardial pressure for 45 minutes
12/1/19	2:50	15.92	14.92	8.69	6.23	54.6	86.0	47.7	105	22.3	358	Normal for 35 minutes

* Five and one-half hours after anesthesia.

TABLE 2

Experimental traumatic shock

NUMBER, WEIGHT, DATE	TIME OF SAMPLE	O_2 OF ARTERIAL BLOOD		O_2 OF VENOUS BLOOD			HEMOGLOBIN CALCULATED	CO_2 COMBINING POWER	BLOOD PRESSURE	METABOLIC RATE O_2 ABSORBED PER MINUTE	BLOOD FLOW PER MINUTE	REMARKS
		Capacity	Content	Content	Consumption	Saturation						
		vol. per cent	vol. per cent	vol. per cent	vol. per cent	per cent	per cent	vol. per cent	mm. Hg.	cc.		
LI	2:35	17.3	18.1	14.8	3.3	85.6	95.0	36.0	124			Normal
4.1 kgm.	4:20	13.9	14.2	5.5	8.7	39.6	75.4	34.1	56			Mild shock for 1 hour
10/22/19	5:00	15.3	13.8	5.9	7.9	38.5	82.7	40.6	81			After transfusion 43 cc. blood
LII	3:30	23.3	21.6	14.0	7.6	60.2	120.3	40.2	143			Normal
4.9 kgm.	6:05	18.1	14.2	8.3	9.8*	45.9	98.0	37.1	68			Shock for 1 hour
10/29/19												
	12:55	17.46	16.16	10.32	5.84	59.1	94.5	40.4	120	31.3	536	Normal
LIII	3:08	14.76	13.46	2.69	10.77	18.2	79.8	33.8	62	36.4	337	Shock for 30 minutes
4.4 kgm.	4:29	17.46	16.17	6.73	9.44	38.5	94.5	40.4	125	31.0	328	Recovery after transfusion of 100 cc. blood
11/24/19	4:34	15.59	2.69	0.89	1.8	5.7	89.6	43.3	70			Asphyxia 3 minutes by clamping trachea
LV	12:55	15.02	13.30	8.99	4.31	59.9	81.1	41.9	80			Normal. Transfused 27 cc.
3.1 kgm.	2:35	11.32	9.73	1.87	7.86	16.5	61.1	25.6	44			Very severe shock for 30 minutes
12/4/19												
LVI	12:35	15.77	14.54	12.27	2.27	77.8	85.1	48.2	132	32.0	1390	Normal
4.3 kgm.	3:02			4.55	7.70†				94	30.3	400†	Before shock developed
12/5/19	4:00	13.16	Clotted	3.18	9.98†	24.2	69.4	45.4	52	24.3	272	Severe shock
LVII	12:47	18.09	17.78	13.68	4.10	75.6	97.8		120	31.0	756	Normal
4.6 kgm.	1:58			6.64					84	27.5	308†	Before shock developed
12/10/19	3:25	15.81		3.65	12.16†	23.1	85.5	39.3	70	24.5	206	Mild shock

* Animal stopped breathing just before taking sample.

† Capacity substituted for oxygen content. These figures therefore approximate.

CONCLUSIONS

1. There is a markedly diminished oxygen content of the venous blood in experimental traumatic shock. This change occurs before the blood pressure falls to a shock level, and is still present after apparent recovery from shock.
2. The blood flow is also greatly decreased in the development of, during and after shock.
3. The resulting anoxemia of the tissues may be the cause of the decreased metabolism.
4. The sequence of these events in traumatic shock is discussed.

BIBLIOGRAPHY

(1) Gesell: This Journal, 1918, xlvii, 468.
(2) Henderson: Ibid., 1910, xxvii, 152.
(3) Aub: This Journal, 1920, liv, 388.
(4) Van Slyke: Journ. Biol. Chem., 1918, xxxiii, 127.
(5) Stadie: Journ. Exper. Med., 1919, xxx, 215.
(6) Cannon, Fraser and Hooper: Report of Shock Committee, English Medical Research Committee, 1917, no. 25, 76; Journ. Amer. Med. Assoc., 1918, lxx, 526.
(7) Morawitz and Röhmer: Deutsch. Arch. f. klin. Med., 1908, xciv, 529.
(8) Lundsgaard: Journ. Exper. Med., 1919, xxx, 147.
(9) Means and Newburgh: Trans. Assoc. Amer. Phys., 1915, xxx, 51; Journ. Pharm. Exper. Therap., 1915, vii, 449.
(10) Verzar: Journ. Physiol., 1912, xlv, 39.
(11) Cannon: Journ. Amer. Med. Assoc., 1918, lxx, 616.
(12) Krogh: Journ. Physiol., 1919, lii, 457.

STUDIES IN EXPERIMENTAL TRAUMATIC SHOCK

III. Chemical Changes in the Blood

JOSEPH C. AUB and HSIEN WU

From the Laboratories of Physiology and Biochemistry in Harvard Medical School

Received for publication August 12, 1920

In experimental traumatic shock there is a marked decrease in the rate of blood flow and of general metabolism. Decreased blood flow and blood pressure result in a diminished secretion by the kidney (1). It is of interest to know what are the effects of such acute abnormal conditions upon the chemical constituents of blood, especially as a chemical cause of shock is now being seriously considered.

Some work in this field has been done by French investigators. Duval and Grigaut (2) studied the non-protein nitrogen of the blood in shock and concluded from their results that in the war-wounded there was an increase in the non-protein nitrogen of the blood, which started promptly after the wounding, was at its height during the second day and then gradually returned to normal. This increase was slight in unshocked cases, whether the wounds were infected or not. The retention differed from that found in nephritis in that the nitrogen increase in blood occurred not markedly in the urea portion but in the remainder of the non-protein nitrogen.

Whipple and his collaborators (3) studied the blood in the intoxication following intestinal obstruction, and after injection of the toxic proteoses which developed in obstructed intestines or in closed intestinal loops. The response to these injections was one which in many ways resembled traumatic shock,—with a fall in temperature and blood pressure. The injection was followed by a large increase (40 per cent or more) in the non-protein nitrogen of the blood, but this increase was found chiefly in the blood urea nitrogen, although the amino- and peptid-nitrogen also showed slight increases.

It is thus seen that the conclusions of the French and of the American investigators are somewhat contradictory, though it may be conceded that the response obtained by proteose injection is not a true shock.

At any rate, neither of these investigators have found any chemical change in blood other than rise in non-protein nitrogen which may be regarded as characteristic of traumatic shock.

The method of analysis used in our experiments was that of Folin and Wu (4). The urea was always determined by means of urease and aeration, as hydrolysis with the autoclave would also decompose the urethane used as an anesthetic. The figures obtained by the latter method were 10 to 15 mgm. too high, and it may therefore be concluded that the blood in our experiments contained about this amount of urethane N per 100 cc. The urethane contributed but little to the non-protein nitrogen as actually determined. It is so volatile that most of it is expelled in the course of the digestion. Experiments with a pure urethane solution containing 10 to 15 mgm. N per liter (i.e., as much urethane N as the blood filtrate might contain) have shown that only 3 to 4 mgm. N were fixed by the acid digestion mixture. The values of the total non-protein N obtained are, therefore, only 3 to 4 mgm. higher than the actual total non-protein nitrogen minus urethane nitrogen.

The creatin N represents as usual the difference between the total creatinine and the preformed creatinine multiplied by 0.37. In the first few experiments both the total creatinine and the preformed creatinine were determined, but as the latter showed no appreciable variation during anesthesia,—averaging 2 mgm. creatinine per 100 cc. blood, in control as well as in shocked animals[1]—its separate determination was discontinued in later experiments in order to economize the blood filtrate. Its average value was used for the calculation of the creatin.

In tables 1 and 2 are shown the results of our experiments. It is clear that in the control experiments there was no marked rise in any of the chemical constituents studied. This is true even in the experiments where the blood pressure and the blood flow were reduced by mechanical means but without muscle trauma (exper. LIV). In the animals in shock, however, there was usually a marked increase of all the constituents which we determined, over what was present before

[1] In a control experiment, 1 hour and 10 minutes after anesthesia the blood contained 5.2 mgm. total creatinine and 2.1 preformed creatinine per 100 cc. blood. Five hours later the total creatinine was again 5.2 mgm. and the preformed creatinine was 1.8 mgm. In another experiment (2 hours after traumatization) the blood contained 15 mgm. total creatinine and only 2.3 mgm. preformed creatinine.

TABLE 1

Control experiments; blood analyses in untraumatized animals

EXPERIMENT NUMBER, DATE	TIME OF BLOOD SAMPLE	BLOOD PRESSURE	TIME OF BLOOD PRESSURE BELOW 80 MM. Hg.	BLOOD ANALYSES, MILLIGRAMS PER 100 CC. OF BLOOD					BASAL METABOLISM		REMARKS
				Total non-protein nitrogen	Urea: Nitrogen	Urea: Per cent	Creatin nitrogen	Sugar	Time	Calories per hour	
		mm. Hg.									
XXVII 3/31/19	12:49	158		48	26	54	1.2	282	—	—	Normal control
									1:28	7.34	
	5:10	141		47	30	64	1.2	280	4:30	7.19	
									5:30	6.84	
7/15/19	10:44	110		52	29	56	1.9	206	11:00	4.10	Normal control
									11:22	4.19	
	5:30	94		55	32	58	1.8	286	4:19	3.43	
									5:11	3.20	
11/18/19	11:34	114		52	28	54	1.4	276			Blood pressure reduced by intrapericardial pressure. No muscle trauma
	1:10	60	90	58	29	50	1.7	328			
LIV 12/1/19	12:40	114		48	26	54	1.2	310	12:15	6.75*	Blood pressure reduced by intrapericardial pressure
	1:45 2:00	65	40	47	28	60	1.2	324			Pericardial pressure removed. Cat transfused. Good recovery of original blood pressure
	2:50	116		50	28	56	1.1	282	2:25	6.31*	

11/19/19	11:16	146		58	29	50	1.3	320			Under ether anesthesia
	12:35	70	20	66	32	49	1.3	334			Under urethane for 1 hour 15 minutes
XXXIV 4/19/19	11:30	106		48	28	58	1.5	250	11:11	5.73	Hemorrhage alone. Blood pressure markedly reduced by taking blood sample. No trauma
									11:42	5.16	
	2:25	108		43	29	67	1.6	276	1.51	5.69	
									2.35	5.32	

* Average.

TABLE 2

Blood analyses after muscle trauma

Experiment number, date	Time of blood sample	Blood pressure	Time of blood pressure below 80 mm. Hg.	Blood analyses, milligrams per 100 cc. of blood: Total non-protein nitrogen	Urea: Nitrogen	Urea: Per cent	Creatin nitrogen	Sugar	Basal metabolism: Time	Basal metabolism: Calories per hour	Remarks
		mm. Hg.									
6/9/19	11:10	155		60	42	70	2.0	286			Cat severely traumatized but no true shock. Blood pressure never below 83
	1:40	93		53	34	64	2.2	400			
6/19/19	11:17	126		53	39	74	1.8	296			After trauma to both legs blood taken as cat seemed about to go into shock
	1:00	80		65	42	65	1.3	334			
6/14/19	11:26	158		55	32	58	2.0	222			Muscles severely traumatized. Marked drop in pressure but no true shock level
	2:40	85		57	37	65	3.0	258			
10/21/19	2:34	110		60	35	58	2.4	320			Severe muscle trauma at 3:00 with prompt drop of blood pressure below 80. Transfusion at 4:26 with only partial recovery (46 cc. blood)
	4:15	60	70	70	40	57	2.8	440			
	4:50	82		71	40	56	2.8	440			
XXXIII 4/15/19	11:15	115		55	35	64	1.3	196	10:50	7.10	Legs smashed at 12:08. Very mild shock and no marked drop in respiratory metabolism
									11:37	5.55	
	2:48	80	140	64	43	67	3.5	400	2:42	6.15	
XXXV 4/22/19	12:40	84		53	25	47	1.5	222	12:27	5.28	Marked reduction of blood pressure from hemorrhage alone. Legs smashed at 2:12 with prompt shock developing
									12:51	4.84	
	3:58	42	280	77	42	55	6.1	364	3:53	3.76	

XL 5/6/19	1:00	100	Few	53	25	47	1.9	242			Very sudden onset of shock after severe resmashing of muscles with prompt death
	3:20	60	mins.	52	28	54	3.7	392			
XXXVII 4/28/19									1:36	8.06	Legs smashed at 2:25 and 3:25. Severe shock
	1:55	126		50	28	56	2.2	250	2:06	8.16	
	6:20	52	80	70	42	60	5.7	400	6:02	5.35	
XXXVIII 5/1/19									12:24	5.08	Both legs smashed at 1:35 and 1:55. Severe shock
	1:00	80–100		51	35	67	2.2	296	1:17	4.63	
	3:55	62	70	74	49	66	6.0	400	3:55	2.74	
XXXIX 5/5/19									12:02	6.30	1:05. Both legs smashed. Mild shock
	12:22	104		47	25	53	1.8	306	12:51	6.07	
	2:40	74	90	59	33	48	4.5	550	1:59	5.61	
XLI 5/8/19	12:55	116		46	20	43	1.5	188	12:39	7.30	1:00. Both legs smashed. Shock developed on removing blood for analysis. Transfusion at 4:00 with 20 cc. blood. Sample IV is blood from femoral vein leaving traumatized muscle. Sample V is taken from carotid artery at same time
									3:00	7.50	
	3:28	84		50	23	46	4.2	250	3:35	5.04	
	Blood used for transfusion			51	29	57	2.2	276			
	5:00			49			4.8				
	5:00	80		50	24	48	3.7	333	4:49	5.40	
6/25/19	11:10	125		50	28	56	2.2	296			Blood CO_2 combining power 36.5 at 12:06. Rapidly developing very severe shock. After muscle trauma blood CO_2 combining power 22.3 volumes per cent
	2:15	70	20	57	32	56	3.2	400			

trauma. This increase was not marked in traumatized animals which did not go into shock,—and, in fact, the rise tended to run parallel with the severity of the shock.

The most significant result of the blood analysis is that in connection with the creatin. In control animals the creatin content of blood remained practically unchanged during the five hours of the experiment. In animals which were traumatized but had not gone into shock the blood creatin showed an unmistakable increase. When shock developed, the creatin figure rose frequently to three times the normal. The source of the increased creatin in blood is the injured muscle. This is not only in accord with the known facts but is also shown in experiment XLI. The blood from the femoral vein contained distinctly more creatin than did the carotid blood. According to the views of Folin and Denis (5), creatin does not exist as such in the intact muscle and it is a post-mortem product set free by the dying tissue. While these investigators based their view on indirect though convincing data, the results of our experiments seem to afford direct evidence.

The parallelism between blood creatin and the severity of the shock does not of course indicate that creatin itself is responsible for this condition. Creatin is innocuous even in large doses. Simultaneously with the liberation of creatin from the autolyzing muscle there is probably formed a large number of other nitrogenous substances—possibly histamine and the like, and to these substances may possibly be ascribed the cause of shock. The increased blood creatin is merely an index of the extent of the necrosis which the injured muscle has undergone. Since creatin is derived solely from the injured muscle, the results of our experiment seem to afford suggestive chemical evidence in support of the view already prevalent that the shock is produced by some substance coming from the injured muscle (6), (7).

Although an increase in the total non-protein nitrogen always attended the development of shock, the increase was slight except in cases where the shock was profound. This relatively slight increase of total nitrogen is an excellent check on the increase of creatin, for it shows that the accumulation is due to increased production and not simply to kidney inefficiency, which would probably cause a parallel rise of all constituents. We are inclined not to attach much significance to the variation of the total nitrogen (and the percentage of urea N) on account of the complication by the urethane, but our results agree rather well with those of Whipple and collaborators (3), and it may be concluded that albumoses, as such, could not have played any important rôle in the development of shock.

Some work has been done on the blood sugar content in traumatic shock. Cannon (8) reported that there was surely a normal amount if not a slightly increased blood sugar in wound shock. Fabre, Wertheimer and Clogne (9), however, report a reduced blood sugar content in shock. In our control experiments the blood sugar, while always high on account of anesthesia, did not rise greatly in the second sample. In the traumatized cases, however, there was nearly always definite and marked rise in the sugar content of the blood. Too much stress may not be laid upon the extent of the rise, however, because of the urethane. That this anesthetic may affect the carbohydrate metabolism was suggested by the work of Underhill (10), who showed that adrenalin glycosuria was more readily obtained when urethane was the anesthetic than otherwise. The rise of sugar values which we have found, however, is very striking and difficult to explain. Three possibilities suggest themselves: *a*, It may be the hyperglycemia associated with activity of the sympathetic nervous system; *b*, The reduced total metabolism might be used to explain an accumulation in the blood,—but the respiratory quotients in traumatic shock (11) suggest that at least a normal proportion of carbohydrate is being metabolized; *c*, finally one may look to the liver for an explanation. Several French observers have ascribed shock phenomena to a liver insufficiency, and one might assume that this rise in blood sugar is due to a loss from the glycogen commonly stored there. This might be a direct result of the toxic alterations which may occur in the liver (12).

CONCLUSIONS

1. Animals with marked muscle trauma but without true shock showed only slight changes in total non-protein nitrogen, urea, creatin and sugar in the blood. These constituents, especially the creatin and the sugar, rose markedly as shock developed. In control animals the determined constituents showed no appreciable change.

2. The marked rise in creatin is direct evidence of the presence in the blood of products of muscle necrosis, and is therefore suggestive evidence for the theory of the chemical cause of traumatic shock.

3. The cause of the rise in blood sugar is briefly discussed.

BIBLIOGRAPHY

(1) Cushny: The secretion of urine, London, 1917, 101.
(2) Duval and Grigaut: Compt. rend. d. l. soc. de biol., 1918, lxxxi, 873.
(3) Whipple et al.: Journ. Exper. Med., 1917, xxv, 461, 479; 1918, xxviii, 213.
(4) Folin and Wu: Journ. Biol. Chem., 1919, xxxviii, 81.
(5) Folin and Denis: Ibid., 1914, xvii, 493.
(6) Cannon and Bayliss: Rept. of Shock Committee, English Medical Research Committee, March, 1919, no. 26, 19.
(7) Quenu: Revue de Chirur., 1918, lvi, 204.
(8) Cannon: Rept. of Shock Committee, English Medical Research Committee, December, 1917, no. 25, 93; Journ. Amer. Med. Assoc., 1918, lxx, 531.
(9) Fabre, Wertheimer and Clogne: Bull. soc. chirur., 1919, lxv, 9.
(10) Underhill: Journ. Biol. Chem., 1911, ix, 13.
(11) Aub: This Journal, 1920, liv, 388.
(12) Richet and Flament: Compt. rend. d. l'acad. d. sci., 1918, clxvi, 718.

THE AMERICAN
JOURNAL OF PHYSIOLOGY

VOL. 54 JANUARY 1, 1921 No. 3

EXPERIMENTAL STUDIES IN DIABETES

Series II. The Internal Pancreatic Function in Relation to Body Mass and Metabolism

7. *The Influence of Cold*

FREDERICK M. ALLEN

From the Hospital of The Rockefeller Institute for Medical Research, New York

Received for publication August 10, 1920

According to some earlier literature (1), cold causes hyperglycemia and glycosuria in both warm- and cold-blooded animals, and increases the glycosuria of diabetic dogs. The use of cold and shivering to drive out glycogen from phlorizinized animals was familiarized by Lusk. A single mild test of cold environment in a human patient gave a negative result (2).

A few words may be devoted to the theory of the subject. In a totally phlorizinized dog, it is obvious that a release of carbohydrate which cannot be utilized will result in a temporary rise of glycosuria and of the D : N ratio. A similar mobilization of stored carbohydrate, together with a possible diuretic action of cold, might produce a similar result in a totally depancreatized animal. The extra heat required to maintain body temperature would supposedly be furnished by fat, and there is no reason to expect any increased output of sugar derived from protein, either in the sense of any appreciable increase of protein decomposition or any genuine alteration of the D : N ratio. In a partially depancreatized animal, the increased carbohydrate mobilization or increased total metabolism may impose an additional burden upon the pancreas remnant, and any lasting increase of glycosuria must be interpreted in the sense of a true aggravation of the diabetes. At the same time complicating factors come into play. If the animal fasts, the extra sugar loss and fat combustion impose a sharper under-nutrition treatment in a cold than in a warm environment. Likewise a diet which is adequate in warmth becomes under-nutrition in the cold. On the other hand an increase of diet to meet the increased requirement complicates the problem still further. Shivering is a form of muscular exercise, and may possibly have a metabolic effect opposed to the effect of cold *per se*.

Normal dogs can live without artificial heat in the ordinary winter weather of New York if merely sheltered, but their metabolism evidently is considerably higher than that of dogs kept in warm rooms. The first experiments were therefore planned to determine whether there is any practical difference in the ease of producing diabetes in dogs kept in outdoor cages in winter and in others kept in a room specially warmed to a high summer temperature. This method was considered better for the purpose than the plan of using severely diabetic dogs and following the variations in their glycosuria, because it was important to distinguish a tendency to the production of mere glycosuria and hyperglycemia (such as cold may excite even in normal animals, which are certainly not diabetic from this cause) from a tendency to the production of actual diabetes. If cold has any diabetogenic action, equivalent to the removal of a small fraction of a gram of pancreatic tissue, this action should be demonstrable in such tests.

Twenty-five dogs were used for this investigation, with removal of such portions of pancreas as were known to produce a close approach to diabetes.[1] These experiments included fasting and fixed diets, also single and repeated operations, the latter as usual removing successive bits of tissue till diabetes resulted. Comparisons were made between dogs kept in the warmth and others kept in the cold, and also in the same animals by sudden changes from one environment to the other. The animals chosen ranged from small short-haired dogs which were highly sensitive to the cold and might sometimes be unduly depressed by it, to large woolly dogs which scarcely shivered in the winter weather. The general technic of such experiments is sufficiently clear from the preceding papers, so that brevity may be served by omitting protocols. In two instances the change from warmth to cold seemed responsible for a definite but transitory glycosuria. Otherwise the results were negative, and the conclusion was established positively that there is no demonstrable difference in the amount of pancreatic tissue that

[1] All operations were performed under ether anesthesia.

must be removed to produce diabetes in dogs in warm or cold environment. An effect of cold upon the islands of Langerhans was also not observable.

Although cold has no diabetogenic influence whatever in the sense of this test, it thus merely conforms to the rule that the most powerful functional influences avail little in comparison with the smallest fraction of a gram of healthy pancreas tissue. As agencies which are negative in this respect sometimes appreciably influence the course of an existing diabetes, some experiments concerning hyperglycemia and glycosuria were performed upon dogs with various grades of carbohydrate tolerance. For this purpose the animals' cages were transferred from a comfortably warm room to a refrigerator room kept at approximately freezing temperature. The observations are arranged in a series chiefly according to descending assimilative capacity.

Dog C3–36

TIME	PLASMA SUGAR	REMARKS
	per cent	
August 6		
10:00 a.m.	0.128	At summer temperature
3:40 p.m.	0.116	Immediately after this bleeding, transferred to ice room
5:50 p.m.	0.098	
August 7		
10:00 a.m.	0.113	
4:00 p.m.	0.100	Immediately after this bleeding, transferred from ice room to summer temperature
6:00 p.m.	0.095	
9:25 p.m.	0.105	

The normal dog C3-36, weighing 17 kilos, was placed in the ice room after the bleeding at 3:40 p.m. on August 6, and left there until after the bleeding at 4 p.m. on August 7. The usual diet of bread and soup was fed each evening after the final blood sample was taken. The dog was in excellent condition and powerfully muscled, but very short haired, and shivered continuously in the cold. The plasma sugar seemed to be affected very slightly if at all. At any rate, no elevation by cold was observed.

Dog B2-00, mentioned several times in previous papers, in August, 1915 was close to the verge of diabetes, but had been free from glycosuria on fixed bread diet for several months. Exercise had proved able to modify the blood sugar and the glucose assimilation considerably, and an experiment with cold was therefore performed under similar conditions. The diet was fed each evening after the last blood test. There was no glycosuria. The plasma sugar was slightly lower at the low temperature.

TIME	PLASMA SUGAR	REMARKS
	per cent	
August 5		
11:30 a.m.	0.111	
2:30 p.m.	0.117	At summer temperature
August 6		
9:30 a.m.	0.110	
3:30 p.m.	0.098	Immediately after this bleeding, transferred to ice room
5:45 p.m.	0.085	
August 7		
9:30 a.m.	0.098	
3:30 p.m.	0.107	Immediately after this bleeding, transferred from ice room to summer temperature
6:00 p.m.	0.125	
9:30 p.m.	0.112	

Dog B2-01

PLASMA SUGAR			TIME
September 21, Cold	September 29, Control	October 6, Exercise	
per cent	*per cent*	*per cent*	
0.116	0.106	0.105	Blood before feeding
0.192	0.256	0.147	1 hour after feeding
0.106	0.147	0.148	3 hours after feeding
0.131	0.103		6 hours after feeding

Dog B2-01, likewise near the verge of diabetes, received 56 grams Merck anhydrous glucose (4 grams per kilo) in 30 per cent solution by stomach tube on three days, respectively in the cold, in warmth at rest, and with treadmill running. The control day showed the highest plasma sugar curve, while both cold and exercise seemed to depress it.

Dog B2–02

PLASMA SUGAR			URINE SUGAR		TIME
July 20, Control	September 23, Cold	October 15, Exercise	July 20, Control	September 23, Cold	
per cent	*per cent*	*per cent*	*per cent*	*per cent*	
0.144	0.118	0.114	0	0	Before feeding
0.270	0.228	0.111	4.50 (13 cc.)	Slight	1 hour after feeding
0.149	0.115	0.100	1.85 (84 cc.)	0	3 hours after feeding
0.112	0.100		0	0	6 hours after feeding

Dog B2–02 was known to have very mild latent diabetes, but was continuously free from glycosuria on bread diet. Tests similar to those of dog B2–01 were carried out with the giving of 30.5 grams Merck glucose (3 grams per kilo) by stomach tube. Cold seemed to reduce hyperglycemia and glycosuria as compared with the control day. On the exercise day there was by far the lowest plasma sugar and no glycosuria.

Dog D4–29

PLASMA SUGAR			TIME
October 4, Control	October 9, Cold	October 10, Control	
per cent	*per cent*	*per cent*	
0.093	0.120	0.147	Blood before feeding
0.307	0.357	0.256	1 hour after feeding
0.307	0.455	0.202	2 hours after feeding
0.322	0.400	0.235	3 hours after feeding
0.307	0.416	0.222	4 hours after feeding
0.313	0.364	0.250	5 hours after feeding
	0.322	0.206	8 hours after feeding
	0.125	0.200	13 hours after feeding

Dog D4–29. Female; mongrel; age 2 years; good condition; weight 11.5 kilos. September 28, 1916, removal of pancreatic tissue weighing 26.9 grams. Remnant about main duct estimated at 3.8 grams ($\frac{1}{8}$). The removal of 0.65 gram additional tissue on October 16 was necessary to produce diabetes. In the interval the tests shown in the table were performed, with the feeding of 200 grams bread and 150 grams glucose on each occasion (together with 200 grams talcum powder as a precaution against diarrhea). On October 9 the dog was transferred to the cold room immediately after feeding. The plasma sugar curve ran noticeably higher on this day than on the control days, but yet was lower at the end of 13 hours, as if more of the available carbohydrate had either been excreted or consumed by shivering. An accident prevented comparison of the glycosuria.

Dog B2–86. The history of this animal was given in paper 2 of the preceding series (3). The animal had been on the verge of diabetes with an unusually large pancreas remnant, and enormous quantities of bread and glucose had been necessary to keep up glycosuria, but by July 21 this was disappearing and the appetite was failing. Therefore the expedient was adopted of raising the animal's metabolism to the highest level possible, by exercising him on the treadmill to the limit of his strength daily, and keeping him in the ice room all the rest of the time, in the endeavor to bring on diabetes either by stimulation of appetite or by any direct influence upon the pancreas. July 22 was occupied in this manner. July 23, exercise was deferred until a feeding experiment with 400 grams bread and 500 grams glucose could be carried out in the ice room in comparison with the one at summer temperature on July 21.

TIME	PLASMA SUGAR	
	July 21, at summer temperature	July 23, at freezing temperature
	per cent	*per cent*
Before feeding	0.124	0.100
2 hours after	0.147	0.128
7 hours after	0.141	0.141

The lower sugar curve on July 23 may have been partly the result of the preceding day's exercise, but at least augured failure for the undertaking. The program of combined exercise and cold was continued daily, with addition of as much as 600 grams of glucose to the bread diet, up to the time of the second operation on August 7. The strong animal merely thrived on the program, and such diabetic tendency as had seemed to be present disappeared.

Dog B2–71. June 3, 1914, at a normal weight of 14.7 kilos, nine-tenths of the pancreas were removed. In July, 1915 the dog was still in a state of moderate diabetes, kept sugar-free on meat diet, at a weight of 12.5 kilos, and was used for exercise and other experiments. Some tests were then performed with feeding 50 grams of bread, following only the urine without blood analyses. The regular lung diet was given each evening after completion of the test.

TIME	URINE		REMARKS
	Volume	Glucose	
	cc.	*per cent*	
July 28			
2:30 p.m.		0	Fed 50 grams bread
5:00 p.m.	38	0.28	
July 29			
2:30 p.m.		0	Fed 50 grams bread and placed in ice room
5:00 p.m.	47	0	Returned to summer temperature
July 30			
10:00 a.m.		0	Fed 50 grams bread and placed in ice room
5:00 p.m.	214	Trace	Returned to summer temperature
July 31			
10:00 a.m.		0	Fed 50 grams bread
5:00 p.m.	275	0.4	

In this experiment there was distinctly greater glycosuria on July 28 and 31 in warm summer weather than on July 29 and 30 at freezing temperature.

Dog C3–00. Female; fox terrier mongrel; white and brown; age 5 years; good condition; weight 4.5 kilos. May 6, 1915, removal of pancreatic tissue weighing 11 grams. Remnant about main duct estimated at 1.25 grams ($\frac{1}{10}$). As sometimes happens in small dogs, glycosuria was absent on full meat diet even with this small pancreas remnant. On May 15 a change to bread and soup promptly brought heavy glycosuria, which ceased with a return to meat diet on May 21. A fixed diet of 750 grams lung was then given daily, but was not always eaten completely. After continuous absence of glycosuria, the dog was transferred to the ice room on May 29, and in the following 24 hours excreted 0.45 per cent sugar in 375 cc. urine. Glycosuria then continued absent on the same diet as before, until on June 7 the dog was removed from the ice room. At summer temperature a return to bread and soup diet produced immediate heavy glycosuria. Accordingly, in this experiment cold failed to maintain glycosuria on meat diet in a dog which was demonstrably diabetic as proved by glycosuria on bread diet.

In August the same dog was tested with the aid of plasma sugar analyses on a regular diet of 500 grams lung and 50 grams suet. There was no glycosuria.

TIME	PLASMA SUGAR	REMARKS
	per cent	
August 10		
10:45 a.m.	0.135	Immediately after this bleeding, transferred to ice room
12:00 noon	0.122	
4:45 p.m.	0.141	
August 15		
12:30 p.m.	0.182	
August 16		
12:45 p.m.	0.098	
4:45 p.m.	0.112	Immediately after this bleeding, transferred from ice room to summer temperature
August 18		
12:00 noon	0.167	Summer temperature
5:25 p.m.	0.143	

Dog B2–88

PLASMA SUGAR					TIME
November 15, Control	November 18, Control	November 20, Cold	November 23, Cold	November 26, Exercise	
per cent	*per cent*	*per cent*	*per cent*	*per cent*	
0.128	0.189	0.131	0.122	0.162	Blood before feeding
	0.250	0.222		0.263	½ hour after feeding
	0.257	0.233		0.189	2 hours after feeding
0.286			0.271		4 hours after feeding

Dog B2–88, with mild diabetes, received test meals of 200 grams bread and 100 grams beef lung. The plasma sugar curve seemed to vary chiefly according to the initial figure, without much influence of any of the special measures employed. Thus, both figures on November 15 are a trifle higher than on November 23 in the refrigerator. Also the differences between November 18, 20 and 26 seemed to be governed chiefly by the level on which the plasma sugar started. Cold at least did not elevate the plasma sugar.

Dog B2–58. Female; mongrel; yellow; age 3 years; good condition; weight 11.8 kilos. Fasting was begun May 4, 1914, and by May 21 the weight was reduced to 9.1 kilos. It was thus possible to remove $\frac{11}{12}$ of the pancreas on this date with only a moderate degree of diabetes resulting. After various tests, the tolerance was spared by a low protein diet, which could be gradually increased by October 20 to 1 kilo of beef lung daily, without glycosuria. The weight gradually rose by December 24 to 12.3 kilos, on which date the first glycosuria appeared. About the same time the dog began to leave part of the diet uneaten, and the weight thus fluctuated and in general fell. The partial checking of glycosuria, and its daily variations, are thus accounted for. Beginning January 6, 1915, the dog's cage was kept outdoors, in order to test the effect of cold upon the diabetes either directly, through stimulation of appetite or in any other way. The dog had time to become acclimated because the weather was fairly mild at first, but after January 20 it turned decidedly colder, and there were several days with considerable snow and ice. As the dog was short-haired, she was shivering practically continuously while outdoors, but passed through even the coldest weather without actual impairment of health. The rectal temperature remained normal. Contrary to expectation, the amount of food eaten was not appreciably different in the cold environment. After February 12 the glycosuria was checked by fasting. The experiment seems to indicate a slight increase of glycosuria by cold, but the influence certainly was not great.

Dog B2–58

DATE	WEIGHT	URINE	
		Volume	Glucose
	kgm.	*cc.*	*per cent*
December 24		320	1.0
25		585	0.5
26	12.8	470	Faint
27		385	0.2
28		950	Faint
29		355	0
30	12.7	384	0
January 1		360	0
2		500	0
3		632	0
4		650	Faint

Dog B2-58—Concluded

DATE		WEIGHT	URINE	
			Volume	Glucose
		kgm.	cc.	per cent
January	5		480	0
	6	12.7	330	0
	7	12.4	502	0
		Today placed	in cage outdoors	
	8		431	0
	9		307	0
	10		575	0
	11	11.1	713	0
	12		766	0
	13	11.2	646	0
	14		954	0
	15	10.9	698	0
	16		382	0
	17	Not	collected	
	18	11.1	1849	0
	19		988	0.6
	20	11.3	995	0
	21		965	0.7
	22	11.1	781	0.9
	23	11.2	609	0.5
	24		740	0.9
	25	10.9	700	Faint
	26	11.1	749	0
	27	11.0	900	V. Faint
	28	11.3	731	1.5
	29	11.5	630	1.0
	30	11.5	156	2.0
	31		820	1.1
February	1	11.3	1036	1.0
	2	11.3	1300	0.8
	3	11.0	950	2.0
	4	11.1	785	1.8
	5	11.4	1157	2.0
	6	11.8	605	2.5
		Today moved into	animal room	
	7		650	1.0
	8	11.5	973	0.9
	9	11.5	649	0.4
	10	11.7	733	0.7
	11	11.5	815	Faint
	12		600	Faint

Dog B2–89. This female mongrel, weighing 13 kilos, underwent partial pancreatectomy on April 12, 1915, leaving a remnant of $\frac{1}{11}$. Under regulated diets, the condition by the end of June was such that glycosuria was absent at a weight of 10.3 kilos on a diet of 1 kilo of lung, but substitution of 250 grams lung by 50 grams bread (making 750 grams lung and 50 grams bread) caused glycosuria of 0.75 per cent in 462 cc. urine on June 30 and 0.71 per cent in 542 cc. urine on July 1. On the latter date the diet of 1 kilo of lung without bread was resumed, and glycosuria immediately ceased (4). On July 2 the dog was transferred to the ice room, in order to test whether the influence of cold would amount to as much as the above difference between carbohydrate and protein. The dog was left in the ice room until July 26. Traces of glycosuria were present on most days during this time, but only twice reached titratable amounts (0.33 per cent on July 14, 0.25 per cent on July 21). A single day of exercise on July 22 abolished the glycosuria, which returned on July 24. It was present also on July 25 and 26, and then was continuously absent during a control period up to August 5 at summer temperature. As the weight fell to 9.7 kilos during the period in the refrigerator, the experiment seems to indicate a slight increase of diabetic tendency due to cold. The difference due to temperature, however, was evidently less than the difference between the preformed carbohydrate of 50 grams of bread and its approximate equivalent of potential carbohydrate in protein. The tolerance had fallen somewhat, for the giving of 50 grams of bread on August 15 resulted in a glycosuria of 1.4 per cent.

Glycosuria remained absent on the lung diet to September 17. On that day at 9:30 a.m. the plasma sugar was 0.143 per cent, the rectal temperature 101.4° F. The dog was then placed in the ice room fasting. At 4 p.m. the plasma sugar was 0.151 per cent, the rectal temperature 100.7°F. The usual lung diet was then fed and the dog left in the ice room. The next morning there was a glycosuria of 0.42 per cent in 567 cc. urine, and the plasma sugar at 9:30 a.m. was 0.164 per cent. The urine of the next 24 hours was 492 cc., with 1.9 per cent sugar. At 9:30 a.m. on September 19 the rectal temperature was 101.5°F. Glycosuria then ceased abruptly, as though the reserve of extra carbohydrate had been exhausted. At 9:30 a.m. on September 20 the plasma sugar was 0.146 per cent. The dog was then transferred to the warm animal room, and at 9:30 a.m. on September 21 the plasma sugar was 0.133 per cent, the rectal temperature 101.7°F.

During the following days the weather turned colder. The night of September 23–24 was particularly sharp, and the door of the animal room blew open, so that the room was cold and the dogs all shivering. This dog was one of five potentially diabetic animals (out of about twenty) which had been kept sugar-free on regulated diets and which showed sudden glycosuria on this night.

Subsequently, at a body weight of 15 kilos and correspondingly reduced tolerance, a comparison was made in this dog of the feeding of 1 kilo of meat in a warm room and in the ice room.

TIME	PLASMA SUGAR	
	November 26, (warm room)	December 3, (ice room)
	per cent	*per cent*
Before feeding	0.200	0.208
2 hours after feeding	0.218	0.278
5 hours after feeding	0.208	0.313
Glycosuria for the period	0	4.08 grams

The later observations showed a decided influence of cold for the production of hyperglycemia and glycosuria. It is possible that this effect became greater as the diabetes became more severe.

Dog B2–79

PLASMA SUGAR		URINE SUGAR		TIME
November 23, Warm	November 30, Cold	November 23, Warm	November 30, Cold	
per cent	*per cent*	*per cent*	*per cent*	
0.133	0.250	0	Faint	Blood before feeding
0.213	0.416	Faint	5.00	1 hour after feeding
0.159	0.525	Faint	5.90	4 hours after feeding
0.189	0.435	0	3.53	6 hours after feeding

Dog B2–79 was an animal which had long been kept in a stage of diabetes such that there was marked hyperglycemia and occasional glycosuria on a diet of 1 kilo of beef lung, the condition being held in check by fasting when necessary. The above record shows a strong contrast in hyperglycemia and glycosuria on days spent in a warm room and in the ice room respectively. The rise of blood sugar after eating the usual kilo of lung was somewhat similar on the two days, but the entire curve was on a much higher level in the cold environment. It was not established that this difference was due entirely to the temperature, because no comparison was made of the blood sugar before and after moving into the refrigerator on November 30. Therefore on December 2 the plasma sugar was determined fasting at 11:40 a.m. and found to be 0.164 per cent. The dog was then moved into the cold room, and at 5:40 p.m. the plasma sugar (still fasting) was found to be 0.185 per cent.

Likewise dog C3–19, weighing 13.8 kilos, was partially depancreatized on June 23, 1915, leaving a remnant of $\frac{1}{11}$ to $\frac{1}{12}$. In August at a weight of 11 kilos, the degree of diabetes was such that a diet of 500 grams lung was slightly in excess of the tolerance. On August 7 the fasting plasma sugar at 10:30 a.m. was 0.156 per cent and at 4:30 p.m. 0.120 per cent. The dog, still fasting, was then moved to the ice room, where the plasma sugar was found to be 0.167 per cent at 7 p.m. and 0.133 per cent at 9:45 p.m. Here a falling blood sugar due to fasting was evidently raised by cold, and then continued to fall slightly.

DISCUSSION

The elevation of blood sugar by cold is so generally accepted as a truism that it was a surprise to encounter instances in which the sugar was little changed or actually lower in a cold environment. It was not feasible to extend the investigation further into the physiological reaction to cold. Supposedly the blood sugar is governed by two factors, namely the mobilization and the disposal of carbohydrate. It is conceivable that in a perfectly smoothly working reaction the two may exactly balance. Under some conditions shivering may perhaps reduce the blood sugar like other forms of muscular activity. Under other conditions hyperglycemia may occur, particularly when the cold stimulus is sufficiently violent, as for example in the case of plunging into ice water. Here the stimulation is so powerful, sometimes to a pathological degree, that a correspondingly excessive sugar discharge may be expected, and in the most extreme cases possibly the utilization of sugar suffers somewhat. Hyperglycemia and glycosuria may be more readily produced when the utilization of sugar is specifically impaired, as in the more severe grades of diabetes. In a similar way exercise sometimes raises the blood sugar instead of lowering it.

Violent or pathological stimulation by cold was not applicable in experiments designed to produce diabetes, because the animals' health would suffer and ill health would be the surest way to spoil the result and prevent diabetes. A more powerful temporary discharge of sugar might occur, but it would cease as soon as the immediate store was exhausted. Such discharge and cessation was actually seen in certain of these experiments, without any lasting diabetogenic effect. As usual, clear thinking requires a distinction between diabetes, which is deficiency of the pancreatic function, and mere glycosuria. The mere excessive discharge of sugar from the glycogen depots is not diabetes, for the power of utilization may remain unimpaired. This has been abundantly proved, for example, in such a condition as epinephrin glycosuria (5). It is also not diabetes if the utilization of sugar is depressed by any extraneous mechanism, such as the chilling of the muscles or their nervous supply, but only if the impairment of utilization is due to impairment of the pancreatic function. If the glycosuria produced by cold is regarded as a diabetes, cold must be a very powerful diabetogenic agent to cause even a temporary diabetes in a normal animal, for it must thus temporarily paralyze about nine-tenths of the function of the dog's pancreas. Trial of this agent in animals depancreatized almost to the point of diabetes proves that it possesses no such power; and as the effect in these animals is not greatly different from that in normal animals, cold evidently does not act by direct depression of the pancreatic function. Its indirect influence upon diabetes through increasing metabolism is a much more delicate point to demonstrate, and the question is answered only somewhat doubtfully in the affirmative by some of the above experiments.

CONCLUSIONS

1. Cold environment, such as did not lower the rectal temperature to any important extent, in some instances failed to affect the plasma sugar of dogs or slightly lowered it, but in the majority of experiments produced hyperglycemia and sometimes glycosuria. These were produced more easily and in higher degree in proportion as the power of sugar utilization was impaired, i.e., as the diabetes was more severe.

2. The power to produce glycosuria is to be distinguished from the power to produce diabetes. There is no demonstrable difference in the proportion of pancreatic tissue that must be removed to produce diabetes in dogs in warm or cold environment, and it was proved by successive operations upon the same animals that the influence of cold is not equivalent to the removal of the smallest fraction of a gram of pancreatic tissue. In animals already diabetic, the course of the diabetes in a few instances seemed to be influenced slightly for the worse, so as perhaps to warrant the conclusion that cold imposes an increased burden upon the pancreatic function by increasing metabolism. But the slightness of this influence is emphasized by control experiments; for example, it amounts to less than the difference between the preformed carbohydrate of 50 grams of bread and the approximate equivalent of potential carbohydrate in protein.

3. The impression that diabetic patients do worse in cold weather is probably explainable by the discomfort of chilliness when they are undernourished, the tendency to take more food, and sometimes by the limitation of exercise. These may be important sometimes from a practical standpoint, but any direct influence of climate upon diabetes must be very slight if it exists.

BIBLIOGRAPHY

(1) ALLEN: Studies concerning glycosuria and diabetes, 1913, 562.
(2) ALLEN, STILLMAN AND FITZ: Rockefeller Inst. Monograph no. 11, 1919, 471.
(3) ALLEN: Journ. Exper. Med., 1920, xxxi, 385.
(4) For the greater glycosuric effect of preformed carbohydrate as compared with protein in mild diabetes. See Journ. Exper. Med., 1920, xxxi, 555 and 397 to 399.
(5) LUSK: Proc. Soc. Exper. Biol. and Med., 1913–14, xi, 49. Cf. also paper 12 of this series.

EXPERIMENTAL STUDIES IN DIABETES

Series II. The Internal Pancreatic Function in Relation to Body Mass and Metabolism

8. The Influence of Extremes of Age upon the Production of Diabetes

FREDERICK M. ALLEN

From the Hospital of The Rockefeller Institute for Medical Research, New York

Received for publication August 10, 1920

An influence upon the production of diabetes may conceivably be expected from the conditions of extreme age or youth.

Senility. The relation of senility to experimental diabetes may have interest from at least three standpoints: *a*, The total metabolism is known to be slightly lowered in old age; *b*, diabetes in elderly patients is generally characterized by a mild and prolonged course; *c*, the increasing incidence of diabetes with the advance of age suggests the possibility of functional or organic impairment of the pancreas.

Toothless decrepit senility is familiar in dogs, and there is reason to expect as great metabolic changes as in aged human beings. Obesity is also common in such animals, so that a number of them had to be included in a previous paper (1). A comparison of the relation of pancreas weight to body weight was made in fourteen dogs, which showed extreme senility together with an average nutritive state.

From a comparison of table 1 with a similar study of normal adult dogs (2), it may be inferred that there is no gross change, in particular no atrophy of the pancreas accompanying senility.

The susceptibility of obese senile dogs to diabetes could seldom be determined, owing to the sudden death to which they are subject following pancreas operations, as previously mentioned (3). Such operations were performed without accidents in senile dogs without obesity, and these were used for diabetic experiments in the same way as younger dogs. No experiments were performed to determine the precise proportion of pancreas that must be removed to produce diabetes, but the incidental observations were sufficient to exclude any marked differences from average adult dogs. The senile animals were somewhat weaker and more subject to loss of appetite and cachexia. Otherwise their diabetes ran a course indistinguishable from that of younger animals. The experimental answers may therefore be stated in the following form, corresponding to the questions raised above.

TABLE 1

Relation of pancreas weight to body weight in senile dogs

NUMBER	BODY WEIGHT	PANCREAS WEIGHT	PANCREAS PER KILOGRAM BODY WEIGHT
	kgm.	*grams*	*grams*
1	4.0	15.0	3.75
2	4.4	7.0	1.59
3	5.8	9.5	1.64
4	8.8	23.1	2.62
5	11.3	19.6	1.73
6	11.3	24.4	2.16
7	11.5	25.6	2.23
8	11.7	32.1	2.74
9	14.2	53.6	3.78
10	15.0	33.6	2.24
11	16.0	20.2	1.26
12	21.3	46.4	2.18
13	21.8	39.6	1.81
14	25.1	41.4	1.65

a. The lowered metabolism characteristic of senility does not render dogs less susceptible to diabetes from pancreatic resection. As the reduction of metabolism with age is slight, and the method of judging susceptibility by the size of the pancreas remnant with which diabetes occurs is a crude one according to former observations, too much stress need not be laid upon these negative findings.

b. A more decisive observation is that diabetes does not run any slower course in senile animals, but follows the same rapid progress which is generally characteristic of diabetes in dogs.

c. If there were any anatomic or functional deterioration of the pancreas with age, a remnant of a given size might be expected to be less efficient in preventing diabetes than in younger animals. An increased susceptibility to diabetes in this sense is excluded by the observations. The microscopic study, as reported in subsequent papers, showed no visible abnormalities resulting from simple senility. Pancreatitis is much rarer in dogs than in human beings, and is apparently due to causes independent of age. Also there is no such arteriosclerosis in senile dogs as in man, and it can by no means be said that a dog "is as old as his arteries." Also, as previously mentioned (2), the pancreas remnant of a senile dog may possess as great power of hypertrophy as that of any younger animal.

Numerous glucose tolerance tests have been performed indiscriminately upon old and young adult dogs, and no indications of alteration of assimilation with age have been found.

In general these observations, made upon a species practically free from the pancreatic changes to which man is subject with advancing years, indicate that the rising incidence and special characteristics of diabetes in older persons are due to the changes in question and not to senility *per se*.

Youth. The outstanding feature of experimental interest is the characteristically rapid and fatal course of diabetes in children. This has often been attributed hypothetically to their high metabolism, which imposes a heavier burden upon the pancreatic function. There is also good evidence that this rapid downward progress indicates a susceptibility of the islands of Langerhans to rapid destruction by hydropic degeneration. As there are occasional cases of acute and severe diabetes in the aged and of mild and prolonged diabetes in children, there is no absolute distinction on the basis of either the level of metabolism or the island changes.

Diabetes is also less frequent in children than in older persons. In seeking possible reasons, it might be imagined that the youthful pancreas is larger in proportion to the body, that it is anatomically richer in islands or that these have stronger functional power, or that the capacity for regeneration after injuries is greater. According to work previously reviewed (4), especially that of Bensley, the pancreas at birth probably contains as many islands as the adult organ, but during early life there is probably a loss followed by a gradual new formation of islands. Observations on the gross relations of the pancreas in puppies are contained in tables 2 to 6. They indicate, in comparison with those on adult dogs (2), that the ratio of pancreas weight to body weight in puppies is not large but rather small in proportion to what might be expected from the small size of the animals; that the tendency to regeneration is often marked but yet not in excess of that often found in adults; and that the tendency to diabetes is at least no greater and often is distinctly less than in adult dogs.

In qualification of this statement, it should be noticed that the observations do not exclude possible alterations of the ratio of pancreas

TABLE 2

Litter of black and tan mongrel pups. Weight of mother, 17 kilos

NUMBER	SEX	AGE	BODY WEIGHT	PANCREAS WEIGHT	PANCREAS WEIGHT PER KILOGRAM
			kgm.	*gram*	*grams*
1	Male	Newborn	0.3	0.6	2.0
2	Male	Newborn	0.3	0.6	2 0
3	Female	Newborn	0.2	0.4	2.0
4	Female	Newborn	0.3	0.5	1.67
5	Male	Newborn	0.3	0.6	2.0
6	Female	Newborn	0.3	0.7	2.33
7	Male	Newborn	0.4	0.8	2.0
8	Female	Newborn	0.3	0.9	3.0
9	Male	Newborn	0.3	0.6	2.0
10	Male	Newborn	0.3	0.8	2.66
11	Female	Newborn	0.3	0.6	2.0

TABLE 3

Litter of harrier mongrel pups. Weight of mother 13 kilos

NUMBER	SEX	AGE	BODY WEIGHT	PANCREAS WEIGHT	PANCREAS WEIGHT PER KILOGRAM
			kgm.	*gram*	*grams*
1	Female	1 day	0.2	0.3	1.5
2	Male	1 day	0.2	0.3	1.5
3	Male	1 day	0.3	0.6	2.0
4	Male	1 day	0.3	0.4	1.33
5	Male	1 day	0.3	0.7	2.33
6	Male	1 day	0.2	0.7	3.50

TABLE 4

Litter of spaniel mongrel pups. Weight of mother, 16 kilos

NUMBER	AGE	BODY WEIGHT	PANCREAS WEIGHT	PANCREAS WEIGHT PER KILOGRAM
		kgm.	*grams*	*grams*
1	Slightly premature	0.2	0.7	3.5
2	Slightly premature	0.2	0.6	3.0
3	Slightly premature	0.3	0.8	2.67
4	Slightly premature	0.3	0.6	2.0
5	2 days	0.3	0.9	3.0
6	3 weeks	0.6	2.1	3.5

weight to body weight with age. In other words, there is no proof that a puppy having a certain ratio will maintain this same ratio up to adult age. In tables 4 and 5 no great change was noticed in the

TABLE 5

Litter of yellow and brown mongrel pups. Weight of mother, 21.5 kilos

NUMBER	AGE	BODY WEIGHT	PANCREAS WEIGHT	PANCREAS WEIGHT PER KILOGRAM
		kgm.	*grams*	*grams.*
1	$\frac{1}{2}$ week	0.3	1.1	3.67
2	$\frac{1}{2}$ week	0.4	1.7	4.25
3	$\frac{1}{2}$ week	0.4	1.3	3.25
4	2 weeks	0.6	2.6	4.33
5	2 weeks	0.7	2.8	4.00

TABLE 6

Relation of pancreas weight to body weight in puppies

NUMBER	AGE	BODY WEIGHT	PANCREAS WEIGHT	PANCREAS WEIGHT PER KILOGRAM
		kgm.	*grams*	*grams*
1	1 week premature	0.1	0.2	2.0
2	1 week premature	0.1	0.2	2.0
3	1 month	0.7	2.2	3.14
4	1 month	1.5	7.1	4.74
5	$1\frac{1}{2}$ months	2.1	4.1	1.95
6	$1\frac{1}{2}$ months	1.3	2.6	2.00
7	2 months	0.9	3.5	3.89
8	2 months	2.3	5.1	2.22
9	2 months	2.0	5.9	2.95
10	2 months	1.8	5.8	3.22
11	2 months	4.3	8.4	1.95
12	2 months	2.3	7.4	3.21
13	$2\frac{1}{2}$ months	1.8	7.4	4.10
14	$2\frac{1}{2}$ months	2.5	5.7	2.28
15	3 months	2.5	12.2	4.89
16	3 months	2.3	5.2	2.26
17	5 months	3.9	13.8	3.54
18	7 months	2.5	11.4	4.55

ratio up to 2 or 3 weeks of age, using other pups of the same litter as controls. The ratios varied widely among the different pups in table 6. They were sometimes larger in the smaller breeds, as found for adult dogs (2), but the rule was not uniform. The state of nutrition

TABLE 7

Partial pancreatectomies in puppies

NUMBER	AGE	BODY WEIGHT	PANCREAS WEIGHT	PANCREAS WEIGHT PER KILOGRAM	WEIGHT OF REMNANT	SIZE OF FRACTION	HYPERTROPHY	REMARKS
	months	*kgm.*	*grams*	*grams*	*grams*		*grams*	
1	1	3.0	13.2	4.4	0.8	$\frac{1}{16}$–$\frac{1}{17}$	0.8–1.02	
2	2	1.9	9.7	5.1	1.3	$\frac{1}{4}$–$\frac{1}{8}$	1.3–5.7	Transitory glycosuria. Mild diabetes produced by removal of additional 1.2 grams
3	2	1.7	8.9	5.2	0.7	$\frac{1}{13}$–$\frac{1}{14}$	0.7–0.4	Cachexia. Weight 1 kgm. at autopsy. Probably mild diabetes
4	3	2.5	11.0	4.4	0.5	$\frac{1}{22}$	0.5–0.6	Cachexia. Mild diabetes
5	3	2.1	10.8	5.1	3.0	$\frac{1}{3}$–$\frac{1}{4}$		Diabetes not produced even by circulatory stasis
6	3	3.9	17.8	4.6	5.7	$\frac{1}{3}$		Diabetes not produced even by circulatory stasis
7	3	2.0	16.0	8.0	2.7	$\frac{1}{6}$	2.7–5.3	No diabetes
8	3	2.1	8.3	3.9	0.8	$\frac{1}{10}$		Thin, no glycosuria
9	4	3.7	15.8	4.3	1.5	$\frac{1}{10}$		Assimilated 5 grams of glucose per kilogram
10	4	8.4	27.6	3.3	4.6	$\frac{1}{5}$		Removal of 3.6 grams additional tissue in 6 operations required to bring on diabetes. Remnant at autopsy was then 1.1 grams
11	5	1.9	7.8	4.1	0.6	$\frac{1}{3}$	0.6–1.0	
12	5½	5.3	25.8	4.9	4.4	$\frac{1}{6}$	5.4–8.4	No diabetes
13	6	8.0	22.5	2.8	9.3	$\frac{1}{2}$–$\frac{1}{3}$		
14	6	3.8	8.5	2.2	1.0	$\frac{1}{8}$–$\frac{1}{9}$		
15	7	5.9	20.1	3.4	1.7	$\frac{1}{12}$		Peritonitis, no glycosuria
16	7	5.9	15.0	2.54	1.6	$\frac{1}{9}$–$\frac{1}{10}$		Diabetes stopped by distemper
17	7	3.4	9.3	2.74	1.5	$\frac{1}{6}$		Cachexia, no glycosuria
18	7	4.4	8.9	2.02	1.0	$\frac{1}{10}$		Diabetes, mild, transitory
19	8	7.2	19.8	2.75	1.8	$\frac{1}{11}$		

TABLE 7—*Concluded*

NUMBER	AGE	BODY WEIGHT	PANCREAS WEIGHT	PANCREAS WEIGHT PER KILOGRAM	WEIGHT OF REMNANT	SIZE OF FRACTION	HYPERTROPHY	REMARKS
	months	*kgm.*	*grams*	*grams*	*grams*		*grams*	
20	9	5.8	21.5	3.71	1.3	$\frac{1}{17}$		Diabetes prevented by preliminary fast
21	9	2.7	10.5	3.90	1.0	$\frac{1}{10}$		Peritonitis, no diabetes
22	9	7.4	24.8	3.36	2.5	$\frac{1}{10}$		Severe diabetes even during fasting
23	9	7.1	26.2	3.69	3.0	$\frac{1}{9}$	3.0–1.95	Severe diabetes checked by cachexia. Emaciated to 5.3 kgm.
24	9	10.3	30.9	3.00	3.1	$\frac{1}{10}$	Considerable	
25	11	4.1	14.3	3.50	1.1	$\frac{1}{13}$	1.1–2.2	Cachexia, no diabetes

or rate of growth is probably an important factor. The differences found among animals of the same litter at the same age in tables 2 and 3 interfere seriously with studies based on any method of controls.

Partially depancreatized puppies are especially liable to cachexia from respiratory infections or diarrhea, so that diabetes is often thus suppressed and the experiments spoiled. The above statement concerning the relatively slight disposition to diabetes is based on animals which remained vigorous and thriving after operation. It is the more striking in view of the fact that the sugar tolerance of the young is distinctly less than that of adult normal animals (5). A series of observations was made upon the question whether partial pancreatectomy short of diabetes interferes with the growth or health of puppies, with negative results except for the temporary backset due to the operation, and a possible specific inhibition of development of sexual and other adult characters. Anything in the nature of a masked diabetes or other fatal metabolic deficiency seemed to be excluded.

As explained in a subsequent publication on acidosis, the expectation that puppies might prove more susceptible than adult dogs to diabetic acidosis was entirely disappointed. Acidosis was absent throughout the reported experiments except where specially mentioned.

As puppies approach adult age, they approach more closely to the adult behavior respecting diabetes. After about the ninth month they generally react like adults except for susceptibility to distemper. Nevertheless in pup 18 in table 7 it is noticeable that diabetes was transitory with a pancreas remnant of only $\frac{1}{10}$. Some typical records of younger puppies are the following.[1]

No. G7–49. Male; mongrel; black and white; age 1 month; well nourished; weight 3 kilos. June 25, 1918, removal of pancreatic tissue weighing 12.4 grams. Remnant about main duct estimated at 0.8 gram ($\frac{1}{16}$ to $\frac{1}{17}$). Following operation there was diarrhea and loss of weight but no glycosuria, though the pup lived on bread and milk. July 4, 0.32 gram additional pancreatic tissue was removed. The condition was still cachexia without glycosuria, up to death on July 11. The pancreas remnant weighed 0.7 gram, and was too badly autolyzed for microscopic study. In the tissue removed on July 4, the acini were normal and well filled; islands were present in normal number and size but showed slight distinct vacuolation. This hydropic change makes it probable that hyperglycemia was present, and possibly only the animal's weakness prevented a frank diabetes. Acidosis was absent as usual.

No. D4–35. Female; mongrel; age 3 months; brown and white; well nourished; weight 2.5 kilos. November 9, 1916, removal of pancreatic tissue weighing 10.5 grams. Remnant about main duct estimated at 0.5 gram ($\frac{1}{22}$). Glycosuria was brought on by the feeding of 20 grams meat and 20 cc. milk, but ceased readily with fasting. Death occurred from weakness, notwithstanding a low meat diet, on November 20. The pancreas remnant weighed 0.6 gram, and was not examined microscopically. The pup obviously had a potentially severe diabetes, but differed from an adult dog in that glycosuria did not begin spontaneously and was promptly checked by fasting and low diet, with such a very small pancreas remnant.

No. D4–34 similarly underwent removal of 8.2 grams pancreatic tissue, leaving a remnant estimated at 0.65 gram ($\frac{1}{13}$ to $\frac{1}{14}$). Glycosuria could readily be checked by fasting, but on full meat diet was as high as 1.2 per cent. Notwithstanding the liveliness following operation and the meat diet, the weight and strength failed rapidly. The animal was killed when moribund on the tenth day after operation, when the plasma sugar was 0.05 per cent. The rapid cachexia was the chief point of difference from an adult dog.

No. G7–25. Female; Boston terrier; brindle; age 6 weeks; good nutrition; weight 3.8 kilos. June 17, 1918, removal of pancreatic tissue weighing 13.1 grams. Remnant about main duct estimated at 1.1 gram ($\frac{1}{13}$). Glycosuria remained absent, first on beef lung, then on bread and soup diet, then with addition of 50 grams glucose. June 25, at a weight of 3.5 kilos, 1 gram additional pancreatic tissue was removed, the remnant having undergone marked hypertrophy. Glycosuria remained absent on bread and milk diet, though weight was lost. July 4, 0.95 gram additional pancreatic tissue was removed. The animal was lively and ate considerable lung on July 5, then gradually lost appetite and weight while retaining spirits up to death on July 9. Glycosuria remained absent. The plasma sugar on June 17 was 0.143 per cent, on July 8, 0.162 per cent. The pancreas remnant weighed 0.8 gram. In the various specimens of pancreas from June 17 and July 4 and 9, inflammation and fibrosis were limited to the peripheral areas. In the central portions the acini were well filled, sometimes large and

[1] All operations were performed under ether anesthesia.

irregular. Islands were normal in number and free from vacuolation. Here the persistent absence of diabetes is perhaps attributable to the hypertrophy of the pancreas remnant.

No. E5–40. Male; mongrel, part Newfoundland; age $3\frac{1}{2}$ months; good nutrition; weight 8.4 kilos. May 14, 1917, removal of pancreatic tissue weighing 23 grams. Remnant about main duct estimated at 4.6 grams ($\frac{1}{6}$). Glycosuria was absent on bread and soup diet, and only transitory with addition of 100 grams glucose.

May 24, additional pancreatic tissue weighing 0.9 gram was removed. There was obvious hypertrophy of the remnant in all three dimensions. Thereafter glycosuria was absent on bread diet, and could be maintained only by increasing additions of glucose, first 50, then 100, then 200 grams daily. The dosage of 200 grams was continued from June 6 to 27 with only traces of glycosuria and with a gain of weight to 9.3 kilos.

June 27, 0.6 gram additional tissue was removed from the pancreas remnant. which again was obviously hypertrophic. Thereafter heavy but transitory glycosuria resulted first from 100 and then from 200 grams glucose added to the bread diet.

July 12, an additional 0.35 gram of pancreatic tissue was removed, the weight then being 9.8 kilos. Glycosuria was then heavy with addition of 200 grams glucose to the bread diet, but ceased July 19.

July 20, an additional 0.4 gram of pancreatic tissue was removed. Glycosuria was then heavy on bread and soup diet, next with addition of glucose up to 200 grams, but was absent after July 29.

August 31, at a weight of 10.6 kilos, glycosuria being still absent on the bread diet with 200 grams glucose, an additional 0.52 gram of pancreatic tissue was removed. Glycosuria was again transitory.

September 7, an additional 0.3 gram of pancreatic tissue was removed with a similar result, glycosuria ceasing September 18.

September 28, an additional 0.55 gram of pancreatic tissue was removed. Glycosuria was then continuous, first with glucose, then on plain bread and soup, till stopped by a change to meat diet on October 22. It may be noted that the downward progress was slow rather than rapid, for the glycosuria of many adult dogs after 3 weeks reaches a point where it cannot be stopped by fasting.

The pup did not thrive on carbohydrate-free diet, suffered from indigestion, diarrhea and loss of weight, and died in cachexia November 16 at a weight of 7 kilos. The blood sugar was low during this period, and there was the usual absence of acidosis.

The pancreas remnant weighed 1.1 gram. Nothing significant was found in the gross autopsy, or in the microscopic examination of the liver, kidneys, adrenals, thyroid and parathyroids. Sections from the pancreas at all the operations and at autopsy showed normal parenchyma and absence of hydropic degeneration. Though the hypertrophy may have gone far toward preventing diabetes, it is evident from the repeated operations and the prolonged carbohydrate excess that this puppy was difficult rather than easy to make diabetic.

No. D4–21. Male; mongrel; age 7 months; good nutrition; weight 6.7 kilos. September 15, 1916, removal of pancreatic tissue weighing 24 grams. Remnant about main duct estimated at 2.9 grams ($\frac{1}{9}$). Glycosuria at first was absent on moderate quantities of milk, but was heavy on bread feeding September 18. It was then checked by fasting, and kept absent on a diet of lung, suet and 100 grams bread. The animal thrived and maintained a weight of about 7 kilos.

December 5, a full bread diet was resumed, and heavy glycosuria returned promptly. After 4 days this was stopped as before. The animal grew to adult life on a diet of 400 grams lung, 100 grams suet, and part of the time 100 grams bread or 100 cc. milk. Yeast was added part of the time, with the idea that it and the milk might supply needed vitamines; also an admixture of bonemeal assured adequate salts. The animal became plump and strong at a weight of 8.7 kilos, but remained always undeveloped in mentality, in the size of the sexual organs and the absence of any apparent sexual function; urination was performed squatting, and the puppy contour of the body and puppy-like behavior toward other dogs were retained. Pratt (6) has made similar observations in young dogs with pancreatic atrophy.

November 16, 1917, it was found that the addition of 100 grams bread to the diet produced a glycosuria of 1.3 per cent in 820 cc. of urine. The tolerance was thus evidently lower than before, and thereafter the diet was kept carbohydrate-free (400 to 600 grams of lung and 100 grams of suet). April 6, 1918, the fasting plasma sugar was found to be 0.250 per cent, indicating that hyperglycemia was now continuous. The weight at this time was 9.15 kilos. Traces of glycosuria began in July, at first intermittently, but by July 30 they were continuous and increasing, so that fasting had to be used. The weight at this time had reached its maximum of 9.5 kilos. The animal appeared not obese but in excellent nutrition.

The diet was then gradually built up to 200 grams lung and suet ad libitum, without glycosuria. This diet continued while the writer was in military service. At a visit on September 16, 1918, the animal was found in excellent strength and spirits, weighing 8.3 kilos, with intense glycosuria and hyperglycemia and heavy nitroprusside reactions in urine and plasma. Notwithstanding the fat-rich diet and acidosis, there was no visible lipemia. The condition was ideal for the development of coma, but under the circumstances there was nothing to do but to kill the animal for autopsy.

The body appeared in excellent condition and retained much fat. Except for a very fatty liver and the puppy-like characters noted above, the gross autopsy was negative. The pancreas remnant weighed 3.1 grams. The practical absence of hypertrophy may be noticed.

Microscopically, the liver was crammed with fat even to the periphery of the lobules. Stains with Best's carmine showed absolutely no glycogen except in occasional leukocytes, which stood out prominently in the capillaries by reason of their stuffing of red granules.

The kidneys were normal except for maximal Armanni vacuolation, as seen in routine Zenker specimens stained with methylene blue and eosin. Best's carmine applied to the alcohol fixed specimens showed only a sparse sprinkling of glycogen, so that the vacuoles evidently represented chiefly fat deposit, as demonstrated by fat stains in some other animals but not in this one.

The adrenals showed no more than the average lipoid vacuolation in the cortex, and were normal in other respects.

The thyroid and parathyroids were normal, with average colloid content in the former.

The pancreas remnant was normal in structure and fullness of acini and number and size of islands, but a minority of island cells were maximally swollen and vacuolated.

This puppy, in respect to "spontaneous" downward progress and other features, behaved practically like an adult animal, and most of the history actually represented an adult period of life. Many long experiments of this character were begun for the purpose of testing whether a partial pancreatectomy which did not suffice to produce immediate diabetes in a puppy might result in diabetes after a certain stage of growth had been reached. In other words, the problem was whether a damaged pancreas might lag behind in development so as finally to become inadequate for the demands of a growing body. The best observations would have been those upon much younger animals, but all these failed for one cause or another. It is evident that in many cases the hypertrophy of the pancreas remnant fully compensates for any bodily growth. It is also very doubtful whether an animal which is actually non-diabetic will become diabetic by simple growth. But when the injury results in such a mild diabetes that there are no symptoms on whatever dietary régime is followed, it is entirely possible that diabetes may develop openly at a much later period under the strain of growth and gain of weight. Such a result is exemplified in this experiment, which covers a rather long period in proportion to a dog's life. Such experimental evidence makes it easily comprehensible that diabetic symptoms may follow either soon or late after an injury of the human pancreas; in particular, that glycosuria may be present immediately after an infection, or may be delayed to a time when there is no plain clinical connection with a long antecedent infection which may have been the real cause.

CONCLUSIONS

1. An influence of senility upon carbohydrate assimilation or diabetes is conceivable from a quantitative reduction or other alterations of metabolism, or from functional or anatomic changes in the pancreas. The observations upon senile dogs failed to show any departures from the normal in the glucose tolerance, the ratio of pancreas weight to body weight, the microscopic structure of the pancreas, the size of the pancreatic remnant with which diabetes occurs, the capacity of such a remnant for hypertrophy, or the clinical course of the diabetes.

2. An investigation was also made of the possible influence of the elevated metabolism or the pancreatic peculiarities of youth. Previous work had indicated that the glucose tolerance of puppies is less than that of adult dogs. No exact studies were made of the most important point in the microscopic anatomy, namely the richness in islands, but no striking departure from the adult average was noticeable in numerous routine observations. The ratio of pancreas weight to body weight was somewhat irregular, and the question of possible changes in an individual during growth could not be accurately decided, but the general average in puppies did not differ appreciably from that in adults, particularly with consideration of the small body weight. The remnant left after partial pancreatectomy generally grows considerably in puppies; the hypertrophy on the whole is greater than in adult dogs, but does not surpass what is found in occasional mature or adult animals, and may be slight or absent especially in older puppies. The tendency to diabetes is distinctly less in puppies than in adult dogs, partly on account of weakness and cachexia, partly because of hypertrophy of the pancreas remnant, and perhaps sometimes because of a high functional efficiency of a small remnant. There is no specific tendency to rapidity of downward progress or to diabetic acidosis in puppies.

3. An example is given of long delayed onset of diabetic symptoms on a fixed diet after gain of weight, this gain being largely growth instead of mere obesity. With a still milder diabetic tendency it is readily conceivable that the delay might be longer and might occur on an ordinary diet, also that the diet might in large measure determine the onset of symptoms. In this way it is possible that childhood infections injuring the pancreas may be responsible for some cases of diabetes which make their appearance at a much later period.

BIBLIOGRAPHY

(1) Allen: Amer. Journ. Med. Sci., paper 2 of this series (in press).
(2) Allen: Journ. Exper. Med., 1920, xxxi, 363.
(3) Allen: Amer. Journ. Med. Sci., paper 2 of this series (in press).
(4) Allen: Studies concerning glycosuria and diabetes, 1913, 905.
(5) Allen: Studies concerning glycosuria and diabetes, 1913, 34.
(6) Pratt: Journ. Amer. Med. Assoc., 1912, lix, 322.

EXPERIMENTAL STUDIES IN DIABETES

Series II. The Internal Pancreatic Function in Relation to Body Mass and Metabolism

9. *The Influence of Pregnancy upon Experimental Diabetes*

FREDERICK M. ALLEN

From the Hospital of The Rockefeller Institute for Medical Research, New York

Received for publication August 10, 1920

Diabetes may conceivably be aggravated by the increased metabolism of pregnancy, which involves both additional food assimilation and the formation of considerable new tissue. Unknown toxic or metabolic factors may possibly have an influence. An opposite possibility is suggested especially by the work of Carlson and collaborators (1), namely, that diabetes in the latter part of pregnancy may be prevented by the internal secretory activity of the fetal pancreas. The chief question here is whether internal secretions pass in appreciable quantities through the placenta. In clinical practice pregnancy has long been regarded as decidedly injurious, to such an extent that therapeutic abortion was commonly recommended in women suffering from any serious grade of diabetes. The most comprehensive and recent survey of clinical experience is by Joslin (2), who considers that the supposed injurious effects are largely explained by the higher diet taken. One case of apparent gain of tolerance during pregnancy (3) is inconclusive, partly because the blood sugar rose during gestation and partly because it is uncertain whether the changes observed were due strictly to the pregnancy.

Partially depancreatized animals offer the most accurate obtainable conditions for studying the effect of pregnancy upon the internal pancreatic function. Before proceeding to the principal experiments, it is desirable to mention briefly some controls and unsuccessful attempts relating to this problem.

One control to be thought of is the possible effect of changes in the sexual organs themselves upon the pancreas or its function. This is part of the larger question of the interrelation of the sex glands with the pancreas and diabetes. A few extirpation experiments were performed as follows.[1]

Dog B2–89, a female mongrel aged 4 years, had been close to the verge of diabetes since the first operation on April 12, 1915, so that the removal of 0.25 gram additional pancreatic tissue on March 16, 1916 brought on mild diabetes. By repeated tests up to May 18 it was proved that glycosuria was regularly absent on a measured bread and soup diet, and was present to the amount of about 5 grams daily with the addition of 75 grams glucose. May 18, both ovaries were removed, together with the tubes and part of the uterine horns. A trace of glycosuria followed the operation, and another trace when the regular bread diet was fed. The addition of 75 grams glucose resulted in glycosuria of 12.5 grams one day and 13 grams another day. By May 27 glycosuria was again absent on the plain bread and soup diet and the glycosuria from glucose was no higher than before operation. The absence of any perceptible influence upon the diabetes, other than the transient effects of the trauma, was also confirmed by the animal's later history.

Dog D4–62. Female; mongrel; long haired; age 6 to 8 years; well nourished; weight 19.2 kilos. December 16, 1916, removal of pancreatic tissue weighing 27.5 grams. Remnant about main duct estimated at 3.2 grams ($\frac{1}{10}$). After fasting, glycosuria was found consistently absent on a diet of 1 kilo of beef lung, and moderate (0.5 to 1 per cent) with addition of 50 grams bread. January 17, 1917, both ovaries were removed. A trace of glycosuria followed the operation, but ceased on the lung diet. With addition of 50 grams bread it was distinctly greater than before (2.8 to 4.8 per cent, in larger urine volumes), but ceased when the bread was omitted on January 26. Thereafter the diabetic tendency was no greater than before the oöphorectomy.

Dog C3–67. Male; Dalmatian; age $1\frac{1}{2}$ years; in excellent nutrition; weight 17.6 kilos. March 14, 1916, castration, and removal of pancreatic tissue weighing 28.5 grams. Remnant about main duct estimated at 2.6 grams ($\frac{1}{14}$ to $\frac{1}{15}$). The dog was used for a few tests (especially feeding of pure fat or talcum powder, as described elsewhere) which had no influence upon the glycosuria. Otherwise no food was given, but heavy glycosuria continued until death occurred from weakness on April 1, at a weight of 11 kilos. The pancreas remnant, weighing 3.1 grams, was normal except for the usual vacuolation of island cells. The bladder urine contained 0.61 per cent of sugar, and the autopsy otherwise was negative. Such irrepressible glycosuria with a pancreas remnant of this size is so unusual that the possibility of an aggravating influence of the castration was suggested.

Dog D4–63. Male; mongrel; long haired; age 3 years; medium nutrition; weight 15.25 kilos. After removal of pancreatic tissue on February 14 and March 7, 1917, glycosuria was maintained almost continuously on bread and soup diet with addition of 200 grams glucose to March 23, after which it was absent. Such a duration of glycosuria is evidence that an animal is very close to diabetes, which will be produced by the removal of a trifle more pancreatic tissue. The actual absence of diabetes was confirmed by blood sugar tests, the plasma sugar being

---

[1] All operations were performed under ether anesthesia.

0.087 per cent before feeding and 0.145 per cent at the highest point afterward, and down to 0.122 per cent by evening even on the bread and glucose diet. March 28, castration was performed. Glycosuria remained absent on bread diet to April 2, and therafter also with addition of 200 grams glucose. The attempts to induce diabetes by diet were continued through May, with merely the usual slight gain in tolerance. The removal of 0.5 gram pancreatic tissue on May 8 proved inadequate, but mild diabetes followed the removal of 0.65 gram additional on June 1.

This single experiment with dog D4-63 probably suffices to prove that removal of the testes has no influence for or against the production of diabetes. Aggravation of an existing diabetes, which is a separate question, was not produced by removal of the ovaries in dogs B2-89 and D4-62. The apparent aggravation after removal of the testes in dog C3-67 may have been purely accidental, and any specific influence remains improbable. Circumstances prevented further experiments of this sort.

Numerous attempts were made to determine the size of pancreas remnant with which diabetes occurs in pregnant animals, with uniform failure on account of abortion or death. Efforts to immunize by one or several preliminary subcutaneous or intraperitoneal injections of aqueous extract of fresh sterile dog pancreas gave no protection. Trials were made with removal of five-sixths to nine-tenths of the pancreas in single operations, performed as quickly and easily as possible so as to be over in half an hour or less, but the animals always became unwell and aborted within a few days or at most a week. Such an interval, especially when glycosuria is prevented by malaise and refusal of food, can decide nothing with the pancreas remnants mentioned, though permitting some observations after total pancreatectomy as in Carlson's experiments. Other attempts were made with successive operations, in the hope that each might be so easy as to avoid abortion, also by leaving a duodenal remnant and a subcutaneous graft early in pregnancy, with the idea that diabetes might be brought on later in pregnancy by simple removal of the graft. All such attempts failed for one cause or another. It is sometimes possible to remove considerable portions of pancreas, even in the later stages of pregnancy, without accident, just as other abdominal operations are often feasible; but any pancreatic resection to the point of diabetes seems absolutely incompatible with continuance of gestation. The possibility that this disturbance may be due to the sudden deficit of the internal pancreatic function was excluded by two sets of controls; first, the results are just as bad when the entire uncinate process is left as a subcutaneous graft in addition to the usual pancreatic remnant; second, pregnant dogs ordinarily survive a week of fasting and phlorizination without abortion, though the glycosuria and acidosis apparently represent a greater disturbance of carbohydrate metabolism than that following the pancreatic operations mentioned.

An attempt to test the influence of the increased food requirement and lactose formation of the lactation period was made as follows.

Dog C3–90, mongrel, in excellent condition, weighing 20.5 kilos, was found pregnant in an operation on May 25, 1916, when the splenic process and body of the pancreas down to the main duct were removed, with the idea that diabetes might later be produced by a very easy operation for removal of the uncinate process. The pregnancy continued uneventfully, but by mistake too long an interval was allowed, and on June 22 the dog gave birth to eight healthy puppies. She was an excellent mother and the puppies all thrived until, on June 29, the uncinate process was removed in an operation requiring only a few minutes. There was quick recovery from the brief etherization, and the dog showed the usual devotion and nursed the puppies immediately on being returned to the cage. She acted well and lively but ate very little on the following days, during which time the pups continued to nurse though the mother paid less attention to them. By July 4 her appetite was fully restored, but she refused to have anything further to do with the pups, and even injured them if they approached to nurse. Part of the trouble may have been due to tenderness about the abdominal wound, but there seemed also to be a genuine breaking up of the physiology and psychology of lactation by the operation. Milk rapidly disappeared from the breasts. Diabetes remained absent notwithstanding glucose feeding. Whether the disturbances observed were peculiar to the pancreatic operation or might follow any other abdominal interference, the experience showed that this method was not applicable for studying the influence of lactation upon diabetes.

Numerous microscopic examinations have been made of the pancreas of dogs in various stages of pregnancy and of a few during lactation, without the finding of any departure from the normal in any respect.

It was evident that a satisfactory study was possible only through the occurrence of pregnancy in animals already diabetic, so as to reproduce exactly the conditions encountered in diabetic women. Properly prepared animals with potential diabetes are normal in their entire behavior, and only the unfavorable laboratory conditions made the experiment difficult. It was hoped that cats might be particularly suitable for the purpose, but in the only instance in which a partially depancreatized cat became pregnant the experiment ended in failure, as follows.

Cat A1–84. Female; strong adult; weight 3.5 kilos. December 20, 1913, pancreatic tissue was removed, not quite to the point of producing diabetes. The cat remained continuously free from glycosuria on meat, bread and milk diets thereafter, but had a permanently lowered tolerance, as shown by the production of glycosuria in subcutaneous glucose tests by doses between 1 and 1.5 grams per kilo. Impregnation occurred February 18, 1914. Thereafter the diet was meat and milk, mixed with as much lactose as the animal could be induced to take. Considerable carbohydrate could thus be given, though cats usually object strongly to the sweetness of glucose or saccharose. About the middle of March the animal was noticed to be weak and unwell. Abortion occurred March 16 and death March 18. There was no diabetes and the pancreas remnant was normal. The fatal outcome was almost certainly a sugar intoxication (4), with no specific relation to the partial pancreatectomy or to diabetes. Cats may possibly prove to be well suited to pregnancy experiments in diabetes, but they are as a rule an unfavorable species for carbohydrate over-feeding.

Far more numerous attempts were made with partially depancreatized dogs during three years, but all failed owing to the unfavorable environment. Finally a successful experiment became possible in dog B2-00, which was particularly valuable for the purpose because of the long previous records which had established the tolerance accurately. These observations have been reported in previous papers, especially no. 3 of series I (5) and no. 1 of series II (6).

A series of operations beginning in 1913 had made the dog nearly diabetic, but after the removal of an additional 0.8 gram of pancreatic tissue on September 6, 1916, it was still impossible to maintain glycosuria with the heaviest bread and glucose feeding. Pregnancy then became evident, though the exact time of its beginning was unknown. Tests of the tolerance were performed by feeding, as described below. As diabetes remained absent with advancing pregnancy, there was danger that the entire result would be negative.

Accordingly, on December 16, 1916, 0.1 gram pancreatic tissue was removed, in an operation so short and easy that the dog did not even lose appetite for the day. Diabetes resulted, as proved by the fact that plain bread and soup feeding now maintained slight glycosuria (0.4 to 0.8 per cent, in 400 to 680 cc. urine). December 26 on this diet the plasma sugar was 0.091 per cent before feeding, 0.182 per cent four hours after. The special feeding test was repeated in late pregnancy on December 30.

As an additional experiment, it was attempted to learn whether the pregnant dog with latent diabetes had any special tendency to acidosis. Therefore nothing was fed on December 31, and only 300 grams suet daily on January 1, 2 and 3 (1917). Abortion then occurred, though the dog appeared only slightly unwell and remained free from acetone bodies in urine and blood, both before and afterward. The plasma sugar was constantly normal (0.089 to 0.105 per cent) after omission of carbohydrate, both before and after abortion. The carbohydrate tests had seemed harmless, and it may be possible that the fat feeding was responsible for the abortion even without acidosis.

January 27, the special feeding test was repeated as a control in the non-pregnant condition. The existence of diabetes was unmistakable. The diet was then changed to meat to prevent downward progress, and the dog was left most of the

Dog B2-00. Tests with feeding 100 grams beef lung, 200 grams bread and 150 grams glucose

DATE	WEIGHT	PLASMA SUGAR	Hb.	URINE		REMARKS
				Volume	Glucose	
1916	*kgm.*	*per cent*	*per cent*	*cc.*	*per cent*	
November 21	13.4	0.106	101	18	0	Before feeding
		0.123	97	16	0	2 hours after feeding
		0.156	98	24	Faint	4 hours after feeding
		0.128	96	38	Faint	6 hours after feeding
November 23		0.092	95		0	Before feeding same diet as Nov. 21
		0.095	88	13	Faint	2 hours after feeding
		0.139	92	No	urine	4 hours after feeding
		0.130	93	105	Faint	6 hours after feeding
December 16	Removed 0.1 gm. pancreatic tissue. Dog pregnant					
December 30	15.6	0.085			0	Before feeding
		0.345		212	3.45	2 hours after feeding
		0.455		192	6.46	4 hours after feeding
		0.500		68	5.89	6 hours after feeding
1917						
January 7	12.9	0.125		7	0	Before feeding. After abortion
		0.400		25	7.13	2 hours after feeding
		0.400		35	6.68	4 hours after feeding
		0.333		33	8.00	6 hours after feeding
February 23	16.3	0.116			0	Before feeding
		0.238		18	0.63	2 hours after feeding
		0.244		17	0.57	4 hours after feeding
		0.232		22	0.69	6 hours after feeding
May 17	15.6	0.130			0	Before feeding. (Early pregnancy)
		0.346		39	4.16	2 hours after feeding
		0.435		73	7.32	4 hours after feeding
		0.384		44	4.82	6 hours after feeding
July 11	14.9	0.106			0	Before feeding. (Late pregnancy.)
		0.322		35	4.72	2 hours after feeding
		0.304		65	3.95	4 hours after feeding
		0.312		68	5.58	6 hours after feeding
July 19	13.0	0.077		0	0	Before feeding. (After delivery)
		0.200		23	0.72	2 hours after feeding
		0.218		16	0.92	4 hours after feeding
		0.232		13	0.95	6 hours after feeding

DATE	WEIGHT	PLASMA SUGAR	Hb.	URINE		REMARKS
				Volume	Glucose	
1917	*kgm.*	*per cent*	*per cent*	*cc.*	*per cent*	
August 9	12.9	0.081			0	Before feeding
		0.164		18	Very faint	2 hours after feeding
		0.109		36	Faint	4 hours after feeding
		0.135		17	Faint	6 hours after feeding
October 5	13.5	0.109			0	Before feed'ng
		0.159		17	0	2 hours after feeding
		0.145		36	Faint	4 hours after feeding
		0 152		46	0.31	6 hours after feeding
November 22	14.0	0.109			0	Before feeding
		0.204		24	Faint	2 hours after feeding
		0.238		36	0.39	4 hours after feeding
		0.125		24	0.44	6 hours after feeding

time with a male in the hope of a second pregnancy. The plasma sugar meanwhile remained normal (0.087 to 0.113 per cent) on the carbohydrate-free diet. The special feeding test was repeated on February 23 and May 17.

Pregnancy then became manifest, and the feeding test was repeated in this condition on July 11. June 28 and July 2, the plasma sugar on the meat diet was normal (between 0.075 per cent before feeding and 0.105 per cent after feeding).

July 12, less than 0.1 gram of pancreatic tissue was removed without appreciable disturbance.

Three pups were born on July 16. They were probably 2 or 3 days premature, and were all dead by July 19 owing to failure to nurse properly. This result may have been independent of the experimental conditions, for the dog was of a type which often has troubles with puppies.

The special feeding test was repeated on August 9, October 5 and November 22.

Owing to the perfect manner in which the dog bore the experiments through two pregnancies, the questions at issue received very satisfactory answers as follows:

a. In the first instance, pregnancy failed to produce diabetes in an animal which was so close to the verge that diabetes resulted from the removal of 0.1 gram additional pancreatic tissue. Against an assumption that the diabetes here was due largely to the pregnancy and only partially to the pancreas operation is the fact that diabetes persisted after termination of the pregnancy. Also in the second instance, when the dog was known to have mild diabetes but was free from symptoms on meat diet, pregnancy failed to produce either glycosuria or hyperglycemia on this diet.

b. The removal of a bit of pancreatic tissue in the latter part of each pregnancy supplemented the observations of the negative effects of gestation and especially demonstrated the absence of vacuolation of the islands first when the animal was not quite diabetic and second when she was mildly diabetic. The absence of such hydropic changes with latent diabetes corresponds fully to the experience in non-pregnant animals.

c. The passage of any appreciable quantity of pancreatic internal secretion from the fetuses to the mother is disproved by two facts. First, the occurrence of diabetes following the operation of December 16, 1916, was not prevented; in other words, there was no transfer of pancreatic hormone sufficient to compensate for the loss of 0.1 gram of maternal pancreatic tissue. Second, the feeding tests demonstrated an actual aggravation of the diabetes during pregnancy. Test meals were used instead of intravenous glucose injections because according to previous experience (7) they afford a more accurate index of the diabetic condition and also because they seemed to promise less danger of abortion or other accidents. Attention may be called to the results of these tests as shown in the table.

The test meal consisted of 100 grams beef lung, 200 grams bread and 150 grams glucose. Only slight hyperglycemia and faint glycosuria resulted from this diet on November 21 and 23, when the dog was non-diabetic. The removal of 0.1 gram pancreatic tissue on December 16 produced a radical change, so that the hyperglycemia and glycosuria in the test of December 30 were of plainly diabetic character. The tolerance was fully as low on January 7, after termination of pregnancy, but the dog was still unwell from the recent abortion. The test of February 23 showed a considerably better tolerance as judged by both blood and urine.

May 17, early in the second pregnancy, the test showed a well-marked fall in the assimilation, and the result was not greatly different in the late stage of pregnancy on July 11. The bit of pancreas removed on July 12 was so tiny that it apparently had little effect upon the tolerance. At any rate, in spite of this operation, the assimilation on July 19, three days after normal delivery, showed a decided improvement. This improvement was still greater on August 9, after all puerperal disturbance had subsided. It was also maintained up to October 5, the length of the experiment and the uniformity of results being thus sufficient to exclude accidental fluctuations of tolerance.

CONCLUSIONS

1. No positive influence of the sex glands upon diabetes was demonstrable by extirpation experiments. Also no anatomic changes in the pancreas were perceptible with pregnancy or lactation.

2. Observations upon a partially depancreatized dog during pregnancy are opposed to the view that any appreciable quantity of internal pancreatic secretion passes from the fetus to the mother.

3. A distinct lowering of carbohydrate assimilation was shown during pregnancy. This was not clearly associated with the increase of metabolism, in the sense either of increased food requirement or new tissue formation, for it seemed approximately the same in early and late pregnancy and was also evident during the illness following abortion. It may therefore be regarded chiefly as a toxic manifestation and thus classifiable with the influence of infection. The effect is relatively slight, because pregnancy failed to produce diabetes in a dog where the removal of 0.1 gram pancreatic tissue sufficed for the purpose, and also after the dog was demonstrably diabetic on carbohydrate diet pregnancy gave rise to neither glycosuria nor hyperglycemia on carbohydrate-free diet.

The tests with partial pancreatectomy, which affords the most exact method of study, suggest that Carlson's results in totally depancreatized dogs are to be interpreted as cachexia. Clearer information of the influence of pregnancy upon the internal pancreatic function is also afforded by the freedom from the variables which enter into clinical cases. The slight tendency to aggravation of the diabetes and the ready control by diet support Joslin's experience of the feasibility of completion of pregnancy by diabetic women under suitable conditions of treatment. If the toxic factor is the principal one, as suggested, the possibility remains that the injurious action in some women may be considerably greater than in dogs and accordingly may require more radical measures.

BIBLIOGRAPHY

(1) Carlson and Drennan: This Journal, 1911, xxviii, 391.
Carlson and Ginsburg: Ibid., 1914, xxxvi, 217.
(2) Joslin: Treatment of diabetes mellitus, 1917, 448.
(3) Joslin: Treatment of diabetes mellitus, 1917, 456.
(4) Allen: Journ. Exper. Med., 1920, xxxi, 393.
(5) Allen: Journ. Exper. Med., 1920, xxxi, 563.
(6) Allen: Amer. Journ. Med. Sci., 1920, clx, 781.
(7) Allen and Wishart: Journ. Biol. Chem., 1920, xlii, 415.

RHYTHMICITY OF THE PYLORIC SPHINCTER

HOMER WHEELON AND J. EARL THOMAS

From the Department of Physiology of the St. Louis University School of Medicine, St. Louis, Missouri

Received for publication August 19, 1920

The functions of the pyloric sphincter are usually considered dependent upon the physical condition and relative degree of acidity of the gastric content. Such an explanation fails in great part to account for certain phenomena associated with the processes of gastric evacuation both in health and disease. It also fails to consider the purpose of gastric motility save for mixing the gastric contents and discharging them into the duodenum at irregular periods of opening of the sphincter. However, recent work tends to show that the opening and closing of the sphincter is related, not only to the degree of fluidity and acidity of the gastric content, but also to peristalsis and the degree of tonicity demonstrated in the stomach.

Our present interest in the physiology of the sphincter was stimulated by our inability to explain, upon accepted theories, radiographic observations made upon the human stomach. We therefore undertook to study, upon laboratory animals under easily controllable conditions, the motility of the pyloric sphincter. In this study the term pyloric sphincter means that narrow band of muscle constituting the last portion of the stomach.

METHODS

Forty-four experiments were performed upon dogs in this series. All operative procedures were carried out under ether anesthesia. Unanesthetized dogs were studied radiographically. In 14 experiments records were obtained immediately following operation and while the animal was under the influence of a light anesthesia. Six dogs were studied from 5 to 18 hours after operation, no anesthesia being used during the taking of records. One animal was studied 3 days after operation, another after an interval of 2 weeks. Four animals were operated under ether and morphine (10 mgm. per kilo) and studied at once, ether being discontinued during the observations. This procedure gave a quiet animal with a very active stomach. Although the type of sphincter action under this anesthesia was similar to that obtained under other anesthesias, it was discontinued because of the known action of morphine upon the gastro-intestinal tract. The most constant graphic results were obtained with only sufficient ether to abolish voluntary movements. Under such an anesthesia the behavior of the sphincter is more constant and uniform than in the unanesthetized animal under experimental conditions.

The operations in most cases consisted in opening the abdomen by a midline incision, entering the fundic portion of the stomach and sewing the recording apparatus in place. The gastric incision was then closed with a pursestring suture about the rubber tube leading from the anchored balloon. The opening in the abdomen was closed with a running suture. Aseptic precautions were observed in all cases in which the animal was permitted to survive 12 hours or longer. In 3 animals the muscle on either side of the pyloric sphincter was cut, thus confining action upon the apparatus to the sphincter proper.

All apparatus except the recording instruments was designed and constructed especially for this work. The apparatus is the equivalent of a balloon and is so constructed that it can be placed and maintained within the lumen of the pyloric sphincter. These balloons, or as we have termed them, *pylorographs*, are of three types: *a*, flexible, closed pylorograph; *b*, rigid, closed pylorograph, and *c*, open, flexible pylorograph.

The closed flexible pylorograph (fig. 1, *a*) consists of a short section of finger cot stretched over two cones of hard rubber the apices of which face each other. One cone is perforated by a small hole which leads out through a nipple on its base for the attachment of a rubber tube. When in position the rubber is pressed down upon the sloping surfaces of the cones by the tonus of the sphincter to such an extent that the recording apparatus is affected by the contraction of a width of muscle not exceeding 5 mm. This device when placed in position tends to remain there because of the V-shaped surfaces offered to the pyloric ring. Complete fixation of the pylorograph was obtained by passing a ligature around the base of each cone and securing it in the muscle.

The rigid pylorograph is similar to the one described above save that the two cones remain connected (fig. 1, *b*).

The open, flexible pylorograph (fig. 1, *c*) is constructed on the same principle as the flexible, closed pylorograph except that an open tunnel 4 mm. in diameter runs throughout its entire length. The apices of the two cones are connected by means of a piece of rubberdam tubing.

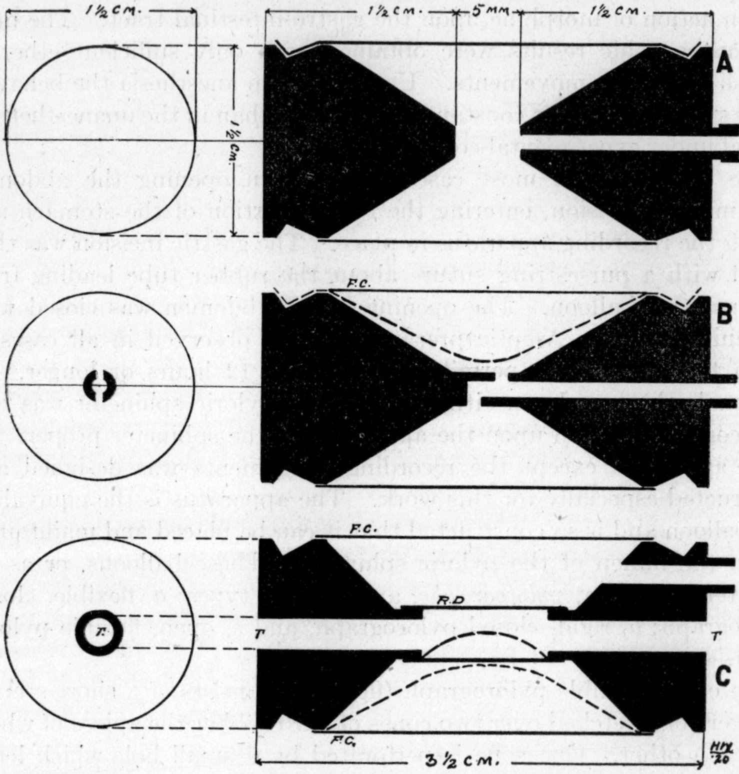

Fig. 1. Illustrations of the various types of pylorographs. *A*, Closed flexible pylorograph. *B*, Closed rigid pylorograph. *C*, Open flexible pylorograph. *V*, Air transmission vent for tube connection with water manometer. *F.C.*, Flexible wall of pylorograph made of finger cot. *T.*, Opening connecting stomach with duodenum. *R.D.*, Tube of rubber dam composing inner wall of air chamber. Dotted lines indicate positions of the rubber surfaces during contraction of the sphincter.

The bases are connected by a section of finger cot. This device, the equivalent of a tunnelled cylindrical balloon, permits the sphincter to demonstrate its motility and at the same time permits material to leave the stomach.

Graphic records were obtained with tambours, and piston and bellows recorders. The pylorograph was connected with the recording apparatus through a water manometer. The manometer was adjusted to a pressure (3 to 30 cm.) which gave best results in any given case. Air transmission was used throughout.

RESULTS

The pyloric sphincter demonstrates two types of motility; *a*, active rhythmic contractions (figs. 2 and 3), and *b*, tone waves (figs. 5 and 6). The characteristics of these two types of action are as follows.

a. Rhythmic contractions. The rhythmic movements of the sphincter are characterized by contractions and relaxations each followed by a quiescent period or pause (fig. 3). These contractions occur at the rate of from 3 to 5 per minute; that is, each cycle is completed in an interval of from 12 to 20 seconds. The phase of contraction is 4 to 5 seconds, the phase of relaxation 3 to 7 seconds; the quiescent phase plus the period of inhibition prior to contraction occupy the remainder of the cycle. These figures are necessarily only relative because of the different rates of contraction shown by various animals, the depth of the anesthesia, and also because of the general motility of the stomach and small intestines. During periods of rhythmic action of the sphincter the contractions and relaxations are uniform in degree; that is, the movements are initiated and consummated from a constant level (figs. 2 and 3). There is usually a definite degree of relaxation (inhibition) of tone immediately preceding a contraction. At times relaxation continues from the completion of contraction until the beginning of a second contraction, no definite phase of quiesence or inhibition being shown. Similar results were obtained both from the filled and recently emptied stomach.

The cycles of the sphincter are definitely altered under various conditions; also, periods of increased activity may occur; however, as will be shown in a later communication, such alterations bear a definite relation to anesthetics, trauma and the activities of the gastro-intestinal canal.

Rhythmicity of the sphincter is not lost following denervation of the stomach (fig 4).

b. Tonicity of the sphincter. The tonicity of the pyloric sphincter is gained or lost during a series of rhythmic contractions of which the heights of the individual contractions vary in proportion to the degree

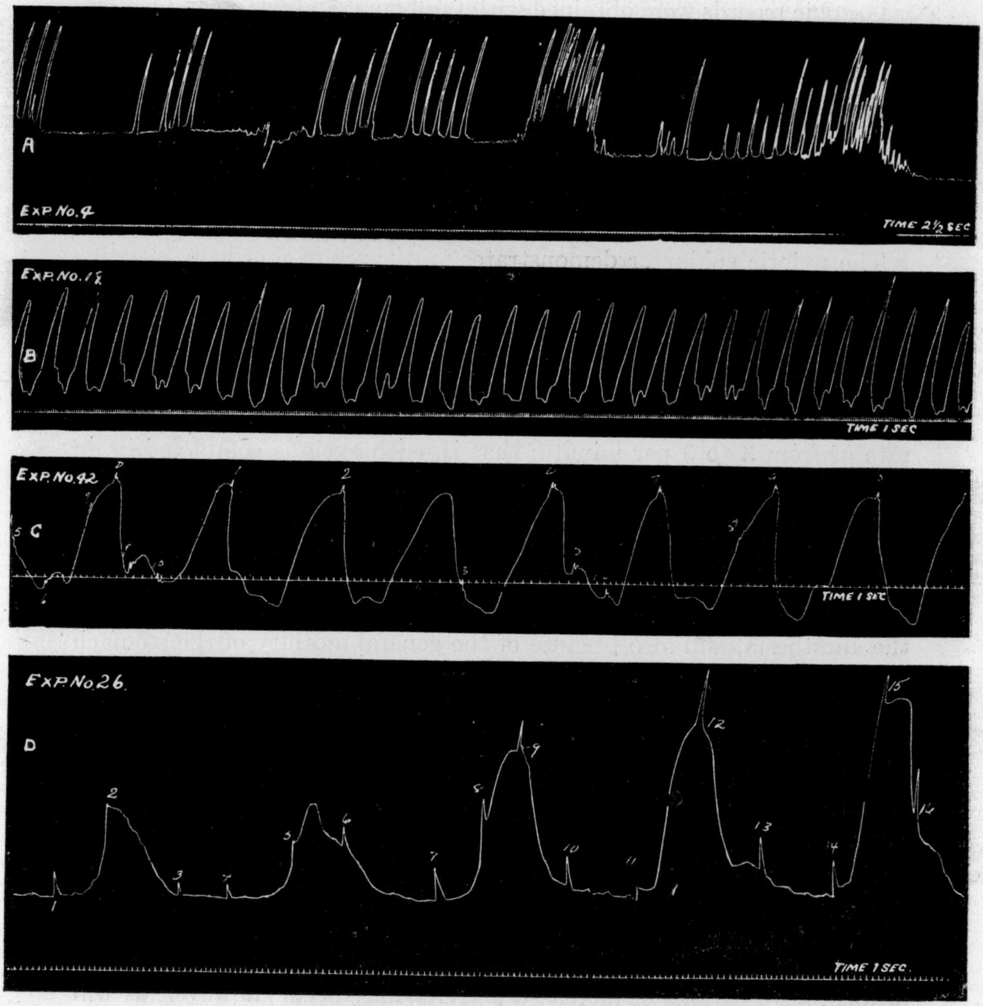

Fig. 2. Pylorograms obtained from four different experiments; *A*, experiment 4; *B*, experiment 19; *C*, experiment 42; *D*, experiment 26. Animals under ether anesthesia. Graph *A* obtained with tambour, *B* and *C* with piston recorder, *D* with bellows recorder. Time, 2½ seconds in trace *A*, 1 second in *B*, *C* and *D*.

Trace *A* shows periods of inactivity followed by rhythmic contractions and alterations in tonicity. Traces *B*, *C* and *D* demonstrate periods of constant rhythmic activity. Note the variation in the height of contractions in traces *A* and *D*. The four graphs are typical of the entire series of experiments.

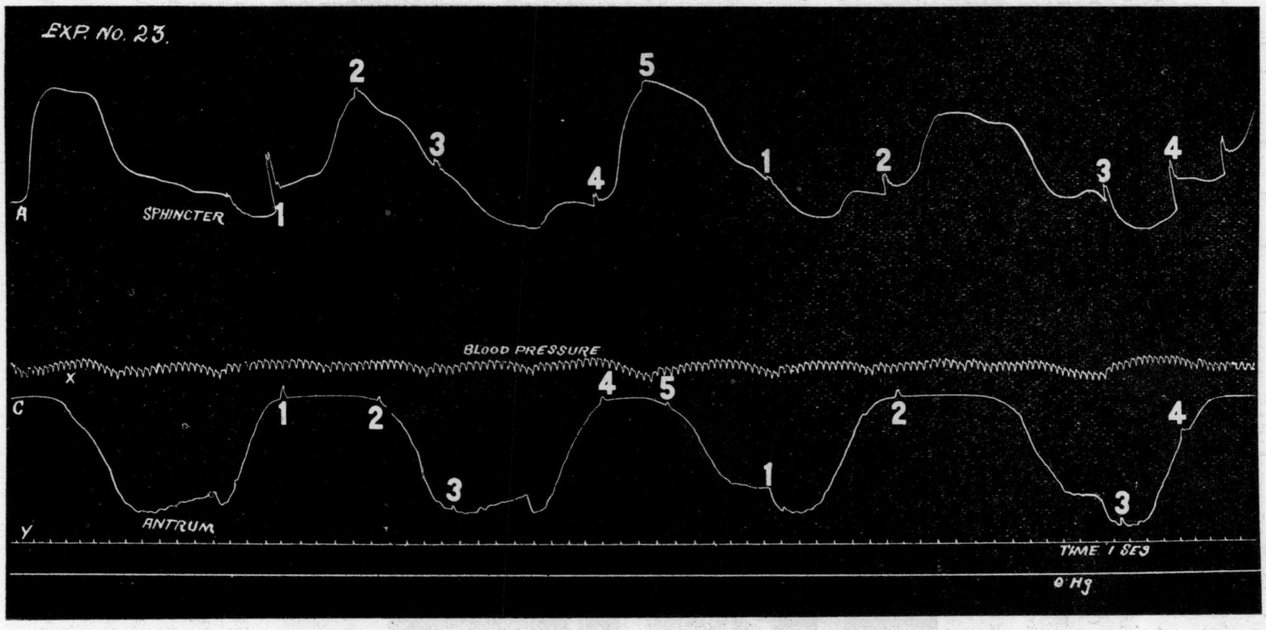

Fig. 3. Experiment 23; February 7 1920. Ether used throughout experiment. Records begun immediately following operation. Double rigid enterograph used. *A*, Sphincteric contractions. *X*, Blood pressure tracing *C*, Antral contractions. *Y*, Time in seconds. Numerals denote synchronous points.

Note that the antrum has reached its maximum at the beginning of the sphincter's contraction, the latter reaching its greatest degree of contraction just as the antrum begins to relax.

of tonicity gained (figs. 5 and 6). On the other hand, periods of increased or decreased rhythmic contractions may appear at a time of constant tonicity (fig. 5, trace *C*). Waves of increased tonicity appear to result because of a lengthening in the time required for complete relaxation; that is, a second wave of contraction appears during the relaxation phase of the previous cycle. A reduction in the degree of tonicity accompanies an increased degree of lengthening of the relaxation phase of the rhythmic cycles, the rate of the rhythmic contractions remaining constant.

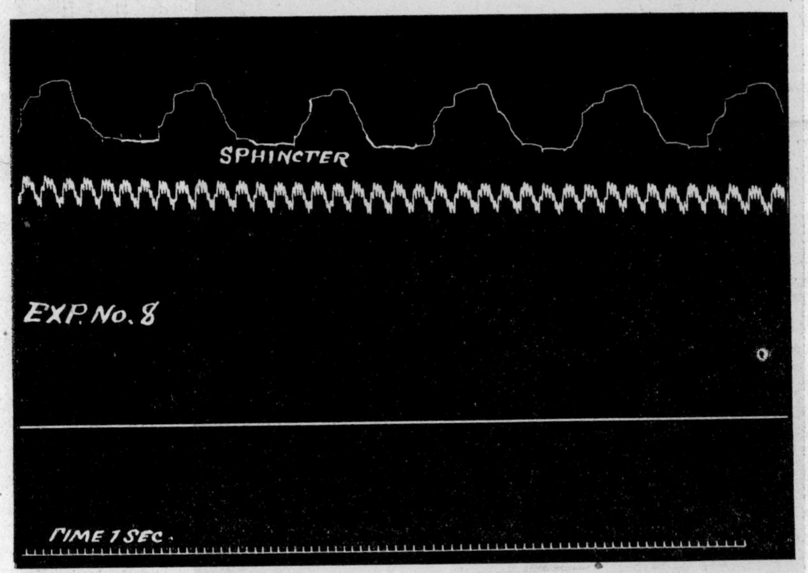

Fig. 4. Experiment 8; January 17, 1920. Rhythmic contractions of the pyloric sphincter following denervation of the stomach. Ether anesthesia. Time in seconds.

The rhythmicity and type of sphincter action are not altered by increasing or decreasing, within limits, the pressure within the pylorograph. However, if the pressure is greatly increased the height of the individual contractions is decreased. Longer excursions of the writing lever are recorded when the pressure in the pylorograph is low (3 to 10 cm. of water). In other words, the greater the degree of resistance offered by the pylorograph to the force of the sphincter's action the smaller becomes the excursion of the muscle while acting. The primary effect of distention of the balloon in the pyloric canal is to excite the sphincter to rhythmic action. Following this there usually appears a gradual loss in tone for several moments after which the rhythmic contractions appear from a constant level. The rapidity with which the sphincter adapts its tonicity to an alteration in resistance is remark-

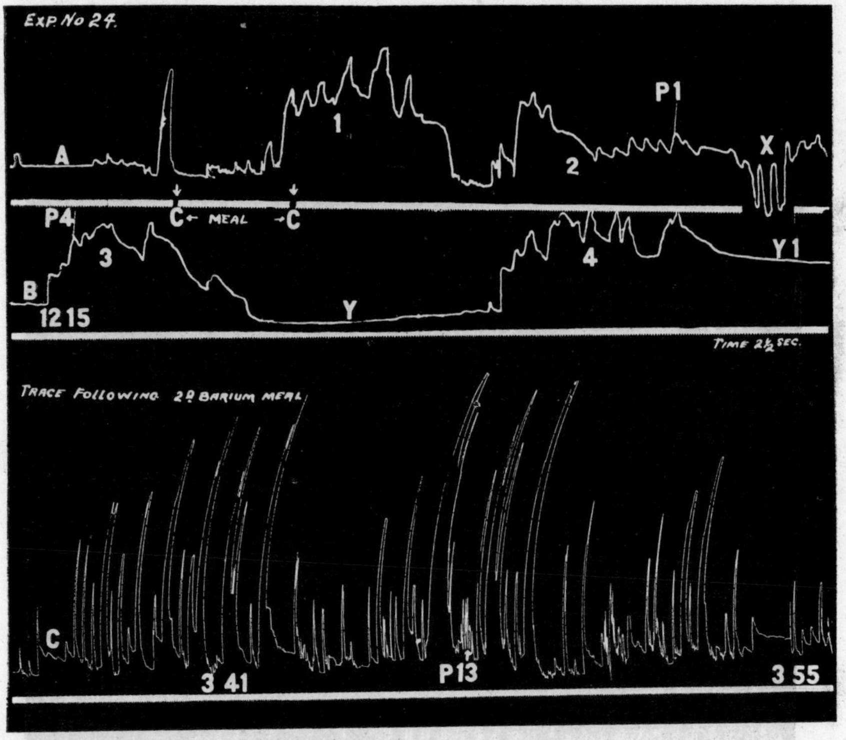

Fig. 5. Experiment 24; February 9, 1920. Pylorograms obtained by use of open pylorograph. Animal operated under ether. Records begun 18 hours later. Piston recorder used for registration. Experiment checked by radiographic records. *A*, *B* and *C*, Sphincter action. *C–C*, Administration of 8 ounces of barium mixture by stomach tube. *1*, *2*, *3* and *4*, Tone waves carrying contraction waves. Trace *C* shows three active and four reduced phases of activity.

able. Apparently, the normal tonicity is only sufficient to close the sphincter or to approximate its surfaces against those of a body in its lumen. Non-resisting materials permit of complete occlusion of the lumen during the positive phase of the sphincteric cycle. Tonicity of the sphincter appears to be unusually high immediately following the ingestion of food, either normally or by means of the stomach tube. Tonicity is also high immediately following the opening of the abdominal cavity. Doubtless this is reflexly the result of peritoneal irritation. Tonicity is not lost by reason of operative procedures on the stomach.

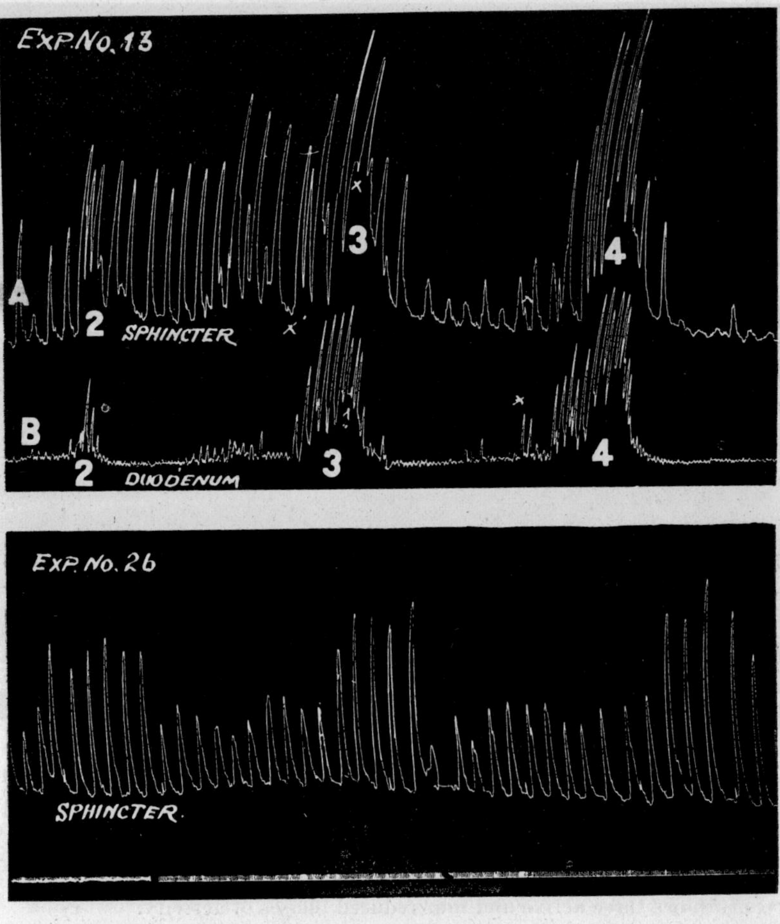

Fig. 6. Experiment 13; January 9, 1920. Ether anesthesia for operation. Double flexible enterograph. Records obtained 3 days after operation upon the conscious animal. *A*, Sphincter contractions. *B*, Duodenal contractions. Note periods of heightened tone of the sphincter at times of pronounced activity on the part of the duodenum (*3* and *4*). *X*, Synchronous points. Time in seconds.

The approach of the pylorograph or examining finger to the antral region causes marked contraction of the pars pylorica. Only under the influence of a deep or surgical anesthesia does the sphincter lose tone completely.

SPECIAL EXPERIMENTS

In dog 25 in which a permanent gastric fistula had been established, it was possible to insert the finger into the antrum and even through the pyloric canal into the duodenum without placing the animal under ether or causing it much discomfort. The primary effect of the finger in the antrum was to excite a state of violent and maintained contraction. Under a constantly applied pressure contracture passed off and the finger was finally permitted to pass through the sphincteric canal. With the finger in the canal one could distinctly feel pressure applied rhythmically during the positive phases of the sphincteric cycles. The sphincter never relaxed completely nor drew away from the finger during the relaxation phase or the period of quiescence. The observation that an initial irritation of the antrum causes a heightened degree of tonicity in the pars pylorica corroborates the generally accepted views as to the functions of these parts in relation to solid objects in the stomach.

In an effort to throw more light on the function of the sphincter the following experiment was performed. An open pylorograph (fig. 1, *c*), as described above, was anchored in the pyloric canal. Graphic records were begun 18 hours following operation (fig. 5). At this time the sphincter demonstrated powerful contractions which occurred irregularly. The animal was then placed on the radiographic table and given an 8-ounce meal of barium sulphate and milk by means of the stomach tube. Immediately following the withdrawal of the tube a marked tone wave appeared on the graphic tracing, superimposed upon which was a series of contractions of varying degree (fig. 5, *A-1*). This was followed by a series of smaller waves each of which lasted from 3 to 7 minutes. Four such tone waves are shown in tracings *A* and *B* of the same figure. As previously stated, these tone waves are built up during a series of rhythmic contractions and lost through a series of gradual and prolonged relaxations. At *X* in figure 5 a series of relaxations permitted the recording lever to drop below the tone level held by the sphincter prior to the administration of the meal. At points marked *Y* and *Y-1* there is a total absence of rhythmic contraction although the tonicity of the sphincter at *Y-1* is markedly above that at *Y* where the level is lower than the pre-meal normal. A radiogram taken at the height of a rhythmic contraction (*P.1*), and at a time of relatively high tonicity, showed the antrum in a state of high tonicity with the pyloric canal closed. As time went on these severe tonic contractions gradually gave way to a constant tone level and rhythmic contractions of varying height (fig. 5, *c*). The stomach emptied itself of the barium mixture in less than 80 minutes. At the end of this time a second meal was given. Rapid distention of the operated stomach easily produces vomiting. This difficulty was overcome by using a small catheter as a stomach tube. The type of sphincter action shown in tracing *C* was continued for 4 hours, at the end of which time the stomach was completely free from the second meal.

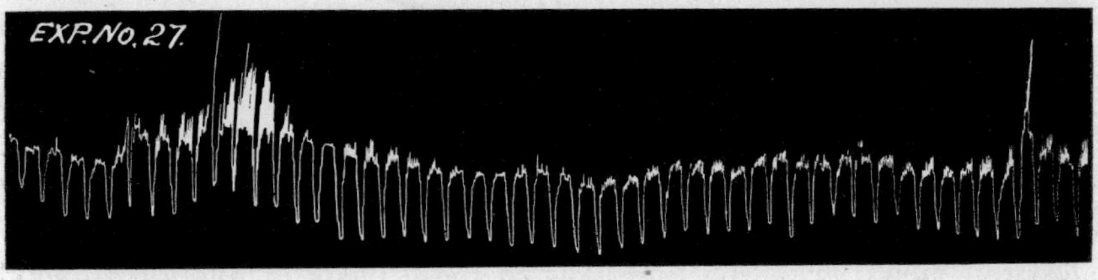

Fig. 7. Experiment 27; February 19, 1920. Ether used throughout experiment. Records begun immediately following operative procedures. Tambour myograph and piston recorder used to obtain graph. Because of construction of the myograph the contraction phase is recorded as the downstroke; relaxation the upstroke. Note the regularity of contraction and the tone level changes.

This experiment seems of special interest because it demonstrates that a foreign body in the pyloric canal through which the gastric contents may pass does not alter the normal progress of gastric evacuation. Further, it supplies information from both the experimental and the radiographic standpoint which indicates that the sphincter is rhythmical in its activities. The development of tone waves in this case does not differ in character from those observed by other types of recording apparatus through which the gastric contents may not pass.

A third type of experiment was performed to check the graphs obtained by means of the closed and open types of pylorographs. In these experiments, three in number, a tambour myograph was attached to the exterior of the sphincter, the animal being immersed in a tank of warm saline solution. The type of rhythmic contractions and tone waves shown in figure 7 are common to the three experiments, and they show no fundamental variation from tracings obtained with other types of apparatus. The animal (no. 27) from which this figure was obtained had been fed about an hour before the experiment started. Often a gurgling noise was audible as material was forced from the antrum into the duodenum, these occurring during a wave of contraction of the pars pylorica.

The results obtained from the various types of experiments and radiographic studies are similar to each other, therefore the movements described for the pyloric sphincter may be considered as representative of normal functioning of this organ.

DISCUSSION

The closure of the pyloric sphincter, according to the prevailing theories, results because of: *a*, the presence of solid masses in the antrum which mechanically excite the mucosa of this region; *b*, an insufficient acidification of the gastric content; and *c*, the presence of acid chyme in the duodenum. Following liquefaction and acidification of the gastric contents these mechanical and chemical stimulants cease and the sphincter relaxes to permit the ejection of chyme into the duodenum.

The theory of an "acid control of the pylorus" (Cannon) does not account for the rapid discharge of water and solutions of neutral egg white from the stomach, neither does it explain the rapid clearance of the stomach in certain pathological conditions. In part the theory of fluidity accounts for the rapid evacuation of the stomach following the ingestion of fluid masses. However, this does not explain the processes involved in the control of the sphincter. Granting that the two theories do explain a certain number of facts relative to the control of the pylorus, we still have to account for pyloric activity when functioning in the absence of acid. That is, something more than fluidity and acid is necessary to open the sphincter to permit the passage of material into the duodenum. Granting that the sphincter is open, all theories agree that peristaltic contractions in the stomach are directly responsible for the discharge of gastric contents. Hence it may be assumed that intragastric pressure and peristalsis bear some definite relation to the activities of the sphincter. That posture and peristalsis do act in such a manner as to facilitate the emptying of the stomach has been pretty definitely shown.

Neilson and Lipsitz (5) have shown that posture to a great extent determines the time of retention of water in the stomach. Individuals lying on their right side retain less of a given amount of water at the end of a stipulated time than individuals assuming other positions. Cole (2), from a study of serial radiograms of the human stomach, has shown that the activities of the sphincter bear a definite relationship to the activities of the antrum in that the amount of contraction of the sphincter is in proportion to the activity of the gastric waves. He has also shown that during the active phase (contraction) of every gastric cycle the pyloric ring is open and a small portion of the gastric contents is propelled through its lumen into the reservoir cap. The terminal wave (peristaltic) which has meanwhile been advancing toward the sphincter, upon attaining it, effects its closure. The recent article by Luckhardt, Phillips and Carlson (4) clearly demonstrates that both in man and dogs the pyloric sphincter opens for the ejection of chyme with the arrival at the sphincter of powerful advancing rings of contraction and a general increase in the tone of the musculature of the stomach as a whole. Their observations demonstrate that a more definite relation exists between the muscular activity and the opening of the sphincter than between the opening of the sphincter and the reaction of the gastric contents. Ivy (3) made the suggestion prior to the appearance of the paper by Luckhardt, Phillips and Carlson, that the rhythmic discharge of water from the dog's stomach is such that it could very well correspond to peristaltic activity.

Such observations clearly demonstrate that the functions of the pyloric sphincter are dependent, in part at least, upon gastric motility. Our observations also tend to show that the sphincter because of its rhythmic type of motility acts in such a manner as to supplement gastric motility. Further observations to be reported later also show that the rhythmic contractions of the sphincter bear a definite and constant relation to the motility of the stomach (fig. 3).

SUMMARY AND CONCLUSION

1. A method is described for recording the motility of the pyloric sphincter.

2. The pyloric sphincter of the dog demonstrates rhythmic activity or cycles of motility which occur at the rate of from 3 to 5 per minute.

3. A single cycle of motility is characterized by a phase of contraction, relaxation and quiescence followed by a definite phase of inhibition prior to a subsequent contraction.

4. The sphincter demonstrates tone changes, such changes being gained or lost because of shortening or lengthening of the relaxation phase of the rhythmic cycles.

5. The observations here reported, therefore, show that the pyloric sphincter of the dog possesses the property of rhythmic contractility, the degree of which is influenced because of changes in tonicity.

BIBLIOGRAPHY

(1) Cannon: This Journal, 1898, i, 359; The mechanical factors of digestion, Longmans, Green and Co., New York, 1911; This Journal, 1907, xx, 283.
(2) Cole: Journ. Amer. Med. Assoc., 1913, lxi, 762; This Journal, 1916, xlii, 618.
(3) Ivy: This Journal, 1918, xlvi, 420.
(4) Luckhardt, Phillips and Carlson: This Journal, 1919, l, 57
(5) Neilson and Lipsitz: Journ. Amer. Med. Assoc., 1915, lxiv, 1052.

A DIFFERENCE BETWEEN THE MECHANISM OF HYPERGLYCEMIA PRODUCTION BY ETHER AND BY CHLOROFORM

ELLISON L. ROSS AND L. H. DAVIS

From the Department of Physiology and Pharmacology, Northwestern University Medical School

Received for publication August 21, 1920

It has already been reported that there are grounds for believing that the hyperglycemia produced by ether anesthesia is due chiefly to the action of ether to reduce the influence of the internal secretion of the pancreas (1). It is considered that this reduction of the action of the internal secretion of the pancreas is a reduction of the inhibitor influence on glycolysis. Since the primary source of blood dextrose is liver glycogen, any injury to the liver should affect the ease with which glycogen is set free. Whether the injury to the liver cells should make the liberation of dextrose easier or more difficult there is no way to foretell. It is well known that chloroform is capable of producing liver pathology. Davis and Whipple (2) showed that chloroform anesthesia produced injury to liver cells and this injury could be increased by fasting before the administration of chloroform. It was thought worth while to compare the hyperglycemia from ether and from chloroform with special reference to the injury produced in the liver.

Experimental work. A group of five normal undieted dogs was given ether for half an hour. Anesthesia was induced by inserting the animal's head into a cylinder into which air that had passed through ether was forced. The animals were bled before anesthesia and after fifteen minutes of anesthesia. The blood sugar was determined by Benedict's method (3). The next day the same procedure was repeated except that the animals were kept under the anesthetic only fifteen minutes. The results are given in tables 1 and 2.

A second group of dogs was given chloroform to the surgical anesthetic stage and kept at this degree of anesthesia for half an hour and the following day the response to fifteen minutes of ether anesthesia was determined. The bleeding, analyses and administration of the anesthetic were carried out as before. The results are given in table 3.

TABLE 1

Ether hyperglycemia of a group of normal dogs

ANIMAL	GLYCEMIA BEFORE ETHER	GLYCEMIA AFTER 15 MINUTES ETHER ANESTHESIA	INCREASE
1	0.113	0.143	0.030
2	0.084	0.111	0.027
3	0.116	0.127	0.011
4	0.096	0.141	0.045
5	0.105	0.132	0.027
Average..........	0.1028	0.1308	0.028

TABLE 2

Ether hyperglycemia of same group of dogs, day following half an hour ether

ANIMAL	GLYCEMIA BEFORE ETHER	GLYCEMIA AFTER 15 MINUTES ETHER ANESTHESIA	INCREASE
1	0.100	0.166	0.066
2	0.093	0.106	0.013
3	0.117	0.140	0.023
4	0.097	0.129	0.032
5	0.085	0.144	0.049
Average..........	0.1004	0.1370	0.0366

TABLE 3

Ether hyperglycemia one day following half hour chloroform anesthesia

ANIMAL	GLYCEMIA BEFORE ETHER	GLYCEMIA AFTER 15 MINUTES ETHER ANESTHESIA	INCREASE
6	0.095	0.106	0.011
7	0.092	0.116	0.024
8	0.099	0.120	0.021
9	0.097	0.136	0.039
10	0.097	0.106	0.009
Average..........	0.0960	0.1168	0.0208

TABLE 4

Ether hyperglycemia following half hour chloroform anesthesia after fast

ANIMAL	GLYCEMIA BEFORE ETHER	GLYCEMIA AFTER 15 MINUTES ETHER ANESTHESIA	INCREASE
11	0.094	0.097	0.003
12	0.093	0.134	0.041
13	0.088	0.094	0.006
14	0.094	0.116	0.022
15	0.095	0.115	0.020
Average..........	0.0928	0.1112	0.0184

A third group of animals fasted two days. Then these dogs were put through the same treatment as the second group. The results are given in table 4.

Discussion. When a drug is administered repeatedly the later reactions usually differ in degree from the first one. This may be due to decreased or increased sensitiveness of nerves, glands or tissue, or injury to cells. To determine whether or not ether had less power to produce hyperglycemia the second day than the first, the first two series of tests were made.

According to tables 1 and 2, the average glycemia before ether the first day was 0.1028 and the second day 0.1004 per cent. This small difference is negligible. Half an hour of ether anesthesia did not change the amount of blood sugar found the following day. This harmonizes with the general impression that ether anesthesia causes very little if any injury to the subject. The first day fifteen minutes of ether anesthesia brought the glycemia up to 0.1308 per cent and the following day the same procedure produced an average glycemia of 0.1370 per cent. The average increase the first day was 0.028 per cent and the average increase the next day was 0.0366 per cent. There was apparently an increased tendency for ether to liberate dextrose the day following half an hour of ether anesthesia. The reason for this increase we do not attempt to give at this time. However, we are able to make the important deduction that ether did not injure the mechanism involved in the production of ether hyperglycemia. If such an injury had occurred the reaction to ether the second day would have been less than that of the first day and the normal glycemia before anesthesia the second day would have been less than that of the first day.

The effect of chloroform on the glycemia of the following day is shown in tables 3 and 4. The average blood sugars before ether of the first and second groups of animals on the day following the chloroform anesthesias were 0.096 and 0.0928 per cent respectively. These values compared with those of normal dogs shown in tables 1 and 2—0.1028 and 0.1004 per cent—indicate a decided tendency of chloroform to partially paralyze the mechanism of sugar mobilization. This phase of the action of chloroform is of great importance. In view of the conclusion of Cannon that blood sugar is the most satisfactory source of energy in emergency, it is of the greatest importance that the mobilization of blood dextrose be not interfered with at a time such as that following an operation when often every vital function is strained to the limit in order to sustain life.

Fifteen minutes of ether anesthesia the day following a chloroform anesthesia of half an hour produced an average glycemia of 0.1168 per cent for the group of non-fasting dogs and a glycemia of 0.1112 per cent for the group of fasting animals. These glycemias compared with those of the group of normal dogs (0.1308 per cent) and of the group which had an ether anesthesia of half an hour the preceding day (0.1370 per cent), show a decided inability of the animals given chloroform the previous day to develop as great a hyperglycemia as normal animals.

The increases in blood sugar due to fifteen minutes of ether anesthesia of the groups of animals which received a chloroform anesthesia the preceding day, were 0.0208 and 0.0184 per cent. The average increase due to ether anesthesia of untreated dogs given in table 1 was 0.028 per cent and the average increase of a group of 17 dogs, given in a previous publication (4), was 0.037 per cent. A comparison of these increases from ether anesthesia obtained the day following a chloroform anesthesia with the increases of normal dogs shows a considerable decrease in the power of the animals to mobilize dextrose after chloroform anesthesia.

There were two groups of animals that were given ether the day following chloroform anesthesia of half an hour. These animals differed in that the second group fasted two days before the tests were made. The day following chloroform anesthesia the non-fasting animals had an average glycemia of 0.0960 per cent and the fasted animals a glycemia of 0.0928 per cent. Fifteen minutes of ether anesthesia of unfasted dogs produced an average increase of blood dextrose of 0.0208 per cent, making a glycemia of 0.1168 per cent. A similar ether anesthesia of the fasting animals produced an increase of 0.0184 per cent making the average blood dextrose value 0.1112 per cent. A comparison of the normal glycemias, the increases due to fifteen minutes of ether anesthesia, and the glycemias after the ether anesthesia of the group of fasting animals and of the group of non-fasting animals, shows greater values for blood dextrose in every case for the non-fasting group. These differences are small but constantly in favor of the one group.

SUMMARY AND CONCLUSIONS

A group of dogs was anesthetized with ether for half an hour. The next day the dogs were anesthetized with the same drug for fifteen minutes. The blood sugar changes were measured for the first fifteen minutes of anesthesia both times.

A second group of dogs was anesthetized with chloroform for half an hour and the following day each was given fifteen minutes of ether anesthesia. The blood dextrose changes the second day were measured.

A third group of animals fasted two days and was then treated the same as the second group.

Half an hour of ether anesthesia did not alter the glycemia of the following day, and did not decrease the hyperglycemia resulting from fifteen minutes of ether anesthesia.

Half an hour of chloroform anesthesia produced on the following day a glycemia lower than normal, an increase in blood dextrose due to fifteen minutes of anesthesia less than normal, and a hyperglycemia from fifteen minutes of ether anesthesia lower than normal.

A fast of two days preceding half an hour of chloroform anesthesia produced on the following day a still lower glycemia and still less reaction to fifteen minutes of ether anesthesia than occurred in non-fasting dogs.

These results in conjunction with the conclusions of Davis and Whipple (2) that the liver injury produced by chloroform is increased by a fast preceding anesthesia leads us to the following conclusions:

1. Ether anesthesia does not produce any injury to the mechanism of dextrose mobilization that can be detected the following day.

2. The injury to the liver cells produced by chloroform anesthesia reduces the glycemia of the following day and injures the mechanism of dextrose mobilization according to the degree of injury.

3. The hyperglycemia due to chloroform anesthesia is not due primarily to the direct action of chloroform on the liver. Probably chloroform, like ether, produces hyperglycemia chiefly through its depressing action on the internal secretion of the pancreas.

BIBLIOGRAPHY

(1) Ross and Davis: This Journal, 1920, liii, 391.
(2) Davis and Whipple: Arch. Int. Med., 1919, xxiii, 612.
(3) Benedict: Journ. Biol. Chem., 1918, xxxiv, 203.
(4) Ross: Journ. Pharm. Exper. Therap., 1919, xii, 377.

DIGESTIBILITY OF SOME HYDROGENATED OILS[1]

ARTHUR D. HOLMES AND HARRY J. DEUEL, Jr.

From the Office of Home Economics, U. S. Department of Agriculture[2]

Received for publication August 28, 1920

Until quite recent times table and culinary fats used in the United States were obtained almost wholly from the animal kingdom—dairy butter being the universal table fat and lard the principal culinary fat. The constantly decreasing per capita supply of animal fats has caused a very rapid increase in the use of vegetable oils for food, until olive, cottonseed, peanut and corn oils are now more or less generally used not only for salad but also for cooking purposes. Except for salad purposes, in the past the housewife apparently preferred fats which were very nearly, if not actually, solid at ordinary temperatures. To meet this demand for solid fats, vegetable oils were hardened either by removing a portion of their low melting constituents or by the addition of stearin or a fat rich in stearin, and fats prepared by one or the other of these methods came into quite general use under a variety of trade names. These processes for hardening vegetable oils have now been largely replaced by the hydrogenation process which is based on the discovery that hydrogen may be added, under proper conditions of temperature and pressure, to the glycerides of the unsaturated fatty acids by means of a catalytic agent, such as nickel in a finely divided state. When the process is carefully controlled it is possible to prepare hydrogenated oils having any desired melting point.

Since it is well known that some metals when taken into the alimentary tract under certain conditions are toxic, it has been very properly questioned whether the ingestion of hydrogenated oils containing appreciable amounts of a metallic catalyst might not be followed by harmful physiological disturbances. Recent investigations (1) indicate that properly prepared hydrogenated oils do not contain sufficient nickel to produce toxic effects. The Federal Meat Inspection Division (2) shares

[1] Published with permission of the Secretary of Agriculture.

[2] Prepared under the direction of C. F. Langworthy, Chief, Office of Home Economics.

this opinion and permits the sale for edible purposes of those hardened oils which do not contain over two parts of the catalyzer per million parts of oil—an amount about five times that ordinarily found in normal hydrogenated oils produced in this country.

The literature contains relatively little information regarding the digestibility of hydrogenated oils. Thoms and Muller (3) found that a hardened oil melting below body temperature was more satisfactory than one in which more complete saturation occurred and a harder fat obtained. Smith, Miller and Hawk (4) determined the relative digestibility of lard (melting at 45°C.) and hydrogenated cottonseed oil (melting at 36°C.) and found the lard to be 94.7 per cent and the hardened oil 93.4 per cent digested—a difference, which in the opinion of the authors, is well within the limits of experimental error. Pekelharing and Schut (5) found that on a diet which contained no fat other than hydrogenated cottonseed oil, mice maintained a steady body increment. They also determined the digestibility of some hydrogenated cottonseed oils in feeding experiments on a dog. On the average the dog digested about 90 per cent of the hydrogenated oils and increased its weight by about one-third the original weight. From the results of the four months' experiment they found that the digestibility of the hydrogenated oils was inversely proportional to their melting points, that mixtures of lard and hardened oils were more completely digested than the hardened oils alone, that no physiological disturbances occurred, and that the feces of the hydrogenated oil diets contained more fat and more fatty acids than those resulting from the lard diet. Erlandsen, Fridricia and Elgstrom (6) report studies of hardened whale oil in which the digestibility varied from 91.6 per cent to 94.9 per cent for butter and whale oil; the difference in digestibility of the two fats did not exceed 0.9 per cent.

The present paper reports a series of digestion experiments with hydrogenated cottonseed, peanut and corn oils in which the entire sample was subjected to the hydrogenation process. Material is also available for reporting the results of experiments on the digestibility of blended hydrogenated oils, in which some hydrogenated oil, hardened to a high melting point, was mixed with enough untreated oil to give a fat of the desired hardness. This investigation is a continuation of an extended series of digestion experiments which has been conducted by this office with about fifty more or less common animal and vegetable fats. The general conclusions from these studies are that edible fats are highly digestible, that they do not unfavorably influence the digestibility of other constituents of the diet, and that when eaten in normal amounts they do not cause any pronounced laxative effects.

Experimental. In these experiments the hydrogenated oils under consideration were included in the diet by being incorporated in the usual specially prepared cornstarch blancmange (7) or pudding. The basal ration, which was nearly fat-free, consisted of wheat biscuit, fruit, sugar and clear tea or coffee. The subjects of the experiments reported below were young men, apparently in normal health, from 20 to 40 years old, students in local universities, who as a result of their previous experience in this type of studies were familiar with the experimental procedure and who were thoroughly trustworthy. The experimental methods for separation and collection of feces and analysis of foods and feces outlined in earlier papers (8) were followed in the experiments below.

The presence of ether-soluble metabolic products in the feces has been taken into account and a suitable correction introduced in calculating results. Since the feces of a given day do not necessarily represent the residue of the food for the preceding day, it has seemed best in these experiments as in all the preceding ones to identify the feces of the experimental period with charcoal or carmine markers and to retain all the feces belonging to the period for analysis. Since the experimental procedure has been uniform throughout the tests on the animal and vegetable fats, the results obtained in these experiments are directly comparable with each other and with the results of our earlier studies.

Results of studies of the digestibility of common fats and oils indicate that their digestibility varies inversely with their melting points in the case of those melting above body temperature. In order to study the relationship between the digestibility and melting points of hydrogenated oils, those considered here were so chosen that some melted above and some below the temperature of the body (37°C.).

The majority of the samples of hydrogenated oil were hardened in the laboratory of Carleton Ellis by one of us (H. J. D.). J. R. Kuhn, of that laboratory, assisted in their preparation.

The melting points of the hydrogenated cottonseed oil were 35°C., 38.6°C. and 46°C.; the melting points of hydrogenated peanut oil were 37°C., 39°C., 43°C., 50°C. and 52.4°C.; and the melting points of hydrogenated corn oil were 33°C., 43°C. and 50°C. The iodine numbers of the samples are given in table 4.

All the hydrogenated oils included in this study were of a white color, solid or practically so at ordinary room temperature, and without any characteristic odor or flavor. When melted they were of a straw yellow color resembling melted tallow. They were very homogeneous and if heated sufficiently they boiled without any sputtering and did not smoke until a relatively high temperature was reached. On cooling, in some instances, different portions of the resulting mass differed slightly in physical appearance, quite likely because of a partial separation of the softer and harder constituents of the hydrogenated oils.

The experiments made with the hydrogenated corn, cottonseed and peanut oils were carried out under conditions essentially the same as those of experiments with the same kinds of oil untreated. As earlier reports show, those oils had coefficients of digestibility as follows: corn oil (9), 96.9 per cent; cottonseed oil (10), 97.8 per cent and peanut oil (11), 98.3 per cent.

Digestibility of hydrogenated corn oil. Fifteen digestion experiments were conducted with hydrogenated corn oil, five each with hardened fats having a melting point of 33°C., 43°C. and 50°C. These fats were prepared by one of the authors (H. J. D.) at a large commercial research laboratory and are believed to be typical of commercial hardened corn oil.

The same group of subjects assisted in each series of experiments with hydrogenated corn oils and the usual standardized experimental conditions were employed.

This report of the individual experiments with hydrogenated corn oil and other oils included in this investigation is somewhat condensed, but the experimental data in full are on file in the Office of Home Economics, States Relations Service, U. S. Department of Agriculture.

The data which were obtained from the study of hydrogenated corn oils are summarized in table 1.

The average amount of hydrogenated corn oil eaten per man per day was 78 grams for the fat melting at 33°C., 74 grams for the 43°C. fat, and 44 grams for the 50°C. fat. The digestibility of the hardened corn oils studied was for 33°C. oil, 94.7 per cent and for 43°C. oil, 95.4 per cent; thus from the standpoint of practical dietetics there was no material difference in the digestibility of these oils. The digestibility of hydrogenated corn oil melting at 50°C. was 88.5 per cent which is identical with that of mutton fat (12) (88 per cent) melting at 50°C. The coefficients of digestibility obtained in these experiments are somewhat lower than 96.8 per cent (13) reported in an earlier paper for the digestibility of commercial, edible corn oil.

The experimental diet as a whole was well utilized, the carbohydrates being very completely absorbed, which would indicate that hydrogenated corn oils having melting points a very little higher than body temperature did not have any unfavorable effect on the digestibility of the other constituents of the diet.

TABLE 1

Summary of digestion experiments with hydrogenated corn oil in a simple mixed diet

EXPERIMENT NUMBER	MELTING POINT OF HYDROGENATED CORN OIL	SUBJECT	DIGESTIBILITY OF ENTIRE RATION			DIGESTIBILITY OF HYDROGENATED CORN OIL
			Protein	Fat	Carbohydrate	
	°C.		*per cent*	*per cent*	*per cent*	*per cent*
1022	33	W. V. D.	75.3	90.8	97.8	93.5
1023	33	H. L. G.	71.0	93.6	96.8	96.7
1024	33	E. L. M.	69.6	91.5	97.4	94.5
1025	33	G. S. M.	72.2	87.6	98.1	90.7
1026	33	J. C. W.	72.0	95.0	96.9	97.9
Average			72.0	91.7	97.4	94.7
1037	42	W. V. D.	83.0	92.5	98.3	95.0
1038	42	H. L. G.	81.0	93.8	97.1	96.8
1039	42	E. L. M.	70.3	89.4	96.6	93.6
1040	42	G. S. M.	70.5	92.5	97.3	96.9
1041	42	J. C. W.	76.6	90.7	95.9	94.6
Average			76.3	91.8	97.0	95.4
1042	50	W. V. D.	65.2	84.8	97.8	90.2
1043	50	H. L. G.	65.9	81.6	95.9	87.9
1044	50	E. L. M.	86.2	91.2	98.3	94.0
1045	50	G. S. M.	60.7	78.9	97.5	85.6
1046	50	J. C. W.	69.9	79.4	97.0	84.9
Average			69.6	83.2	97.3	88.5

Digestibility of hydrogenated cottonseed oils. The experiments made with hydrogenated cottonseed oil were conducted under experimental conditions identical with those employed in the study of the digestibility of cottonseed oil which was found to be 97.8 per cent digested (14). The hydrogenated oils which have received attention in this investigation were not all prepared from the same lot of cottonseed oil; one lot melting at 35°C. (used in experiment 512) was a well-known commercial product which was purchased in the open market; the fat melting at 38.6°C. was specially prepared for our studies in the research laboratories of a concern manufacturing edible hydrogenated oils; the fats melting at 35°C. (used in experiments 1027–1031) and 46°C. were prepared by one of us in a large consulting laboratory. While these products were not all of commercial origin it is believed that they are, nevertheless, typical of the commercial article.

Table 2 summarizes the data from the experiments with hydrogenated cottonseed oil.

TABLE 2

Summary of digestion experiments with hydrogenated cottonseed oil in a simple mixed diet

EXPERIMENT NUMBER	MELTING POINT OF HYDROGENATED COTTONSEED OIL	SUBJECT	DIGESTIBILITY OF ENTIRE RATION: Protein	Fat	Carbohydrate	DIGESTIBILITY OF HYDROGENATED COTTONSEED OIL
	°C.		per cent	per cent	per cent	per cent
512	35	P. K.	67.0	92.6	96.6	96.2
1027	35	W. V. D.	84.8	96.9	99.0	98.3
1028	35	H. L. G.	61.5	94.4	95.2	98.6
1029	35	E. L. M.	70.2	94.4	97.9	97.0
1031	35	J. C. W.	63.6	89.7	95.7	93.9
Average			69.2	93.6	96.9	96.8
459	38.6	R. L. S.	69.5	92.7	97.3	95.5
1052	46	W. V. D.	75.9	93.8	98.4	96.3
1053	46	H. L. G.	69.5	93.2	96.7	96.4
1054	46	E. L. M.	68.7	91.0	97.7	91.9
Average			71.7	92.7	97.6	94.9

The average digestibility of the entire ration in the above experiments indicates that this diet was quite well digested. The daily consumption of hydrogenated oil in these experiments was on the average about 84 grams. In the last group of experiments with hydrogenated cottonseed oil melting at 46°C., 89 grams of the fat were eaten daily without causing any physiological disturbances, which would indicate that the limit of tolerance for this fat was in excess of 89 grams. The coefficients of digestibility, 96.8 per cent for hydrogenated oil having a melting point of 35°C., 95.5 per cent for hydrogenated oil having a melting point of 38.6°C. and 94.9 per cent for hydrogenated oil having a melting point of 46°C., indicate that the hydrogenated cottonseed oils having these melting points are well utilized by the body.

Digestibility of hydrogenated peanut oil. Twenty digestion experiments were made with hydrogenated peanut oils having melting points of 37°C., 39°C., 43°C., 50°C. and 52.4°C. under the usual uniform experimental conditions. The peanut oils melting at 39°C. and 52.4°C. were prepared for us through the courtesy of the chief chemist of a large manufacturing concern. The oils melting at 37°C., 43°C. and 50°C. were hydrogenated by one of us at a commercial fat and oil research laboratory. The results of the experiments with hydrogenated peanut oil are given in table 3.

The average amounts of hydrogenated peanut oil eaten daily in the above groups of experiments were: 37°C. fat, 76 grams; 39°C. fat, 78 grams; 43°C. fat, 91 grams; 50°C. fat, 59 grams; and 52.4°C. fat, 62 grams. No instance of intestinal disturbance resulted which indicates that the above quantities of these hardened oils are well tolerated by the average adult.

A comparison of the melting points and digestibility of these hardened oils is of interest. An increase of 2 degrees in the melting point (from 37°C. to 39°C.) was accompanied by a 2 per cent decrease in digestibility, an increase of 4 degrees from 39°C. to 43°C. caused no significant change in digestibility, an increase of 7 degrees from 43°C. to 50°C. caused a decrease of 4.5 per cent in digestibility, while an increase of 2.4 degrees from 50°C. to 52.4°C. caused a decrease of 13 per cent in digestibility. The coefficient of digestibility of 79 per cent for peanut oil melting at 52.4°C. is the lowest value obtained for any fat of this series; the digestibility (15) of mutton fat (melting point 50°C.) being 88 per cent and that of oleo stearin (16), 80 per cent. Since the melting point, 52.4°C., of this hardened oil is considerably higher than 37°C., the temperature of the human body, it is probable that in the process of digestion saponification takes place only on the exterior of the particles of hardened oil which decrease in size as the process of digestion continues. If surface area be thus a factor, then the rate of digestion and possibly the extent of digestion of a hydrogenated fat having a high melting point is governed to some extent by the size of the particles of hydrogenated oil ingested. Additional experiments are necessary to supply conclusive evidence on this point.

The hydrogenated oil melting at 37°C. was as completely digested (98.1 per cent) as the untreated peanut oil which was found to be 98.3 per cent absorbed (17) by the body. As a group the hydrogenated peanut oils were well digested and well tolerated by the subjects of this investigation.

TABLE 3

Summary of digestion experiments with hydrogenated peanut oil in a simple mixed diet

EXPERIMENT NUMBER	MELTING POINT OF HYDROGENATED PEANUT OIL	SUBJECT	DIGESTIBILITY OF ENTIRE RATION			DIGESTIBILITY OF HYDROGENATED PEANUT OIL
			Protein	Fat	Carbohydrate	
	°C.		*per cent*	*per cent*	*per cent*	*per cent*
1012	37	W. V. D.	74.7	95.1	97.5	97.6
1013	37	H. L. G.	78.3	96.9	97.5	99.1
1014	37	E. L. M.	68.3	94.3	97.4	97.4
1015	37	G. S. M.	57.7	94.0	96.3	97.9
1016	37	J. C. W.	66.7	94.9	95.8	98.6
Average			69.1	95.0	96.9	98.1
464	39	H. R. G.	74.0	95.4	98.1	97.8
466	39	P. K.	81.3	94.2	97.8	96.3
467	39	R. L. S.	66.7	90.2	96.8	93.7
Average			74.0	93.3	97.6	95.9
1032	43	W. V. D.	87.0	95.9	98.3	97.6
1033	43	H. L. G.	71.0	93.7	95.0	97.5
1034	43	E. L. M.	74.6	91.1	97.2	94.1
1035	43	G. S. M.	51.6	90.1	96.8	94.7
1036	43	J. C. W.	84.6	96.5	96.9	98.6
Average			73.8	93.5	96.8	96.5
1057	50	W. V. D.	70.0	87.0	98.2	90.6
1058	50	H. L. G.	65.4	88.5	96.1	93.1
1059	50	E. L. M.	69.9	90.3	97.8	93.6
1060	50	G. S. M.	69.0	86.6	98.1	90.7
Average			68.6	88.1	97.6	92.0
472	52.4	D. D. G.	65.0	65.8	96.4	71.6
473	52.4	H. R. G.	61.0	73.7	96.3	79.5
475	52.4	P. K.	41.7	81.8	98.9	85.9
Average			55.9	73.8	97.2	79.0

SUMMARY

Three vegetable oils, cottonseed, peanut and corn, have been partially hydrogenated to obtain hardened oils having different melting points and their digestibility studied. The results are summarized in table 4.

With the exception of peanut oil melting at 52.4°C. and the corn oil melting at 50°C. all of the hydrogenated oils were 92.0 per cent or more digested. They did not cause any observed digestive disturbances nor did they decrease the digestibility of the experimental diet as a whole. In general, the results showed uniformly that as the melting point of the oil was increased the coefficient of digestibility was decreased. The coefficient of digestibility decreased at a much faster rate in the case of fats with melting points above 46°. The number of experiments conducted with the majority of the hydrogenated oils under consideration, it is believed, is sufficient to permit of fairly definite conclusions regarding the digestibility of each of the oils in question.

TABLE 4

Summary of digestion experiments with hydrogenated vegetable oils in a simple diet

KIND OF HYDROGENATED VEGETABLE OIL	MELTING POINT OF HYDROGENATED VEGETABLE OILS	IODINE NUMBER	NUMBER OF EXPERIMENTS	DIGESTIBILITY OF ENTIRE RATION			DIGESTIBILITY OF HYDROGENATED VEGETABLE OILS
				Protein	Fat	Carbohydrate	
	°C.			*per cent*	*per cent*	*per cent*	*per cent*
Cottonseed	35	89.6	5	69.2	93.6	96.9	96.8
	38.6		1	69.5	92.7	97.3	95.5
	46	72.8	3	71.7	92.7	97.6	94.9
Peanut	37	81.3	5	69.1	95.0	96.9	98.1
	39		3	74.0	93.3	97.6	95.9
	43	78.8	5	73.8	93.5	96.8	96.5
	50	58.5	4	68.6	88.1	97.6	92.0
	52.4		3	55.9	73.8	97.2	79.0
Corn	33	89.0	5	72.0	91.7	97.4	94.7
	43	74.9	5	76.3	91.8	97.0	95.4
	50	55.4	5	69.6	83.2	97.3	88.5

The results of these experiments indicate that these hydrogenated oils are as well utilized as natural fats of corresponding melting points.

BIBLIOGRAPHY

(1) Sufsmann: Arch. Hyg., 1915, lxxxiv, 121.
Lackey and Sayre: Journ. Amer. Pharm. Assoc., 1917, vi, 348.
Lehmann: Chem. Ztg., 1914, xxxviii, 798.
(2) Kerr: Personal communication.
(3) Thoms and Muller: Arch. Hyg., 1915, lxxxiv, 54.

(4) Smith, Miller and Hawk: Journ. Biol. Chem., 1915, xxiii, 505.
(5) Pekelharing and Schut: Pharm. Weeklad., 1916, liii, 769.
(6) Erlandsen, Fridricia and Elgstrom: Tidskr. Kem., 1918, xv, 109.
(7) Langworthy and Holmes: U. S. Dept. Agric. Bull. 310, 1915.
(8) Langworthy and Holmes: U. S. Dept. Agric. Bull. 310, 1915.
Langworthy and Holmes: U. S. Dept. Agric. Bull. 505, 1917.
Langworthy and Holmes: U. S. Dept. Agric. Bull. 507, 1917.
Holmes: U. S. Dept. Agric. Bull. 613, 1919.
Holmes: U. S. Dept. Agric. Bull. 630, 1918.
Holmes: U. S. Dept. Agric. Bull. 687, 1918.
Holmes: U. S. Dept. Agric. Bull. 781, 1919.
Deuel and Holmes: Journ. Biol. Chem., 1920, xli, 227.
(9) Holmes: U. S. Dept. Agric. Bull. 687, 1918, 20.
(10) Langworthy and Holmes: U. S. Dept. Agric. Bull. 505, 1917, 18.
(11) Langworthy and Holmes: Ibid.
(12) Langworthy and Holmes: U. S. Dept. Agric. Bull. 310, 1915, 21.
(13) Holmes: U. S. Dept. Agric. Bull. 687, 1918, 20.
(14) Langworthy and Holmes: U. S. Dept. Agric. Bull. 505, 1917, 18.
(15) Langworthy and Holmes: U. S. Dept. Agric. Bull. 310, 1915, 21.
(16) Holmes: U. S. Dept. Agric. Bull. 613, 1919, 16.
(17) Langworthy and Holmes: U. S. Dept. Agric. Bull. 505, 1917, 18.

INDEX TO VOLUME LIV

ACACIA, effect of intravenous injection of, on blood, 1.
Acid and alkali tolerance in planarians, 138.
Adrenalin, effect of, on venous blood pressure, 96.
——, —— —— subcutaneous injection of, 248.
Age, influence of extremes of, on production of diabetes, 439.
Alkali tolerance in planarians, acid and, 138.
Alkaline reserve of blood of insane, 147.
ALLEN, F. M. Experimental studies in diabetes. Series II. The internal pancreatic function in relation to body mass and metabolism:
5. The influence of fever and intoxication, 375.
7. The influence of cold, 425.
8. The influence of extremes of age upon the production of diabetes, 439.
9. The influence of pregnancy upon experimental diabetes, 451.
Atropin, effects of, on volume-flow of blood, 204.
AUB, J. C. Studies in experimental traumatic shock. I. The basal metabolism, 388.
—— and T. D. CUNNINGHAM. Studies in experimental traumatic shock. II. The oxygen content of the blood, 408.
—— and H. WU. Studies in experimental traumatic shock. III. Chemical changes in the blood, 416.

BARR, D. P., and J. P. PETERS, JR. Studies of the respiratory mechanism in cardiac dyspnea. III. The effective ventilation in cardiac dyspnea, 345.
——. See PETERS and BARR, 307, 335.
Blood analyses following acacia-glucose injection, 1.
——, chemical changes in, in experimental traumatic shock, 416.
—— of insane, alkaline reserve of, 147.
——, oxygen content of, in experimental traumatic shock, 408.
—— pressure, arterial, relation of cerebral hemispheres and thalamus to, 355.
—— ——, venous, effect of adrenalin on, 96.
——, sugar of, under chloroform and ether anesthesia, 474.
——, volume-flow of, 166, 185, 204.
Brain stem, studies on, 355.

CAPILLARIES and venules, functional activity of, 30.
Carbon dioxide, low alveolar, of cardiac dyspnea, 307.
Cardiac dyspnea, respiratory mechanism in, 307, 335, 345.
CARLSON, A. J., and A. B. LUCKHARDT. Studies on the visceral sensory nervous system:
I. Lung automatism and lung reflexes in the frog (R. pipiens and R. catesbiana), 55.
III. Lung automatism and lung reflexes in reptilia (turtles: Chrysemys elegans and Malacoclemmys lesueurii. Snake: Eutenia elegans), 261.
——. See LUCKHARDT and CARLSON, 122.
Cerebral hemispheres, relation of, to arterial blood pressure, 355.
Cold, influence of, on diabetes, 425.
CONNET, H. The effect of adrenalin on venous blood pressure, 96.

CRUICKSHANK, E. W. H. The distribution and quantitative action of the vagi as determined by the electrical changes arising in the heart upon vagus stimulation, 217.

CUNNINGHAM, T. D. See AUB and CUNNINGHAM, 408.

DAVIS, L. H. See ROSS and DAVIS, 474.

DEUEL, H. J., JR. See HOLMES and DEUEL, 479.

Diabetes, experimental studies in, 375, 382, 425, 439, 451.

Digestibility of some hydrogenated oils, 479.

ERLANGER, J. See WHITE and ERLANGER, 1.

FEVER and intoxication, influence of, on diabetes, 375.

GASTRIC hunger contractions, 153.

GESELL, R. Studies on the submaxillary gland:

VI. On the dependence of tissue activity upon volume-flow of blood and on the mechanism controlling the volume-flow of blood, 166.

VII. On the effects of increased salivary pressure on the electrical deflections, the volume-flow of blood and the secretion of the submaxillary gland of the dog, 185.

VIII. On the effects of atropin upon volume-flow of blood, electrical deflections and oxidations of the submaxillary gland, 204.

Glucose, effect of intravenous injection of, on blood, 1.

HEART, vagus action on, 217.

HOLMES, A. D., and H. J. DEUEL, JR. Digestibility of some hydrogenated oils, 479.

HOOKER, D. R. The functional activity of the capillaries and venules, 30.

Hyperglycemia, production of, by chloroform and by ether, 474.

LENHART, C. H. See MARINE and LENHART, 248.

LUCKHARDT, A. B., and A. J. CARLSON. Studies on the visceral sensory nervous system. II. Lung automatism and lung reflexes in the salamanders (necturus, axolotl), 122.

——. See CARLSON and LUCKHARDT, 55, 261.

Lung automatism and lung reflexes in the frog, 55.

—— —— —— —— —— in reptilia, 261.

—— —— —— —— —— in the salamanders, 122.

—— volume, effective, in cardiac dyspnea, 335.

MACARTHUR, J. W. Changes in acid and alkali tolerance with age in planarians. With a note on catalase content, 138.

MARINE, D., and C. H. LENHART. The influence of glands with internal secretions on the respiratory exchange. I. Effect of the subcutaneous injection of adrenalin on normal and thyroidectomized rabbits, 248.

Metabolism, basal, in experimental traumatic shock, 388.

NERVOUS system, visceral sensory, 55, 122, 261.

OILS, hydrogenated, digestibility of, 479.

PANCREATIC function, internal, in relation to body mass and metabolism, 375, 382, 425, 439, 451.

PATTERSON, T. L. Gastric tonus of the empty stomach of the frog. Comparative studies IV, 153.

PETERS, J. P., JR., and D. P. BARR. Studies of the respiratory mechanism in cardiac dyspnea:
I. The low alveolar carbon dioxide of cardiac dyspnea, 307.
II. A note on the effective lung volume in cardiac dyspnea, 335.
——. See BARR and PETERS, 345.
Planarians, acid and alkali tolerance in, 138.
Pregnancy, influence of, on experimental diabetes, 451.
PRITCHETT, I. W. See WISHART and PRITCHETT, 382.
Pyloric sphincter, rhythmicity of, 460.

RESPIRATORY exchange, influence of glands with internal secretions on, 248.
—— mechanism in cardiac dyspnea, 307, 335, 345.
ROGERS, F. T. Studies on the brain stem. IV. On the relation of the cerebral hemispheres and thalamus to arterial blood pressure, 355.
ROSS, E. L., and L. H. DAVIS. A difference between the mechanism of hyperglycemia production by ether and by chloroform, 474.

SALIVARY pressure, increased, effects of, on volume-flow of blood, 185.
Shock, studies in experimental traumatic, 388, 408, 416.
Submaxillary gland, studies on, 166, 185, 204.
SUITSU, N. Studies on the alkaline reserve of the blood of the insane, 147.

THALAMUS, relation of, to arterial blood pressure, 355.
THOMAS, J. E. See WHEELON and THOMAS, 460.

VAGUS action on heart, 217.
Venous blood pressure, effect of adrenalin on, 96.
Ventilation, effective, in cardiac dyspnea, 345.
Venules, capillaries and, functional activity of, 30.
Visceral sensory nervous system, 55, 122, 261.

WHEELON, H., and J. E. THOMAS. Rhythmicity of the pyloric sphincter, 460.
WHITE, H. L., and J. ERLANGER. The effect on the composition of the blood of maintaining an increased blood volume by the intravenous injection of a hypertonic solution of gum acacia and glucose in normal, asphyxiated and shocked dogs, 1.
WISHART, M. B., and I. W. PRITCHETT. Experimental studies in diabetes. Series II. The internal pancreatic function in relation to body mass and metabolism. 6. Gas bacillus infections in diabetic dogs, 382.
WU, H. See AUB and WU, 416.